INSTRUCTOR'S MANUAL WITH VIDEO GUIDE

EFFECTIVE SMALL BUSINESS MANAGEMENT

INSTRUCTOR'S MANUAL WITH VIDEO GUIDE

James V. Dupree with Norman M. Scarborough

Grove City College   Presbyterian College

EFFECTIVE SMALL BUSINESS MANAGEMENT

Sixth Edition

Norman M. Scarborough
Thomas W. Zimmerer

Prentice Hall
Upper Saddle River, New Jersey 07458

Acquisitions editor: Stephanie Johnson
Managing editor: Melissa Steffens
Associate editor: Hersch Doby
Project editor: Richard Bretan
Manufacturer: Technical Communication Services

Printed in the United States of America

10   9   8   7   6   5   4

ISBN 0-13-999442-4

Prentice-Hall International (UK) Limited, London
Prentice-Hall of Australia Pty. Limited, Sydney
Prentice-Hall Canada Inc., Toronto
Prentice-Hall Hispanoamericana, S.A., Mexico
Prentice-Hall of India Private Limited, New Delhi
Prentice-Hall of Japan, Inc., Tokyo
Prentice-Hall (Singapore) Pte Ltd
Editora Prentice-Hall do Brasil, Ltda., Rio de Janeiro

Table of Contents

Section IV - Marketing for the Small Business: Building a Competitive Edge

Prentice Hall Video Guide

Chapter 1 - Entrepreneurs: The Driving Force Behind Small Business

Real success is finding your lifework in the work that you love.
--David McCullough

An entrepreneur is the kind of person who will work 16 hours a day
just to avoid having to work 8 hours a day for someone else.
--Anonymous

Teaching Objectives
Students will be able to:
1. Define the role of the entrepreneur in business--in the United States and across the globe.
2. Describe the entrepreneurial profile.
3. Describe the benefits and opportunities of owning a small business.
4. Describe the potential drawbacks of owning a small business.
5. Explain the forces that are driving the growth in entrepreneurship.
6. Discuss the role of diversity in small business and entrepreneurship.
7. Describe the contributions small businesses make to the U.S. economy.
8. Describe the small business failure rate and explain why small businesses fail.
9. Put business failure into the proper perspective.
10. Analyze the major pitfalls involved in managing a small business and understand how small business owners can avoid them.

Instructor's Outline
I. Introduction
    A. The dramatic resurgence of the entrepreneurial spirit
        1. A study showed that 35 million households, 37% have an intimate connection with small business.
        2. 18 million households include someone running a small business.
        3. This resurgence of the entrepreneurial spirit is the most significant economic development in recent business history.

    B. A record number of entrepreneurs launch new businesses.
        1. Figure 1.1.
        2. A survey of college seniors shows 49% of men and 31 % of women are interested in pursuing entrepreneurship.
        3. Current conditions suggest this is just the crest of a new wave of entrepreneurship.
        4. Technology, downsizing, and the move to a knowledge-based economy all favor the development of small business and entrepreneurial endeavors.
        5. The trend is benefiting not just the U.S., but also China, Russia, and many other countries.

II. What is an entrepreneur?
    A. Definition
        1. An entrepreneur is one who creates a new business in the face of risk and uncertainty for the purpose of achieving profit and growth opportunities and assembles the necessary resources to capitalize on those opportunities.

IN THE FOOTSTEPS OF AN ENTREPRENEUR - Creativity and Opportunity: Hallmarks of the Entrepreneur

Two characteristics common to entrepreneurs are creativity and an eye for opportunity. When Dennis Gabrick started Preserved Tree-scapes International, Inc. [PTIJ in 1987, he had difficulty explaining to the architects and interior designers he was targeting exactly what he was selling. Preserved Trees International takes branches and leaves from live trees [without killing the trees] and preserves them in a special solution. Workers attach the limbs and leaves to a metal-core trunk covered with real bark. The result: a "pickled" tree that looks real but never needs watering. Tree prices range from $100 to $300 a foot, but PTI has been successful by showing customers how preserved trees actually save them money. PTI has sold more than 10,000 trees, some as tall as 72 feet, and generates sales of $6.5 million a year.

A Song of Love. Joanna and David, thinking that there might be a market for serenading, set up Serenading Service, a business that keeps alive a practice that started in sixteenth-century Italy and spread across Europe. Complete with guitars, mandolin, a ladder, champagne, and a dozen roses, the serenade usually brings a tear to the eye of the recipient as the singer expresses "a vocal celebration of love that can make the stiffest upper lip tremble. "Even the serenade business has occupational hazards, however. While David serenades, Joanna sometimes must convince overzealous neighbors that the serenaders are not burglars.

A Hopping Business. In 1953, Richard Fluker bought a cricket farm. In the early days of the business, the only market for crickets was for fish bait. Today, however, Fluker Farms ships boxes of live crickets, mealworms, and other insects to pet stores, zoos, and universities all over the world. Now under the leadership of David Fluker Richard's son, Fluker Farms generates more than $6 million in revenues a year.

1. Assume that you are a banker and each of these three entrepreneurs approaches you with a loan request to start these companies. What questions will you ask them? Would you approve the loan? Explain.
    Answer - Students' questions should focus on the evidence of the viability of these businesses and what personal commitment the entrepreneurs have in them, i.e., personal investment.
2. Using these business ventures as a source of inspiration, work in a team with two or three of your classmates to generate ideas for unusual business ventures that you could start.
    Answer - Students' answer will vary.
3. Select one idea from those that your team generated in question 2. What could you do to convince skeptical lenders or investors to put money into your company and to increase the probability of its success?
    Answer - Students' answer will vary.

B. Entrepreneurial profile
1. Desire for responsibility.
2. Preference for moderate risk.
3. Confidence in their ability to succeed.
4. Desire for immediate feedback.
5. High level of energy.
6. Future orientation.

       7.   Skill at organizing.

       8.   Value achievement over money.

C. Hayberg Consulting Group's 10 characteristics of an entrepreneur.

       1.   Table 1.1

D. Other characteristics

       1.   High degree of commitment.

       2.   Tolerance for ambiguity.

       3.   Flexibility.

       4.   Tenacity.

E. Conclusions from research on entrepreneurs

       1.   There is no mold, no one set of characteristics.

       2.   Diversity seems a central characteristic.

III. Benefits and opportunities of small business ownership

    A. Opportunity to gain control over your own destiny

       1.   Reap the rewards.

       2.   Achieve independence.

    B. Opportunity to make a difference

       1.   Opportunity to do what is important to you.

       2.   Example of Mike Riebel.

    C. Opportunity to reach your full potential

       1.   Escape from boring and unchallenging work.

       2.   Entrepreneurship is a vehicle for self-expression.

    D. Opportunity to reap unlimited profits

       1.   Money is not the primary motivator, but owning your own business is a great way to create wealth.

       2.   Typical American millionaire is first-generation wealthy, owns a small business and works 45-55 hours a week.

       3.   Greg Brophy example.

    E. Opportunity to make a contribution to society and be recognized for your efforts

       1.   Often small business owners are among the most trusted and respected members of their communities.

       2.   Entrepreneurs enjoy the recognition they get from customers for doing a job well.

    F. Opportunity to do what you enjoy doing

       1.   Their work is not really work; it's their avocation turned into a vocation.

       2.   Example of Ed Krech.

IV. Potential drawbacks of entrepreneurship

    A. Uncertainty of income

       1.   The regularity of income from working for someone is gone.

       2.   "The entrepreneur is the last one to be paid."

B. Risk of losing your entire invested capital
   1. 24% fail within 2 years.
   2. 51% shut down within 4 years.
   3. 63% fold within 6 years.
   4. Consider the risk-reward trade-off.
      a) What is the worst thing that could happen if my business fails?
      b) How likely is it that the worst to happen?
      c) What can I do to lower the risk that my business will fail?
      d) What is my contingency plan for coping if my business fails?

WIRED TO THE WEB - The Wedding Planner

During her senior year in college, the sister of Margaret Ellen Pender's boyfriend, Christian got married, Margaret offered to help the family "manage" the wedding. She created a process for planning and managing any wedding. She observed others planning weddings, took notes, and learned. After testing her wedding planner and finding it worked she is now trying to find a way to market it on the World Wide Web.

1. How should Margaret Ellen use the World Wide Web to market her business? What other methods might she use to market her wedding planner?
   Answer - Students' answer will vary.
2. Using one of the search engines on the WWW, find at least three sites with which Margaret Ellen should establish links. Did you find any competitors already on the Web?
   Answer - Students' answer will vary.
3. Work with a team of your classmates to develop a design for a Web site for Margaret Ellen's business.
   Answer - Students' answer will vary.
4. Would you recommend that Margaret Ellen operate this business from her home? Explain. If so, what pitfalls would you warn her to avoid? Use the WWW to identify the steps she should take to avoid those pitfalls.
   Answer - Students' answer will vary.

C. Long hours and hard work
   1. Most new owners put in 60 hours a week.
   2. One-forth put in 70 hours a week.
   3. See Figure 1-3.

D. Lower quality of life until the business gets established
   1. The workload can take a toll on the entrepreneur's personal life and family.
   2. Most launch their business when they are between 25 and 39, just as their families are starting.
   3. Figure 1.3.

E. High levels of stress
   1. Running your own business is highly stressful.
   2. Failure can mean total financial ruin.

   F. Complete responsibility
      1. Entrepreneurs end up taking on issues with which they are not knowledgeable.
      2. The owner is the business.

V. Why the boom? The fuel feeding the entrepreneurial fire
   A. Entrepreneurs as heroes
      1. Americans have very positive attitudes towards entrepreneurs.

   B. Entrepreneurial education
      1. More colleges and universities are offering courses, more students see entrepreneurship as a career option.
      2. 1,500 colleges and universities offer courses to 15,000 students.

   C. Demographic and economic factors
      1. Most start their businesses between ages 25 to 39.

   D. Shift to a service economy
      1. By 2000, the service sector will produce 90 % of the jobs and 85 % of the GNP in the U.S.

   E. Technological advancements
      1. Make it easier for entrepreneurs to start and run a business, faxes, computers, voice mail, etc.
      2. Example of Paul Wenner.

   F. Independent lifestyles
      1. Entrepreneurship fits the American life, independence and self-sufficiency.

   G. The World Wide Web (WW)
      1. Electronic commerce will have grown from $518 million in 1996 and $6.6 billion in 2000.
      2. 141,000 small businesses have web-sites.
      3. Amazon.com story.

   H. International opportunities
      1. Small business is able to do business outside U.S. borders.
      2. 95% of the world's population lives outside of U.S. borders.
      3. Changing political conditions favor going international.
      4. Robert Bizzell story.

VI. The Cultural Diversity of Entrepreneurship
   A. Women entrepreneurs
      1. Women are launching new businesses at a rate twice the rate of men.
         a) 72% is concentrated in retail and services.
      2. 8 million women own their own businesses, employing 18.5 million workers, 25% of the labor force in the U.S.
      3. Women, generating $2.5 trillion in sales own 37% of all U.S. businesses.
         a) See Figure 1.5.

        4.   Key differences between companies started by women and those started by men. Women-owned businesses:

           a) typically start smaller, grow slower but steadier.

           b) have a high survival rate.

           c) face more of a capital barrier and are more likely to rely on personal credit.

           d) are run differently, more family friendly benefits.

        5.   Example of Carolee Friedlander.

SMALL BUSINESS ACROSS THE GLOBE - A Rush to Entrepreneurship in Russia

Entrepreneurship is not a uniquely American phenomenon. The desire to create businesses is taking root all across the globe, even in nations whose economies were, for many years, centrally planned. In Russia, for instance, small businesses are playing an important role in rebuilding an economy that collapsed in the early 1990s. Small companies account for 12 percent of all of the goods produced in Russia, and that proportion is growing rapidly.

Of course, many Russian start-ups, like those in any country, fail. The obstacles entrepreneurs must overcome are substantial. Tatyana Zeleranskaya and Irina Koroleva, both former reporters for Soviet State radio, were willing to brave the obstacles when they launched Moscow's Radio Nadezhda. They decided to forgo the usual political shows and popular music that are the mainstay of so many Russian radio stations, opting instead for programs on topics such as family and health.

Olga Romashko is another entrepreneur who grew tired of a grueling state job and left to start her own business. She quit her post as a researcher at a top-secret biophysics lab to launch a company selling a line of skin-care products. Her Olga line now carries 14 products, and sales are coming in at $20,000 a month.

1. How do the entrepreneurial experiences described above differ from those of the typical American enterprise? In what ways are they similar?
   Answer - Americans have a national culture that supports entrepreneurship, and while they face some bureaucracy, they do not face as much bureaucracy as the Russians. Taxes are higher for the Russians.

2. What impact do you predict the small business sector will have on the Russian economy over the next 10 to 20 years?
   Answer - It is the future of Russia. The collapse of the Russian economy is the result of state controlled economies and bureaucracies. The faster growth and adaptability of small businesses will result in more and faster growth.

3. What impact do you think entrepreneurship will have on Russia's women over the next 10 to 20 years?
   Answer - It is their major entrée into economic equality. They are probably likely to succeed due to a different attitude toward women working in Russia than traditional American families.

   B. Minority enterprises

      1. African-Americans own 3.6% of U.S. businesses and account for 1% of total U.S. commercial revenues.

      2. Discrimination in corporations is the number one motivator for the minority entrepreneur.

       3. African-American owned businesses grew twice as fast as most businesses. Hispanic owned businesses grew even faster.

       4. Yla Eason story.

C. Immigrant entrepreneurs
1. Many are lured to the U.S. by its economic freedom.
2. Come with few assets but lots of drive and dreams.
3. Marty and Helen Shih from Taiwan.

D. Part-time entrepreneurs
1. Permits people to try it with low-risk.
2. 13 million Americans are self-employed part-time.
3. Use it to "test the waters."

E. Home-based business owners
1. 30.7 million businesses operate from homes.
2. 14.9 million are full-time.
3. These companies generate $383 billion in revenue and create 8,219 new jobs each day.
    a) See Figure 1.6.
4. 57% of home-based business involve white-collar work.
    a) Work 61 hours per week.
    b) $50,250 in annual income, a third earn more than $60,000 a year.
    c) 85% are surviving after 3 years.
5. See Table 1.2 - guidelines for home-based businesses.

F. Family business owners
1. Two or more family members are in financial control.
2. 90% of the 22 million businesses in the U.S. are family owned.
3. These companies employ 50 million people and generate 55% of the GDP.
4. Survival rate of these businesses is not good.
    a) Only 33% make it to the second generation.
    b) Only 15% make it to the third generation.
5. One-third of the Fortune 500 companies are "family businesses."
6. Example of Jim Henson Productions.

G. Copreneurs
1. Husband and wife entrepreneurial teams.
2. Characteristics of successful husband-wife teams include:
    a) personalities that mesh.
    b) mutual respect.
    c) compatible goals.
    d) equal partnership.
    e) open communication.
    f) clear division of roles and authority.
    g) ability to encourage each other.
    h) separate work spaces.
    i) boundaries between work and personal life.
    j) a sense of humor.
3. Story of Bob and Cindy Maynard.

H. Corporate castoffs
1. As major U.S. companies have "trimmed their ranks," many of these displaced workers have launched their own companies.
2. 15% of these managers start their own companies.
3. An entrepreneurial offense is the best defense to corporate layoffs.
4. David Barry after 18 years with a corporation.

I. Corporate dropouts
1. Downsizing has diminished employee loyalties.
2. Many are striking out on their own for more opportunity, better income, and more "job security."
3. 64% of those starting a business have some college, 16% have advanced degrees.
4. 77% of businesses started since the mid-eighties were still in business three years later.

VII. The Contributions of Small Business
A. Introduction
1. 22.1 million businesses, 98.5% of all businesses in the U.S. would qualify as small businesses.
2. Small business employs more than 53% of the private sector work force.
3. Virtually all job growth in 1990s came from small business, creating 75% of new jobs.
4. Small companies bear the heaviest load of training new workers.
5. Small businesses produce 50% of the GDP and 47% of business sales.
6. They also generate 20% more innovations per employee than large companies.
7. See Figure 1.7.

VIII. The Failure Record: Can You Beat the Odds?
A. Small businesses have a much higher failure rate than larger businesses.
1. 63% will fail in six years.
2. See Figure 1.8.
3. Causes of small business failure

B. Managerial incompetence
1. The chief problem.
2. The owner-leader lacks the knowledge or ability needed.
3. Andrew Kay story.

C. Lack of experience
1. Small business managers need experience in the field, not just general experience.

D. Poor financial control
1. The margin for error is small, controls need to be tight.

E. Lack of strategic planning.
1. Owners neglect the strategic planning process, because they "don't have the time."
2. Small businesses need a strategy in order to maintain a clear competitive advantage.

F. Uncontrolled growth

1. They will outgrow their capital base with every 40 to 50% increase in sales.
2. Ideally the business should expand on retained earnings.
3. Growth also requires structural and other changes.

G. Inappropriate location
    1. Location is part art and part science.
    2. Owners need to investigate before they locate.
       a) It's critical in retail.
    3. Keys to location.
       a) What it costs.
       b) What revenues it generates.

IN THE FOOTSTEPS OF AN ENTREPRENEUR - Never Too Young

According to the following entrepreneurs, you're never too young [or too old] to launch your own business. A recent study of 1,200 business owners found that the highest percentage of entrepreneurs starting businesses was in the 25 to 35 age group. Twenty-something entrepreneurs are not unusual, especially with more college courses in entrepreneurship and small business management available and poor job prospects in big companies. The World Wide Web has created a tremendous opportunity for young, computer-savvy entrepreneurs because it offers low financial barriers to entry. Also popular with young entrepreneurs are "knowledge-based businesses;" such as public relations, telemarketing, consulting, and others.

After Annette Quintana had a dispute with her employer, she decided to start a business of her own. Annette and her sister Victoria founded Excel Professional Services, a computer consulting company. First-year sales were $250,000, and within five years, their company was bringing in sales of $15 million.

Some entrepreneurs don't wait until they're in their twenties to start their companies; they start even earlier. Before graduating from elementary school, Richie Stachowski was an entrepreneur. While on a Hawaiian vacation with his family 10-year-old Richie was frustrated by his inability to talk to his father while they were snorkeling. Researching the problem on the Internet, Richie discovered that sound travels better underwater than through air. Using $267 of his own savings, he invented the Water Talkie, a cone-shaped device that allows users to talk underwater, patented his new product, and formed a limited liability company, Short Stack, to sell it. Major retailers such as Toys "R" Us and Sportmart have purchased more than 50,000 Water Talkies from Short Stack.

When K-K Gregory was 10 years old, while playing in the snow outside her Bedford, Massachusetts, home, her wrists became cold from the snow that had gotten up the sleeves of her jacket. K-K went inside and sewed a piece of fleece fabric into a tubular shape; she added a thumbhole to keep it from sliding up her arm. A few weeks later, she sewed fleece tubes of the same design for her Girl Scout troop, and they were a big hit. Recognizing a business opportunity K-K and her mother created a company named after their trademark product, Wristles.

1. In addition to the normal obstacles of starting a business, what other barriers do young entrepreneurs face?
Answer - Discrimination or not being taken seriously due to their age. Difficulty in raising capital. Difficulty in hiring and supervising help.

> 2. What factors do you think contribute to a young person's taking the risk of starting a business.
>   **Answer** - Supportive parents, the ability to fail and try again, imagination, etc.

   H. Lack of inventory control
- 1. Many small firms have too much money tied up in inventory.
- 2. On the other hand, insufficient inventory leads to stock outs and lost sales.

   I. Inability to make the "entrepreneurial transition"
- 1. Businesses are most likely to fail in the first five years.
- 2. The ability to start a business is often what contributes to its demise as the founder can't make the transition.

IX. Putting Failure into Perspective
- 1. It is a natural part of the process. The only way to not fail is to not do anything.
- 2. Learn from failures and be more successful the next time. It's not mistake avoidance but learning from mistakes that counts.
- 3. Entrepreneurship requires persistence and resilience.
- 4. The Bryn Kaufman example.
- 5. See Table 1.3 - strategies for the life cycle of a company.

X. How to avoid the pitfalls

   A. Know your business in depth
- 1. Get the best education and experience before you start.
- 2. Example of Suzanne Clifton.

   B. Prepare a business plan.
- 1. Planning replaces "I think" with "I know."
- 2. Most entrepreneurs don't have a solid plan.

   C. Manage financial resources.
- 1. Develop a practical information system and use it to make decisions.
- 2. Estimate capital needed then double it.
- 3. Cash is your most valuable resource.

   D. Understand your financial statements.
- 1. These documents are reliable indicators of the small business's health. Know them.
- 2. Know the financial danger signs to look for.

   E. Learn to manage people effectively.
- 1. Your hires will determine where your company will go.
- 2. Share information.

   F. Set your business apart from the competition
- 1. Differentiate your company and products.
- 2. Convince your customers that you are different from competitors.

   G. Keep in tune with yourself.
- 1. Manage yourself.

2. Keep a positive attitude.
3. Keep your passion.

Chapter Summary

♦ Define the role of the entrepreneur in business--in the United States and across the globe.
- Record numbers of people have launched companies over the past decade. The boom in entrepreneurship is not limited solely to the United States; many nations across the globe are seeing similar growth in the small business sector. A variety of competitive, economic, and demographic shifts have created a world in which "small is beautiful."
- Society depends on entrepreneurs to provide the drive and risk-taking necessary for the business system to supply people with the goods and services they need.

♦ Describe the entrepreneurial profile.
- Entrepreneurs have some common characteristics, including a desire for responsibility, a preference for moderate risk, confidence in their ability to succeed, a desire for immediate feedback, a high energy level, a future orientation, skill at organizing, and a value of achievement over money. In a phrase, they are high achievers.

♦ Describe the benefits and opportunities of owning a small business.
- Driven by these personal characteristics, entrepreneurs establish and manage small businesses to gain control over their lives, become self-fulfilled, reap unlimited profits, contribute to society, and do what they enjoy doing.

♦ Describe the potential drawbacks of owning a small business.
- Small business ownership has some potential drawbacks. There are no guarantees that the business will make a profit or even survive. The time and energy required to manage a new business may have dire effects on the owner and family members.

♦ Explain the forces that are driving the growth in entrepreneurship.
- Several factors are driving the boom in entrepreneurship, including the portrayal of entrepreneurs as heroes, better entrepreneurial education, economic and demographic factors, a shift to a service economy, technological advancements, more-independent lifestyles, and increased international opportunities.

♦ Discuss the role of diversity in small business and entrepreneurship.
- Several groups are leading the nation's drive toward entrepreneurship: women, minorities, immigrants, "part-timers," home-based business owners, family business owners, copreneurs, corporate castoffs, and corporate dropouts.

♦ Describe the contributions small businesses make to the U.S. economy.
- The small business sector's contributions are many. They make up 99 percent of all businesses, employ 53 percent of the private sector workforce, create most of the new jobs in the economy, produce 50 percent of the country's gross domestic product (GDP), and account for 47 percent of business sales.

♦ Describe the small business failure rate and explain why small businesses fail.
- The failure rate for small businesses is higher than for big businesses, and profits fluctuate with general economic conditions. Small Business Administration statistics show that 63 percent of new businesses will have failed within six years. The primary cause of business failure is incompetent management. Other reasons include poor financial control, failure to plan, inappropriate location, lack of inventory control, improper managerial attitudes, and inability to make the "entrepreneurial transition."

♦ Put business failure into the proper perspective.
- Because they are building businesses in an environment filled with uncertainty and shaped by rapid change, entrepreneurs recognize that failure is likely to be a part of their lives, but they

are not paralyzed by that fear. Successful entrepreneurs have the attitude that failures are simply stepping stones along the path to success.

♦ Analyze the major pitfalls involved in managing a small business and understand how the small business owner can avoid them.

- There are several general tactics the small business owner can use to avoid failure. The entrepreneur should know the business in depth, develop a solid business plan, manage financial resources effectively, understand financial statements, learn to manage people effectively, set the business apart from the competition, and keep in tune with himself.

Discussion Questions

1. What forces have led to the boom in entrepreneurship in the United States and across the globe?
   Answer - Corporate downsizing flooding the market with corporate cast-offs, an attitude that small is beautiful, international economic development due to the fall of communism and the "capitalization" of former state-owned industries, a dream of freedom and independence, perseverance in achieving results, and the opportunities presented by an ever-changing environment.

2. What is an entrepreneur? Give a brief description of the entrepreneurial profile.
   Answer - One who creates a new business in the face of risk and uncertainty for the purpose of achieving profit and growth by identifying opportunities and assembling the necessary resources to capitalize on them. Profile - a) desire for responsibility, b) preference for moderate risk, c) confidence in personal success, d) desire for immediate feedback, e) high level of energy, f) possess a future orientation, g) skill in organization, h) money is a great way to keep score but it is not as important as achievement.

3. *Inc.* magazine claims, "Entrepreneurship is more mundane than it's sometimes portrayed . . . you don't need to be a person of mythical proportions to be very, very successful in building a company." Do you agree? Explain.
   Answer - will vary according to the student.

4. What are the major benefits of business ownership?
   Answer - a) opportunity to gain control over your destiny, b) opportunity to make a difference, c) opportunity to reach your full potential, d) opportunity to reap unlimited profits, e) opportunity to make a contribution to society and receive recognition for your efforts.

5. Which of the potential drawbacks to business ownership are most critical?
   Answer - Student's responses will vary but should cover the following drawbacks: a) uncertainty of income, b) risk of losing invested capital, c) long hours and hard work, d) lower quality of life until the business gets established, d) complete responsibility.

6. Briefly describe the role of the following groups in entrepreneurship: women, minorities, immigrants, "part-timers," home-based business owners, family business owners, copreneurs, corporate castoffs, and corporate dropouts.
   Answer - For women see pages 16-17, for minorities see pages 18-19, for immigrants and "part-timers" see pages 19, for home-based business owners see pages 20-21, for family business owners see pages 21, and for copreneurs, corporate castoffs, and corporate dropouts see pages 21-24.

7. What is a small business? What contributions do they make to our economy?

Answer - There is no set definition of a small business. SBA criteria vary by industry, see page 36. 98% of U.S. businesses could be considered small. They've contributed almost all of the recent job growth, employ over 50% of the private workforce, and contribute 48% of our GNP and 42% of all business sales.

8. Describe the small business failure rate.
   Answer - See Figure 1.8 for failure rate.

9. Outline the causes of business failure. Which problems cause most business failures?
   Answer - <u>Management incompetence</u> - This one causes the most problems. The manager lacks the capacity to operate a small business successfully. <u>Lack of experience</u> - Many owners who start businesses in fields in which they have no prior experience fail. Some owners lack the right kind of experience. <u>Poor financial control</u> - Undercapitalization - Starting the business on a "shoestring"-- often leads to failure. <u>Lack of strategic planning</u> - Too many owners neglect it because they think it only benefits large companies. <u>Uncontrolled growth</u> - Growth is natural and healthy, but unplanned growth can be fatal to the business. <u>Inappropriate location</u> - Owners who choose a business location without proper analysis, investigation, and planning often fail. Too often, owners seek "cheap" sites and locate themselves straight into failure. <u>Lack of inventory control</u> - Although inventory is typically the largest investment for the owner, inventory control is one of the most neglected duties. The result is loss through crime and pressure on cash flows from handling the wrong items. <u>Inability to make the "entrepreneurial transition"</u> - Having started the business, some entrepreneurs lack the ability to manage it when it gets larger and fail to turn it over to a different management team.

10. How can the small business owner avoid the common pitfalls that often lead to business failure?
    Answer - Doing the following will help to avoid pitfalls. a) know the business in depth, b) prepare a business plan, c) manage financial resources, d) understand financial statements and know how to use them, e) learn to manage people effectively, f) keep in tune with yourself.

11. Why is it important to study the small business failure rate?
    Answer - It provides a realistic picture for potential entrepreneurs to consider prior to their launching of their businesses. It provides understanding of why businesses fail and offers insight into ways to prevent it.

12. Explain the typical entrepreneur's attitude toward failure.
    Answer - He/she learn from the mistakes and tries again. He/she takes moderate, considered risks, has a positive upbeat attitude, and doesn't avoid failure; he/she learn from it.

13. One entrepreneur says that too many people "don't see that by spending their lives afraid of failure, they become failures. But when you go out there and risk as I have, you'll have failures along the way, but eventually the result is great success if you are willing to keep risking. For every big yes in life, there will be 199 nos." Do you agree? Explain.
    Answer - Students' responses will vary.

14. What advice would you offer an entrepreneurial friend who has just suffered a business failure?
    Answer - Students' responses will vary but the advice should include a reality check, long hours, high failure rate, and a dose of the positive, persist, learn, don't give up.

Step into the Real World

1. Choose an entrepreneur in your community and interview him or her. What's the "story" behind the business? What advantages and disadvantages does the owner see in owning a business? What advice would he or she offer to someone considering launching a business?

2. Search through recent business publications (especially those focusing on small companies such as *Inc.*, *Entrepreneur*, *Business Start-Ups*, *Nation's Business*, or *Your Company*) and find an example of an entrepreneur--past or present--who exhibits the entrepreneurial spirit of striving for success in the face of failure as Gail Borden did. Prepare a brief report for your class.

3. Select one of the categories under the section "The Diversity of Entrepreneurship" in this chapter and research it in more detail. Find examples of the entrepreneurial profile. Prepare a brief report for your class.

4. Interview a local banker who has experience lending to small companies. What factors does he or she believe are important to a small company's success? What factors has he or she seen to cause business failures? What does the lender want to see in a business start-up before agreeing to lend any money?

Chapter 2 - Strategic Management and the Entrepreneur

*To accomplish great things, we must not only act, but we must also dream;
not only plan but also believe.*
Anatole France

You either have to be first, best, or different.
Loretta Lynn

Teaching Objectives
Students will be able to:
1. Understand the importance of strategic management to a small business.
2. Explain why and how a small business must create a competitive advantage in the market.
3. Develop a strategic plan for a *business* using the 10 steps in the strategic planning process.
4. Understand the Entrepreneurial Strategy Matrix and how to apply it.
5. Discuss the characteristics of three basic strategies: low-cost, differentiation, and focus.
6. Understand the importance of controls, such as the balanced scorecard, in the planning process.

Instructor's Outline
I. Introduction
   A. Strategy Necessary for Success
      1. Vital and often over-looked.
      2. Too often, entrepreneurs launch businesses destined for failure because their founders never stop to define a workable strategy that sets them apart from their competition.
      3. Entrepreneurs often find the process of developing a strategy dull and unnecessary.
         a) Their tendency is to start a business, try several approaches, and see what works.
      4. Companies lacking clear strategies may achieve some success, but as competition stiffens or an unanticipated threat arises, they usually "hit the wall" and fold.
      5. Without a basis for differentiating itself, the best a company can hope for is mediocrity.

   B. Today's Global Competitive Environment
      1. Any business not thinking and acting strategically is extremely vulnerable.
      2. Every business is exposed to the forces of a rapidly changing competitive environment, and in the future small business executives can expect even greater uncertainty.
         a) Sweeping political changes.
         b) Technological advances.
         c) More intense competition and newly emerging global markets.
      3. The biggest change business owners face is unfolding now.
         a) The shift in the world's economy from a base of financial to intellectual capital.
         b) "Knowledge is no longer just a factor of production," says futurist Alvin Toffler. "It is the critical factor-of production."
      4. The Knowledge Revolution will spell disaster for companies that are not prepared for it, but it will spawn tremendous opportunities for entrepreneurs who are equipped with the strategies to exploit it.
         a) The rules of the competitive game have been dramatically altered.
         b) To be successful, entrepreneurs can no longer do things in .the way they have always clone them.
      5. Strategic management involves developing a game plan to guide the company as it strives to accomplish its vision, mission, goals, and objectives and to keep it from straying off its desired course.

          a)   It is a blueprint for matching the company's strengths and weaknesses to the opportunities and threats in the environment.

C.   Building a Competitive Advantage
    1.   The goal of developing a strategic plan is to create for the small company a competitive advantage.
        a)   The aggregation of factors that sets the small business apart from its competitors and gives it a unique position in the market.
    2.   No business can be everything to everyone.
        a)   Example of No Kidding, a small toy store in Brookline, Massachusetts.
    3.   Small companies have a variety of natural advantages over their larger competitors.
        a)   Fewer product lines.
        b)   A better-defined customer base.
        c)   A specific geographic market area.
        d)   Close contact with their markets, providing valuable knowledge on how to best serve customers' needs and wants.
    4.   Consequently, strategic management may come more naturally to small businesses than to larger companies.
    5.   Strategic management can increase a small firm's effectiveness, but owners first must have a procedure designed to meet their needs and their business's special characteristics.
    6.   The strategic management procedure for a small business should include:
        a)   a relatively short planning horizon: two years or less for most small companies.
        b)   informality and not overly structured; a shirtsleeve approach is ideal.
        c)   participation of employees and outside parties to improve the reliability and creativity of the plan.
        d)   not beginning with setting objectives; extensive objective setting early on may interfere with the creative process.
        e)   strategic thinking, not just on planning, linking long-range goals to day-to-day operations.

II.   The Strategic Management Process
  A.   Strategic planning is a continuous process that consists of 10 steps:
    1.   Step 1. Develop a clear vision and translate it into a meaningful mission statement.
    2.   Step 2. Define the firm's core competencies and target market segment, and position the business to compete effectively.
    3.   Step 3. Assess the company's strengths and weaknesses.
    4.   Step 4. Scan the environment for significant opportunities and threats.
    5.   Step 5. Identify the key factors for success.
    6.   Step 6. Analyze the competition.
    7.   Step 7. Create company goals and objectives.
    8.   Step 8. Formulate strategic options and select the appropriate strategies.
    9.   Step 9. Translate strategic plans into action plans.
    10.   Step 10. Establish accurate controls.

  B.   Step 1. Develop a Clear Vision and Translate it into a Meaningful Mission Statement
    1.   Vision.
        a)   The vision touches everyone associated with the company--employees, investors, lenders, customers, the community.
        b)   It is an expression of what the owner stands for and believes in.

(1) One study of more than 500 "hidden champions"--little-known superperforming companies that hold worldwide market shares of at least 50 percent--identified having a clear vision as an important factor in their competitive edge.

   c) Vision is based on an entrepreneur's values.

   d) Successful entrepreneurs build their businesses around a set of three to six core values.

   e) The best way to put values into action is to create a written mission statement.

2. Mission.

   a) The mission statement addresses the first question of any business venture: What business am I in?

   b) Establishing the purpose of the business in writing gives the company a sense of direction.

   c) The mission makes clear "why we are here" and "where we are going."

   d) Without it a small business risks wandering aimlessly in the marketplace.

   e) The mission statement essentially sets the tone for the entire company.

3. Elements of a mission statement.

   a) What are the basic beliefs and values of the organization? What do we stand for?

   b) Who are the company's target customers?

   c) What are our basic products and services? What customer needs and wants do they satisfy?

   d) How can we better satisfy those needs and wants?

   e) Why should customers do business with us rather than with the competitor down the street (or across town, on the other coast, on the other side of the globe)?

   f) What constitutes value to our customers? How can we offer them better value?

   g) What is our competitive advantage? What is its source?

   h) In which markets (or market segments) will we choose to compete?

   i) Who are the key stakeholders in our company, and what effect do they have on it?

   j) What benefits should we be providing our customers five years from now?

   k) What business do we want to be in five years from now?

4. By answering these basic questions, the company will have a much clearer picture of what it is and what it wants to be.

   a) The firm's mission statement maybe its most essential and basic communication.

   b) To be effective, a mission statement must become a natural part of the organization, embodied in the minds, habits, attitudes, and decisions of everyone in the company every day.

5. A company may have a powerful competitive advantage, but it is wasted unless:

   a) the owner has communicated that advantage to workers, who, in turn, are working hard to communicate it to customers and potential customers.

   b) customers are recommending the company to their friends because they understand the benefits they are getting from it that they cannot get elsewhere.

C. Step 2: Define the firm's core competencies and its target market segment, and position the business to compete effectively

1. Core competencies are what sets a company apart from its competition.

2. Core competencies are a unique set of capabilities that a company develops in key operational areas, such as quality, service, innovation, team building, flexibility, responsiveness, and others that allow it to vault past competitors.

   a) A company is likely to build core competencies in no more than five or six areas.

   b) Competencies should be difficult for competitors to duplicate, and provide customers with some kind of perceived benefit.

c) Small companies' core competencies often have to do with the advantages of their size: agility, speed, closeness to their customers, superior service, and ability to innovate.

IN THE FOOTSTEPS OF AN ENTREPRENEUR - Grading the Mission Statement

SUMMARY

Alan Lewis' mission statement for his travel agency Grand Circle Travel [GCT]--the company's responsibilities to "our customers, our associates, our stakeholders, and our world." The company hit a huge growth spurt, going from 150 to 230 employees, making it much more difficult for Lewis to measure how well GCT was performing in regard to its mission. To gauge how well GCT measured up to the standards set forth in its mission statement, Lewis asked the people who knew best--his employees [or associates, as GTC calls them]--to grade the company's performance in each of the four major areas the mission statement covered.

Employees said that the company's rapid growth had created confusion about how the business worked, etc. Lewis established an open-book management program called BusinessWorks. Employees saw a need to improve the quality of customers' travel experiences. etc. Lewis created teams of employees to study existing processes and procedures and improve them. Associates noted loose financial controls and unnecessary expenses. Lewis established a new financial reporting system. Employees wanted to know more about which charitable organizations GTC was supporting. Lewis created a monthly newsletter.

1. What benefits does GTC reap from its associate report card?
   Answer - It reinforces the mission statement and makes the employees feel they have a part in the business. It helps Lewis to "fix" potential problems, i.e., loose financial controls before they become a problem.
2. What impact do you think this report card will have on the company? On its mission statement?
   Answer - It will increase employee commitment, provide a feedback loop that will foster continually improvement. It will make the company a better community citizen and model social responsibility. There will be an increase in customer satisfaction and profitability.
3. Use the World Wide Web to find examples of two organizational mission statements, one you think is effective and the other ineffective. Discuss the differences between the two mission statements. Explain in your own words why it is important for a company to have a mission statement.
   Answer - Students responses will vary based on their experience with the net.

---

3. The key to success is building core competencies (or identifying the ones a company already has) and then concentrating on them.
   a) Building a company's strategy around its core competencies allows the business to gain a sustainable competitive edge over its rivals and to ride its strategy to victory.
4. Table 2.1 defines a small company's core competencies.
   a) Successful small businesses know the market segment in which they compete and build and retain core competencies that directly contribute to their long-term effectiveness.
5. Key questions for creating or reinforcing their companies' core competencies.
   a) What are our target customers' characteristics (e.g., age, income, buying habits, location)?
   b) Why do they buy our goods or use our service?
   c) Which characteristics that our industry takes for granted should we eliminate?
   d) Which ones should we reduce well below the current industry standard?

e) Which ones should we raise well above the current industry standard?

f) What characteristics should we create that the industry has never offered?

g) What unique skills, knowledge, service, or other resources do we possess that would improve our target customers' lives?

h) How can we use those resources to offer value to customers that our competitors cannot? How loyal are they to their present suppliers?

i) What factors cause them to increase or decrease purchases?

j) To what extent does our market focus build on skills that we already have?

k) What skills must we develop to serve our customers in the future?

6. Market Segmentation.

  a) Market segmentation simply means carving up the mass market into smaller, more homogeneous units and then attacking each segment with a specific marketing strategy designed to appeal to its members.

    (1) Know who the firm's customers are, their characteristics, and their likes and dislikes.

    (2) Identify the characteristics of two or more groups of customers with similar needs or wants.

    (3) Develop a basis for segmenting the market--benefits sought, product usage, brand preference, purchase patterns, and so on--and use this basis to identify the various submarkets to enter.

    (4) Verify that the segments are large enough and have enough purchasing power to generate a profit.

    (5) Reach the market, a segment must be accessible.

7. Positioning.

  a) Positioning involves influencing customers' perceptions to create the desired image for the business and its goods and services.

    (1) Position by differentiating products from those of competitors using some characteristic important to the customer, such as price, quality, service, or performance.

    (2) Example - Bruce Wilson, Healthy Planet Products.

8. Proper positioning gives the small business a foundation for developing a competitive advantage.

  a) Lower prices are a common method of establishing a competitive advantage, but this can be especially dangerous for small businesses, which cannot rely on the economies of scale that larger businesses can.

  b) A smarter tactic for the small business owner is to rely on a natural advantage, such as the small firm's flexibility in reaching the market, a wider variety of customer services, or special knowledge of the good or service.

D. Step 3: Assess the Company's Strengths and Weaknesses

  1. Building a successful competitive strategy demands that a business magnify its strengths and overcome or compensate for its weaknesses.

    a) Strengths are positive internal factors that contribute to the accomplishment of a company's mission, goals, and objectives.

    b) Weaknesses are negative internal factors that inhibit the accomplishment of its mission, goals, and objectives.

  2. Identifying strengths and weaknesses helps the owner understand her business as it exists (or will exist).

  3. The key to building a successful strategy is to use the company's strengths as its foundation and to match those strengths against competitors' weaknesses.

4. One effective technique for taking this strategic inventory is to prepare a balance sheet of the company's strengths and weaknesses.
    a) See Table 2.2.

E. Step 4: Scan the Environment for Significant Opportunities and Threats
    1. Opportunities.
        a) Opportunities are positive external factors that the firm could employ to accomplish its objectives. The number of potential opportunities is limitless, so managers need analyze only factors significant to the business (probably two or three at most).
        b) When identifying opportunities, a business owner must pay close attention to new potential markets.
    2. Threats.
        a) Threats are negative external forces that inhibit the firm's ability to achieve its objectives.
        b) Threats to the business can take a variety of forms.
            (1) New competitors might enter the local market.
            (2) The government might issue a new mandate regulating a business activity.
            (3) There could be an economic recession; interest rates might rise.
            (4) Technological advances could make a company's product obsolete.
    3. Figure 2.1 illustrates that opportunities and threats are products of the interactions of forces, trends, and events outside the direct control of the business.
    4. Table 2.3 provides a form that enables business owners to take a strategic inventory of the opportunities and threats facing their companies.

F. Step 5: Identify the Key Success Factors
    1. In every industry there are controllable variables that determine the relative success of market participants.
    2. Identifying and manipulating these variables is how a small business gains a competitive advantage.
    3. Key success factors are relationships between a controllable variable (e.g., plant size, size of sales force, advertising expenditures, product packaging) and a critical factor influencing the firm's ability to compete.
        a) Which factors will be key depends on the industry.
        b) Many are based on cost factors, some are less tangible and less obvious, but just as important, such as product quality, services offered, store location, customer credit.
    4. Example restaurant owner identified key success factors.
        a) These controllable variables determine the ability of any restaurant in his market segment to compete.
    5. Table 2.4 presents a form to help the owner identify the most important success factors and their implications for the company.

G. Step 6: Analyze the Competition
    1. Keeping tabs on rivals' movements through competitive intelligence programs is a vital a strategic activity.
    2. The primary goals of a competitive intelligence program.
        a) Avoiding surprises from existing competitors' new strategies and tactics
        b) Identifying potential new competitors
        c) Improving reaction time to competitors' actions
        d) Anticipating rivals' next strategic moves
    3. Many small companies fail to gather competitive intelligence because their owners mistakenly assume that doing so is too costly or simply unnecessary.

4. A competitive intelligence exercise enables entrepreneurs to update their knowledge of competitors by answering the following questions:

    a) Who are your major competitors? Where are they located? (The Yellow Pages is a great place to start.)

    b) What distinctive competencies have they developed?

    c) How do their cost structures compare with yours? Their financial resources?

    d) How do they market their products and services?

    e) What do customers say about them? How do customers describe their products or services; their way of doing business; the additional services they supply?

    f) What are their key strategies?

    g) What are their strengths? How can your company surpass them?

    h) What are their primary weaknesses? How can your company capitalize on them?

    i) Are new competitors entering the business?

5. A small business owner can collect a great deal of information about competitors through low-cost methods including the following:

    a) Read industry trade publications for announcements from competitors.

    b) Ask questions of customers and suppliers.

    c) Attend trade shows and collect the competitors' sales literature.

    d) If appropriate, benchmark competitors' products against yours.

    e) Obtain credit reports from firms such as Dun & Bradstreet on each of your major competitors to evaluate their financial condition.

    f) Check out the resources of your local library, including articles, computerized databases, and on-line searches.

    g) Use the vast resources of the World Wide Web to learn more about your competitors.

6. A business owner can set up teams of managers and employees to evaluate each competitor and to make recommendations on specific strategic actions that will improve the firm's competitive position against each.

7. The owner can construct a competitive profile matrix for each market segment.

    a) First, list the key success factors identified in step 5 of the strategic planning process and to attach weights to them reflecting their relative importance.
        (1) See Table 2.5.

    b) Next, identify the company's major competitors and to rate each one (and your company) on each of the key success factors.

    c) If factor is a: Rating is:

If factor is a:	Rating is:
Major weakness	1
Minor weakness	2
Minor strength	3
Major strength	4

    d) Finally, simply multiply the weight by the rating for each factor to get a weighted score and then adds up each competitor's weighted scores to get a total weighted score. Table 2.5 shows a sample competitive profile matrix for a small company. The results should show which company is strongest, which is weakest, and which of the key success factors each one is best and worst at meeting. By carefully studying and interpreting the results, the small business owner can begin to envision the ideal strategy for building a competitive edge in her market segment.

    e) By this stage of the planning, the owner has begun to compare her firm's strengths with those of her competitors and to formulate ways of magnifying her strengths and exploiting their weaknesses. In other words, the entrepreneur is looking toward the future and planning ahead.

IN THE FOOTSTEPS OF AN ENTREPRENEUR - What's the Difference?

SUMMARY

The worst nightmare for many small retailers is the announcement that a large "category killer" retail store such as Home Depot, Wal-Mart, or Toys "R" Us is opening in their local market. Yet many of these small companies thrive in the shadow of the giants. Example of two small companies, one a small nursery and the other a small soft drink bottler.

The Nursery Josh and Michael Bracken's Nicholson-Hardie Nursery and Garden Center operates in an industry where giant retailers now control two-thirds of the $71 billion lawn-and-garden market. Opened in 1938 as a seed store and purchased in 1974 by the Bracken brothers' parents, Nicholson-Hardie grew until the 1980s, when the big chain stores began hurting its business. The two brothers realized that the only way their company could survive was to change its strategy. Their new strategy was to avoid taking on their larger rivals head-to-head. The Brackens began to define ways to set themselves apart. They do not even try to match the prices of the chain retailers. Instead, they stock more than 1,000 plant varieties, far more than the chains. The Brackens sell their extensive knowledge of plants. They even make house calls! The company's radio ads reinforce its image.

The Soft Drink Bottler Pierce Sears grew up helping his father and his grandfather in the family's Rockport, Massachusetts, soda-bottling business. Today Sears run the business alone. 79-cent bottles of Twin Lights collect dust on the bottom shelves of a few local stores, outflanked by a bevy of canned sodas, etc. Sears company is on the verge of being crushed by the rapid expansion and cutthroat competition. Critics of the bottling industry say the mass closings stemmed from bottlers' failure to change their businesses as their customers' tastes and habits shifted. And because their bottling volume is so small, drinks such as Twin Lights do not offer good value to bargain hunters used to purchasing Coke or Pepsi at big discounts.

1.   What similarities and differences exist between these two companies' competitive situations? In their strategic positions?
     Answer - Both faced competitors with economies of scale, both were in industries and served customers who had changed in their preferences. The nursery sought an upscale market, the bottler remained a commodity.
2.   Using the World Wide Web and other resources, develop a profile of the industries in which these two companies compete. What strategic changes would you suggest these entrepreneurs make?
     Answer - Students' responses will vary based on the web site they access. Basic principles would be to avoid price competition, differentiate their product; in the case of the bottle, probably reengineer his processes and modernized his plant.

H. Step 7. Create Company Goals and Objectives
    1. Business goals and objectives provide targets to aim for and provide a basis for evaluating company's performance.
        a) Creating goals and objectives is an essential part of the strategic management process.
    2. Goals.
        a) Goals are the broad, long-range attributes that a business seeks to accomplish; they tend to be general and sometimes even abstract.
        b) Goals are not intended to be specific enough for a manager to act on, but simply state the general level of accomplishment sought.
    3. Objectives.
        a) Objectives are specific targets of performance.

      b) Common objectives concern profitability, productivity, growth, efficiency, markets, financial resources, physical facilities, organizational structure, employee welfare, and social responsibility.

      c) Because some objectives might conflict with one another, the manager must establish priorities.

      d) Well-written objectives.

         (1) Are specific. Objectives should be quantifiable and precise. For example, "to increase retail sales by 12 percent and wholesale by 10 percent in the next fiscal year."

         (2) Are measurable. Managers should be able to plot the organization's progress toward its objectives.

         (3) Are assignable. Creating objectives without giving someone responsibility for accomplishing them is futile.

         (4) Are realistic yet challenging. Objectives must be within the reach of the organization.

         (5) Are timely. A time frame for achievement is important.

         (6) Are written down. The manager should make the number of objectives relatively small, from five to fifteen.

GAINING THE COMPETITIVE EDGE - The Power of Written Goals and Objectives

SUMMARY

Emmit Smith firmly believes in their power. The various businesses that Smith, the famous Dallas Cowboy running back, owns have a record for running past their. J.J Stupp founder of TableTalk, credits the success of her company to goal setting and objective achievement.

Successful goal setting requires an entrepreneur to:
- Dare to dream and then set your sights.
- Take the time to write down your goals and objectives.
- Make sure your targets are measurable.
- Take one step at a time toward your ultimate goal.
- Reward yourself for achieving success.
- Pause periodically to review your progress so that you can improve your future performance.
- Focus on the golden ring not on tile hole inside it.

1. Use the guidelines above to create a set of meaningful goals and objectives for a task you want to complete. What can you do this week [or today] that would have a positive impact on your long-term goal?
Answer - Students' responses will vary, but they should tie into the seven goal setting steps outlined above. Consider putting students into small groups to share their action plan for the week and to hold each accountable. Hold follow-up small group meetings one week later.

---

    4. The strategic planning process works best when managers and employees are actively involved jointly in setting objectives.

I. Step 8. Formulate Strategic Options and Select the Appropriate Strategies
    1. The next step is to evaluate strategic options and then prepare a game plan designed to achieve the business's objectives.
    2. Strategy.

a) A strategy is a road map of the actions the entrepreneur draws up to fulfill the firm's mission, goals, and objectives.
   (1) The mission, goals, and objectives spell out the ends.
   (2) The strategy defines the means for reaching them.

b) A strategy is the master plan that covers all of the major parts of the organization and ties them together into a unified whole.
   (1) The plan must be action-oriented.
   (2) Uses the company's core competencies as the springboard to success.

c) A successful strategy is comprehensive and well integrated.

3. The Entrepreneurial Strategy Matrix.

a) Matthew C. Sonfield and Robert N. Lussier developed a model using a four-cell matrix that outlines various strategic alternatives for entrepreneurs.
   (1) See Figure 2.2.

b) The matrix is built on two independent variables: innovation, the creation of something new and different; and risk, the probability of a major financial loss.

4. At the different combinations of innovation and risk levels (low to high), an entrepreneur will find that certain strategies will be more effective than others.

a) High Innovation, Low Risk. These ventures involve a truly novel idea that carries with it very little risk for an entrepreneur, usually because they require small amounts of start-up capital.
   (1) Software producer McAfee Associates, the leader in programs that prevent, detect, and cure computer viruses, is a company that fits into the I-r quadrant of the matrix.
   (2) Companies in high innovation, low risk situations tend to have a "first-mover advantage." Because they are often pioneers in a market, they tend to capture it before competitors can move in or, in some cases, before competitors are aware that a market exists.
   (3) Entrepreneurs should focus their strategic moves on keeping costs (and therefore risk) low and competitors out.
   (4) Acquiring patent protection when possible, establishing brand names, and using techniques to encourage customer loyalty are effective strategies for companies in this quadrant.

b) High Innovation, High Risk. These businesses also market highly innovative products or services, but the risk associated with them is high, often because the initial financial requirement is high or because competition in the market is stiff.
   (1) The strategic prescription--reduce the level of risk without sacrificing the ability to innovate.
   (2) Lowering risk might involve outsourcing operations with high investment requirements or operating expenses or forming a joint venture with an already established company.

c) Low Innovation, High Risk. The most common environment in which small companies operate. Most entrepreneurs launch conventional businesses in well-established industries. Innovation is minimal.
   (1) Amy Nye's company, AltiTunes Partner, LP.

d) Low Innovation, Low Risk. For many modern business start-ups, the investment required is low; therefore, the risk level is also low. In other cases, the investment required may be higher, but market demand is strong or competition is weak, creating low levels of risk.
   (1) Many service, part-time, and home-based businesses fall into this cell of the matrix.

(2) Dave Wiggins and American Wilderness Experience, a tiny $20,000 a year operation offering Western-style horseback vacations.

5.   Three Strategic Options.

  a)   In his classic book *Competitive Strategy*, Michael Porter defines these three strategies: cost leadership, differentiation, and focus.

6.   Cost Leadership.

  a)   A company pursuing a cost leadership strategy strives to be the lowest-cost producer relative to its competitors in the industry.

  b)   Low-cost leaders have a competitive advantage in reaching buyers whose primary purchase criterion is price, and they have the power to set the industry's price floor.

     (1) Such a strategy works well when buyers are sensitive to price changes.

     (2) When competing firms sell the same commodity products.

     (3) When companies can benefit from economies of scale.

  c)   The most successful cost leaders know where they have cost advantages over their competitors, and they use these as the foundation for their strategies.

  d)   Dangers in following a cost leadership strategy.

     (1) Sometimes, a company focuses exclusively on lower manufacturing costs without considering the impact of purchasing, distribution, or overhead costs.

     (2) Misunderstanding the firm's true cost drivers.

     (3) A firm may pursue a low-cost leadership strategy so zealously that it essentially locks itself out of other strategic choices.

7.   Differentiation.

  a)   A company following a differentiation strategy seeks to build customer loyalty by positioning its goods or services in a unique or different fashion.

  b)   There are many ways to create a differentiation strategy, but the key concept is to be special at something that is important to the customer.

     (1) If a small company can improve the product's (or service's) performance, reduce the customer's cost and risk of purchasing it, or both, it has the potential to differentiate.

  c)   The key to a successful differentiation strategy is to build it on a distinctive competence, something the small company is uniquely good at doing in comparison with its competitors.

     (1) Common bases for differentiation include superior customer service, special product features, complete product lines, instantaneous parts availability, absolute product reliability, supreme product quality, and extensive product knowledge.

     (2) To be successful, a differentiation strategy must create the perception of value in the customer's eyes.

  d)   There are risks in pursuing a differentiation strategy.

     (1) One danger is trying to differentiate a product or service on the basis of something that does not boost its performance or lower its cost to the buyer.

     (2) Another pitfall is overdifferentiating and charging so much that the company prices its products out of the market.

     (3) The final risk is focusing only on the physical characteristics of a product or service and ignoring important psychological factors: status, prestige, image, and customer service.

8.   Focus.

  a)   The principal idea of this strategy is to select one or more segments, identify customers' special needs, wants, and interests, and approach the customers with a good or a service designed to excel in meeting those needs, wants, and interests.

  b)   Focus strategies build on differences among market segments.

      c) A successful focus strategy depends on a small company's ability to identify the changing needs of its targeted customer group and to develop the skills required to serve them.

        (1) Rather than attempting to serve the total market, the focusing firm specializes in serving a specific target segment or niche.

        (2) A focus strategy is ideally suited to many small businesses, which often lack the resources to reach a national market.

      d) The most successful focusers build a competitive edge by concentrating on specific market niches and serving them better than any other competitor can.

        (1) Essentially, this strategy depends on creating value for the customer either by being the lowest-cost producer or by differentiating the product or service in a unique fashion, but doing it in a narrow target segment.

      e) Pursuing a focus strategy is not without risk.

        (1) Companies sometimes must struggle to capture a large enough share of a small market to be profitable.

        (2) There is also the danger that larger competitors will enter the market and erode market share.

        (3) Sometimes a company with a successful niche strategy gets distracted by its success and tries to branch out into other areas.

      f) An effective strategic plan identifies a complete set of success factors--financial, operating, and marketing--that, taken together, produce a competitive advantage for the small business.

   9. Strategy in Action.

      a) A business that has a well-defined strategic advantage can aggressively attempt to deepen its market penetration, especially if the business has achieved a "first-mover" advantage with little direct competition.

      b) Some firms use a "specialist" strategy in which they build a highly defensible market position through product uniqueness, or service, or knowledge that competitors cannot easily duplicate.

        (1) An example of this strategy is Red Adair, the world-famous fighter of oil well fires.

      c) Small companies develop strategies that exploit all of the competitive advantages of their size by:

        (1) responding quickly to customers' needs.

        (2) remaining flexible and willing to change.

        (3) continually searching for new emerging market segments.

        (4) building and defending market niches.

        (5) erecting "switching costs" through personal service and loyalty.

        (6) remaining entrepreneurial and willing to take risks and act with lightning speed.

        (7) constantly innovating

J. Step 9 Translate Strategic Plans into Action Plans

   1. To make the plan workable, the business owner should divide the plan into projects, carefully defining each one by the following:

      a) Purpose. What is the project designed to accomplish?

      b) Scope. Which areas of the company will be involved in the project?

      c) Contribution. How is the project related to other projects and to the overall strategic plan?

      d) Resource requirements. What human and financial resources are needed to complete the project successfully?

      e) Timing. Which schedules and deadlines will ensure project completion?

2. Once managers assign priorities to these projects, they can begin to implement the strategic plan by involving employees and delegating adequate authority to them.
3. Early involvement of the total workforce in the strategic management process is a luxury that larger businesses cannot achieve.
    a) It is important to remember that without committed, dedicated employees, an organization's strategies usually fail.

WIRED TO THE WEB - Bookstore Wars

SUMMARY

Across the country, the explosion of book super-stores has put intense pressure on small independent booksellers, threatening to squeeze them out of existence. The number of bookstore failures has increased in recent years, and the independents' share of the market has slipped. Yet, many independent bookstores are thriving in the face of the giants.

The most successful independents are analyzing their larger competitors to identify their weaknesses and then are focusing their resources in those areas. Because they are locally owned and operated, small bookstores are better at stocking books that are unique to a particular community or region. Other independents are settling successfully into niches and by focusing on just one category of book titles, these stores can offer their customers a wide selection of books of interest to them.

Virtually every small bookstore has at its disposal a powerful competitive weapon that often turns out to be a dandy giant slayer: customer service and lots of little "extras" that keep customers coming back.

The newest battle zone in the bookstore wars is in cyberspace. Amazon.com, billing itself as "the world's largest bookstore exists only on the World Wide Web.

1. What advice would you offer the owner of a small bookstore located in a town where one of the book superstores has just announced it will open an outlet?
    Answer - Students' responses should focus on differentiating or focus strategies, serving niches in ways large retailers can't afford to.
2. Visit Amazon.com's World Wide Web site at <http://www. amazon.com> and Barnes & Noble's site at <http://www. barnesandnoble.com>. What benefits do these companies' Web sites offer customers? What weaknesses do booksellers on the Web experience?
    Answer - The strengths are low price, variety, and convenience--shopping without leaving home or the dorm. The drawbacks are, you can't handle the merchandise, having to wait for the product, and the social experience involved in retail shopping.
3. What advice would you offer the owner of a small bookstore about conducting business on the World Wide Web?
    Answer - Students' responses should focus on management and marketing issues. Some students will get into web page design, which is valid, but not covered in the text. Making web sites easy to find and use, not to get into price competition, to still find a niche to serve, etc.

K. Step 10 Establish Accurate Controls
    1. Rarely, if ever, will the company's actual performance match stated objectives.
    2. Hence the need to control actual results that deviate from plans.
    3. The measures created in the control-planning process become the standards against which actual performance is compared.
    4. To control projects and keep them on schedule, employees must identify and track key performance indicators.

          a)   The source of these indicators is the operating data from the company's normal business activity.

          b)   Accounting, production, sales, inventory, and other operating records are primary sources of data the manager can use for controlling activities.

5.   Some companies are developing balanced scorecards--a set of measurements unique to a company that includes both financial and operational measures.

          a)   The premise behind such a scorecard is that relying on any single measure of company performance is dangerous.

          b)   The complexity of managing a business demands that an entrepreneur be able to see performance measures in several areas simultaneously.

6.   The balanced scorecard looks at a business from four important perspectives.

          a)   Figure 2.3.

7.   Customer perspective: how do customers see us?

          a)   Customers judge companies by at least four standards: time, quality, performance, and service.

8.   Internal business perspective: what must we excel at?

          a)   The internal factors that managers should focus on are those that have the greatest impact on customer satisfaction and retention and on company effectiveness and efficiency.

9.   Innovation and learning perspective: can we continue to improve and create value?

          a)   A company's ability to innovate, learn, and improve determines its future.

10. Financial perspective: how do we look to shareholders?

          a)   These measures focus on such factors as profitability, growth, and shareholder value.

          b)   On balanced scorecards, companies often break their financial goals into three categories: survival, success, and growth.

11. Figure 2.4 shows a sample-balanced scorecard for a hypothetical company, Electronic Circuits Inc. (ECI).

12. Although the balanced scorecard is a vital tool that helps managers keep their companies on track, it is also an important tool for changing behavior in an organization and for keeping everyone focused on what really matters.

L. Conclusion and Beginning

1.   The strategic planning process is an ongoing procedure that the small business owner must repeat.

2.   No small business should be burdened with an elaborate, detailed formal planning process that it cannot easily use.

3.   What does this strategic planning process lead to?

          a)   It teaches discipline that is important to his business's survival.

          b)   It helps the small business owner in learning about his business, his competitors, and, most importantly his customers.

4.   A recent survey of family businesses by Arthur Andersen Consulting and Mass Mutual Life Insurance Company found that just 30 percent of the companies had a written strategic plan.

Chapter Summary

◆ Understand the importance of strategic management to a small business.

    ■   Strategic planning, often ignored by small companies, is a crucial ingredient in business success. The planning process forces potential entrepreneurs to subject their ideas to an objective evaluation in the competitive market.

◆ Explain why and how a small business must create a competitive advantage in the market.

- The goal of developing a strategic plan is to create for the small company a competitive advantage--the aggregation of factors that sets the small business apart from its competitors and gives it a unique position in the market. Every small firm must establish a plan for creating a unique image in the minds of its potential customers.

♦ Develop a strategic plan for a business using the 10 steps in the strategic planning process. · Small businesses need a strategic planning process designed to suit their particular needs. It should be relatively short, be informal and not structured, encourage the participation of employees, and not begin with extensive objective setting. Linking the purposeful action of strategic planning to an entrepreneur's little ideas can produce results that shape the future.

  - Step 1. Develop a clear vision and translate it into a meaningful mission statement. Highly successful entrepreneurs are able to communicate their vision to those around them. The firm's mission statement answers the first question of any venture: What business am I in? The mission statement sets the tone for the entire company.

  - Step 2. Define the firm's core competencies and its target market segments, and position the business to compete effectively. Core competencies are a unique set of capabilities that a company develops in key operational areas, such as quality, service, innovation, team building, flexibility, responsiveness, and others that allow it to vault past competitors. They are what the company does best and are the focal point of the strategy. This step must identify target market segments and determine how to position the firm in those markets. The owner must identify some way to differentiate her business from its competitors.

  - Step 3. Assess the company's strengths and weaknesses. Strengths are positive internal factors; weaknesses are negative internal factors.

  - Step 4. Scan the environment for significant opportunities and threats facing the business. Opportunities are positive external options; threats are negative external forces.

  - Step 5. Identify the key factors for success in the business. In every business, key factors determine the success of the firms in it, so they must be an integral part of a company' strategy. Key success factors are relationships between a controllable variable (e.g., plant size, size of sales force, advertising expenditures, product packaging) and a critical factor influencing the firm's ability to compete in the market.

  - Step 6. Analyze the competition. Business owners should know their competitors' businesses almost as well as they know their own. A competitive profile matrix is a helpful tool for analyzing competitors' strengths and weaknesses.

  - Step 7. Create company goals and objectives. Goals are the broad, long-range attributes that the firm seeks to accomplish. Objectives are quantifiable and more precise; they should be specific, measurable, assignable, realistic, timely, and written down. The process works best when subordinate managers and employees are actively involved.

  - Step 8. Formulate strategic options and select the appropriate strategies. A strategy is the game plan the firm will use to achieve its objectives and mission. It must center on establishing for the firm the key success factors identified earlier.

  - Step 9. Translate strategic plans into action plans. No strategic plan is complete until the owner puts it into action.

  - Step 10. Establish accurate controls. Actual performance rarely, if ever, matches plans exactly. Operating data from the business serve as guideposts for detecting deviations from plans. Such information is helpful when plotting future strategies.

  - The strategic planning process does not end with these 10 steps; rather, it is an ongoing process.

♦ Understand the Entrepreneurial Strategy Matrix and how to apply it.

  - The Entrepreneurial Strategy Matrix helps entrepreneurs develop appropriate strategies given the different levels of risk and innovation associated with their businesses.

♦ Discuss the characteristics of three basic strategies: low-cost, differentiation, and focus.

- Three basic strategic options are cost leadership, differentiation, and focus. A company pursuing a cost leadership strategy strives to be the lowest-cost producer relative to its competitors in the industry.
- A company following a differentiation strategy seeks to build customer loyalty by positioning its goods or services in a unique or different fashion. In other words, the firm strives to be better than its competitors at something that customers value.
- A focus strategy recognizes that not all markets are homogeneous. The principal idea of this strategy is to select one or more segments; identify customers' special needs, wants, and interests; and approach them with a good or service designed to excel in meeting those needs, wants, and interests. Focus strategies build on differences among market segments.

♦ Understand the importance of controls such as the balanced scorecard in the planning process.
- Just as a pilot in command of a jet cannot fly safely by focusing on a single instrument, an entrepreneur cannot manage a company by concentrating on a single measurement. The balanced scorecard is a set of measurements unique to a company that includes both financial and operational measures and gives managers a quick yet comprehensive picture of the company's total performance.

Discussion Questions

1. Why is strategic planning important to a small company?
    Answer - Companies lacking clear strategies may achieve some short-term success, but as competition stiffens or an unanticipated threat arises, they usually "hit the wall" and fold. Without a basis for differentiating itself, the best a company can hope for is mediocrity. Any business not thinking and acting strategically is extremely vulnerable to global competitors. Every business is exposed to the forces of a rapidly changing competitive environment, and in the future, small business executives can expect even greater uncertainty. The biggest change business owners face is the shift in the world's economy from a base of financial to intellectual capital. It is a blueprint for matching the company's strengths and weaknesses to the opportunities and threats in the environment.

2. What is a competitive advantage? Why is it important for a small business to establish one?
    Answer - The goal of developing a strategic plan is to create for the small company a competitive advantage. The aggregation of factors that sets the small business apart from its competitors and gives it a unique position in the market. It helps the small business focus on its best markets and develop the strengths that will help it dominate that market.

3. What are the steps in the strategic management process?
    Answer - Strategic planning is a continuous process that consists of 10 steps. Step 1. Develop a clear vision and translate it into a meaningful mission statement. Step 2. Define the firm's core competencies and target market segment, and position the business to compete effectively. Step 3. Assess the company's strengths and weaknesses. Step 4. Scan the environment for significant opportunities and threats. Step 5. Identify the key factors for success. Step 6. Analyze the competition. Step 7. Create company goals and objectives. Step 8. Formulate strategic options and select the appropriate strategies. Step 9. Translate strategic plans into action plans. Step 10. Establish accurate controls.

4. What are strengths, weaknesses, opportunities, and threats? Give an example of each.
    Answer - Strengths are positive internal factors that contribute to the accomplishment of a company's mission, goals, and objectives. Weaknesses are negative internal factors that inhibit the accomplishment of its mission, goals, and objectives. The key to building a successful strategy is to use the company's strengths as its foundation and to match those strengths against competitors'

weaknesses. Opportunities are positive external factors that the firm could employ to accomplish its objectives. The number of potential opportunities is limitless, so managers need analyze only factors significant to the business (probably two or three at most). Threats are negative external forces that inhibit the firm's ability to achieve its objectives.

5. Explain the characteristics of effective objectives. Why is setting objectives important?
    Answer - Business goals and objectives provide targets to aim for and provide a basis for evaluating company's performance. Goals are the broad, long-range attributes that a business seeks to accomplish; they tend to be general and sometimes even abstract. Objectives are specific targets of performance.

6. What are business strategies?
    Answer - A strategy is a road map of the actions the entrepreneur draws up to fulfill the firm's mission, goals, and objectives. A strategy is the master plan that covers all of the major parts of the organization and ties them together into a unified whole.

7. Explain the concept of the Entrepreneurial Strategy Matrix and how entrepreneurs can use it to develop appropriate strategies.
    Answer - Matthew C. Sonfield and Robert N. Lussier developed a model using a four-cell matrix that outlines various strategic alternatives for entrepreneurs. See Figure 2.2. The matrix is built on two independent variables: innovation, the creation of something new and different, and risk, the probability of a major financial loss. At the different combinations of innovation and risk levels (low to high), an entrepreneur will find that certain strategies will be more effective than others.

8. Describe the three basic strategies available to small companies. Under what conditions is each most successful?
    Answer - In his classic book *Competitive Strategy*, Michael Porter defines these three strategies: cost leadership, differentiation, and focus. A company pursuing a cost leadership strategy strives to be the lowest-cost producer relative to its competitors in the industry. A company following a differentiation strategy seeks to build customer loyalty by positioning its goods or services in a unique or different fashion. Focus, the principal idea of this strategy is to select one or more segments, identify customers' special needs, wants, and interests, and approach the customers with a good or a service designed to excel in meeting those needs, wants, and interests.

9. How is the controlling process related to the planning process?
    Answer - Rarely, if ever, will the company's actual performance match stated objectives. Hence the need to control actual results that deviate from plans. The measures created in the control-planning process become the standards against which actual performance is compared. To control projects and keep them on schedule, employees must identify and track key performance indicators.

10. What is a balanced scorecard? What value does it offer entrepreneurs who are evaluating the success of their current strategies?
    Answer - The balanced scorecard looks at a business from four important perspectives; Figure 2.3 lists them. Although the balanced scorecard is a vital tool that helps managers keep their companies on track, it is also an important tool for changing behavior in an organization and for keeping everyone focused on what really matters.
    - Customer perspective: how do customers see us?
    - Internal business perspective: what must we excel at?
    - Innovation and learning perspective: can we continue to improve and create value?
    - Financial perspective: how do we look to shareholders?

Step into the Real World

1. Choose an entrepreneur in your community and interview him or her. Does the company have a strategic plan? A mission statement? Why or why not? What does the owner consider the company's strengths and weaknesses to be? What opportunities and threats does the owner perceive? What image is the owner trying to create for the business? Does the owner think the effort has been successful? (Do you agree?) Which of the generic competitive strategies is the company following? Who are the company's primary competitors? On a scale of 1 to 10, how does the owner rate his or her chances for success in the future?

2. Using the resources on your campus (such as magazines in the library focusing on entrepreneurship and small business or the World Wide Web) or in your community (such as your knowledge of local businesses), find an example of a company in each of the four quadrants in the Entrepreneurial Strategy Matrix. Prepare a brief report on each company explaining why it fits in a particular cell. What strategic recommendations would you make to each business owner?

3. Contact a local entrepreneur and help him or her devise a balanced scorecard for his or her company. What goals did you and the owner establish in each of the four perspectives? What measures did you use to judge progress toward those goals?

4. Contact the owner of a small business that competes directly with an industry giant (such as Home Depot, Wal-Mart, Barnes & Noble, or others). What does the owner see as his or her competitive advantage? How does the business communicate this advantage to its customers? What competitive strategy is the owner using? How successful is it? What changes would you suggest the owner make?

5. Use the strategic tools provided in this chapter to help a local small business owner discover his or her firm's strengths, weaknesses, opportunities, and threats; identify the relevant key success factors; and analyze its competitors. Help the owner devise a strategy for success for his or her business.

Chapter 3 Choosing a Form of Ownership

Nothing in fine print is ever good.
Anonymous

There is no trap so deadly as the trap you set for yourself.
Phillip Marlowe

Teaching Objectives

Students will be able to:
1. Describe the advantages and disadvantages of the sole proprietorship.
2. Describe the advantages and disadvantages of the partnership.
3. Describe the advantages and disadvantages of the corporation.
4. Describe the features of the alternative forms of ownership such as the S corporation, the limited liability company, and the joint venture.

Instructor's Outline

I. Introduction
  A. One of the first decisions
    1. Selecting the form of ownership for the new business venture.
    2. Entrepreneurs give little thought to choosing a form of ownership and simply select the form that is most popular.
    3. Changing from one form of ownership to another once a business is up and running can be difficult, expensive, and complicated, so it is important for an entrepreneur to make the right choice at the outset.
    4. There may be a form of ownership that is best suited to each entrepreneur's circumstances.
    5. Considerations that every entrepreneur should review before choosing the form of ownership
      a) Tax considerations. Because of the graduated tax rates under each form of ownership, the government's constant tinkering with the tax code, and the year-to-year fluctuations in a company's income, an entrepreneur should calculate the firm's tax bill under each ownership option every year.
      b) Liability exposure. Certain forms of ownership offer business owners greater protection from personal liability due to financial problems, faulty products, and a host of other difficulties.
      c) Start-up and future capital requirements. Forms of ownership differ in their ability to raise start-up capital.
      d) Control. Entrepreneurs must decide early on how much control they are willing to sacrifice in exchange for help from other people in building a successful business.
      e) Managerial ability. If an entrepreneur lack skills or experience in certain areas, he/she may need to select a form of ownership that allows him/her to bring into the company people who possess those skills and experience.
      f) Business goals. How big and how profitable an entrepreneur plans for the business to become will influence the form of ownership chosen.
      g) Management succession plans. Some forms of ownership make this transition much smoother than others. In other cases, when the owner dies, so does the business.
      h) Cost of formation. Some forms of ownership are much more costly and involved to create than others. Entrepreneurs must weigh carefully the benefits and the costs of the particular form they choose.

6. As a business grows and changes, the founders may discover the need to modify the form of ownership.
7. As their companies' needs change, the entrepreneurs behind them must reexamine the factors that determine the "best" form of ownership for them and be willing to change when necessary.
8. Business owners have traditionally had three major forms of ownership from which to choose: the sole proprietorship, the partnership, and the corporation.
   a) See Figure 3.1.
   b) In recent years, various hybrid forms of business ownership have emerged; the S corporation, the limited liability company, and the joint venture.

II. The Sole Proprietorship
   A. Defined
      1. The sole proprietorship is a business owned and managed by one individual. This form of ownership is by far the most popular.
      2. Approximately 74 percent of all businesses in the United States are sole proprietorships.

   B. Advantages of a Sole Proprietorship
      1. Simple to create. One attractive feature of a proprietorship is the ease and speed of its formation. An entrepreneur can complete all of the necessary paperwork in a single day.
      2. Least costly form of ownership to establish. It is generally the least expensive form of ownership to establish, as there is no need to create and file the legal documents that are recommended for partnerships and are required for corporations.
         a) In many jurisdictions, entrepreneurs planning to conduct business under a trade name are usually required to acquire a Certificate of Doing Business under an Assumed Name from the secretary of state.
         b) In a proprietorship, the owner is the business.
      3. Profit incentive. Once the owner has paid all of the company's expenses, she can keep the remaining profits (less taxes, of course).
      4. Total decision-making authority. The sole proprietor is in total control of operations and can respond quickly to changes. The ability to respond quickly is an asset in a rapidly shifting market.
      5. No special legal restrictions. The proprietorship is the least regulated form of business ownership.
      6. Easy to discontinue. If the entrepreneur decides to discontinue operations, he can terminate the business quickly, even though he will still be liable for all of the business's outstanding debts and obligations.

   C. Disadvantages of a Sole Proprietorship
      1. Unlimited personal liability. The sole proprietor is personally liable for all of the business's debts.
      2. Limited access to capital. Many proprietors have already put all they have into their businesses and have used their personal resources as collateral on existing loans, so it is difficult for them to borrow additional funds.
      3. Limited skills and abilities. A sole proprietor may not have the wide range of skills running a successful business requires. Many business failures occur because owners lack skills, knowledge, and experience in areas that are vital to business success.
      4. Feelings of isolation. Running a business alone allows an entrepreneur maximum flexibility, but it also creates feelings of isolation most small business owners report that they sometimes feel alone and frightened when they must make decisions knowing that they have nowhere to turn for advice or guidance.

5. Lack of continuity for the business. If the proprietor dies, retires, or becomes incapacitated, the business automatically terminates.

GAINING THE COMPETITIVE EDGE - What's in a Name?

SUMMARY

Aron Benon recently changed his flower shop's name from The French Flower Market to Floral and Hardy, and the impact amazed him. Sales immediately picked up. The right name for a company can convey exactly what the business does, create the right image in customers' minds, and deliver a subtle message about its unique features. For small companies, which often lack the financial resources to embark on costly advertising campaigns, the right business name can be a powerful tool.

- How can you find the perfect name for your business?
- Decide what you want your business name to convey about your company.
- Conduct a brainstorming session.
- Pick a name that will be an effective marketing tool.
- Test the name on people before you commit to it.
- Once you find a suitable name, conduct a fictitious name search to make sure that no one else in your jurisdiction has already claimed it.

1. Review the following company names to see if you can figure out what businesses they are in?

Name	Business
Salvador Deli	_____
Bait and Tackle	_____
Tender Lubing Care	_____
Wok and Roll	_____
Hair It Is	_____
The Filling Station	_____
Blazing Salads	_____
Hannah and Her Sissors	_____
The Ferret and Firkin	_____

Answer - delicatessen, lingerie shop, auto service center, Chinese takeout restaurant, hairstyling salon, dental center, vegetarian restaurant, hairstyling salon, and British pub.

III. The Partnership
   A. Defined
       1. A partnership is an association of two or more people who co-own a business for the purpose of making a profit. In a partnership the co-owners (partners) share the business's assets, liabilities, and profits according to the terms of a previously established partnership agreement.
       2. The law does not require a written partnership agreement (also known as the articles of partnership), but it is wise to work with an attorney to develop one.
           a) The partnership agreement is a document that states in writing all of the terms of operating the partnership for the protection of each partner involved.
           b) Every partnership should be based on a written agreement.
       3. When no partnership agreement exists, the Uniform Partnership Act governs the partnership, but its provisions may not be as favorable as a specific agreement hammered out among the partners.
       4. Probably the most important feature of the partnership agreement is that it addresses in advance sources of conflict that could result in partnership battles and the dissolution of a business that could have been successful.

5. Unfortunately, the tendency for partners just starting out is to ignore writing a partnership agreement as they ride the emotional high of launching a company together.
6. The standard partnership agreement will likely include the following:
   a) Name of the partnership.
   b) Purpose of the business. What is the reason the partners created the business?
   c) Domicile of the business. Where will the principle business be located?
   d) Duration of the partnership. How long will the partnership last?
   e) Names of the partners and their legal addresses.
   f) Contributions of each partner to the business, at the creation of the partnership and later. This would include each partner's investment in the business.
   g) Agreement on how the profits or losses will be distributed.
   h) Agreement on salaries or drawing rights against profits for each partner.
   i) Procedure for expansion through the addition of new partners.
   j) Distribution of the partnership's assets if the partners voluntarily dissolve the partnership.
   k) Sale of partnership interest. How can partners sell their interests in the business?
   l) Absence or disability of one of the partners.
   m) Voting rights. In many partnerships, partners have unequal voting power. The partners may base their voting fights on their financial or managerial contributions to the business.
   n) Decision-making authority. When can partners make decisions on their own, and when must other partners be involved?
   o) Financial authority. Which partners are authorized to sign checks, and how many signatures are required to authorize bank transactions?
   p) Handling tax matters. The Internal Revenue Service requires partnerships to designate one person to be responsible for handling the partnership's tax matters.
   q) Alterations or modifications of the partnership agreement. As a business grows and changes, partners often find it necessary to update their original agreement.

B. The Uniform Partnership Act
   1. The Uniform Partnership Act (UPA) codifies the body of law dealing with partnerships in the United States.
   2. Under the UPA, the three key elements of any partnership are common ownership interest in a business, sharing the business's profits and losses, and the fight to participate in managing the operation of the partnership.
   3. Under the act, each partner has the right to:
      a) Share in the management and operations of the business.
      b) Share in any profits the business might earn from operations.
      c) Receive interest on additional advances made to the business.
      d) Be compensated for expenses incurred in the name of the partnership.
      e) Have access to the business's books and records.
      f) Receive a formal accounting of the partnership's business affairs.
   4. The UPA also sets forth the partners' general obligation. Each partner is obligated to:
      a) Share in any losses sustained by the business.
      b) Work for the partnership without salary.
      c) Submit differences that may arise in the conduct of the business to majority vote or arbitration.
      d) Give the other partner complete information about all business affairs.
      e) Give a formal accounting of the partnership's business affairs.
   5. A partnership is based above all else on mutual trust and respect.

C. Advantages of the Partnership

1. Easy to establish. Like the proprietorship, the partnership is easy and inexpensive to establish. In most states, partners must file a Certificate for Conducting Business As Partners if the business is run under a trade name.

2. Complementary skills. In successful partnerships, the parties' skills and abilities complement one another, strengthening the company's managerial foundation.

3. Division of profits. The partnership agreement should articulate the nature of each partner's contribution and proportional share of the profits. If the partners fail to create an agreement, the UPA says that the partners share equally in the partnership's profits, even if their original capital contributions are unequal.

4. Larger pool of capital. The partnership form of ownership can significantly broaden the pool of capital available to a business. Undercapitalization is a common cause of business failures.

5. Ability to attract limited partners. Every partnership must have at least one general partner (although there is no limit on the number of general partners a business can have).

    a) General partners have unlimited personal liability for the company's debts and obligations and are expected to take an active role in managing the business.

    b) Limited partners, on the other hand, cannot take an active role in the operation of the company. They have limited personal liability for the company's debts and obligations. Essentially, limited partners are financial investors who do not participate in the day-to-day affairs of the partnership.

6. Little governmental regulation.

7. Flexibility. Partnerships can generally react quickly to changing market conditions, because no giant organization stifles quick and creative responses to new opportunities.

8. Taxation. The partnership itself is not subject to federal taxation. The partnership, like the proprietorship, avoids the "double taxation" disadvantage associated with the corporate form of ownership.

D. Disadvantages of the Partnership

1. Unlimited liability of at least one partner. At least one member of every partnership must be a general partner. The general partner has unlimited personal liability, even though he is often the partner with the least personal resources.

2. Capital accumulation. It is generally not as effective as the corporate form of ownership, which can raise capital by selling shares of ownership to outside investors.

3. Difficulty in disposing of partnership interest without dissolving the partnership. Often, a partner is required to sell his interest to the remaining partner. Even if the original agreement contains such a requirement and clearly delineates how the value of each partner's ownership will be determined, there is no guarantee that the other partners will have the financial resources to buy the seller's interest.

4. Lack of continuity. Partners can make provisions in the partnership agreement to avoid dissolution due to death if all parties agree to accept as partners those who inherit the deceased's interest.

5. Potential for personality and authority conflicts. Being in a partnership is much like being married. Making sure partners' work habits, goals, ethics, and general business philosophy are compatible is an important step in avoiding a nasty business divorce. The demise of many partnerships can often be traced to interpersonal conflicts and the lack of a partnership agreement for resolving those conflicts.

6. The law of agency binds partners. A partner is like a spouse in that decisions made by one, in the name of the partnership, bind all. Each partner is an agent for the business and can legally bind the other partners to a business agreement.

E. Dissolution and Termination of Partnership
1. Partnership dissolution is not the same as partnership termination.
    a) Dissolution occurs when a general partner ceases to be associated with the business.
    b) Termination is the final act of winding up the partnership as a business. Termination occurs after the partners have expressed their intent to cease operations and all affairs of the partnership have been concluded.

GAINING THE COMPETITIVE EDGE - How to Avoid a Business Divorce

SUMMARY
Co-owners of businesses are very much like marriage partners. Unfortunately, like some marriages, business relationships can end in divorce. Although every business dispute is unique, most have one common element: no written agreement spelling out the fights, duties, privileges, and obligations of the owners. In a start-ups early phases, co-founders are immersed in details and believe that they can work out any disputes that arise; after all, that's what friends do, right?

How can co-owners avoid such disputes?
1. Make sure that you and your business partners have common business objectives.
2. Divide responsibilities on the basis of ability and interest and stick to the agreement.
3. Share and share alike.
4. Don't lie. Resist the temptation to "protect" the other owners from bad news.
5. Get it in writing. Avoid the tendency to go into business with nothing more than high hopes and a handshake.
6. Realize that conflict will occur. Conflict is a natural part of any business relationship; co-owners will never agree on everything.

How do you know when it's time to leave? One counselor suggests asking yourself the following questions:
▪ Do you and your co-owners still share the goals that brought you together?
▪ Have you resolved difficult problems before?
▪ Do you still basically respect and trust each other?
▪ When you imagine the future, does it seem brighter if you see yourself working with your partners than without them?

If the answer to at least three of these questions is yes, the co-owners can probably salvage their relationship.

---

2. Dissolution occurs as a result of one or more of the following events:
    a) Expiration of a time period or completion of the project undertaken as delineated in the partnership agreement.
    b) Expressed wish of any general partner to cease operation.
    c) Expulsion of a partner under the provisions of the agreement.
    d) Withdrawal, retirement, insanity, or death of a general partner (except when the partnership agreement provides for a method of continuation).
    e) Bankruptcy of the partnership or of any general partner.
    f) Admission of a new partner resulting in the dissolution of the old partnership and establishment of a new partnership.
    g) Any event that makes it unlawful for the partnership to continue operations or for any general partner to participate in the partnership.

h) A judicial decree that a general partner is insane or permanently incapacitated, making performance or responsibility under the partnership agreement impossible.

i) Mounting losses that make it impractical for the business to continue.

j) Impropriety or improper behavior of any general partner that reflects negatively on the business.

F. Limited Partnerships

1. A limited partnership, which is a modification of a general partnership, is composed of at least one general partner and at least one limited partner.

2. In a limited partnership the general partner is treated, under the law, exactly as in a general partnership. Limited partners are treated as investors in the business venture, and they have limited liability. They can lose only the amount they have invested in the business.

3. Most states have ratified the Revised Uniform Limited Partnership Act. To form a limited partnership, the partners must file a Certificate of Limited Partnership in the state in which the limited partnership plans to conduct business.

4. The Certificate of Limited Partnership should include:

a) The name of the limited partnership.

b) The general character of its business.

c) The address of the office of the firm's agent authorized to receive summonses or other legal notices.

d) The name and business address of each partner, specifying which ones are general partners and which are limited partners.

e) The amount of cash contributions actually made, and agreed to be made in the future, by each partner.

f) A description of the value of noncash contributions made or to be made by each partner.

g) The times at which additional contributions are to be made by any of the partners.

h) Whether and under what conditions a limited partner has the right to grant limited partner status to an assignee of his or her interest in the partnership.

i) If agreed upon, the time or the circumstances when a partner may withdraw from the firm (unlike the withdrawal of a general partner, the withdrawal of a limited partner does not automatically dissolve a limited partnership).

j) It agreed upon, the amount of, or the method of determining, the funds to be received by a withdrawing partner.

k) Any right of a partner to receive distributions of cash or other property from the firm, and the times and circumstances for such distributions.

l) The time or circumstances when the limited partnership is to be dissolved.

m) The rights of the remaining general partners to continue the business after withdrawal of a general partner.

n) Any other matters the partners want to include.

5. Limited partners can make management suggestions to the general partners, inspect the business, and make copies of business records.

6. A limited partner is, of course, entitled to a share of the business's profits as agreed on and specified in the Certificate of Limited Partnership.

7. The primary disadvantage of limited partnerships is the complexity and the cost of establishing them.

G. Master Limited Partnerships

1. A relatively new form of business structure, master limited partnerships (MLPs), are just like regular limited partnerships, except their shares are traded on stock exchanges.

    2. They provide most of the same advantages to investors as a corporation--including limited liability.

    3. Master limited partnership profits typically must be divided among thousands of partners.

H. Limited Liability Partnerships

    1. Many states now recognize limited liability partnerships (LLPs) in which all partners in the business are limited partners, having only limited liability for the debts and obligations of the partnership. Most states restrict LLPs to certain types of professionals such as attorneys, physicians, dentists, accountants, and others. Just as with any limited partnership, the partners must file a Certificate of Limited Partnership in the state in which the partnership plans to conduct business. Also, like every partnership, an LLP does not pay taxes; its income is passed through to the limited partners, who pay taxes on their shares of the company's net income.

IV. The Corporation

  A. Definition

    1. The Supreme Court has defined a corporation as "an artificial being, invisible, intangible, and existing only in contemplation of the law."

      a) It is the most complex of the three major forms of business ownership.

      b) It is a separate entity apart from its owners and may engage in business, make contracts, sue and be sued, and pay taxes.

      c) Because the life of the corporation is independent of its owners, the shareholders can sell their interest in the business without affecting its continuation.

    2. Corporations (also known as C corporations) are creations of the state.

      a) When a corporation is founded, it accepts the regulations and restrictions of the state in which it is incorporated and any other state in which it chooses to do business.

      b) A corporation doing business in the state in which it is incorporated is a domestic corporation.

      c) When a corporation conducts business in another state, that state considers it to be a foreign corporation.

      d) Corporations that are formed in other countries but do business in the United States are alien corporations.

    3. Corporations have the power to raise large amounts of capital by selling shares of ownership to outside investors, but many corporations have only a handful of shareholders.

      a) Publicly held corporations are those that have a large number of shareholders, and their stock is usually traded on one of the large stock exchanges.

      b) Closely held corporations are those whose shares are in the control of a relatively small number of people, often family members, relatives, or friends. Their stock is not traded on any stock exchange.

    4. In general, a corporation must report annually its financial operations to its home state's attorney general.

      a) There are substantially more reporting requirements for a corporation than for the other forms of ownership.

  B. Requirements for Incorporation

    1. Most states allow entrepreneurs to incorporate without the assistance of an attorney.

      a) In some states, the application process is complex, and the required forms are confusing.

b) The price for filing incorrectly can be high.

2. Once the owners decide to form a corporation, they must choose the state in which to incorporate.

    a) States differ--sometimes dramatically--in the requirements they place on the corporations they charter and in how they treat corporations chartered in other states.

3. Every state requires a Certificate of Incorporation or charter to be filed with the secretary of state.

    a) The corporation's name. Different from any other firm in that state to avoid confusion or deception and include a term such as corporation, incorporated, company, or limited to notify the public that they are dealing with a corporation.

    b) The corporation's statement of purpose. The incorporators must state in general terms the intended nature of the business.

    c) The corporation's time horizon. Most corporations are formed with no specific termination date; they are formed "for perpetuity." However, it is possible to incorporate for a specific duration (e.g., 50 years).

    d) Names and addresses of the incorporators. The incorporators must be identified in the articles of incorporation and are liable under the law to attest that all information in the articles of incorporation is correct.

    e) Place of business. The post office address of the corporation's principal office must be listed.

    f) Capital stock authorization. The articles of incorporation must include the amount and class (or type) of capital stock the corporation wants to be authorized to issue.

    g) Capital required at the time of incorporation. Some states require a newly formed corporation to deposit in a bank a specific percentage of the stock's par value before incorporating.

    h) Provisions for preemptive rights, if any, that are granted to stockholders.

    i) Restrictions on transferring share. Many closely held corporations require shareholders interested in selling their stock to offer it first to the corporation. (Shares the corporation itself owns are called treasury stock.)

    j) Names and addresses of the officers and directors of the corporation.

    k) Rules under which the corporation will operate. Bylaws are the rules and regulations the officers and directors establish for the corporation's internal management and operation.

4. Once incorporation is approved and the fees are paid, the approved articles of incorporation become its charter.

    a) The next order of business is to hold an organizational meeting for the stockholders to formally elect directors, who, in turn, will appoint the corporate officers.

C. Advantages of the Corporation

1. Limited liability of stockholders. The primary reason most entrepreneurs choose to incorporate is to gain the benefit of limited liability, which means that investors can limit their liability to the total amount of their investment.

    a) This legal protection of personal assets beyond the business is of critical concern to many potential investors.

    b) Courts are increasingly holding entrepreneurs personally liable for environmental, pension, and legal claims against their corporations--much to the surprise of the owners, who chose the corporate form of ownership to shield themselves from such liability.

        c) Courts will pierce the corporate veil and hold owners liable for the company's debts and obligations if the owners deliberately commit criminal or negligent acts when handling corporate business.

        d) Corporate shareholders most commonly lose their liability protection, however, because owners and officers have commingled corporate funds with their personal funds.

2. Ability to attract capital.
    a) Corporations have proved to be the most effective form of ownership for accumulating large amounts of capital.

3. Ability to continue indefinitely.
    a) Unless limited by its charter, a corporation is a separate legal entity and can continue indefinitely.

4. Transferable ownership.
    a) If stockholders so desire, they may transfer their shares through sale or bequeath to someone else.

D. Disadvantages of the Corporation

1. Cost and time involved in the incorporation process. Creating a corporation can cost between $500 and $2,500, typically averaging around $1,000.

2. Double taxation. Because a corporation is a separate legal entity, it must pay taxes on its net income to the federal, most state, and some local governments before issuing any net income as dividends.
    a) Then, stockholders must pay taxes on the dividends they receive from these same profits at the individual tax rate.
    b) Thus, a corporation's profits are taxed twice.

GAINING THE COMPETITIVE EDGE - How to Avoid Corporate Woes

SUMMARY

The main reason entrepreneurs choose the corporate form of ownership is to avoid having unlimited personal liability for their companies' debts. Some entrepreneurs, however, have discovered that their limited liability protection crumbles if they fail to maintain certain standards of behavior. Courts call it "piercing the corporate veil" and will hold shareholders personally responsible for the debts and obligations of the corporation. For instance, if an individual forms a corporation for fraudulent purposes; if they form the corporation without sufficient capital to operate; if they fail to observe corporate formalities; or if they fail to keep separate the corporation's assets and their personal assets, they can be and have been held liable by the courts.

To avoid problems entrepreneurs need to:
- File all of the reports and pay all of the necessary fees required by the state in a timely manner.
- Hold annual meetings to elect officers and directors.
- Keep minutes of every meeting of the officers and directors.
- Make sure that the corporation's board of directors makes all major decisions.
- Make it clear that the business is a corporation by having all officers sign contracts, loan agreements purchase orders and other legal documents in the corporation's name rather than in their own names.
- Keep corporate assets and the personal assets of the owners separate.

3. Potential for diminished managerial incentives.
   a) Because they created their companies and often have most of their personal wealth tied up in them, entrepreneurs have an intense interest in ensuring their success and are willing to make sacrifices for their businesses.
   b) Professional managers an entrepreneur brings in to help run the business as it grows do not always have the same degree of interest in or loyalty to the company.
4. Legal requirements and regulatory red tape.
   a) Corporations are subject to more legal and financial requirements than other forms of ownership. Managers may be required to submit some major decisions to the stockholders for approval. Corporations that are publicly held must file quarterly and annual reports with the Securities and Exchange Commission (SEC).
5. Potential loss of control by the founders.
   a) When entrepreneurs sell shares of ownership in their companies, they relinquish some control, especially when they need large capital infusions for start-up or growth.

E. The Professional Corporation
   1. A professional corporation is designed to offer professionals such as lawyers, doctors, dentists, accountants, and others the advantage of the corporate form of ownership.
   2. It is ideally suited for licensed professionals, who must always be concerned about malpractice lawsuits, because it offers limited liability.
   3. They often are identified by the abbreviation P.C. (professional corporation), P.A. (professional association), or S.C. (service corporation).

V. Alternative Forms of Ownership
   A. The S Corporation
      1. In 1954 the Internal Revenue Service Code created the Subchapter S corporation.
      2. In recent years the IRS has changed the title to S corporation and has made a few modifications in its qualifications.
      3. An S corporation is a distinction that is made only for federal income tax purposes and is, in terms of legal characteristics, no different from any other corporation.
      4. An S corporation criteria.
         a) It must be a domestic (U.S.) corporation.
         b) It cannot have a nonresident alien as a shareholder.
         c) It can issue only one class of common stock, which means that all shares must carry the same fights (e.g., the fight to dividends or liquidation rights). The exception is voting rights, which may differ. In other words, an S corporation can issue voting and nonvoting common stock.
         d) It cannot have more than 75 shareholders (increased from 35).
      5. By increasing the number of shareholders allowed in S corporations to 75, the new law makes succession planning easier for business owners.
      6. The new law also permits them to sell shares of their stock to certain tax-exempt organizations such as pension funds.
         a) Previous rules limited ownership strictly to individuals, estates, and certain trusts.
      7. Violating any of the requirements for an S corporation automatically terminates a company's S status.
         a) If a corporation satisfies the definition for an S corporation, the owners must actually elect to be treated as one. Filing IRS Form 2553 (within the first 75 days of the tax year) makes the election, and all shareholders must consent.
      8. Advantages of an S Corporation.

   a) S corporations retain all of the advantages of a regular corporation, such as continuity of existence, transferability of ownership, and limited personal liability for its owners.
   b) It passes all of its profits or losses through to the individual shareholders, and its income is taxed only once at the individual tax rate.
      (1) Thus avoiding double taxation.
   c) Another advantage of the S corporation is that it avoids the tax C corporations pay on assets that have appreciated in value and are sold.
      (1) Also, owners of S corporations enjoy the ability to make year-end payouts to themselves if profits are high.
9. Disadvantages of an S Corporation.
   a) When the Tax Reform Act (TRA) of 1986 restructured individual and corporate tax rates, many business owners switched to S corporations to lower their tax bills.
   b) In 1993, Congress realigned the tax structure by raising the maximum personal tax rate to 39.6 percent from 31 percent.
   c) Entrepreneurs must consider the total impact of tax implications, the size of company net profits, shareholder tax rates, etc., when choosing their corporate form.

IN THE FOOTSTEPS OF AN ENTREPRENEUR - Which Form of Ownership Is Best?

SUMMARY

When Deborah Williams started Black Cat Computer Wholesale as a home-based business, she had no idea that her company would grow so fast. She selected the simplest form of ownership available: the sole proprietorship. Black Cat, now with annual sales of $7 million, went through three forms of ownership in its first five years of operation. Williams has spent the last two years trying to undo the mistakes that resulted from selecting the wrong forms of ownership in the past.

One business consultant says he sees the same story played out all the time. "Clients come in and don't even want to think about [choosing a form of ownership]. All they want is for me to tell them quickly what's the best form for them. But there's no quick answer to that question. We absolutely need to discuss their goals for the company and all kinds of other issues"

As soon as she saw Black Cat's sales climb rapidly, Williams knew that she needed to make some changes in her business. "The big thing I was worried about was limiting my personal liability;' she recalls." After a year of operation, I switched to S corporation status..." The company continued to experience rapid growth there is a need for external financing, Williams recently switched to a C corporation. "My real goal was to create a broader base of financing for the company, which I'm convinced is easier with C corporation structure."

1. In the early stages of her business, what benefits did a sole proprietorship offer Williams? What disadvantages did she face?
   Answer - Maximum control, less paperwork and cost incorporating, plus all the advantages of being incorporated.
2. What factors prompted Williams' to switch to an S corporation? What benefits did she give up, and what advantages did she gain by switching to a C corporation?
   Answer - The changing nature of the business, especially the increased liability exposure. She lost some control, moves to double taxation, has more regulatory concerns with local, state, and federal governments.

10. When Is an S Corporation a Wise Choice?
   a) Choosing S Corporation status is usually beneficial to start-up companies anticipating net losses and to highly profitable firms with substantial dividends to pay out to shareholders.
      (1) The owner can use the loss to offset other income or to remain in a lower tax bracket than the corporation, thus saving money in the long run.
   b) Companies that plan to reinvest most of their earnings to finance growth also find S corporation status favorable.
   c) Small business owners who intend to sell their companies in the near future will prefer S over C status, because the taxable gains on the sale of an S corporation are generally lower than those on the sale of a C corporation.
   d) On the other hand, small companies with the following characteristics are not likely to benefit from S corporation status:
      (1) Highly profitable personal-service companies with large numbers of shareholders, in which most of the profits are passed on to shareholders as compensation or retirement benefits.
      (2) Fast-growing companies that must retain most of their earnings to finance growth and capital spending.
      (3) Corporations in which the loss of fringe benefits to shareholders exceeds tax savings.
      (4) Corporations in which the income before any compensation to shareholders is less than $100,000 a year.
      (5) Corporations with sizable net operating losses that cannot be used against S corporation earning.

B. The Limited Liability Company (LLC}
   1. A relatively new creation, it is a cross between a partnership and a corporation.
   2. Originating in Wyoming in 1977.
   3. Combines benefits of the partnership and the corporate forms of ownership but is not subject to many of the restrictions imposed on S corporations.
      a) An LLC can have one owner, most have multiple owners (called members).
      b) An LLC offers its owners limited liability without imposing any requirements on their characteristics or any ceiling on their numbers.
      c) An LLC does not restrict its members' involvement in managing the company.
      d) LLCs also avoid the double taxation imposed on C corporations.
      e) Like an S corporation, an LLC does not pay income taxes; its income flows through to the members, who are responsible for paying income taxes on their shares of the LLC's net income.
      f) LLCs offer entrepreneurs flexibility. Like a partnership, an LLC permits its members to divide income (and thus tax liability) as they see fit.
      g) These advantages make the LLC an ideal form of ownership for small companies in virtually any industry.
         (1) They are becoming especially popular among family-owned businesses because of the benefits they offer.
   4. Creating an LLC
      a) Forming an LLC requires an entrepreneur to file two documents with the secretary of state: the articles of organization and the operating agreement.
      b) The LLCs articles of organization, similar to the corporation's articles of incorporation, establish the company's name, its method of management (board-managed or member-managed), its duration, and the names and addresses of each organizer.

c) In most states, the company's name must contain the words limited liability company, limited company, or the letters L.L.C. or L.C.

d) An LLC's charter may not exceed 30 years.

    (1) The same factors that would cause a partnership to dissolve would also cause an LLC to dissolve before its charter expired.

e) The operating agreement, similar to a corporation's bylaws, outlines the provisions governing the way the LLC will conduct business.

    (1) The operating agreement must create an LLC that has more characteristics of a partnership than of a corporation to maintain this favorable tax treatment.

f) Specifically, an LLC cannot have any more than two of the following four corporate characteristics:

    (1) Limited liability. Limited liability exists if no member of the LLC is personally liable for the debts or claims against the company.

    (2) Continuity of life. To avoid continuity of life, any LLC member must have the power to dissolve the company.

    (3) Free transferability of interest. To avoid this characteristic, the operating agreement must state that a recipient of a member's LLC stock cannot become a substitute member without the consent of the remaining members.

    (4) Centralized management. To avoid this characteristic, the operating agreement must state that the company elects to be "member-managed."

5. LLC Disadvantages.

    a) They can be expensive to create, often costing between $1,500 and $5,000.

        (1) It may pose problems for business owners who are considering converting an existing business to an LLC.

    b) The biggest disadvantage of the LLC stems from its newness.

        (1) As yet, no uniform legislation for LLCs exists (although a Uniform Limited Liability Act is pending at the federal level).

        (2) Two states (Vermont and Hawaii) still do not recognize LLCs as a legal form of ownership.

C. The Joint Venture

1. A joint venture is very much like a partnership, except that it is formed for a specific, limited purpose.

    a) Example. Suppose that you have a 500-acre tract of land 60 miles from Chicago. This land has been cleared and is normally used for farming. One of your friends has solid contacts among major musical groups and would like to put on a concert. You expect prices for your agricultural products to be low this summer, so you and your friend form a joint venture for the specific purpose of staging a three-day concert. Your contribution will be the exclusive use of the land for one month, and your friend will provide all the performers as well as technicians, facilities, and equipment. All costs will be paid out of receipts, and the net profits will be split, with you receiving 20 percent for the use of your land. When the concert is over, the facilities removed, and the accounting for all costs completed, you and your friend will split the profits 20-80, and the joint venture will terminate.

2. The "partners" form a new joint venture for each new project they undertake. The income derived from a joint venture is taxed as if it had arisen from a partnership.

3. In any endeavor in which neither party can effectively achieve the purpose alone, a joint venture becomes a common form of ownership.

VI. Summary of the Major Forms of Ownership
    A. Figure 3.2
        1. Shows the liability features of the major forms of ownership discussed in this chapter.

    B. Table 3.1
        1. Summarizes of the key features of the sole proprietorship, the partnership, the C
           corporation, the S corporation, and the limited liability company.

WIRED TO THE WEB - A Plan for the Future

SUMMARY
When he was just five years old, Kirk Sweeney began ice-skating with a pair of skates his older brother had outgrown. As Kirk grew older, his love for skating did not fade. He became an accomplished hockey player and was a key member of every team he joined. While in college, Kirk became interested in owning his own business and decided to major in entrepreneurship. During his senior year, Kirk went home to attend a special ceremony at his high school alma mater; the hockey team was going to retire his No. 13 jersey! While he was at home, Kirk learned that the Swensens, the couple who had run the skating rink for as long as he could remember, were going to retire next year and wanted to sell the rink. Kirk couldn't believe the opportunity unfolding before him! He began to explore the possibility of buying the skating rink and transforming it into a complete sports complex. Kirk threw himself into developing the business plan for what he hoped would become his skating complex with as much enthusiasm as he had for skating. Although Kirk didn't have the financial resources to purchase the skating rink outright, he knew that his father did. On Friday night, Kirk handed his plan to his father and asked him to read it. Saturday afternoon, Kirk and his father sat at the kitchen table to discuss the plan. "Dad, I want you to be my partner in this venture," Kirk said. "I'll run the business, and you can be the investor." "Son, you know I'll help you buy that skating rink. I think we need to be very careful how we set up this business, though. I'm at the stage in my life where I've accumulated some pretty valuable assets, and I don't want to put them at risk in case something bad happens. Plus, if things go according to your plan, in a couple of years, you're going to need more money than I have access to. We've got to think about these things as we choose a form of ownership."

1. Use the resources in this chapter and on the World Wide Web to help Kirk and his father decide which form of ownership would be best suited for them. Use the WWW to find out how much it would cost to create the form of ownership you recommend in your state.
    Answer - The key here is having students think through each form of ownership, it will serve as a chapter review as well as cement their learning. You can either turn the students loose or pre-research several Internet sites and provide them with the URLs.
2. What factors should Kirk and his father consider in their choice of a form of ownership? Explain.
    Answer - They should consider, control, the need for additional financing in the future, liability, tax considerations [it sounds like it would be a major concern for the father, etc.]

Chapter Summary
♦ Describe the advantages and the disadvantages of the sole proprietorship.
    ▪ A sole proprietorship is a business owned and managed by one individual and is the most popular form of ownership.
    ▪ Sole proprietorships offer these advantages: They are simple to create; they are the least costly form to begin; the owner has total decision-making authority; there are no special legal restrictions; and they are easy to discontinue.
    ▪ They also suffer from these disadvantages: unlimited personal liability of owner; limited: managerial skills and capabilities; limited access to capital; lack of continuity.

♦ Describe the advantages and the disadvantages of the partnership.
  ▪ A partnership is an association of two or more people who co-own a business for the purpose of making a profit. Partnerships offer these advantages: ease of establishment; complementary skills of partners; division of profits; larger pool of capital available; ability to attract limited partners; little government regulation; flexibility; and tax advantages.
  ▪ Partnerships suffer from these disadvantages: unlimited liability of at least one partner; difficulty in disposing of partnership interest; lack of continuity; potential for personality and authority conflicts; and partners bound by the law of agency.
  ▪ A limited partnership operates like any other partnership except that it allows limited partners (who are primarily investors and cannot take an active role in managing the business) to become owners without subjecting themselves to unlimited personal liability for the company's debts.
♦ Describe the advantages and disadvantages of the corporation.
  ▪ A corporation, the most complex of the three basic forms of ownership, is a separate legal entity. To form a corporation, an entrepreneur must file the articles of incorporation with the state in which the company will incorporate.
  ▪ Corporations offer these advantages: limited liability of stockholders; ability to attract capital; ability to continue indefinitely; and transferable ownership.
  ▪ Corporations suffer from these disadvantages: cost and time involved in incorporating; double taxation; potential for diminished managerial incentives; legal requirements and regulatory red tape; and potential loss of control by the founders.
♦ Describe the advantages and the disadvantages of the alternative forms of ownership such as the S corporation, the limited liability company, and the joint venture.
  ▪ An S corporation offers its owners limited liability protection but avoids the double taxation of C corporations.
  ▪ A limited liability company, like an S corporation, is a cross between a partnership and a corporation, yet it operates without the restrictions imposed on an S corporation. To create an LLC, an entrepreneur must file the articles of organization and the operating agreement with the secretary of state.
  ▪ A joint venture is like a partnership, except that it is formed for a specific purpose.

Discussion Questions

1. What factors should an entrepreneur consider before choosing a form of ownership?
   Answer - Tax considerations. Because of the graduated tax rates under each form of ownership, the government's constant tinkering with the tax code, and the year-to-year fluctuations in a company's income, an entrepreneur should calculate the firm's tax bill under each ownership option every year. Liability exposure. Certain forms of ownership offer business owners greater protection from personal liability due to financial problems, faulty products, and a host of other difficulties. Start-up and future capital requirements. Forms of ownership differ in their ability to raise start-up capital. Control. Entrepreneurs must decide early on how much control they are willing to sacrifice in exchange for help from other people in building a successful business. Managerial ability. If an entrepreneur lack skills or experience in certain areas, he/she may need to select a form of ownership that allows him/her to bring into the company people who possess those skills and experience. Business goals. How big and how profitable an entrepreneur plans for the business to become will influence the form of ownership chosen. Management succession plans. Some forms of ownership make this transition much smoother than others. In other cases, when the owner dies, so does the business. Cost of formation. Some forms of ownership are much more costly and involved to create than others. Entrepreneurs must weigh carefully the benefits and the costs of the particular form they choose.

2. Why are sole proprietorships so popular as a form of ownership?
    Answer - The sole proprietorship is a business owned and managed by one individual. This form of ownership is by far the most popular. Approximately 74 percent of all businesses in the United States are sole proprietorships. It is very popular for several reasons; the ease and speed of its formation, it is the least costly form of ownership to establish, the owner can keep the profits (less expenses and taxes, of course), total control of operations and can respond quickly to changes, it is the least regulated form of business ownership, and it is easy to discontinue.

3. How does personal conflict affect partnerships? How can co-owners avoid becoming sparring partners?
    Answer - Being in a partnership is much like being married. Making sure partners' work habits, goals, ethics, and general business philosophy are compatible is an important step in avoiding a nasty business divorce. The demise of many partnerships can often be traced to interpersonal conflicts and the lack of a partnership agreement for resolving those conflicts.

4. What issues should the articles of partnership address? Why are the articles important to a successful partnership?
    Answer - There are two answers, the most complete is related to the partnership agreement drawn up by the partners. The second is the generic issues covered by the UPA when no written agreement exists.

    The standard partnership agreement will likely include the following: name of the partnership, purpose of the business, domicile of the business, duration of the partnership, names of the partners and their legal addresses, contributions of each partner to the business at the creation of the partnership and later, agreement on how the profits or losses will be distributed, agreement on salaries or drawing rights against profits for each partner, procedure for expansion through the addition of new partners, distribution of the partnership's assets if the partners voluntarily dissolve the partnership, sale of partnership interest, absence or disability of one of the partners, voting rights, decision-making authority, financial authority, handling tax matters, and how alterations or modifications of the partnership agreement will be made.

    Under the UPA, the three key elements of any partnership are common ownership interest in a business, sharing the business's profits and losses, and the fight to participate in managing the operation of the partnership. Under the act, each partner has the right to: share in the management and operations of the business, share in any profits the business might earn from operations, receive interest on additional advances made to the business, be compensated for expenses incurred in the name of the partnership, have access to the business's books and records, and receive a formal accounting of the partnership's business affairs.

5. Can one partner commit another to a business deal without the other's consent? Why?
    Answer - Partners are bound by the law of agency. A partner is like a spouse in that decisions made by one, in the name of the partnership, bind all. Each partner is an agent for the business and can legally bind the other partners to a business agreement.

6. Explain the differences between a domestic corporation, a foreign corporation, and an alien corporation.
    Answer - A corporation doing business in the state in which it is incorporated is a domestic corporation. When a corporation conducts business in another state, that state considers it to be a foreign corporation. Corporations that are formed in other countries but do business in the United States are alien corporations.

7. What issues should the Certificate of Incorporation cover?

    Answer - Every state requires a Certificate of Incorporation or charter to be filed with the secretary of state. It includes: the corporation's name, the corporation's statement of purpose, the corporation's time horizon, names and addresses of the incorporators, place of business, capital stock authorization, capital required at the time of incorporation, provisions for preemptive rights, if any. that are granted to stockholders, restrictions on transferring share, names and addresses of the officers and directors of the corporation, and the rules under which the corporation will operate.

8. How does an S corporation differ from a regular corporation?

    Answer - An S corporation is a distinction that is made only for federal income tax purposes and is, in terms of legal characteristics, no different from any other corporation. An S corporation criteria: it must be a domestic (U.S.) corporation, it cannot have a nonresident alien as a shareholder, it can issue only one class of common stock, which means that all shares must carry the same fights (e.g., the fight to dividends or liquidation rights). The exception is voting rights, which may differ. In other words, an S corporation can issue voting and nonvoting common stock, and it cannot have more than 75 shareholders.

9. How does a joint venture differ from a partnership?

    Answer - A joint venture is very much like a partnership, except that it is formed for a specific, limited purpose. The "partners" form a new joint venture for each new project they undertake. The income derived from a joint venture is taxed as if it had arisen from a partnership. In any endeavor in which neither party can effectively achieve the purpose alone, a joint venture becomes a common form of ownership.

10. What role do limited partners play in a partnership? What will happen if a limited partner takes an active role in managing the business?

    Answer - A limited partnership, which is a modification of a general partnership, is composed of at least one general partner and at least one limited partner. In a limited partnership the general partner is treated, under the law, exactly as in a general partnership. Limited partners are treated as investors in the business venture, and they have limited liability. They can lose only the amount they have invested in the business. Limited partners can make management suggestions to the general partners, inspect the business, and make copies of business records. A limited partner is, of course, entitled to a share of the business's profits as agreed on and specified in the Certificate of Limited Partnership. The primary disadvantage of limited partnerships is the complexity and the cost of establishing them.

11. What advantages does a limited liability company offer over an S corporation? Over a partnership?

    Answer - Many states now recognize limited liability partnerships (LLPs) in which all partners in the business are limited partners, having only limited liability for the debts and obligations of the partnership. Most states restrict LLPs to certain types of professionals such as attorneys, physicians, dentists, accountants, and others. Just as with any limited partnership, the partners must file a Certificate of Limited Partnership in the state in which the partnership plans to conduct business. Also, like every partnership, an LLP does not pay taxes; its income is passed through to the limited partners, who pay taxes on their shares of the company's net income.

12. How is an LLC created?

    Answer - Forming an LLC requires an entrepreneur to file two documents with the secretary of state: the articles of organization and the operating agreement. The LLCs articles of organization, similar to the corporation's articles of incorporation, establish the company's name, its method of management (board-managed or member-managed), its duration, and the names and addresses of each organizer. In most states, the company's name must contain the words limited liability company, limited company, or the letters L.L.C. or L.C. An LLC's charter may not exceed 30 years. The operating agreement, similar to a corporation's bylaws, outlines the provisions governing the way the LLC will conduct business. The operating agreement must create an LLC that has more characteristics of a partnership than of a corporation to maintain this favorable tax treatment.

13. What criteria must an LLC meet to avoid double taxation?
   Answer - An LLC <u>cannot</u> have any more than two of the following four corporate characteristics:
   - Limited liability. Limited liability exists if no member of the LLC is personally liable for the debts or claims against the company.
   - Continuity of life. To avoid continuity of life, any LLC member must have the power to dissolve the company.
   - Free transferability of interest. To avoid this characteristic, the operating agreement must state that a recipient of a member's LLC stock cannot become a substitute member without the consent of the remaining members.
   - Centralized management. To avoid this characteristic, the operating agreement must state that the company elects to be "member-managed."

14. Briefly outline the advantages and disadvantages of the major forms of ownership.
   Answer - Refer to Table 3.1, pages 96-98.

Step into the Real World

1. Interview five local small business owners. What form of ownership did they choose? Why? Prepare a brief report summarizing your findings, and explain advantages and disadvantages those owners face because of their choices.
2. Contact your secretary of state to determine the status of limited liability companies in your state. Are they recognized? How does an entrepreneur create one? What requirements must an LLC meet? Report your findings to the class.
3. Invite entrepreneurs who operate as partners to your classroom. Do they have a written partnership agreement? Are their skills complementary? How do they divide responsibility for running their company? How do they handle decision making? What do they do when disputes and disagreements arise?
4. Find in the Yellow Pages of your local telephone book the names of four businesses that you think are effective marketing tools. Also find four companies whose names do little or nothing to help market their products or services. Explain the reasons for your choices. Select a business with the "wrong" name and work with a team of your classmates to brainstorm a better name.

Chapter 4 - Franchising and the Entrepreneur

Teaching Objectives

Students will be able to:

1. Explain the importance of franchising in the U.S. economy.
2. Define the concept of franchising.
3. Describe the different types of franchises.
4. Explain the forces behind franchising's popularity.
5. Describe the benefits of franchising for the franchisor.
6. Describe the benefits and limitations of franchising for the franchisee.
7. Discuss what franchisors look for in a franchisee.
8. Describe the legal aspects of franchising, including the protection offered by the FTC's Trade Regulation Rule.
9. Explain the right way to buy a franchise.
10. Describe a typical franchise contract and some of its provisions.
11. Understand current trends shaping modern franchising.

Instructor's Outline

I. Introduction
   A. The Growth of Franchising
      1. Since 1990, sales by franchised businesses have grown 10 times as fast as the U.S. economy as a whole.
      2. Today, some 4,500 franchisors operate more than 600,000 franchise outlets throughout the world, and more are opening at an incredibly fast pace.
         a) A new franchise opens somewhere in the United States every eight minutes and somewhere in the world every six-and-a-half minutes.
         b) Franchises account for 43 percent of all retail sales, totaling more than $810 billion, and they employ more than 8 million people in more than 70 major industries.
      3. Franchising's impressive growth will continue into the new millennium.
         a) Experts predict that, by 2004, franchises will be ringing up sales of $2.5 trillion worldwide.

II. What is Franchising?
   A. Described
      1. Franchising can be traced to Civil War times, when Isaac M. Singer devised a more efficient, less expensive way to sell his Singer sewing machines through franchised outlets.
      2. Retail outlets dominate franchising, accounting for about 85 percent of all franchise sales, but increasing demand for consumer and business services is producing a boom among service-oriented franchises.
      3. In franchising, semi-independent business owners (franchisees) pay fees and royalties to a parent company (franchisor) in return for the right to sell its products or services and often to use its business format and system.
         a) Franchisees buy a "success package" from the franchisor, who shows them how to use it.
         b) Franchisees, unlike independent business owners, do not have the freedom to change the way they run their businesses.
      4. Successful franchisors claim that neglecting to follow the formula is one of the chief reasons that franchisees fail.

     5. Because franchisors develop the business systems their franchisees use and direct their distribution methods, they maintain substantial control over their franchisees.

III. Types of Franchising
    A. Trade-Name Franchising
        1. Involves a brand name such as True Value Hardware or Western Auto.
        2. The franchisee buys the right to become identified with the franchisor's trade name without distributing particular products exclusively under the manufacturer's name.

    B. Product Distribution Franchising
        1. Involves licensing the franchisee to sell specific products under the manufacturer's brand name and trademark through a selective, limited distribution network.
        2. This system is commonly used to market automobiles, soft drinks, bicycles (Schwinn), appliances, cosmetics, and other products.

    C. Pure (or comprehensive or business format) Franchising
        1. Involves providing the franchisee with a complete business format, including a license for a trade name, the products or services to be sold, the physical plant, the methods of operation, a marketing strategy plan, a quality control process, a two-way communications system, and the necessary business services.
        2. The franchisee purchases the right to use all the elements of a fully integrated business operation.
        3. Pure franchising is the most rapidly growing of all types of franchising and is common among fast-food restaurants, hotels, business service firms, car rental agencies, educational institutions, beauty aid retailers, and many others.

IV. What's Behind Franchising's Popularity?
    A. Reasons
        1. The rekindling of the entrepreneurial spirit in the United States.
        2. Demographic factors and shifting lifestyles, such as the baby boom and the proliferation of the dual-career couple, have put a premium on convenience and service--two of franchising's specialties.
        3. The rapidly growing number of women entering the workforce.
            a) Career women, tired of bumping against the glass ceiling in large corporations, are choosing to open their own businesses in record numbers.
        4. Executives jumping off the corporate ladder in search of job security and control over their careers and lives.
        5. Downsizing at major companies is also feeding the growth of franchising.
            a) As companies reorganize and downsize their operations, more former "pinstripers" are becoming franchisees.
        6. Franchisors are also seeing young, well-educated people take greater interest in franchising.
            a) Rather than risk joining a large corporation only to become victims of downsizing, recent college graduates are building their careers around franchising.
        7. Perhaps the most important reason franchising has been so successful is the mutual benefits it offers franchisors and franchisees.
            a) In a franchising relationship, each party depends on the other for support.
            b) The ideal franchising relationship is a partnership based on trust and a willingness to work together for mutual success.

V. The Franchisor
  A. Benefits
    1. Franchising offers franchisors a relatively quick way to expand a distribution system with minimum capital.
    2. The franchisor can grow his/her business without the cost and inconvenience of locating and developing key managers internally.
    3. Franchisors receive income from franchisees through franchise fees and ongoing royalties.
    4. A franchisor gains the opportunity to grab a share of a regional or national market relatively quickly without having to invest huge amounts of her own money, and she gets paid while she does it.
      a) Approximately 70 percent of all franchisors have fewer than 50 locations.
      b) Sales begin slowly but accelerate by the fourth year.

SMALL BUSINESS ACROSS THE GLOBE - The King's; Global Market

SUMMARY
During the next 24 hours, McDonald's, the king of franchising, will open three more shiny new restaurants. Chances are good that two of them will be outside the United States. As same-store sales at outlets in the United States have climbed only slightly over the past several years, McDonald's has increasingly looked to foreign markets to fuel its growth. Cantalupo uses the following formula to guesstimate how many stores a particular country can support. Using "Cantalupo's theorem" to compute the number of franchises McDonald's could build worldwide produces an estimate of about 42,000, twice as many as it currently has. McDonald's success going global is based on several simple strategies.
- Gather people together often for face-to-face meetings to learn from each other.
- Put employees through arduous and repetitive management training.
- Develop long-term relationships with the best suppliers.
- Understand a country's culture before locating there.
- Hire local employees whenever possible.
- Maximize workers' autonomy.
- Tweak the standard menu only slightly to adapt it to local tastes.
- Keep prices low to build market share; profits will follow.

McDonald's success is also built on blanketing the world with advertising and promotion. CEO Mike Quinlan knows that sustaining the company's phenomenal growth record forever will be no easy task, so he has placed a premium on innovation and is scouring the globe for new ideas. Much of McDonald's success in global markets comes from its intense preparation for entering a foreign market. Going global can pose risks for any company, especially those stepping into foreign markets for the first time. However, in this global economy failing to expand into foreign markets is an even greater risk.

1. What advantages does McDonald's global strategy provide for the company?
   Answer - New markets to grow into, new ideas from foreign franchisees, diversifying economic risk by being in multiple different markets, etc.
2. What risks does the company's global expansion entail?
   Answer - Mistakes can be made due to lack of understanding of other cultures and governments. Investment in other countries where facilities could be taken by the government, a dilution of its image and way of doing things due to foreign expansion, a greater need for managerial expertise.

VI. The Franchisee
   A. Benefits
      1. A franchisee gets the opportunity to own a small business relatively quickly.
      2. A franchise often reaches the break-even point faster than an independent business.
         a) Most new franchise outlets don't break even for at least 6 to 18 months.
      3. Franchisees also benefit from the franchisor's business experience.
         a) Experience is the essence of what a franchisee is buying from a franchisor.
      4. Franchisees also earn a great deal of satisfaction from their work.
         a) A Gallup survey of franchise owners--82 percent of franchisees said they were "somewhat satisfied," to "very satisfied" with their work.
         b) 75 percent said they would purchase their franchises again.
      5. Before jumping at a franchise opportunity, an entrepreneur should consider carefully the question "What can a franchise do for me that I cannot do for myself?"
      6. Management training and support.
         a) The leading cause of business failure is incompetent management.
         b) Many franchisors, especially the well-established ones, also provide follow-up training and counseling services.
         c) Training programs often involve both classroom and on-site instruction to teach franchisees the basic operations of the business--from producing and selling the good or service
      7. Brand name appeal.
         a) A licensed franchisee purchases the right to use a nationally known and advertised brand name for a product or service.
      8. Standardized quality of goods and services.
         a) The quality of the goods and services sold determines the franchisor's reputation. To build a good reputation requires both high quality and consistent quality delivery.
      9. National advertising programs.
         a) An effective advertising program is essential to the success of virtually all franchise operations.
         b) A regional or national advertising program benefits all franchisees.
         c) Normally, such an advertising campaign is organized and controlled by the franchisor and financed by each franchisee's contribution of a percentage of monthly sales.
         d) Most franchisors also require franchisees to spend a minimum amount on local advertising.
      10. Financial assistance.
         a) Because they rely on their franchisees' money to grow their businesses, franchisors typically do not provide any extensive financial help for franchisees.
         b) Franchisors rarely make loans to enable franchisees to pay the initial franchise fee. However, once a franchisor locates a suitable prospective franchisee, he may offer the qualified candidate direct financial assistance in specific areas, such as purchasing equipment, inventory, or even the franchise fee.
      11. Nearly half of the International Franchise Association's members indicate that they offer some type of financial assistance to their franchisees; however, only one-fourth offer direct financial assistance.
      12. Proven products and business formats.
         a) What a franchisee essentially is purchasing is the franchisor's experience, expertise, and products.
         b) Standardized procedures and operations greatly enhance the franchisee's chances of success and avoid the most inefficient type of learning--trial and error.

        c) A franchisee does not have to struggle for recognition in the local marketplace as much as an independent owner might.

        d) Reputable franchisors also invest resources in researching and developing new products and services.

13. Centralized buying power.

        a) A significant advantage is participation in the franchisor's centralized and large-volume buying power.

        b) If franchisors sell goods and materials to franchisees, they may pass on to franchisees any cost savings from quantity discounts they earn by buying in volume.

14. Site selection and territorial protection.

        a) A proper location is critical to the success of any small business, and franchises are no exception. In fact, franchise experts consider the three most important factors in franchising to be location, location, and location.

        b) Many franchisors will make an extensive location analysis for each new outlet (for a fee), including studies of traffic patterns, zoning ordinances, accessibility, and population density.

        c) Franchisors also may offer a franchisee territorial protection, which gives the franchisee the right to exclusive distribution of brand-name goods or services within a particular geographic area.

        d) As the competition for top locations has escalated over the past decade, the placement of new franchise outlets has become a source of friction between franchisors and franchisees.

           (1) Existing franchisees charge that franchisors are encroaching on their territories by granting new franchises so close to them that their sales are diluted.

15. Greater chance for success.

        a) Investing in a franchise is not risk-free. Between 200 and 300 new franchise companies enter the market each year, and not all of them survive.

        b) But franchising is less risky than building a business from the ground up.

           (1) Approximately 24 percent of new businesses fail by the second year of operation; in contrast, only about 7 to 10 percent of all franchises will fail by the second year.

           (2) After five years, about 85 percent of franchises are still in business compared with less than 50 percent of independent businesses.

           (3) These statistics must be interpreted carefully, however, because when a franchise is in danger of failing, the franchisor often repurchases or relocates the outlet and does not report it as a failure.

        c) The risk of purchasing a franchise is two-pronged.

           (1) Success depends on the entrepreneur's managerial skills and motivation.

           (2) And on the franchisor's business experience and system.

B. Limitations

  1. The franchisees must sacrifice some freedom to the franchisor.

        a) The prospective franchisee must explore other limitations of franchising before undertaking this form of ownership.

  2. Franchise fees and profit sharing.

        a) Virtually all franchisors impose some type of fees and demand a share of the franchisee's sales revenues in return for the use of the franchisor's name, products or services, and business system.

        b) The Commerce Department reports that total investments for franchises range from $1,000 for business services up to $10 million for hotel and motel franchises.

    c) The average start-up cost for a franchise is between $150,000 and $200,000.

    d) Start-up costs for franchises sometimes include numerous additional fees not included in the franchise fee.

        (1) Most franchises impose a franchise fee ranging from $5,000 to $50,000 up front for the right to use the company name.

    e) Additional start-up costs might include site purchase and preparation, construction, signs, fixtures, equipment, management assistance, and training.

    f) Franchisors also impose continuing royalty fees as profit-sharing devices.

        (1) The royalty usually involves a percentage of gross sales with a required minimum or a flat fee levied on the franchise.

        (2) Royalty fees typically range from 1 percent to 15 percent of sales (the average royalty fee is between 5 and 7 percent) and can increase the franchisee's overhead expenses significantly.

        (3) Because franchisors' royalties and fees are calculated as a percentage of a franchisee's sales, they get paid even if the franchisee fails to earn a profit.

3. Strict adherence to standardized operations.

    a) The terms of the franchise agreement govern the franchisor/franchisee relationship.

    b) That agreement requires franchisees to operate their outlets according to the principles spelled out in the franchisor's operations manual.

        (1) Typical topics covered in the manual include operating hours, dress standards, operating policies and procedures, product or service specifications, and confidentiality requirements.

    c) To protect its public image, the franchisor requires that the franchisee maintain certain operating standards.

4. Restrictions on purchasing.

    a) In the interest of maintaining quality standards, franchisees may be required to purchase products or special equipment from the franchisor, and perhaps other items from an "approved" supplier.

    b) Under some conditions, these purchase arrangements may be challenged in court as a violation of antitrust laws, but generally the franchisor has a legal right to see that franchisees maintain acceptable quality standards.

    c) A franchisor can legally set the prices paid for such products but cannot establish the retail prices to be charged on products sold by the franchisee. A franchisor legally can suggest retail prices but cannot force the franchisee to abide by them.

5. Limited product line.

    a) In most cases, the franchise agreement stipulates that the franchise can sell only those products approved by the franchisor.

    b) Some companies allow franchisees to modify their product or service offerings to suit regional or local tastes, but only with the franchisor's approval.

    c) A franchise may be required to carry an unpopular product or be prevented from introducing a desirable one by the franchise agreement.

    d) A franchisee's freedom to adapt a product line to local market conditions is restricted.

6. Unsatisfactory training programs.

    a) Every would-be franchisee must be wary of the unscrupulous franchisor who promises extensive services, advice, and assistance but delivers nothing.

7. Market saturation.

    a) Some franchisors offer franchisees territorial protection, others do not.

    b) Territorial encroachment has become a hotly contested issue in franchising as growth-seeking franchisors have exhausted most of the prime locations and are now setting up new franchises close to existing ones.

   c) The biggest challenge to the growth potential of franchising is the lack of
      satisfactory locations.
8. Less freedom.
   a) When a franchisee signs a contract, he agrees to sell the franchisor's product or
      service by following its prescribed formula.
   b) Franchisors want to ensure success, and most monitor their franchisees'
      performances closely.
   c) Strict uniformity is the rule rather than the exception.
9. Table 4.1 offers a Franchise Evaluation Quiz designed to help potential franchisees
   decide whether a franchise is right for them.

IN THE FOOTSTEPS OF AN ENTREPRENEUR - Choosing the Right Franchise

SUMMARY
A Costly Lesson.
Wayne Flesier discovered that the fast-food business wasn't for him. Unfortunately, he didn't make that discovery until after he had invested $135,000 in a Subway sandwich franchise. It was an expensive lesson. Flesier began to have doubts about his choice in franchises after he got to know the owners of an American Fastsigns franchise located next door to his Subway franchise. He was amazed to learn that they were making more money than he was, and they were working fewer hours and no nights or weekends. Flesier realizes that he made a mistake that is all too common in franchising: buying a franchise without really understanding what the day-to-day business is like.

A Good Fit.
Manuel Morales Jr. didn't work for an HQ Business Center franchise before he bought one, but he did analyze the franchise thoroughly before he made the purchase. He visited 22 HQ Centers and talked with seven owners before he bought one. He questioned franchisees extensively about their operations, the system, the support from the franchisor, and what made them successful. Today, Morales is on track to reach his target of opening 57 HQ Business Centers in his territories.

Franchisees who have made both wise and ill-advised franchise purchases offer the following advice:
- Start by evaluating your own personal and business interests.
- Establish a budget.
- Do your research.
- Identify potential franchise candidates and narrow your search to the top five or six.
- Get these companies' UFOCs and review them thoroughly.
- Study your local market.

1. Develop a list of the mistakes franchisees commonly make when selecting and purchasing their outlets.
   Answer - The list is basically the reverse of the advice given above. Students might add things like getting emotionally involved in the decision, unrealistic expectations as to profitability, etc.
2. What can a franchisee do to avoid making those mistakes?
   Answer - Response is outlined above under franchisee advice.
3. Use the World Wide Web and your local library to compile a list of resources that would help potential franchisees as they evaluate franchise opportunities.
   Answer - There are a number of sites available. Consider researching several and providing them to the students to help direct and limit their efforts. Students also tend to show great creativity in finding information on the web.

VII. What Do Franchisors Look for in a Franchisee?
   A. What does the typical franchisor look for?
      1. A "good franchisee" is willing to follow the franchisor's business system.
      2. He/she has adequate financing to make the business work.
      3. The franchisee understands the importance of quality and superior customer service.
         a) Table 4.1 A Franchise Evaluation Quiz
      4. The portrait of the typical franchisee is diverse.
         a) Studies show that the average franchisee is 40 years old with a net worth of $329,704 (before investing in a franchise).
         b) Some 90 percent are college-educated, 20 percent are women, 11 percent are minorities, and more than 33 percent are corporate castoffs or dropouts.
      5. Characteristics a franchisor looks for.
      6. Experienced?
         a) Not necessarily.
         b) "No experience necessary" is a key selling point of franchising.
         c) Most franchisees find that a certain level of business know-how and savvy is crucial to a successful franchise operation. A basic understanding of business law, finance, marketing, and general management is useful.
      7. Hard working?
         a) Definitely.
         b) Most franchisees work long hours.
         c) A franchisee must be willing to do any job that needs to be done: preparing paperwork, reconciling the bank statement, sweeping the floor, and selling merchandise.
      8. Team player?
         a) Yes. Franchisors are looking for people who are willing to work hard not only for their own success but for the success of the entire franchise.
         b) Although franchisors expect franchise owners to be loyal to the franchise and to follow the format, many encourage franchisees to use their creativity to generate new ideas for improving the system.
      9. Leadership and management skills?
         a) No doubt. Managing people is a significant part of every successful business operation.
         b) Franchisees must realize that they are in the people business and that their workforce is often unskilled and transitory.
      10. Risk-Averse?
         a) Definitely not. Although franchises have a much lower failure rate than do independent businesses, they are not without risks.
      11. Educated?
         a) Yes, but a franchisee does not have to have an MBA and a Ph.D. in management to run a franchise successfully.
      12. Financially Stable?
         a) Certainly. Some franchises have breathtakingly high capital requirements; others, especially the new growth-oriented service franchises, are much more affordable.
         b) Still, every franchisor requires each applicant to submit a personal financial statement proving that he is financially sound.
      13. A desire to succeed?
         a) Absolutely. A burning desire to succeed and a healthy dose of enthusiasm can carry a franchisee through may difficult situations.
      14. One business writer summarizes what franchisors look for in a franchisee.

a) "[Franchisors] want franchisees who think for themselves and aggressively seek new ways to improve business. At the same time, they want someone who's willing to follow the franchisor's format. In other words, the ideal franchisee is a creative, outgoing person who's eager to succeed, but not so independent that he resents other people's advice."

VIII. Franchising and the Law
   A. Key Issues
      1. The explosion of legitimate franchises also ushered in with it several fly-by-night franchisors who defrauded their franchisees.
      2. In response to these specific incidents and to the potential for deception inherent in a franchise relationship, California, in 1971, enacted the first Franchise Investment Law.
         a) The law (and similar laws subsequently passed by 16 other states) requires franchisors to register a Uniform Franchise Offering Circular (UFOC) and deliver a copy to prospective franchisees before any offer or sale of a franchise.
      3. In October 1979, the Federal Trade Commission (FTC) enacted the Trade Regulation Rule, requiring all franchisors to disclose detailed information on their operations at the first personal meeting or at least 10 days before a franchise contract is signed or any money is paid.
         a) The FTC rule covers all franchisors, even those in the 33 states lacking franchise disclosure laws.
      4. In 1994, the FTC modified the requirements for the UFOC, making more information available to prospective franchisees and making the document easier to read and understand.

   B. The Trade Regulation Rule
      1. Requires 23 major topics in its disclosure statement:
         a) Information identifying the franchisor and its affiliates and describing their business experience and the franchises being sold.
         b) Information identifying and describing the business experience of each of the franchisor's officers, directors, and management personnel responsible for the franchise program.
         c) A description of the lawsuits in which the franchisor and its officers, directors, and managers have been involved.
         d) Information about any bankruptcies in which the franchisor and its officers, directors, and managers have been involved.
         e) Information about the initial franchise fee and other payments required to obtain the franchise, including the intended use of the fees.
         f) A description of any other continuing payments franchisees are required to make after start-up, including royalties, service fees, training fees, lease payments, advertising charges, and others.
         g) A detailed description of the payments a franchisee must make to fulfill the initial investment requirement and how and to whom they are made. The categories covered are initial franchise fee, equipment, opening inventory, initial advertising fee, signs, training, real estate, working capital, legal, accounting, and utilities.
         h) Information about quality restrictions on goods and services used in the franchise and where they may be purchased, including restricted purchases from the franchises.
         i) Information covering requirements to purchase goods, services, equipment, supplies, inventory, and other items from approved suppliers (including the franchisor).

    j)   A description of-any financial assistance available from the franchisor in the purchase of the franchise.

    k)   A description of all obligations the franchisor must fulfill in helping a franchisee prepare to open, open, and operate a unit. Plus, information covering location selection methods and the training program provided to franchisees.

    l)   A description of any territorial protection that will be granted to the franchise and a statement as to whether the franchisor may locate a company-owned store or other outlet in that territory.

    m)   All relevant information about the franchisor's trademarks, service marks, trade names, logos, and commercial symbols, including where they are registered.

    n)   Similar information on any patents and copyrights the franchisor owns and the rights to these transferred to franchisees.

    o)   A description of the extent to which franchisees must participate personally in the operation of the franchise.

    p)   A description of any restrictions on the goods or services franchises are permitted to sell and with whom franchisees may deal.

    q)   A description of the conditions under which the franchise may be repurchased or refused renewal by the franchisor, transferred to a third party by the franchisee, and terminated or modified by either party.

    r)   A description of the involvement of celebrities and public figures in the franchise.

    s)   A complete statement of the basis for any earnings claims made to the franchisee, including the percentage of existing franchises that have actually achieved the results that are claimed. New rules put two requirements on franchisors making earnings claims:

        (1)   Any earnings claim must be included in the UFOC, and

        (2)   the claim must "have a reasonable basis at the time it is made." However, franchisors are not required to make any earnings claims at all; in fact, 80 percent of franchisors don't make earnings claims in their circulars, primarily because of liability concerns about committing such numbers to paper.

    t)   Statistical information about the present number of franchises; the number of franchises projected for the future; the number of franchises terminated; the number the franchisor has not renewed; the number repurchased in the past; and a list of the names and addresses of other franchises.

    u)   The financial statements of the franchisors.

    v)   A copy of all franchise and other contracts (leases, purchase agreements, etc.) the franchisee will be required to sign.

    w)   A standardized, detachable "receipt" to prove that the prospective franchisee received a copy of the UFOC.

2.   The typical UFOC is about 100 pages long, but every potential franchisee should take the time to read and understand it.

    a)   The information contained in the UFOC does not fully protect a potential franchise from deception, nor does it guarantee success.

    b)   It does, however, provide enough information to begin a thorough investigation of the franchisor and the franchise deal.

    c)   Many experts recommend that potential franchisees have an experienced franchise attorney or consultant review a company's UFOC before they invest.

IX. How to Buy a Franchise

   A. Clues that Should Arouse Suspicion

      1. The UFOC is a powerful tool designed to help potential franchisees avoid dishonest franchisors.

2. The best defenses a prospective entrepreneur has against unscrupulous franchisors are preparation, common sense, and patience.
3. The following clues should arouse the suspicion of an entrepreneur about to invest in a franchise:
    a) Claims that the franchise contract is a standard one and that "you don't need to read it."
    b) A franchisor who fails to give you a copy of the required disclosure document at your first face-to-face meeting.
    c) A marginally successful prototype store or no prototype at all.
    d) A poorly prepared operations manual outlining the franchise system or no manual (or system) at all.
    e) Oral promises of future earnings without written documentation.
    f) A high franchisee turnover rate or a high termination rate.
    g) An unusual amount of litigation brought against the franchisor.
    h) Attempts to discourage you from allowing an attorney to evaluate the franchise contract before you sign it.
    i) No written documentation to support claims and promises.
    j) A high-pressure sale: sign the contract now or lose the opportunity.
    k) Claiming to be exempt from federal laws requiring complete disclosure of franchise details.
    l) "Get-rich-quick schemes," promises of huge profits with only minimum effort.
    m) Reluctance to provide a list of present franchisees for you to interview.
    n) Evasive, vague answers to your questions about the franchise and its operation.
4. Not every franchise "horror story" is the result of dishonest franchisors.
5. More often than not, the problems that arise in franchising have more to do with franchisees who buy legitimate franchises without proper research and analysis.

B. Evaluate Yourself
1. Before looking at any franchise, an entrepreneur should study her own personality, experiences, likes, dislikes, goals, and expectations.
2. According to the president of the International Franchise Association (IFA), potential franchisees should "not only do thorough research of the prospective franchise opportunity, but more importantly, they [should] take a complete inventory of themselves and their capabilities."

C. Research the Market
1. Before shopping for a franchise, an entrepreneur should research the market in the area she plans to serve.
2. Solid market research should tell a prospective franchisee whether a particular franchise is merely a passing fad.
    a) The president of the IFA advises franchisees to "go with a product [or a service] that [is] established in the marketplace and is going to fit with the demographic trends and basic American tastes for the next 15 or 20 years."

D. Consider Your Franchise Options
1. The International Franchise Association publishes the Franchise Opportunities Guide, which lists its members and some basic information about them.
2. Many cities host franchise trade shows throughout the year, where hundreds of franchisors gather to sell their franchises.

E. Get a Copy of the Franchisor's UFOC and Study it
    1. Once you narrow down your franchise choices, you should contact each franchise and get a copy of its UFOC.
    2. This document is an important tool in your search for the right franchise, and you should make the most of it.
    3. It is best to have an attorney experienced in franchising review the UFOC and discuss it with you.
        a) The franchise contract summarizes the details that will govern the franchisor]franchisee relationship over its life.
        b) It outlines exactly the rights and the obligations of each party and sets the guidelines that govern the franchise relationship.
    4. Particular items in the UFOC that entrepreneurs should focus on include the franchisor's experience (items 1 and 2), fees and total investment (items 5, 6, and 7), the franchisee turnover rate for the past three years (item 20), and the current and past litigation against the franchisor (item 3).
        a) If the turnover rate is less than 5 percent, the franchise is probably sound.
        b) Virtually every franchisor has been involved in lawsuits but an excessive amount of litigation against a franchisor should alert a prospective franchisee to potential problems.

F. Talk to Existing Franchisees
    1. Perhaps the best way to evaluate the reputation of a franchisor is to interview (in person) several franchise owners who have been in business at least one year about the positive and the negative features of the agreement and whether the franchisor delivered what it promised.
        a) Item 20 of the UFOC lists all of a company's franchisees and their addresses by state, making it easy for potential franchisees to contact them.
    2. It is also wise to interview past franchisees to get their perspectives on the franchisor/franchisee relationship.
        a) Why did they leave?
        b) Table 4.2 offers some important questions to ask existing franchisees.

G. Ask the Franchisor Some Tough Questions
    1. Visit the franchisor's headquarters and ask plenty of questions about the company and its relationship with its franchisees.

H. Make Your Choice
    1. The first lesson in franchising is "Do your homework before you get out your checkbook."
    2. Once you have done your research, you can make an informed choice about which franchise is right for you.
    3. Then it is time to put together a solid business plan that will serve as your road map to success in the franchise you have selected.

X. Franchise Contracts
  A. Introduction
    1. The amount of franchisor/franchisee litigation has risen steadily since the 1980s.
    2. A common source of much of this litigation is the interpretation of the franchise contract's terms.
    3. Courts have relatively little statutory law and few precedents on which to base decisions in franchise disputes, so there is minimal protection for franchisees.

    4. The contract summarizes the details that will govern the franchisor/franchisee
       relationship over its life.
       a) It outlines exactly the rights and the obligations of each party and sets the
          guidelines that govern the franchise relationship.
       b) The Federal Trade Commission requires that the franchisee be allowed to hold the
          completed contract with all revisions for at least five business days before having to
          sign it.
       c) Despite such protection, one study by the FTC suggests that 40 percent of new
          franchisees sign contracts without reading them.
    5. Every potential franchisee should have an attorney evaluate the franchise contract and
       review it with him before he signs anything.
    6. Most large, established franchisors are not willing to negotiate the franchise contract's
       terms, many smaller franchises will, especially for highly qualified candidates.

B. Termination
    1. Probably the most litigated subject of a franchise agreement is the termination of the
       contract by either party.
       a) Most contracts prohibit termination "without just cause."
    2. In general, the franchisor has the right to cancel a contract if a franchisee declares
       bankruptcy, fails to make required payments on time, or fails to maintain quality
       standards.
    3. Terminations usually are costly to both parties and are seldom conducted in an
       atmosphere of goodwill.

C. Renewal
    1. Franchisors usually retain the right to renew or refuse to renew franchisees' contracts.
    2. In a recent dispute over a franchisor's refusal to renew a franchisee's contract a
       Michigan court of appeals held that a franchisor "cannot discriminate between
       franchisees--renewing one while refusing to renew another who has a similar record of
       performance."
    3. When a franchisor grants renewal, the two parties must draw up a new contract.
       a) Frequently, the franchisee must pay a renewal fee and may be required to fix any
          deficiencies of the outlet or to modernize and upgrade it.
       b) The FTC's Trade Regulation Rule requires the franchisor to disclose these terms
          before any contracts are signed.

D. Transfer and Buybacks
    1. At any given time, about 10 percent of the franchisees in a system have their outlets up
       for sale.
    2. Under most franchise contracts, a franchisee cannot sell his franchise to a third party or
       will it to a relative without the franchisor's approval.
    3. Most franchisors retain the right of first refusal in franchise transfers; the franchisee
       must offer the franchise to the franchisor first.

XI. Trends in Franchising
  A. Franchising's Three Major Growth Waves
    1. The first wave occurred in the early 1970s when fast-food restaurants used the concept
       to grow rapidly.
       a) The fast-food industry was one of the first to discover the power of franchising, but
          other businesses soon took notice and adapted the franchising concept to their
          industries.

2. The second wave took place in the mid-1980s as our nation's economy shifted heavily toward the service sector.
   a) Franchises followed suit, springing up in every service business imaginable--from maid services and copy centers to mailing services and real estate.
3. The third wave began in the early 1990s and continues today.
   a) It is characterized by new, low-cost franchises that focus on specific market niches. These companies feature start-up costs in the $2,000 to $250,000 range and span a variety of industries, from leak detection in homes to auto detailing to day care to tile glazing.
4. Other significant trends affecting franchising include international opportunities, nontraditional ways of locating and creating a franchise, and changing demographics.

B. International Opportunities
   1. Currently, the biggest trend in franchising is the globalization of U.S. franchise systems.
   2. Increasingly, franchising is becoming a major export industry for the United States because markets outside U.S. borders offer most franchisors the greatest potential for growth.
   3. Canada is the primary market for U.S. franchisors, with Mexico, Japan, and Europe following.
      a) These markets are most attractive to franchisors because they have features similar to the U.S. market: rising personal incomes, strong demand for consumer goods, growing service economies, and spreading urbanization.
      b) For franchisors moving into foreign markets, adaptation is one key to success. Although they keep their basic systems intact, franchises that are successful in foreign markets quickly learn how to change their concepts to appeal to local tastes.

C. Smaller, Nontraditional Locations
   1. As the high cost of building full-scale locations continues to climb, more franchisors are searching out nontraditional locations in which to build smaller, less expensive outlets.
   2. Based on the principle of intercept marketing, the idea is to put a franchise's products or services directly in the paths of potential customers, wherever they may be.
   3. Franchises are putting scaled-down outlets on college campuses, in high school cafeterias, in sports arenas, in hospitals, on airline flights, and in zoos.
   4. Many franchisees have discovered that smaller outlets in these nontraditional locations generate nearly the same sales volume as full-sized outlets at just a fraction of the cost.

D. Conversion Franchising
   1. Conversion franchising--owners of independent businesses become franchisees to gain the advantage of name recognition.
   2. In a franchise conversion, the franchisor gets immediate entry into new markets and experienced operators; franchisees get increased visibility and often a big sales boost.
      a) The average sales gain in the first year for converted franchisees is 20 percent.

E. Multiple-Unit Franchising
   1. Multiple-unit franchising (MUF) became extremely popular in the early 1990s, and the trend has accelerated rapidly since then.
   2. In multiple-unit franchising, a franchisee opens more than one unit in a broad territory within a specific time period.
   3. The typical multi-unit franchisee owns between three and six outlets, but some franchisees own many more.

4. For franchisors, multiple-unit franchising is an efficient way to expand into either domestic or international markets quickly.
5. Multiple-unit franchising is an extremely effective strategy for franchisors targeting foreign markets, where having a local representative who knows the territory is essential.
6. For franchisees, multiple-unit franchising offers the opportunity for rapid growth without leaving the safety net of the franchise.
7. Also, because franchisors usually offer discounts of about 25 percent off their standard fees on multiple units, franchisees can get fast-growing companies for a bargain.

SMALL BUSINESS ACROSS THE GLOBE - The Battle of the Menu Boards: Seaweed Soup, Anyone?

SUMMARY
When McDonald's opened its first store in Japan in 1971, it not only launched a campaign to bring the traditional American hamburger and french fries to the Far East but it also sparked the imagination of a local entrepreneur Satoshi Sakurai. Inspired by the fast-food king's instant success in Tokyo, Sakurai launched his own version of a hamburger franchise, Mos Burger the next year. Mos Burger also has outpaced its competitors, including KFC (Japan's second-largest fast-food chain behind McDonald's), Wendy's, McDonald's, and others in adapting its menu to the particular taste of its Japanese customers. Mos Burger also spends more money on its ingredients than its rivals do, but that makes its products more expensive. For years, Mos Burger posed little threat to its much larger competitors from the United States. Thanks to its exotic, localized menu, however, the company grew quietly but rapidly. Now McDonald's and other fast-food chains are having to fight back, launching new menu items to please locals' palates. What's driving this battle of the menu board? Experts point to Japan's maturing fast-food market, which makes impressive sales gains hard to come by.

1. How might a franchise agreement with a Japanese franchisee differ from such an agreement with a U.S.-based franchise?
   Answer - Consider providing a "mini-lecture" on Japanese culture to help students. Things like a longer time frame, relationships with suppliers due to the Japanese focus on those relationships, etc. would probably be very different. Other aspects would remain unchanged.
2. Use the World Wide Web to conduct research on fast-food companies operating in other parts of the world (Eastern Europe and Australia, for example).
   Answer - Consider placing students in teams. Divide teams up by product line, specific franchises or particular countries. Have students report the results of their research in class.
3. McDonald's is locating franchised restaurants in India. Use the Word Wide Web to develop some specific recommendations for modifications McDonald's should make in its locations there.
   Answer - Again, considering preparing students with a "mini-lecture" on Indian culture. Students should research Indian culture--especially social class, business law--it's on an English model, and dietary habits.

F. Master Franchising
   1. A master franchise (or subfranchise) gives a franchisee the right to create a semi-independent organization in a particular territory to recruit, sell, and support other franchisees.
   2. A master franchisee buys the right to develop subfranchises within a broad geographic area or, sometimes, an entire country.

3. It enables franchisors to open outlets in international markets quickly and efficiently because the master franchisees understand local laws and the nuances of selling in local markets.

G. Piggybacking
1. Some franchisors are teaming up with other franchisors selling complementary products or services.
2. A growing number of companies are piggybacking (or co-branding or combination franchising) outlets: combining two or more distinct franchises under one roof.
3. This "buddy system" approach works best when the two franchise ideas are compatible and appeal to similar customers.
4. Properly planned, piggybacked franchises can magnify many times over the sales and profits of individual, self-standing outlets.

H. Serving Aging Baby Boomers
1. Now that dual-career couples have become the norm, especially among baby boomers, the market for franchises offering convenience and time-saving services is booming.
2. Customers are willing to pay for products and services that will save them time or trouble, and franchises are ready to provide them.

WIRED TO THE WEB - The Power of the Web

SUMMARY
The World Wide Web is reshaping the franchise industry allowing franchisors to locate potential franchisees more efficiently, improving communications between franchisors and their franchisees, and giving franchisees the ability to sell their products and services across the globe. Franchise web sites already number in the hundreds, and more are coming on line every day. For entrepreneurs considering investing in franchises, the World Wide Web makes the process of gathering information much easier and faster. The World Wide Web also helps franchisors to keep in close contact with their franchisees and to provide them with better support services. Although franchising experts differ in their opinions about the direction in which the World Wide Web will take franchising, one thing they do agree on is that both franchisors and franchisees have only begun to explore the possibilities the Web offers.

[Answers to the following questions are discussion based, so no suggested responses are offered.]
1. What possibilities do you see for franchising on the World Wide Web? Work with a team of your classmates to brainstorm ways in which franchisors and franchisees could use the Web to improve their businesses.
2. Investigate several franchisors Web sites [such as McDonald's at <http://www.mcdonalds.com>, Ben & Jerry's Homemade at <http://benjerry. com>, Wendy's at <http:wendys.com>, and others you locate with a Web search engine]. Select two franchises and prepare a one-page report comparing the Web sites and how the franchisors use them. How would you score each site on the following factors. [See text for rating scale.]
3. Is each site effective? Why? What recommendations would you make for improving each site?

XII. Conclusion
A. Franchising has prove its viability in the U.S. economy and has become a key part of the small business sector, because it offers many would-be entrepreneurs the opportunity to own and operate a business with a greater chance for success. Despite its impressive growth rate to date, the franchising industry still has a great deal of room left to grow, especially globally.

Describing the future of franchising, one expert says, "Franchising has not yet come close to reaching its full potential in the American marketplace."

Chapter Summary

♦ Explain the importance of franchising in the U.S. economy.
  ▪ Since 1990, sales by franchised businesses have grown 10 times as fast as the U.S. economy as a whole. Through franchised businesses, consumers can buy nearly every good or service imaginable.
  ▪ A new franchise opens somewhere in the United States every eight minutes and somewhere in the world every six-and-a-half minutes. Franchises account for 43 percent of all retail sales, totaling more than $810 billion, and they employ more than 8 million people in more than 70 major industries.

♦ Define the concept of franchising.
  ▪ Franchising is a method of doing business involving a continuous relationship between a franchisor and a franchisee. The franchisor retains control of the distribution system, while the franchisee assumes all of the normal daily operating functions of the business.

♦ Describe the different types of franchises.
  ▪ There are three types of franchising: trade-name franchising, where the franchisee purchases only the right to use a brand name; product distribution franchising, which involves a license to sell specific products under a brand name; and pure franchising, which provides a franchisee with a complete business system.

♦ Explain the forces behind franchising's popularity.
  ▪ Franchising has been a successful business format, in part, because of the mutual benefits it provides to franchisors and franchisees.
  ▪ Describe the benefits of franchising for the franchisor.
  ▪ The franchisor has the benefits of expanding his business on limited capital and growing without developing key managers internally.

♦ Describe the benefits and limitations of franchising for the franchisee.
  ▪ The franchisee receives many key benefits: management training and counseling, customer appeal of a brand name, standardized quality of goods and services, national advertising programs, financial assistance, proven products and business formats, centralized buying power, territorial protection, and greater chances for success.
  ▪ The limitations involved in buying a franchise include franchise fees and profit sharing, strict adherence to standardized operations, restrictions on purchasing, limited product lines, possible ineffective training programs, and less freedom than independent owners have.

♦ Discuss what franchisors look for in a franchisee.
  ▪ Franchisors look for franchisees who are hardworking team players with leadership and management skills, are educated and financially stable, and have a strong desire to succeed.

♦ Describe the legal aspects of franchising, including the protection offered by the FTC's Trade Regulation Rule.
  ▪ The FTC's Trade Regulation Rule is designed to help the franchisee evaluate a franchising package. It requires each franchisor to disclose information covering 23 topics at least 10 days before accepting payment from a potential franchisee. This document, the Uniform Franchise Offering Circular (UFOC) is a valuable source of information for anyone considering investing in a franchise.

♦ Explain the right way to buy a franchise.
  ▪ Evaluate yourself; research your market; consider your franchise options; get a copy of the franchisor's UFOC and study it; talk to existing franchisees; ask the franchisor some tough questions; and make your choice.

♦ Describe a typical franchise contract and some of its provisions.

- The amount of franchisor-franchisee litigation has risen steadily over the past decade. Three items are responsible for most franchisor-franchisee disputes: termination of the contract, contract renewal, and transfer and buy-back provisions.
♦ Understand current trends shaping modern franchising.
  - Trends influencing franchising include low-cost franchises that target specific market niches, international opportunities, the emergence of smaller nontraditional locations, conversion franchising, multiple-unit franchising, master franchising, piggyback (or combination) franchising, and products and services targeting aging baby boomers.

Discussion Questions

1. What is franchising?
    Answer - In franchising, semi-independent business owners (franchisees) pay fees and royalties to a parent company (franchisor) in return for the right to sell its products or services and often to use its business format and system. Franchisees buy a "success package" from the franchisor, who shows them how to use it. Franchisees, unlike independent business owners, do not have the freedom to change the way they run their businesses. Retail outlets dominate franchising, accounting for about 85 percent of all franchise sales, but increasing demand for consumer and business services is producing a boom among service-oriented franchises.

2. Describe the three types of franchising and give an example of each.
    Answer - Trade-name franchising involves a brand name such as True Value Hardware or Western Auto. The franchisee buys the right to become identified with the franchisor's trade name without distributing particular products exclusively under the manufacturer's name. Product distribution franchising involves licensing the franchisee to sell specific products under the manufacturer's brand name and trademark through a selective, limited distribution network. This system is commonly used to market automobiles, soft drinks, bicycles (Schwinn), appliances, cosmetics, and other products. Pure (or comprehensive or business format) franchising involves providing the franchisee with a complete business format, including a license for a trade name, the products or services to be sold, the physical plant, the methods of operation, a marketing strategy plan, a quality control process, a two-way communications system, and the necessary business services. The franchisee purchases the right to use all the elements of a fully integrated business operation. Pure franchising is the most rapidly growing of all types of franchising and is common among fast-food restaurants, hotels, business service firms, car rental agencies, educational institutions, beauty aid retailers, and many others.

3. How does franchising benefit the franchisor?
    Answer - Franchising offers franchisors a relatively quick way to expand a distribution system with minimum capital. The franchisor can grow his/her business without the cost and inconvenience of locating and developing key managers internally. Franchisors receive income from franchisees through franchise fees and ongoing royalties. A franchisor gains the opportunity to grab a share of a regional or national market relatively quickly without having to invest huge amounts of her own money, and she gets paid while she does it. Approximately 70 percent of all franchisors have fewer than 50 locations.

4. Discuss the advantages and the disadvantages of franchising for the franchisee.
    Answer - Have students refer to Table 4.1 which offers a Franchise Evaluation Quiz designed to help potential franchisees decide whether a franchise is right for them. Benefits. A franchisee gets the opportunity to own a small business relatively quickly. Franchisees also benefit from the franchisor's business experience. Franchisees also earn a great deal of satisfaction from their work. Plus the franchisor provides guidance and help through--management training and support, proven products and business formats, centralized buying power, site selection and territorial protection.

Limitations. The franchisees must sacrifice some freedom to the franchisor, he/she pays franchise fees and profit sharing with the franchisor, there must be strict adherence to standardized operations, there are restrictions on purchasing, in most cases, the franchise agreement stipulates that the franchise can sell only those products approved by the franchisor, and some franchisors offer franchisees territorial protection, others do not. Territorial encroachment has become a hotly contested issue in franchising as growth-seeking franchisors have exhausted most of the prime locations and are now setting up new franchises close to existing ones.

5.   How beneficial to the franchisee is a quality training program? Why?
Answer - The leading cause of business failure is incompetent management. Training programs are the key to success because this is how the success system with its processes and procedures is communicated to the franchisee and his/her employees. It is the means by which standardization is reinforced. Many franchisors, especially the well-established ones, also provide follow-up training and counseling services. Training programs often involve both classroom and on-site instruction to teach franchisees the basic operations of the business--from producing to selling the good or service.

6.   Compare the failure rates for franchises with those of independent businesses.
Answer - Investing in a franchise is not risk-free. Between 200 and 300 new franchise companies enter the market each year, and not all of them survive. But franchising is less risky than building a business from the ground up. Approximately 24 percent of new businesses fail by the second year of operation; in contrast, only about 7 to 10 percent of all franchises will fail by the second year. After five years, about 85 percent of franchises are still in business compared with less than 50 percent of independent businesses. These statistics must be interpreted carefully, however, because when a franchise is in danger of failing, the franchisor often repurchases or relocates the outlet and does not report it as a failure. The risk of purchasing a franchise is two-pronged. Success depends on the entrepreneur's managerial skills and motivation, and on the franchisor's business experience and system.

7.   Why might an independent entrepreneur be dissatisfied with a franchising arrangement?
Answer - The franchisees must sacrifice some freedom to the franchisor. When a franchisee signs a contract, he agrees to sell the franchisor's product or service by following its prescribed formula. Franchisors want to ensure success, and most monitor their franchisees' performances closely. Strict uniformity is the rule rather than the exception. The prospective franchisee must explore other limitations of franchising before undertaking this form of ownership.

8.   What do franchisors look for in a franchisee?
Answer - There are a number of characteristics but the most important are: willingness to follow the franchisor's business system, adequate financing to make the business work, and an understanding of the importance of quality and superior customer service. Table 4.1 A Franchise Evaluation Quiz. The portrait of the typical franchisee is diverse. Studies show that the average franchisee is 40 years old with a net worth of $329,704 (before investing in a franchise). Some 90 percent are college-educated, 20 percent are women, 11 percent are minorities, and more than 33 percent are corporate castoffs or dropouts. See pages 115-116 for the complete list.

9.   What are the clues in detecting an unreliable franchisor?
Answer - The UFOC is a powerful tool designed to help potential franchisees avoid dishonest franchisors. The best defenses a prospective entrepreneur has against unscrupulous franchisors are preparation, common sense, and patience. There are numerous clues, refer to pages 118-119 for a complete list, but here are a few things to watch out for. 1) Claims that the franchise contract is a standard one and that "you don't need to read it." 2) A franchisor who fails to give you a copy of the required disclosure document at your first face-to-face meeting. 3) A marginally successful

prototype store or no prototype at all. 4) A poorly prepared operations manual outlining the franchise system or no manual (or system) at all. 5) Oral promises of future earnings without written documentation. 6) No written documentation to support claims and promises. 7) A high-pressure sale: sign the contract now or lose the opportunity. 8) "Get-rich-quick schemes," promises of huge profits with only minimum effort.

10. How and in what areas should a prospective franchisee investigate before investing in a franchise?
    Answer - The entrepreneur should study her own personality, experiences, likes, dislikes, goals, and expectations. Before shopping for a franchise, an entrepreneur should research the market in the area she plans to serve. The franchisee should consider your franchise options. The franchisee should contact each franchise and get a copy of its UFOC. Particular items in the UFOC that entrepreneurs should focus on include the franchisor's experience (items I and 2), fees and total investment (items 5, 6, and 7), the franchisee turnover rate for the past three years (item 20), and the current and past litigation against the franchisor (item 3). Perhaps the best way to evaluate the reputation of a franchisor is to interview (in person) several franchise owners who have been in business at least one year about the positive and the negative features of the agreement and whether the franchisor delivered what it promised. It is also wise to interview past franchisees to get their perspectives on the franchisor/franchisee relationship. Visit the franchisor's headquarters and ask plenty of questions about the company and its relationship with its franchisees. Once you have done your research, you can make an informed choice about which franchise is right for you.

11. What is the function of the FTC's Trade Regulation Rule?
    Answer - The Trade Regulation Rule is to protect the franchisee by requiring disclosure of key information by the franchisor. It requires 23 major topics in its disclosure statement: 1) Information identifying the franchisor and its affiliates and describing their business experience and the franchises being sold, and, 2) Information identifying and describing the business experience of each of the franchisor's officers, directors, and management personnel responsible for the franchise program. See pages 116-117 for a complete list of what is to be in the UFOC.

12. Outline the rights given all prospective franchisees by the Trade Regulation Rule.
    Answer - In October 1979, the Federal Trade Commission (FTC) enacted the Trade Regulation Rule, requiring all franchisors to disclose detailed information on their operations at the first personal meeting or at least 10 days before a franchise contract is signed or any money is paid. The FTC rule covers all franchisors, even those in the 33 states lacking franchise disclosure laws. In 1994, the FTC modified the requirements for the UFOC, making more information available to prospective franchisees and making the document easier to read and to understand.

    Also, see pages 116-118. There are 23 key topic areas that must be covered. The typical UFOC is about 100 pages long, but every potential franchisee should take the time to read and to understand it. The information contained in the UFOC does not fully protect a potential franchise from deception, nor does it guarantee success. It does, however, provide enough information to begin a thorough investigation of the franchisor and the franchise deal. Many experts recommend that potential franchisees have an experienced franchise attorney or consultant review a company's UFOC before they invest.

13. What are the causes of most franchisor-franchisee litigation? Whom does the standard franchise contract favor?
    Answer - The amount of franchisor/franchisee litigation has risen steadily since the 1980s. A common source of much of this litigation is the interpretation of the franchise contract's terms. Courts have relatively little statutory law and few precedents on which to base decisions in franchise disputes, so there is minimal protection for franchisees. The contract summarizes the details that

will govern the franchisor/franchisee relationship over its life. It outlines exactly the rights and the obligations of each party and sets the guidelines that govern the franchise relationship. The Federal Trade Commission requires that the franchisee be allowed to hold the completed contract with all revisions for at least five business days before having to sign it. Despite such protection, one study by the FTC suggests that 40 percent of new franchisees sign contracts without reading them.

14. Describe the current trends of franchises.
   Answer - There have been three major growth waves. The first wave occurred in the early 1970s when fast-food restaurants used the concept to grow rapidly. The fast-food industry was one of the first to discover the power of franchising, but other businesses soon took notice and adapted the franchising concept to their industries. The second wave took place in the mid-1980s as our nation's economy shifted heavily toward the service sector. Franchises followed suit, springing up in every service business imaginable--from maid services and copy centers to mailing services and real estate. The third wave began in the early 1990s and continues today. It is characterized by new, low-cost franchises that focus on specific market niches. These companies feature start-up costs in the $2,000 to $250,000 range and span a variety of industries, from leak detection in homes to auto detailing to day care to tile glazing. Other significant trends affecting franchising include international opportunities, nontraditional ways of locating and creating a franchise, and changing demographics.

   Other relevant trends include a move into international markets. Also, as the high cost of building full-scale locations continues to climb, more franchisors are searching out nontraditional locations in which to build smaller, less expensive outlets. There is a move to conversion franchising--owners of independent businesses become franchisees to gain the advantage of name recognition. Multiple-unit franchising (MUF) became extremely popular in the early 1990s, and the trend has accelerated rapidly since then. There are also master franchises (or subfranchise) which gives a franchisee the right to create a semi-independent organization in a particular territory to recruit, sell, and support other franchisees. And, some franchisors are teaming up with other franchisors selling complementary products or services. Finally, now that dual-career couples have become the norm, especially among baby boomers, the market for franchises offering convenience and time-saving services is booming. Customers are willing to pay for products and services that will save them time or trouble, and franchises are ready to provide them.

15. What areas of franchising offer the greatest growth potential in the near future? Why?
   Answer - Currently, the biggest trend in franchising is the globalization of U.S. franchise systems. Increasingly, franchising is becoming a major export industry for the United States because markets outside U.S. borders offer most franchisors the greatest potential for growth. Canada is the primary market for U.S. franchisors, with Mexico, Japan, and Europe following. These markets are most attractive to franchisors because they have features similar to the U.S. market: rising personal incomes, strong demand for consumer goods, growing service economies, and spreading urbanization. For franchisors moving into foreign markets, adaptation is one key to success. Although they keep their basic systems intact, franchises that are successful in foreign markets quickly learn how to change their concepts to appeal to local tastes.

16. One franchisee says, "Franchising is helpful because it gives you somebody [the franchisor] to get you going, nurture you, and shove you along a little. But, the franchisor won't make you successful. That depends on what you bring to the business, how hard you are prepared to work, and how committed you are to finding the right franchise for you." Do you agree? Explain.
   Answer - In this discussion question, students' responses will vary.

Step into the Real World

1. Visit a local franchise operation. Is it a trade name, product distribution, or pure franchise? To what extent did the franchisee investigate before investing? What assistance does the franchisor provide?

2. Consult a copy of the International Franchise Association publication *Franchise Opportunities Handbook* (the library should have a copy). Write several franchisors in a particular business category and ask for their franchise packages. Write a report comparing their treatment of the topics covered by the Trade Regulation Rule.

3. Analyze the terms of the franchise contracts of the franchisors found in exercise 2. What are the major differences? Are some terms more favorable than others? If you were about to invest in the franchise, which terms would you want to change?

4. Ask a local franchisee to ask his or her regional franchise representative to lead a class discussion on franchising.

5. Contact the International Franchise Association (1350 New York Avenue, N.W., Suite 900, Washington, D.C., 20005-4709 [202]628-8000) for a copy of *Investigate before Investing.* Also search the resources on the World Wide Web for information on franchising. Prepare a report outlining what a prospective franchisee should do before buying a franchise.

6. Working with several of your classmates, select a franchise concept with which you are familiar. Conduct a brainstorming session in which your goal is to identify as many nontraditional locations for franchised outlets as possible. Prepare a short report on your ideas and the justification for them.

Chapter 5 - Buying an Existing Business

Teaching Objectives

Students will be able to:

1. Understand the advantages and disadvantages of buying an existing business.
2. Define the steps involved in the right way to buy business.
3. Explain the process of evaluating an existing business.
4. Describe the various ways of determining the value of a business.
5. Understand the seller's side of the buyout decision and how to structure the deal.
6. Understand how the negotiation process works and identify the factors that affect it.

Instructor's Outline

I. Introduction
    A. Secondhand Entrepreneurs
        1. These individuals are buying existing businesses rather than starting them "from scratch."
        2. Experts estimate that the market for U.S. small businesses is about $200 billion a year. Each year, more than 500,000 companies are sold, and 90 percent if those are valued at less than $5 million.
        3. The average sale price of these companies is less than $200,000.
        4. Problems often arise when entrepreneurs are in a hurry to close a deal. Be patient, and do the necessary homework. Be sure that you have answers to all of the following questions.
            a) Is the right type of business for sale in the market in which you want to operate?
            b) What experience do you have in a particular business and the industry in which it operates? How critical is experience in the business to your ultimate success?
            c) What price and payment methods are reasonable for you and acceptable to the seller?
            d) Should you start a business and build it from the ground up, or should you shop around to buy an existing company?
            e) What is each purchase candidate's potential for success?
            f) Are you willing to consider a business in decline with the intention of turning it around?
            g) What kinds of changes will you have to make--and how extensive will they be--to realize the business's full potential?

II. Buying an Existing Business
    A. Advantages of Buying an Existing Business
        1. A successful business may continue to be successful.
            a) The previous management already has established a customer base, built supplier relationships, and set up a business system.
            b) The new owner's objective should be to make modifications that will attract new customers while retaining the firm's existing customers.
        2. An existing business may already have the best location.
            a) When the location of the business is critical to its success, it may be wise to purchase a business that is already in the right place.
        3. Employees and suppliers are in place.
            a) You already have experienced employees who can help the company earn money while you learn the business.

        b) An existing business has an established set of suppliers with a history of business dealings.

    4. Equipment is installed and productive capacity is known.

        a) Acquiring and installing new equipment exerts a tremendous strain on a fledgling company's financial resources.

        b) In an existing business, a potential buyer can determine the condition of the plant and equipment and its capacity before he buys.

    5. Inventories are in place, and trade credit has been established.

        a) The proper amount of inventory is essential to both cost control and sales volume.

        b) Previous owners also have established trade credit relationships of which the new owner can take advantage.

        c) The business's proven track record gives the new owner leverage in negotiating favorable trade credit terms.

    6. The new business owner hits the ground running.

        a) The entrepreneur who purchases an existing business saves the time, costs, and energy required to plan and launch a new business.

    7. The new owner can use the experience of the previous owner.

        a) In many business sales, the previous owner spends time in an orientation period with the new owner, which gives the new manager the opportunity to question him about the policies and procedures he developed and the reasons for them.

        b) Previous owners also can be extremely helpful in unmasking the unwritten rules of business in the area: what types of behavior are acceptable, whom to trust, and other important intangibles.

    8. It's a bargain.

        a) If the current owners want to sell quickly, they may sell the business at a low price.

        b) The more specialized the business is, the greater the likelihood is that a buyer will find a bargain.

    9. Finding financing usually is easier.

        a) Because the risk associated with buying an existing business is lower than that of a start-up, financing for the purchase is easier.

B. Disadvantages of Buying an Existing Business

    1. It's a Loser.

        a) A business may be for sale because it has never been profitable.

        b) Such a situation may be disguised.

        c) The reason that a business is for sale will seldom be stated honestly.

        d) Although buying a money-losing business is risky, it is not necessarily taboo. If your analysis of a company indicates that it is poorly managed or suffering from neglect, you may be able to turn it around.

    2. The previous owner may have created ill will.

        a) Just as proper business dealings create goodwill, improper business behavior creates ill will.

        b) The business may look great on the surface, but customers, suppliers, creditors, or employees may have extremely negative feelings about it.

        c) The best way to avoid these problems is to investigate a prospective purchase target thoroughly before closing a deal.

    3. Employees inherited with the business may not be suitable.

        a) If the new owner plans to make changes in a business, the present employees may not suit her needs.

        b) Some workers may have a difficult time adapting to the new owner's management style and vision for the company.

4. The business location may have become unsatisfactory.
   a) What was once or is currently an ideal location may become obsolete as market and demographic trends change.
5. Equipment and facilities may be obsolete or inefficient.
   a) Potential buyers sometimes neglect to have an expert evaluate a company's building and equipment before they purchase it.
   b) Modernizing equipment and facilities is seldom inexpensive.
6. Change and innovation are difficult to implement.
   a) Methods and procedures the previous owner used created precedents that can be difficult or awkward for a new owner to change.
   b) Implementing changes to reverse a downward sales trend in a turnaround business can be just as difficult as eliminating unprofitable procedures.
7. Inventory may be obsolete.
   a) Inventory is valuable only if it is salable.
   b) Too many owners make the mistake of trusting a company's balance sheet to provide them with the value of its inventory.
8. Accounts receivable may be worth less than face value.
   a) Like inventory, accounts receivable rarely are worth their face value.
   b) The prospective buyer should age the accounts receivable to determine their collectibility.
9. The business may be overpriced.
   a) Most business sales are asset purchases rather than stock purchases, and a buyer must be sure that he knows which assets are included in the deal and what their real value is.
   b) Table 5.1 Valuing Accounts Receivable

III. How to Buy a Business
   A. A Method to the Purchase
      1. Studies show that more than 50 percent of all business acquisitions fail to meet the buyer's expectations.
         a) Analyze your skills, abilities, and interests to determine what kinds of businesses you should consider.
         b) Develop a list of criteria that defines the "ideal business" for you.
         c) Prepare a list of potential candidates.
         d) Investigate those candidates and evaluate the best ones.
         e) Negotiate the deal.
         f) Explore financing options.
         g) Ensure a smooth transition.

   B. Analyze Your Skills, Abilities, and Interests
      1. The first step in buying a business is conducting a self-audit:
         a) What business activities do you enjoy most? Least?
         b) Which industries interest you most? Least? Why?
         c) What kind of business do you want to buy?
         d) What kinds of businesses do you want to avoid?
         e) In what geographic area do you want to live and work?
         f) What do you expect to get out of the business?
         g) How much can you put into the business in both time and money?
         h) What business skills and experience do you have? Which ones do you lack?
         i) How easily can you transfer your existing skills and experience to other types of businesses? In what kinds of businesses would that transfer be easiest?

       j)   How much risk are you willing to take?

       k)   What size company do you want to buy?

  2. Answering those and other questions beforehand will allow you to develop a list of criteria that a company must meet before you will consider it to be a purchase candidate.

C. Develop a List of Criteria

  1. The next step is to develop a list of criteria that a potential business acquisition must meet.

  2. The goal is to identify the characteristics of the "ideal business" for you.

D. Prepare a List of Potential Candidates

  1. Now begin your search.

  2. One technique is to start at the macro level and work down.

       a)   Drawing on the resources in the library, the World Wide Web, government publications, and industry trade associations and reports, buyers can discover which industries are growing fastest and offer the greatest potential in the future.

       b)   For entrepreneurs with a well-defined idea of what they are looking for, another effective approach is to begin searching in an industry in which they have experience or one they understand well.

  3. Typical sources for identifying potential acquisition candidates include the following:

       a)   Business brokers.

       b)   Bankers.

       c)   Accountants.

       d)   Investment bankers.

       e)   Industry contacts: suppliers, distributors, customers, and others.

       f)   Knocking on the doors of businesses you'd like to buy.

       g)   Newspaper and trade journal listings of businesses for sale.

       h)   Trade associations.

       i)   The World Wide Web, where several sites include listings of companies for sale.

       j)   "Networking": social and business contact with friends and relatives.

  4. Buyers should consider every business that meets their criteria, even those that may not be listed for sale.

       a)   The hidden market of companies that might be for sale but are not advertised as such is one of the richest sources of top-quality businesses.

       b)   About 85 percent of [purchase] opportunities are tucked away in the unadvertised hidden market.

  5. Finding the right business often takes months.

E. Investigate and Evaluate Candidate Businesses and Determine the Value of the Best Ones

  1. This is known as due diligence.

  2. Due diligence involves studying, reviewing, and verifying all of the relevant information concerning your top acquisition candidates.

  3. The goal is to discover exactly what you will be buying and to avoid any unpleasant surprises after the deal is closed.

  4. Important questions to investigate include:

       a)   What are the company's strengths? Weaknesses?

       b)   What major threats is the company facing? Are there hidden threats you don't yet know about?

       c)   Is the company profitable? What is its overall financial condition?

       d)   What growth rate can you expect from the company in the near future?

e) What is its cash flow cycle?
f) Who are its major competitors?
g) How large is the company's customer base? Is it growing or shrinking?
h) Are the current employees suitable? Will they stay?
i) Will the seller stay on as a consultant to help you make a smooth transition?
j) What is the physical condition of the business, its equipment, and its inventory?
k) What is the company's reputation in the community and among customers and vendors?

5. Conducting a thorough analysis of a potential acquisition candidate usually requires an entrepreneur to assemble a team of advisers.
   a) Many entrepreneurs bring in an accountant, an attorney, an insurance agent, a banker, and a business broker to serve as consultants during the due diligence process.

F. Negotiate the Deal
1. The price paid for a company typically is not as crucial to its continued success as the terms on which the purchase is made.
   a) The structure of the deal is more important than the actual price the seller agrees to pay.
   b) The buyer's primary concern should be to make sure that the deal does not endanger the company's financial future and that it preserves the company's cash flow.

G. Explore Financing Options
1. Traditional lenders often shy away from deals involving the purchase of an existing business.
2. Those that are willing to finance business purchases normally lend only a portion of the value of the assets.
3. An important source of financing built into the deal: the seller.
4. Typically, a deal is structured so that the buyer makes a down payment to the seller, who then finances a note for the balance.
5. In most business sales, the seller is willing to finance 40 percent to 70 percent of the purchase price over time, usually across 3 to 10 years.

H. Ensure a Smooth Transition
1. No matter how well planned the sale is, there are always surprises.
2. Charged with emotion and uncertainty, the transition phase is always difficult and frustrating--and sometimes painful.
3. To avoid a bumpy transition, a business buyer should do the following:
   a) Concentrate on communicating with employees.
   b) Be honest with employees.
   c) Listen to employees.
   d) Devote time to selling your vision for the company to its key stakeholders, including major customers, suppliers, bankers, and others.
   e) Consider asking the seller to serve as a consultant until the transition is complete.
4. Figure 5.1 illustrates the sequence of events leading up to a successful negotiation with a seller.

IV. Evaluating an Existing Business
A. Five critical areas
1. Why does the owner want to sell?
2. What is the physical condition of the business?

3. What is the potential for the company's products or services?
4. What legal aspects are important?
5. Is the business financially sound?

B. Why does the Owner Want to Sell?
   1. A recent study by the Geneva Corporation found that the most common reasons that owners of small and medium-sized businesses gave for selling were boredom and burnout.
   2. Others decided to cash in their business investments and diversify into other types of assets.
   3. Other less obvious reasons that a business owner might have for selling his venture include a major competitor's moving into the market, highway rerouting, frequent burglaries and robberies, expiring lease agreements, cash flow problems, and a declining customer base.
   4. Some owners think ethical behavior requires only not making false or misleading statements.
      a) Visiting local business owners may reveal general patterns about the area and its overall vitality.
      b) The local chamber of commerce also may have useful information.
      c) Suppliers and competitors may be able to shed light on why the business is up for sale.

C. What is The Physical Condition of the Business?
   1. A prospective buyer should evaluate the business's assets to determine their value.
   2. It may be necessary to hire a professional to evaluate the major components of the building: its structure and its plumbing, electrical, and heating and cooling systems.
      a) Renovations are rarely inexpensive or simple.
   3. How fresh is the firm's inventory?
      a) A potential buyer may need to get an independent appraisal to determine the value of the firm's inventory and other assets because the current owner may have priced them far above their actual value.
      b) Book value is not the same as market value.
   4. Important factors that the potential buyer should investigate.
      a) Accounts receivable.
         (1) If the sale includes accounts receivable, the buyer should check their quality before purchasing them.
      b) Lease arrangements.
         (1) Is the lease included in the sale? When does it expire?
         (2) What restrictions does it have on renovation or expansion?
      c) Business records.
         (1) Many business owners are sloppy record keepers.
         (2) Consequently, the potential buyer and his team may have to reconstruct some critical records.
      d) Intangible assets.
         (1) Does the sale include any intangible assets such as trademarks, patents, copyrights, or goodwill?
      e) Location and appearance.
         (1) The location and the overall appearance of the building are important.
         (2) What kinds of businesses are in the area?
         (3) Every buyer should consider the location's suitability several years into the future.

(4) The potential buyer should also check local zoning laws to ensure that any changes he wants to make are legal.

D.   What is the potential for the company's products or services?
1.   A thorough market analysis can lead to an accurate and realistic sales forecast.
2.   Customer characteristics and composition.
a)   Discovering why customers buy from the business and developing a profile of the entire customer base can help the buyer identify a company's strengths and weaknesses.
b)   The entrepreneur should determine the answers to the following questions:
(1) Who are my customers in terms of race, age, gender, and income level?
(2) What do the customers want the business to do for them?
(3) How often do customers buy? Do they buy in seasonal patterns?
(4) How loyal are present customers?
(5) Will it be practical to attract new customers?
(6) Does the business have a well-defined customer base? Is it growing or shrinking?
3.   Analyzing the answers to those questions can help the potential owner implement a marketing plan.

IN THE FOOTSTEPS OF AN ENTREPRENEUR - In Search of the Perfect Business: Part I

SUMMARY

After becoming a victim of corporate downsizing, Hendrix Neimann decided to buy an existing business rather than start one from scratch. He had no idea what kind of business he was looking for, but he believed he would know the right company when he found it. For months, Neimann found nothing, so he began calling business brokers. He found a promising company through a blind ad in the Wall Street Journal: an access control and security company with sales of nearly $2 million whose owner was retiring. He met with the owner was told that there was nothing wrong with the company that a little salesmanship and marketing muscle wouldn't cure. On his first visit to Automatic Door Specialists [ADS], Neimann was shocked. Still, the business intrigued him. The price was affordable, and Neimann's severance pay was about to run out. Klosky sent Neimann a proposal showing how he could buy ADS with 100 percent financing, while keeping the debt service at manageable levels and taking out 7.5 percent of what his previous salary was. He and Klosky signed a letter of intent. Neimann met with ADS employees and what they told him was unsettling. Despite his reservations, Neimann went ahead with the purchase but only after offering Kiosk, just 50 percent of the amount stated in the letter of intent. Klosky accepted the offer. Neimann was astonished when Klosky and his attorney suddenly wanted to rewrite the entire deal at the closing. Both Neimann and Klosky came close to walking out, but seven hours--and more negotiations--later, they signed the deal. Hendrix Neimann had bought himself a business.

1.   Critique the way in which Neimann went about buying Automatic Door Specialists.
Answer - Neimann did ask questions and did inspect the site. He had the framework of a proper search he simply wasn't thorough or systematic. It seemed that the pressure of the ending of severance pay and the emotional desire to own a business drove him.
2.   Suppose that Neimann is a friend of yours and that he has come to you for advice about whether to purchase ADS. What will you tell him? Explain.
Answer - Students' answers will vary. Whether they recommend he not buy or buy, they should justify their answers in terms of an analysis of the business based on the facts of the case.

4. Competitor Analysis.
   a) The potential profitability and survival of the business may well depend on the behavior of these competitors.
   b) In addition to analyzing direct competitors, the buyer should identify businesses that compete indirectly.
   c) A potential buyer should also evaluate the trend in the competition. How many similar businesses have entered the market in the past five years? How many similar businesses have closed in the past five years? What caused these failures? Has the market already reached the saturation point? Being a late comer in an already saturated market is not the path to long-term success.
5. When evaluating the competitive environment, the prospective buyer should answer other questions:
   a) Which competitors have survived, and what characteristics have led to the success of each?
   b) How do the competitors' sales volumes compare with those of the business the entrepreneur is considering?
   c) What unique services do the competitors offer?
   d) How well organized and well coordinated are the marketing efforts of competitors?
   e) What are the competitors' reputations?
   f) What are the strengths and weaknesses of the competitors?
   g) How can you gain market share in this competitive environment?

E. What Legal Aspects are Important?
1. Liens.
   a) The key legal issue in the sale of any asset is typically the proper transfer of good title from seller to buyer.
   b) Some business assets may have liens (creditors' claims) against them, and unless those liens are satisfied before the sale, the buyer must assume them and become financially responsible for them.
   c) One way to reduce this potential problem is to include a clause in the sales contract stating that any liability not shown on the balance sheet at the time of sale remains the responsibility of the seller.
2. Bulk transfers.
   a) A bulk transfer is a transaction in which a buyer purchases all or most of a business's inventory (as in a business sale).
   b) To protect against surprise claims from the seller's creditors after purchasing a business, the buyer should meet the requirements of a bulk transfer under Section 6 of the Uniform Commercial Code.
   c) Without the protection of a bulk transfer, those creditors could make claim (within six months) to the assets that the buyer purchased in order to satisfy the previous owner's debts.
   d) To be effective, a bulk transfer must meet the following criteria:
      (1) The seller must give the buyer a sworn list of existing creditors.
      (2) The buyer and the seller must prepare a list of the property included in the sale.
      (3) The buyer must keep the list of creditors and the list of property for six months.
      (4) The buyer must give notice of the sale to each creditor at least 10 days before he takes possession of the goods or pays for them (whichever is first).
   e) By meeting these criteria, a buyer acquires free and clear title to the assets purchased.

3. Contract Assignments.
   a) A buyer must investigate the rights and the obligations he would assume under existing contracts with suppliers, customers, employees, lessors, and others.
   b) In general, the seller can assign any contractual right, unless the contract specifically prohibits the assignment or the contract is personal in nature.
   c) The prospective buyer also should evaluate the terms of any other contracts.
      (1) Patent, trademark, or copyright registrations
      (2) Exclusive agent or distributor contracts
      (3) Real estate leases
      (4) Insurance contracts
      (5) Financing and loan arrangements
      (6) Union contracts
4. Covenants not to compete.
   a) One of the most important and most often overlooked legal considerations for a prospective buyer.
   b) Under a restrictive covenant, the seller agrees not to open a new competing store within a specific time period and geographic area of the existing one. (The covenant should be negotiated with the owner, not the corporation, because if the corporation signs the agreement, the owner may not be bound.)
   c) However, the covenant must be a part of a business sale and must be reasonable in scope in order to be enforceable.
5. Ongoing legal liabilities.
   a) These typically arise from three sources: (1) physical premises, (2) product liability claims, and (3) labor relations.
   b) First, the buyer must examine the physical premises for safety.
   c) Second, the buyer must consider whether the product contains defects that could result in product liability lawsuits, which claim that a company is liable for damages and injuries caused by the products or services it sells.
   d) Third, what is the relationship between management and employees?
6. The existence of such liabilities does not necessarily eliminate the business from consideration.
   a) Insurance coverage can shift such risks from the potential buyer, but the buyer should check to see whether the insurance covers lawsuits resulting from actions taken before the purchase.
   b) Despite conducting a thorough search, a buyer may purchase a business only to discover later the presence of hidden liabilities, such as unpaid back taxes or delinquent bills, unpaid pension fund contributions, undisclosed lawsuits, or others.
      (1) Including a clause in the purchase agreement that imposes the responsibility for such hidden liabilities on the seller can protect a buyer from unpleasant surprises after the sale.

F. Is the Business Financially Sound?
   1. The prospective buyer must analyze the financial records of the business to determine its health.
      a) Current profits can be inflated by changes in the accounting procedure or in the method for recording sales.
      b) For the buyer, the most dependable financial records are audited statements, those prepared by a certified public accountant in accordance with generally accepted accounting principles (GAAP).
   2. A buyer also must remember that he is purchasing the future profit potential of an existing business.

         a) To evaluate the firm's profit potential, a buyer should review past sales, operating expenses, and profits as well as the assets used to generate those profits.

    3. Financial records that a potential buyer should examine.

         a) Income statements and balance sheets for the past three to five years.

            (1) It is important to review data from several years because creative accounting techniques can distort financial data in any single year.

         b) Income tax returns for the past three to five years.

            (1) Comparing basic financial statements with tax returns can reveal discrepancies of which the buyer should beware.

            (2) Some small business owners "skim" from their businesses; that is, they take money from sales without reporting it as income.

         c) Owner's compensation (and that of relatives).

            (1) The smaller the company is, the more important this will be.

            (2) Buyers must consider the impact of fringe benefits--company cars, insurance contracts, country club memberships, and the like.

         d) Cash flow.

            (1) Few buyers recognize the need to analyze its cash flow.

               (a) They assume that if profits are adequate, there will be sufficient cash to pay all of the bills and to fund an adequate salary for themselves.

            (2) Before closing any deal, a buyer should sit down with an accountant and convert the target company's financial statements into a cash flow forecast.

            (3) A potential buyer must look for suspicious deviations from the average (in either direction) for sales, expenses, profits, assets, and liabilities.

            (4) This financial information gives the buyer the opportunity to verify the seller's claims about the business's performance.

         e) Finally, a potential buyer should always be wary of purchasing a business if the present owner refuses to disclose his financial records.

            (1) Table 5.2 lists the records that a potential buyer should review before making a final decision about buying a business.

V. Methods for Determining the Value of a Business

  A. The Art and Science of Business Valuation

    1. What makes establishing a reasonable price for a privately owned business so difficult is the wide variety of factors that influence its value.

         a) The nature of the business itself.

         b) Its position in the market or industry.

         c) The outlook for the market or industry.

         d) The company's financial status and stability.

         e) Its earning capacity.

         f) Any intangible assets it may own (e.g., patents, trademarks, and copyrights).

         g) The value of other similar companies that are publicly owned.

         h) And many other factors.

    2. Computing the value of the company's tangible assets normally poses no major problem, but assigning a price to the intangibles, such as goodwill, almost always creates controversy.

    3. There are few hard-and-fast rules in establishing the value of a business, but the following guidelines can help.

         a) There is no single best method for determining a business's worth, because each business sale is unique.

         b) The deal must be financially feasible for both parties.

         c) Both the buyer and the seller should have access to the business records.

   d)   Valuations should be based on facts, not fiction.
   e)   No surprise is the best surprise.
4. The main reason that buyers purchase existing businesses is to get their future earnings potential.
5. The second most common reason is to obtain an established asset base.
   a)   It is often much easier to buy assets than to build them.
6. The best rule of thumb to use when valuing businesses is "Don't use rules of thumb to value businesses."

IN THE FOOTSTEPS OF AN ENTREPRENEUR - In Search of the Perfect Business: Part 2

SUMMARY

Two years after purchasing Automatic Door Specialists [ADS], Hendrix Neimann was well aware of the dark side of buying a business. Neimann discovered that a substantial portion of ADS sales came from government contracts, where the lowest bidder got the job. Under Neimann, however, ADS was focusing on quality product lines and full installation and service practices. Unfortunately, Neimann also discovered that potential customers saw ADS's products as commodities and made their purchase decisions on the basis of price, not quality and service. Neimann's attempts to change the company's culture met with no more success than did his marketing strategies. As in many small companies, cash flow was a constant problem. Looking back on his purchase of ADS, Neimann says, "Before I bought the business, I never really, truly assembled enough information. Neimann felt trapped.

1. Review the sections in this chapter entitled "How to Buy a Business" and "In Search of the Perfect Business: Part 1" Which steps did Neimann violate?
   Answer - Neimann violated: analyze your skills, abilities, and interests to determine what kinds of businesses you should consider, develop a list of criteria that defines the "ideal business," and investigate those candidates and evaluate the best ones.
2. What could Neimann have done to avoid the problems at ADS?
   Answer - Basically not violate the process and stop the purchase when he kept getting unpleasant surprises.
3. What is your forecast for ADS and Hendrix's future?
   Answer - Students' answers will vary, most will think he will fail. Some will think he will tough it out. Others will read ahead. ☺

   B.   Balance Sheet Method: Net Worth = Assets - Liabilities
      1.   Balance sheet technique.
         a)   One of the most commonly used methods of evaluating a business.
         b)   It is not highly recommended, because it oversimplifies the valuation process.
         c)   This method computes the book value of company's net worth, or owner's equity (net worth = assets - liabilities) and uses this figure as the value.
         d)   The problem with this technique is that it fails to recognize reality. Most small businesses have market values that exceed their reported book values.
         e)   The first step is to determine which assets are included in the sale.
            (1)   In most cases, the owner has some personal assets that he does not want to sell.
            (2)   Net worth on a financial statement will likely differ significantly from actual net worth in the market.
            (3)   Figure 5.2 shows the balance sheet for Lewis Electronics.
      2.   Variation: Adjusted balance sheet technique.
         a)   A more realistic method for determining a company's value.

b) Typical assets in a business sale include notes and accounts receivable, inventories, supplies, and fixtures.

c) If a buyer purchases notes and accounts receivable, he should estimate the likelihood of their collection and adjust their value accordingly.

d) In manufacturing, wholesale, and retail businesses, inventory is usually the largest single asset in the sale.

   (1) The sale may include three types of inventory, each having its own method of valuation: raw materials, work-in-process, and finished goods.

e) The buyer and the seller must arrive at a method for evaluating the inventory.

f) First-in-first-out (FIFO), last-in-first-out (LIFO), and average costing are three frequently used techniques, but the most common methods use the cost of last purchase and the replacement value of the inventory.

g) Before accepting any inventory value, the buyer should evaluate the condition of the goods.

h) Some buyers insist on having a knowledgeable representative on an inventory team to count the inventory and check its condition.

i) Fixed assets transferred in a sale might include land, buildings, equipment, and fixtures.

   (1) Appraisals of these assets on insurance policies are helpful guidelines for establishing market value.

3. Business evaluations based on balance sheet methods suffer one major drawback:

a) They do not consider the future earnings potential of the business.

C. Earnings Approach

1. The earnings approach is more refined than the balance sheet method, because it considers the future income potential of the business.

2. Variation 1: Excess earnings method.

a) This method combines both the value of the firm's existing assets (over its liabilities) and an estimate of its future earnings potential to determine a business's selling price.

b) One advantage of the excess earnings method is that it offers an estimate of goodwill.

   (1) Goodwill is an intangible asset that often creates problems in a business sale.

   (2) In essence, goodwill is the difference between an established, successful business and one that has yet to prove itself.

   (3) It is based on the company's reputation and its ability to attract customers.

3. The excess earnings method provides a fairly consistent and realistic approach for determining the value of goodwill.

a) Step 1. Compute adjusted tangible net worth.

b) Step 2. Calculate the opportunity costs of harvesting in the business.

   (1) Opportunity costs represent the cost of forgoing a choice.

   (2) There are three components in the rate of return used to value a business.

      (a) the basic, risk-free return.

      (b) an inflation premium.

      (c) the risk allowance for investing in the particular business.

   (3) A normal-risk business typically indicates a 25 percent rate of return.

   (4) The second part of the buyer's opportunity cost is the salary that she could have earned working for someone else.

c) Step 3. Project net earnings.

   (1) The buyer must estimate the company's net earnings for the upcoming year before subtracting the owner's salary.

(2) Averages can be misleading, so the buyer must be sure to investigate the trend of net earnings.

d) Step 4. Compute extra earning power.

(1) A company's extra earning power is the difference between forecasted earnings (step 3) and total opportunity costs (step 2).

e) Step 5. Estimate the value of intangibles.

(1) The owner can use the business's extra earning power to estimate the value of its intangible assets, that is, its goodwill.

(2) Multiplying the extra earning power by a years-of-profit figure yields an estimate of the intangible assets value.

(3) The years-of-profit figure for a normal-risk business ranges from three to four.

f) Step 6. Determine the value of the business.

(1) To determine the value of the business, the buyer simply adds together the adjusted tangible net worth (step 1) and the value of the intangibles (step 5).

g) Both the buyer and seller should consider the tax implications of transferring goodwill.

(1) The amount that the seller receives for goodwill is taxed as ordinary income.

h) The success of this approach depends on the accuracy of the buyer's estimates of net earnings and risk, but it does offer a systematic method for assigning a value to goodwill.

4. Variation 2: Capitalized earnings approach.

a) Another earnings approach capitalizes expected net profits to determine the value of a business.

b) The buyer should prepare his own pro forma income statement and should ask the seller to prepare one also.

c) The greater the perceived risk, the higher the return the buyer will require.

d) The capitalized earnings approach divides estimated net earnings (after subtracting the owner's reasonable salary) by the rate of return that reflects the risk level.

e) Clearly, firms with lower risk factors are more valuable than are those with higher risk factors.

5. Variation 3. Discounted future earnings approach.

a) This variation of the earnings approach assumes that a dollar earned in the future will be worth less than that same dollar today.

b) Present value represents the cost of the buyers' giving up the opportunity to earn a reasonable rate of return by receiving income in the future instead of today.

(1) To visualize the importance of the time value of money, consider two $1 million sweepstakes winners. Rob wins $1 million in a sweepstakes, and he receives it in $50,000 installments over 20 years.

(2) If Rob invests every installment at 15 percent interest, he will have accumulated $5,890,505.98 at the end of 20 years.

(3) Lisa wins $1 million in another sweepstakes, but she collects her winnings in one lump sum.

(4) If Lisa invests her $1 million today at 15 percent, she will have accumulated $16,366,537.39 at the end of 20 years.

(5) The difference in their wealth is the result of the time value of money.

6. The discounted future earnings approach has five steps:

a) Step 1. Project earnings for five years into the future.

(1) The buyer must remember that the further into the future he forecasts, the less reliable the estimates will be.

b) Step 2. Discount these future earnings using the appropriate present value factor.

(1) The appropriate present value factor can be found by looking in published present value tables, by using modem calculators or computers, or by solving the equation $I/(1 + k)t$, where k = rate of return and t = time (year 1, 2, 3 ..... n).

c) Step 3. Estimate the income stream beyond five years.

(1) One technique suggests multiplying the fifth-year income by $I/$(rate of return).

d) Step 4. Discount the income estimate beyond five years using the present value factor for the sixth year.

e) Step 5. Compute the total value of the business.

7. The primary advantage of this technique is that it evaluates a business solely on the basis of its future earnings potential, but its reliability depends on making forecasts of future earnings and on choosing a realistic present value factor.

8. The discounted future earnings approach is especially well-suited for valuing service businesses (whose asset bases are often small) and for companies experiencing high growth rates.

D. Market Approach

1. The market (or price/earnings) approach uses the price/earnings ratios of similar businesses to establish the value of a company.

a) The buyer must use businesses whose stocks are publicly traded in order to get a meaningful comparison.

b) A company's price/earnings ratio (or P/E ratio) is the price of one share of its common stock in the market divided by its earnings per share (after deducting preferred stock dividends).

2. To compute the company's value, the buyer multiplies the average price/earnings ratio by the private company's estimated earnings.

3. The biggest advantage of the market approach is its simplicity.

4. Disadvantages.

a) Necessary comparisons between publicly traded and privately owned companies.

b) Underrepresented earnings estimates.

c) Finding similar companies for comparison.

d) Applying the after-tax earnings of a private company to determine its value.

5. Despite its drawbacks, the market approach is useful as a general guideline to establishing a company's value.

E. The Best Method

1. Which of these methods is best for determining the value of a small business?

2. Simply stated, there is no single best method.

VI. Understanding the Seller's Side

A. Introduction

1. Few events are more anticipated--and emotional--than selling your business.

2. Many entrepreneurs who sell out experience a tremendous void in their lives.

3. Letting go is not easy, and putting a price on what they have worked most of their lives to build is even more difficult.

B. Pick the Right Time

1. Too often, business owners put off the selling process until the last minute: at retirement age or when a business crisis looms.

2. Advance planning and maintaining accurate financial records is key to a successful sale.

3. Important questions before selling a business.

a) Do I want to walk away from the business completely, or do I plan to stay on after the sale?
b) If I decide to stay on, how involved do I want to be in running the company?
c) How much can I realistically expect to get for the business?
d) Is this amount of money sufficient to maintain my desired lifestyle?
e) Rather than sell the business to an outsider, should I be transferring ownership to my children or to my employees?
f) Who are the professionals (business brokers, accountants, attorneys, tax advisers, and others) I will need to help me close the sale successfully?
g) How do I expect the buyer to pay for the company?
h) Am I willing to finance at least part of the purchase price? If so, on what terms?

WIRED TO THE WEB - Planning for a Purchase

SUMMARY
Tony Kurtz and Randa Alexander wanted to purchase the Bettendorf, Iowa, branch of the wholesale heating, air-conditioning, and refrigeration supply chain where Kurtz had worked for the past 11 years. Although the branch was currently losing money, Kurtz and Alexander had confidence that they could turn the business around.

They attended a seminar sponsored by the Small Business Association's Service Corps of Retired Executives program on how to write a business plan. Kurtz and Alexander signed a letter of intent and began analyzing the company's records and market potential as part of their due diligence. The asking price of $350,000, about twice what the pair was hoping to pay. They could come up with almost $58,000 in cash. Alexander suggested that they apply for a Small Business Administration loan guarantee, and Kurtz thought that the present owner might be willing to finance part of the sale.

1. Use the resources on the World Wide Web to assemble a plan for Kurtz and Alexander as they prepare to purchase this business. What specific pitfalls should they watch for?
    Answer - Students' responses will depend on the resources they find on the Internet. Consider offering them the SBA, SCOPE, etc., as starting points. Refer to pages 144-147 for considerations.
2. Search the World Wide Web for negotiating tips that will help Kurtz and Alexander as they work to strike a bargain with the current owner.
    Answer - Students' responses will depend on the resources they find on the Internet.
3. How should Kurtz and Alexander go about determining the value of the business?
    Answer - Refer to pages 157-160. Students should argue for their choice based on what they think it will do for Kurtz and Alexander. The earnings approach might be best, because it looks as if they will be carrying heavy debt and need to be sure they can service it. Other approaches are viable.

C. Plot an Exit Strategy and Structure the Deal
    1. Now the focus shifts to structuring the most beneficial deal.
    2. Planning the structure of the deal is the most important decision a seller can make after the choice of buyer.
        a) Entrepreneurs who sell their companies without considering the tax implications of the deal can wind up paying as much as 70 percent of the proceeds in the form of capital gains and other taxes?
    3. Straight business sale.
        a) A recent study of small business sales in 60 categories found that 94 percent were asset sales; the remaining 6 percent involved the sale of stock.

b) About 22 percent were for cash, and 75 percent included a down payment with a note carried by the seller. The remaining 3 percent relied on a note from the seller with no down payment.

c) When the deal included a down payment, it averaged 33 percent of the purchase price. Only 40 percent of the business sales studied included covenants not to compete.

4. Although selling a business outright is often the safest exit path for an entrepreneur, it is usually the most expensive.

5. Form a family limited partnership.
   a) For entrepreneurs who want to pass their businesses on to their children.
   b) The owner takes the role of general partner while her children become limited partners.
      (1) The general partner keeps just 1 percent of the company, but the partnership agreement gives her total control over the business. The children own 99 percent of the company but have little or no say over how to run the business.

6. Sell controlling interest.
   a) Sometimes, business owners sell the majority interest in their companies to investors, competitors, suppliers, or large companies with an agreement that they will stay on after the sale.

7. Restructure the company.
   a) Another way for business owners to cash out gradually is to replace the existing corporation with a new one, formed with other investors.
   b) The owner essentially is performing a leveraged buyout of his own company.
   c) See Figure 5.4 for an example.

8. Sell to an international buyer.
   a) Small U.S. businesses have become attractive buyout targets for foreign companies.
   b) Foreign buyers--mostly European--buy more than 1,000 U.S. businesses each year.
      (1) England leads the list of nations acquiring U.S. companies.
   c) In most instances, foreign companies buy U.S. businesses to gain access to a lucrative, growing market.
   d) Disadvantages.
      (1) They typically purchase 100 percent of a company.
      (2) Relationships with foreign owners also can be difficult to manage.

9. Use a two-step sale.
   a) For owners wanting the security of a sales contract now but not wanting to step down from the company's helm for several years, a two-step sale may be ideal.
   b) The buyer purchases the business in two phases, getting 20 to 70 percent today and agreeing to buy the remainder within a specific time period.

10. Establish an employee stock ownership plan (ESOP).
    a) Some owners cash out by selling to their employees through an employee stock ownership plan (ESOP).
    b) An ESOP is a form of employee benefit plan in which a trust created for employees purchases their employers' stock.
       (1) See Figure 5.5.
    c) To use an ESOP successfully, a small business should be profitable (with pretax profits exceeding $100,000) and should have a payroll of more than $500,000 a year.

VII. Negotiating the Deal
   A. The Seller is Looking To
      1. Get the highest price possible for the company.

      2. Sever all responsibility for the company's liabilities.

      3. Avoid unreasonable contract terms-that might limit her future opportunities.

      4. Maximize the cash she gets from the deal.

      5. Minimize the tax burden from the sale.

      6. Make sure the buyer will make all future payments.

B. The Buyer Seeks To

      1. Get the business at the lowest price possible.

      2. Negotiate favorable payment terms, preferably over time.

      3. Get assurances that he is buying the business he thinks he is getting.

      4. Avoid enabling the seller to open a competing business.

      5. Minimize the amount of cash paid up front.

IN THE FOOTSTEPS OF AN ENTREPRENEUR - In Search of the Perfect Business: Part 3

SUMMARY

"How could I possibly have been so foolish." asks Hendrix Neimann. After Neimann and his accountant discovered the unpaid bills, inflated inventory values, and past-due accounts receivable, they discounted heavily the price they offered Peter Klosky for the company. "I really thought it was a smart, talented, hardworking guy and that I could fix whatever was wrong with the company. Never mind that I didn't have a technical bone in my body and that this was a technical business in a technical industry. Never mind that the company turned out to be struggling and, in fact, losing money when I bought it."

But he couldn't. On February 12, 1997, Neimann closed the company, now called **ADS Systems**, that he had purchased nearly eight years before. He contacted the company's banker and its creditors and told them that he was ceasing operations. For Neimann, the next few months were a nightmare. From the time Neimann had bought **ADS**, the company was struggling financially and was never able to recover. The company was constantly in a cash flow bind, was usually behind in paying its bills, and rarely had a payables-to-receivables ratio of less than 2.5 to 1. Neimann reflected on the path that had brought him to this point. Looking around at the condition he had allowed his company to degenerate into, Neimann was embarrassed. "Like the former owner, I no longer had noticed the dirt, the grease, the grime, the disorganization. I had allowed the men's offices, their desks, their vans to become no better than the inside of garbage cans. I had let the shop remain in a state of chaos since we had moved in there. The technicians and I never connected--ever."

1. Using Hendrix Neimann's experience with ADS, develop a list of "red flags" that should alert a buyer that a particular business is not for him or her.
    Answer - Neimann missed almost every sign. First, why does the owner want to sell? It was clearly in decline in a competitive industry. Second, what is the physical condition of the business? The physical condition was deployable and stayed that way. Third, what is the potential for the company's products or services? Here he should have noted the mismatch between his abilities and the nature of both the product and the market, i.e., a technical market and product. Fourth, what legal aspects are important? This was not a factor. Fifth, is the business financially sound? This was a major red flag that he simply didn't dig far enough to discover.
2. Looking back at Neimann's experience, what advice would you give to someone who is considering buying a business?
    Answer - Refer to pages 139-144 as the students' offer their suggestions.

C. Factors Affecting the Negotiation Process

      1. Before beginning negotiations, a buyer should take stock of some basic issues.

    a) How strong is the seller's desire to sell?
    b) Is the seller willing to finance part of the purchase price?
    c) What terms does the buyer suggest? Which ones are most important to him?
    d) Is it urgent that the seller close the deal quickly?
    e) What deal structure best suits your needs?
    f) What are the tax consequences for both parties?
    g) Will the seller sign a restrictive covenant?
    h) Is the seller willing to stay on with the company for a time as a consultant?
    i) What general economic conditions exist in the industry at the time of the sale?

2. Sellers tend to have the upper hand in good economic times.
3. Buyers will have an advantage during recessionary periods in an industry.

D. The Negotiation Process
    1. On the surface, the negotiation process appears to be strictly adversarial.
    2. The negotiation process will go much more smoothly and much faster if the two parties work to establish a cooperative relationship based on honesty and trust from the outset.
    3. A successful deal requires both parties to examine and to articulate their respective positions while trying to understand the other party's position.
    4. Negotiating tips that can help parties reach a mutually satisfying deal.
        a) Know what you want to have when you walk away from the table.
        b) Develop a negotiation strategy.
        c) Recognize the other party's needs.
        d) Be an empathetic listener.
        e) Focus on the problem, not on the person.
        f) Avoid seeing the other side as "the enemy."
        g) Educate; don't intimidate.
        h) Be patient.
        i) Remember that "no deal" is an option.
        j) Be flexible and creative.

Chapter Summary

♦ Understand the advantages and disadvantages of buying an existing business.
- The advantages of buying an existing business include: successful business may continue to be successful; the business may already have the best location; employees and suppliers are already established; equipment is installed and its productive capacity known; inventory is in place and trade credit established; the owner hits the ground running; the buyer can use the expertise of the previous owner; the business may be a bargain.
- The disadvantages of buying an existing business include: an existing business may be for sale because it is deteriorating; the previous owner may have created ill will; employees inherited with the business may not be suitable; its location may have become unsuitable; equipment and facilities may be obsolete; change and innovation are hard to implement; inventory may be outdated; accounts receivable may be worth less than face value; the business may be over-priced.

♦ Define the steps involved in the right way to buy a business.
- Buying a business can be a treacherous experience unless the buyer is well-prepared. The right way to buy a business is: analyze your skills, abilities, and interests to determine the ideal business for you; prepare a list of potential candidates, including those that might be in the "hidden market'; investigate and evaluate candidate businesses and evaluate the best one; explore financing options before you actually need the money; and, finally, ensure a smooth transition.

♦ Explain the process of evaluating an existing business.

- Rushing into a deal can be the biggest mistake a business buyer can make. Before closing a deal, every business buyer should investigate five critical areas: (1) Why does the owner wish to sell? Look for the real reason. (2) Determine the physical condition of the business. Consider both the building and its location. (3) Conduct a thorough analysis of the market for your products or services. Who are the present and potential customers? Conduct an equally thorough analysis of competitors, both direct and indirect. How do they operate and why do customers prefer them? (4) Consider all of the legal aspects that might constrain the expansion and growth of the business. Did you comply with the provisions of a bulk transfer? Negotiate a restrictive covenant? Consider ongoing legal liabilities? (5) Analyze the financial condition of the business, looking at financial statements, income tax returns, and especially cash flow.

♦ Describe the various ways of determining the value of a business.
  - Placing a value on a business is partly an art and partly a science. There is no single best method for determining the value of a business. The following techniques (with several variations) are useful: the balance sheet technique (adjusted balance sheet technique); the earnings approach (excess earnings method, capitalized earnings approach, and discounted future earnings approach); and the market approach.

♦ Understand the seller's side of the buyout decision and how to structure the deal.
  - Selling a business takes time, patience, and preparation to locate a suitable buyer, strike a deal, and make the transition. Sellers must always structure the deal with tax consequences in mind. Common exit strategies include a straight business sale, forming a family limited partnership, selling a controlling interest in the business, restructuring the company, selling to an international buyer, using a two-step sale, and establishing an employee stock ownership plan (ESOP).

♦ Understand how the negotiation process works and identify the factors that affect it.
  - The first rule of negotiating is never confuse price with value. In a business sale, the party who is the better negotiator usually comes out on top. Before beginning negotiations, a buyer should identify the factors that are affecting the negotiations and then develop a negotiating strategy. The best deals are the result of a cooperative relationship based on trust.

Discussion Questions

1. What advantages can an entrepreneur who buys a business gain over one who starts a business from scratch?

   Answer - There are a number of advantages. 1) A successful business may continue to be successful. 2) An existing business may already have the best location. 3) Employees and suppliers are in place. 4) Equipment is installed and productive capacity is known. 5) Inventories are in place and trade credit has been established. 6) The ability to hit the ground running is running. 7) Use the experience of the previous owner. 8) If the current owners want to sell quickly, they may sell the business at a low price. 9) Because the risk associated with buying an existing business is lower than that of a start-up, financing for the purchase is easier.

2. How would you go about determining the value of the assets of a business if you were unfamiliar with them?

   Answer - Studies show that more than 50 percent of all business acquisitions fail to meet the buyer's expectations. To avoid this buyers should look at the following.
   - Analyze your skills, abilities, and interests to determine what kinds of businesses you should consider.
   - Develop a list of criteria that defines the "ideal business" for you.
   - Prepare a list of potential candidates.
   - Investigate those candidates and evaluate the best ones.
   - Negotiate the deal.

- Explore financing options.
- Ensure a smooth transition.

3. Why do so many entrepreneurs run into trouble when they buy an existing business? Outline the steps involved in the right way to buy business.
    Answer - Buying a business can be a treacherous experience unless the buyer is well-prepared. The right way to buy a business is: analyze your skills, abilities, and interests to determine the ideal business for you; prepare a list of potential candidates, including those that might be in the "hidden market;" investigate and evaluate candidate businesses and evaluate the best one; explore financing options before you actually need the money; and, finally, ensure a smooth transition.

4. When evaluating an existing business that is for sale, what areas should an entrepreneur consider? Briefly summarize the key elements of each area.
    Answer - There are five key elements. 1) Why does the owner want to sell? A recent study by the Geneva Corporation found that the most common reasons that owners of small and medium-sized businesses gave for selling were boredom and burnout. 2) What is the physical condition of the business? A prospective buyer should evaluate the business's assets to determine their value. It may be necessary to hire a professional to evaluate the major components of the building: its structure and its plumbing, electrical, and heating and cooling systems. 3) What is the potential for the company's products or services? A thorough market analysis can lead to an accurate and realistic sales forecast. Buyers should examine customer characteristics and composition. Analyzing the answers to those questions can help the potential owner implement a marketing plan. 4) What legal aspects are important? 5) Who are the competitors? The potential profitability and survival of the business may well depend on the behavior of these competitors. In addition to analyzing direct competitors, the buyer should identify businesses that compete indirectly. 6) The buyer needs to look at what legal aspects are important. The key legal issue in the sale of any asset is typically the proper transfer of good title from seller to buyer. To protect against surprise claims from the seller's creditors after purchasing a business, the buyer should meet the requirements of a bulk transfer under Section 6 of the Uniform Commercial Code. A buyer must investigate the rights and the obligations he would assume under existing contracts with suppliers, customers, employees, lessors, and others. 7) Finally, is the business financially sound? The prospective buyer must analyze the financial records of the business to determine its health.

5. How should a buyer evaluate a business's goodwill?
    Answer - Computing the value of the company's tangible assets normally poses no major problem, but assigning a price to the intangibles, such as goodwill, almost always creates controversy. The excess earnings method combines both the value of the firm's existing assets (over its liabilities) and an estimate of its future earnings potential to determine a business's selling price. One advantage of the excess earnings method is that it offers an estimate of goodwill. Goodwill is an intangible asset that often creates problems in a business sale. In essence, goodwill is the difference between an established, successful business and one that has yet to prove itself. It is based on the company's reputation and its ability to attract customers. The excess earnings method provides a fairly consistent and realistic approach for determining the value of goodwill.

6. What is a restrictive covenant? Is it fair to ask the seller of a travel agency located in a small town to sign a restrictive covenant for one year covering a 20-square-mile area? Explain.
    Answer - It is a form of covenants not to compete. It is one of the most important and most often overlooked legal considerations for a prospective buyer. Under a restrictive covenant, the seller agrees not to open a new competing store within a specific time period and geographic area of the existing one. (The covenant should be negotiated with the owner, not the corporation, because if the corporation signs the agreement, the owner may not be bound.) However, the covenant must be a

part of a business sale and must be reasonable in scope in order to be enforceable. It depends if the travel agency draws clients from that large an area.

7. How much negative information can you expect the seller to give you about the business? How can a prospective buyer find out such information?
    Answer - One should not expect the seller to reveal much. Some owners think ethical behavior requires only not making false or misleading statements. A recent study by the Geneva Corporation found that the most common reasons that owners of small and medium-sized businesses gave for selling were boredom and burnout. Others decided to cash in their business investments and diversify into other types of assets. Other less obvious reasons that a business owner might have for selling his venture include a major competitor's moving into the market, highway rerouting, frequent burglaries and robberies, expiring lease agreements, cash flow problems, and a declining customer base. There are several ways to gather this information. Visiting local business owners may reveal general patterns about the area and its overall vitality. The local chamber of commerce also may have useful information. Suppliers and competitors may be able to shed light on why the business is up for sale.

8. Why is it so difficult for buyers and sellers to agree on a price for a business?
    Answer - The two parties have different goals. Few events are more anticipated--and emotional-- than selling your business. Many entrepreneurs who sell out experience a tremendous void in their lives. Letting go is not easy, and putting a price on what they have worked most of their lives to build is even more difficult. Also, too often, business owners put off the selling process until the last minute: at retirement age or when a business crisis looms.

9. Which method of valuing a business is best? Why?
    Answer - There is no one best method. Students' answers should reference pages 151-160. There is no right answer, students' responses should address the particular value of each method.

10. Outline the different exit strategies available to a seller.
    Answer - Planning the structure of the deal is the most important decision a seller can make, after the choice of buyer.
    - Straight business sale.
    - Form a family limited partnership.
    - Sell controlling interest.
    - Restructure the company.
    - Sell to an international buyer.
    - Use a two-step sale.
    - Establish an employee stock ownership plan (ESOP).

11. Explain the buyer's position in a typical negotiation for a business. Explain the seller's position. What tips would you offer a buyer about to begin negotiating the purchase of a business?
    Answer - The seller is looking to:
    - Get the highest price possible for the company.
    - Sever all responsibility for the company's liabilities.
    - Avoid unreasonable contract terms-that might limit her future opportunities.
    - Maximize the cash she gets from the deal.
    - Minimize the tax burden from the sale.
    - Make sure the buyer will make all future payments.
    The buyer seeks to:
    - Get the business at the lowest price possible.
    - Negotiate favorable payment terms, preferably over time.

- Get assurances that he is buying the business he thinks he is getting.
- Avoid enabling the seller to open a competing business.
- Minimize the amount of cash paid up front.

Before beginning negotiations, a buyer should take stock of some basic issues.

- How strong is the seller's desire to sell?
- Is the seller willing to finance part of the purchase price?
- What terms does the buyer suggest? Which ones are most important to him?
- Is it urgent that the seller close the deal quickly?
- What deal structure best suits your needs?
- What are the tax consequences for both parties?
- Will the seller sign a restrictive covenant?
- Is the seller willing to stay on with the company for a time as a consultant?
- What general economic conditions exist in the industry at the time of the sale?

Sellers tend to have the upper hand in good economic times.

Buyers will have an advantage during recessionary periods in an industry.

Step into the Real World

1. Ask several new owners who purchased existing businesses the following questions.
   a) How did you determine the value of the business?
   b) How close was the price paid for the business to the value assessed before purchase?
   c) What percentage of the accounts receivable was collectible?
   d) How accurate were the projections concerning customers (sales volume and number of customers, especially)?
   e) Did you encounter any surprises after buying the business?
   f) If you were negotiating the deal again, what would you do differently?
2. Visit a business broker and ask him how he brings a buyer and seller together. What does he do to facilitate the sale? What methods does he use to determine the value of a business?
3. Ask a local attorney about the legal aspects of buying a business. What recommendations does she have for someone considering the purchase of an existing business? What negotiating tips can she offer? Prepare a brief report on what you learned for your class.
4. Use some of the following resources on the World Wide Web (or conduct your own search) to locate two businesses for sale that interest you:

BizQuest	http://www.bizQuest.com/
BizBuySell	http://www.bizbuysell.com/
Be The Boss	http://www.betheboss.com/
Internet Business Multiple Listing Site	http://www.bbn-net.com/

Write a brief synopsis of these businesses and explain why they interest you. Create a plan outlining the steps you would take to actually evaluate and purchase one of these companies.

Chapter 6 - Creating the Marketing Plan

Teaching Objectives
Students will be able to:
1. Describe the components of a marketing plan and explain the benefits of preparing one.
2. Discuss the role of market research.
1. Outline the market research process.
2. Explain how small businesses can pinpoint their target markets.
3. Describe the factors on which a small business can build a competitive edge.
4. Discuss the marketing opportunities the World Wide Web offers entrepreneurs and how to best take advantage of them.
5. Discuss the "four Ps' of marketing-product, place, price, and promotion-and their role in building a successful marketing strategy.

Instructor's Outline
I. Introduction
    A. We now shift our focus for the next three chapters to the business plan.
        1. A statement of <u>what</u> the entrepreneur plans to accomplish in both quantitative and qualitative terms.
        2. How it will be accomplished.
        3. The business plan consolidates many of the areas discussed in preceding chapters.

    B. The challenges in creating the business plan.
        1. Entrepreneurs often create business plans with great detail on the entrepreneur's intentions.
        2. But neglect the strategies to achieve those intentions.
        3. Sometimes entrepreneur's fail to adequately identify and research their target markets.
        4. And, sometimes entrepreneurs forget to create any business plan at all.

    C. An effective business plan
        1. Contains both a financial plan and a marketing plan.
        2. Like the financial plan, an effective marketing plan projects numbers and analyzes them, but from a different perspective. Rather than focus on cash flow, net profits, and owner's equity, the marketing plan concentrates on the *customer*.

II. Market-driven companies and the Marketing Plan
    A. Described
        1. Marketing is the process of creating and delivering goods and services to customers.
        2. It involves all of the activities associated with winning and retaining loyal customers.
        3. The secrets to successful marketing
            a) Understand the company's target customers' needs, demands, and wants before competitors.
            b) Offer them the products and services that will satisfy those needs, demands, and wants.
            c) Provide those customers with quality, service, convenience, and value so that they will keep coming back.
        4. The marketing function influences every aspect of its operation from finance and production to hiring and purchasing.

B. Small business owners must understand the importance of developing relevant marketing strategies.
   1. While small with correspondingly small marketing budgets, entrepreneurial companies can develop effective marketing strategies.
   2. Using "guerrilla marketing strategies"-unconventional, low-cost, creative techniques-small companies can wring as much or more "bang" from their marketing bucks.
      a) See example page 172, Just Books.

C. Winning marketing strategies are built on three vital resources: people, information, and technology.
   1. The entrepreneur needs to be able to recruit people with talent and form them into a team.
   2. Second, successful marketing relies on a company's ability to capture data and transform them into useful, meaningful information.
      a) Collecting more data than competitors.
      b) Putting it into a meaningful form faster.
      c) Disseminating the information to everyone in the business.
   3. Finally, technology has prove to be a powerful marketing weapon, but one easily matched by competitors.
      a) See Craig Heard, Gateway Outdoor Advertising, page 173.

D. The Marketing Plan
   1. Focuses on the customer.
   2. It builds a strategy of success for a business from the customer's point of view.
      a) Theodore Levitt, the primary purpose of a business is not to earn a profit; instead, it is "to create and keep a customer.
   3. A marketing plan should accomplish four objectives:
      a) determine customer needs and wants through market research.
      b) pinpoint a specific target market.
      c) analyze a firm's competitive advantages and builds a marketing strategy around them.
      d) create a marketing mix that meets customer needs and wants.

III. The Value of Market Research
   A. The value of market research
      1. Change in the U.S. population is a potent force altering the business environment.
      2. Market research is particularly valuable in tracking demographic trends in the population.
      3. The vehicle for gathering information for the marketing plan.
      4. It involves collecting, analyzing, and interpreting data about the company's market, customers, and competitors.
         a) See Larry Work and Michael Sternberg's story, pages 174-175.
      5. Market research does not have to be time consuming, complex, or expensive to be effective. Faith Popcorn encourages small business owners to be their own "trend trackers" by:
         a) reading as many current publications as possible.
         b) watching the top ten TV shows and the top ten movies.
         c) talking to at least 150 customers each year about what they are buying and why.
         d) talking with the 10 smartest people you know.
         e) listening to your children.
         f) engage in brainstorming with employees, customers, outsides, etc.
      6. Create a list and match your products and services against the trends. Adjust accordingly.

7. See Table 6.1 - Sixteen Trends Shaping the Business Environment for the Next Decade.

IV. How to Conduct Market Research
    A. The goal
        1. To reduce the risks inherent to business decisions.

    B. Define the problem
        1. The critical step in the process is being clear and concise about what the problem is.
            a) It is common to confuse the symptom and the problem.
            b) Example--declining sales is a symptom not a problem. To properly research it the owner must consider the factors that could cause it and then focus on investigating the most likely ones.
        2. This process can also uncover potential market opportunities.

    C. Collect the data
        1. The 1990s trend in market research is individualized marketing, increasing the importance of market research.
        2. Databases and PCs have become central to this process.
        3. There are three types of data the owner must collect:
            a) Geographic - Where are customers?
            b) Demographic - Customer characteristics.
            c) Psychographic - What drives customer buying behavior?
        4. Figure 6.1 - How to Become an Effective One-to-One Marketer, outlines the process for developing customer relation marketing.
        5. Also, see Table 6.2 - Building and Using a Consumer Database.

    D. Analyze and interpret the data
        1. Market research does not provide solutions to the problems; the owner must decide what the information means.

    E. Act on the data
        1. Decide how to use the information, what changes need to be made?

V. Market Diversity: Pinpointing the Target Market
    A. Objectives
        1. The primary objective of market research is to identify the target market.
        2. The more a business learns from market research about its local markets its customers, and their buying habits and preferences the more precisely it can focus its marketing efforts on the groups of prospective and existing customers who are most likely to buy its products or services.
        3. Small businesses' number one mistake is failing to define clearly the target market to be served; they tend to use a "shotgun approach" to marketing; firing marketing blasts at every customer they see, hoping to capture just some of them.
        4. Most small companies simply cannot use shotgun marketing to compete successfully with larger rivals and their deep pockets.
            a) Small businesses often develop new products that do not sell because they failed to target them at a specific audience's needs.
            b) They broadcast ads that attempt to reach everyone and end up reaching no one.

B. The irony
    1. Failing to pinpoint their target markets is ironic, because small firms are ideally suited to reaching market segments that their larger rivals overlook or consider too small to be profitable.
    2. The shotgun approach is popular, because it is easy and does not require market research or a marketing plan.
        a) The shotgun approach is a sales-driven rather than a customer-driven strategy.
        b) To be customer-driven, a marketing program must be based on a clear, concise definition of the firm's targeted customers.

C. "One-size-fits-all"
    1. This approach to business no longer works, because the mass market is rapidly disappearing.
    2. The mass market that dominated the business world of 25 years ago has been replaced by an increasingly fragmented market of multicultural customers.
        a) Hispanic.
        b) African American.
        c) Asian Pacific.
        d) Native American.

WIRED TO THE WEB - Coffee + Computers: A Cybercase

SUMMARY
While studying for a semester abroad a few years ago, Larissa Janus saw other groups of college students and young professional workers reading their mail and chatting with friends. Mentioning her observation to one of her friends, who was from France. "Oh yes!" the friend commented, "the tradition of stopping by a cafe to read your mail started in Europe in the last century."

Later Larissa thought back to the days in the café and thought "Why not set up a cybercafe in the European tradition where people could come to check their e-mail. Larissa began to list the questions she would have to answer as she developed a business plan for her idea. As her list of questions grew, Larissa said to herself, "Surely I can find some information on the World Wide Web."

1. What other questions must Larissa address as she begins to plan to launch her cybercafe? Help her by adding to her list of questions.
    Answer - Students should reference the items listed on pages 177-178. The need is to define the behavior of her potential customers.

2. Use the resources of the World Wide Web to locate some Web sites that would help Larissa. On the basis of what you learn from your Web search, outline the issues Larissa should address in her marketing plan. What types of customers should she target?
    Answer - Students' responses will vary based on their discoveries.

---

3. The most successful businesses have well-defined portraits of their target customers. They know their customers':
    a) income.
    b) lifestyle.
    c) buying patterns.

        d) likes and dislikes.

        e) etc.

   4. Growing diversity in the population is offering tremendous marketing opportunities. See Bill O'Gara's success story on page 183.

VI. Plotting a Marketing Strategy: How to Build a Competitive Edge
  A. Competitive edge
    1. A competitive edge is the customer's perception that the products or services of a business are superior to those of its competitors.
    2. Successful entrepreneurs build a competitive edge by creating value through:
      a) being closer to the customer.
      b) personal attention.
      c) a focus on service.
      d) organizational and managerial flexibility.
    3. Relationship marketing is the future--developing a long-term relationship with customers so they will keep coming back.

  B. Relationship marketing involves four levels of customer service.
    1. Level 1 - Customer awareness - know there's a customer "out there" but knows little about him/her.
    2. Level 2 - Customer sensitivity - there's better knowledge of the customer but still a barrier, and the company doesn't solicit feedback from its customers.
    3. Level 3 - Customer alignment - managers and employees understand the customers' central role in the business.
    4. Level 4 - Customer partnership - customers are part of every major issue. Employees at every level receive information about the customer.
    5. Small businesses rely on six sources to develop a competitive edge:
      a) focus on the customer.
      b) devotion to quality.
      c) attention to convenience.
      d) concentration on innovation.
      e) dedication to service.
      f) emphasis on speed.

  C. Focus on the customer
    1. U.S. companies lose about 1/2 of their customer base every five years.
    2. Everything depends on a satisfied customer.
    3. Poor customer service costs.
      a) 67% stop patronizing a store because of an indifferent employee.
      b) 96% of dissatisfied customers never complain.
      c) 91% never buy from the business again.
      d) 100% tell their "horror" stories to 9 other people.
      e) 13% of unhappy customers tell at least 20 other people.
    4. 70% of company sales come from present customers.
    5. The typical business loses 20% of its customers each year.
    6. A retention of just 5% more customers would raise profits 25%.
      a) See the example on the bottom of page 186.
      b) See Table 6.3 for The High Cost of Lost Customers.
    7. Principles for developing and maintaining a customer orientation.

a) When you create a dissatisfied customer, fix the problem fast. 95 percent of customers will buy again if a business handles their complaints promptly and effectively.

b) Encourage customer complaints. See Table 6.4 for Ways to Turn Complaints into Satisfied Customers.

c) Ask employees for feedback on improving customer service.

d) Get total commitment to superior customer service from top managers-and allocate resources appropriately.

e) Allow managers to wait on customers occasionally.

f) Carefully select and train everyone who will deal with customers. *Never* let rude employees work with customers.

g) Develop a service theme that communicates your attitude toward customers.

h) Reward employees "caught" providing exceptional service to the customer.

8. Remember: The customer pays the bills. Special treatment wins customers and keeps them coming back.

D. Devotion to quality

1. In the intensely competitive global business environment, quality goods and services are a prerequisite for success-and even survival.

   a) See Table 6.4, Ways to Turn Complaints into Satisfied Customers.

2. Manufacturers were the first to apply TQM techniques, but retail, wholesale, and service organizations have seen the benefits of becoming champions of quality.

   a) Tracking customer complaints.

   b) Contacting "lost" customers.

   c) Finding new ways to track the cost of quality and the return on quality (ROQ).

3. The ROQ measure recognizes that although any improvement in quality may improve a company's competitive ability, only the improvements that produce a reasonable rate of return are worthwhile.

4. The key to developing a successful TQM philosophy is seeing the world from the customer's point of view. How do customers define quality?

5. Guidelines used by world-class companies to "get it right the first time."

   a) Build quality into the process; don't rely on inspection to obtain quality.

   b) Foster teamwork and dismantle the barriers that divide disparate departments.

   c) Establish long-term ties with select suppliers; don't award contracts on low price alone.

   d) Provide managers and employees the training needed to participate fully in the quality improvement program.

   e) Empower workers at all levels of the organization; give them authority and responsibility for making decisions that determine quality.

   f) Get managers' commitment to the quality philosophy. Otherwise, the program is doomed.

   g) Rethink the processes the company uses now to get its products or services to its customers.

   h) Reward employees for quality work. Link workers' compensation clearly and directly to key measures of quality and customer satisfaction.

   i) Develop a companywide strategy for constant improvement of product and service quality.

6. The goal is to achieve 100 percent quality. Table 6.5 shows the consequences of 99.9% quality.

E. Attention to convenience
    1. Convenience is now critical in our busy, fast-paced world of dual-career couples and lengthy commutes to and from work; customers increasingly are looking for convenience.
    2. Customers rank easy access to goods and services at the top of their purchase criteria.
    3. Successful companies go out of their way to make sure that it is easy for customers to do business with them. The business owner can increase the convenience level of his/her business by conducting a "convenience audit" from the customer's point of view to get an idea of its ETDBW ("Easy To Do Business With") index:
        a) Is your business located near your customers? Does it provide easy access?
        b) Are your business hours suitable to your customers? Should you be open evenings and weekends to serve them better?
        c) Would customers appreciate pickup and delivery service?
        d) Does your company make it easy for customers to purchase on credit or with credit cards?
        e) Are your employees trained to handle business transactions quickly, efficiently, and politely?
        f) Does your company handle telephone calls quickly and efficiently?

F. Concentration on innovation
    1. Innovation is the key to future success. Markets change too quickly and competitors move too fast for a small company to stand still and remain competitive.
    2. Small business, because of its inherent organizational and managerial flexibility, often detects and acts on new opportunities faster than large companies. Despite financial constraints, small businesses frequently are leaders in innovation. For example:
        a) microcomputers (Apple Computer).
        b) minicomputers (Digital).
        c) supercomputers (Cray Research).
        d) pharmaceutical industry, the dominant drugs in most markets were discovered by small companies.
    3. Companies of all sizes are feeling the pressure to develop new products and get them to market faster than ever before. More intense competition, often from across the globe, as well as rapid changes in technology and improvements in communication have made innovation crucial to business success.
        a) One survey of U.S. companies found that executives expected new products to account for 39 percent of profits in the next five years compared with just 25 percent in the previous five.
    4. Small businesses manage to maintain their leadership role in innovating new products and services by using their size to their advantage and maintaining their speed and flexibility much as a martial arts expert does against a larger opponent.
    5. Their closeness to their customers enables them to read subtle shifts in the market and to anticipate trends as they unfold.
    6. The ability to concentrate their efforts and attention in one area also gives small businesses an edge in innovation.
    7. The small companies have an advantage: a dedicated management team totally focused on a new product or market.
    8. To be an effective innovator, an entrepreneur should:
        a) Make innovation a priority in the company by devoting management time and energy to it.

b) Measure the company's innovative ability. The number of new products or services introduced and the proportion of sales generated by products less than five years old can be useful measures of a company's ability to innovate.

c) Set goals and objectives for innovation. Establishing targets and rewarding employees for achieving them can produce amazing results.

d) Encourage new product and service ideas among employees.

e) Always be on the lookout for new product and service ideas.

f) Keep a steady stream of new products and services coming.

9. Table 6.6 describes a screening device for testing the viability of new product ideas.

G. Dedication to service and customer satisfaction

1. Successful companies go beyond customer satisfaction, striving for customer astonishment.

2. In the new economy, companies are discovering that unexpected innovative, customized service can be a powerful strategic weapon.

3. Small companies that lack the financial resources of their larger rivals have discovered that offering exceptional customer service is one of the most effective ways to differentiate themselves and to attract and maintain a growing customer base.

4. Most Americans still rate U.S. companies low on customer service.

5. Stellar superior customer service is characterized by the following.

a) Listening to customers.

b) Defining superior service.

c) Setting standards and measure performance.

d) Examining your company's service cycle.

e) Hiring the right employees.

f) Training employees to deliver superior service.

g) "Empower" employees to offer superior service.

h) Use technology to provide superior service.

i) Reward superior service.

j) Get top manager's support.

H. Emphasis on speed

1. Today's world is one of instantaneous expectations. Customers now expect an immediate response from companies, whatever products or services they may be buying.

a) McKinsey and Company found that high-tech products that come to market on budget but six months late will earn 33 percent less profit over five years than products that are on schedule.

b) Bringing the product out on time but 50 percent over budget cuts profits just 4 percent!

2. Service companies also know that they must build speed into their business systems if they are to satisfy their impatient, time-sensitive customers.

3. This philosophy of speed is called time compression management (TCM), and it involves three aspects:

a) speeding new products to market.

b) shortening customer response time in manufacturing and delivery.

c) reducing the administrative time required to fill an order.

4. Most businesses waste 85 to 99 percent of the time it takes to produce products or services without ever realizing it!

5. Companies relying on TCM need to:

      a) reengineer the entire production and delivery process rather than attempt to do the same things in the same way only faster.

      b) create cross-functional teams of workers and give them the power to attack and solve problems.

      c) set aggressive goals for time reduction and stick to the schedule.

      d) instill speed in the culture.

      e) use technology to find shortcuts wherever possible.

I. In the Footsteps of an Entrepreneur
    1. See "Are we making the grade?" page 201 for both how to measure a company's value-added success and the ultimate in customer-orientation.

VII. Marketing on the World Wide Web
  A. The hope
    1. The World Wide Web promises to become a revolutionary business tool.
      a) 50 million people are now on line.
      b) Electronic commerce has soared from $518 million in 1996 to $6.6 billion in 2000.
      c) The management consulting firm Booz, Allen and Hamilton estimates that by 2007 as much as 20 percent of all household expenditures will occur in cyberspace .
    2. Most entrepreneurs are still struggling to understand what it is, how it can work for them, and how they can establish a presence on it.
      a) By establishing a creative, attractive Web site, the "electronic storefront' for a company on the Web, even the smallest companies can market their products and services to customers across the globe.
      b) Although small companies cannot match the marketing efforts of their larger competitors, a creative Web page can be "the Great Equalizer" in a small company's marketing program, giving it access to markets all across the globe. The Web gives small businesses the power to broaden their scope to unbelievable proportions.
    3. Well-designed "home pages," include interactive features that allow customers to access information about a company, its products and services, its history, and other features such as question-and-answer sessions with experts or the ability to conduct electronic conversations with company officials.
    4. The Web also allows business owners to link their companies' home pages to other related Web sites, something advertisements in other media cannot offer.
    5. Currently about 141,000 small businesses have Web sites."
    6. Small companies have plenty of incentive to set up shop on the World Wide Web. The number of cybershoppers is growing rapidly, and the demographic profile of the typical Web user is very attractive to entrepreneurs: young (See Figure 6.2), educated, and wealthy. And:
      a) The average age is 35.
      b) Sixty-four percent have college degrees.
      c) Average annual household income is $69,000, and 25 percent earn more than $80,000 per year.
      d) Sixty percent are male.
      e) Seventy-seven percent browse the Web at least once a day.
    7. Although the current profile of Web customers is decidedly slanted toward affluent, well-educated males, the fact is that the Web is rapidly becoming a mainstream marketing medium, one that small business owners cannot afford to ignore.

8. The key to successful marketing on the World Wide Web is selling the right product or service at the right price to the right target audience.
9. For ideas on gaining a competive edge with a web site, see page 199, Designing a Killer Web Site.

GAINING THE COMPETITIVE EDGE - Designing a Killer Web Site

World Wide Web users are not a patient lot. How can an entrepreneur design a Web site that will capture and hold potential customers' attention long enough to make a sale? There's no sure-fire formula for stopping surfers in their tracks but the following suggestions will help.
- Be easy to find.
- Give customers what they want.
- Promote your web site in other media ad.
- Establish "hot links" with other businesses, preferably those selling products or services that complement yours.
- Include an E-Mail option in your site.
- Offer web shoppers a special all their own.
- Use a simple design.

Specific design tips include:
1. Avoid clutter. The best designs are simple and elegant with a balance of text and graphics.
2. Include a menu bar at the top of the page that makes it easy for customers to find their way around your site.
3. Include navigation buttons at the bottom of pages that enable customers to return to the top of the page or to the menu bar.
4. Avoid fancy typefaces and small fonts because they are too hard to read.
5. Don't put small fonts on "busy" backgrounds; no one will read them.
6. Use contrasting colors of text and graphics.
7. Be careful with frames.
8. Avoid automated music that plays continuously and cannot be cut off.
9. Make sure the overall look of the page is appealing.
10. Remember: Simpler usually is better.
- Assure customers that their on-line transactions are secure.
- Keep your site updated.

Small business owners must remember that on the World Wide Web every company, no matter how big or small, has the exact same screen size for its site. What matters most is not the size of your company but how you put that screen size to use.

VIII. The Marketing Mix
    A. The major elements of marketing are product, place, pricing, and promotion.
       1. These four elements are self-reinforcing and, when coordinated, they increase the salability of the product or service.

    B. Product
       1. Any good or service that satisfies the need of a consumer. The product must be viewed from the point of view of the consumer.

2. The product life cycle (See Figure 6.3) measures these stages of growth, and these measurements enable the company's management to make decisions about whether to continue selling the product and when to introduce new follow-up products.
   a) Introductory stage--Product "breaks into" the market; marketing is intensive and costs are high; profits are very low or, more likely, negative. Advertising and promotion help the new product gain recognition. Potential customers must get information about the product and the needs it can satisfy.
   b) Growth and Acceptance stage--consumers begin to experiment with the product, if successful, sales and profits continue to rise; otherwise, product disappears. Products that reach this stage, however, do not necessarily become successful. For successful products, sales and profit margins continue to rise through the growth stage.
   c) Maturity and Competition stage--sales volume continues to rise, but profit margins peak and then begin to fall as competitors enter the market. Normally, the selling price is lowered to meet competition and to hold its share of the market.
   d) Market Saturation stage--sales peak and give the marketer fair warning that it is time to begin product innovation.
   e) Product decline stage is the final stage. Sales continue to drop, and profit margins fall drastically. A product does not have to eventually fail. Products that have remained popular are always being revised.
3. The time span of the stages in the product life cycle depends on the type of products involved.
   a) High-fashion and fad clothing have a short product life cycle, lasting for only four to six weeks.
   b) Products that are more stable may take years to complete a life cycle.
   c) The typical product's life cycle lasts 10 to 14 years. See Figure 6.4, Time between Introduction of Products.
4. Understanding the product life cycle can help a business owner plan the introduction of new products to the company's product line.
   a) Often, companies wait too late into the life cycle of one product to introduce another.
   b) The result, they are totally unprepared for a competitor's innovation.
   c) The ideal time to develop new products is early on in the life cycle of the current product (See Figure 6.4).
5. Launching successful new products is no easy task. The most commonly cited reasons for product failures are:
   a) Too little differentiation from existing products.
   b) Inadequate knowledge of the market.
   c) Poor planning and execution of the introduction.
   d) Failure to adjust product strategy when changes dictate.
   e) Inadequate funding for, or lack of commitment to the new product.

C. Place
   1. The method of distribution.
   2. The channel of distribution is the path that goods or services and their titles take in moving from producer to consumer.
   3. "Middlemen" perform valuable services, providing:
      a) time utility.
      b) place utility.
   4. Four channels of distribution for consumer goods (see Figure 6-5).
      a) Manufacturer to consumer.

      b)   Manufacturer to retailer to consumer.
      c)   Manufacturer to wholesaler to retailer to consumer.
      d)   Manufacturer to wholesaler to wholesaler to retailer to consumer.
  5. 5.   Two channels of distribution for industrial goods (see Figure 6-6).
      a)   Manufacturer to industrial user.
      b)   Manufacturer to wholesaler to industrial user.

IN THE FOOTSTEPS OF AN ENTREPRENEUR - Are We Making the Grade?

SUMMARY
Granite Rock Company looks like any other small, family-owned construction material supplier. But closer examination reveals a highly sophisticated, quality-conscious, customer-oriented industry leader in what is ordinarily considered a "commodity business." Selling "value" can be a successful marketing strategy, but only if customers recognize and are willing to pay for it. Granite Rock concentrates on understanding exactly how its customers define such nebulous terms as value, quality and service.

The company also monitors its performance regularly and feeds all of this information directly to its workforce. Every year, Granite Rock sends a "report card" to customers, asking them to "grade" their top three suppliers on these factors. Granite Rock then combines the results of the survey with those from the report cards to generate a Customer Service Graph. Granite Rock's customer surveys led the company to create its "automatic loadout system" at its crushed rock quarry. The systems works like a bank's ATM machine. The company's attitudes toward customer satisfaction and its system for measuring it have helped Granite Rock maintain its profitability and nearly double its marketshare, even through a severe recession.

1.   What benefits does Granite Rock's customer satisfaction system offer customers? What are its benefits to the company itself?
    Answer - This is one way to build a competitive edge, the customer's perception that the products or services of a business are superior to those of its competitors. This is a prime example of relationship marketing--developing a long-term relationship with customers so they will keep coming back. Granite Rock seems to be at level 3--Customer alignment--managers and employees understand the customers' central role in the business.
2.   Which areas of the Customer Service Graph would be most important to Granite Rock? Least important. Why?
    Answer - On-time delivery, product quality, scheduling, and problem-resolution.

  D. Price
    1.   Price is a key factor affecting both sales volume and profits.
    2.   The right price for a product or service depends on three factors.
       a)   the company's cost structure.
       b)   an assessment of what the market will bear.
       c)   the desired image the company wants to create in its customers' minds.
    3.   Many small companies need to focus on nonprice competition because it is more effective against larger competitors. Such as:
       a)   free trial offers.
       b)   free delivery.
       c)   lengthy warranties.

         d) money-back guarantees.
    4. Nonprice competition plays down the product's price and stresses its durability, quality, reputation, or special features.

   E. Promotion
     1. Informing and persuading consumers is the role of promotion. Promotion is divided into advertising and personal selling.
     2. The goals of a small company's promotional efforts are:
        a) to create a brand image.
        b) to persuade customers to buy.
        c) to develop brand loyalty

Chapter Summary

♦ Describe the components of a marketing plan and explain the benefits of preparing one.
- A major part of the entrepreneur's business plan is the marketing plan, which focuses on a company's target customers and how best to satisfy their needs and wants. A solid marketing plan should:
  - Determine customer needs and wants through market research.
  - Pinpoint the specific target markets the company will serve.
  - Analyze the firm's competitive advantages and build a marketing strategy around them.
  - Create a marketing mix that meets customer needs and wants.

♦ Discuss the role of market research.
- Market research is the vehicle for gathering the information that serves as the foundation of the marketing plan. Good research does *not* have to be complex and expensive to be useful.

♦ Outline the market research process.
- The steps in conducting market research include:
  - Defining the problem: "What do you want to know?"
  - Collecting the data from either primary or secondary sources.
  - Analyzing and interpreting the data.
  - Acting on the data.

♦ Explain how small businesses can pinpoint their target markets.
- Sound market research helps the owner pinpoint his target market. The most successful businesses have well-defined portraits of the customers they are seeking to attract.

♦ Describe the factors on which a small business can build a competitive edge.
- When plotting a marketing strategy, owners must strive to achieve a competitive advantage some way to make their companies different from and better than the competition. Successful small businesses rely on six sources to develop a competitive edge:
  - Focus on the customer
  - Devotion to quality
  - Attention to convenience
  - Concentration on innovation
  - Dedication to service
  - Emphasis on speed

♦ Discuss the marketing opportunities the World Wide Web offers entrepreneurs and how to best take advantage of them.
- The Web offers small business owners tremendous marketing potential, on a par with their larger rivals. Entrepreneurs are just beginning to uncover the Web's profit potential. which is growing rapidly. Establishing a presence on the Web is important for companies targeting educated,

wealthy, young customers. Successful Web sites are attractive, easy to navigate, and interactive, and they offer users something of value.

♦ Discuss the "four Ps" of marketing-product, place, price, and promotion-and their role in building a successful marketing strategy.
   ● Product. Entrepreneurs should understand where in the product life cycle their products are.
   ● Place. The focus is on choosing the appropriate channel of distribution and using it most efficiently.
   ● Price. The right price depends on the company's cost structure and image and what the market will bear.
   ● Promotion. Promotion helps create a company image, persuades customers to buy, and develops customer loyalty.

Discussion Questions

1. Define the marketing plan. What lies at its center?
   Answer - The marketing plan is a subset of the business plan; it complements the financial section of the plan. While the financial plan focuses on cash flow and profits. The center of the marketing plan is the customer.

2. What objectives should a marketing plan accomplish?
   Answer - An effective marketing plan should accomplish four objectives. 1) Determine customer needs and wants through market research. 2) Pinpoint the specific target markets the company will serve. 3) Analyze the firm's competitive advantages and build a marketing strategy around them. 4) Create a marketing mix to meet customer needs and wants.

3. How can market research benefit a small business owner? List some possible sources of market information.
   Answer - Market research is the tool which aids management in determining who potential customers might be, what they need and want, and how much they are willing to pay. It helps the small business owner track demographic trends. Sources include a wide range of census data from the government, plus publications such as the "Survey of Buying Power," trade association data, and Chambers of Commerce data.

4. Does market research have to be expensive and sophisticated to be valuable? Explain.
   Answer - Market research does not have to be time consuming, complex, or expensive to be effective. Faith Popcorn encourages small business owners to be their own "trend trackers" by: a) reading, b) watching the top ten TV shows, c) seeing the top ten movies, d) talking to 150 customers each year about what they are buying and why, e) talking with the 10 smartest people you know, f) listening to your children. Use this information to make a list of major trends, then write out how well your products or services match those trends.

5. Describe the market trends that are driving markets in the 1990s, and their impact on small businesses.
   Answer - There are a number of trends impacting small businesses. a) Increasing population diversity, b) changing family patterns, c) greater environmental and health concerns, d) emergence of "premium" and "discount" niches, e) surge in "baby boomers" and the elderly.

6. Why is it important for small business owners to define their target markets as part of their marketing strategy?

Answer - The most successful businesses have well-defined portraits of their target customers. They know their customers' income, lifestyle, buying patterns, likes and dislikes, etc.   Growing diversity in the population is offering tremendous marketing opportunities, but small business owners need to know where those markets are in order to exploit them.

7. What is a competitive edge? How might a company gain one?
    Answer - Competitive edge is the customer's perception that the products or services of a business are superior to those of its competitors. Successful entrepreneurs use their special advantages to build a competitive edge over larger rivals. 1) Closer to the customer. 2) Personal attention. 3) Focus on service. 4) Organizational and managerial flexibility. A key competitive edge for small businesses is relationship marketing--developing a long-term relationship with customers so they will keep coming back.

8. Describe how a small business owner could use each of the following to gain a competitive advantage:
    - Focus on the customer
    - Devotion to quality
    - Attention to convenience
    - Concentration on innovation
    - Dedication to service
    - Emphasis on speed

    Answer - Focus on the customer--U.S. companies lose about 1/2 of their customer base every five years. Everything depends on a satisfied customer. A retention of just 5% more customers would raise profits 25%. Devotion to quality--Manufacturers were the first to apply TQM techniques, but retail, wholesale, and service organizations have seen the benefits of becoming champions of quality. The ROQ measure recognizes that although any improvement in quality may improve a company's competitive ability, only the improvements that produce a reasonable rate of return are worthwhile. The key to developing a successful TQM philosophy is seeing the world from the customer's point of view. How do customers define quality? Attention to convenience--Customers rank easy access to goods and services at the top of their purchase criteria. The business owner can increase the convenience level of his/her business by conducting a "convenience audit" from the customer's point of view to get an idea of its ETDBW ("Easy To Do Business With") index. Concentration on innovation--Innovation is the key to future success. Markets change too quickly and competitors move too fast for a small company to stand still and remain competitive. Dedication to service and customer satisfaction--In the new economy, companies are discovering that unexpected innovative, customized service can be a powerful strategic weapon. Small companies that lack the financial resources of their larger rivals have discovered that offering exceptional customer service is one of the most effective ways to differentiate themselves and to attract and maintain a growing customer base. Emphasis on speed--Customers now expect an immediate response from companies, whatever products or services they may be buying. Service companies also know that they must build speed into their business systems if they are to satisfy their impatient, time-sensitive customers. This philosophy of speed is called time compression management (TCM), and it involves three aspects.   1) speeding new products to market, 2) shortening customer response time in manufacturing and delivery, and 3) reducing the administrative time required to fill an order.

9. What is the World Wide Web? Describe its marketing potential for small business.
    Answer - The World Wide Web promises to become a revolutionary business tool with 50 million people now on line and electronic commerce at $518 million in 1996 and growing to $6.6 billion in 2000. It is estimated that by 2007 as much as 20 percent of all household expenditures will occur in cyberspace. By establishing a creative, attractive Web site, the "electronic storefront' for a company on

the Web, even the smallest companies can market their products and services to customers across the globe. Although small companies cannot match the marketing efforts of their larger competitors, a creative Web page can be "the Great Equalizer" in a small company's marketing program, giving it access to markets all across the globe. The Web gives small businesses the power to broaden their scope to unbelievable proportions. Currently about 141,000 small businesses have Web sites. Small companies have plenty of incentive to set up shop on the World Wide Web. The number of cybershoppers is growing rapidly, and the demographic profile of the typical Web user is very attractive to entrepreneurs: young (See Figure 6.2), educated, and wealthy.

10. Explain the concept of the marketing mix. What are the four Ps?
    Answer - The marketing mix consists of four elements; product, place, price, and promotion. <u>Product</u> - any good or service that satisfies the need of a consumer. It's managed through a product life cycle. See Figure 7.6 for diagram. <u>Place</u> - the method of distribution. The channel of distribution is the path that goods or services and their titles take in moving from producer to consumer. <u>Price</u> - a key factor affecting both sales volume and profits. Price can be a powerful tool for changing a company's image. But, most small companies need to focus on nonprice competition because it is more effective against larger competitors. <u>Promotion</u> - informing and persuading consumers is the role of promotion. Promotion is divided into advertising and personal selling.

11. List and explain the stages in the product life cycle. How can a small business extend its product's life?
    Answer - The product life cycle goes through four (five) stages. See Figure 7.6 for diagram. 1) Introductory stage - product "breaks into" the market; marketing is intensive and costs are high; profits are very low or, more likely, negative. 2) Growth and acceptance stage--consumers begin to experiment with the product; if successful, sales and profits continue to rise; otherwise, product disappears. 3) Maturity and competition stage--sales rise but profits begin to fall due to intense competition. 4) Market saturation--sales peak, profits drop, and the company must innovate. 5) Product decline stage-- sales continue to fall and profits decline drastically. The time span in each stage varies by product and market. There is no set time cycle in any case. See Figure 7.7 for time between introduction of products. See Table 7.4 for Twelve Ways to Rejuvenate Obsolete Products.

12. With a 70% customer retention rate . . . . What can the typical small business do to increase ints customer rention rate?
    Answer - Businesses can--and should--boost their customer retention rates by: a) focusing on their customers' individual needs and wants, b) producing quality goods and services, c) offering customers greater convenience, d) introducing product and service innovations, e) dedicating themselves to customer service and satisfaction (or, better yet, customer astonishment), f) building an organization that responds quickly to customer needs, wants, and problems.

Step into the Real World

1. Interview the owner of a local restaurant about its marketing strategy. From how large a geographic region does the restaurant draw its clientele? What is the firm's target market? What are the restaurant's characteristics? Does the restaurant have a competitive edge?
2. Select a local small manufacturing operation and evaluate its primary product. What stage of the product life cycle is it in? What channels of distribution does the product follow after leaving the manufacturer?
3. Research current business periodicals such as *Inc., Inc. Technology, Nation's Business, Your Company, Fortune, Forbes,* and others to determine how small companies are using the World Wide Web to market their products and services more effectively. Find at least one example of a company

effectively using the Web as a marketing tool. Visit its Web site and evaluate it use of the criteria described in the "Gaining the Competitive Advantage" feature in this chapter.

4. Using one of the search engines on the World Wide Web, research the current demographic profile of Web users. What is the growth rate for Web users? Prepare a brief report on your findings. What implications do your conclusions have for entrepreneurs considering setting up Web sites?

5. Contact three local small business owners and ask them about their marketing strategies. How have they achieved a competitive edge? Develop a series of questions to determine the sources of their competitive edge: a focus on the customer, devotion to quality, attention to convenience, concentration on innovation, dedication to service, emphasis on speed. How do the businesses compare?

6. Select a local small business owner and work with him or her to develop a "report card" like the one Granite Rock uses. On the basis of this customer feedback, make specific recommendations to improve the business's ability to serve its customers effectively.

Chapter 7 - Creating the Financial Plan

Teaching Objectives
Students will be able to:
1. Understand the importance of preparing a financial plan.
2. Describe how to prepare financial statements and use them to manage the small business.
3. Create pro forma financial statements.
4. Understand the basic financial statements through ratio analysis.
5. Explain how to interpret financial ratios.
6. Conduct a breakeven analysis for a small company.

Instructor's Outline
I. Introduction
    A. Introduction to the Financial Plan
        1. Potential lenders and investors demand such a plan before putting their money into a start-up company.
        2. More important, this financial plan can be a vital tool that helps entrepreneurs manage their businesses effectively, steering their way around the pitfalls that cause failures.
        3. According to one recent survey, more than one-third of all entrepreneurs admitted that they were not spending sufficient time tracking key financial indicators.
        4. To reach profit objectives, small business managers must be aware of their firm's overall financial position.

II. Basic Financial Reports
    A. The Balance Sheet
        1. The balance sheet takes a "snapshot" of a business, providing owners with an estimate of the firm's worth on a given date.
           a) It shows the assets a business owns.
           b) And, the claims creditors and owners have against those assets.
              (1) Figure 7.1 shows a sample balance sheet.
        2. The balance sheet is built on the fundamental accounting equation: assets = liabilities + owner's equity.
           a) The first section of the balance sheet lists the firm's assets (valued at cost, not actual market value) and shows the total value of everything the business owns.
              (1) Current assets consist of cash and items to be converted into cash within one year or within the normal operating cycle of the company, whichever is longer.
           b) The second section shows the business's liabilities, creditors' claims against the firm's assets.
              (1) Current liabilities are those debts that must be paid within one year or within the normal operating cycle of the company, whichever is longer.
              (2) Long-term liabilities are those that come due after one year.
           c) The final section of the balance sheet shows the owner's equity, the value of the owner's investment in the business.
           d) It is the balancing factor on the balance sheet, representing all of the owner's capital contributions to the business plus all accumulated earnings not distributed to the owners.

    B. The Income Statement
        1. The income statement (or profit and loss statement or "P&L") compares expenses against revenue over a certain period of time to show the firm's net profit or loss.

    2. The income statement is a "moving picture" of the firm's profitability over time.
      a) Figure 7.2 shows a sample income statement.
    3. To calculate net profit or loss, the owner records sales revenues for the year, which includes all income that flows into the business from sales of goods and services.
      a) Income from other sources (rent, investments, and interest) also must be included in the revenue section of the income statement.
      b) To determine net sales revenue, owners subtract the value of returned items and refunds from gross revenue.
      c) Cost of goods sold represents the total cost, including shipping, of the merchandise sold during the year.
      d) Subtracting the cost of goods sold from net sales revenue yields a company's gross profit, an important number that many business owners overlook.
      e) Operating expenses include those costs that contribute directly to the manufacture and distribution of goods.
      f) General expenses are indirect costs incurred in operating the business.

  C. The Statement of Cash Flows
    1. The statement of cash flows shows the changes in the firm's working capital since the beginning of the year by listing the sources of funds and the uses of those funds.
    2. Many small businesses never need such a statement; instead, they rely on a cash budget, a less formal managerial tool that tracks the flow of cash into and out of a company over time.
    3. To prepare the statement, the owner must assemble the balance sheets and the income statements summarizing the present year's operations.
      a) She begins with the company's net income for the accounting period (from the income statement).
      b) Then she adds the sources of funds: borrowed funds, owner contributions, decreases in accounts payable, decreases in inventory, depreciation, and any others.
      c) Depreciation is listed as a source of funds because it is a non-cash expense that is deducted as a cost of doing business.
      d) Next the owner subtracts the uses of these funds: plant and equipment purchases, dividends to owners, repayment of debt, increases in accounts receivable, decreases in accounts payable, increases in inventory, and so on.
      e) The difference between the total sources and the total uses of funds is the increase or decrease in working capital.
    4. When these statements are used in conjunction with the analytical tools described in the following sections, they can help small business managers map their firms' financial futures and actively plan for profit.

III. Creating Projected (Pro Forma) Financial Statements
  A. Introduction
    1. Creating projected financial statements via the budgeting process helps the small business owner transform business goals into reality.
    2. Also, because these statements project the firm's financial position through the end of the forecasted period, they help the owner plan the route to improved financial strength and healthy business growth.
    3. Because the established business has a history of operating data from which to construct pro forma financial statements, the task is not nearly as difficult as it is for the beginning business.

4. When creating pro forma financial statements for a brand new business, an entrepreneur typically relies on published statistics summarizing the operation of similar-sized companies in the same industry.
5. One of the most important tasks confronting the entrepreneur launching a new enterprise is to determine the funds needed to begin operation as well as those required to keep going through the initial growth period.
6. Too often entrepreneurs are overly optimistic in their financial plans and fail to recognize that expenses initially exceed income for most small firms.

B. The Pro Forma Income Statement
    1. When creating a projected income statement, an entrepreneur has two options.
       a) Develop a sales forecast and work down.
       b) Set a profit target and work up.
    2. Most businesses target a profit figure and then determine what sales must be achieved to reach it.
    3. The next step is to estimate the expenses the business will incur in securing those sales.
    4. An entrepreneur who earns less in his own business than he could earn working for someone else must weigh carefully the advantages and disadvantages of choosing the path of entrepreneurship.
    5. An adequate profit must also include a reasonable return on the owner's total investment in the business.
    6. So, the owner's target income is the sum of a reasonable salary for the time spent running the business and a normal return on the amount invested in the firm. Determining how much this should be is the first step in creating the pro forma income statement.
    7. To calculate net sales from a target profit, the owner needs published statistics for this type of business.
       a) The bookstore example
    8. The next step is to determine whether this required sales volume is reasonable.
       a) One useful technique is to break down the required annual sales volume into daily sales figures.
    9. To determine whether the profit expected from the business will meet or exceed the entrepreneur's target income, the prospective owner should create an income statement based on a realistic sales estimate.
   10. At this stage in developing the financial plan, the owner should create a more detailed picture of the firm's expected operating expenses.
   11. One common method is to use the operating statistics data found in Dun & Bradstreet's Cost of Doing Business reports.
      a) These booklets document typical selected operating expenses (expressed as a percentage of net sales) for 190 lines of business.
   12. Entrepreneurs should list all of the initial expenses they will incur and have an accountant review the list.
      a) Figures 7.4 and 7.5 show two useful forms designed to help assign dollar values to anticipated expenses.
   13. Entrepreneurs who follow the other approach to building an income statement, developing a sales forecast and working down to net income, must be careful to avoid falling into the trap of excessive optimism.
      a) To avoid this problem divide revenues by two multiply expenses by two, and if the business can still make it, it's a winner.

C. The Pro Forma Balance Sheet
1. In addition to projecting the small firm's net profit or loss, the entrepreneur must develop a pro forma balance sheet outlining the fledgling firm's assets and liabilities.
2. Assets.
   a) Cash is one of the most useful assets the business owns; it is highly liquid and can quickly be converted into other tangible assets.
   b) But how much cash should a small business have at its inception? One practical rule of thumb suggests that the company's cash balance should cover its operating expenses (less depreciation, a noncash expense) for one inventory turnover period.
      (1) There is an inverse relationship between the small firm's average inventory turnover ratio and its cash requirements.
   c) Another decision facing the entrepreneur is how much inventory the business should carry. A rough estimate of the inventory requirement can be calculated from the information found on the projected income statement and from published statistics.
      (1) The owner can use the planning forms shown in Figures 7.4 and 7.5 to estimate fixed assets (land, building, equipment, and fixtures).
3. Liabilities.
   a) To complete the projected balance sheet, the owner must record all of the small firm's liabilities, the claims against the assets.
4. The final step is to compile all of these items into a projected balance sheet, as shown in Figure 7.6.

IV. Ratio Analysis
A. Introduction
1. Many small business owners never take the time to check the vital signs of their businesses using their "financial dashboards."
   a) The result: Their companies develop engine trouble, fail, and leave them stranded along the road to successful entrepreneurship.
2. Establishing these controls--and using them consistently--is one of the keys to keeping a business vibrant and healthy.
   a) A smoothly functioning system of financial controls can serve as an early warning device for underlying problems that could destroy a young business.
   b) They allow an entrepreneur to step back and see the big picture and to make adjustments in the company's direction when necessary.
3. A company's financial accounting and reporting system will provide signals, through comparative analysis, of impending trouble, such as:
   a) decreasing sales and falling profit bargains.
   b) increasing corporate overheads.
   c) growing inventories and accounts receivable.
4. These are all signals of declining cash flows from operations. As cash flows decrease, the squeeze begins.
   a) Payments to vendors become slower.
   b) Maintenance on production equipment lags.
   c) Raw material shortages appear.
   d) Equipment breakdowns occur.
5. One extremely helpful tool is ratio analysis.
6. Ratio analysis, a method of expressing the relationship between any two accounting elements, provides a convenient technique for performing financial analysis.
   a) When analyzed properly, ratios serve as barometers of a company's financial health.

b) These comparisons allow the small business manager to determine if the firm is carrying excessive inventory, experiencing heavy operating expenses, overextending credit, and paying its debts on time and to answer other questions relating to the efficient operation of the firm.

GAINING THE COMPETITIVE EDGE - Between the Lines of Financial Statements

SUMMARY
When he was president and owner of a small medical equipment firm, Dan Cronin knew how important it was to stay focused on the basics of business success. Cronin's simple system allowed him to maintain control over the most important aspects of his business.

Turnaround specialist Raleigh Minor offers five rules for setting up proper financial controls.
1. Generate numbers quickly and accurately. For financial statements to be of any value to managers, growing businesses must compile them no more than 10 days after the end of each month.
2. Establish different timetables for different numbers. All companies must establish priorities concerning which numbers to monitor monthly and which to watch weekly. Minor offers these guidelines:
   Monthly updates on:
   - inventory
   - accounts receivable [aging of accounts and average collection period]
   - accounts payable [aging of accounts and average payable period]
   Weekly updates on:
   - current cash position
   - cash disbursements by major category
   - cash receipts
   - new sales
   - order backlogs
   - number of employees [with productivity measures such as sales per employee ratio]
3. Compare results with projections.
4. Prioritize.
5. Circulate financial reports to responsible managers.

Although analyzing financial data intimidates some business owners, it is an integral part of running a business successfully. Analyzing the numbers over time and comparing them with industry standards is one of the most practical ways of putting them to work to make a business better. And, as many business owners have found, that is the best way to read between the lines of financial statements.

1. Which financial summaries should small business owners prepare to improve control over their companies?
   Answer - Students' responses should focus on justification. Pages 210-219 show examples. Basic to any business would be a balance sheet and income statement. Students will need to justify cash flow.
2. Why do some business owners fail to prepare adequate financial summaries and reports?
   Answer - A fear of numbers, a concern with the time it will take, a focus on "fire fighting" and the immediate needs of running the business versus planning, sitting and reviewing the past, etc.
3. What are the benefits of conducting the type of financial analysis described here?
   Answer - It tells owners where to place an emphasis in their control efforts, it will signal problems while they can still be fixed, etc.

7. Clever business owners use financial ratio analysis to identify problems in their businesses while they are still problems, not business-threatening crises.
8. Business owners also can use ratio analysis to increase the likelihood of obtaining bank loans.
   a) By analyzing his financial statements with ratios, an owner can identify weaknesses and strengths in advance.
9. But how many ratios should a small business manager monitor to maintain adequate financial control over the firm?
   a) The secret to successful ratio analysis is simplicity, focusing on just enough ratios to provide a clear picture of a company's financial standing.

B. Twelve Key Ratios
   1. Four categories: liquidity ratios, leverage ratios, operating ratios, and profitability ratios.

C. Liquidity Ratios
   1. Liquidity ratios tell whether the small business will be able to meet its maturing obligations as they come due.
   2. The primary measures of liquidity are the current ratio and the quick ratio.
   3. Current Ratio. The current ratio measures the small firm's solvency by indicating its ability to pay current liabilities from current assets. It is calculated in the following manner:
      a) Current ratio = Current assets/Current liabilities
      b) The current ratio, sometimes called the working capital ratio, is the most commonly used measure of short-term solvency.
         (1) Typically, financial analysts suggest that a small business maintain a current ratio of at least 2:1.
         (2) In general, the higher the firm's current ratio, the stronger its financial position.
   4. Quick Ratio. The current ratio can sometimes be misleading, because it does not show the quality of a company's current assets. The quick ratio (or the acid test ratio) is a more conservative measure of a firm's liquidity, because it shows the extent to which its most liquid assets cover its current liabilities.
      a) Quick ratio = Quick assets/Current liabilities
      b) Quick assets include cash, readily marketable securities, and notes and accounts receivables--assets that can be converted into cash immediately if needed.
         (1) Most small firms determine quick assets by subtracting inventory from current assets because inventory cannot be converted into cash quickly.
      c) The quick ratio is a more specific measure of a firm's ability to meet its short-term obligations and is a more rigorous test of its liquidity than the current ratio.
         (1) In general, a quick ratio of 1:1 is considered satisfactory.
         (2) A ratio of less than 1:1 indicates that the small firm is overly dependent on inventory and on future sales to satisfy short-term debt.
         (3) A quick ratio of more than 1:1 indicates a greater degree of financial security.

D. Leverage Ratios
   1. Leverage ratios measure the financing supplied by the firm's owners against that supplied by its creditors; they are a gauge of the depth of a company's debt.
   2. These ratios show the extent to which an entrepreneur relies on debt capital (rather than equity capital) to finance operating expenses, capital expenditures, and expansion costs.
      a) It is a measure of the degree of financial risk in a company.

3. Debt Ratio. The small firm's debt ratio measures the percentage of total assets financed by creditors.
    a) Debt ratio = Total debt (or liabilities)/Total assets
        (1) Total debt includes all current liabilities and any outstanding long-term notes and bonds.
        (2) Total assets represent the sum of the firm's current assets, fixed assets, and intangible assets.
    b) Clearly, a high debt ratio means that creditors provide a large percentage of the firm's total financing. Owners generally prefer a high leverage ratio; the owner is able to generate profits with a smaller personal investment.
    c) However, creditors typically prefer moderate debt ratios because a lower debt ratio indicates a smaller chance of creditor losses in case of liquidation.
4. Debt to Net Worth Ratio. The small firm's debt to net worth ratio also expresses the relationship between the capital contributions from creditors and those from owners.
    a) It is a measure of the small firm's ability to meet both its creditor and owner obligations in case of liquidation.
    b) Debt to net worth ratio = Total debt (or liabilities)/Tangible net worth
    c) Total debt is the sum of current liabilities and long-term liabilities, and tangible net worth represents the owners' investment in the business (capital + capital stock + earned surplus + retained earnings) less any intangible assets (e.g., goodwill) the firm owns.
        (1) The higher this ratio, the lower the degree of protection afforded creditors if the business should fail.
        (2) Also, a higher debt to net worth ratio means that the firm has less capacity to borrow.
        (3) As a firm's debt to net worth ratio approaches 1:1, the creditors' interest in the business approaches that of the owners.
            (a) If the ratio is greater than 1:1, the creditors' claims exceed those of the owners, and the business may be undercapitalized.
5. Times interest earned ratio. The times interest earned ratio is a measure of the small firm's ability to make the interest payments on its debt.
    a) It tells how many times the company's earnings cover the interest payments on the debt it is carrying.
    b) Times interest earned = Earnings before interest and taxes (EBIT)/Total interest expense
    c) EBIT is the firm's profit before deducting interest expense and taxes; the denominator measures the amount the business paid in interest over the accounting period.
        (1) A high ratio suggests that the company would have little difficulty meeting the interest payments on its loans; creditors would see this as a sign of safety for future loans.
        (2) Many creditors look for a times interest earned ratio of at least 4:1 to 6:1 before pronouncing a company a good credit risk.
    d) Trouble looms on the horizon for companies whose debt loads are so heavy that they must starve critical operations.
    e) Debt is a powerful financial tool, but companies must handle it carefully.
        (1) Unfortunately, some companies have gone on borrowing binges, pushing their debt loads beyond the optimal zone.
        (2) See Figure 7.7.

E. Operating Ratios
    1. Operating ratios help the owner evaluate the small firm's performance and indicate how effectively the business uses its resources.
    2. The more effectively its resources are used, the less capital a small business will require.
    3. Average Inventory Turnover Ratio. The small firm's average inventory turnover ratio measures the number of times its average inventory is sold out, or turned over, during the accounting period.
        a) This ratio tells the owner whether the firm's inventory is being managed properly.
        b) It apprises the owner of whether the business inventory is understocked, over-stocked, or obsolete.
        c) Average inventory turnover ratio = Cost of goods sold/Average inventory
    4. Average inventory is found by adding the firm's inventory at the beginning of the accounting period to the ending inventory and dividing the result by 2.
        a) This ratio tells the owner how fast the merchandise is moving through the business and helps to balance the company on the fine line between oversupply and undersupply.
        b) To determine the average number of days units remain in inventory, the owner can divide the average inventory turnover ratio into the number of days in the accounting period (e.g., 365 + average inventory turnover ratio).
            (1) The result is called days' inventory.
            (2) An above-average inventory turnover indicates that the small business has a healthy, salable, and liquid inventory and a supply of quality merchandise supported by sound pricing policies.
            (3) A below-average inventory turnover suggests an illiquid inventory characterized by obsolescence, overstocking, and stale merchandise.
        c) Businesses that turn their inventories rapidly require a relatively small inventory investment to produce a particular sales volume.
        d) The inventory turnover ratio can be misleading, however.
        e) Financial analysts suggest that a favorable turnover ratio depends on the type of business, its size, its profitability, its method of inventory valuation, and other relevant factors.
    5. Average Collection Period Ratio. The small firm's average collection period ratio (or days' sales outstanding, DSO) tells the average number of days it takes to collect accounts receivable.
        a) To compute the average collection period ratio, you must first calculate the firm's receivables turnover.
        b) Receivables turnover ratio = Credit sales (or net sales)/Accounts receivable
        c) This ratio measures the number of times the firm's accounts receivable turn over during the accounting period.
            (1) The higher the firm's receivables turnover ratio, the shorter the time lag between making a sale and collecting the cash from it.
        d) Use the following equation to calculate the firm's average collection period ratio:
            (1) Average collection period ratio = Number of days in accounting period
                                                    Receivables turnover ratio
        e) One of the most useful applications of the collection period ratio is to compare it with the industry average and with the firm's credit terms.
            (1) Such a comparison will indicate the degree of the small company's control over its credit sales and collection techniques.
            (2) One rule of thumb suggests that the firm's collection period ratio should be no more than one-third greater than its credit terms.

   f) Slow payers represent great risk to many small businesses.
6. Average Payable Period Ratio. The converse of the average collection period ratio, the average payable period ratio, tells the average number of days it takes a company to pay its accounts payable.
   a) Like the average collection period, it is measured in days.
      (1) Payables turnover ratio = Accounts payable/Cost of purchases
   b) To find the average payable period, use the following computation:
   c) Average payable period ratio = <u>Number of days in accounting period</u>
                                      Payables turnover ratio
   d) An excessively high average payable period ratio indicates the presence of a significant amount of past-due accounts payable.
      (1) Ideally, the average payable period would match (or exceed) the time it takes to convert inventory into sales and ultimately into cash.
      (2) In this case, the company's vendors would be financing its inventory and its credit sales.
   e) One of the most meaningful comparisons for this ratio is against the credit terms offered by suppliers (or an average of the credit terms offered).
      (1) If the average payable ratio slips beyond vendors' credit terms, it is an indication that the company is suffering from cash shortages or a sloppy accounts payable procedure and its credit rating is in danger.
7. Net Sales to Total Assets. The small company's net sales to total assets ratio (also called the total assets turnover ratio) is a general measure of its ability to generate sales in relation to its assets.
   a) It describes how productively the firm uses its assets to produce sales revenue.
   b) Total assets turnover ratio = Net sales/Net total assets
   c) The denominator of this ratio, net total assets, is the sum of all of the firm's assets (cash, inventory, land, buildings, equipment, tools, everything owned) less depreciation.
      (1) This ratio is meaningful only when compared with that of similar firms in the same industry category.
      (2) A total assets turnover ratio below the industry average may indicate that the small firm is not generating an adequate sales volume for its asset size.
8. Net Sales to Working Capital. The net sales to working capital ratio measures how many dollars in sales the business generates for every dollar of working capital (working capital = current assets - current liabilities).
   a) Also called the turnover of working capital ratio, this proportion tells the owner how efficiently working capital is being used to generate sales.
   b) Net sales to working capital ratio = Net sales/Current assets - current liabilities
   c) An excessively low net sales to working capital ratio indicates that the small firm is not using its working capital efficiently or profitably.
   d) It is critical for the small firm to keep a satisfactory level of working capital to nourish its expansion, and the net sales to working capital ratio helps define the level of working capital required to support higher sales volume.

F. Profitability Ratios
   1. Profitability ratios indicate how efficiently the small firm is being managed and how successfully it is conducting business.
   2. Net Profit on Sales Ratio. The net profit on sales ratio (also called the profit margin on sales) measures the firm's profit per dollar of sales.
      a) The computed percentage shows the number of cents of each sales dollar remaining after deducting all expenses and income taxes.

b)   Net profit on sales ratio = Net profit/Net sales

c)   To evaluate this ratio properly, the owner must consider the firm's asset value, its inventory and receivables turnover ratios, and its total capitalization.

d)   If the firm's profit margin on sales is below the industry average, it may be a sign that its prices are relatively low or that its costs are excessively high, or both.

e)   If a company's net profit on sales ratio is excessively low, the owner should check the gross profit margin (net sales minus cost of goods sold expressed as a percentage of net sales).

3.   Net Profit to Equity. The net profit to equity ratio (or the return on net worth ratio) measures the owners' rate of return on investment.

a)   Because it reports the percentage of the owners' investment in the business that is being returned through profits annually, it is one of the most important indicators of the firm's profitability or a management's efficiency.

b)   Net profit to equity ratio = Net profit/Owners' equity (or net worth)

c)   This ratio compares profits earned during the accounting period with the amount the owner has invested in the business during that time.

V.   Interpreting Business Ratios
    A.   Introduction

1.   Key performance ratios vary dramatically among industries and even within different segments of the same industry.

2.   Another valuable way to utilize ratios is to compare them with those of similar businesses in the same industry.

3.   The principle behind calculating these ratios and comparing them with industry norms is the same as that of most medical tests.

a)   Just as a healthy person's blood pressure and cholesterol levels should fall within a range of normal values, so should a financially healthy company's ratios.

b)   A company cannot deviate too far from these normal values and remain successful for long.

c)   When deviations from "normal" do occur (and they will), a business owner should focus on determining the cause of the deviations.

4.   Several organizations regularly compile and publish operating statistics, including key ratios.

a)   Robert Morris Associates publishes its *Annual Statement Studies*, showing ratios and other financial data for more than 350 industrial, wholesale, retail, and service categories.

b)   Dun & Bradstreet, Inc., publishes *Key Business Ratios*, which covers 22 retail, 32 wholesale, and 71 industrial business categories. Dun & Bradstreet also publishes *Cost of Doing Business*, a series of operating ratios compiled from the IRS's Statistics of Income.

c)   *Vest Pocket Guide to Financial Ratios* is published by Prentice Hall, gives key ratios and financial data for a wide variety of industries.

d)   Bank of America. Periodically, the Bank of America publishes many documents relating to small business management, including the *Small Business Reporter*, which details costs of doing business ratios.

e)   Trade associations. Virtually every type of business is represented by a national trade association, which publishes detailed financial data compiled from its membership.

f)   Government agencies. Several government agencies (the Federal Trade Commission, Interstate Commerce Commission, Department of Commerce, Department of Agriculture, and Securities and Exchange Commission) offer a great deal of financial operating data on a variety of industries, although the categories are more general than those used by other organizations. In addition, the IRS annually publishes *Statistics of Income*, which includes income r statement and balance sheet statistics compiled from income tax returns. The IRS also publishes the *Census of Business*, which gives a limited amount of ratio information.

IN THE FOOTSTEPS OF AN ENTREPRENEUR - Good News in the Grocery Business

SUMMARY
As part of a training program for new employees in his supermarket business, Norman Mayne gives a quiz: How much profit does a $25 grocery order yield? The correct answer is 25 cents. For the first time, Mayne's company, Dorothy Lane Market <http://www. dorothylane.com>, based in Dayton, Ohio, is operating at a 2 percent profit margin. For many years, supermarket owners have lived with profit margins of just 1 percent of sales. Mayne explains that the chain has come a long way in its management techniques since his father rang up total sales of $35 on his first day in business in 1944. Taking a cue from the major discounters, supermarkets have learned how to increase the number of times they turn their inventory, have streamlined their distribution systems, and have adopted serious cost-cutting strategies to become more efficient. Combining technology such as checkout scanners with new marketing techniques, including frequent-shopper cards, has reduced the need for constant sales, which cut into profit margins. The results are going straight to the bottom line. Like airlines with their frequent-flier clubs, grocery stores are creating frequent-shopper cards that allow them to track exactly what and when their best customers are buying.

The company's direct mail ads are customized with coupons tied specifically to each customer's buying habits. The card program has helped Dorothy Lane Market reduce its investment in inventory, increase the number of items it turns in inventory, and speed up distribution. Using the card system, store managers can tell exactly which items are selling fast and which ones are not. Employees at Dorothy Lane Market are happy about the brighter profit picture because they share in the gains. The company routinely pays out bonuses equal to 20 percent of its profits.

1. How successfully can small supermarkets use the techniques that Dorothy Lane Market is using to boost profitability? Explain. What benefits can stores that use these techniques expect?
    Answer - They are more closely managing their resources reducing waste, increasing return on each dollar.
2. Work with a team of your classmates to brainstorm other profit-boosting techniques for grocers.
    Answer - Place students in teams of four. Perhaps have them tour a local store and then brainstorm together. "Step Into the Real World" has an exercise related to this case/question, consider using it in conjunction with answering this question.

B. What do All of These Numbers Mean?
  1. Learning to interpret financial ratios just takes a little practice.
  2. This section will show you how it's done by comparing the ratios from the operating data already computed for Sam's Appliance Shop with those taken from Robert Morris Associates' Annual Statement Studies. (The industry median is the ratio falling exactly in the middle when sample elements are arranged in ascending or descending order.)
  3. Current ratio. Sam's: 1.87:1   Industry median 1.50:1
      a) By this measure, the company's liquidity is solid.
  4. Quick ratio. Sam's 0.63:1   Industry median 0.50:1
      a) A sales slump could cause liquidity problems for Sam's.
  5. Debt ratio. Sam's 0.68:1   Industry median 0.64:1

        a) Although Sam's does not appear to be overburdened with debt, the company might have difficulty borrowing additional money, especially from conservative lenders.

6. Debt to net worth ratio. Sam's 2.20:1   Industry median 1.90:1

        a) Borrowing capacity is somewhat limited because creditors' claims against the business are more than twice what the owners have invested.

7. Times interest earned ratio. Sam's 2.52:1   Industry median 2.0:1

        a) Sam's Appliance Shop has a cushion (although a small one) in meeting its interest payments.

8. Average inventory turnover ratio.

        Sam's 2.05 times/year   Industry median 4.0 times/year

        a) Inventory is moving through Sam's at a very slow pace, half that of the industry median.

9. Average collection period ratio.

        Sam's 50.0 days   Industry median 19.3 days

        a) Sam's Appliance Shop collects the average accounts receivable at more than two-and-a-half times as long.

10. Average payable period ratio.

        Sam's 59.3 days   Industry median 43 days

        a) Sam's payables are nearly 40 percent slower than those of the typical firm in the industry.

11. Net sales to total assets ratio.

        Sam's 2.21:1   Industry median 2.7:1

        a) Sam's Appliance Shop is not generating enough sales, given the size of its asset base.

12. Net sales to working capital ratio. Sam's 5.86:1   Industry median 10.8:1

        a) Sam's generates just $5.86 in sales for every $I in working capital, just over half of what the typical firm in the industry does.

13. Net profit on sales ratio. Sam's 3.24%   Industry median 7.6%

        a) After deducting all expenses, 3.24 cents of each sales dollar remains as profit for Sam's: less than half the industry median.

14. Net profit to equity ratio. Sam's 22.65%   Industry median 12.6%

        a) Sam's Appliance Shop's yield is nearly twice that of the industry median.

15. When comparing ratios for their individual businesses with published statistics, small business owners must remember that the comparison is made against averages.

        a) The owner must strive to achieve ratios that are at least as good as these average figures.

        b) The goal should be to manage the business so that its financial performance is above average.

16. In addition to comparing ratios with industry averages, owners should analyze their firms' financial ratios over time.

17. By themselves, these ratios are "snapshots" of the firm's finances at a single instant; by examining these trends over time, the owner can detect gradual shifts that otherwise might go unnoticed until a financial crisis is looming.

        a) See Figure 7.9.

VI. Breakeven Analysis

    A. The Breakeven Analysis.

        1. The small firm's breakeven point is the level of operation (sales dollars or production quantity) at which it neither earns a profit nor incurs a loss.

        2. At this level of activity, sales revenue equals expenses; that is, the firm "breaks even."

3. By analyzing costs and expenses, the owner can calculate the minimum level of activity required to keep the firm in operation.
    a) Most potential lenders and investors will require the potential owner to prepare a breakeven analysis to assist them in evaluating the earning potential of the new business.
    b) It can also serve as a planning device for the small business owner.

WIRED TO THE WEB - A Recipe for Financial Control

SUMMARY

Ilene Polansky owns two trendy restaurants in Montreal, Canada. Since starting with her first restaurant, Polansky has been juggling multiple roles shortchanging a focus on profitability. Although her restaurants' net profit margin of 10 to 15 percent is within the industry average and loyal patrons pack both locations virtually every night, Polansky continues to experience periodic financial problems.

Polansky counts on what she learned in a 10-week bookkeeping course to manage her company's finances. Her secretary writes all the checks, but she does not track the restaurants' expenses over time. Once a month, the secretary goes to Polansky's father's accounting firm to use his computer to input invoices. Polansky is planning to open a third location within a year, but she knows she has to get her financial "plate" in order first.

1. Critique the existing financial control system Polansky has in place for her restaurants. What recommendations can you make for improving it? Which financial reports would you advise Polansky to prepare? How should she use them to manage her restaurants?
    Answer - She needs to stop being driven by the tyranny of the urgent and do what's important. Her problem is more self- and business-management than it is financial management. She needs to surrender some control to others, hire expertise and stop trying to control everything herself. Her lack of financial controls is largely a function of her management.
2. Would you recommend that Polansky computerize her financial records? If so, use the resources of the World Wide Web and your library to provide her with suggestions for accounting packages designed for small businesses such as Maestro's.
    Answer - Only if she hires and trusts someone to do this for her. If she does, it will simply add to her stress and overload. Prentice Hall has several excellent small paperbacks on Managing Information on the Web, etc. Ask your rep. for one of these in preparing to lead students through this question.
3. Search the World Wide Web for sources of information that could help Polansky gain better financial control over her business. (Hint: Check out sites such as the National Restaurant Association, Dun & Bradstreet, and Robert Morris Associates.
    Answer - Also refer to #2 and contact your Prentice Hall rep. Consider requiring one of these texts as a supplement, as the web is becoming a more important element in small business.

B. Calculating the Breakeven Point
    1. A small business owner can calculate a firm's breakeven point by using a simple mathematical formula.
        a) Determine fixed expenses and variable expenses.
            (1) Fixed expenses are those that do not vary with changes in the volume of sales or production (e.g., rent, depreciation expense, interest payments).
            (2) Variable expenses, on the other hand, vary directly with changes in the volume of sales or production (e.g., raw materials costs, and sales commissions).

2. Some expenses cannot be neatly categorized; these semivariable expenses change, although not proportionately, with changes in the level of sales or production (electricity would be one example).
3. Steps using an example of a typical small business, The Magic Shop:
   a) Step 1. Determine the expenses the business can expect to incur.
      (1) With the help of a budget, an entrepreneur can develop estimates of sales revenue, cost of goods sold, and expenses for the upcoming accounting period.
   b) Step 2. Categorize the expenses estimated in Step 1 into fixed expenses and variable expenses.
      (1) Separate semivariable expenses into their component parts.
   c) Step 3. Calculate the ratio of variable expenses to net sales.
   d) Step 4. Compute the breakeven point by inserting this information into the following formula.
      (1) Breakeven sales (\$) = $\dfrac{\text{Total fixed costs}}{\text{Contribution margin expressed as a percentage of sales}}$

C. Adding in a Profit
   1. What if the Magic Shop's owner wants to do better than just break even?
   2. His analysis can be adjusted to consider such a possibility.
   3. He can calculate this by treating the desired profit as if it were a fixed cost.
      a) Breakeven sales (\$) = $\dfrac{\text{Total fixed expenses + Desired net income}}{\text{Contribution margin expressed as a percentage of sales}}$

D. Breakeven Point in Units
   1. Some small businesses may prefer to express the breakeven point in units produced or sold instead of in dollars.
      a) Manufacturers often find this approach particularly useful.
      b) Breakeven volume = $\dfrac{\text{Total fixed costs}}{\text{Sales price per unit - Variable cost per unit}}$
   2. Computation of contribution margin.
      a) Contribution margin = Price per unit - Variable cost per unit
   3. Computation of breakeven volume.
      a) Breakeven volume (units) = $\dfrac{\text{Total fixed costs}}{\text{Per unit contribution margin}}$
   4. To convert this number of units to breakeven sales dollars, simply multiply it by the selling price per unit.

E. Constructing a Breakeven Chart
   1. Step 1. On the horizontal axis, mark a scale measuring sales volume in dollars (or in units sold or some other measure of volume).
      a) The breakeven chart for the Magic Shop--Figure 7.10.
   2. Step 2. On the vertical axis, mark a scale measuring income and expenses in dollars.
   3. Step 3. Draw a fixed expense line intersecting the vertical axis at the proper dollar level parallel to the horizontal axis.
   4. Step 4. Draw a total expense line that slopes upward beginning at the point where the fixed cost line intersects the vertical axis.
      a) The precise location of the total expense line is determined by plotting the total cost incurred at a particular sales volume.
      b) Total cost for a given sales level = Fixed expenses + (Variable expenses expressed as a percentage of sales ÷ sales level)

5. Step 5. Beginning at the graph's origin, draw a 45 degree revenue line showing where total sales volume equals total income.
6. Step 6. Locate the breakeven point by finding the intersection of the total expense line and the revenue line.

F. Using Breakeven Analysis
1. Breakeven analysis is a useful planning tool for the potential small business owner, especially when approaching potential lenders and investors for funds.
2. It provides an opportunity for integrated analysis of sales volume, expenses, income, and other relevant factors.
3. Breakeven analysis is a simple, preliminary screening device for the entrepreneur faced with the business start-up decision.
4. Breakeven analysis does have certain limitations.
   a) It is too simple to use as a final screening device because it ignores the importance of cash flows.
   b) Also, the accuracy of the analysis depends on the accuracy of the revenue and expense estimates.
   c) Finally, the assumptions pertaining to breakeven analysis may not be realistic for some businesses.

Chapter Summary
♦ Understand the importance of preparing a financial plan.
  ▪ Launching a successful business requires an entrepreneur to create a solid financial plan. Not only is such a plan an important tool in raising the capital needed to get a company off the ground, but it also is an essential ingredient in managing a growing business.
  ▪ Earning a profit does not occur by accident; it takes planning.
♦ Describe how to prepare the basic financial statements and use them to manage the small business.
  ▪ The balance sheet. Built on the accounting equation Assets = Liabilities + Owner's equity (capital). It provides an estimate of the company's value on a particular date.
  ▪ The income statement. Compares the firm's revenues against its expenses to determine its net profit (or loss). It provides information about the company's bottom line.
  ▪ The statement of cash flow. Shows the change in the company's working capital over the accounting period by listing the sources and the uses of funds.
♦ Create pro forma financial statements.
  ▪ Projected (pro forma) financial statements are a basic component of a sound financial plan. They help the manager plot the company's financial future by setting operating objectives and by analyzing the reasons for variations from targeted results. Also, the small business in search of start-up funds will need these pro forma statements to present to prospective lenders and investors. They also assist in determining the amount of cash, inventory, fixtures, and other assets the business will need to begin operation.
♦ Understand the basic financial statements through ratio analysis.
  ▪ The 12 key ratios described in this chapter are divided into four major categories: liquidity ratios, which show the small firm's ability to meet its current obligations, leverage ratios, which tell how much of the company's financing is provided by owners and how much by creditors; operating ratios, which show how effectively the firm uses its resources; and profitability ratios, which disclose the company's profitability.
  ▪ Many agencies and organizations regularly publish such statistics. If there is a discrepancy between the small firm's ratios and those of the typical business, the owner should investigate the reason for the difference. A below-average ratio does not necessarily mean that the business is in trouble.

♦ Explain how to interpret financial ratios.
  ▪ To benefit from ratio analysis, the small company should compare its ratios with those of other companies in the same line of business and look for trends over time.
  ▪ When business owners detect deviations in their companies' ratios from industry standards, they should determine the cause of the deviations. In some cases, such deviations are the result of sound business decisions; in other instances, however, ratios that are out of the normal range for a particular type of business are indicators of what could become serious problems for a company.
♦ Conduct a break-even analysis for a small company.
  ▪ Business owners should know their firm's break-even point, the level of operations at which total revenues equal total costs; it is the point at which companies neither earn a profit nor incur a loss. Although just a simple screening device, break-even analysis is a useful planning and decision-making tool.

Discussion Questions

1. Why is it important for entrepreneurs to develop financial plans for their companies?
   Answer - Potential lenders and investors demand such a plan before putting their money into a start-up company. More important, this financial plan can be a vital tool that helps entrepreneurs manage their businesses effectively, steering their way around the pitfalls that cause failures. According to one recent survey, more than one-third of all entrepreneurs admitted that they were not spending sufficient time tracking key financial indicators. To reach profit objectives, small business managers must be aware of their firm's overall financial position.

2. How should a small business manager use the ratios discussed in this chapter?
   Answer - Establishing financial controls through ratio analysis--and using them consistently--is one of the keys to keeping a business vibrant and healthy. A smoothly functioning system of financial controls can serve as an early warning device for underlying problems that could destroy a young business. They allow an entrepreneur to step back and see the big picture and to make adjustments in the company's direction when necessary. Ratio analysis, a method of expressing the relationship between any two accounting elements, provides a convenient technique for performing financial analysis.

3. Outline the key points of the 12 ratios discussed in this chapter. What signals does each give a business owner?
   Answer - Liquidity ratios tell whether the small business will be able to meet its maturing obligations as they come due. The primary measures of liquidity are the current ratio and the quick ratio. The current ratio measures the small firm's solvency by indicating its ability to pay current liabilities from current assets. The quick ratio (or the acid test ratio) is a more conservative measure of a firm's liquidity, because it shows the extent to which its most liquid assets cover its current liabilities. Leverage ratios measure the financing supplied by the firm's owners against that supplied by its creditors; they are a gauge of the depth of a company's debt. The small firm's debt ratio measures the percentage of total assets financed by creditors. The small firm's debt to net worth ratio also expresses the relationship between the capital contributions from creditors and those from owners. The times interest earned ratio earned is a measure of the small firm's ability to make the interest payments on its debt. Operating ratios help the owner evaluate the small firm's performance and indicate how effectively the business uses its resources. The small firm's average inventory turnover ratio measures the number of times its average inventory is sold out, or turned over, during the accounting period. The small firm's average collection period ratio (or days' sales outstanding, DSO) tells the average number of days it takes to collect accounts receivable. The converse of the average collection period ratio, the average payable period ratio, tells the average number of days it takes a company to pay its accounts payable. The small company's net sales to total assets ratio (also

called the total assets turnover ratio) is a general measure of its ability to generate sales in relation to its assets. The net sales to working capital ratio measures how many dollars in sales the business generates for every dollar of working capital (working capital = current assets - current liabilities). Profitability ratios indicate how efficiently the small firm is being managed and how successfully it is conducting business. The net profit on sales ratio (also called the profit margin on sales) measures the firm's profit per dollar of sales. The net profit to equity ratio (or the return on net worth ratio) measures the owners' rate of return on investment. Because it reports the percentage of the owner's investment in the business that is being returned through profits annually, it is one of the most important indicators of the firm's profitability or a management's efficiency.

4. Describe the method for building a projected income statement and a projected balance sheet for a beginning business.
Answer - See pages 210-213. Because the established business has a history of operating data from which to construct pro forma financial statements, the task is not nearly as difficult as it is for the beginning business. When creating pro forma financial statements for a brand new business, an entrepreneur typically relies on published statistics summarizing the operation of similar-sized companies in the same industry.

5. Why are pro forma financial statements important to the financial planning process?
Answer - Creating projected financial statements via the budgeting process helps the small business owner transform business goals into reality. Also, because these statements project the firm's financial position through the end of the forecasted period, they help the owner plan the route to improved financial strength and healthy business growth. One of the most important tasks confronting the entrepreneur launching a new enterprise is to determine the funds needed to begin operation as well as those required to keep going through the initial growth period. Too often entrepreneurs are overly optimistic in their financial plans and fail to recognize that expenses initially exceed income for most small firms.

6. How can break-even analysis help an entrepreneur planning to launch a business?
Answer - The small firm's breakeven point is the level of operation (sales dollars or production quantity) at which it neither earns a profit nor incurs a loss. At this level of activity, sales revenue equals expenses; that is, the firm "breaks even." By analyzing costs and expenses, the owner can calculate the minimum level of activity required to keep the firm in operation. Most potential lenders and investors will require the potential owner to prepare a breakeven analysis to assist them in evaluating the earning potential of the new business. It can also serve as a planning device for the small business owner.

Step into the Real World
1. Ask the owner of a small business to provide your class with copies of the firm's financial statements (current or past) or go to the SEC's Edgar file at <http://www.sec.gov/edgarhp.htm> to find the financial statements of a publicly held company that interests you.
   a) Using these statements, compute the 12 key ratios described in this chapter.
   b) Compare the firm's ratios with those of the typical firm in this line of business.
   c) Interpret the ratios and make suggestions for operating improvements.
   d) Prepare a breakeven analysis for the owner.
2. Use "In the Footsteps of an Entrepreneur: Good News in the Grocery Business" as a guide to develop a set of interview questions for the owner or manager of a local grocery store. What is the store's net profit margin? Is the local store using any of the techniques Dorothy Lane Market is using to boost its profitability? Is the store using any other strategies to enhance its profits? Prepare a brief report on your findings for your class.

Chapter 8 - Managing Cash Flow

Teaching Objectives
Students will be able to:
1. Explain the importance of cash management to the success of the small business.
2. Differentiate between cash and profits.
3. Understand the five steps in creating a cash budget and use them to create a cash budget.
4. Describe fundamental principles involved in managing the "Big Three" of cash management: accounts receivable, accounts payable, and inventory.
5. Explain the techniques for avoiding a cash crunch in a small company.

Instructor's Outline
I. Introduction
    A. Cash
        1. A four-letter word that has become a curse for many small businesses.
        2. Developing a cash forecast is essential for new businesses because in the early stages businesses usually do not generate sufficient cash to keep afloat.
        3. Controlling the financial aspects of a business with the techniques described in the previous chapter is immensely important.
        4. However, by themselves, those techniques are insufficient to achieve business success. Entrepreneurs are prone to focus on their companies' income statements--particularly sales and profits.
            a) It is entirely possible for a business to have a solid balance sheet and to make a profit and still go out of business by running out of cash.

II. Cash Management
    A. Introduction
        1. Cash is the most important yet least productive asset that a small business owns.
            a) A business must have enough cash to meet its obligations or it will be declared bankrupt.
            b) But some firms retain an excessive amount of cash to meet any unexpected circum- stances that might arise.
        2. Proper cash management enables the owner to adequately meet the cash demands of the business, to avoid retaining unnecessarily large cash balances, and to stretch the profit- generating power of each dollar the business owns.
        3. One survey asking small business owners to identify their "greatest financial obstacle" found that the most common response was "uneven cash flow."
            a) See Figure 8.1. What Is Your Greatest Financial Obstacle?
            b) Managing cash flow is an acute problem, especially for rapidly growing businesses.
        4. The head of the National Federation of Independent Businesses says that many small business owners "wake up one day to find that the price of success is no cash on hand."
        5. The cash flow cycle.
            a) The time lag between paying suppliers for merchandise and receiving payment from customers.
            b) See Figure 8.2 as an example.
            c) The longer this cash flow cycle, the more likely the business owner is to encounter a cash crisis.
        6. It is important to begin cutting down the length of the cash flow cycle.

III. Cash and Profits Are Not the Same
   A. Described
      1.   Profit (or net income) is the difference between a company's total revenue and its total expenses. It measures how efficiently the business is running.
         a)   As important as earning a profit is, no business owner can pay creditors, employees, and lenders in profits; those payments require cash.
         b)   Profits are tied up in many forms, such as inventory, computers, or machinery.
      2.   Cash is the money that flows through a business in a continuous cycle without being tied up in any other asset.
      3.   Figure 8.3 shows the flow of cash through a typical small business.
         a)   Cash flow is the volume of cash that comes into and goes out of the business during an accounting period.
         b)   Decreases in cash occur when a business purchases, on credit or for cash, goods for inventory or materials for use in production.
         c)   When cash is taken in or when accounts receivable are collected, the firm's cash balance increases.

IN THE FOOTSTEPS OF AN ENTREPRENEUR - The Price of Success

SUMMARY

Rochelle Zabarkes is a classic entrepreneur. Before she opened her specialty food store in Manhattan in 1991, she put together a detailed business plan, lined up financing, and rented space on one of New York City's busiest streets. With its universal mix of gourmet foods and spices from around the world, ethnic takeout food, and exotic gift items, Adriana's Bazaar was an instant hit with customers.

Despite her company's success, its rapid growth has devoured all of her start-up capital and then some. When she launched Adriana's Bazaar, Zabarkes raised $245,000. Unfortunately, the rapid growth of the company pushed cash requirements closer to $350,000. Failing to forecast cash requirements accurately during the volatile start-up period almost cost Zabarkes her business. At one point, Zabarkes was so desperate for cash that she used the proceeds of a check a state agency had made out to her for work a consultant did for her.

So far, her efforts to rescue her store from the cash crisis have been successful. Zabarkes has mollified most of her creditors with repeated phone calls and letters explaining her situation, asking for their patience, and promising eventual payment. She also has convinced the Small Business Administration into being flexible about her loan repayment schedule.

1. What factors caused the cash crises affecting Adriana's Bazaar?
    Answer - Rapid growth and not forecasting her cash flow needs. Her success buried her.
2. Evaluate the manner in which Zabarkes has handled the cash crisis in her business.
    Answer - She neglected to plan ahead. She may have confused profit with cash. She lacked any cash flow forecast or management tools.
3. What ethical dilemmas does Zabarkes face as a result of her company's cash crisis? How should she handle them?
    Answer - Who should she pay, when, and who does she keep "stringing" along? Snagging the consultant's check was unethical; she could have caused him financial difficulties. How much does she tell her creditors? How bleak or rosy a picture does she paint? What kind of time lines does she negotiate for repaying debt, etc.?

IV. Cash Budget
   A. Described
      1. Every small business manager should track the flow of cash through her business so she can project the cash balance available throughout the year.
      2. One recent study of 230 fast-growing companies by TEC, an international organization of CEOs, found that 73 percent tracked cash flow either daily or weekly.
      3. How much cash is enough?
         a) What is suitable for one business may be totally inadequate for another, depending on each firm's size, nature, and particular situation.
         b) The small business manager should prepare a cash budget, which is nothing more than a "cash map," showing the amount and timing of cash receipts and cash disbursements day by day, week by week. or month by month.
         c) The cash budget is used to predict the amount of cash the firm will need to operate smoothly over a specific period of time, and it is a valuable tool in managing a company successfully.

V. Preparing the Cash Budget
   A. Introduction
      1. Typically, a small business should prepare a projected monthly cash budget for at least one year into the future and a quarterly estimate several years in advance.
      2. It must cover all seasonal sales fluctuations.
         a) The more variable the firm's sales pattern, the shorter its planning horizon should be.
      3. Regardless of the time frame selected, the cash budget must be in writing for the small business owner to properly visualize the firm's cash position.
      4. The cash budget is based on the cash method of accounting, which means that cash receipts and cash disbursements are recorded in the forecast only when the cash transaction is expected to take place.
      5. The cash budget is nothing more than a forecast of the firm's cash inflows and outflows for a specific time period, and it will never be completely accurate.
         a) It does give the small business manager a clear picture of the firm's estimated cash balance for the period, pointing out where external cash infusions may be required or where surplus cash balances may be available for investing.
         b) By comparing actual cash flows with projections, the owner can revise his forecast so that future cash budgets will be more accurate.
      6. Formats for preparing a cash budget vary depending on the pattern of a company's cash flow.
         a) See Table 8.2 for a monthly cash budget for a small department store over a four-month period.
      7. There are five basic steps in completing a cash budget:
         a) Determine an adequate minimum cash balance.
         b) Forecast sales.
         c) Forecast cash receipts.
         d) Forecast cash disbursements.
         e) Determine the end-of-month cash balance.

   B. Step 1. Determine an Adequate Minimum Cash Balance
      1. What is considered an excessive cash balance for one small business may be inadequate for another, even though the two firms are in the same trade.
      2. Some financial analysts suggest that a firm's cash balance should equal at least one-fourth of its current debts, but this clearly will not work for all small businesses.

   3. The most reliable method of deciding cash balance is based on experience.
C. Step 2. Forecast Sales
   1. The heart of the cash budget is the sales forecast.
   2. For most businesses, sales constitute the major source of the cash flowing into the business.
   3. The sales forecast can be based on past sales, but the owner must be careful not to be excessively optimistic in projecting sales.
   4. The task of forecasting sales for a new firm is difficult but not impossible.
      a) Conduct research on similar firms and their sales patterns in the first year of operation to come up with a forecast.
      b) Marketing research is another source of information that may be used to estimate annual sales for the fledgling firm.
      c) Table 8.3 gives an example of how one entrepreneur used such marketing information to derive a sales forecast for his first year of operation.
   5. Even the best sales estimate will be wrong.
      a) Many financial analysts suggest that the owner create three estimates--an optimistic, a pessimistic, and a most likely sales estimate--and then make a separate cash budget for each forecast.

D. Step 3. Forecast Cash Receipts
   1. Sales constitute the major source of cash receipts.
   2. To project accurately the firm's cash receipts, the owner must analyze the accounts receivable to determine the collection pattern.
   3. In addition to cash and credit sales, the small business may receive cash in a number of forms: interest income, rental income, dividends, and others.
   4. Some small business owners never discover the hidden danger in accounts receivable until it is too late for their companies.
      a) Receivables act as cash sponges, tying up valuable dollars until the entrepreneur collects them.
      b) Figure 8.4 demonstrates how vital it is to act promptly once an account becomes past due.
      c) Table 8.4 illustrates the high cost of failing to collect accounts receivable on time.

E. Step 4. Forecast Cash Disbursements
   1. Most owners of established businesses have a clear picture of the firm's pattern of cash disbursements.
   2. The key factor in forecasting disbursements for a cash budget is to record them in the month in which they will be paid, not when the obligation is incurred.
   3. Usually, an owner's tendency is to underestimate cash disbursements, which can result in a cash crisis.
      a) A cushion is particularly important for entrepreneurs opening new businesses.
      b) Some financial analysts recommend that a new owner estimate cash disbursements as best he can and then add on another 25 to 50 percent.
   4. One of the most effective techniques for overcoming the "I don't know where to begin" hurdle is to make a daily list of the items that generated cash (receipts) and those that consumed it (disbursements).

F. Step 5. Determine the End-of-Month Cash Balance
   1. To estimate the firm's cash balance for each month, the small business manager first must determine the cash balance at the beginning of each month.

2. The beginning cash balance includes cash on hand as well as cash in checking and savings accounts.
3. As development of the cash budget progresses, the cash balance at the end of a month becomes the beginning balance for the succeeding month.
4. A firm's cash balance might fluctuate from month to month, reflecting seasonal sales patterns.
   a) Such fluctuations are normal, but the small business owner must watch closely any increases and decreases in the cash balance over time.
5. A cash budget not only illustrates the flow of cash into and out of the small business, but it also allows the owner to anticipate cash shortages and cash surpluses.
6. By planning cash needs ahead of time, the small business is able to do the following:
   a) Take advantage of money-saving opportunities, such as economic order quantities and cash discounts.
   b) Make the most efficient use of cash.
   c) Finance seasonal business needs.
   d) Develop a sound borrowing program.
   e) Develop a workable program of debt repayment.
   f) Provide funds for expansion.
   g) Plan for the investment of surplus cash.
7. Manage cash flow effectively, and the business works.
8. One recent study reported that just 26 percent of all small businesses used formal techniques for tracking the level of their cash balances.

VI. The "Big Three" of Cash Management
   A. Accounts Receivable
      1. Selling merchandise and services on credit is a necessary evil for most small businesses.
      2. However, selling to customers on credit is more expensive than cash sales; it requires more paperwork, more staff, and more cash to service accounts receivable.
      3. Selling on credit is a common practice in business.
         a) One recent survey of small businesses in a variety of industries reported that 77 percent extend credit to their customers.
            (1) An assertive collection program is essential to managing a company's cash flow.
      4. How to establish a credit and collection policy.
         a) Screen customers carefully before granting credit.
            (1) According to one survey, nearly 95 percent of small firms that sell on credit sell to anyone who wants to buy; most have no credit-checking procedure.
         b) The first line of defense against bad-debt losses is a detailed credit application.
         c) At a minimum, this credit profile should include:
            (1) Name, address, Social Security number, and telephone number.
            (2) Form of ownership (proprietorship, S corporation, limited liability company, corporation, etc.) and number of years in business
            (3) Credit references (e.g., other suppliers) including contact names, addresses, and telephone numbers
            (4) Bank and credit card references
      5. After collecting this information, the business owner should use it by checking the potential customer's credit references.
         a) On the Web, entrepreneurs can gain access to potential customers' credit information at many sites.
            (1) The cost to check a potential customer's credit at reporting services such as these ranges from $10 to $35.

    b) The next step involves establishing a firm written credit policy and letting every customer know in advance the company's credit terms.

        (1) The credit agreement should specify each customer's credit limit (limits usually vary among customers, depending on their credit ratings) and any deposits required (often stated as a percentage of the purchase price).

        (2) It should state clearly all the terms the business will enforce if the account goes bad, including interest, late charges, attorney's fees, and others.

    c) The third step in an effective credit policy is to send invoices promptly because customers rarely pay before they receive their bills.

IN THE FOOTSTEPS OF AN ENTREPRENEUR - Coping with the Ups and Downs of Business

SUMMARY

Managing cash flow is no easy task in any small business, but the challenge becomes even greater when the business is highly seasonal.

Joe Sergio, co-owner of Sergio's Pools and Spas in South Bend, Indiana, says, "Managing cash flow is my number one stress. To survive in business, Sergio and his partners knew that they had to find a way to increase sales during the winter months, when pool construction and maintenance in Indiana come to a screeching halt. Sergio and his two partners came up with the idea of starting First Response Construction, a business that repairs fire damage. A few employees specialize in pool construction and maintenance, others work to restore fire-damaged buildings, and most constitute a "swing force" that does both.

Because both businesses are growing rapidly, he and his partners know that they must monitor their cash balance constantly. To make that task easier, Sergio generates weekly and monthly cash flow forecasts on a computer.

For Chris Batalis, a significant part of cash management is maintaining a balance between the size of his workforce and the volume of work his advertising agency attracts from clients. Since starting his agency Heptagon, in 1979, Batalis has seen revenues grow steadily at rates between 4 and 9 percent a year. However, he also knows that the advertising business is prone to large swings in revenues and, hence, cash flow. When managing Heptagon's cash, Batalis relies heavily on the experience he gained early in his career as a bank loan officer. Batalis also is careful to keep his company's growth rate reined in to a steady rate because he knows the cash flow dangers of growing too fast. To the amazement of some of his competitors, Batalis also has turned away business from major companies, those he calls "gorilla accounts" A gorilla account is any account that's simply too big for your business." Batalis also sees that Heptagon collects its accounts receivable on time because he recognizes the danger in letting receivables spiral out of control. "Our philosophy of business is to deal only with people who pay their bills on time" says Batalis.

1. Contact the owner of a highly seasonal business in your community, and interview him or her about the problems of managing cash flow. What similarities do you see to the stories told here? What strategies is the owner using to cope with the problems of uneven cash flow?
    Answer - No suggested answer as the answer is based on student interviews.

2. Work with a team of your classmates to brainstorm other strategies for helping the business owner cope with the seasonal swings in cash flow. Prepare a short report of your recommendations and present them to the business owner.
    Answer - No suggested answer as the answer is based on student interviews.

6. Small business owners can take several steps to encourage prompt payment of invoices:
    a) Ensure that all invoices are clear, accurate, and timely.
    b) State clearly a description of the goods or services purchased and an account number, if possible.
    c) Make sure that prices on invoices agree with the price quotations on purchase orders or contracts.
    d) Highlight the terms of sale (e.g., "net 30') on all invoices and reinforce them, if necessary.
    e) Include a telephone number and a contact person in your organization in case the customer has a question or a dispute.

WIRED TO THE WEB - A Blessing or a Curse?

SUMMARY

Dona McKenzie, owner of a graphics design company, thought she had it made when she landed a contract with a major bank to design some marketing brochures. She saw the contract as a doorway to other lucrative jobs with the bank and to work with other large corporate clients. Four months after completing the job, the bank got around to paying the $11,302 it owed her. Now, she's fallen behind on payments to some suppliers and vendors. This job turned out to be more of a curse than the blessing. The bank's slow payment devastated McKenzie's business, but what really annoyed her was the bank's attitude toward the past-due bill.

1. Use the resources of the World Wide Web to research ideas that will help small business owners such as Dona McKenzie collect their accounts payable promptly. [Hint: In addition to conducting your own searches, visit some of the sites listed on the Scarborough/Zimmerer Web site at <http://www. prenhall.com/scarbzim>.
    Answer - No suggested answer since response depends on students' Internet research.
2. What other cash management techniques would you suggest business owners use to avoid the problems that Dona McKenzie encountered?
    Answer - Avoiding the "gorilla" account as mentioned in the early box, estimating the costs and getting clients to pay in increments, collecting enough up front to at least cover expenses of the job.

---

f) Invoices that are well-organized, easy to read, and allow customers to identify what is being billed are much more likely to get paid than those that are not. The key to creating "user-friendly" invoices is to design them from the customer's perspective.
7. When an account becomes overdue, small business owners must take immediate action. The longer an account is past due, the lower is the probability of collecting it.
    a) Send a "second notice" letter requesting immediate payment.
    b) If that fails to produce results, the next step is a telephone call.
    c) If the customer still refuses to pay the bill after 30 days, collection experts recommend the following:
        (1) Send a letter from the company's attorney.
        (2) Turn the account over to a collection agency.
        (3) Hire a collection attorney.
8. Although collection agencies and attorneys will take a portion of any accounts they collect, they are often worth the price paid.
    a) Only 5 percent of accounts over 90 days delinquent will be paid voluntarily.
9. Business owners must be sure to abide by the provisions of the federal Fair Debt Collection Practices Act, which prohibits any kind of harassment when collecting debts

(e.g., telephoning repeatedly, issuing threats of violence, telling third parties about the debt, or using abusive language).

 a) Table 8.5 offers practical insights into building a successful collection system.

10. Other techniques for accelerating accounts receivable.

 a) Speed up orders by having customers fax them to you.

 b) Send invoices when goods are shipped rather than a day or a week later; consider faxing invoices to reduce "in transit" time to a minimum.

 c) Indicate in conspicuous print the invoice due date and any late payment penalties. (Check with an attorney to be sure all finance charges comply with state laws.)

 d) Restrict the customer's credit until past-due bills are paid.

 e) Deposit customer checks and credit card receipts daily.

 f) Identify the top 20 percent of your customers (by sales volume), create a separate file system for them, and monitor them closely. Twenty percent of the typical company's customers generate 80 percent of all accounts receivable.

 g) Ask customers to pay a portion of the purchase price up front.

 h) Watch for signs that a customer may be about to declare bankruptcy.

 i) Consider using a bank's lockbox collection service (located near customers) to reduce mail time on collections.

  (1) In a lockbox arrangement, customers send payments to a post office box the bank maintains.

  (2) The bank collects the payments several times each day and deposits them immediately into the company account.

11. Combining a lockbox with other cash management services from banks--such as zero balance accounts (ZBAs) and sweep accounts--can dramatically improve a small firm's ability to get the most out of its available cash.

 a) A zero balance account is a checking account that technically never has funds in it but is tied to a master account such as payroll.

B. Accounts Payable

 1. The second element of the Big Three of cash management is accounts payable.

 2. The timing of payables is just as crucial to proper cash management as the timing of receivables, but the objective is exactly the opposite.

 3. An entrepreneur should strive to stretch out payables as long as possible without damaging the company's credit rating.

 4. A simple five-point accounts payable system.

  a) Set scheduling goals.

  b) Keep paperwork organized.

  c) Prioritize.

  d) Be consistent.

  e) Look for warning signs.

 5. Business owners should verify all invoices before paying them.

 6. In general, it is a good idea for owners to take advantage of cash discounts that vendors offer.

  a) A clever cash manager also will negotiate the best possible credit terms with his suppliers.

  b) Almost all vendors grant their customers trade credit, and the small business owner should take advantage of it.

 7. Favorable credit terms can make a tremendous difference in a firm's cash flow.

  a) Table 8.6 shows the same most likely cash budget as that shown in Table 8.2, with one exception: Instead of purchasing on C.O.D. terms (Table 8.2), the owner has negotiated "net 30" payment terms (Table 8.6). Notice the drastic improvement in the company's cash flow resulting from improved credit terms.

8. Owners who do find themselves financially strapped should discuss openly the situation with the vendor.

SMALL BUSINESS ACROSS THE GLOBE - Collecting International Accounts

SUMMARY

Selling globally is an excellent strategy for boosting sales and profits, but only if you get paid for what you sell! Collecting accounts receivable from U.S. companies takes an average of 42 days; collecting from foreign customers usually takes a good deal longer. For example, the countries with the worst payment records are Iran (310 days], Syria [175 days], Chile [109 days], and Ecuador [107 days].

Uniform laws giving businesses the right to pursue late payers and to add interest charges to their accounts do not exist across Europe. Before they send thousands of dollars of merchandise halfway around the world, U.S. entrepreneurs must take some basic precautions to make sure their foreign customers will pay their bills.
- Require cash in advance.
- Purchase export credit insurance.
- Secure a letter of credit.
- Research a company's payment norms and creditor protection laws before shipping goods.
- Conduct thorough credit checks on all prospective foreign customers.
- Bill only in U.S. dollars and insist on payment in U.S. dollars.

---

9. Small business owners also can improve their firm's cash flow by scheduling controllable cash disbursements so that they do not come due at the same time.
   a) Scheduling insurance premiums monthly or quarterly rather than annually also improves cash flow.
10. Wise use of business credit cards is another way to stretch the firm's cash balance.
   a) However, owners should avoid cards that charge transaction fees.

C. Inventory
   1. Inventory is a significant investment for many small businesses and can create a severe strain on cash flow.
   2. Although inventory represents the largest capital investment for most businesses, few owners use any formal methods for managing it.
   3. Surplus inventory yields a zero rate of return and unnecessarily ties up the firm's cash.
      a) A typical manufacturing company pays 25 percent to 30 percent of the value of the inventory for the cost of borrowed money, warehouse space, materials handling, staff, lift-truck expenses, and fixed costs.
      b) Only 20 percent of a typical business's inventory turns over quickly, so the owner must watch constantly for stale items.
   4. Carrying too much inventory increases the chances that a business will run out of cash.
   5. The cash flow trick is to commit just enough cash to inventory to meet demand.

VII. Avoiding tile Cash Crunch
   A. Bartering
      1. Bartering, the exchange of goods and services for other goods and services, is an effective way to conserve cash.

2. An ancient concept, bartering began to regain popularity during recent recessions. Over the last decade, nearly 700 barter exchanges have cropped up, catering primarily to small and medium-sized businesses.

3. More than 400,000 companies--most of them small--engage in more than $9.1 billion worth of barter each year.
   a) See Figure 8.5.

4. There is a cost associated with bartering, but the real benefit is that entrepreneurs "pay" for products and services at their wholesale cost of doing business and get in the barter exchange for the retail price.

5. In a typical arrangement, businesses accumulate trade credits when they offer goods or services through the exchange. Then, they can use their trade credits to purchase other goods and services from other members of the exchange.

6. The typical exchange charges a $500 membership fee and a 10 percent transaction fee (5 percent from the buyer and 5 percent from the seller) on every deal. The exchange tracks the balance in each member's account and typically sends a monthly statement summarizing account activity.

7. Rather than join a barter exchange, many enterprising entrepreneurs choose to barter on an individual basis.
   a) The place to start is with the people the company normally does business with.

B. Trimming Overhead Costs
   1. When practical, lease instead of buy.
      a) By leasing automobiles, computers, office equipment, machinery, and other assets rather than buying them, an entrepreneur can conserve valuable cash.
      b) The value of such assets is not in owning them but in using them.
      c) Approximately 80 percent of U.S. companies use leasing as a cash management strategy.
      d) Although total lease payments typically are greater than those for a conventional loan, most leases offer 100 percent financing, which means the owner avoids the large capital outlays required as down payments on most loans.
      e) Also, leasing is an "off-the-balance-sheet" method of financing; the lease is considered an operating expense on the income statement, not a liability on the balance sheet.
      f) Lease agreements also are flexible.
   2. Avoid nonessential outlays.
      a) By forgoing costly indulgences such as ostentatious office equipment, first-class travel, and flashy company cars, business owners can make efficient use of the company's cash.
      b) Before putting scarce cash into an asset, every business owner should put the decision to the acid test: What will this purchase add to the company's ability to compete and to become more successful?
   3. Negotiate fixed loan payments to coincide with your company's cash flow cycle.
      a) Many banks allow businesses to structure loans so that they can skip specific payments when their cash flow ebbs to its lowest point.
      b) Negotiating such terms gives businesses the opportunity to customize their loan repayments to their cash flow cycles.
   4. Buy used or reconditioned equipment, especially if it is "behind-the-scenes" machinery.
   5. Hire part-time employees and freelance specialists whenever possible.
      a) Hiring part-timers and freelancers rather than full-time workers saves on the cost of both salaries and benefits.
   6. Control employee advances and loans.

      a) A manager should grant only those advances and loans that are necessary and should keep accurate records on payments and balances.

7. Establish an internal security and control system.

      a) Reconciling the bank statement monthly and requiring special approval for checks over a specific amount, say $1,000, will help minimize losses.

      b) Separating recordkeeping and check-writing responsibilities, rather than assigning them to a single employee also offers protection.

8. Develop a system to battle check fraud.

      a) Merchants take in more than $13 billion in bad checks each year.

      b) Losses from check fraud will grow by 25 percent annually in the coming years.

      c) About 70 percent of all "bounced" checks occur because nine out of ten customers fail to keep their checkbooks balanced; the remaining 30 percent of bad checks are the result of fraud.

9. Change your shipping terms.

      a) Changing the firm's shipping terms from "FOB (free on board) buyer," in which the seller pays the cost of freight, to "FOB seller," in which the buyer absorbs all shipping costs, will improve cash flow.

10. Switch to zero-based budgeting.

      a) Zero-based budgeting (ZBB) primarily is a shift in the philosophy of budgeting.

      b) ZBB starts from a budget of zero and evaluates the necessity of every item.

11. Keep your business plan current.

      a) Smart owners keep their plans up to date in case an unexpected cash crisis forces them to seek emergency financing.

      b) Revising the plan annually also forces the owner to focus on managing the business more effectively.

C. Investing Surplus Cash

1. Because of the uneven flow of receipts and disbursements, a company will often temporarily have more cash than it needs a for a week, a month, a quarter, or longer.

2. Entrepreneurs who put surplus cash to work immediately rather than allowing it to sit idle soon discover that the yield adds up to a significant amount over time.

3. However, when investing surplus cash, the owner's primary objective should not be to earn the maximum yield (which usually carries with it maximum risk); instead, the focus should be on the safety and the liquidity of the investments.

4. Asset-management accounts, which integrate checking, borrowing, and investing services under one umbrella and were once available only to large businesses, now help small companies conserve cash.

VIII. Conclusion

1. Successful owners-run their businesses "lean and mean." Trimming wasteful expenditures, investing surplus funds, and carefully planning and managing the company's cash flow enables them to compete effectively in a hostile market.

2. The simple but effective techniques covered in this chapter can improve every small company's cash position. One business writer says, "In the day-to-day course of running a company, other people's capital flows past an imaginative CEO as opportunity."

3. By looking forward and keeping an analytical eye on your cash account as events unfold (remembering that if there's no real cash there when you need it, you're history), you can generate leverage as surely as if that capital were yours to keep.

Chapter Summary

♦ Explain the importance of cash management to the success of the small business.
  - Cash is the most important but least productive asset the small business has. The manager must maintain enough cash to meet the firm's normal requirements (plus a reserve for emergencies) without retaining excessively large, unproductive cash balances.
  - Without adequate cash, a small business will fail.
♦ Differentiate between cash and profits.
  - Cash and profits are not the same. More businesses fail for lack of cash than for lack of profits.
  - Profits, the difference between total revenue and total expenses, are an accounting concept. Cash flow represents the flow of actual cash (the only thing businesses can use to pay bills) through a business in a continuous cycle. A business can be earning a profit and be forced out of business because it runs out of cash.
♦ Understand the five steps in creating a cash budget and use them to create a cash budget.
  - The cash budgeting procedure tracks the flow of cash through the business and enables the owner to project cash surpluses and cash deficits at specific intervals.
  - The five steps in creating a cash budget are determining an adequate minimum cash balance, forecasting sales, and forecasting cash receipts, forecasting cash disbursements, and determining the end-of-month cash balance.
♦ Describe fundamental principles involved in managing the "Big Three" of cash management: accounts receivable, accounts payable, and inventory.
  - Controlling accounts receivable requires business owners to establish clear, firm credit and collection policies and to screen customers before granting them credit. Sending invoices promptly and acting on past-due accounts quickly also improve cash flow. The goal is to collect cash from receivables as quickly as possible.
  - When managing accounts payable, a manager's goal is to stretch out payables as long as possible without damaging the company's credit rating. Other techniques include verifying invoices before paying them, taking advantage of cash discounts, and negotiating the best possible credit terms.
  - Excess inventory earns a zero rate of return and ties up a company's cash unnecessarily. Owners must watch for stale merchandise.
♦ Explain the techniques for avoiding a cash crunch in a small company.
  - Trimming overhead costs by bartering, leasing assets, avoiding nonessential outlays, using zero-based budgeting, and implementing an internal control system boost a firm's cash flow position.
  - Investing surplus cash maximizes the firm's earning power. The primary criteria for investing surplus cash are security and liquidity.

Discussion Questions

1. Why must small business owners concentrate on effective cash flow management?
   Answer - Cash is the most important yet least productive asset that a small business owns. A business must have enough cash to meet its obligations or it will be declared bankrupt. Proper cash management enables the owner to adequately meet the cash demands of the business, to avoid retaining unnecessarily large cash balances, and to stretch the profit-generating power of each dollar the business owns.

2. Explain the difference between cash and profit.
   Answer - Profit (or net income) is the difference between a company's total revenue and its total expenses. It measures how efficiently the business is running. As important as earning a profit is, no business owner can pay creditors, employees, and lenders with the business' profits; those payments require cash. Profits are tied up in many forms, such as inventory, computers, or machinery. Cash is

the money that flows through a business in a continuous cycle without being tied up in any other asset.

3.   Outline the steps involved in developing a cash budget.
     Answer - There are five basic steps in completing a cash budget:
     • Determine an adequate minimum cash balance.
     • Forecast sales.
     • Forecast cash receipts.
     • Forecast cash disbursements.
     • Determine the end-of-month cash balance.

4.   How can an entrepreneur launching a new business forecast sales?
     Answer - The heart of the cash budget is the sales forecast. For most businesses, sales constitute the major source of the cash flowing into the business. The sales forecast can be based on past sales, but the owner must be careful not to be excessively optimistic in projecting sales. The task of forecasting sales for a new firm is difficult but not impossible. The owner can conduct research on similar firms and their sales patterns in the first year of operation to come up with a forecast. Or he/she can use marketing research as another source of information that may be used to estimate annual sales for the fledgling firm. See Table 8.3 for an example of how one entrepreneur used such marketing information to derive a sales forecast for his first year of operation.

5.   Outline the basic principles of managing a small firm's receivables, payables, and inventory.
     Answer - Managing receivables. Selling merchandise and services on credit is a necessary evil for most small businesses. One recent survey of small businesses in a variety of industries reported that 77 percent extend credit to their customers. An assertive collection program is essential to managing a company's cash flow. The owner should have a credit and collection policy. Small business owners can take several steps to encourage prompt payment of invoices.
     • Ensure that all invoices are clear, accurate, and timely.
     • State clearly a description of the goods or services purchased and an account number, if possible.
     • Make sure that prices on invoices agree with the price quotations on purchase orders or contracts.
     • Highlight the terms of sale (e.g., "net 30") on all invoices and reinforce them, if necessary.
     • Include a telephone number and a contact person in your organization in case the customer has a question or a dispute.

The second element of the Big Three of cash management is accounts payable. The timing of payables is just as crucial to proper cash management as the timing of receivables, but the objective is exactly the opposite. An entrepreneur should strive to stretch out payables as long as possible without damaging the company's credit rating. Business owners should verify all invoices before paying them. In general, it is a good idea for owners to take advantage of cash discounts that vendors offer. Small business owners also can improve their firm's cash flow by scheduling controllable cash disbursements so that they do not come due at the same time. Inventory is a significant investment for many small businesses and can create a severe strain on cash flow. Surplus inventory yields a zero rate of return and unnecessarily ties up the firm's cash. A typical manufacturing company pays 25 percent to 30 percent of the value of the inventory for the cost of borrowed money, warehouse space, materials handling, staff, lift-truck expenses, and fixed costs. Only 20 percent of a typical business's inventory turns over quickly, so the owner must watch constantly for stale items. Carrying too much inventory increases the chances that a business will run out of cash.

6. How can bartering improve a company's cash position?
    Answer - Bartering, the exchange of goods and services for other goods and services, is an effective way to conserve cash. There is a cost associated with bartering, but the real benefit is that entrepreneurs "pay" for products and services at their wholesale cost of doing business and get credit in the barter exchange for the retail price. In a typical arrangement, businesses accumulate trade credits when they offer goods or services through the exchange. Then, they can use their trade credits to purchase other goods and services from other members of the exchange. The typical exchange charges a $500 membership fee and a 10 percent transaction fee (5 percent from the buyer and 5 percent from the seller) on every deal. The exchange tracks the balance in each member's account and typically sends a monthly statement summarizing account activity. Rather than join a barter exchange, many enterprising entrepreneurs choose to barter on an individual basis. The place to start is with the people the company normally does business with.

7. What steps should business owners take to conserve cash in their companies?
    Answer - Business owners can take a number of steps to conserve cash.
    - When practical, lease instead of buy.
    - Avoid nonessential outlays.
    - Negotiate fixed loan payments to coincide with your company's cash flow cycle.
    - Buy used or reconditioned equipment, especially if it is "behind-the-scenes" machinery.
    - Hire part-time employees and freelance specialists whenever possible.
    - Control employee advances and loans.
    - Establish an internal security and control system.
    - Develop a system to battle check fraud.
    - Change shipping terms.
    - Switch to zero-based budgeting.

8. What should be a small business owner's primary concerns when investing surplus cash?
    Answer - Because of the uneven flow of receipts and disbursements, a company will often temporarily have more cash than it needs a for a week, a month, a quarter, or longer. Entrepreneurs who put surplus cash to work immediately rather than allowing it to sit idle soon discover that the yield adds up to a significant amount over time. However, when investing surplus cash, the owner's primary objective should not be to earn the maximum yield (which usually carries with it maximum risk); instead, the focus should be on the safety and the liquidity of the investments. Asset-management accounts, which integrate checking, borrowing, and investing services under one umbrella and were once available only to large businesses, now help small companies conserve cash.

Step into the Real World

1. Ask several local small business owners about their cash management policies. Do they know how much cash their businesses have during the month? How do they track their cash flows? Do they use some type of cash budget? If not, ask if you can help the owner develop one. Does the owner invest surplus cash?
2. Volunteer to help a small business owner develop a cash budget for his or her company. What patterns do you detect? What recommendations can you make for improving the company's cash management system?
3. Use the resources available in your local library and on the World Wide Web to prepare a brief report on bartering. What benefits does barter offer business owners? How does the typical barter exchange operate? What fees are involved? How are barter transactions taxed? A useful source of information is the International Reciprocal Trade Association's Web site at <http://www. irta.com>.
4. Interview several local business owners about their policies on accepting payments by check. How much do they typically lose each year to bad checks? What safeguards do they use to combat check

fraud? Contact the American Collectors Association at P.O. Box 39106, Minneapolis, MN 55439-0106 or access the ACA's Web site at <http://www.collector.com/>. How prevalent is check fraud? What can business owners do to prevent it'? Using these resources and those in your local library, develop a set of recommendations for the owners you interviewed to reduce their losses to check fraud.

Chapter 9 - Crafting a Winning Business Plan

Teaching Objectives
Students will be able to:
1. Explain the two essential functions and the value of a business plan.
2. Describe the elements of a solid business plan.
3. Explain the three tests that a business plan must pass.
4. Understand the keys to making an effective business plan presentation.
5. Explain the five Cs of credit and why they are important to potential lenders and investors reading business plans.

Instructor's Outline
I. Introduction
    A. A Business Plan Is
        1. A systematic, realistic evaluation of a venture's chances for success in the market.
        2. A way to determine the principal risks facing the venture.
        3. A game plan for managing the business successfully.
        4. A tool for comparing actual results against targeted performance.
        5. An important tool for attracting capital in the challenging hunt for money

II. Why Develop a Business Plan?
    A. Functions of a Business Plan
        1. A business plan is a written summary of an entrepreneur's proposed business venture, its operational and financial details, its marketing opportunities and strategy, and its managers' skills and abilities.
           a) It describes the direction the company is taking, what its goals are, where it wants to be, and how it's going to get there.
           b) The plan is written proof that the entrepreneur has performed the necessary research and has studied the business opportunity adequately.
        2. The business plan serves two essential functions.
           a) First and most important, it guides the company's operations by charting its future course and devising a strategy for following it.
               (1) The plan provides a battery of tools--a mission statement, goals, objectives, budgets, financial forecasts, target markets, strategies--to help managers lead the company successfully.
           b) The second function of the business plan is to attract lenders and investors.
               (1) Too often small business owners approach potential lenders and investors without having prepared to sell themselves and their business concept.
               (2) Preparing a solid plan demonstrates that the entrepreneur has taken the time to commit the idea to paper.
               (3) Building a plan also forces the entrepreneur to consider both the positive and the negative aspects of the business.
        3. An entrepreneur should not allow others to prepare a business plan for him because outsiders cannot understand the business or envision the proposed company as well as he can.
           a) Investors want to feel confident that an entrepreneur has realistically evaluated the risk involved in the new venture and has a strategy for addressing it.
           b) They also want to see proof that a business will become profitable and produce a reasonable return on their investment.

   4. Perhaps the best way to understand the need for a business plan is to recognize the validity of the "two-thirds rule," which says that only two-thirds of the entrepreneurs with a sound and viable new business venture will find financial backing.
   5. Sometimes the greatest service a business plan provides an entrepreneur is the realization that "it just won't work."
   6. The real value in preparing a business plan is the process the entrepreneur goes through to create the plan.
   7. During the process, the entrepreneur replaces "I thinks" with "I knows" and makes mistakes on paper, which is much cheaper than making them in reality.
       a) Table 9.1 describes the four bases every business plan should cover.

III. The Elements of a Business Plan
   A. Introduction
       1. The elements of a business plan may be standard, but how the entrepreneur tells her story should be unique and reflect her personal excitement about the new venture.
       2. Many entrepreneurs would rather launch their companies and "see what happens" than invest the necessary time and energy defining and researching their target markets, defining their strategies, and mapping out their finances.
       3. A business plan typically ranges from 25 to 55 pages in length.
           a) Shorter plans usually are too sketchy.
           b) A longer plan might never get used.
           c) "It should take less than an hour to read your plan, and in that time, readers should be able to understand the entire concept--where you're going and how you're going to get there."

   B. The Executive Summary
       1. Presents the essence of the plan in a capsulized form.
       2. A maximum of two pages.
       3. It should explain the dollar amount requested, how the funds will be used, and how (and when) any loans will be repaid.

   C. Mission Statement
       1. Expresses in words the entrepreneur's vision for what her company is and what it is to become.
       2. It is the broadest expression of a company's purpose and defines the direction in which it will move.
       3. It serves as the thesis statement for the entire business plan.

   D. Company History
       1. A brief history of the operation, highlighting the significant financial and operational events in the company's life.
       2. It should describe when and why the company was formed, how it has evolved over time, and what the owner envisions for the future.
       3. It should highlight the successful accomplishment of past objectives and should convey the firm's image in the marketplace.

   E. Business and Industry Profile
       1. The owner should describe the nature of the business.
           a) It begins with a statement of the company's general business goals and a narrower definition of its immediate objectives.
               (1) "Why am I in business?"

      b)   Both goals and objectives should be related to the company's basic mission.
2.   Describe the present state of the art in the industry and what is needed to succeed in the market segment in which her business will compete.
3.   Identify the current applications of the product or service in the market and include projections for future applications.
4.   This section should provide the reader with an overview of the industry or market segment in which the new venture will operate.
      a)   Industry data such as market size, growth trends, and the relative economic and competitive strength of the major firms in the industry.
      b)   Strategic issues such as ease of market entry and exit, the ability to achieve economies of scale or scope, and the existence of cyclical or seasonal economic trends.
      c)   Significant industry trends and an overall outlook for its future.
5.   The industry analysis should also focus on the existing and anticipated profitability of the firms in the targeted market segment.
6.   The entrepreneur also should mention any events that have significantly altered the industry in the past 10 years.

F.   Business Strategy
1.   The strategy needed to meet, and beat, the competition.
2.   This section addresses the question of how to accomplish the goals and objectives of the previous section.
      a)   How the entrepreneur plans to gain a competitive edge in the market.
      b)   The image that the business will try to project.
      c)   What makes the company unique in the eyes of its customers?
3.   This segment of the business plan should outline the methods the company can use to meet the key success factors cited earlier.

G.   Description of Firm's Product/Service
1.   Describe the company's overall product line, giving an overview of how customers use its goods or services.
      a)   Drawings, diagrams, and illustrations may be required if the product is highly technical.
      b)   A statement of a product's position in the product life cycle.
      c)   A summary of any patents, trademarks, or copyrights protecting the product or service from infringement by competitors.
      d)   An honest comparison of the company's product or service with those of competitors, citing specific advantages or improvements.
      e)   What competitive advantage does the venture's product or service offer?
2.   One danger entrepreneurs must avoid in this part of the plan is the tendency to dwell excessively on the features of their products or services.
      a)   Customers, lenders, and investors care less about how much work, genius, and creativity went into a product or service than about what it will do for them.
3.   The emphasis should be on defining the benefits customers get by purchasing the company's products or services.
      a)   A feature is a descriptive fact about a product or service.
      b)   A benefit is what the customer gains from the product or service feature.
4.   Manufacturers should describe their production process, strategic raw materials required, sources of supply they will use and their costs.
      a)   Summarize the production method and illustrate the plant layout.

b) If the product is based on a patented or proprietary process, a description (including diagrams, if necessary) of its unique market advantages is helpful.
c) Explain the company's environmental impact and how the entrepreneur plans to mitigate any negative environmental consequences the process may produce.

GAINING THF COMPETITIVE EDGE - The Right Way to Build a Business Plan

Building a plan forces entrepreneurs to ask--and to answer-questions that are vitally important to their company's ultimate success. Building a solid plan that will help your business become more successful has the following 10 characteristics.

1. Detailed market research. Prove that you know your target customers and the problems your product or service solves for them.
2. Clear and realistic financial projections. Potential lenders and investors often start and end their investigation of a business here. They want to see summaries of a company's financial performance to date [if it is an existing business] and realistic forecasts for the future.
3. A detailed competitor analysis. A plan should show that an entrepreneur understands the competition and its strengths and weaknesses.
4. A description of the management team. The universal factor that potential lenders and investors look for--a sound management team.
5. A distinct vision. Entrepreneurs who have a clear-vision of what they want their companies to stand for and to accomplish create a sense of excitement among investors.
6. An understanding of financial options. A plan should explain why a company needs financing, how much money it needs, how it will use the money, and how it will repay lenders or investors.
7. Proper format and a flowing writing style. "The first requisite of a business plan is that it be interesting to read, well-written, and smooth-flowing."
8. Conciseness. Business plans must include enough detail to answer potential lenders' and investors' questions without overloading them with unnecessary clutter.
9. A killer summary. The executive summary may be the toughest part of a business plan to write. It's the section almost every potential lender or investor reads first. A good executive summary captures the essence of the plan and piques the reader's interest--all in no more than two pages.
10. Customization. Be careful to avoid the cookie cutter look. Use guides and resources as a starting point for your plan. Make sure your plan presents your company in the most favorable way.

H. Marketing Strategy
1. One crucial concern--is there a real market for the proposed good or service?
2. Defining the target market and its potential is one of the most important, and most difficult, parts of building a business plan.
3. Perhaps the worst marketing error an entrepreneur can commit is failing to define her target market and trying to make her business "everything to everybody."
4. Defining a company's target market involves using the techniques described in Chapter 6.
   a) Questions in this part of the business plan should address market issues such as target market, market size and trends, location, advertising and promotion, pricing, and distribution.
5. Proving that a profitable market exists involves two steps: showing customer interest and documenting market claims.
6. Showing customer interest.
   a) The entrepreneur must be able to prove that her target customers need or want her good or service and are willing to pay for it.

    b) This phase is relatively straightforward for a company with an existing product or service but can be quite difficult for one with only an idea or a prototype.

       (1) Getting a product into customers' hands is also an excellent way to get valuable feedback that can lead to significant design improvements and increased sales down the road.

  7. Documenting market claims.

    a) Entrepreneurs must support claims of market size and growth rates with facts, and that requires market research.

    b) Results of market surveys, customer questionnaires, and demographic studies lend credibility to an entrepreneur's optimistic sales projections.

  8. Quantitative market data are important because they form the basis for all of the company's financial projections in the business plan.

  9. One of the essential goals of this section of the plan is to identify the basics for financial forecasts that follow.

  10. An effective market analysis should identify:

    a) Target market. Who are the most promising customers or prospects (demographics)? Where do they live and shop? What are their characteristics?

    b) Advertising and promotion. Which media are most effective in reaching the target market? How will they be used? How much will the promotional campaign cost?

    c) Market size and trends. How large is the potential market? Is it growing or shrinking?

    d) Location. For retailers, wholesalers, and service companies, the best location usually is one that is most convenient to their target customers. Which specific sites put the company in the path of its target customers? Do zoning regulations restrict the use of the site? For manufacturers, the location issue often centers on finding a site near its key raw materials or near its major customers.

    e) Pricing. What does the product or service cost to produce or deliver? What is the company's overall pricing strategy? What image is the company trying to create in the market? Will the company offer discounts? If so, what kinds and how much?

    f) Distribution. How will the product or service be distributed? Will distribution be extensive, selective, or exclusive? What is the average sale? How large will the sales staff be?

  11. This portion of the plan also should describe the channels of distribution that the business will use (mail, in-house sales force, sales agent, and retailers). The owner should summarize the firm's overall pricing and promotion strategies, including the advertising budget, media used, and publicity efforts. The company's warranties and guarantees for its products and services should be addressed as well.

I. Competitor Analysis

  1. Failing to assess competitors realistically makes entrepreneurs appear to be poorly prepared, naive, or dishonest.

  2. Gathering information on competitors' market shares, products, and strategies is usually not difficult.

    a) Trade associations, customers, industry journals, marketing representatives, and sales literature are valuable sources of data.

    b) This section of the plan should focus on demonstrating that the entrepreneur's company has an advantage over its competitors.

J. Officers' and Owners' Resumes

  1. The most important factor in the success of a business venture is its management.

  2. Financial officers and investors weigh heavily the ability and experience of the firm's managers in financing decisions.

       3. Include the resumes of business officers, key directors, and any person with at least 20 percent ownership in the company.
         a) A resume should summarize the individual's education, work history (emphasizing managerial responsibilities and duties), and relevant business experience.
       4. One experienced private investor advises entrepreneurs to remember the following:
         a) Ideas and products don't succeed; people do. Show the strength of your management team. A top-notch management team with a variety of proven skills is crucial.
         b) Show the strength of key employees and how you will retain them. A board of directors or advisers consisting of industry experts lends credibility and can enhance the value of the management team.

K. Plan of Operation
       1. To complete the description of the business, the owner should construct an organizational chart identifying the business's key positions and the personnel occupying them.
       2. Finally, a description of the form of ownership (partnership, joint venture, S corporation, limited liability company) and of any leases, contracts, and other relevant agreements pertaining to the operation is helpful.

L. Financial Data
       1. One of the most important sections --a detailed outline of the loan or investment package of the proposed deal.
       2. Lenders and investors use past financial statements to judge the health of an existing small company and its ability to repay loans or to generate adequate returns.
       3. Supply copies of the firm's major financial statements from the past three years.
         a) Ideally, audited by a certified public accountant.
       4. Carefully prepare monthly projected (or pro forma) financial statements for the operation for the next two to three years (and possibly for two more years by quarters). Use past operating data, published statistics, and judgment to derive three sets of forecasts of the income statement, balance sheet, cash budget, and schedule of planned capital expenditures.
         a) Pessimistic.
         b) Most likely.
         c) Optimistic.
       5. It is essential that all three sets of forecasts be realistic.
         a) Some venture capitalists automatically discount an entrepreneur's financial projections by as much as 50 percent.
         b) Perform a breakeven analysis and a ratio analysis on the projected figures.
       6. It is also important to include a statement of the assumptions on which these financial projections are based.

M. The Request for Funds
       1. The loan proposal section of the business plan should state the purpose of the loan, the amount requested, and the plans for repayment.
         a) One important by-product of preparing a business plan is discovering how much money it will take to launch the business.
       2. When describing the purpose of the loan, the owner must specify the planned use of the funds.
         a) Entrepreneurs should state the precise amount of money they are requesting and include relevant backup data, such as vendor estimates of costs or past production levels.
       3. Another important element is the repayment schedule and exit strategy.

4. A lender's main consideration in granting a loan is the reassurance that the applicant will repay, whereas an investor's major concern is earning a satisfactory rate of return.
5. Financial projections must reflect the firm's ability to repay loans and to produce adequate yields.
    a) Without this proof, a request for additional funds stands little chance of being accepted.
    b) Generally, the equity investor's objective with early-stage funding is to earn a 30 percent to 50 percent annual return over the life of the investment.
6. Finally, the owner should have a realistic timetable for implementing the proposed plan.
7. It is beneficial to include an evaluation of the risks of a new venture.
8. Evaluating risk in a business plan requires an entrepreneur to walk a fine line.
    a) Dwelling too much on everything that can go wrong will discourage potential lenders and investors from financing the venture.
    b) Ignoring the project's risks makes those who evaluate the plan tend to believe that the entrepreneur is either naive, dishonest, or unprepared.
    c) The best strategy is to identify the most significant risks the venture faces and then to describe what plans have been developed to avoid them altogether or to overcome the negative outcome if the event does occur.

IN THE FOOTSTEPS OF AN ENTREPRENEUR - Turning a Dream into Reality

David Cupp, a professional photographer with credits in high-profile magazines such as *National Geographic*, wanted to launch his own stock photography house. An experienced computer and Internet user, Cupp says he "saw that hadn't been done before." Photo stock houses purchase the rights to photographs from photographers and then resell.

Cupp's proposed company, Photos Online, would allow customers to use the World Wide Web to browse through his extensive collection of photographs by topic. Once they had selected the photos they wanted, they could order them through the Web site and receive them by downloading them on-line--all in a single transaction. The only problem was that he needed $25,000 to finance the start-up expenses to launch the company. First stop was the Small Business Administration's office. Officials there asked to see a copy of his business plan. "A what?" Cupp quickly enrolled in a SBA-sponsored.

Cupp found that getting started was the hardest part. For help with his financial projections, Cupp began working with accountant Wayne Logan. Finally, Cupp had a business plan he could take to potential lenders and investors. Given the amount of money he needed, Cupp decided to focus on banks. His first four calls resulted in four rejections, but with each rejection, Cupp went back and revised his plan on the basis of what the lender had told him. The extra work paid off. Bank One not only approved a $26,000 term loan but also extended Photos Online a $24,000 line of credit for short-term needs.

1. Would David Cupp have been able to attract the money he needed to launch Photos Online without a business plan?
   Answer - Apparently not, since it took several revisions to finally get the loan.
2. Assume that you were a private investor whom Cupp approached for the start-up capital he needed. Would you have considered investing in Cupp's business if he had had no business plan? Explain.
   Answer - Students' responses vary but basically they should want some plan to show the use of their money.
3. Which parts of Cupp's business plan would interest you most? Why?
   Answer - Students' responses will vary but if they parallel venture bankers, his financials and plan--product competitive advantage--would probably be of the most interest.

    N. Appearance
        1. A plan is usually the tool that an entrepreneur uses to make a first impression on potential lenders and investors.
        2. To ensure that impression is a favorable one:
            a) Make sure the plan is free of spelling and grammatical errors and typos.
            b) Make it visually appealing. Use color charts, figures, and diagrams to illustrate.
            c) Leave ample white space in margins.
            d) Create an attractive (but not extravagant) cover with the company's name and logo.
            e) Include a table of contents to allow readers to navigate the plan easily.
            f) Write in a flowing, conversational style and use "bullets" to itemize points in lists.
            g) Support claims with facts and avoid generalizations.
            h) Avoid overusing industry jargon and abbreviations.
            i) Make it interesting.
            j) Use computer spreadsheets to generate financial forecasts.
            k) Always include cash flow projections. Entrepreneurs sometimes focus excessively on their proposed venture's profit forecasts and ignore cash flow projections.
            l) The ideal plan is crisp: long enough to say what it should but not so long that it is a chore to read.
            m) Tell the truth. Absolute honesty is critical in a business plan.

IV. Testing the Plan
    A. Reality Test
        1. The external component of the reality test revolves around proving that a market for the product or service really does exist.
            a) It focuses on industry attractiveness, market niches, potential customers, market size, degree of competition, and similar factors.
        2. The internal component of the reality test focuses on the product or service itself.
            a) Can the company really build it for the cost estimates in the business plan?

    B. Competitive Test
        1. The external part of the competitive test evaluates the company's position relative to its key competitors.
            a) How do the company's strengths and weaknesses match up with those of the competition?
        2. The internal competitive test focuses on management's ability to create a company that will gain an edge over existing rivals.
            a) What resources does the company have that can give it a competitive edge in the market?

    C. Value Test
        1. A business plan must prove to lenders and investors that the business offers a high probability of repayment or an attractive rate of return.

V. Making the Business Plan Presentation
    A. Described
        1. The written business plan almost always precedes the opportunity to meet face to face.
            a) If the written plan does pass muster, the time allowed for the personal meeting usually is quite limited--15 to 20 minutes, 30 minutes at the maximum.
            b) It is a mistake to begin by leading the audience into a long-winded explanation about the technology on which the product or service is based.
        2. A business plan presentation should cover five basic areas:

    a) The company's background and its products or services.
    b) A market analysis and a description of the opportunities it presents.
    c) Marketing strategies and tactics.
    d) The management team and its members' qualifications.
    e) A financial analysis that shows lenders and investors an attractive payback or payoff.
3. No matter how good a written business plan is, entrepreneurs who muff the presentation to potential lenders and investors will blow the deal.

IN THE FOOTSTEPS OF AN ENTREPRENEUR - (Boot) Camp Entrepreneur

Entrepreneur Rob Ryan learned two valuable lessons after starting his first company, Softcom, which he sold to a larger competitor when he ran out of money. "First, never start a company without a great team," he says. "Second, raise a lot of money." He put those lessons into practice with his second company, was successful and went public in 1994. Rather than "retire," Ryan decided to devote his life to helping other entrepreneurs become successful. He established Entrepreneur America, a boot camp for budding entrepreneur.

As tactful as a drill sergeant, Ryan challenges the entrepreneurs under his tutelage, questioning the assumptions underlying their plans and cajoling them into improving the quality of their business plans. Although it sounds harsh to outsiders, entrepreneurs love Ryan's tough, straightforward style. In response to one of Ryan's blistering assaults, one entrepreneur practicing his business plan presentation exclaimed, "This is good. It's making my head hurt, which is why I came here." Another of Ryan's students who has launched a highly successful technology company says, "There is a saying, 'There is no progress without the unreasonable man.'"

1. What benefits does Rob Ryan's entrepreneurial boot camp offer aspiring entrepreneurs?
    Answer - It gives them a safe "real world" experience and helps them hone their business plans before they go to venture bankers. It is a condensed way to get a lot of presentation experience.
2. Critique the confrontational style that Ryan uses with his entrepreneurial students. What benefits does it give them?
    Answer - Students will argue both ways. The reality is that finance people see lots of plans and have limited time and resources to invest so they will often be abrupt and "brutal." Therefore Ryan's style helps prepare the entrepreneurs and increases their chance of success.
3. Use the resources in the library and on the World Wide Web to develop a list of suggestions and advice for entrepreneurs presenting their business plans to lenders and investors.
    Answer - Responses will vary based on students' research efforts.

---

4. Tips for making a business plan presentation
    a) Demonstrate enthusiasm, about the venture, but don't be overemotional.
    b) Fight the temptation to launch immediately into a lengthy discourse about the details of your product or service or how much work it took to develop it. Focus instead on communicating the dynamic opportunity your idea offers and how you plan to capitalize on it.
    c) Use visual aids. They make it easier for people to follow your presentation.
    d) Hit the highlights; specific questions will bring out the details later.
    e) Keep the presentation crisp.
    f) Avoid the use of technological terms that will likely be above most of the audience.
    g) Remember that every potential lender and investor you talk to is thinking "What's in it for me?"
    h) Close by reinforcing the nature of the opportunity.

        i)   Be prepared for questions.
        j)   Anticipate and prepare for the questions the audience is most likely to ask.
        k)   Be sensitive to the issues that are most important to lenders and investors by "reading" the pattern of their questions.
        l)   Follow up with every investor you make a presentation to.

VI. Lenders, and What They Look For in a Loan Application
    A. The five Cs
        1. Capital
        2. Capacity
        3. Collateral
        4. Character
        5. Conditions

    B. Capital
        1. A small business must have a stable capital base before a bank will grant a loan.
        2. Most banks refuse to make loans that are capital investments because the potential for return on the investment is limited strictly to the interest on the loan, and the potential loss would probably exceed the reward.
        3. In fact, the most common reasons that banks give for rejecting small business loan applications are undercapitalization or too much debt.

    C. Capacity
        1. A synonym for capacity is cash flow.
        2. The bank must be convinced of the firm's ability meet its regular financial obligations and to repay the bank loan.
        3. The bank studies closely the small company's cash flow position to decide whether it meets the capacity requirement.

    D. Collateral
        1. Collateral includes any assets the owner pledges to the bank as security for repayment of the loan.
        2. If the company defaults on the loan, the bank has the right to sell the collateral and use the proceeds to satisfy the loan.

    E. Character
        1. The banker must be satisfied with the owner's character.
        2. This evaluation of character frequently is based on intangible factors such as honesty, competence, polish, determination, and intelligence.
        3. The business plan and a polished presentation can go far in convincing the banker of the owner's character.

    F. Conditions
        1. The conditions surrounding a loan request also affect the owner's chance of receiving funds.
        2. Banks consider factors relating to the business operation, such as potential growth in the market, competition, location, form of ownership, and loan purpose.
        3. Another important condition influencing the banker's decision is the shape of the overall economy, including interest rate levels, inflation rate, and demand for money.

WIRED TO THE WEB - A Little Help from My Friends and the Web

SUMMARY

Kosha Batel couldn't help but smile smugly as she climbed into her sport utility vehicle. "I can't believe I finally have the money to launch my business." Uncle Cal, himself a successful business owner, had seemed intrigued when she had first pitched her business idea to him five months earlier. He told Kosha then that he liked her idea and her enthusiasm for becoming an entrepreneur and that he would consider bankrolling her business idea. "It certainly sounds like a great business idea. Anyway, you are my favorite niece and $25,000 isn't a lot of money."

Several days later, Kosha ran into Liz, an old friend from college. As they caught up on what had happened in each others' lives since graduation, Liz mentioned that she was now working for a consulting firm that specialized in small and medium-sized businesses. Liz volunteered to look over her business plan, which Kosha didn't have. Liz couldn't disguise her shock. "Kosha, whether you search for capital from lenders or investors or not, you need a business plan. How else are you going to guide your company through all of the crises you'll encounter, especially in the early months of your business venture?"

Kosha couldn't say a word. She just stood there, realizing that her friend was right. Liz told Kosha. "Give me a call, and we'll get together. In the meantime, go to the World Wide Web and search for information on business plans.

1. Use the search engines on the World Wide Web to help Kosha learn more about writing a business plan.
    Answer - Students' responses will vary based on their searches.
2. On the basis of what you learned in this chapter and your Web search, write a two-page report outlining for Kosha some practical advice on assembling a business plan.
    Answer - Students' reports should use both their Web site information and text content.
3. Locate a sample business plan on the WWW that you believe would serve as a good model for Kosha to follow. Record its URL [Web address] and explain why it is a good model.
    Answer - Consider offering students 2-3 key Web sites to look at. The paperback, *Management on the World Wide Web*, and similar books list a number of small business and business planning sites.

VII. Business Plan Format
      1. This format is detailed on pages 300-302 in the text.

Chapter Summary

♦ Explain the two essential functions and the value of a business plan.
  - The business plan guides the company's operations by charting its future course and devising a strategy for following it.
  - The business plan attracts lenders and investors.
  - The real value in preparing a business plan is not so much in the plan itself as it is in the process the entrepreneur goes through to create the plan. Although the finished product is useful, the process of building a plan requires an entrepreneur to subject his idea to an objective, critical evaluation. What the entrepreneur learns about his company, its target market, its financial requirements, and other factors can be essential to making the venture a success.
♦ Describe the elements of a solid business plan.
  - Although a business plan should be unique and tailor-made to suit the particular needs of a small company, it should cover these basic elements: an executive summary, a mission statement, a company history, a business and industry profile, a description of the company's business

strategy, a profile of its products or services, a statement explaining its marketing strategy, a competitor analysis, owners' and officers' resumes, a plan of operation, financial data, and the loan or investment proposal.

♦ Explain the three tests that a business plan must pass.
  ▪ The reality test, externally, proves that a market for the product or service exists. Internally, it proves that the cost estimates in the plan are accurate.
  ▪ The competitive test, externally, proves that the product or service will be able to successfully compete in its market. Internally, it proves that the company's management is competent and that the company has resources to give it a competitive advantage.
  ▪ The value test proves that the business offers a high probability of repayment of a loan or an attractive rate of return on an investment.

♦ Understand the keys to making an effective business plan presentation.
  ▪ Demonstrate enthusiasm about the venture, but don't be overemotional; "hook" investors quickly with an up-front explanation of the new venture, its opportunities, and the anticipated benefits to them; use visual aids; hit the highlights of your venture; don't get caught up in too much detail in early meetings with lenders and investors; avoid the use of technological terms that will likely be above most of the audience; rehearse your presentation before giving it; close by reinforcing the nature of the opportunity; and be prepared for questions.

♦ Explain the five Cs of credit and why they are important to potential lenders and investors reading business plans.
  ▪ Capital. Lenders expect small businesses to have an equity base of investment by the owners that will help support the venture during times of financial strain.
  ▪ Capacity. A synonym for capacity is cash flow. The bank must be convinced of the firm's ability to meet its regular financial obligations and to repay the bank loan, and that takes cash.
  ▪ Collateral. Collateral includes any assets the owner pledges to the bank as security for repayment of the loan.
  ▪ Character. Bankers judge the owner's honesty, competence, polish, determination, and intelligence.
  ▪ Conditions. Bankers consider interest rates, the health of the nation's economy, industry growth rates, form of ownership, location, and other external and internal factors that might affect the business.

Discussion Questions

1. Why should an entrepreneur develop a business plan?
   Answer - A business plan is a written summary of an entrepreneur's proposed business venture, its operational and financial details, its marketing opportunities and strategy, and its managers' skills and abilities. It describes the direction the company is taking, what its goals are, where it wants to be, and how it's going to get there. The plan is written proof that the entrepreneur has performed the necessary research and has studied the business opportunity adequately. Too often small business owners approach potential lenders and investors without having prepared to sell themselves and their business concept. Preparing a solid plan demonstrates that the entrepreneur has taken the time to commit the idea to paper. Investors want to feel confident that an entrepreneur has realistically evaluated the risk involved in the new venture and has a strategy for addressing it. They also want to see proof that a business will become profitable and produce a reasonable return on their investment.

2. Why do entrepreneurs who are not seeking external financing need to prepare business plans?
   Answer - The real value in preparing a business plan is the process the entrepreneur goes through to create the plan. During the process, the entrepreneur replaces "I thinks" with "I knows" and makes mistakes on paper, which is much cheaper than making them in reality. Building a plan also forces the entrepreneur to consider both the positive and the negative aspects of the business. A business plan is

a written summary of an entrepreneur's proposed business venture, its operational and financial details, its marketing opportunities and strategy, and its managers' skills and abilities. Table 9.1 describes the four bases every business plan should cover.

3. Describe the major components of a business plan.
    Answer - The executive summary presents the essence of the plan in a capsulized form. The mission statement expresses in words the entrepreneur's vision for what her company is and what it is to become. A brief history of the operation, highlighting the significant financial and operational events in the company's life. The owner should describe the nature of the business and the present state of the art in the industry and what is needed to succeed in the market segment in which her business will compete. Then there is the business strategy needed to meet, and beat, the competition. A description of the company's overall product line, giving an overview of how customers use its goods or services. The marketing strategy should address one crucial concern--is there a real market for the proposed good or service? Entrepreneurs must support claims of market size and growth rates with facts, and that requires market research. There should be a competitor analysis. The most important factor in the success of a business venture is its management. To complete the description of the business, the owner should construct an organizational chart identifying the business's key positions and the personnel occupying them. Finally, a description of the form of ownership (partnership, joint venture, S corporation, limited liability company) and of any leases, contracts, and other relevant agreements pertaining to the operation is helpful. One of the most important sections--a detailed outline of the loan or investment package of the proposed deal. The loan proposal section of the business plan should state the purpose of the loan, the amount requested, and the plans for repayment.

4. How can an entrepreneur seeking funds to launch a business convince potential lenders and investors that a market for the product or service really does exist?
    Answer - He/she can convince them by showing how the business plan passes three tests. 1) The reality test, externally, proves that a market for the product or service exists. Internally, it proves that the cost estimates in the plan are accurate. 2) The competitive test, externally, proves that the product or service will be able to successfully compete in its market. Internally, it proves that the company's management is competent and that the company has resources to give it a competitive advantage. 3) The value test proves that the business offers a high probability of repayment of a loan or an attractive rate of return on an investment.

5. How would you prepare to make a formal presentation of your business plan to a venture capital forum?
    Answer - There are several keys to making an effective business plan presentation. a) Demonstrate enthusiasm about the venture, but don't be overemotional. b) "Hook" investors quickly with an up-front explanation of the new venture, its opportunities, and the anticipated benefits to them; use visual aids; hit the highlights of your venture. c) Don't get caught up in too much detail in early meetings with lenders and investors. d) Avoid the use of technological terms that will likely be above most of the audience. e) Rehearse your presentation before giving it. f) Close by reinforcing the nature of the opportunity. And, g) be prepared for questions.

6. What are the five Cs of credit? How does a banker use them when evaluating a loan request?
    Answer - They are what potential lenders and investors look for in business plans. 1) Capital. Lenders expect small businesses to have an equity base of investment by the owners that will help support the venture during times of financial strain. 2) Capacity. A synonym for capacity is cash flow. The bank must be convinced of the firm's ability to meet its regular financial obligations and to repay the bank loan, and that takes cash. 3) Collateral. Collateral includes any assets the owner pledges to the bank as security for repayment of the loan. 4) Character. Bankers judge the owner's honesty, competence, polish, determination, and intelligence. 5) Conditions. Bankers consider interest rates,

the health of the nation's economy, industry growth rates, form of ownership, location, and other external and internal factors that might affect the business.

Step into the Real World

1. Interview a local banker or investor who has experience in making loans to or investments in small businesses. Ask him or her the following questions.
   a. How important is a well-prepared business plan?
   b. How important is a smooth presentation?
   c. How do you evaluate the owner's character?
   d. How heavily do you weigh the five Cs of credit?
   e. What percentage of small business owners are well prepared to request loan or investment?
   f. What mistakes do entrepreneurs most commonly make when creating their business plans? When presenting them?
   g. What are the major reasons for rejecting a business plan?
2. Interview a small business owner who has requested a bank loan or an equity investment from external sources. Ask him or her these questions:
   a. Did you prepare a written business plan before approaching the financial officer?
   b. (If the answer is yes), Did you have outside or professional help in preparing it?
   c. How many times have your requests for additional funds been rejected? What reasons were given for the rejections?

Chapter 10 - Pricing for Profit

Teaching Objectives
Students will be able to:
1. Describe effective pricing techniques for both new and existing products and services.
2. Discuss the links among pricing, image, and competition.
3. Explain the pricing techniques used by retailers.
4. Explain the pricing techniques used by manufacturers.
5. Explain the pricing techniques used by service firms.
6. Describe the impact of credit on pricing.

Instructor's Outline
I. Introduction
    A. Setting Prices
1. One of the toughest decisions small business owners face, but it is also one of the most important.
2. Prices that are too high will hurt a company's sales.
3. Pricing products or services too low, a common tendency among start-up businesses, will rob a company of profits, threaten its long-term success, and leave customers with the impression that its products or services are of inferior quality.
4. Improper pricing has destroyed countless businesses.
5. The factors that small business owners must consider when determining the final price:
    a) Product or service costs
    b) Market factors: supply and demand
    c) Sales volume
    d) Competitors' prices
    e) The company's competitive advantage
    f) Economic conditions
    g) Business location
    h) Seasonal fluctuations
    i) Psychological factors
    j) Credit terms and purchase discounts; Customers' price sensitivity; Desired image
6. Price is the monetary value of a product or service.
    a) It is a measure of what customers must give up to get goods and services.
    b) Price also is an indication of a product's or service's value to an individual customer, so different customers assign different values to the same products and services.
7. Setting prices with a customer orientation is more important than trying to choose the ideal price for a product.
    a) For most products, there is an acceptable price range, not a single ideal price.
    b) This price range is the area between the price ceiling defined by customers and the price floor established by the firm's cost structure.
        (1) See Figure 10.1
8. Identifying the price ceiling requires entrepreneurs to understand their customers' characteristics and buying behavior.
    a) The price floor depends on a company's cost structure, which can vary considerably from one business to another.
    b) Owners often assume that their cost structures are the same as their competitors, which is rarely the case.

9. The entrepreneur's goal should be to position the firm's prices within this acceptable price range.
10. The final price that business owners set depends on the desired image they want to create for their products or services: discount (bargain), middle-of-the-road (value), or prestige (upscale).
11. Business owners must walk a fine line when pricing their products and services, setting their prices high enough to cover costs and earn a reasonable profit but low enough to attract customers and generate an adequate sales volume.
12. Furthermore, the right price today may be completely inappropriate tomorrow because of changing market and competitive conditions.
13. Businesses faced with rapidly rising raw materials costs should consider:
    a) Communicate with customers. Let your customers know what's happening.
    b) Focus on improving efficiency everywhere in the company.
    c) Consider absorbing cost increases to save accounts with long-term importance to the company. Saving a large account might be more important than keeping pace with rising costs.
    d) Emphasize the value your company provides to customers. Unless a company reminds them, customers can forget the benefits and value its products offer.
    e) Anticipate rising materials costs and try to lock in prices early. It pays to keep tabs on raw materials prices and to be able to predict cycles of inflation.

II. Pricing Strategies and Tactics
   A. New Products: Penetration, Skimming, or Sliding
      1. Most entrepreneurs approach setting the price of a new product with a great deal of apprehension because they have no precedent.
      2. When pricing any new product, the owner should try to satisfy three objectives:
         a) Get the product accepted. No matter how unusual a product is, its price must be acceptable to the firm's potential customers.
         b) Maintain market share as competition grows. If a new product is successful, competitors will enter the market, and the small company must work to expand or at least maintain its market share.
         c) Earn a profit. Obviously, a small firm must establish a price for the new product that is higher than its cost. Managers should not introduce a new product at a price below cost because it is much easier to lower the price than to increase it once the product is on the market.
      3. Entrepreneurs have three basic strategies to choose from in establishing a new product's price: penetration, skimming, and sliding down the demand curve.
      4. Penetration
         a) If a small business introduces a product into a highly competitive market in which a large number of similar products are competing for acceptance, the product must penetrate the market to be successful.
         b) To gain quick acceptance and extensive distribution in the mass market, a company introduces the product at a low price--just above total unit cost to develop a wedge in the market and quickly achieve a high volume of sales.
         c) The resulting low profit margins may discourage other competitors from entering the market with similar products.
         d) A penetration pricing strategy is used to introduce relatively low-priced goods into a market where no elite segment and little opportunity for differentiation exist.
         e) The introduction is usually accompanied by heavy advertising and promotional techniques, special sales, and discounts.

      f)   The objective of the penetration strategy is to achieve quick access to the market in order to realize high sales volume as soon as possible.

5. Skimming
    a)   A skimming pricing strategy often is used when a company introduces a new product into a market with little or no competition.
    b)   Sometimes a company uses this tactic when introducing a product into a competitive market that contains an elite group that is able to pay a premium price.
    c)   The firm uses a higher-than-normal price in an effort to quickly recover the initial developmental and promotional costs of the product.
    d)   Product development or start-up costs usually are substantial owing to intensive promotional expenses and high initial costs.
    e)   The idea is to set a price well above the total unit cost and to promote the product heavily to appeal to the segment of the market that is not sensitive to price.
    f)   This pricing tactic often reinforces the unique, prestigious image of a store and projects a quality picture of the product.

6. Sliding down the demand curve
    a)   One variation of the skimming pricing strategy is called sliding down the demand curve.
       (1) The small company introduces a product at a high price.
       (2) Then, technological advancements enable the firm to lower its costs quickly and to reduce the product's price sooner than its competition can.
    b)   By beating other businesses in a price decline, the small company discourages competitors and, over time, becomes a high-volume producer.
    c)   Computers are a prime example.
    d)   Sliding is a short-term pricing strategy that assumes that competition will eventually emerge.

B. Established Goods and Services
  1. Odd pricing
    a)   Although studies of consumer reactions to prices are mixed and generally inconclusive, many small business managers use the technique known as odd pricing.
    b)   They set prices that end in odd numbers (frequently 5,7,9) because they believe that an item selling for $12.95 appears to be much cheaper than an item selling for $13.00.
  2. Price lining
    a)   Price lining is a technique that greatly simplifies the pricing function.
    b)   The manager stocks merchandise in several different price ranges or price lines. Each category of merchandise contains items that are similar in appearance, quality, cost, performance, or other features.
    c)   Most lined products appear in sets of three--good, better, and best--at prices designed to satisfy different market segment needs and incomes.
  3. Leader pricing
    a)   Leader pricing is a technique in which the small retailer marks down the customary price (i.e., the price consumers are accustomed to paying) of a popular item in an attempt to attract more customers.
    b)   The company earns a much smaller profit on each unit because the markup is lower, but purchases of other merchandise by customers seeking the leader item often boost sales and profits.

IN THE FOOTSTEPS OF AN ENTREPRENEUR - What Price Success?

After she was fired from her sales job at a downtown Philadelphia bicycle courier firm, Claudia Post started her own courier service, determined to outperform her former company. Using every sales tool she knew, Post took Diamond Courier Service to the $1 million sales level in just 17 months. In addition to the bicycle courier business, Post also owned companies that specialized in driver deliveries, truck deliveries, parts distribution, airfreight services, and a legal service that delivered subpoenas and court papers. Each business had its own employees, manager, customer base, and pricing strategy.

Just when things seemed to be taking off, however, Post's businesses began to experience serious difficulties, careening from one cash crisis to another. By the end of the company's third year, Post was shuffling accounts payable, trying to decide which creditor to pay and when. Her response was the typical entrepreneur's solution: SELL MORE! Knowing she needed help--and fast--Post turned to her friend Al Sloman, a veteran consultant in the courier industry.

After carefully examining the company's financial records, Sloman delivered his prognosis. "Claudia," he said, "you're headed for the rocks." Sloman knew that Post understood the sales side of the courier business, but his goal was to teach her the "business" side of the business. He saw that she was operating her business from a set of reasonable but untested assumptions. One of the most basic assumptions involved pricing. Post assumed that because her prices were equivalent to her competitors' prices, the more she sold, the more money she would make. From his review of the company's financial records, Sloman suspected that Diamond was losing money on most of the deliveries it made because its prices were too low. They isolated each of Post's six businesses as a separate profit center and began to allocate labor, operating, and administrative costs to each one. The biggest challenge they faced was allocating the indirect (i.e., overhead) cost accurately to each profit center. Sloman turned to activity-based costing. As the weeks went by Post began to see her business from a different perspective and to realize that many of the assumptions on which she had been running her company were not valid. Nowhere had her assumptions been more invalid than in her original bicycle courier business. Post had assumed that if she kept her delivery prices in line with competitors [in fact, her prices were above those of some competitors], she would have to earn a profit. She had never calculated what it actually cost her to make a delivery!

What Post thought of as Diamond's core business actually contributed only 10 percent of the company's total revenues and was not even generating enough to cover its costs! Post decided that she had to close that business. Her decision to close the bicycle courier business became easier after she discovered that her driver- and truck-delivery divisions were highly profitable, generating an average of $6.37 per delivery in profit. Post knows exactly what Diamond's costs are and that its prices are appropriate.

1. Describe the pricing mistakes that Post made with her courier service. What caused these mistakes?
    Answer - Post didn't know what her price floor was or how high her price ceiling should be. She never gathered any market research to find out.
2. How common are these mistakes among small business owners? Explain.
    Answer - These are common mistakes because owners focus on running the business, making decisions, taking action, not gathering information, and doing analysis. Also, its the old confusion between profit and cash flow.

4. Geographic pricing
    a) Small businesses whose pricing decisions are greatly affected by the costs of shipping merchandise to customers across a wide range of geographic regions frequently employ one of the geographic pricing techniques.

   b) Zone pricing--a small company sells its merchandise at different prices to
       customers located in different territories.
       (1) The small business must be able to show a legitimate basis (e.g., difference in
            selling or transportation costs) for the price discrimination or risk violating
            Section 2 of the Clayton Act.
   c) Uniform-delivered pricing--a technique in which the firm charges all of its
       customers the same price regardless of their location, even though the cost of
       selling or transporting merchandise varies.
   d) The firm calculates the proper freight charges for each region and combines them
       into a uniform fee.
   e) F.O.B. factory--the small company sells its merchandise to customers on the
       condition that they pay all shipping costs.
5. Opportunistic pricing
   a) When products or services are in short supply, customers are willing to pay more
       for products they need.
   b) Some businesses use such circumstances to maximize short-term profits by
       engaging in price gouging.
   c) Opportunistic pricing may backfire, however, because customers know that a
       company that charges unreasonably high prices is exploiting them.
6. Discounts
   a) Many small businesses use discounts, or markdowns, reductions from normal list
       prices, to move stale, outdated, damaged, or slow-moving merchandise.
   b) A seasonal discount is a price reduction designed to encourage shoppers to
       purchase merchandise before an upcoming season.
   c) Some firms grant purchase discounts to special groups of customers.
7. Multiple pricing
   a) Multiple pricing is a promotional technique that offers customers discounts if they
       purchase in quantity.
8. Bundling
   a) Bundling is the grouping together of several products or services, or both, into a
       package that offers customers extra value at a special price.
9. Suggested retail prices
   a) Many manufacturers print suggested retail prices on their products or include them
       on invoices or in wholesale catalogs.
   b) Small business owners frequently follow these suggested retail prices because
       doing so eliminates the need to make a pricing decision.
       (1) Following prices established by a distant manufacturer may create problems for
            the small firm.
       (2) Another danger of accepting the manufacturer's suggested price is that it does
            not take into consideration the small firm's cost structure or competitive
            situation.

III. Two Potent Pricing Forces: Image and Competition
   A. Price Conveys Image
       1. A company's pricing policies offer potential customers important information about its
           overall image.
           a) High prices frequently convey the idea of quality, prestige, and uniqueness.
       2. Accordingly, when developing a marketing approach to pricing, business owners must
           establish prices that are compatible with what their customers expect and are willing to
           pay.

       a) Too often, small business owners underprice their goods and services, believing that low prices are the only way they can achieve a competitive advantage.

3. Business owners must recognize that the prices they set for their company's goods and services send clear signals to customers about quality and value.

       a) The secret to setting prices properly is based on understanding a company's target market.

4. Target market, business image, and price are closely related.

WIRED TO THE WEB - (Home Made for the Web)

SUMMARY

For years, people had been telling Sasha and Seth Dowager that they should package and sell their brownies. After both Sasha and Seth had graduated from college and had gotten established in their careers, they opened a brownie business. At first, it was a part-time venture focusing primarily on local customers who already knew about the Dowagers' brownies. Their business began to earn greater notoriety and name recognition across the region. Their orders skyrocketed after a local television celebrity did a story on their brownies. Within a year of the television program, Sasha and Seth had quit their jobs to devote their time and energy to developing their brownie business. They renamed the company Grandma's Brownies and moved into a new location. The volume of traffic in their store was enough to generate a solid profit in the first year of business.

Nearing the end of their second year of operation, Sasha and Seth see the potential to expand their business. The primary issue they face is how to expand the market for their product. Seth and Sasha are seriously considering building a page on the World Wide Web from which to sell their brownies. They have talked to a student at the local college who has built Web sites for several small and medium-sized companies within the past year and is willing to build their site for $700. "Before we build a Web site, we've got to develop our Web marketing strategy," says Seth.

1. Use the resources of the World Wide Web to help Sasha and Seth conduct some basic market research on competitors who are selling brownies over the Web. [You may find it helpful to review the "Gaining the Competitive Edge," feature titled "Designing a Killer Web site" in Chapter 6 first.] Develop a chart that shows all the competitors you find, their prices, their competitive edge, and any other relevant marketing information you discover. Include a column in your chart that rates the quality of each company's Web site on a 1 [low] to 10 [high] scale.
Answer - Response depends on students' research efforts.
2. Use the information gathered in question 1 to recommend a pricing strategy to the Dowagers. What factors should they consider when establishing prices for their brownies?
Answer - Competition and competitions' goals/purposes, their own goals and strategy, the market, how they are differentiating their brownies.
3. On the basis of the characteristics of the Web sites you discovered, write a one-page memo to Sasha and Seth with your recommendations for designing an effective Web site.
Answer - Response depends on students' research efforts.

  B. Competition and Prices

1. An important part of setting appropriate prices is tracking competitors' prices regularly; however, what the competition is charging is just one variable in the pricing mix.
2. Businesses that offer customers extra quality, value, service, or convenience can charge higher prices as long as customers recognize the "extras" they are getting.
3. Two factors are vital to studying the effects of competition on the small firm's pricing policies.

a) The location of the competitors.
b) The nature of the competing goods.

4. In most cases, unless a company can differentiate the quality and the quantity of extras it provides, it must match the prices charged by nearby competitors for identical items.

   a) Although the prices that distant competitors charge are not nearly as critical to the small business as are those of local competitors, it can be helpful to know them and to use them as reference points.
   b) Before matching any competitor's price change, however, the small business owner should consider the rival's motives.

5. The nature of competitors' goods also influences the small firm's pricing policies.

   a) The manager must recognize which products are substitutes for those he sells and then strive to keep prices in line with them.

6. In general, the small business manager should avoid head-to-head price competition with other firms that can more easily achieve lower prices through lower cost structures.

7. One of the deadliest games a small business can get into with competitors is a price war.

   a) Price wars usually begin when one competitor thinks it can achieve higher volume instantaneously by lowering prices. Rather than sticking to their strategic guns, competitors believe they must follow suit.

8. Entrepreneurs usually overestimate the power of price cuts.

   a) Sales volume rarely rises enough to offset the lower profit margins of a lower price.

9. In a price war, a company may cut its prices so severely that it is impossible to achieve the volume necessary to offset the lower profit margins.

   a) "If you have a 25 percent gross [profit] margin, and you cut your price 10 percent, you have to roughly triple your sales volume just to break even."

10. The underlying forces that dictate how a business prices its goods or services vary greatly among industries.

IV. Pricing Techniques for Retailers
   A. Markup
      1. The basic premise of a successful business operation is selling a good or service for more than it costs to produce it.
      2. The difference between the cost of a product or service and its selling price is called markup (or markon).
      3. Markup can be expressed in dollars or as a percentage of either cost or selling price:
         a) Dollar markup = Retail price - Cost of the merchandise
         b) Percentage (of retail price) markup = $\frac{\text{Dollar markup}}{\text{Retail price}}$
      4. Percentage (of cost) markup = $\frac{\text{Dollar markup}}{\text{Cost of unit}}$
      5. The cost of merchandise used in computing markup includes not only the wholesale price of the merchandise but also any incidental costs (e.g., selling or transportation charges) that the retailer incurs and a profit minus any discounts (quantity, cash) that the wholesaler offers.
      6. Once business owners have a financial plan in place, including sales estimates and anticipated expenses, they can compute the firm's initial markup.
      7. The initial markup is the average markup required on all merchandise to cover the cost of the items, all incidental expenses, and a reasonable profit.
      8. Initial dollar markup = $\frac{\text{Operating expenses + Reductions + Profits}}{\text{Net Sales + Reductions}}$

9. Operating expenses are the cost of doing business, such as rent, utilities, and depreciation; reductions include employee and customer discounts, markdowns, special sales, and the cost of stockouts.
10. Some businesses use a standard markup on all of their merchandise.
    a) Usually used in retail stores carrying related products, it applies a standard percentage markup to all merchandise.
    b) Most stores find it much more practical to use a flexible markup, which assigns various markup percentages to different types of products.
11. Once owners determine the desired markup percentage, they can compute the appropriate retail price.
12. Finally, retailers must verify that the computed retail price is consistent with their planned initial markup percentage.
    a) Figure 10.2 illustrates the concept of markup by showing the price breakdown on a common item, a concert T-shirt.

B. Follow-the-Leader Pricing
    1. Some small companies simply follow the prices that their competitors establish.
    2. Managers wisely monitor their competitors' pricing policies and individual prices by reviewing their advertisements or by hiring part-time or full-time comparison shoppers.

C. Below-Market Pricing
    1. By setting prices below those of their competitors, these firms hope to attract a sufficient level of volume to offset the lower profit margins.
    2. Many retailers using a below-market pricing strategy eliminate most of the extra services that their above-market-pricing competitors offer.

V. Pricing Techniques for Manufacturers
    A. Cost-plus Pricing
        1. The most commonly used pricing technique for manufacturers is cost-plus pricing.
        2. Using this method, manufacturers establish a price composed of direct materials, direct labor, factory overhead, selling and administrative costs, plus the desired profit margin.
        3. The main advantage of the cost-plus pricing method is its simplicity.
        4. Given the proper cost accounting data. computing a product's final selling price is relatively easy.
        5. Also, because it adds a profit onto the top of the firm's costs, the manufacturer is guaranteed the desired profit margin.
        6. It does not encourage the manufacturer to use its resources efficiently.
        7. Finally, because manufacturers' cost structures vary so greatly, cost-plus pricing fails to consider the competition sufficiently.

    B. Direct Costing and Price Formulation
        1. One requisite for a successful pricing policy in manufacturing is a reliable cost accounting system that can generate timely reports to determine the costs of processing raw materials into finished goods.
        2. The traditional method of product costing is called absorption costing because all manufacturing and overhead costs are absorbed into the finished product's total cost.
            a) Absorption costing includes direct materials and direct labor, plus a portion of fixed and variable factory overhead costs, in each unit manufactured.
        3. A more useful technique for managerial decision making is variable (or direct) costing, in which the cost of the products manufactured includes only those costs that vary directly with the quantity produced.

a)   Variable costing encompasses direct materials, direct labor, and factory overhead costs that vary with the level of the firm's output of finished goods.
4.   A manufacturer's goal in establishing prices is to discover the cost combination of selling price and sales volume that exceeds the variable costs of producing a product and contributes enough to cover fixed costs and earn a profit.
   a)   Full-absorption costing is that it clouds the true relationships among price, volume, and costs by including fixed expenses in unit cost.
   b)   Direct-costing basis yields a constant unit cost of the product no matter what the volume of production is.
5.   The starting point for establishing product prices is the direct-cost income statement.
   a)   As Table 10.1 indicates, the direct-cost statement yields the same net profit as does the full-absorption income statement.
   b)   The only difference between the two statements is the format.

C. Computing a Breakeven Selling Price
   1.   A manufacturer's contribution percentage tells what portion of total revenues remains after covering variable costs to contribute toward meeting fixed expenses and earning a profit.
   2.   This manufacturer's contribution percentage is 36.5 percent, which means that variable costs absorb 63.5 percent of total revenues.
      a)   In other words, variable costs represent 63.5 percent (1.00 - 0.365 = 0.635) of the product's selling price.
      b)   Suppose that this manufacturer's variable costs include the following:

Material	$2.08/unit
Direct labor	$4.12/unit
Variable factory overhead	$0.78/unit
Total variable cost	$6.98/unit

   3.   The minimum price at which the manufacturer would sell the item is $6.98. Any price below that would not cover variable costs.
   4.   To compute the breakeven selling price for this product, find the selling price using the following equation:

$$\text{Profit} = \frac{(\text{Selling price} \times \text{Quantity produced}) + (\text{Variable cost per unit} \times \text{Quantity produced}) + \text{Total fixed cost}}{\text{Quantity produced}}$$

   which becomes:

$$\text{Profit} = \frac{\text{Profit} + (\text{Variable Cost per unit} \times \text{Quantity produced}) + \text{Total fixed cost}}{\text{Quantity produced}}$$

   5.   Because the manufacturer's capacity in the short run is fixed, pricing decisions should be aimed at using its resources most efficiently.
   6.   The fixed cost of operating the plant cannot be avoided, and the variable costs can be eliminated only if the firm ceases to offer the product.
   7.   Therefore, the selling price must be at least equal to the variable costs (per unit) of making the product. Any price above that amount contributes to covering fixed costs and providing a reasonable profit.
   8.   Over the long run, the selling price must cover total product costs--both fixed and variable--and generate a reasonable profit.

SMALL BUSINESS ACROSS THE GLOBE - A Different Perspective on Pricing

SUMMARY

Japan's unique approach to pricing, and with it, a cost management system that stands conventional thinking on its head. The methods are simple and very effective, encouraging companies to design and build new products in the shortest time possible and at the lowest possible cost.

The typical U.S. company researching and developing a new product designs the product first and then estimates the cost to determine the final price. Japanese approach, however, is to start with a target cost for the product based on the price most customers are likely to accept; then, designers and manufacturers engineer the product to meet that target price.

The Japanese system focuses on pinning down the key cost elements of the product in the planning and design stage. Rather than depending on the disjointed efforts in various departments, the Japanese approach relies on a team of workers from a wide variety of disciplines to bring a new product idea to market. The Japanese use the word taraku, which means "to beat down" to describe the battle over costs with their suppliers. The battle is an intense negotiation process between the company and outside suppliers to push down costs to meet the overall target cost.

The contrast is striking. U.S. companies design a product by throwing it over the wall from one department to another--from engineering, to marketing. At the end of the design phase, after something like 85 percent of the product's costs have been built in, the specifications are given to the accountants, who tell you what the product will cost. The Japanese turn it around. They say, "It's got to sell for X, Let's work backwards to make sure we can achieve it."

1. What are the key differences between the U.S. and Japanese companies' approaches to pricing new products?
    Answer - The Japanese consider price up front, in the design process and collaborate among those involved in developing and marketing the product. Americans consider price an aftereffect and tend to work in isolation, one department from another.
2. What advantages does the Japanese system offer? Disadvantages?
    Answer - It gives them a competitive advantage, close tight controls on costs and pricing so there are few if any profitability surprises, and it would seem to minimize failing products due to price. It results in over planning, new products that are untried may be mispriced, pricing strategies are only as good as the market research they have.
3. What kinds of changes in their management systems would U.S. companies have to make to implement the Japanese pricing approach successfully?
    Answer - More empowerment of employees, more up-front research on products, reengineering of production processes to permit closer cost controls, a change in accounting procedures, etc.

VI. Pricing Techniques for Service Firms
   A. The Basis for Pricing
      1. Service businesses must establish their prices on the basis of the materials used to provide the service, the labor employed, an allowance for overhead, and a profit.
      2. A service firm must have a reliable, accurate accounting system to keep a tally of the total costs of providing the service.
         a) Most service firms base their prices on an hourly rate, usually the actual number of hours required to perform the service.
         b) Some companies, however, base their fees on a standard number of hours, determined by the average number of hours needed to perform the service.

    c) For most firms, labor and materials constitute the largest portion of the cost of the service.

    d) To establish a reasonable, profitable price for service, the small business owner must know the cost of materials, direct labor, and overhead for each unit of service.

    e) Using these basic cost data and a desired profit margin, the owner of the small service firm can determine the appropriate price for the service.

3. Consider a simple example for pricing a common service--television repair.

    a) Ned's TV Repair Shop uses the direct-costing method to prepare an income statement for exercising managerial control.

    b) See Table 10.2.

4. Smart service shop owners compute the cost per production hour at regular intervals throughout the year because they know that rising costs can eat into their profit margins very quickly.

5. Rapidly rising labor costs and materials prices dictate that the service firm's price per hour be computed even more frequently.

VII. The Impact of Credit on Pricing

  A. Introduction

    1. The pricing of goods and services must take into account how the business will be paid. The straight exchange of cash for goods or services is becoming a thing of the past.

    2. Companies that do sell on credit incur additional expenses for offering this convenience.

    3. Small companies have three options for selling to customers on credit: credit cards, installment credit, and trade credit.

  B. Credit Cards

    1. Approximately 70 percent of the U.S. adult population uses credit cards to make purchases, and 36 percent of consumer debt is credit-card debt.

       a) There are more than 1 billion credit cards in circulation in the United States.

       b) An average of about four cards per person.

       c) Customers use credit cards to pay for $28 out of every $100 spent.

    2. Business owners cite the following advantages of accepting credit cards:

       a) Customers prefer to carry credit cards instead of cash for the sake of both convenience and safety.

       b) Credit card users are more likely to spend and to spend in higher amounts than nonusers.

       c) Accepting credit cards enhances a business's image.

       d) Businesses that fail to display that they accept credit cards (even when they might) lose revenues because customers are too embarrassed to ask and simply leave without buying.

       e) Customers rate businesses offering credit higher on key performance measures than those that do not.

          (1) See Table 10.3.

    3. The convenience of credit cards is not free to business owners.

       a) Companies must pay to use the system, typically 1 to 6 percent.

       b) They also pay a transaction fee of 5 to 50 cents per charge and must purchase or lease equipment to process transactions.

       c) Fees operate on a multistep process.

          (1) On a $100 Visa or MasterCard purchase at a typical business, a processing bank buys the credit card slip from the retailer for $97.44.

          (2) Then, that bank sells the slip to the bank that issued the card for about $98.80.

(3) The remaining $1.20 discount is called the interchange fee, which is what the processing bank passes along to the issuing bank.

4. More small businesses also are equipping their stores to handle debit-card transactions, which act as electronic checks, automatically deducting the purchase amount from a customer's checking account.
   a) The equipment is easy to install and to set up, and the cost to the company is negligible.
   b) The payoff can be big, however, in the form of increased sales.

GAINING THE COMPETITIVE EDGE - How to Obtain Merchant Status

Acquiring merchant status enables a small business to accept credit-card payments for goods and services. Offering customers the convenience of paying with credit cards enhances a company's reputation and translates directly into higher sales. Qualifying for merchant status is not easy for many small companies, however, because banks view it in the same manner as making a loan to a business.

What can business owners do to increase their chances of gaining merchant status so that they can accept customers' credit cards without driving their costs sky high?
- Recognize that business start-ups and companies that have been in business less than three years face the greatest obstacles to getting merchant status.
- Apply with your own bank first. If your banker cannot set up a credit-card account for your business, ask for a referral to an ISO that might be interested.
- Know what information the bank or ISO is looking for and be prepared to provide it.
- Make sure you understand the costs involved. When merchants accept credit cards, they do not receive the total amount of the sale; they must pay a transaction charge to the bank.
- Shop around. Too often, business owners take the first deal offered them, only to regret it later.
- Have a knowledgeable attorney look over your contract before you sign it. Otherwise, you may not discover clauses that work a hardship on your business until it's too late.

Accepting credit cards is not important for every business, but for those whose customers expect that convenience, acquiring merchant status can spell the difference between making a sale and losing it.

1. Use the World Wide Web to research how businesses on the Web conduct credit-card transactions. How do they secure the privacy of these transactions?
    Answer - Students' responses determined by their Web research.

C. Installment Credit
   1. Small companies that sell big-ticket consumer durables--major appliances, cars, and boats--frequently rely on installment credit.
   2. The time horizon may range from just a few months up to 30 or more years.
      a) Most companies require the customer to make an initial down payment.
      b) One advantage of installment loans for a small business is that the owner retains a security interest as collateral on the loan.
      c) If the customer defaults on the loan, the owner still holds the title to the merchandise.
      d) Because installment credit absorbs a small company's cash, many rely on financial institutions such as banks and credit unions to provide the installment credit.
D. Trade Credit
   1. Companies that sell small-ticket items frequently offer their customers trade credit; that is, they create customer charge accounts.

2. The typical small business bills its credit customers each month.
3. To speed collections, some offer cash discounts.
4. The small business owner must make sure that the firm's cash position is strong enough to support that additional pressure.
5. For manufacturers and wholesalers, trade credit is traditional.
6. Small businesses must be willing to grant credit to purchasers in order to get, and keep, their business; they must work extremely hard, and often be very tough, with debtors who do not pay as they agreed to.

Chapter Summary

- Describe effective pricing techniques for both new and existing products and services.
  - Pricing a new product is often difficult for the small business manager, but it should accomplish three objectives: getting the product accepted; maintaining market share as the competition grows; and earning a profit.
  - There are three major pricing strategies generally used to introduce new products into the market: penetration, skimming, and sliding down the demand curve.
  - Pricing techniques for existing products and services include odd pricing, price lining, leader pricing, geographic pricing, opportunistic pricing, discounts, multiple pricing, bundling, and suggested retail pricing.
- Discuss the links among pricing, image, and competition.
  - A company's pricing policies offer potential customers important information about its overall image. Accordingly, when developing a marketing approach to pricing, business owners must establish prices that are compatible with what their customers expect and are willing to pay. Too often, small business owners underprice their goods and services, believing that low prices are the only way they can achieve a competitive advantage. They fail to identify the extra value, convenience, service, and quality they give their customers--all things many customers are willing to pay for.
  - An important part of setting appropriate prices is tracking competitors' prices regularly; however, what the competition is charging is just one variable in the pricing mix. When setting prices, business owners should take into account their competitors' prices, but they should not automatically match or beat them. Businesses that offer customers extra quality, value, service, or convenience can charge higher prices as long as customers recognize the "extras" they are getting. Two factors are vital to studying the effects of competition on the small firm's pricing policies: the location of the competitors and the nature of the competing goods.
- Explain the pricing techniques used by retailers.
  - Pricing for the retailer means pricing to move merchandise. Markup is the difference between the cost of a product or service and its selling price. Most retailers compute their markup as a percentage of retail price, but some retailers put a standard markup on all their merchandise; more frequently, they use a flexible markup.
- Explain the pricing techniques used by manufacturers.
  - A manufacturer's pricing decision depends on the support of accurate cost accounting records. The most common technique is cost-plus pricing, in which the manufacturer charges a price that covers the cost of producing a product plus a reasonable profit. Every manufacturer should calculate a product's breakeven price, the price that produces neither a profit nor a loss.
- Explain the pricing techniques used by service firms.
  - Service firms often suffer from the effects of vague, unfounded pricing procedures and frequently charge the going rate without any idea of their costs. A service firm must set a price based on the cost of materials used, labor involved, overhead, and a profit. The proper price reflects the total cost of providing a unit of service.

◆ Describe the impact of credit on pricing.
  ▪ Offering consumer credit enhances a small company's reputation and increases the probability, speed, and magnitude of customers' purchases. Small firms offer three types of consumer credit: credit cards, installment credit, and trade credit (charge accounts).

Discussion Questions

1. What does a price represent to the customer? Why is a customer orientation to pricing important?
    Answer - Price is the monetary value of a product or service. It is a measure of what customers must give up to get goods and services. Price also is an indication of a product's or service's value to an individual customer, so different customers assign different values to the same products and services. Setting prices with a customer orientation is more important than trying to choose the ideal price for a product. Identifying the price ceiling requires entrepreneurs to understand their customers' characteristics and buying behavior.

2. How does pricing affect a small firm's image?
    Answer - One of the toughest decisions small business owners face, but it is also one of the most important. Prices that are too high will hurt a company's sales. Pricing products or services too low, a common tendency among start-up businesses, will rob a company of profits, threaten its long-term success, and leave customers with the impression that its products or services are of inferior quality. Improper pricing has destroyed countless businesses.

3. What competitive factors must the small firm consider when establishing prices?
    Answer - Most entrepreneurs approach setting the price of a new product with a great deal of apprehension because they have no precedent. When pricing any new product, the owner should try to satisfy three objectives. 1) Get the product accepted. No matter how unusual a product is, its price must be acceptable to the firm's potential customers. 2) Maintain market share as competition grows. If a new product is successful, competitors will enter the market, and the small company must work to expand or at least maintain its market share. 3) Earn a profit. Obviously, a small firm must establish a price for the new product that is higher than its cost. Managers should not introduce a new product at a price below cost because it is much easier to lower the price than to increase it once the product is on the market.

4. Describe the strategies a small business could use in setting the price of a new product. What objectives should the strategy seek to achieve?
    Answer - Entrepreneurs have three basic strategies to choose from in establishing a new product's price: penetration, skimming, and sliding down the demand curve. Penetration--introducing a product into a highly competitive market in which a large number of similar products are competing for acceptance, the product must penetrate the market to be successful. The objective is to gain quick acceptance and extensive distribution in the mass market; a company introduces the product at a low price--just above total unit cost to develop a wedge in the market and quickly achieve a high volume of sales. Skimming--often is used when a company introduces a new product into a market with little or no competition. The objective is to quickly recover the initial developmental and promotional costs of the product. This pricing tactic often reinforces the unique, prestigious image of a store and projects a quality picture of the product. Sliding down the demand curve--a variation of the skimming pricing strategy is called sliding down the demand curve. The objective is to beat other businesses in a price decline; the small company discourages competitors and, over time, becomes a high-volume producer.

5. Define the following pricing techniques: odd pricing, price lining, leader pricing, geographic pricing, and discounts.

Answer - Although studies of consumer reactions to prices are mixed and generally inconclusive, many small business managers use the technique known as odd pricing. They set prices that end in odd numbers (frequently 5,7,9) because they believe that an item selling for $12.95 appears to be much cheaper than an item selling for $13.00. Price lining is a technique that greatly simplifies the pricing function. The manager stocks merchandise in several different price ranges or price lines. Each category of merchandise contains items that are similar in appearance, quality, cost, performance, or other features. Leader pricing is a technique in which the small retailer marks down the customary price (i.e., the price consumers are accustomed to paying) of a popular item in an attempt to attract more customers. Geographic pricing. Small businesses whose pricing decisions are greatly affected by the costs of shipping merchandise to customers across a wide range of geographic regions frequently employ one of the geographic pricing techniques. a) Zone pricing--a small company sells its merchandise at different prices to customers located in different territories. b) Uniform delivered pricing--a technique in which the firm charges all of its customers the same price regardless of their location, even though the cost of selling or transporting merchandise varies. c) F.O.B. factory--the small company sells its merchandise to customers on the condition that they pay all shipping costs. Opportunistic Pricing. When products or services are in short supply, customers are willing to pay more for products they need. Many small businesses use discounts, or markdowns, reductions from normal list prices, to move stale, outdated, damaged, or slow-moving merchandise. Multiple pricing is a promotional technique that offers customers discounts if they purchase in quantity. Bundling is the grouping together of several products or services, or both, into a package that offers customers extra value at a special price.

6. Why do many small businesses use the manufacturer's suggested retail price? What are the disadvantages of this technique?

Answer - Many manufacturers print suggested retail prices on their products or include them on invoices or in wholesale catalogs. Small business owners frequently follow these suggested retail prices because doing so eliminates the need to make a pricing decision. Following prices established by a distant manufacturer may create problems for the small firm such as it does not take into consideration the small firm's cost structure or competitive situation.

7. What is a markup? How is it used to determine prices?

Answer - The basic premise of a successful business operation is selling a good or service for more than it costs to produce it. The difference between the cost of a product or service and its selling price is called markup (or markon). Markup can be expressed in dollars or as a percentage of either cost or selling price:

a) Dollar markup = Retail price - Cost of the merchandise

b) Percentage (of retail price) markup = $\dfrac{\text{Dollar markup}}{\text{Retail price}}$

c) Percentage (of cost) markup = $\dfrac{\text{Dollar markup}}{\text{Cost of unit}}$

The cost of merchandise used in computing markup includes not only the wholesale price of the merchandise but also any incidental costs (e.g., selling or transportation charges) that the retailer incurs and a profit minus any discounts (quantity, cash) that the wholesaler offers. Once business owners have a financial plan in place, including sales estimates and anticipated expenses, they can compute the firm's initial markup. The initial markup is the average markup required on all merchandise to cover the cost of the items, all incidental expenses, and a reasonable profit. Figure 10.2 illustrates the concept of markup by showing the price breakdown on a common item, a concert T-shirt.

8. What is a standard markup? A flexible markup?
    Answer - Some businesses use a standard markup on all of their merchandise. Usually used in retail stores carrying related products, it applies a standard percentage markup to all merchandise. Most stores find it much more practical to use a flexible markup, which assigns various markup percentages to different types of products. Once owners determine the desired markup percentage, they can compute the appropriate retail price.

9. What is follow-the-leader pricing? Why is it risky?
    Answer - It is when small companies simply follow the prices that their competitors establish. Managers wisely monitor their competitors' pricing policies and individual prices by reviewing their advertisements or by hiring part-time or full-time comparison shoppers. It doesn't take into consideration cost differences and it is a "me-too" strategy eliminating some differentiation.

10. What is cost-plus pricing? Why do so many manufacturers use it? What are the disadvantages of using it?
    Answer - The most commonly used pricing technique for manufacturers is cost-plus pricing. Using this method, manufacturers establish a price composed of direct materials, direct labor, factory overhead, selling and administrative costs, plus the desired profit margin. The main advantage of the cost-plus pricing method is its simplicity. Given the proper cost accounting data. computing a product's final selling price is relatively easy. Also, because it adds a profit onto the top of the firm's costs, the manufacturer is guaranteed the desired profit margin. However, it does not encourage the manufacturer to use its resources efficiently. And, because manufacturers' cost structures vary so greatly, cost-plus pricing fails to consider the competition sufficiently.

11. Explain the difference between full-absorption costing and direct costing. How does absorption costing help a manufacturer determine a reasonable price?
    Answer - One requisite for a successful pricing policy in manufacturing is a reliable cost accounting system that can generate timely reports to determine the costs of processing raw materials into finished goods. The traditional method of product costing is called absorption costing because all manufacturing and overhead costs are absorbed into the finished product's total cost. Absorption costing includes direct materials and direct labor, plus a portion of fixed and variable factory overhead costs, in each unit manufactured. A more useful technique for managerial decision making is variable (or direct) costing, in which the cost of the products manufactured includes only those costs that vary directly with the quantity produced. A manufacturer's goal in establishing prices is to discover the cost combination of selling price and sales volume that exceeds the variable costs of producing a product and contributes enough to cover fixed costs and earn a profit. Full-absorption costing is that it clouds the true relationships among price, volume, and costs by including fixed expenses in unit cost. Direct-costing basis yields a constant unit cost of the product no matter what the volume of production is.

12. Explain the techniques for a small service firm setting an hourly price.
    Answer - Service businesses must establish their prices on the basis of the materials used to provide the service, the labor employed, an allowance for overhead, and a profit. Most service firms base their prices on an hourly rate, usually the actual number of hours required to perform the service. Some companies, however, base their fees on a standard number of hours, determined by the average number of hours needed to perform the service. For most firms, labor and materials constitute the largest portion of the cost of the service. To establish a reasonable, profitable price for service, the small business owner must know the cost of materials, direct labor, and overhead for each unit of service. Using these basic cost data and a desired profit margin, the owner of the small

service firm can determine the appropriate price for the service. Smart service shop owners compute the cost per production hour at regular intervals throughout the year because they know that rising costs can eat into their profit margins very quickly.

13. What is the relevant price range for a product or service?
    Answer - Setting prices with a customer orientation is more important than trying to choose the ideal price for a product. For most products, there is an acceptable price range, not a single ideal price. This price range is the area between the price ceiling defined by customers and the price floor established by the firm's cost structure. Identifying the price ceiling requires entrepreneurs to understand their customers' characteristics and buying behavior. The price floor depends on a company's cost structure, which can vary considerably from one business to another. The entrepreneur's goal should be to position the firm's prices within this acceptable price range. The final price that business owners set depends on the desired image they want to create for their products or services: discount (bargain), middle-of-the-road (value), or prestige (upscale). Business owners must walk a fine line when pricing their products and services, setting their prices high enough to cover costs and earn a reasonable profit but low enough to attract customers and generate an adequate sales volume. Furthermore, the right price today may be completely inappropriate tomorrow because of changing market and competitive conditions.

14. What advantages and disadvantages does offering trade credit provide to a small business?
    Answer - Companies that sell small-ticket items frequently offer their customers trade credit; that is, they create customer charge accounts. The typical small business bills its credit customers each month. The small business owner must make sure that the firm's cash position is strong enough to support that additional pressure. For manufacturers and wholesalers, trade credit is traditional. Small businesses must be willing to grant credit to purchasers in order to get, and keep, their business; they must work extremely hard, and often be very tough, with debtors who do not pay as they agreed to.

15. What advantages does accepting credit cards provide a small business? What costs are involved?
    Answer - Approximately 70 percent of the U.S. adult population uses credit cards to make purchases, and 36 percent of consumer debt is credit-card debt. Customers prefer to carry credit cards instead of cash for the sake of both convenience and safety. Credit card users are more likely to spend and to spend in higher amounts than nonusers. Accepting credit cards enhances a business's image. Businesses that fail to display that they accept credit cards (even when they might) lose revenues because customers are too embarrassed to ask and simply leave without buying. Customers rate businesses offering credit higher on key performance measures than those that do not. But credit cards cost business owners. Companies must pay to use the system, typically 1 to 6 percent. They also pay a transaction fee of 5 to 50 cents per charge and must purchase or lease equipment to process transactions.

16. What steps should a small business owner take to earn merchant status?
    Answer - See "Gaining a Competitive Edge," page 330.

Step into the Real World
1. Interview two successful small retailers in your area and ask the following questions: Do you seek a specific image through your prices? What role do your competitors play in pricing? Do you use specific pricing techniques such as odd pricing, price lining, leader pricing, or geographic pricing? How are discounts calculated? What markup percentage does the firm use? What is your cost structure?

2. Select an industry that has several competing small firms in your area. Contact these firms and compare their approaches to determining prices. Do prices on identical or similar items differ? Why?

3. Contact two local small businesses: one that does accept credit cards and one that doesn't. Ask the owner of the business that does accept credit cards why he or she does. What role do customers' expectations play? Does the owner believe that accepting credit cards leads to increased sales? What does it cost the owner to accept credit cards? How difficult was it to gain merchant status? Ask the owner of the business that does not accept credit cards why he or she does not. Has the business lost sales because it does not accept credit cards? What would it take and how much would it cost for the owner to be able to accept credit cards?

Chapter 11 - Creative Use of Advertising and Promotion

Teaching Objectives

Students will be able to:

1. Describe the steps in developing an advertising strategy.
2. Explain the differences among promotion, publicity, personal selling, and advertising.
3. Describe the advantages and disadvantages of the various advertising media.
4. Identify four basic methods for preparing an advertising budget.
5. Explain practical methods for stretching a small business's advertising budget.

Instructor's Outline

I. Introduction
    A. Introduction
        1. Some small business owners believe that because of limited budgets they cannot afford the "luxury" of advertising.
        2. Advertising is not just an expense; it is an investment in a company's future. Without a steady advertising and promotional campaign, a small business's customer base will soon vanish.
        3. Advertising can be an effective means of increasing sales by informing customers of the business and its goods or services; by improving the image of the firm and its products; or by persuading customers to purchase the firm's goods or services.
        4. With a little creativity and ingenuity, a small company can make its voice heard above the clamor of its larger competitors and still stay within a limited budget.
        5. Developing an effective advertising program has become more of a challenge for business owners in recent years because of media overflow, overwhelming ad clutter, increasingly fragmented audiences, and more skeptical consumers.

II. Developing an Advertising Strategy
    A. The Strategy
        1. An advertising strategy ensures that money isn't wasted.
        2. A well-developed strategy increases the likelihood of good results.
        3. The first step is to define the purpose of the company's advertising program by creating specific, measurable objectives.
            a) Some ads are designed to stimulate immediate response.
            b) Other ads seek to build name recognition.
            c) Still other ads strive to draw new customers, build mailing lists, increase foot traffic in a store, or introduce a company or a product into a new territory.
        4. The next step is to identify the company's target customers.
            a) Before considering either the advertising message or the media by which to send it, business owners must understand their target customers.
            b) Business owners should address the following questions:
                (1) What business are we in?
                (2) What image do we want to project?
                (3) Who are our target customers and what are their characteristics? Where can we best reach them?
                (4) What do my customers really purchase from us?
                (5) What benefits can the customer derive from our goods or services?
                (6) How do I want to position our company in the market?
                (7) What advertising approach do our competitors take?

5. Answering those questions will help business owners define their business, profile their customers, and focus their advertising messages on their specific target market to get more for their advertising dollars.
6. Once the small business owner has defined her target audience, she can design an advertising message and choose the media for transmitting it.

B. The USP
1. Owners should build their ads around a unique selling proposition (USP), a key customer benefit of a product or service that sets it apart from its competition.
2. To be effective, a USP must be unique, something the competition does not (or cannot) provide--and strong enough to encourage the customer to buy.
3. A successful USP answers the critical question every customer asks:
    a) "What's in it for me?"
    b) It should express in 10 words or less exactly what a business can do for its customers.
    c) The USP becomes the heart of the advertising message.
4. Sometimes, the most powerful USPs are the intangible or psychological benefits a product or service offers customers: e.g., safety, security, acceptance, or status.
5. The best way to identify a meaningful USP is to describe the primary benefit your product or service offers customers and then to list secondary benefits it provides.
    a) Building an ad around a USP spells out for customers the specific benefit they will get if they buy that product or service.
6. A company's target audience and the nature of its message determine the advertising media it will use.
    a) Some messages are much more powerful in some media than in others.
7. The final step involves evaluating the ad campaign's effectiveness.
    a) Did it accomplish the objectives it was designed to accomplish?
    b) One advertising executive claims that a successful ad for a special sale should generate at least two to three times the amount invested in the campaign.
8. Immediate response ads can be evaluated in a number of ways.
    a) Coupons that customers redeem.
    b) Dated coupons identify customer responses over certain time periods.
    c) Hidden offers--statements hidden somewhere in an ad that offer customers special deals if they make a special request.
9. A business owner can also gauge an ad's effectiveness by measuring the volume of store traffic generated.
10. Ad tests can help determine the most effective methods of reaching potential customers.
    a) Owners can design two different ads (or use two different media or broadcast times) that are coded for identification and see which one produces more responses.
11. Table 11.2 offers 12 tips for creating an effective advertising campaign.

III. Advertising versus Promotion
A. Definition
1. The terms advertising and promotion are often confused.
2. Promotion is any form of persuasive communication designed to inform consumers about a product or service and to influence them to purchase these goods or services.
    a) It includes publicity, personal selling, and advertising.

B. Publicity
1. Publicity is any commercial news covered by the media that boosts sales but for which the small business does not pay.

2. Tactics any small business owner can use to stimulate publicity.
   a) Write an article that will interest your customers or potential customers.
   b) Contact local TV and radio stations and offer to be interviewed.
   c) Publish a newsletter.
   d) Contact local business and civic organizations and offer to speak to them.
   e) Offer or sponsor a seminar.
   f) Write news releases and fax them to the media.
   g) Volunteer to serve on community and industry boards and committees.
   h) Sponsor a community project or support a nonprofit organization or charity.
   i) Promote a cause.
3. Sometimes publicity is a matter of knowing a celebrity or, as in the case of Drake Bakeries, having a celebrity who knows and loves your product.

C. Personal Selling
   1. Personal selling is the personal contact between salespeople and potential customers resulting from sales efforts.
   2. Effective personal selling can give the small company a definite advantage over its larger competitors by creating a feeling of personal attention.
   3. Recent studies of top salespeople found that they:
      a) Are enthusiastic and are alert to opportunities.
      b) Concentrate on select accounts.
      c) Plan thoroughly.
      d) Use a direct approach.
      e) Work from the customer's perspective.
      f) Spend 60 to 70 percent of a sales call letting the customer talk while they listen.
      g) See customers' objections for what they really are--a source of valuable information.
      h) Focus on building a rapport with prospects before attempting to sell them anything.
      i) Don't offer product or service recommendations until 40 percent or more of the time in the sales call has elapsed.
      j) Emphasize customer benefits, not product or service features, when selling.
      k) Use "past success stories."
      l) Leave sales material with clients.
      m) See themselves as problem solvers, not just vendors.
      n) Measure their success not just by sales volume but also by customer satisfaction.
   4. One extensive study of salespeople found that just 20 percent of all salespeople have the ability to sell and are selling the "right" product or service.
      a) That 20 percent makes 80 percent of all sales.
      b) The study also concluded that 55 percent of sales representatives have "absolutely no ability to sell."
      c) The remaining 25 percent have sales ability but are selling the wrong product or service.
   5. A study by Dartnell Corporation found that it takes an average of 3.9 sales calls to close a deal.
   6. Common causes of sales rejections include the representative's failure to determine customers' needs, talking too much, and neglecting to ask for the order.
      a) Studies show that 60 percent of the time, salespeople never ask the customer to buy.
      b) The cost of making a sales call exceeds $225.
      c) Figure 11.1 shows how sales representatives spend their time in an average 45.5-hour workweek.

7. Improving sales representatives' "batting averages."
    a) Develop a selling system. One sales consultant recommends a six-step process to increase the likelihood of closing a sale:
        (1) Approach. Establish rapport with the prospect.
        (2) Interview. Get the prospect to do most of the talking; the goal is to identify his needs, preferences, and problems.
        (3) Demonstrate, explain, and show the features and benefits of your product or service and point out how they meet the prospect's needs or solve his problems.
        (4) Validate. Prove the claims about your product or service.
        (5) Negotiate. Listen for objections from the prospect.
        (6) Close. Ask for a decision.
    b) Be empathetic. The best salespeople look at the sale from the customer's viewpoint, not their own.
    c) Set multiple objectives. Before making a sales call, salespeople should set three objectives:
        (1) The primary objective. The most reasonable outcome expected from the meeting. It may be to get an order or to learn more about a prospect's needs.
        (2) The minimum objective. The very least the salesperson will leave with. It may be to set another meeting or to identify the prospect's primary objections.
        (3) The visionary objective. The most optimistic outcome of the meeting. This objective forces the salesperson to be open-minded and to shoot for the top.
    d) Monitor sales efforts and results. Selling is just like any other business activity and must be controlled. At a minimum, small business managers should know:
        (1) Actual sales versus projected sales
        (2) Sales generated per call made
        (3) Total sales costs
        (4) Sales by product, salesperson, territory, customer, etc.
        (5) Profit contribution by product, salesperson, territory, customer, etc.

D. Advertising
    1. Advertising is any sales presentation that is nonpersonal in nature and is paid for by an identified sponsor.
    2. One recent study on the effectiveness of advertising concluded that ads influence purchases of some products for six to nine months.

IV. Selecting Advertising Media
    A. Introduction
        1. One of the most important decisions a small business manager must make is which media to use in disseminating the advertising message.
        2. The medium used to transmit the message influences the consumer's perception--and reception--of it.
            a) Choosing the proper advertising means, a small business owner can reach his target audience effectively at minimum cost.
        3. No formula exists for determining the ideal medium to use; there are several important characteristics that make some media better suited than others.
        4. Understanding the qualities of the various media available can simplify an owner's decision.

IN THE FOOTSTEPS OF AN ENTREPRENEUR - Wanted: Dedicated Sales Force

SUMMARY
Twins Karen Hilderbrand and Kim Thompson started Twin Sisters, a company that produces educational products for children, in 1987. Their-tapes, activity books, and CD-ROM-book sets use original music and songs to teach children from ages 1 to 11 the alphabet, colors and shapes, math, foreign languages, social studies, and science. Although the company's products are now sold in more than 21,500 stores, Hilderbrand and Thompson know they are missing out on a large volume of sales. Sales of children's educational products in the United States are growing by 5 percent a year and the sisters believe their company could generate revenue of more than $2 million--if only they had a top-notch sales force.

To supplement their small sales force, the sisters have hired 350 independent sales representatives who earn 10 to 15 percent sales commissions to cover the country and selected foreign markets. The approach has been only marginally successful. Unfortunately, Twin Sisters' experience with independent sales representatives is not uncommon. High turnover and handling large numbers of products from different companies make selling through independent reps a risky venture for many small companies. In 1994, Twin Sisters hired a sales management group, hoping to overcome many of the problems of using an independent sales force. Unfortunately, that experiment failed too.

By 1995, Hilderbrand and Thompson had come up with a new sales strategy: hiring a sales manager to coordinate selling activities. Shortly afterward, they hired a second sales manager. One concentrates on toy stores, school-supply chains, and distributors while the other takes care of museums, hobby shops, and bookstores. Hilderbrand and Thompson direct international sales and take care of all of the large accounts themselves. The new sales strategy is starting to pay off.

1. What advice would you give Hilderbrand and Thompson on the following issues?
■   Hiring sales representatives.
■   Retaining sales representatives.
■   Motivating the sales force.
■   Compensating the sales force.
■   Controlling the sales force.
   Answer - As the text doesn't provide sufficient direct information, students should try searching the World Wide Web for ideas.
2. What advice would you offer the sisters about promoting their products and increasing customers' awareness of them? What kind of unique selling proposition would you suggest for Twin Sisters?
   Answer - Their budget is limited so publicity would be a good place to start. Accomplished writers they should consider writing press releases themselves. Promotions should go to the independent reps to help them focus on Twin Sisters' products. Their advertising needs to be national but their budget limitations hinder that. Perhaps buying spot ads on local cable channels in their major markets/cities. They should also try getting on Sesame Street and similar children's programs as part of their publicity efforts.

5.   The owner should consider several questions.
   a) How large is my firm's trading area? How big is the geographic region from which the firm will draw its customers?
   b) Who are my target customers, and what are their characteristics? A customer profile often points to the appropriate medium to get the message across most effectively.
   c) What budget limitations do I face?

        d) What media do my competitors use? It is helpful to know the media competitors use.

        e) How important are repetition and continuity of my advertising message? In general, an ad becomes effective only after it is repeated several times, and many ads must be continued for some time.

        f) What does the advertising medium cost? Business owners must consider two types of advertising costs: absolute cost and relative cost.

            (1) Absolute cost is the actual dollar outlay a business owner must make to place an ad in a particular medium for a specific time period.

            (2) An even more important measure is an ad's relative cost, the ad's cost per potential customer reached.

    6. Example of placing an ad in a newspaper.

B. Media Options

    1. Figure 11.2 gives a breakdown of U.S. business advertising expenditures by medium.

        a) Newspapers and television are the most popular advertising media.

    2. Newspapers

        a) Traditionally, the local newspaper has been the medium that most advertisers rely on.

        b) The number of newspapers has declined but it still attracts 22.7 percent of all advertising dollars nationwide, establishing it as a leader among all media.

        c) Newspaper advertisement advantages

            (1) Selected geographic coverage. Newspapers are geared to a specific geographic region, and they reach potential customers in all demographic classes.

            (2) Flexibility. Newspaper advertisements can be changed readily; the owner can select the size of the ad, its location in the paper, and the days on which it runs.

            (3) Timeliness. Papers almost always have very short publication deadlines.

            (4) Communication potential. Newspaper ads can convey a great deal of information by employing attractive graphics and copy.

            (5) Low costs. Newspapers normally offer advertising space at a low absolute cost and, because of their blanket coverage of a geographic area, at a low relative cost as well.

            (6) Prompt responses. Newspaper ads typically produce relatively quick customer responses.

        d) Newspaper advertisement disadvantages

            (1) Wasted readership. At least a portion of an ad's coverage will be wasted on those who are not potential customers.

            (2) Reproduction limitations. The quality of reproduction in newspapers is limited.

            (3) Lack of prominence. The typical newspaper is 65 percent advertising. This disadvantage can be overcome by increasing the size of the ad or by adding color to it.

                (a) Proper ad placement in the newspaper can increase an ad's effectiveness.

            (4) Declining readership. Newspaper ads would be least effective for small businesses targeting young people, who are least likely to read newspapers.

            (5) Short ad life. The typical newspaper is soon discarded and, as a result, an ad's life is extremely short.

        e) Buying newspaper space.

            (1) Newspapers typically sell ad space by lines and columns or inches and columns.

            (2) Most papers offer discounts for bulk, long-term, and frequency contracts and for full-page ads.

(3) Advertising rates vary from one paper to another, depending on such factors as circulation and focus.

3. Radio
   a) Radio permits advertisers to appeal to specific audiences over large geographic areas.
   b) By choosing the appropriate station, program, and time for an ad, a small company can reach virtually any target market.
   c) Radio advertising advantages
      (1) Universal infiltration. Virtually every home and car in the United States is equipped with a radio. Radio reaches 77 percent of all customers each day and 95 percent of customers each week.
      (2) Market segmentation. Radio stations design their formats to appeal to specific types of audiences. Stations have listener profiles that give entrepreneurs the ability to pinpoint virtually any advertising target.
      (3) Flexibility and timeliness. Radio commercials have short closing times and can be changed quickly.
      (4) Friendliness. Radio ads are more "active" than ads in printed media because they use the spoken word to influence customers.
   d) Table 11.3 offers a guide to producing effective radio copy.
   e) Radio advertisements disadvantages
      (1) Poor listening. Customers will hear ads, but they may not listen to them.
      (2) Need for repetition. Listeners usually do not respond to radio ads after a single exposure to them.
      (3) Limited message. Radio ads are limited to one minute or less, so small business owners must keep their messages simple, covering only one or two points.
   f) Buying Radio Time
      (1) Stations follow various formats--from rap to rhapsodies---to appeal to specific audiences.
      (2) Radio advertising time usually sells in 10-second, 20-second, 30-second, and 60-second increments, with the last being the most common.
      (3) Fixed spots are guaranteed to be broadcast at the times specified in the owner's contract with the station.
      (4) Preemptible spots are cheaper than fixed spots, but the advertiser risks being preempted by an advertiser willing to pay the fixed rate for a time slot.
      (5) Floating spots are the least expensive, but the advertiser has no control over broadcast times.
      (6) Many stations offer package plans, using flexible combinations of fixed, preemptible, and floating spots.
      (7) Radio rates vary depending on the time of day they are broadcast
      (8) See page 349 for time classifications.
      (9) Some stations may also have different rates for weekend time slots.

4. Television
   a) In advertising dollars spent, television is tied with newspapers in popularity.
   b) A 30-second commercial on network television may cost well over $500,000.
      (1) A 30-second spot on a local cable station may go for $200 or less.
   c) Television advertising advantages
      (1) Broad coverage. About 97 percent of the homes in any area will have a television, and those sets are on an average of 7 hours and 8 minutes each day.
         (a) The nation's 200-plus cable channels now draw 50 percent of television viewership.

(b) Cable television offers advertisers the ability to reach specific target markets much as radio ads do.

(2) Visual advantage. Research shows that 46 percent of television ads result in long-term sales increases and that 70 percent of campaigns boost sales immediately. The ability to use sight, sound, and motion makes TV ads a powerful selling tool.

(3) Flexibility. Television ads can be modified quickly to meet the rapidly changing conditions in the marketplace. Advertising on TV is a close substitute for personal selling.

(4) Design assistance. The television station from which a manager purchases the airtime often is willing to help design and produce the ad very inexpensively.

d) Television advertising disadvantages

(1) Brief exposure. Nearly half of all adults engage in other activities during television commercials and are likely to miss them.

(2) Clutter. The typical person sees 1,500 advertising messages a day.

(3) "Zapping." "Zappets" are television viewers who flash from one channel to another, especially during commercials, pose a real threat to TV advertisers.

(4) Cost. A 30-second ad can cost several thousand dollars to develop, even before the owner purchases airtime.

e) Table 11.4 offers some suggestions for developing creative television commercials.

5. The World Wide Web

a) The Web draws customers with attractive demographic profiles--young, educated, and wealthy.

b) It also gives small companies the ability to reach growing numbers of customers outside the United States very inexpensively.

c) Nearly 27 percent of Web surfers are located outside U.S. borders.

d) Experts estimate that about 141,000 of those Web sites belong to small businesses.

e) Companies that normally advertise through direct mall can bring the two-dimensional photos and product descriptions in their print catalogs to life and avoid the expense of mailing them at the same time.

f) One study shows that 80 percent of Web users log on at least once a day and that 36 percent of them go on line instead of watching television.

g) The Web offers advertisers many of the same advantages as television ads but at a lower cost.

(1) For instance, a restaurant might place on its Web site reviews from local publications, comments from patrons, its menu, photographs of popular dishes, a map showing its location, and video clips of its chef at work--in short, everything but the aroma.

(2) The Web site is a way to display merchandise to a larger audience while simultaneously reducing costs.

h) Advertisements on the Web take four basic forms: banner ads, cookies, full-page ads, and "push" technology ads.

(1) Banner ads are small, rectangular ads that reside on Web sites, much like roadside billboards, touting a company's product or service.

(2) Cookies are small programs that attach to users' computers when they visit a Web site.

(3) Full-page ads are those that download to Web users' screens before they can access certain Web sites.

(4) Push technology ads appear on users' screens when they download information such as news, sports, or entertainment from another site.

i) Table 11.5 offers guidelines for Internet ad campaigns.

6. Magazines
    a) Nearly 9 out of 10 adults read an average of seven magazines each month.
    b) The average magazine attracts 6 hours and 3 minutes of total adult reading time.
    c) The reader is exposed to 89 percent of the ads in the average issue.
    d) Magazines' advertising advantages
        (1) Long life spans. Few people read an entire magazine at one sitting. Instead, most pick it up, read it at intervals, and come back to it later.
        (2) Multiple readership. The average magazine has a readership of 3.9 adult readers, and each reader spends about one hour and 33 minutes with each copy. And magazines have a high "passalong" rate; they are handed down from reader to reader.
        (3) Target marketing. Once business owners define their target markets, they can select magazines whose readers most closely match their customer profiles.
        (4) Ad quality. Photographs and drawings can be reproduced very effectively, and color ads are readily available. Advertisers can also choose the location of their ads in a magazine and can design creative ads that capture readers' attention.
    e) Magazines advertising disadvantages
        (1) Costs. Magazine advertising rates vary according to their circulation rates; the higher the circulation, the higher the rate.
        (2) Long closing times. For a weekly periodical, the closing date for an ad may be several weeks before the actual publication date.
        (3) Lack of prominence. The effectiveness of a single ad may be reduced because of a lack of prominence. Proper ad positioning, therefore, is critical to an ad's success. Research shows that readers "tune out" right-hand pages and look mainly at left-hand pages.
7. Direct Mail
    a) Direct mail includes such tools as letters, postcards, catalogs, discount coupons, brochures, computer disks, and videotapes mailed to homes or businesses.
        (1) Fifteenth-century printers printed the earliest known catalogs.
    b) Customers purchase more than $420 billion worth of goods and services through mail order each year.
    c) Direct mail advantages
        (1) Selectivity. Its greatest strength. Depending on mailing list quality, an owner can select an audience with virtually any set of characteristics.
        (2) Flexibility. The advertiser's presentation to the customer can be as simple or as elaborate as necessary. With direct mail, the tone of the message can be personal, creating a positive psychological effect. In addition, the advertiser controls the timing of the campaign; she can send the ad when it is most appropriate.
        (3) Reader attention. An advertiser's message does not have to compete with other ads for the reader's attention. Recipients opened and read 48 percent of their direct mail.
            (a) Table 11.6 describes common categories of direct mail campaigns with examples of each.
        (4) Rapid feedback. In most cases, the ad will generate sales within three or four days after customers receive it.
        (5) Measurable results and testable strategies. Direct marketers can readily measure the results their ads produce. Also, direct mail allows advertisers to test different ad layouts, designs, and strategies (often within the same "run") to see which one "pulls" the greatest response.
    d) Table 11.7 offers guidelines for creating direct mail ads that really work.

e) Direct mail disadvantages
   (1) Inaccurate mailing lists. 60 percent of the success of direct marketing is based on the quality of the mailing list.
   (2) High relative costs. Direct mail has a higher cost per thousand (cpm) than any other advertising medium. A typical direct mailing costs $400 or more per thousand customers reached.
       (a) Figure 11.3 shows the breakdown of costs for a typical 3,000-piece mailing.
       (b) But if the mailing is well planned and properly executed, it can produce a high percentage of returns, making direct mail one of the least expensive advertising methods in terms of results.
   (3) Rising postal rates. One of the primary causes of the high costs of direct mail ads is postage costs, which continue to rise.
   (4) High throwaway rate. The average family receives 10 pieces of direct mail each week.
       (a) To boost returns, small business owners can supplement their traditional direct mail pieces with toll-free (800) numbers (an increase of 1 to 2 percent) and carefully timed follow-up phone calls (an increase of 2 to 14 percent).
   (5) Creative entrepreneurs have found other ways to boost their direct mail response rates, including three-dimensional mailers, computer diskettes, and compact disks.

IN THE FOOTSTEPS OF AN ENTREPRENEUR - A Tough Market to Reach

About 33 percent of American men and 36 percent of American women are considered overweight. For years, marketers ignored this plus-sized segment of the population. Now companies of all sizes are providing products and services aimed at this target audience. In 1989, Jan Herrick began publishing Royal Resources, a directory of companies offering plus-sized products and services.

One small company focusing on the plus-sized market is Anne Kelly's Junonia Ltd., a maker of active-wear that sells its products through a mail-order catalog. Kelly's direct mail catalog carries items such as bike shorts, swimsuits, sports bras, ski jackets, leggings, and many others. Within three years, Junonia's mailing list topped 350,000, and sales surged past $2 million. Like Kelly many companies targeting the plus-sized market have discovered that direct mail is an excellent avenue for reaching their customers. For many large people, shopping in retail stores can be frustrating, embarrassing, and painful.

Companies selling to the plus-sized market must exercise caution, however. The problem stems from America's obsession with thinness. One way many have found to work well is by placing ads in magazines such as BBW, Radiance, and Dimension and other media that invite customers to write, fax, call, or e-mail for a catalog.

1. Working with a team of your classmates, develop at least five methods small companies targeting the plus-sized market could use to reach their customers.
    Answer - Using positive ads about having a "real" woman's or man's figure/physique, piggyback on recent stories about "large" major TV/film stars.
2. What kinds of unique selling propositions should they consider?
    Answer - Think of terms that convey "largeness" in positive terms, etc. Focus on benefits such as convenience, privacy, style, etc.

8. High-tech direct mail
    a) Sending out ads on computer diskettes is an excellent way to reach upscale households and businesses. They grab and hold the audience's attention. Studies show that recipients of a computer diskette ad spend an average of 26 to 30 minutes interacting with it and that their retention rate is twice that of other ads.
    b) Compact discs (CDs) offer advertisers the same benefits as computer disks with one extra--more space to do it in. Companies are using CDs with interactive ads to sell everything from cars to computers.
        (1) One expert explains the appeal of multimedia ads, "You remember 20 percent of what you see, 30 percent of what you see and hear, and 60 percent of what you interact with."
9. How to use direct mail
    a) The key to a direct mailing's success is the right mailing list.
    b) Owners can develop lists themselves, using customer accounts, telephone books, city and trade directories, and other sources.
10. Outdoor advertising
    a) National advertisers have long used outdoor ads, and small firms (especially retailers) are now using this medium.
    b) Very few small businesses rely solely on outdoor advertising; instead, they supplement other advertising media with billboards.
    c) With a creative outdoor campaign, a small company can make a big impact, even on a small budget.
    d) Outdoor advertising advantages
        (1) High exposure. Outdoor advertising offers a high-frequency exposure; studies suggest that the typical billboard reaches an adult 29 to 31 times each month.
        (2) Broad reach. The people outdoor ads reach tend to be younger, wealthier, and better educated than the average person.
        (3) Flexibility. Advertisers can buy outdoor advertising units separately or in a number of packages. Through its variety of graphics, design, and unique features, outdoor advertising enables the small advertiser to match his message to the particular audience.
        (4) Cost efficiency. Outdoor advertising offers one of the lowest costs per thousand customers reached of all the advertising media.
    e) Outdoor ads' disadvantages
        (1) Brief exposure. Because billboards are immobile, the reader is exposed to the advertiser's message for only a short time, typically no more than five seconds.
        (2) Legal restrictions. Outdoor billboards are subject to strict regulations and to a high degree of standardization.
        (3) Lack of prominence. More than 450,000 billboards now line the nation's highways.
    f) Using outdoor ads. Because the outdoor ad is stationary and the viewer is in motion, the small business owner must pay special attention to its design.
        (1) Identify the product and the company clearly and quickly.
        (2) Use a simple background. The background should not compete with the message.
        (3) Rely on large illustrations that jump out at the viewer.
        (4) Include clear, legible type.
        (5) Use black-and-white designs. Research shows that black-and-white outdoor ads are more effective than color ads.
        (6) Emphasize simplicity; short copy and short words are best.
        (7) Use sharp, eye-catching graphics.

        (8) Be located on the right-hand side of the highway. Studies show that ads located there draw higher recall scores than those located on the left-hand side.

        (9) Use billboards as a reinforcement for other methods of advertising and to remind prospects of where you are and what you do.

    g) A spin-off of the billboard is the cold-air balloon--those giant balloons shaped like King Kong or Godzilla that sit atop businesses holding signs that promote a special sale or event.

11. Transit advertising

    a) Transit advertising includes advertising signs inside and outside some 70,000 public transportation vehicles throughout the country's urban areas.

    b) The medium is likely to grow as more cities look to public transit systems to relieve transportation problems.

    c) Transit ads advantages

        (1) Wide coverage. Transit advertising offers advertisers mass exposure to a variety of customers.

        (2) Repeat exposure. The typical transit rider averages 24 rides per month and spends 61 minutes per day riding.

        (3) Low cost. One study shows that transit advertising costs on average only 30 cents per thousand.

        (4) Flexibility. With transit ads, an owner can select an individual market or any combination of markets across the country.

    d) Transit ads' disadvantages

        (1) Generality. It cannot target a particular segment of the market through transit advertising.

        (2) Limited appeal. Unlike many media, transit ads are not beamed into the potential customer's residence or business.

        (3) Brief message. Transit ads do not permit the small advertiser to present a detailed description or a demonstration of the product or service for sale.

12. Directories

    a) Directories are an important advertising medium for reaching customers who have already made purchase decisions. The directory simply helps these customers locate the specific product or service they have decided to buy.

    b) Directory advantages

        (1) Prime prospects. Directory listings reach customers who have already decided to purchase an item.

        (2) Long life. A typical directory may be published annually.

    c) Directory disadvantages

        (1) Lack of flexibility. Listings and ads in many directories offer only a limited variety of design features.

        (2) Obsolescence. Because directories are commonly updated only annually, some of their listings become obsolete.

    d) Using directories. When choosing a directory, the small business owner should evaluate several criteria:

        (1) Completeness. Does the directory include enough listings that customers will use it?

        (2) Convenience. Are the listings well organized and convenient?

        (3) Evidence of use. To what extent do customers actually use the directory?

        (4) Age. Is the directory well established, and does it have a good reputation?

        (5) Circulation. Is there an audited circulation statement?

13. Trade shows.
   a) Trade shows provide manufacturers and distributors with a unique opportunity to advertise to a preselected audience of potential customers who are inclined to buy.
   b) Nearly 5,000 thousand trade shows are sponsored each year.
   c) Trade show advantages
      (1) A natural market. Comparative shopping is easy, and the buying process is efficient.
      (2) Preselected audience. Trade exhibits attract potential customers with a specific interest in the goods or services being displayed.
      (3) New customer market. Trade shows offer exhibitors a prime opportunity to reach new customers and to contact people who are not accessible to sales representatives.
      (4) Industry information. Trade shows provide excellent opportunities for entrepreneurs to find out what is happening in their industries and to size up their competitors--all in one place. Observant entrepreneurs can spot key trends.
      (5) International contacts. Many small companies make their first international sales at trade shows, which are extremely popular with foreign businesses.
      (6) Cost advantage. As the cost of making a field sales call continues to escalate, more companies are realizing that trade shows are an economical method for making sales contacts and presentations.
   d) Disadvantages of trade shows
      (1) Increasing costs. The cost of exhibiting at trade shows is rising quickly.
      (2) Wasted effort. A poorly planned exhibit ultimately costs the small business more than its benefits are worth.
   e) To avoid these disadvantages, business owners should:
      (1) Study the profile of trade show guests and compare it with their target customers before committing to a show.
      (2) Consider less expensive local or regional trade shows.
      (3) Communicate with key potential customers before the show; send them invitations.
      (4) Have knowledgeable salespeople staffing the booth.
      (5) Demonstrate the product or service; let customers see it in action.
      (6) Learn to distinguish between serious customers and "tirekickers." Ask probing questions to weed out those who are not good prospects.
      (7) Distribute literature that clearly communicates the product or service sold.
      (8) Project a professional image at all times.
      (9) Follow up promptly on sales leads.
14. Specialty Advertising.
   a) As advertisers have shifted their focus to "narrow casting" their messages to target audiences and away from "broadcasting," specialty advertising has grown in popularity.
   b) Advertisers now spend more than $3 billion annually on specialty items.
   c) Specialty advertising offers several advantages:
      (1) Reaching select audiences. Advertisers can reach specific audiences with well-planned specialty items.
      (2) Personalized nature. A small business owner should choose items that are un-usual, related to the nature of the business, and meaningful to customers.
      (3) Versatility. The rich versatility of specialty advertising is limited only by the business owner's imagination.
   d) Disadvantages to specialty advertising:
      (1) Potential for waste.

(2) Costs. Some specialty items can be quite expensive.

WIRED TO THE WEB - The Advertising Puzzle

Four years ago, Lisa and Isaac Sineath launched The Chef's Companion, a small retail shop selling an up-scale line of condiments, kitchen accessories, and food-related gift items on Hilton Head Island, South Carolina. "When we started, we underestimated the amount of money it would take to run a company, and nearly went out of business. We didn't have enough money to spend on advertising and promotion."

In those days, they advertised occasionally in the local newspaper. They eventually rented a booth during a celebration and sales took off. Although business is good and the company is successful, the Sineaths suspect that they are missing out on opportunities to sell their products and services. Based on customer feedback and conversations, they are now working on setting up a Web site that will allow visitors to order more product once they return home. "Their problem is that we really don't have an integrated advertising and promotion strategy for the Chef's Companion."

1. Use the resources of the World Wide Web and the resources in the library to research the demographics of the population of Hilton Head Island, South Carolina, and to learn about the island's tourist trade. Prepare a brief summary of your findings
   Answer - Students' responses will vary based on their research.
2. On the basis of your summary, help the Sineaths develop an advertising and promotion strategy for the Chef's Companion. Which advertising media would you suggest they use to advertise? Why? Use the Web to learn more about the media you suggest.
   Answer - Students' responses will vary based on their research.
3. Would the Chef's Companion benefit from a mail-order catalog? If it would, how could the Sineaths get a mailing list?
   Answer - It would but the Internet would probably be cheaper. They are obviously selling to an upscale audience who would have access to computers. They might use the catalog to reach older upscale customers who are not computer literate. They could generate a mailing list from customers as they buy product. They could get mailing list information local, from the Chamber of Commerce etc., of people who only winter in Hilton Head, etc.

---

15. Special events and promotions
    a) A growing number of small companies are finding that special events and promotions attract a great deal of interest and provide a lasting impression of the company.
    b) Creativity and uniqueness are essential ingredients in any special event promotion, and most entrepreneurs excel at those.
16. Point-of-purchase ads
    a) In the last several years, in-store advertising has become more popular as a way of reaching the customer at a crucial moment--the point of purchase.
    b) Research suggests that consumers make two-thirds of all buying decisions at the point of sale.
    c) Self-service stores are especially well suited for in-store ads.

V. Preparing an Advertising Budget
   A. Approaches
      1. One of the most challenging decisions confronting a small business owner is how much money to invest in advertising.

2. There are four methods of determining an advertising budget: what is affordable, matching competitors, percentage of sales, and objective-and-task.
3. What-is-affordable method
    a) The owner sees advertising as a luxury, advertising is an expense, not as an investment that produces sales and profits in the future.
    b) The advertising budget is allocated funds only after all other budget items have been financed.
    c) The result is an inadequate advertising budget.
4. Match the advertising expenditures of competitors
    a) Match in a flat dollar amount or as a percentage of sales.
    b) This method assumes that a firm's advertising needs and strategies are the same as those of its competitors.
    c) Relying on this technique can lead to blind imitation instead of a budget suited to the small firm's circumstances.
5. Percentage-of-sales approach
    a) The most commonly used method.
    b) This method relates advertising expenditures to actual sales results.
        (1) It is preferred to relating them to profits because sales tend to fluctuate less than profits.
    c) A useful rule of thumb when establishing an advertising budget: 10 percent of projected sales the first year in business; 7 percent the second year; and at least 5 percent each year after that.
6. The objective-and-task method
    a) Is the most difficult and least used technique.
    b) It also is the method most often recommended by advertising experts.
    c) The owner links advertising expenditures to specific objectives.
    d) The task method builds up the advertising funds by analyzing what it will cost to accomplish the specific objectives.
    e) A common problem with the method is that managers tend to be overly ambitious in setting advertising objectives, and, consequently, they set unrealistically high advertising expenditures.
7. Most small companies find it useful to plan in advance their advertising expenditures on a weekly basis.
    a) A calendar like the one pictured in Figure 11.5 can be one of the most valuable tools in planning a small company's advertising program.

VI. How to Advertise Big on a Small Budget
   A. Introduction
       1. The typical small business cannot afford to hire a professional ad agency.
       2. Unless a small company spends more than $10,000 a year on advertising, it probably doesn't need an ad agency.
       3. For most, hiring freelance copywriters and artists on a per-project basis is a much better bargain.

   B. Cooperative Advertising
       1. In cooperative advertising, a manufacturing company shares the cost of advertising with a small retailer if the retailer features its products in those ads.
       2. Both the manufacturer and the retailer get more advertising per dollar by sharing expenses.
       3. Most small business owners fail to take advantage of manufacturers' cooperative advertising programs.

4. Manufacturers offer cooperative advertising programs in almost every medium.
5. Cooperative advertising not only helps small businesses stretch their advertising budgets; it also offers another source of savings: the free advertising packages that many manufacturers supply to retailers.
6. These packages usually include photographs and illustrations of the product as well as professionally prepared ads to use in different media.

GAINING THE COMPETITIVE EDGE - The "Scoop" on Successful Promotions

SUMMARY

Entrepreneurs Ben Cohen and Jerry Greenfield, founders of the world-famous Ben & Jerry's Homemade Inc., mixed a dash of irreverence with a pinch of optimism and a dollop of social activism to produce a business that scoops more than $167 million a year in ice cream. Cohen and Greenfield's attitude that business should be fun has led them to develop a host of fun--and very successful--promotions.

Here are some lessons from these pundits of promotion:
▪ Offer special off-season promotion.
▪ Give away product samples. Product sampling is one of the promotions Ben and Jerry have relied on most often.
▪ Encourage your customers to take part in your business.
▪ Throw a party.
▪ Build a relationship with your customers.
▪ Run your business in a socially responsible fashion, and let customers know you're doing it.

Business owners who want to take a lesson from Ben & Jerry's Homemade should consider the following tips:
▪ Create an event that is related to your business.
▪ Consider a nontraditional holiday to run a promotion.
▪ Choose a local charity or nonprofit organization with which your company can get involved.
▪ Find ways to get your customers involved in and excited about your business.
▪ Offer a scholarship.
▪ Sponsor a contest.
▪ Conduct a seminar.
▪ Create a "frequent buyer" program.
▪ Create an award for your community.

1. Visit Ben and Jerry's Homemade Web site at <http://www. benjerry.com>. Write a one-page paper summarizing some of the company's current promotional campaigns.
   Answer - Students' responses will vary based on their research.
2. Working with a team of your classmates, select a local business and develop ideas for special promotions that would benefit that company.
   Answer - Students' responses will vary.

C. Shared Advertising
   1. In shared advertising, a group of similar businesses forms a syndicate to produce generic ads that allow the individual businesses to dub in local information.
   2. The technique is especially useful for small businesses that sell relatively standardized products or services such as legal assistance, autos, and furniture.

D. Publicity
1. The press can be either a valuable friend or a fearsome foe to a small business, depending on how well the owner handles her firm's publicity.
2. However, wise small business managers recognize that investing time and money in public relations (publicity) benefits both the community and the company.
3. The community gains the support of a good business citizen, and the company earns a positive image in the marketplace.
4. Many small businesses rely on media attention to get noticed, and getting that attention takes a coordinated effort.
5. One successful publicity technique is cause marketing, in which a small business sponsors and promotes fund-raising activities of nonprofit groups and charities while raising its own visibility in the community.

E. Other Ways to Save
1. Other cost-saving suggestions for advertising expenditures include the following:
a) Repeat ads that have been successful.
b) Use identical ads in different media.
c) Hire independent copywriters, graphic designers, photographers, and other media specialists.
d) Concentrate advertising during times when customers are most likely to buy.

Chapter Summary

♦ Describe the steps in developing an advertising strategy.
- Define the purpose of the company's advertising program by creating specific, measurable objectives.
- Analyze the firm and its target audience.
- Decide what to say and how to say it, making sure to build the message around the company's unique selling proposition (USP).
- Evaluate the ad campaign's effectiveness.
♦ Explain the differences among promotion, publicity, personal selling, and advertising.
- Promotion is any form of persuasive communication designed to inform consumers about a product or service and to influence them to purchase those goods or services.
- Publicity is any commercial news covered by the media that boosts sales but for which the small business does not pay.
- Personal selling is the personal contact between salespeople and potential customers resulting from sales efforts.
- Advertising is any sales presentation that is nonpersonal in nature and is paid for by an identified sponsor.
♦ Describe the advantages and disadvantages of the various advertising media.
- The medium used to transmit an advertising message influences the consumer's perception--and reception--of it.
- Media options include newspapers, radio, television, magazines, direct mail, the World Wide Web, outdoor advertising, transit advertising, directories, trade shows, special events and promotions, and point-of-purchase ads.
♦ Identify four basic methods for preparing an advertising budget.
- Establishing an advertising budget presents a real challenge to the small business owner. There are four basic methods: what is affordable; matching competitors; percentage of sales; objective-and-task.
♦ Explain practical methods for stretching a small business's advertising budget.

- Despite their limited advertising budgets, small businesses do not have to take a second-class approach to advertising. Three techniques that can stretch a small company's advertising dollars are cooperative advertising, shared advertising, and publicity.

Discussion Questions

1. What are the three elements of promotion? How do they support one another?
   Answer - Promotion is any form of persuasive communication designed to inform consumers about a product or service and to influence them to purchase these goods or services. It includes publicity, personal selling, and advertising. The difference in audiences and forms broaden the reach and offer variety to the promotional message.

2. What factors should a small business manager consider when selecting advertising media?
   Answer - Before considering either the advertising message or the media by which to send it, business owners must understand their target customers. Business owners should address the following questions.
   - What business are we in?
   - What image do we want to project?
   - Who are our target customers and what are their characteristics? Where can we best reach them?
   - What do my customers really purchase from us?
   - What benefits can the customer derive from our goods or services?
   - How do I want to position our company in the market?
   - What advertising approach do our competitors take?

3. What is a unique selling proposition? What role should it play in a company's advertising strategy?
   Answer - A successful USP answers the critical question every customer asks, "What's in it for me?" It should express in 10 words or less exactly what a business can do for its customers. The USP becomes the heart of the advertising message. Owners should build their ads around a unique selling proposition (USP), a key customer benefit of a product or service that sets it apart from its competition.

4. Create a table to summarize the advantages and disadvantages of the following advertising media:
   Newspapers - Page 346   Direct mail - Page 353
   Radio - Page 347   Outdoor advertising - Pages 358-359
   Television - Page 349   Transit advertising - Pages 360-361
   Magazines - Pages 351-2   Directories - Page 361
   Specialty advertising - Page 366   Trade shows - Pages 362-364

5. What are fixed spots, preemptible spots, and floating spots in radio advertising?
   Answer - Fixed spots are guaranteed to be broadcast at the times specified in the owner's contract with the station. Preemptible spots are cheaper than fixed spots, but the advertiser risks being preempted by an advertiser willing to pay the fixed rate for a time slot. Floating spots are the least expensive, but the advertiser has no control over broadcast times.

6. Describe the characteristics of an effective outdoor advertisement.
   Answer - Identify the product and the company clearly and quickly. Use a simple background. The background should not compete with the message. Rely on large illustrations that jump out at the viewer. Include clear, legible type. Use black-and-white designs. Research shows that black-and-white outdoor ads are more effective than color ads. Emphasize simplicity; short copy and short words are best. Use sharp, eye-catching graphics. Be located on the right-hand side of the highway.

7. Briefly outline the steps in creating an advertising plan. What principles should the small business owner follow when creating an effective advertisement?
   Answer - An advertising strategy ensures that money isn't wasted. A well-developed strategy increases the likelihood of good results. The first step is to define the purpose of the company's advertising program by creating specific, measurable objectives. The next step is to identify the company's target customers. Answering those questions will help business owners define their business, profile their customers, and focus their advertising messages on their specific target market to get more for their advertising dollars. Once the small business owner has defined her target audience, she can design an advertising message and choose the media for transmitting it.

8. Describe the common methods of establishing an advertising budget. Which method is most often used? Which technique is most often recommended? Why?
   Answer - There are four methods of determining an advertising budget: what is affordable, matching competitors, percentage of sales, and objective-and-task. What-is-affordable method--The advertising budget is allocated funds only after all other budget items have been financed. Match the advertising expenditures of competitors. This method assumes that a firm's advertising needs and strategies are the same as those of its competitors. Percentage-of-sales approach--The most commonly used method. This method relates advertising expenditures to actual sales results. A useful rule of thumb when establishing an advertising budget: 10 percent of projected sales the first year in business; 7 percent the second year; and at least 5 percent each year after that. The objective-and-task method--is the most difficult and least used technique. It also is the method most often recommended by advertising experts.

9. What techniques can small businesses use to stretch their advertising budgets?
   Answer - How to advertise big on a small budget. In cooperative advertising, a manufacturing company shares the cost of advertising with a small retailer if the retailer features its products in those ads. Both the manufacturer and the retailer get more advertising per dollar by sharing expenses. In shared advertising, a group of similar businesses forms a syndicate to produce generic ads that allow the individual businesses to dub in local information. The technique is especially useful for small businesses that sell relatively standardized products or services such as legal assistance, autos, and furniture. Publicity--the press can be either a valuable friend or a fearsome foe to a small business, depending on how well the owner handles her firm's publicity. However, wise small business managers recognize that investing time and money in public relations (publicity) benefits both the community and the company. Other cost-saving suggestions for advertising expenditures include the following--repeat ads that have been successful, use identical ads in different media, hire independent copywriters, graphic designers, photographers, and other media specialists, and concentrate advertising during times when customers are most likely to buy.

Step into the Real World
1. Contact a small retailer, a manufacturer, and a service firm and interview each one about his or her advertising program.
   a. Are there specific advertising objectives?
   b. What media does the owner employ? Why?
   c. How does the manager evaluate an ad's effectiveness?
   d. What assistance does the manager receive in designing ads?
2. Contact several small business owners and determine how they establish their advertising budgets, and why do they use the method they do.
3. Collect two or three advertisements for local small businesses and evaluate them on a scale of 1 (low) to 10 (high) using the following criteria: attention-getting, distinctive, interesting, concise, appealing, credible, USP-focused, convincing, motivating, and effective. How would you change the ads to make them more effective?

4. Browse through a magazine and find two ads that use sex to sell a good or service--one that you consider effective and one that you consider offensive. Compare your ads and reasoning with those of your classmates. What implications does your discussion have for advertisers?

Chapter 12 - International Opportunities for Small Business

It is easier to go to the moon than it is to enter the world of another civilization.
Culture--not space--is the greatest distance between two people.
Jamake Highwater

Knowledge, learning, information, and skilled intelligence are the raw materials
of international commerce and are today spreading throughout the world
as vigorously as miracle drugs, synthetic fertilizers, and blue jeans did earlier.
From A Nation at Risk

Teaching Objectives
Students will be able to:
1. Explain why "going global" has become an integral part of many small companies' strategies.
2. Describe the eight principal strategies small businesses have for going global.
3. Explain how to build a thriving export program.
4. Discuss the major barriers to international trade and their impact on the global economy.
5. Describe the trade agreements that will have the greatest influence on foreign trade into the twenty-first century.

Instructor's Outline
I. Introduction
    A. A Copernican Perspective
        1. Until recently, the world of international business was much like the world of astronomy before Copernicus, who revolutionized the study of the planets and the stars with his theory of planetary motion.
        2. In the sixteenth century, his Copernican system replaced the Polemic system, which held that the earth was the center of the universe, with the sun and all the other planets revolving around it.
        3. The Copernican system, however, placed the sun at the center of the solar system with all of the planets, including the earth, revolving around it. Astronomy would never be the same.
        4. In the same sense, business owners across the globe have had a Polemic perspective when it came to viewing international business opportunities.
            a) Owners have thought in terms of an economy that revolved around their national home base.
            b) Global trade was only for giant corporations.
        5. Today, the global marketplace is as much the territory of small, upstart companies as it is that of giant multinational corporations.
        6. Just a few years ago, military might governed world relationships; today, commercial trade has become the force that drives global interaction.
            a) Developing countries account for about 25 percent of world trade, up from 20 percent a decade ago.
            b) In the United States alone, international trade now accounts for 25 percent of gross domestic product.
            c) The Organization for Economic Cooperation and Development (OECD) projects the growth rate of global business at 3.5 to 4 percent per year over the next two decades. At that rate of growth, global trade will double by the year 2020.
        7. Political, social, cultural, and economic changes are sweeping the world.

8. Expanding a business beyond its domestic borders may actually enhance a small company's performance.
    a) A recent study by Coopers and Lybrand found that small companies that export grow at an average rate of 31.2 percent a year compared with just 24.9 percent for companies that operate domestically.
    b) Another study, by the Conference Board, concluded that U.S. manufacturers with global operations grow faster than do those that remain purely domestic.
    c) See Figure 12.1.

II. Why Go Global?
    A. Reasons
        1. Going global is a matter of survival, not preference.
        2. Competitors are forcing the small business to think globally.
        3. Failure to cultivate global markets can be a lethal mistake for modern businesses.

    B. The Benefits
        1. Offset sales declines in the domestic market.
        2. Increase sales and profits.
        3. Extend their products' life cycle.
        4. Lower manufacturing costs.
        5. Improve competitive position and enhance reputation.
        6. Raise quality levels.
        7. Become more customer oriented.
        8. Unfortunately, not enough entrepreneurs have learned to see their companies from a global perspective.
        9. Gaining a foothold in newly opened foreign markets or maintaining a position in an existing one is no easy task.
        10. Success in the global economy also requires:
            a) Constant innovation.
            b) Staying nimble enough to use speed as a competitive weapon.
            c) Maintaining a high level of quality and constantly improving it.
            d) Being sensitive to foreign customers' unique requirements.
            e) Adopting a more respectful attitude toward foreign habits and customs.
            f) Hiring motivated, multilingual employees.
            g) Retaining a desire to learn constantly about global markets.
        11. Before venturing into the global marketplace, a small business owner should consider five questions.
            a) Are we willing to commit adequate resources of time, people, and capital to our international campaign?
            b) Can we make money there?
            c) If so, can we get it out? (i.e., Is the currency convertible?)
            d) Will we feel comfortable doing business there? (i.e., Are we sensitive to the cultural differences of conducting international business?)
            e) Can we afford not to go global?

III. Going Global: Strategies for Small Businesses
    A. Introduction
        1. A growing number of small businesses are recognizing that going global is not a strategy reserved solely for industry giants.
        2. In the global economy the competitive edge is swiftness to market and innovation. Small units are much better at speed to market and innovation.

3. Their agility and adaptability give small firms the edge in today's highly interactive, fast-paced global economy.

GAINING THE COMPETITIVE EDGE - Assessing Your Company's Global Potential

SUMMARY
A.T. Kearney Inc., a Chicago-based management consulting firm, recently developed a matrix to help businesses assess the level of their global business competitiveness. The matrix describes the characteristics of companies at each of four stages of global development. "The stages are a reflection of management's leadership and ability to advance its [international] capabilities."

- Stage I. These are firms whose main focus is the domestic market Any exporting is likely to be an attempt to increase revenues at low cost; products designed for domestic consumption are marketed through international distribution channels. As a result, these companies have little or no presence in overseas markets.
- Stage II. These international companies recognize the need to adapt products to local markets but are slow to do so-or to manufacture or make major investments overseas. Senior management is conversant with, but not fluent in, the ways of international business.
- Stage III. These multinational firms are experienced in tailoring products to overseas markets and in offshore research, development, and production. Service needs are likely to be fulfilled locally.
- Stage IV. These global companies, operating with worldwide strategies, are at home in every market. There is so much foreign presence at the senior management and board levels that the companies could be dubbed country-neutral.

A.T. Kearney designed this matrix to help businesses assess their capacity for global competitiveness. Best suggests using it to help companies answer five key questions:
1. How worldly is management's orientation?
2. What is the firm's approach to products, service, and quality?
3. Is the company's financial perspective short- or long-term?
4. How is the company organized for foreign business?
5. What foreign constraints on business exist?

1. At what level in the matrix do most U.S. small businesses fall? Why?
    Answer - Probably Stage I, largely because they are thinking short term, survival mode. Most think they don't have the resources to go international.
2. What steps can a small business take to advance to higher levels on the matrix?
    Answer - Finding someone with international expertise to help advise them. Learn more about global markets. Begin thinking globally as they develop new products.

---

4. Small companies go global for a variety of reasons.
    a) Some move into foreign markets because their domestic sales have sagged.
    b) Other small businesses have discovered soaring demand for their products and services among foreign customers.
    c) Still other entrepreneurs realize that their future success depends on their ability to go global.
5. Becoming a global business depends on instilling a global culture throughout the organization that permeates everything the company does.
6. Small companies pursuing a global presence have eight principal strategies available: the World Wide Web, relying on trade intermediaries, joint ventures, foreign licensing,

franchising, countertrading and bartering, exporting, and establishing international locations.
   a)   See Figure 12.2

B.   The World Wide Web
   1.   Perhaps the simplest and least expensive way for a small business to begin conducting business globally.
   2.   With a well-designed Web site, a small company can extend its reach to customers anywhere in the world and without breaking the budget.
   3.   Most small companies follow a four-step evolutionary process to conducting global business on the Web:
      a)   Step 1. Connecting to e-mail. Even though it lacks the ability to provide the wealth of visual images and sounds available on the WWW, e-mail gives entrepreneurs the ability to communicate with customers anywhere in the world quickly and easily.
      b)   Step 2. Building an informational Web site. Companies soon see the need to educate their international customers about the features and the benefits of their products and services and thus set up Web sites.
      c)   Step 3. Conducting international market research electronically. Once business owners begin to see the power of the Web and its ability to attract customers across the globe, they become interested in using it as a more proactive tool to generate sales, researching markets in other countries.
      d)   Step 4. Establishing a secure ordering and payment system for on-line customers. Currently, the most common purchase pattern on the WWW is for customers to tap a company's Web site for product or service information and then to use the fax or phone to place orders. Their primary concerns involve on-line security.

C.   Trade Intermediaries
   1.   Another relatively easy way to break into international markets.
   2.   Trade intermediaries are domestic agencies that serve as distributors in foreign countries for domestic companies of all sizes.
   3.   They rely on their networks of contacts, their extensive knowledge of local customs and markets, and their experience in international trade to market products effectively and efficiently all across the globe.
   4.   Trade intermediaries account for about 10 percent of all U.S. exports.
      a)   Export management companies. An important channel of foreign distribution for small companies just getting started in international trade or for those lacking the resources to assign their own people to foreign markets.
         (1) Most EMCs are merchant intermediaries, working on a buy-and-sell arrangement with domestic small companies.
      b)   Export trading companies. Export trading companies are businesses that buy and sell products in a number of countries, and they typically offer a wide range of services such as exporting, importing, shipping, storing, distributing, and others to their clients.
         (1) ETCs usually perform both import and export trades across many countries' borders.
         (2) However, like EMCs, ETCs lower the risk of exporting for small businesses.
         (3) In 1982, Congress passed the Export Trading Company Act to allow producers of similar products to form ETC cooperatives without the fear of violating antitrust laws. The goal was to encourage U.S. companies to export more goods by allowing businesses in the same industry to band together to form export trading companies.

   c) Manufacturer's export agents. MEAs act as international sales representatives in a limited number of markets for various noncompeting domestic companies.
     (1) The relationship between an MEA and a small company is a short-term one, and the MEA typically operates on a commission basis.

IN THE FOOTSTEPS OF AN ENTREPRENEUR - Blasting Their Way into International Markets

SUMMARY
Engineered Demolition, a family business with 20 employees that operates in a unique niche market that spans the globe: explosive demolition. The Minneapolis-based company is one of just a handful of businesses worldwide that uses implosion to destroy old buildings in metropolitan areas to make way for new ones. Chong and Kelly spend a great deal of time educating clients about the implosion process, dispelling the misconceived images people have of debris shooting out for hundreds of yards from the work site. After studying the blueprints of the target building, Engineered Demolition workers plan the blast, emphasizing four key elements: the direction of the fall, how straight the fall is, the material structure of the building, and the proximity and location of adjoining buildings.

As one might imagine, implosion is a highly specialized field that requires extensive training. Both Kelly and Chong hold blaster's licenses valid in the United States and internationally. Engineered Demolition currently averages about 75 jobs a year, but business is doubling about every four years. Chong says that the number of jobs from international customers is increasing rapidly. Currently, about one-third of the company's contracts come from international clients.

Although used for years in the United States and Canada, demolition by implosion has caught on in Asia, Europe, and Latin America only recently. Performing an implosion in these countries is more difficult because of the time required to get the necessary permits. As their international clientele increases, Chong and Kelly have learned to be more sensitive to their customers' cultural preferences and customs.

Engineered Demolition is actively pursuing business in European markets. Chong was one of 22 women who participated in a recent Women in Trade mission to Europe led by the U.S. Commerce Department. The exposure has already paid off. Not long after Chong returned from the trip, Engineered Demolition landed one of its most unusual jobs in Europe. Not only are Chong and Kelly successful, but they also love their work.

1. What factors are contributing to the growth of Engineered Demolition's international business? Which countries should the company target? Why?
Answer - A growing need for a specific service that serves a niche market. A reputation for quality and safety--i.e. doing the job right--and their sensitivity to national cultural issues related to the service they provide.
2. Work with a team of your classmates to brainstorm ways that Engineered Demolition can locate international customers.
Answer - Students' responses will vary but should take the Web, direct mail to construction and architectural firms, large city governments, etc., into consideration.

---

    5. Export merchants. Export merchants are domestic wholesalers who do business in foreign markets. They buy goods from many domestic manufacturers and then market the goods in foreign markets. They often carry competing lines, which means they have little loyalty to suppliers.
    6. Resident buying offices. A government-owned or privately owned operation of one country established in another country for the purpose of buying goods made there.

7. Foreign distributors. They handle all of the marketing, distribution, and service functions in the foreign country.
8. The value of using trade intermediaries.
    a) Trade intermediaries make the transition to global markets much faster and easier.
    b) The key to establishing a successful relationship with a trade intermediary is conducting a thorough screening to determine what type of intermediary--and which one in particular-will best serve a small company's needs.
    c) A company looking for an intermediary should compile a list of potential candidates using some of the sources listed in Table 12.1.

D. Joint Ventures
    1. Lower the risk of entering global markets for small businesses. They also give small companies more clout in foreign lands.
    2. In a domestic joint venture, two or more U.S. small businesses form an alliance for the purpose of exporting their goods and services.
        a) For export ventures, participating companies get antitrust immunity, allowing them to cooperate freely.
        b) The businesses share the responsibility and the costs of getting export licenses and permits, and they split the venture's profits.
    3. In a foreign joint venture, a domestic small business forms an alliance with a company in the target nation.
        a) The host partner brings to the joint venture valuable knowledge of the local market and its method of operation as well as of the customs and the tastes of local customers, making it much easier to conduct business in the foreign country.
        b) Sometimes foreign countries place certain limitations on joint ventures. Some nations, for example, require host companies to own at least 51 percent of the venture.
    4. The most important ingredient in the recipe for a successful joint venture is choosing the right partner.
    5. A second key to creating a successful alliance is to establish common objectives.
        a) Defining exactly what each party in the joint venture hopes to accomplish at the outset.
    6. Unfortunately, most joint ventures fail.
        a) The average success rate is just 43 percent.
        b) The average life of a joint venture is only 3.5 years.
    7. Common problems leading to failure include improper selection of partners, incompatible management style, failure to establish common goals, inability to be flexible, and failure to trust one another.
    8. What can entrepreneurs do to avoid these pitfalls in joint ventures?
        a) Define at the outset important issues such as each party's contributions and responsibilities, the distribution of earnings, the expected life of the relationship, and the circumstances under which the parties can terminate the relationship.
        b) Understand in depth their partner's reasons and objectives for joining the venture.
        c) Select a partner who shares their company's values and standards of conduct.
        d) Spell out in writing exactly how the venture will work and where decision-making authority lies.
        e) Select a partner whose skills are different from but compatible with those of their own companies.
        f) Prepare a "prenuptial agreement" that spells out what will happen in case of a business "divorce."

E. Foreign Licensing
1. Some small companies enter foreign markets by licensing businesses in other nations to use their patents, trademarks, copyrights, technology, processes, or products.
2. In return, the small company collects royalties from the sales of its foreign licenses.
3. Licensing is relatively simple.
    a) They find someone who can capture the market, who is already at home in that market.
4. Although many business owners consider licensing only their products, the licensing potential for intangibles such as processes, technology, copyrights, and trademarks often is greater.
5. Foreign licensing enables a small business to enter foreign markets quickly, easily, and with virtually no capital investment.
6. Risks to the company include the potential of losing control over its manufacturing and marketing and creating a competitor if the licensee gains too much knowledge and control.
7. Securing proper patent, trademark, and copyright protection beforehand can minimize those risks, however.

F. International Franchising
1. Franchising has become a major export industry for the United States.
2. More than 20 percent of the nation's 4,000-plus franchisors have outlets in foreign countries.
3. International franchisors sell virtually every kind of product or service imaginable--some identical to those sold in the United States. However, most franchisors have learned that they must modify their products and services to suit local tastes and customs.
4. Although franchise outlets span the globe, Canada is the primary market for U.S. franchisors, with Japan and Europe following.
5. These markets are most attractive to franchisors because they are similar to the U.S. markets.
6. Europe also holds special interest for many U.S. franchises as trade barriers there continue to topple, opening up the largest--and one of the most affluent--markets in the world.
    a) Growth potential is the primary attraction.
    b) Eastern European countries that recently have thrown off the chains of communism are turning to franchising to help them move toward a market economy.
    c) Southeast Asian countries such as Indonesia, Malaysia, and Vietnam hold promise for franchising in the future, as do India and Russia, with their large populations and blooming economies.
    d) Because of its growing middle class and recent free-trade agreement with the United States, Mexico is becoming a popular target for franchises.

G. Countertrading and Bartering
1. Another problem global businesses face when selling to some countries is that their currencies are virtually worthless outside their borders, so getting paid in a valuable currency is a real challenge.
    a) 70 percent of all countries do not have either convertible currencies or sufficient cash flow to pay for imported goods.
    b) Companies wanting to reach these markets must countertrade or barter.
2. A countertrade is a transaction in which a company selling goods or services in a foreign country agrees to help promote investment and trade in that country.

3. The goal of the transaction is to help offset the capital drain from the foreign country's purchases.
    a) Experts estimate that countertrading accounts for 20 to 30 percent of all global trade, and its use will continue to escalate.
4. Countertrading does suffer from numerous drawbacks.
    a) Countertrade transactions can be complicated, cumbersome, and time-consuming.
    b) They also increase the chances that a company will get stuck with merchandise that it cannot move.
    c) They can lead to unpleasant surprises concerning the quantity and quality of products required in the countertrade.
5. Still, countertrading offers one major advantage.
    a) Sometimes it's the only way to make a sale.
6. Because of its complexity and the risks involved, countertrading is not the best choice for a novice entrepreneur looking to break into the global marketplace.
7. Bartering, the exchange of goods and services for other goods and services, is another way of trading with countries lacking convertible currency.
    a) Barter transactions require finding a business with complementary needs, but they are much simpler than countertrade transactions.

H. Exporting
    1. Small companies increasingly are looking toward exporting as a global business strategy.
    2. Small companies account for 97 percent of the companies involved in exporting but only generate one-third of the dollar value of the nation's exports.
    3. A recent study by Grant Thornton LLP reported that the percentage of small and medium-sized exporters that generate at least 10 percent of their revenue from exports doubled to 51 percent in just two years.
    4. Approximately 100,000, U.S. companies currently export; however, experts estimate that at least twice as many are capable of exporting but are not doing so.
        a) The biggest barrier facing companies that have never exported is not knowing where or how to start.
        b) Most entrepreneurs in the United States envision markets only within domestic and sometimes even state borders.
        c) Breaking the psychological barrier to exporting is the first, and most difficult, step in setting up a successful program.
    5. Steps an entrepreneur must take to get an export program under way.
        a) Recognize that even the tiniest companies and least experienced entrepreneurs have the potential to export.
        b) Exporting can not only boost a small company's sales, but it also can accelerate its growth rate.
        c) Analyze your product or service.
        d) Analyze your commitment.
        e) Research markets and pick your target.
            (1) Research shows export entrepreneurs whether they need to modify their existing products and services to suit the tastes and preferences of their foreign target customers.
        f) Develop a distribution strategy.
        g) Find your customer.
            (1) Refer to Table 12.1 for a list of some of the resources available from the government.
        h) Find financing. One of the biggest barriers to small business exports is lack of financing.

       (1) Several federal, state, and private programs are operating to fill the export-financing void.

   i) Ship your goods. Export novices usually rely on international freight forwarders and custom-house agents--experienced specialists in overseas shipping for help in navigating the bureaucratic morass of packaging requirements and paperwork demanded by customs.

       (1) These specialists, also known as transport architects, are to exporters what travel agents are to passengers and normally charge relatively small fees for a valuable service.

WIRED TO THE WEB - Where Do We Start?

Specialty Building Supplies is a small company with $6.4 million in annual sales that manufactures and sells a line of building products such as foundation vents, insulation materials, and fireplace blowers to building supply stores in the Northeastern United States.

Meyers was a homebuilder who observed the increasing costs of heating fuels. As a result he began installing simple, inexpensive ways to save on heating costs. He launched Specialty Building Supplies on the basis of his first product, an automatic foundation vent that was thermostatically controlled. Simple and inexpensive Autovent was a big hit in newly constructed homes in the Northeast.

Due to lack luster domestic sales, Tad Meyers is considering a move into international markets due to the comments of his marketing manager.

1. What advice would you offer Meyers and the other managers at Specialty Building Supplies about their prospects of going global?
   Answer - Their chances are very good, and they probably should go for it. But they need to get help from someone with experience.
2. How would you suggest these managers go about finding the answers to the questions they have posed? What other questions would you recommend they ask?
   Answer - Refer students to Table 12.2 for the questions the managers need to ask. Refer students to Table 12.1 for finding a trade intermediary.
3. Using the resources of the World Wide Web, develop an outline of the steps these managers should take to assemble an international marketing plan.
   Answer - While the Web will provide ideas students' plans should follow the form of the marketing plan in the text's appendix beginning at page A-1. Their plans should also address the questions listed in Tables 12.2 and 12.3

---

   j) Collect your money. Collecting foreign accounts can be more complex than collecting domestic ones, but by picking their customers carefully and checking their credit references closely, entrepreneurs can minimize bad-debt losses.

       (1) Financing foreign sales often involves special credit arrangements such as letters of credit and bank (or documentary) drafts.

       (2) A letter of credit is an agreement between an exporter's bank and the foreign buyer's bank that guarantees payment to the exporter for a specific shipment of goods.

       (3) A bank draft is a document the seller draws on the buyer, requiring the buyer to pay the face amount (the purchase price of the goods) either on sight (a sight draft) or on a specified date (a time draft) once the goods have been shipped.

(4) Rather than use letters of credit or drafts, some exporters simply require cash in advance or cash on delivery (COD).

6. Planned carefully and taken one step at a time, exporting can be a highly profitable route for small businesses.

7. Many small companies are forming foreign sales corporations (FSCs, pronounced "risks") to take advantage of a tax benefit that is designed to stimulate exports.

    a) By forming an FSC, a company can shelter about 15 percent of its profits on foreign sales from federal--and in some cases state--income taxes.

    b) Setting up an FSC requires a company to establish a shell corporation in the Virgin Islands, Barbados, or one of another 40 tax-friendly offshore locations that have tax treaties with the United States.

    c) The company also must have fewer than 25 shareholders and one non-U.S.-resident board member.

    d) Because it costs about $2,500 to establish an FSC and about $1,500 a year to maintain one, a business should earn at least $50,000 a year to make the savings from an FSC worthwhile.

I. Establishing International Locations

1. Establishing an office or a factory in a foreign land can require a substantial investment reaching beyond the budgets of many small companies.

2. Plus, setting up an international office can be an incredibly frustrating experience in some countries. Business infrastructures are in disrepair or are nonexistent.

3. Finding the right person to manage an international office is crucial to success; it also is a major challenge, especially for small businesses.

4. Few small businesses begin their global ventures by establishing international locations, preferring, instead, to build a customer base through some of the strategies already covered.

5. Small companies that do establish international locations can reap significant benefits.

6. Start-up costs are lower in some foreign countries, and lower labor costs can produce significant savings as well.

IV. Barriers to International Trade

  A. Domestic Barriers

    1. Sometimes the biggest barriers potential exporters face are right here at home.

    2. Three major domestic roadblocks are common: attitude, information, and financing.

    3. Perhaps the biggest barrier to small businesses exporting is the attitude.

      a) The first lesson of exporting is "Take nothing for granted about who can export and what you can and cannot export."

    4. Entrepreneurs neglect international markets because of a lack of information about how to get started.

      a) The key to success in international markets is choosing the correct target market and designing the appropriate strategy to reach it. That requires access to information and research.

    5. Another significant obstacle is the lack of export financing available.

      a) A recent survey of exporters found that 53 percent said they had lost export business because they couldn't get financing.

  B. International Barriers

    1. Two types of international barriers are common: tariff and nontariff.

    2. Tariff barriers

     a) A tariff is a tax, or duty, that a government imposes on goods and services imported into that country.

     b) Imposing tariffs raises the price of the imported goods--making them less attractive to consumers--and protects the makers of comparable domestic products and services.

     c) Established in the United States in 1790 by Alexander Hamilton, the tariff system generated the majority of federal revenues for about 100 years. Today, the U.S. tariff code lists duties on 8,862 items--from brooms and olives to flashlights and teacups.

   3. Nontariff barriers

     a) Quotas. Rather than impose a direct tariff on certain imported products, nations often use quotas to protect their industries.

     b) A quota is a limit on the amount of a product imported into a country.

     c) Embargoes. An embargo is a total ban on imports of certain products.

     d) Dumping. In an effort to grab market share quickly, some companies have been guilty of dumping products: selling large quantities of them in foreign countries below cost.

WIRED TO THE WEB - On To Japan

"It's hard to believe how far we've come in just 14 months," said Tad Meyers, president of Specialty Building Supplies. "Which one of us would have thought we would be trying to sell our products in Japan?"

Planning a trip to meet with distributors Tad, Dee, and Hal discuss what they will take and do. They tried to learn a few phrases, selected some gifts, and studied how the Japanese do business. They took some brochures detailing the product line, emphasizing its unique nature and superb quality, printed in Japanese. They plan to get right down to business since time will be at a premium on their trip. They anticipate a big payday just around the corner.

1. Evaluate the preparations Meyers and Rada have made for their upcoming trip to Japan.
   Answer - These two questions are closely interlinked. Students may have to do #2 to answer #1. Students should find both positive and negative things in these preparations. Clearly they are trying to think about adjusting to the Japanese. Their time focus will be a problem in Japan where there is little rush and lots of relationship building.

2. Using the library and the WWW as resources, read about Japanese culture and Japanese business practices. On the basis of what you learned, would you advise them to change any of their plans? Explain.
   Answer - This question is tied to #1. Students should discover that relationships are very important to the Japanese and that entertaining is a major form for doing business. The Japanese will not respond well to Dee Rada; often traditional upper level Japanese managers will not even speak with a woman.

  C. Political Barriers

    1. Entrepreneurs who go global quickly discover a labyrinth of political tangles.

    2. The complex web of governmental and legal regulations and barriers they encounter in foreign countries often astounds them.

    3. Companies doing business in politically risky lands face the very real dangers of government takeovers of private property; attempts at coups to overthrow ruling parties; kidnappings, bombings, and other violent acts against businesses and their employees; and other threatening events.

4. Their investments of millions of dollars may evaporate overnight in the wake of a government coup or the passage of a law nationalizing an industry (giving control of an entire industry to the government).
5. Some nations welcome foreign business investment; others do everything they can to discourage competition from foreign companies.

D. Business Barriers
1. Business practices and regulations in foreign lands can be quite different from those in the United States.
2. The biggest shock comes in the area of human resources management, where international managers discover that practices common in the United States, such as overtime, women workers, and employee benefits are restricted, disfavored, or forbidden in other cultures.
3. Business owners new to international business sometimes are shocked at the wide range of labor costs they encounter and the accompanying wide range of skilled labor available.
4. In some countries, what appear to be "bargain" labor rates turn out to be excessively high after accounting for the quality of the labor force and the benefits their governments mandate.

E. Cultural Barriers
1. The culture of a nation includes the beliefs, values, views, and mores that its inhabitants share.
2. The diversity of languages, business philosophies, practices, and traditions make international trade more complex than selling to the business down the street.
3. Consider the following examples:
    a) A U.S. entrepreneur, eager to expand into the European Union, arrives at his company's potential business partner's headquarters in France. Confidently, he strides into the meeting room, enthusiastically pumps his host's hand, slaps him on the back, and says "Tony, I've heard a great deal about you; please, call me Bill." Eager to explain the benefits of his product, he opens his briefcase and gets right down to business. The French executive politely excuses himself and leaves the room before negotiations ever begin, shocked by the American's rudeness and ill manners. Rudeness and ill manners? Yes--from the French executive's perspective.
    b) Another American business owner flies to Tokyo to close a deal with a Japanese executive. He is pleased when his host invites him to play a round of golf shortly after he arrives. He plays well and manages to win by a few strokes. The Japanese executive invites him to play again the next day, and again he wins by a few strokes. Invited to play another round the following day, the American asks, "But when are we going to start doing business?" His host, surprised by the question, says, "But we have been doing business."
4. When American businesspeople enter international markets for the first time, they often are amazed at the differences in foreign cultures' habits and customs.
5. Understanding and heeding these often subtle cultural differences is one of the most important keys to international business success.
6. Entrepreneurs who fail to learn the differences in the habits and customs of the cultures in which they hope to do business are at a distinct disadvantage.

V. International Trade Agreements
A. Introduction
1. In an attempt to boost world trade, nations have created a variety of trade agreements over the years. While hundreds of agreements are paving the way for freer trade across

the world, two stand out with particular significance: the General Agreement on Tariffs and Trade (GATT) and the North American Free Trade Agreement (NAFTA).

B. GATT
    1. Created in 1947, the General Agreement on Tariffs and Trade (GATT) became the first global tariff agreement.
    2. It was designed to reduce tariffs among member nations and to facilitate trade across the globe.
    3. Originally signed by the United States and 22 other nations, GATT has grown to include 124 member countries today.
    4. Together, they account for nearly 90 percent of world trade.

GAINING THE COMPETITIVE EDGE - The Secret Language of International Business

SUMMARY
When U.S. businesspeople enter international markets for the first time, they often are amazed at the differences in foreign cultures' habits and customs. The key for entrepreneurs is learning to be sensitive to the business cultures in which they operate. Consider these pointers.

♦ Patience is a must for doing business in Spain.
♦ Appearance and style are important to Italian businesspeople; they judge the polish and the expertise of the company's executives as well as the quality of its products and services.
♦ In Great Britain, businesspeople consider it extremely important to conduct business "properly"--with formality and reserve.
♦ In China, entrepreneurs will need an ample dose of the "three Ps": patience, patience, patience.
♦ In the Pacific Rim, entrepreneurs must remember that each country has its own unique culture and business etiquette. Starting business relationships with customers in the Pacific Rim usually requires a third-party contact because Asian executives prefer to do business with people they know.
♦ American entrepreneurs doing business in the Pacific Rim should avoid hard-sell techniques, which are an immediate turnoff to Asian businesspeople. Harmony, patience, and consensus make good business companions in this region.
♦ Japanese executives conduct business much like the British: with an emphasis on formality, thoughtfulness, and respect.
♦ In Japan and South Korea, exchanging business cards, known in Japan as meishi, is an important business function, unlike Great Britain, where exchanging business cards is less popular.
♦ Greeting a Japanese executive properly includes a bow and a handshake--showing respect for both cultures.
♦ In Mexico, making business appointments through a well-connected Mexican national will go a long way to assuring successful business deals.

1. What can an entrepreneur do to avoid committing cultural blunders when conducting global business?
    Answer - He/she can avoid mistakes by studying the culture, traveling with someone who knows the culture, take his/her cues from his host, etc. "Common sense" is culture bound and unreliable.

---

    5. The latest round of GATT negotiations, called the Uruguay Round, was completed in December 1993 and took effect on July I, 1995.
        a) Negotiators reduced the remaining industrial tariffs by 40 percent, established new rules governing dumping goods at unfairly low prices, strengthened the global protection of patents, and cut the level of government subsidies on agricultural products.

b)   In addition, negotiators agreed to form a World Trade Organization (WTO) with more power to settle trade disputes among member nations than GATT had.
6.   Although the agreement failed to topple trade barriers for services as much as managers had hoped, GATT will benefit a wide variety of businesses.

C. NAFTA
1.   The North American Free Trade Agreement (NAFTA) created a free trade area among Canada, Mexico, and the United States.
2.   A free trade area is an association of countries that have agreed to knock down trade barriers, both tariff and nontariff, among partner nations. Under the provisions of NAFTA, these barriers were eliminated for trade among the three countries, but each remained free to set its own tariffs on imports from nonmember nations.
3.   NAFTA forged a unified United States-Canada-Mexico market of 380 million people with a total annual output of more than $6.5 trillion dollars of goods and services.
4.   Before NAFTA took effect on January 1, 1994, the average tariff on U.S. goods entering Mexico was 10 percent. Under NAFTA, these tariffs will be reduced to zero on most goods over the next 10 to 15 years.
5.   Among NAFTA's provisions are:
a)   Tariff reductions.
b)   Elimination of nontariff barriers.
c)   Simplified border processing.
d)   Tougher health and safety standards.

D. Conclusion
1.   To remain competitive, businesses must assume a global posture. Global effectiveness requires managers to be able to leverage workers' skills, company resources, and customer know-how across borders and throughout cultures across the world. Managers also must concentrate on maintaining competitive cost structures and a focus on the core of every business: the customer! Robert G. Shaw, CEO of International Jensen Inc., a global maker of home and automobile stereo speakers, explains the importance of retaining that customer focus as his company pursues its global strategy: "We want [our customers] to have the attitude of [our] being across the street. If we're going to have a global company, we have to behave in that mode, whether [the customer is] across the street or seven miles, seven minutes, or 7,000 miles away." The manager of one global business discourages the use of the word domestic among its employees, asking, "Where's domestic when the world is your market?" Although there are no surefire rules for going global, small businesses wanting to become successful international competitors should observe these guidelines:
a)   Make yourself at home in all three of the world's key markets: North America, Europe, and Asia.
b)   Appeal to the similarities within the various regions in which you operate but recognize the differences in their specific cultures.
c)   Develop new products for the world market. Make sure your products and services measure up to world-class quality standards.
d)   Familiarize yourself with foreign customs and languages; constantly scan, clip, and build a file on other cultures: their lifestyles, values, customs, and business practices.
e)   Learn to understand your customers from the perspective of their culture, not your own.
f)   "Globalize," make global decisions about products, markets, and management but allow local employees to make tactical decisions about packaging, advertising, and service.

g) Train employees to think globally, send them on international trips, and equip them with state-of-the-art communications technology.

h) Hire local managers to staff foreign offices and branches.

i) Do whatever seems best wherever it seems best, even if people at home lose jobs or responsibilities.

j) Consider using partners and joint ventures to break into foreign markets you cannot penetrate on your own.

2. By its very nature, going global can be a frightening experience. Most entrepreneurs who have already made the jump, however, have found that the benefits outweigh the risks and that their companies are much stronger because of it.

Chapter Summary

♦ Explain why "going global" has become an integral part of many small companies' strategies.

- Companies that move into international business can reap many benefits, including offsetting sales declines in the domestic market; increasing sales and profits; extending their products' life cycles; lowering manufacturing costs; improving competitive position; raising quality levels; and becoming more customer-oriented.

♦ Describe the eight principal strategies small businesses have for going global.

- Perhaps the simplest and least expensive way for a small business to begin conducting business globally is to establish a site on the World Wide Web (WWW). Companies wanting to sell goods on the Web should establish a secure ordering and payment system for on-line customers.

- Trade intermediaries such as export management companies, export trading companies, manufacturer's export agents, export merchants, resident buying offices, and foreign distributors can serve as a small company's "export department."

- In a domestic joint venture, two or more U.S. small companies form an alliance for the purpose of exporting their goods and services abroad. In a foreign joint venture, a domestic small business forms an alliance with a company in the target nation.

- Some small businesses enter foreign markets by licensing businesses in other nations to use their patents, trademarks, copyrights, technology, processes, or products.

- Franchising has become a major export industry for the United States. The International Franchise Association estimates that more than 20 percent of the nation's 4,000 franchisors have outlets in foreign countries.

- Some countries lack a hard currency that is convertible into other currencies, so companies doing business there must rely on countertrading or bartering. A countertrade is a transaction in which a

- business selling its goods in a foreign country agrees to promote investment and trade in that country. Bartering involves trading goods and services for other goods and services.

- Although small companies account for 97 percent of the companies involved in exporting, they generate only 33 percent of the dollar value of the nation's exports. However, small companies, realizing the incredible profit potential it offers, are making exporting an ever-expanding part of their marketing plans. Nearly half of U.S. companies with annual revenues under $100 million export goods.

- Once established in international markets, some small businesses set up permanent locations there. Although they can be very expensive to establish and maintain, international locations give businesses the opportunity to stay in close contact with their international customers.

♦ Explain how to build a thriving export program.

- Building a successful export program takes patience and research. Steps include: realize that even the tiniest firms have the potential to export; analyze your product or service; analyze your commitment to exporting; research markets and pick your target; develop a distribution strategy; find your customer; find financing; ship your goods; and collect your money.

- ♦ Discuss the major barriers to international trade and their impact on the global economy.
  - ▪ Three domestic barriers to international trade are common: the attitude that "we're too small to export," lack of information on how to get started in global trade, and a lack of available financing.
  - ▪ International barriers include tariffs, quotas, embargoes, dumping, and political business, and cultural barriers.
- ♦ Describe the trade agreements that will have the greatest influence on foreign trade into the twenty-first century.
  - ▪ Created in 1947, the General Agreement on Tariffs and Trade (GATT), the first global tariff agreement, was designed to reduce tariffs among member nations and to facilitate trade across the globe.
  - ▪ The North American Free Trade Agreement (NAFTA) created a free trade area among Canada, Mexico, and the United States. The agreement created an association that knocked down trade barriers, both tariff and nontariff, among these partner nations.

Discussion Questions

1. Why must entrepreneurs learn to think globally?

   Answer - Today, the global marketplace is as much the territory of small, upstart companies as it is that of giant multinational corporations. Developing countries now account for about 25 percent of world trade, up from 20 percent a decade ago. The Organization for Economic Cooperation and Development (OECD) projects the growth rate of global business at 3.5 to 4 percent per year over the next two decades. At that rate of growth, global trade will double by the year 2020. Expanding a business beyond its domestic borders may actually enhance a small company's performance. A recent study by Coopers and Lybrand found that small companies that export grow at an average rate of 31.2 percent a year compared with just 24.9 percent for companies that operate domestically. Another study, by the Conference Board, concluded that U.S. manufacturers with global operations and grow faster than do those that remain purely domestic. See Figure 12.1.

2. What forces are driving small businesses into international markets?

   Answer - In the global economy, the competitive edge is swiftness to market and innovation. Small units are much better at speed to market and innovation. Their agility and adaptability give small firms the edge in today's highly interactive, fast-paced global economy. Going global is a matter of survival, not preference. Competitors are forcing the small business to think globally. Failure to cultivate global markets can be a lethal mistake for modern businesses. Small companies go global for a variety of reasons. Some move into foreign markets because their domestic sales have sagged. Other small businesses have discovered soaring demand for their products and services among foreign customers. Still other entrepreneurs realize that their future success depends on their ability to go global.

3. What advantages does going global offer a small business owner? Risks?

   Answer - The benefits are numerous.
   - ▪ Offset sales declines in the domestic market.
   - ▪ Increase sales and profits.
   - ▪ Extend their products' life cycle.
   - ▪ Lower manufacturing costs.
   - ▪ Improve competitive position and enhance reputation.
   - ▪ Raise quality levels.
   - ▪ Become more customer-oriented.

   However there are some risks, as gaining a foothold in newly opened foreign markets or maintaining a position in an existing one is no easy task. Before venturing into the global marketplace, a small business owner should consider five questions.

- Are we willing to commit adequate resources of time, people, and capital to our international campaign?
- Can we make money there?
- If so, can we get it out? (i.e., Is the currency convertible?)
- Will we feel comfortable doing business there? (i.e., Are we sensitive to the cultural differences of conducting international business?)
- Can we afford not to go global?

4. Outline the eight strategies that small businesses can use to go global.
   Answer - Small companies pursuing a global presence have eight principal strategies available: the World Wide Web, relying on trade intermediaries, joint ventures, foreign licensing, franchising, countertrading and bartering, exporting, and establishing international locations. See Figure 12.2.

The World Wide Web is perhaps the simplest and least expensive way for a small business to begin conducting business globally. With a well-designed Web site, a small company can extend its reach to customers anywhere in the world and without breaking the budget.

Trade intermediaries are domestic agencies that serve as distributors in foreign countries for domestic companies of all sizes. They rely on their networks of contacts, their extensive knowledge of local customs and markets, and their experience in international trade to market products effectively and efficiently all across the globe. Trade intermediaries account for about 10 percent of all U.S. exports.

Some small companies enter foreign markets by licensing businesses in other nations to use their patents, trademarks, copyrights, technology, processes, or products. In return, the small company collects royalties from the sales of its foreign licenses. Although many business owners consider licensing only their products, the licensing potential for intangibles such as processes, technology, copyrights, and trademarks often is greater.

International franchisors sell virtually every kind of product or service imaginable--some identical to those sold in the United States. However, most franchisors have learned that they must modify their products and services to suit local tastes and customs. Franchising has become a major export industry for the United States. More than 20 percent of the nation's 4,000-plus franchisors have outlets in foreign countries. Although franchise outlets span the globe, Canada is the primary market for U.S. franchisors, with Japan and Europe following.

Another problem global businesses face when selling to some countries is that their currencies are virtually worthless outside their borders, so getting paid in a valuable currency is a real challenge. A countertrade is a transaction in which a company selling goods or services in a foreign country agrees to help promote investment and trade in that country. Bartering, the exchange of goods and services for other goods and services, is another way of trading with countries lacking convertible currency. The goal of the transaction is to help offset the capital drain from the foreign country's purchases.

Small companies increasingly are looking toward exporting as a global business strategy. Small companies account for 97 percent of the companies involved in exporting but only generate one-third of the dollar value of the nation's exports. Approximately 100,000 U.S. companies currently export; however, experts estimate that at least twice as many are capable of exporting but are not doing so. The biggest barrier facing companies that have never exported is not knowing where or how to start.

Establishing an office or a factory in a foreign land can require a substantial investment reaching beyond the budgets of many small companies. Plus, setting up an international office can be an incredibly frustrating experience in some countries. Business infrastructures are in disrepair or are nonexistent. Few small businesses begin their global ventures by establishing international locations, preferring, instead, to build a customer base through some of the strategies already covered. Small companies that do establish international locations can reap significant benefits.

5. Describe the various types of trade intermediaries small business owners can use. What functions do they perform?
   Answer - Trade intermediaries are domestic agencies that serve as distributors in foreign countries for domestic companies of all sizes. They rely on their networks of contacts, their extensive knowledge of local customs and markets, and their experience in international trade to market products effectively and efficiently all across the globe. Trade intermediaries account for about 10 percent of all U.S. exports.

   Export management companies. An important channel of foreign distribution for small companies just getting started in international trade or for those lacking the resources to assign their own people to foreign markets.

   Export trading companies. Export trading companies are businesses that buy and sell products in a number of countries, and they typically offer a wide range of services such as exporting, importing, shipping, storing, distributing, and others to their clients. ETCs usually perform both import and export trades across many countries' borders.

   Manufacturer's export agents. MEAs act as international sales representatives in a limited number of markets for various noncompeting domestic companies. The relationship between an MEA and a small company is a short-term one, and the MEA typically operates on a commission basis.

   Export merchants. export merchants are domestic wholesalers who do business in foreign markets. They buy goods from many domestic manufacturers and then market them in foreign markets. They often carry competing lines, which means they have little loyalty to suppliers.

   Resident buying offices. A government-owned or privately owned operation of one country established in another country for the purpose of buying goods made there.

   Foreign distributors. They handle all of the marketing, distribution, and service functions in the foreign country.

6. What is a domestic joint venture? A foreign joint venture? What advantages does taking on an international partner through a joint venture offer? Disadvantages?
   Answer - Lower the risk of entering global markets for small businesses. They also give small companies more clout in foreign lands. In a domestic joint venture, two or more U.S. small businesses form an alliance for the purpose of exporting their goods and services. For export ventures, participating companies get antitrust immunity, allowing them to cooperate freely. The businesses share the responsibility and the costs of getting export licenses and permits, and they split the venture's profits. In a foreign joint venture, a domestic small business forms an alliance with a company in the target nation. The host partner brings to the joint venture valuable knowledge of the local market and its method of operation as well as of the customs and the tastes of local customers, making it much easier to conduct business in the foreign country. Sometimes foreign countries place certain limitations on joint ventures. Some nations, for example, require host companies to own at least 51 percent of the venture. The most important ingredient in the recipe for a successful joint venture is choosing the right partner. A second key to creating a successful alliance is to establish common objectives. Unfortunately, most joint ventures fail. The average success rate is just 43 percent. The average life of a joint venture is only 3.5 years. Common problems leading to failure

include improper selection of partners, incompatible management style, failure to establish common goals, inability to be flexible, and failure to trust one another.

7. What mistakes are first-time exporters most likely to make? Outline the steps a small company should take to establish a successful export program.
    Answer - The biggest barrier facing companies that have never exported is not knowing where or how to start. Most entrepreneurs in the United States envision markets only within domestic and sometimes even state borders. Breaking the psychological barrier to exporting is the first, and most difficult, step in setting up a successful program.

    Steps an entrepreneur must take to get an export program under way.
    ▪   Recognize that even the tiniest companies and least experienced entrepreneurs have the potential to export.
    ▪   Analyze your product or service.
    ▪   Analyze your commitment.
    ▪   Research markets and pick your target.
    ▪   Develop a distribution strategy.
    ▪   Find your customer.
    ▪   Ship your goods.
    ▪   Collect your money.

    Planned carefully and taken one step at a time, exporting can be a highly profitable route for small businesses. Many small companies are forming foreign sales corporations (FSCs, pronounced "risks") to take advantage of a tax benefit that is designed to stimulate exports.

8. What are the benefits of establishing international locations? Disadvantages?
    Answer - Establishing an office or a factory in a foreign land can require a substantial investment reaching beyond the budgets of many small companies. Plus, setting up an international office can be an incredibly frustrating experience in some countries. Business infrastructures are in disrepair or are nonexistent. Finding the right person to manage an international office is crucial to success; it also is a major challenge, especially for small businesses. Few small businesses begin their global ventures by establishing international locations, preferring, instead, to build a customer base through some of the strategies already covered. Small companies that do establish international locations can reap significant benefits. Start-up costs are lower in some foreign countries, and lower labor costs can produce significant savings as well.

9. Describe the barriers businesses face when trying to conduct business internationally. How can a small business owner overcome these obstacles?
    Answer - Sometimes the biggest barriers potential exporters face are right here at home, domestic barriers. Three major domestic roadblocks are common: attitude, information, and financing. Two types of international barriers are common: tariff and nontariff. Political barriers--entrepreneurs who go global quickly discover a labyrinth of political tangles. The complex web of governmental and legal regulations and barriers they encounter in foreign countries often astounds them. There are also business barriers. Business practices and regulations in foreign lands can be quite different from those in the United States. The biggest shock comes in the area of human resources management, where international managers discover that practices common in the United States, such as overtime, women workers, and employee benefits are restricted, disfavored, or forbidden in other cultures. Finally there are cultural barriers. The culture of a nation includes the beliefs, values, views, and mores that its inhabitants share. The diversity of languages, business philosophies, practices, and traditions make international trade more complex than selling to the business down the street.

10. What is a tariff? A quota? What impact do they have on international trade?
    Answer - A tariff is a tax, or duty, that a government imposes on goods and services imported into that country. Imposing tariffs raises the price of the imported goods--making them less attractive to consumers--and protects the makers of comparable domestic products and services. Quotas. Rather than impose a direct tariff on certain imported products, nations often use quotas to protect their industries. A quota is a limit on the amount of a product imported into a country. It is a type of nontariff barrier.

11. What impact have the GATT and NAFTA trade agreements had on small companies wanting to go global? What provisions are included in these trade agreements?
    Answer - Created in 1947, the General Agreement on Tariffs and Trade (GATT) became the first global tariff agreement. The latest round of GATT negotiations, called the Uruguay Round, was completed in December 1993 and took effect on July 1, 1995. Negotiators reduced the remaining industrial tariffs by 40 percent, established new rules governing dumping goods at unfairly low prices, strengthened the global protection of patents, and cut the level of government subsidies on agricultural products. In addition, negotiators agreed to form a World Trade Organization (WTO) with more power to settle trade disputes among member nations than GATT had.

    The North American Free Trade Agreement (NAFTA) created a free trade area among Canada, Mexico, and the United States. A free trade area is an association of countries that have agreed to knock down trade barriers, both tariff and nontariff, among partner nations. Under the provisions of NAFTA, these barriers were eliminated for trade among the three countries, but each remained free to set its own tariffs on imports from nonmember nations. NAFTA forged a unified United States-Canada-Mexico market of 380 million people with a total annual output of more than $6.5 trillion dollars of goods and services. Before NAFTA took effect on January 1, 1994, the average tariff on U.S. goods entering Mexico was 10 percent. Under NAFTA, these tariffs will be reduced to zero on most goods over the next 10 to 15 years.

12. What advice would you offer an entrepreneur interested in launching a global business effort?
    Answer - To remain competitive, businesses must assume a global posture. Global effectiveness requires managers to be able to leverage workers' skills, company resources, and customer know-how across borders and throughout cultures across the world. Managers also must concentrate on maintaining competitive cost structures and a focus on the core of every business: the customer. Although there are no surefire rules for going global, small businesses wanting to become successful international competitors should observe these guidelines:
    - Make yourself at home in all three of the world's key markets: North America, Europe, and Asia.
    - Appeal to the similarities within the various regions in which you operate but recognize the differences in their specific cultures.
    - Develop new products for the world market.
    - Familiarize yourself with foreign customs and languages.
    - Learn to understand your customers from the perspective of their culture, not your own.
    - "Globalize," make global decisions about products, markets, and management.
    - Train employees to think globally.
    - Hire local managers to staff foreign offices and branches.
    - Do whatever seems best wherever it seems best, even if people at home lose jobs or responsibilities.
    - Consider using partners and joint ventures to break into foreign markets.

Step into the Real World

1. Go to lunch with a student from a foreign country. What products and services are most needed? How does the business system there differ from ours? How much government regulation affects business? What cultural differences exist? What trade barriers has the government erected?

2. Review several current business publications and prepare a brief report on which nations seem to be the most promising for U.S. entrepreneurs. What steps should a small business owner take to break into those markets? Which nations are the least promising? Why?

3. Select a nation that interests you and prepare a report on its business customs and practices. How are they different from those in the United States? How are they similar?

Chapter 13 - Sources of Equity Financing

Always try to rub up against money, for if you rub up against money long enough,
some of it may rub off on you.
Damon Runyon, *Guys and Dolls*

It's like having someone go through your panty drawer.
You have to explain why you wear cotton on Monday and lace on Wednesday.
Lannie Bernhard, describing what it's like to take her company, Nursing Management, public

Teaching Objectives
Students will be able to:
1. Explain what seed capital is and why it is so important to the entrepreneurial process.
2. Explain the differences in the three types of capital small businesses require: fixed, working, and growth.
3. Describe the various sources of equity financing available to entrepreneurs.
4. Explain the various simplified registrations, exemptions from registration, and other alternatives available to small businesses wanting to sell securities to investors.

Instructor's Outline
I. Raising Money
   A. Four "secrets" to successful business financing for 2000 and beyond:
      1. Choosing the right sources of capital for a business can be just as important as choosing the right form of ownership or the right location.
        a) It is a decision that will influence a company for a lifetime, so entrepreneurs must weigh their options carefully before committing to a particular funding source.
      2. The money is out there; the key is knowing where to look.
        a) "The problem is not a lack of funding sources but a lack of knowledge of how to find them," says Bruce Blechman, coauthor of *Guerrilla Financing*.
        b) Entrepreneurs must do their homework before embarking on their search for capital.
      3. Creativity counts.
        a) Entrepreneurs must use as much ingenuity in financing their businesses as they do in generating their product and service ideas.
        b) Entrepreneurs cannot overestimate the importance of making sure the "chemistry" between themselves, their companies, and their funding sources is a good one.
          (1) Too many entrepreneurs get into financial deals because they need the money to keep their businesses growing only to discover that their plans do not match those of their financial partners.
      4. Entrepreneurs have to piece their capital together from multiple sources, a method known as layered financing.

II. The Importance of Seed Capital
   A. Introduction
      1. Becoming a successful entrepreneur requires one to become a skilled fund-raiser, a job that usually requires time and energy.
      2. In start-up companies, raising capital can easily consume as much as half of an entrepreneur's time.
      3. In some cases, the prospective entrepreneur has the creativity and skills required to start and manage an enterprise but lacks the knowledge and the ability to sell himself and his idea to potential lenders and investors.

4. Without adequate financing, a small business never gets off the ground, and the entrepreneur is trapped in a vicious cycle.
   a) Undercapitalization is a contributing factor to many business failures.
   b) Because of the high mortality rate of new small businesses, financial institutions are unwilling to lend to or invest in new ventures.
   c) Lack of start-up capital leaves a small business on a weak financial foundation, vulnerable to the causes of business failure.
5. The money an entrepreneur needs to begin a business is called seed money, adventure capital, or injection capital.
   a) The reward for investing in a successful start-up usually does not come in the form of dividends or interest, the traditional rewards for debt capital.
   b) It comes in the appreciation of the company's value, which can be astounding.
      (1) Ted Waitt started Gateway 2000, drew a very modest salary of $200 a week. Then, in 1993, Gateway 2000 made an initial public offering. Today, Waitt and his brother own Gateway stock worth about $1.4 billion.

III. Types of Capital
   A. Introduction
      1. Most entrepreneurs are seeking less than $1 million.
      2. Most need less than $100,000.
         a) See Figure 13.1.
      3. Where to find this seed money depends, in part, on the nature of the proposed business and on the amount of money required.
      4. It is important to understand the nature of the capital requirement to determine the appropriate sources of capital.

   B. Types of Capital
      1. Capital is any form of wealth used to produce more wealth for the firm.
         a) It exists in many forms in a typical business, including cash, inventory, plant, and equipment.
      2. Fixed capital
         a) Fixed capital is needed to purchase the business's permanent, or fixed, assets, such as buildings, and, computers, and equipment.
         b) Money invested in these fixed assets tends to be frozen because it cannot be used for any other purpose.
         c) Typically, large sums of money are involved in purchasing fixed assets, and credit terms are frequently lengthy.
      3. Working capital
         a) Working capital represents the business's temporary funds; it is the capital used to support the business's normal short-term operation.
         b) Accountants define working capital as current assets minus current liabilities.
         c) The need for working capital is created by the uneven flow of cash into and out of the business due to normal seasonal fluctuations. Just as an individual's income does not exactly match expenditures, a company's revenue does not match its cash outflow.
      4. Growth capital
         a) Growth capital requirements surface when an existing business is expanding or changing its primary direction.
         b) During times of such rapid expansion, a growing company's capital requirements are similar to those of a business start-up.
         c) Like lenders of fixed capital, growth capital lenders expect the funds to improve a company's profitability and cash flow position, thus ensuring repayment.

5.   Table 13.1 lists the various sources of capital for companies in the various stages of the business life cycle and their likelihood of use.

IV. Sources of Equity Financing
   A. Equity Financing Described
      1.   Equity financing is the personal investment of the owner (or owners) in the business and is sometimes called risk capital or equity capital because these investors assume the primary risk of losing their funds if the business fails.
      2.   The primary advantage of equity capital is that it does not have to be repaid as does a loan.
         a)   Equity investors are entitled to share in the company's earnings and usually to have a voice in the company's future direction.
      3.   The primary disadvantage of equity financing is that the entrepreneur is giving up some, perhaps most, of the ownership in the business to others.
         a)   Although 50 percent of something is better than 100 percent of nothing, giving up control of your company can be disconcerting and dangerous.
      4.   Entrepreneurs are most likely to give up more equity in their businesses in the start-up phase than in any other.
      5.   See Figure 13.2.

   B. Personal Savings
      1.   The first place an entrepreneur should look for start-up money is in his own pockets.
      2.   It's the least expensive source of funds available.
      3.   Figure 13.3 shows that the founders of the fastest-growing small companies in the United States tapped their personal savings more often than any other source for their start-up financing.
      4.   As a general rule, an entrepreneur should expect to provide at least half of the start-up funds in the form of equity capital.
         a)   If an entrepreneur is not willing to risk his own money, potential investors are not likely to risk their money in the business either.
      5.   Further, if an owner contributes less than half of the initial capital requirement, he must borrow an excessive amount of capital to fund the business properly, and the high repayment schedule puts intense pressure on cash flows.

   C. Friends and Relatives
      1.   After emptying her own pockets, the entrepreneur should turn to friends and relatives who might be willing to invest in her business venture.
      2.   Often, they are more patient than other outside investors.
      3.   Inherent dangers lurk in family business investments, however.
         a)   Unrealistic expectations or misunderstood risks.
      4.   To avoid such problems, an entrepreneur must honestly present the investment opportunity and the nature of the risks involved.
      5.   And he/she should:
         a)   Keep the arrangement strictly business. The parties should treat all loans and investments in a businesslike manner.
         b)   Settle the details up front. Before any money changes hands, both parties must agree on the details of the deal.
         c)   Create a written contract. Don't make the mistake of closing a financial deal with just a handshake.
         d)   Treat the money as "bridge financing." Consider money from family and friends as a bridge to take your company to the next level of financing.

e)   Develop a payment schedule that suits both the entrepreneur and the lender or investor. Establish a realistic repayment plan that works for both parties without putting excessive strain on the young company's cash flow?

GAINING THE COMPETITIVE EDGE - How to Get the Financing You Need

SUMMARY

Almost every entrepreneur has a start-up financing horror story. But the real reason most entrepreneurs can't get financing for their new business is they're just "not ready for the money." They'd spend it without producing any long-term positive results. The following mistakes will guarantee that your plan is rejected.

- Poor communications. If you won't take the time to prepare a professional, concise business plan that explains your business concept in detail, don't expect to see much interest from outside investors and lenders.
- Insufficient sales and marketing strategies. Investors like to see about 30 percent of a business plan devoted to marketing and selling.
- Ignoring the negatives.
- Overuse of technical jargon. Assume the listener knows nothing about your industry or business and explain it accordingly.
- Overemphasis on the product or service. Initially, spend time selling the entire business concept not just a product or a service to potential lenders and investors.
- No basis for financial projections. Entrepreneurs who cannot explain where they got the numbers.
- Insufficient evidence of a market. Offer evidence of market research, endorsements from prototype users, purchase orders, or other signs of interest from real, live customers.
- Failing to know how much money you need.
- Failing to set yourself and your business apart from the rest.

What can you do to prove you are ready for the financing you're seeking. Satisfy these criteria:
- Your business plan must explain the business and its competitive advantage.
- Your business plan must show you understand the power of the bottom line.
- Your financial projections must be realistic and must make sense.
- You must grab your readers' attention in the executive summary.
- You must have a clear strategy for marketing your product or service and know what it will cost to make or provide.
- You must show exactly how you will use the money to meet your company's goals.
- You must prove that the business concept will work--that customers will buy your good or service.

In short, before starting your search for financing, be sure you're really ready for it!

1.   What mistakes do entrepreneurs searching for financing most often make?
     Answer - Selling the product not its benefits, not knowing their numbers--where they came from or how much they need, and not differentiating themselves/companies from competitors.
2.   What advice would you give an entrepreneur about to begin her search for start-up capital?
     Answer - Follow the pattern offered in the text but avoid friends and relatives. For every success story, there are 100 destroyed relationships. Begin researching sources on the WWW first, and then move to traditional routes. But be sure to check out WWW sources before entering into contracts.

---

6.   A recent study of fast-growing manufacturing and service companies by Coopers and Lybrand discovered that 70 percent of the founders used their own money and that of relatives and friends to launch their companies.

D. Angels
1. Frequently, the next stop on the road to business financing is private investors.
2. Private investors (or angels*) are wealthy individuals, often entrepreneurs themselves, who invest in business start-ups in exchange for equity stakes in the companies.
   a) Angels are a primary source of start-up capital for companies in the embryonic stage through the growth stage, and their role in financing small businesses is significant.
   b) Some experts conservatively estimate that some 250,000 angels invest more than $20 billion a year in 30,000 to 40,000 small companies.
   c) Others contend that private investors may put as much as $30 billion a year into 500,000 small businesses.
   d) The angel market is fragmented and disorganized.
3. Angels fill a significant gap in the seed capital market.
   a) They are most likely to finance start-ups with capital requirements in the $250,000 to $1,000,000 range.
   b) Well below the $3 million minimum investments most professional venture capitalists prefer.
   c) One study of technology firms in New England found that more businesses raised equity capital from private investors than from any other source and that when the financing required was less than $1 million, angels were the primary source of capital.
4. Most private investors have substantial business experience, which they are willing to invest in the businesses where they put their money.
   a) In many cases, an angel's advice can be just as valuable as his money.
   b) Putting an investor on the board of directors or encouraging him to assume the role of informal consultant can make the difference between a moderately successful company and an extremely successful one.
5. The challenge, of course, is finding these angels.
   a) The typical angel is a 47-year-old white male with a college education earning $100,000 a year and having a net worth (excluding a home) of $1 million.
   b) Most have substantial business and financial experience and prefer to invest in companies at the start-up or infant growth stage.
   c) The typical angel accepts 30 percent of the investment opportunities presented; makes an average of two investments every three years; and has invested an average of $131,000 of equity in 3.5 firms.
   d) Ninety percent say they're satisfied with their investment decisions.
6. Locating angels boils down to making the most of networking.
7. Angels almost always invest their money locally, so entrepreneurs should look close to home for them--typically within a 50- to 100-mile radius.
8. Angels also look for businesses they know something about, and most expect to invest their knowledge, experience, and energy as well as their money in a company.
9. Angels tend to invest in clusters as well.
10. Angels are an excellent source of "patient money," often willing to wait seven years or longer to cash out their investments.
    a) They earn their returns through the increased value of the business, not through dividends and interest.
    b) Private investors typically take less than 50 percent ownership, leaving the majority ownership to the entrepreneur.
    c) Venture capitalists, on the other hand, usually own 80 percent of a company by the time it goes public.
    d) Sixty percent of angel investments are in seed capital.
    e) 82 percent involve less than $500,000.

11. If an entrepreneur needs relatively small amounts of money to launch a company, angels are a primary source.

GAINING THE COMPETITIVE EDGE - Angels among Us

Although they are an important source of small business financing, angels can be extremely difficult to locate. How does an entrepreneur needing financing find an angel to help launch or expand a company?
- Start early.
- Have a business plan ready.
- Look close to home.
- Canvas your industry. Angels tend to specialize in particular industries.
- Recognize that in addition to the money they invest angels also want to provide their knowledge and expertise.
- Remember that angels invest for more than lust financial reasons. Angels tend to look at things more spiritually than other investors do often investing in companies for personal reasons.
- Join local philanthropic organizations, chambers of commerce, nonprofit organizations, and advisory boards.
- Ask business professionals such as bankers, lawyers, stockbrokers, accountants, and others for names of potential angels.
- Network, network, network. Finding angel financing initially is a game of contacts.

Networking was the key to finding angel financing for Patrick Laminert and Mark Weber, co-founders of Wisconsin Technology, a color-separation company that serves the printing business.

The Small Business Administration (SBA) is trying to make it easier for angels and entrepreneurs to find one another with its Angel Capital Electronic Network (ACE-Net), a nationwide listing service identifying small, fast-growing companies that angels would be interested in reviewing.

1. What advantages does angel financing offer an entrepreneur?
   Answer - Expertise for building the business, long-term focus on return, more control over the company, etc.
2. What advice would you offer an entrepreneur about locating an angel?
   Answer - The key is networking--via agencies like the SBA, on the Internet, through personal business contacts, through organizations that they are a member of, etc.
3. How would you go about finding an angel to finance a business in your local area?
   Answer - Students' responses will vary. They should refer to the SBA service, the use of the Internet, and personal contacts. Consider finding and bringing an "angel" or two into class. Have the "angel" explain how entrepreneurs find him/her and what they look for in an investment. Contact SCOPE, your local Chamber, or your alumni office. Alumni love to get into the classroom.

---

12. An entrepreneur should avoid potential problems by doing several things.
    a) Investigate the investors and their past deals.
    b) Summarize the details of the deal in a letter of intent. It outlines what the deal will look like and discusses the most sensitive areas being negotiated so that there are no surprises.
    c) Keep the deal simple. It's best to give up straight equity--a percentage of ownership of your business, represented by common stock.
    d) Nail down the angel's exit path. Angels make their money when they sell their ownership interests. Ideally, the exit path should be part of structuring the deal.
    e) Avoid intimidating potential investors.

f)   Always be truthful. Overpromising and underdelivering will kill a deal and spoil future financing arrangements.

g)   Don't take the money and run. Investors appreciate entrepreneurs who keep them informed about how their money is being spent and the results it shows. Prepare periodic reports for them.

h)   Stick to the deal. If you promised to use the funds for specific purposes, do it.

E.   Partners
   1.   An entrepreneur can choose to take on a partner to expand the capital base of the proposed business.
   2.   Before entering into any partnership arrangement, however, the owner must consider the impact of giving up some personal control over operations and of sharing profits with one or more partners.

F.   Corporate Venture Capital
   1.   Large corporations recently have gotten into the business of financing small companies.
   2.   Today, more than 100 large corporations across the globe--from Johnson & Johnson to Genetech--maintain their own venture capital funds to finance projects with small businesses.
   3.   Foreign corporations are also interested in investing in small U.S. businesses.
      a)   Often, these corporations are seeking strategic partnerships to gain access to new technology, new products, or lucrative U.S. markets.
      b)   Companies in the United Kingdom, Germany, Japan, and Malaysia are prime candidates for investments in small U.S. firms.

G.   Venture Capital Companies
   1.   Venture capital companies are private, for-profit organizations that purchase equity positions in young businesses they believe have high growth and profit potential, producing annual returns of 300 to 500 percent over five to seven years.
   2.   Venture capital companies raise money from mutual funds, pension funds, and other institutional investors and buy shares of ownership in promising new businesses.
   3.   They seek to add value to the businesses in which they invest by taking a role in managing them.
   4.   Like all financiers, venture capitalists are interested in reviewing the small firm's financial history, but venture capital companies are more concerned with the future profit potential the business investment offers.
      a)   As a result, they invest funds in return for a share of the ownership and try to develop long-term capital gains.
      b)   Venture capital companies are not charitable organizations; they invest in small companies and hope to make an attractive profit when they sell their equity.
      c)   Table 13.2 offers a humorous look at deciphering the language of venture capitalists.
   5.   Policies and investment strategies. Venture capital firms usually establish stringent policies to implement their overall investment strategies.
      a)   Investment size and screening. Minimum investments range from $10,000 to $3 million.
         (1)   Most firms seek investments in the $1 million to $5 million range to justify the cost of investigating the large number of proposals they receive.
         (2)   The typical venture capital company invests in just one-tenth of 1 percent of the applications it receives.
         (3)   An average venture capital firm screens in excess of 1,000 proposals a year.

(4) 10 percent are investigated more thoroughly at a cost ranging from $2,000 to $3,000 for each proposal.

(5) 10 to 15 proposals are subjected to comprehensive review.

(6) Of the three to five proposals finally remaining, the venture capital firm will invest in one or two.

b) Ownership. Most venture capitalists prefer to purchase ownership in a small business through common stock or convertible preferred stock.

    (1) A typical venture capital company seeks to purchase 30 to 40 percent of the business.

IN THE FOOTSTEPS OF AN ENTREPRENEUR - One Step at a Time

SUMMARY

Phil Garfinkle, Yaacov Ben-Yaacov, and Elliot Jaffe peered into the future and saw the power of blending the Internet and photographic technology. In late 1995, the partners launched PictureVision, a company whose products allow users to share, manipulate, and store photographs on the World Wide Web. After launching PictureVision with their own money, they needed more. Attracting capital from angel investors would be an ideal way to start feeding their company's growth. Within two months, nine angels put up $300,000 in exchange for a 10 percent stake in the company. For the next round of financing, the entrepreneurs knew that PictureVision would need larger amounts of capital. PictureVision raised $9 million in two rounds of equity financing from venture capital companies. They are now planning to attempt an initial public offering IPO. The steps they are taking include:

- Building a stronger, more professional management team.
- Creating benefit plans.
- Enlisting the help of a Big Six accounting firm.
- Building an active board of directors.
- Building bridges to the financial community.

1. Evaluate the step-by-step method these entrepreneurs used to finance their business at each stage of its growth. What are the implications of planning a company's financing in stages?
    Answer - Students' assessments will vary. The implications could be two, they didn't plan far enough ahead so the growth has surprised them. That's not likely. It seems more likely that they are growing the company steadily and in increments so that they can control the growth and simply need additional resources.

2. Evaluate the steps these entrepreneurs are taking to prepare their company for an IPO. Do you predict that they will be successful in their attempted IPO? Explain.
    Answer - They are doing a reasonably thorough job and will probably be successful. They have raised funds three times so far each time, successfully. This will be different however, in that they go from private ownership to stockholders who will tend to have a short-term focus. Plus they are more subject to outside regulation and interference.

---

c) Control. The entrepreneur must sacrifice a portion of the business to the venture capitalist; he usually can maintain a majority interest and control of its operations.

    (1) Most venture capitalists serve as financial and managerial advisers, but some take an active role in managing the company; they recruit employees, provide sales leads, choose attorneys and advertising agencies, and make daily decisions.

    (2) One survey found that 90 percent of venture capitalists eventually either become directly involved in managing or select outside managers for the companies they invest in.

(3) Seventy-five percent of these active venture capitalists say they were forced to step in.
d) Investment Preference. As the industry grows, more venture capital funds are focusing their investments in niches.
6. What venture capitalists look for. Two factors make a deal attractive to venture capitalists: high returns and a convenient (and profitable) exit strategy. Venture capitalists look for:
a) Competent management. The most important ingredient in the success of any business is the ability of the manager or the management team.
b) Competitive edge. Investors are searching for some factor that will enable a small business to set itself apart from its competitors.
c) Growth industry. Profits are not a must for companies seeking venture capital (although they help), but the potential for rapid growth is.
d) Intangible factors. Some other important factors considered in the screening process are not easily measured; they are the intuitive, intangible factors the venture capitalist detects by gut feeling. This feeling might be the result of the small firm's solid sense of direction, its strategic planning process, the chemistry of its management team, or a number of other factors.
7. Table 13.3 presents questions entrepreneurs should answer to determine whether they can qualify for venture capital financing.

H. Public Stock Sale ("Going Public")
1. This is an effective method of raising needed capital, but it can be an expensive and time-consuming process filled with regulatory nightmares.
2. Once a company makes an initial public offering (IPO), nothing will ever be the same again.
a) Managers must consider the impact of their decisions not only on the company and its employees but also on its shareholders and the value of their stock.
3. Few entrepreneurs are able to take their start-up companies public.
a) Only about 20,000 companies in the United States--less than 1 percent--are publicly held, and fewer than 1,000 companies make initial public offerings each year.
b) Few companies with less than $5 million in annual sales manage to go public successfully.
4. Investment bankers who underwrite public stock offerings typically look for:
a) Consistently high growth rates
b) Strong record of earnings
c) Three to five years of audited financial statements
d) A solid position in a rapidly growing market
e) A sound management team and a strong board of directors
5. Figure 13.4 shows the number of U.S. IPOs from 1981 to 1996, along with the amount of capital raised during that time.

6. The advantages of an IPO:
a) Ability to raise large amounts of capital. The biggest benefit of a public offering is the capital infusion the company receives.
b) Improved access for future financing. Going public boosts a company's net worth and broadens its equity base. Its improved financial strength makes it easier for the firm to attract more capital, both debt and equity, and to grow.
c) Improved corporate image. Becoming a public company in some industries improves its prestige and enhances its competitive position, one of the most widely recognized, intangible benefits of going public.

    d) Attracting and retaining key employees. Stock options and bonuses are excellent methods for winning employees' loyalty and for instilling a healthy ownership attitude among them.

    e) Using stock for acquisitions. Acquiring other companies with shares of stock eliminates the need to incur additional debt.

    f) Listing on a stock exchange. Being listed on an organized stock exchange, even a small regional one, improves the marketability of a company's shares and enhances its image.

        (1) Table 13.4 describes the requirements of each of the major markets for listing initial public offerings.

7. The disadvantages of going public include the following:

    a) Dilution of founder's ownership. Most owners retain a majority interest in the business, but they may still run the risk of unfriendly takeovers years later after selling more stock.

    b) Loss of control. If a large block of shares falls into the hands of dissident stockholders, they could vote the existing management team (including the founder) out.

    c) Loss of privacy. Information that was once private must be available for public scrutiny.

    d) Reporting to the SEC. Publicly held companies must file periodic reports with the SEC, which often requires a more powerful accounting system, a larger accounting staff, and greater use of attorneys and other professionals.

    e) Filing expenses. For the typical small company, the cost of a public offering is around 12 percent of the capital raised. On small offerings, costs can eat up as much as 40 percent of the capital raised, whereas on offerings above $20 million, a mere 5 percent will go to cover expenses.

    f) Accountability to shareholders. The law requires that they recognize and abide by a relationship built on trust. Profit and return on investment become the primary concerns for investors.

    g) Loss of focus. As impatient as they can be, entrepreneurs often find the time demands of an initial public offering frustrating and distracting.

    h) Timing. While putting its offering together, a company runs the risk that the market for IPOs or for a particular issue may go sour.

8. The registration process. Taking a company public is a complicated bureaucratic process that usually takes several months to complete.

    a) Choose the underwriter.

        (1) Probably the single most important ingredient in making a successful IPO is selecting a capable underwriter (or investment banker).

        (2) The underwriter's primary role is to sell the company's stock through an underwriting syndicate it develops.

    b) Negotiate a letter of intent.

        (1) The letter of intent spells out what each party will do and also acts as a blueprint or "constitution" for the deal.

        (2) The letter of intent covers a variety of important issues, including the type of underwriting, its size and price range, the underwriter's commission, and any warrants and options included.

        (3) There are two types of underwriting agreements: firm commitment and best efforts.

           (a) In a firm commitment agreement, the underwriter agrees to purchase all of the shares in the offering and then resell them to investors. This agreement guarantees that the company will receive the required funds, and most large underwriters use it.

(b) In a best efforts agreement, the underwriter merely agrees to use its best efforts to sell the company's shares and does not guarantee that the company will receive the needed financing. The managing underwriter acts as an agent, selling as many shares as possible through the syndicate.

(c) Another version of the best efforts agreement is to set a minimum number of shares that must be sold for the issue to be completed.

(4) The company and the underwriter must decide on the size of the offering and the price of the shares.

(a) To keep the stock active in the aftermarket, most underwriters prefer to offer a minimum of 400,000 to 500,000 shares.

(b) Most underwriters recommend selling 25 percent to 40 percent of the company in the IPO.

(c) They also strive to price the issue so that the total value of the offering is at least $8 million to $15 million.

(5) The number of shares offered and prevailing market conditions have a direct impact on the price of the shares. Underwriters typically do not guarantee an offering price and total proceeds amount because the final offering price is not set until shortly before the registration statement becomes effective.

(a) But the underwriter should estimate a range for the stock offering price based on current market conditions.

(6) Most letters of intent include a lock-up agreement that prevents the sale of insider shares--those owned by directors, managers, founders, employees, and other insiders--for 12 to 36 months.

9. Prepare the registration statement.

a) The statement consists of two parts: the prospectus, which is distributed to underwriters and prospective investors as a selling tool, and a section containing information for the SEC.

b) To prepare the statement, the owner must rely on her team of professionals. The statement is extremely comprehensive and may take months to prepare. It includes information on the use of the proceeds, the company's history, its financial position, its capital structure, any risk factors it faces, the managers, and many other details.

c) When the registration statement is completed, the company can ask for a prefiling conference with the SEC to present the statement informally.

10. File with the SEC. When the statement is finished (with the exception of pricing the shares, proceeds, and commissions), the company officially files the statement with the SEC and awaits the review of the division of Corporate Finance.

a) The division sends notice of any deficiencies in the registration statement to the company's attorney in a comment letter (typically set at 20 to 60 days after the initial filing).

b) Very few first-time registrations escape the review process with no SEC comments.

c) Finally, the company files the revised registration statement, along with a pricing amendment (giving the price of the shares, the proceeds, and the commissions).

11. Wait to go effective. While waiting, the underwriters are building a syndicate of other underwriters who will market the company's stock and are approaching investors who might be interested in purchasing shares in the issue.

a) The SEC also limits the publicity and information a company may release during this quiet period.

b) Securities laws do permit a road show, a gathering of potential syndicate members sponsored by the managing underwriter.

(1) Its purpose is to promote interest in the IPO by featuring the company, its management, and the proposed deal.

c) On the last day before the registration statement becomes effective, the company signs the formal underwriting agreement.

d) The final settlement, or closing, takes place within seven business days of the effective date for a firm commitment IPO and within 60 to 120 days after the effective date for a best efforts issue.

WIRED TO THE WEB - Going . . . Going . . . Gone . . . Public?

SUMMARY

Joe Falsetti, founder of ROM Tech, a publisher of multimedia CD-ROM software, knew his company was riding the crest of a wave that was pushing the popularity of CD-ROMs to record levels. Falsetti knew that successfully cracking a market driven by new technology requires large amounts of capital. In his conversations about financing with venture capitalists and private investors, Falsetti noticed a common theme: They all wanted to know about an exit strategy. ROM Tech was profitable with annual sales of $1.2 million, but the investment banker was afraid that ROM Tech was too small to make a successful IPO.

Growth Spiral Kwik Goal, a sports-equipment manufacturer, is constantly experiencing cash shortages because of its tremendous appetite for capital that resulted from the growing popularity of soccer in the United States. Like many fast-growing companies, Kwik Goal's cash demands are simply outstripping its ability to generate cash. Caruso has met with several investment bankers, but because he lacks a strong background in financial management, he does not feel comfortable selling the benefits of his company to strangers who happen to be financial experts.

Go or No Go? Best Programs Inc., a company that develops accounting and human resources software, is flush with cash but is in an industry full of competitors. To establish a stronger position in the industry, managers at Best Programs see the need to buy out some existing companies whose product lines complement their own. To make these acquisitions, however, requires big money. Best Programs has decided to file for a $2.5 million IPO. The company has more than $20 million in annual revenues, attractive pretax profit margins of 14 percent, and an annual growth rate of 30 percent. Because of its impressive record of success, Best has been able to interest two regional underwriters in making its public offering. In their letter of intent, the underwriters have recommended selling 2.1 million shares at $9 to $11 per share.

1. Which of these companies do you think has the greatest chance of making a successful public offering? Why?
   Answer - Probably Go or No Go. It is large enough to be interesting to investors. The money is being raised to expand the company. It shows a strong growth rate. Kwik Goal might go but he will need some significant help on the financials and he needs to allay fears that his company is in too small of a market to be worthwhile.

2. Would you advise any of these companies not to make a public offering? Explain.
   Answer - ROM Tech is clearly too small, the owner will become an employee, and he's not raising enough money to attract investors, nor is there long-term growth potential. It seems growth is on a tech fad. Kwik Goal probably shouldn't go public. They aren't showing sufficient growth. Their cash needs might be address through better collections and inventory control. And, their CEO doesn't have a clear understanding of the IPO, just that he needs money.

3. Use the material in this chapter and the resources of the World Wide Web to draft a memo to each of these entrepreneurs, offering them advice about taking their companies public and about any other options they might have.
   Answer - Students' memos will vary.

12. Figure 13.6 shows a typical timetable for a public offering.
13. Meet state requirements. In addition to satisfying the SEC's requirements, the company also must meet the securities laws in all states in which the issue is sold.
    a) These state laws (or "blue-sky" laws) vary drastically from one state to another.

V. Simplified Registrations and Exemptions
    A. Introduction
        1. The IPO process described above requires maximum disclosure in the initial filing and discourages most small businesses from using it because of its cost and complexity.
        2. Fortunately, the SEC allows several exemptions from this full-disclosure process for small businesses.

    B. Simplified Registration: Regulation S-B
        1. In August 1992, the SEC approved Regulation S-B, which created a simplified registration process for small companies seeking to make initial or subsequent public offerings.
            a) Its primary goal is to open the doors to capital markets to smaller companies by cutting the paperwork and the costs of raising capital.
        2. Companies using the simplified registration process have two options:
            a) Form SB-1, a "transitional" registration statement for companies issuing less than $10 million worth of securities over a 12-month period.
            b) Form SB-2 reserved for small companies seeking more than $10 million in a 12-month period.
        3. To be eligible, a company must:
            a) Be based in the United States or Canada.
            b) Have revenues of less than $25 million.
            c) Have outstanding securities of less than $25 million.
            d) Not be an investment company.
        4. Regulation S-B's simplified registration requirements are intended to enable small companies to go public without incurring the expense of a full-blown registration.

    C. Exemptions
        1. Small businesses can choose from four exemptions from the tedious and expensive registration process: Regulation D (Rule 504); private placements (Regulation D, Rules 505 and 506 and Section 4(6)); intrastate offerings (Rule 147); and Regulation A.
        2. Regulation D (Rule 504): the Small Company Offering Registration (SCOR).
            a) Also known as the Uniform Limited Offering Registration (ULOR) now is available in 46 states.
            b) A little-known tool, the whole process typically costs less than half of what a traditional public offering costs and is possible for companies seeking as little as $200,000.
            c) Entrepreneurs using SCOR will need an attorney and an accountant to help them with the issue, but many can get by without a securities lawyer.
            d) The SEC's objective in creating SCOR was to give small companies the same access to equity financing that large companies have through the stock market without burdening them with the same costs and filing requirements.
            e) The capital ceiling on a SCOR issue is $1 million, and the price of each share must be at least $5.
                (1) That means that a company can sell no more than 200,000 shares (making the stock relatively unattractive to stock manipulators).

f) The company must file a standardized disclosure statement, the U-7, which consists of 50 fill-in-the-blank questions.

g) Entrepreneurs using SCOR may advertise their companies' offerings and can sell them to any investor with no restrictions and no minimums.

h) An entrepreneur can sell practically any kind of security through a SCOR.

3. A SCOR offering offers entrepreneurs needing equity financing several advantages:

a) Access to a huge pool of equity funds without the expense of full registration with the SEC.

b) Few restrictions on the securities to be sold and on the investors to whom they can be sold.

c) The ability to market the offering through advertisements.

d) The ability of new or start-up companies to qualify.

e) No requirement of audited financial statements for offerings of less than $500,000.

f) Faster approval of the issue from regulatory agencies.

g) The ability to make the offering in several states at once.

4. There are, of course some disadvantages to using SCOR to raise needed funds:

a) Not every state recognizes SCOR offerings. (Four states, Alabama, Delaware, Hawaii, and Nebraska, have not yet authorized SCOR offerings.)

b) Partnerships cannot make SCOR offerings.

c) A company can raise no more than $1 million in a 12-month period.

d) Every state in which the offering is to be made must approve it.

e) The process can be time-consuming, distracting the entrepreneur from the daily routine of running the company.

f) A limited secondary market for the securities may limit investors' interest. Currently, SCOR shares must be traded through brokerage firms that make small markets in specific stocks.

5. Regulation D (Rules 505 and 506): Private Placements

a) Rules 505 and 506 are exemptions that give emerging companies the opportunity to sell stock through "private placements" without actually "going public."

b) In a private placement, the company sells its shares directly to private investors without having to register them with the SEC.

c) A Rule 505 offering has a higher capital ceiling ($5 million) than a SCOR offering but imposes more restrictions (no more than 35 "nonaccredited" investors, limits on advertising, and others).

d) Its disclosure requirements also are more stringent, requiring a company to publish information on the company, its operating history, its financial performance, its managers and directors, and the nature of the offering itself.

e) Rule 506 imposes no ceiling on the amount that can be raised, but it does limit the issue to 35 "nonaccredited" investors.

f) There is no limit on the number of accredited investors, however. Rule 506 also requires detailed disclosure of information, but the extent depends on the dollar size of the offering.

g) Private deals typically are in the $8 million to $25 million range, with investors usually buying between 10 percent and 30 percent of a company's stock.

6. These Regulation D rules minimize the expense and the time required to raise equity capital for small businesses. They do impose limitations and demand some disclosure, but they require a company to file only a simple form (Form D) with the SEC within 15 days of the first sale of stock.

7. Section 4(6): Private placements

a) Section 4(6) covers private placements and is similar to Regulation D, Rule 505 and Rule 506.

      b) Like Regulation D Rule 505, its ceiling is $5 million. Unlike Rules 505 and 506, however, Section 4(6) does not place a limit on the number of investors.

      c) A company does not have to register with the SEC on those offerings made only to accredited investors.

  8. Rule 147: Intrastate offerings

      a) Rule 147 governs intrastate offerings: those sold only to investors in a single state by a company doing business in that state.

      b) To qualify, a company must be incorporated in the state, maintain its executive offices there, have 80 percent of its assets there, derive 80 percent of its revenues from the state, and use 80 percent of the offering proceeds for business in the state.

      c) There is no ceiling on the amount of the offering.

  9. Regulation A

      a) Currently not used often, allows an exemption for offerings up to $5 million over a 12-month period.

      b) It imposes few restrictions, but it is more costly than the other types of exempted offerings, usually running between $80,000 and $120,000.

      c) The primary difference between a SCOR offering and a Regulation A offering is that a company must register its SCOR offering only in the states where it will sell its stock; in a Regulation A offering, the company also must file those documents with the SEC.

      d) Like a SCOR offering, a Regulation A offering allows a company to sell its shares directly to investors.

  10. Table 13.5 provides a summary of the major types of simplified registrations and exemptions.

      a) Limited offerings and private placements are most commonly used.

D. Alternatives to the IPO Process

  1. Direct public offerings (DPOs)

      a) Selling shares of their company's stock directly to investors in a direct public offering (DPO) is becoming an increasingly popular financing strategy for entrepreneurs.

      b) A recent study found that 31 percent of all of the companies seeking to raise money through initial public offerings used DPOs, going straight to Main Street instead of going through underwriters.

      c) Entrepreneurs willing to handle the paperwork requirements and to market their own shares can make DPOs for about 6 percent of the total amount of the issue, compared with 13 percent for a traditional underwritten stock offering.

  2. Direct public offerings do have a downside.

      a) The time, energy, and attention needed.

      b) Attracting investors can be challenging.

      c) Because many companies making DPOs are too small to have their shares listed on any stock exchange, they must make arrangements for shareholders to trade their shares.

      d) Also, after making a DPO, a company must keep its investors informed about the company's progress and financial status. For most DPO companies with small offerings, mailing copies of the company's annual report is sufficient.

  3. Table 13.6 provides a 10-question quiz to help entrepreneurs determine whether their company would be a good candidate for a DPO.

  4. Direct stock offerings on the World Wide Web (WWW)

      a) The World Wide Web (WWW) is one the fastest-growing sources of capital for small businesses.

b) Much of the Web's appeal as a fund-raising tool stems from its ability to reach large numbers of prospective investors very quickly and at a low cost.

c) Experts caution Web-based fund-seekers to make sure their electronic prospectuses meet SEC and state requirements.

d) Figure 13.7 shows the number of U.S. DPOs from 1989 to 1997.

IN THE FOOTSTEPS OF AN ENTREPRENEUR - I'll Do It Myself

SUMMARY

After 10 years in business, Michael Quinn wanted to transform Hahnemann Laboratories, a manufacturer of homeopathic all natural medicines, into a national company. Quinn was searching for about $500,000, and investment bankers simply weren't interested. So Quinn decided to make his own direct public offering using Regulation A. Quinn began soliciting his customers by posting ads for the offer in the pharmacy he ran, packed announcements into every mail-order shipment, and told every customer with whom he spoke. Quinn realized that he would have to reach beyond his customer base for potential investors. He swapped mailing lists with a homeopathic bookseller and a homeopathic software company and mailed announcements about the offer to their customers. He also took out ads in homeopathic newsletters and magazines. Only about 15 percent of the investors sent their money in after receiving the prospectus; Quinn had to call the rest. In all, he estimates that he talked with between 700 and 800 potential investors by phone. Costs for the offer totaled $103,000. He ended up with $364,000.

1. What benefits did Quinn realize by choosing to make a direct public offering of his company's stock? What costs (monetary and otherwise) did he incur?
   Answer - Students will review the text content. More importantly, the way Quinn went about this taught him a lot about his business and his customers. He also developed an extensive network within his industry that he didn't have before.

2. What other options besides Regulation A were available to Quinn to raise the capital he needed? Review the features, advantages, and disadvantages of each option you listed. Do you think Quinn made the right choice? Explain.
   Answer - Refer to Table 13.5, pages 444-445.

---

5. Foreign stock markets
   a) Sometimes, foreign stock markets offer entrepreneurs access to equity funds more readily than U.S. markets.

6. United Kingdom offerings have several advantages:
   a) Smaller offerings are very common, are readily accepted by investors, and can be completed relatively quickly.
   b) The costs of U.K. offerings are lower than those in the United States. Underwriting fees there are usually 2 percent of the offering.
   c) U.K. offering prices may be higher than those in the United States because underwriters there use forecasted results, not historical ones, to set prices.
   d) U.K. offerings require less disclosure of information.
   e) Ongoing reporting requirements are less stringent in the United Kingdom.

7. Closer to home, Canada's Vancouver Stock Exchange <http://www.vse.com/> is becoming a popular source of equity capital for U.S. entrepreneurs.
   a) It also encourages listings of small companies, and the costs of offerings are lower than those in the United States.

Chapter Summary

- ◆ Explain what seed capital is and why it is so important to the entrepreneurial process.
  - ▪ The money an entrepreneur needs to begin a business is called seed money, adventure capital, or injection capital. It truly is risk capital because entrepreneurs and investors in new businesses must be prepared for the possibility of losing *everything* in exchange for the chance to earn significant rewards.
  - ▪ Becoming a successful entrepreneur requires one to become a skilled fund-raiser, a job that usually requires more time and energy than most business founders think.
  - ▪ Without the ability to raise capital, many entrepreneurs never get their businesses off the ground.
- ◆ Explain the differences in the three types of capital small businesses require: fixed, working, and growth.
  - ▪ Capital is any form of wealth employed to produce more wealth.
  - ▪ Fixed capital is used to purchase a company's permanent, or fixed, assets; working capital represents the business's temporary funds and is used to support the business's normal short-term operations; growth capital requirements surface when an existing business is expanding or changing its primary direction.
- ◆ Describe the various sources of equity financing available to entrepreneurs.
  - ▪ The most common source of financing a business is the owner's personal savings. After emptying their own pockets, the next place entrepreneurs turn for capital is family members and friends. Angels are private investors who not only invest their money in small companies but also offer valuable advice and counsel to them. Some business owners have success financing their companies by taking on limited partners as investors or by forming an alliance with a corporation, often a customer or a supplier. Venture capital companies are for-profit, professional investors looking for fast-growing companies in hot industries. When screening prospects, venture capital firms look for competent management, a competitive edge, a growth industry, and important intangibles that will make a business successful.
  - ▪ Some owners choose to attract capital by taking their companies public, which requires registering the public offering with the SEC. Going public involves choosing the underwriter, negotiating a letter of intent, preparing the registration statement, filing with the SEC, and meeting state requirements.
  - ▪ Going public offers the advantages of raising large amounts of capital, improved access to future financing, improved corporate image, and gaining a listing on a stock exchange. The disadvantages include dilution of the founder's ownership, loss of privacy, reporting to the SEC, filing expenses, and accountability to shareholders.
- ◆ Explain the various simplified registrations, exemptions from registration, and other alternatives available to small businesses wanting to sell securities to investors.
  - ▪ Rather than go through the complete registration process, some companies use one of the simplified registration options and exemptions available to small companies: Regulation S-B, Regulation D (Rule 504, Small Company Offering Registration (SCOR); Rule 505; and Rule 506), Section 4(6), Rule 147, and Regulation A.
  - ▪ Rather than make a public offering using investment bankers, some entrepreneurs sell shares of stock in their companies directly to investors in a direct public offering. The World Wide Web, with its ability to reach larger numbers of potential investors quickly and at low cost, is making direct public offerings feasible for more entrepreneurs.
  - ▪ Many foreign stock markets have relaxed requirements for small companies making public stock offerings and offer lower registration and filing expenses than those in the United States.

Discussion Questions

1. Why is it so difficult for most small business owners to raise the capital needed to start operate, or expand their ventures?
    Answer - Some entrepreneurs lack the knowledge and the ability to "sell" themselves and their ideas to potential lenders and investors. Also, there seems to be a "vicious cycle." Undercapitalization is a major cause of the high small business failure rate, and because of this failure rate, small firms have difficulty obtaining funds from financial institutions.

2. What is capital? List and describe three types of capital a small business needs for its operations.
    Answer - Capital is any form of wealth a business employs to create more wealth. There are three types of capital. Fixed capital--used to purchase the permanent ("fixed") assets of the business. Working capital--the temporary funds of the business needed to deal with the uneven flow of cash into and out of the business. Growth capital--needed when an existing business is expanding or is changing its primary direction.

3. Define equity financing. What advantage does it offer over debt financing?
    Answer - Equity financing represents the personal investment of the owner (or owners) in the business; it is called "risk capital." The primary advantage of equity capital is that it does not have to be repaid; instead, investors are guaranteed a voice in operating the business and a share of its profits (if there are any).

4. What is the most common source of equity funds in a typical small business? If an owner lacks sufficient equity capital to invest in the firm, what options are available for raising it?
    Answer - The most common source of equity funds in a typical small business is the entrepreneur's personal savings. Few entrepreneurs are able to launch their ventures on their personal assets alone, however. Other sources of equity capital include: a) wealthy friends or relatives, b) "angels"--individuals in search of tax shelters, c) partners, d) public stock offerings, e) venture capital companies.

5. What guidelines should an entrepreneur follow if friends and relatives choose to invest in his/her business?
    Answer - To avoid problems be sure to: a) consider the impact of the investment on everyone involved, b) keep the arrangement strictly business, and c) settle the details up front.

6. What is an "angel"? Put together a brief profile of the typical private investor. Do most angels take an active role in the businesses in which they invest?
    Answer - Angels are private investors who are a primary source of start-up capital. Some estimate that angels put over $15 billion into 30,000 to 40,000 small companies every year. Angels typically invest in start-ups with capital needs of $250,000 to $500,000. Profile: a) 47-year-old white male earning $100,000 a year, b) college educated, c) net worth of $1 million, d) typically accepts 30% of the company, e) averages 2 investments a year,   f) has equity in 3.5 firms with an average investment of $131,000. They take an active role only if they have to.

7. What advice would you offer an entrepreneur about to strike a deal with a private investor to avoid problems?
    Answer - Avoid problems with angels by: a) investigating the investors and their past deals, b) summarizing the details of the deal in a letter of intent, c) keeping the deal simple, d) nailing down the angel's exit path, e) avoid intimidating potential investors, f) always being truthful, g) not taking the money and run, h) sticking to the deal.

8. What types of businesses are most likely to attract venture capital? What investment criteria do venture capitalists use when screening potential businesses? How do these compare with the typical angel's criteria?

    Answer - Venture capital companies are private, for-profit organizations that purchase equity positions in young businesses they believe have high growth and profit potential, producing annual returns of 300 to 500 percent over five to seven years. Venture capital firms usually establish stringent policies to implement their overall investment strategies.

    ◆   Minimum investments range from $10,000 to $3 million. Most firms seek investments in the $1 million to $5 million range to justify the cost of investigating the large number of proposals they receive.

    ◆   Most venture capitalists prefer to purchase ownership in a small business through common stock or convertible preferred stock. A typical venture capital company seeks to purchase 30 to 40 percent of the business.

    ◆   The entrepreneur must sacrifice a portion of the business to the venture capitalist; he usually can maintain a majority interest and control of its operations.

    What venture capitalists look for. Two factors make a deal attractive to venture capitalists: high returns and a convenient (and profitable) exit strategy. Venture capitalists look for:

    ◆   Competent management. The most important ingredient in the success of any business is the ability of the manager or the management team.

    ◆   Competitive edge. Investors are searching for some factor that will enable a small business to set itself apart from its competitors.

    ◆   Growth industry. Profits are not a must for companies seeking venture capital (although they help), but the potential for rapid growth is.

    ◆   Intangible factors. Some other important factors considered in the screening process are not easily measured; they are the intuitive, intangible factors the venture capitalist detects by gut feeling. This feeling might be the result of the small firm's solid sense of direction, its strategic planning process, the chemistry of its management team, or a number of other factors.

    Refer to question #6 for comparison to angels.

9. How do venture capital firms operate? Describe their procedure for screening investment proposals.

    Answer - Venture capital firms usually establish stringent policies to implement their overall investment strategies. Minimum investments range from $10,000 to $3 million.

    ■   Most firms seek investments in the $1 million to $5 million range to justify the cost of investigating the large number of proposals they receive.

    ■   The typical venture capital company invests in just one-tenth of 1 percent of the applications it receives.

    ■   An average venture capital firm screens in excess of 1,000 proposals a year.

    ■   10 percent are investigated more thoroughly at a cost ranging from $2,000 to $3,000 for each proposal.

    ■   10 to 15 proposals are subjected to comprehensive review.

    ■   Of the three to five proposals finally remaining, the venture capital firm will invest in one or two.

    Most venture capitalists prefer to purchase ownership in a small business through common stock or convertible preferred stock. The entrepreneur must sacrifice a portion of the business to the venture capitalist; he usually can maintain a majority interest and control of its operations. Most venture capitalists serve as financial and managerial advisers, but some take an active role in managing the company; they recruit employees, provide sales leads, choose attorneys and advertising agencies, and make daily decisions. As the industry grows, more venture capital funds are focusing their investments in niches.

10. What characteristics make a company an attractive candidate to investment bankers for an initial public offering?
   Answer - Two factors make a deal attractive to venture capitalists: high returns and a convenient (and profitable) exit strategy. Venture capitalists look for:
   - Competent management. The most important ingredient in the success of any business is the ability of the manager or the management team.
   - Competitive edge. Investors are searching for some factor that will enable a small business to set itself apart from its competitors.
   - Growth industry. Profits are not a must for companies seeking venture capital (although they help), but the potential for rapid growth is.
   - Intangible factors. Some other important factors considered in the screening process are not easily measured; they are the intuitive, intangible factors the venture capitalist detects by gut feeling. This feeling might be the result of the small firm's solid sense of direction, its strategic planning process, the chemistry of its management team, or a number of other factors.

   Table 13.3 presents questions entrepreneurs should answer to determine whether they can qualify for venture capital financing.

11. Briefly explain the advantages and disadvantages to a company of making a public stock offering.
   Answer - The advantages of an IPO.
   - Ability to raise large amounts of capital.
   - Improved access for future financing.
   - Improved corporate image.
   - Attracting and retaining key employees.
   - Using stock for acquisitions.
   - Listing on a stock exchange.

   The disadvantages of going public include the following:
   - Dilution of founder's ownership.
   - Loss of control.
   - Loss of privacy.
   - Reporting to the SEC.
   - Filing expenses.
   - Accountability to shareholders.
   - Loss of focus.
   - Timing. While putting its offering together, a company runs the risk that the market for IPOs or for a particular issue may go sour.

12. Outline the registration process entrepreneurs must go through to take their companies public.
   Answer - Refer to Figure 13.6 on pages 439-440.

13. Summarize the simplified registrations and exemptions small businesses can use to raise funds through public and private markets. What is the goal of these simplified registrations and exemptions?
   Answer - Refer to Table 13.5, pages 444-445.

14. What benefits do foreign stock exchanges offer entrepreneurs in search of capital?
   Answer - Sometimes, foreign stock markets offer entrepreneurs access to equity funds more readily than U.S. markets. United Kingdom offerings have several advantages:
   - Smaller offerings are very common, are readily accepted by investors, and can be completed relatively quickly.
   - The costs of U.K. offerings are lower than those in the United States. Underwriting fees there are usually 2 percent of the offering.
   - U.K. offering prices may be higher than those in the United States because underwriters there use forecasted results, not historical ones, to set prices.

- U.K. offerings require less disclosure of information.
- Ongoing reporting requirements are less stringent in the United Kingdom.

Closer to home, Canada's Vancouver Stock Exchange is becoming a popular source of equity capital for U.S. entrepreneurs. It also encourages listings of small companies, and the costs of offerings are lower than those in the United States.

Step into the Real World

1. Interview several local business owners about how they financed their businesses. Where did their initial capital come from? How much money did they need to launch their business? Where did their subsequent capital come from? What advice do they offer others seeking capital?
2. Contact a local private investor and ask him or her to address your class. (You may have to search to locate one.) What kinds of businesses does this angel prefer to invest in? What screening criteria does he or she use? How are the deals typically structured?
3. Contact a local venture capitalist, and ask him or her to address your class. What kinds of businesses does his or her company invest in? What screening criteria does the company use? How are deals typically structured?
4. Invite an investment banker or a financing expert from a local accounting firm to address your class about the process of taking a company public. What does the firm look for in a potential IPO candidate? What is the process, and how long does it usually take?

Chapter 14 - Sources of Debt Financing

It used to be that you'd get a good loan officer, establish a relationship, and then he'd disappear.
Nowadays you get a good bank, establish a relationship, and the bank disappears.
Jeffrey McKeever, MicroAge Inc.

Don't ever borrow a little bit of money because when you borrow a little bit of money, you have a serious
creditor if you run short. And, if you borrow a lot of money,
you have a partner when you get into trouble.
Fred Smith, founder, Federal Express

Teaching Objectives

Students will be able to:
1. Describe the vital role that banks play in providing small business financing and the types of business loans banks make.
2. Explain the types of financing available from nonbank sources of credit.
3. Identify the sources of government financial assistance and the loan programs these agencies offer.
4. Explain the various loan programs the Small Business Administration offers.
5. Discuss state and local development programs.
6. Discuss valuable methods of financing growth and expansion internally with bootstrap financing.
7. Describe how to avoid becoming a victim of a loan scam.

Instructor's Outline

I. Debt Financing
    A. Described
        1. Debt financing involves the funds that the small business owner has borrowed and must repay with interest.
        2. Very few entrepreneurs have adequate personal savings to finance the complete start-up costs of a small business.
        3. Nine instances in which small business owners should consider borrowing money:
            a) Increasing the company's workforce or inventory to boost sales
            b) Gaining market share
            c) Purchasing new equipment
            d) Refinancing existing debt
            e) Taking advantage of cash discounts
            f) Buying the building in which the business is located
            g) Establishing a relationship with a lender
            h) Retiring debt held by a "nonrelationship" creditor
            i) Foreseeing a downturn in business
        4. Lenders of capital are more numerous than investors, although small business loans can be just as difficult (if not more difficult) to obtain.
        5. Although entrepreneurs who use borrowed capital can maintain complete ownership of their businesses, they must carry it as a liability on the balance sheet as well as repay it with interest at some point in the future.
        6. Small businesses are considered to be greater risks than bigger corporate customers; they must pay higher interest rates because of the risk-return trade-off.
            a) The cost of debt financing often is lower than that of equity financing.
            b) Also, unlike equity financing, debt financing does not require entrepreneurs to dilute their ownership interest in their companies.

7. Entrepreneurs seeking debt capital are quickly confronted with an astounding range of credit options.

II. Commercial Banks
    A. Introduction
        1. Commercial banks are the very heart of the financial market, providing the greatest number and variety of loans to small businesses.
        2. Business owners consider banks to be lenders of first resort.
            a) See Figure 14.1.
            b) A recent study by the Federal Reserve concluded that commercial banks provide almost half the financing available to small businesses.
            c) The same study found that 80 percent of all loans to existing small businesses come from banks.
        3. Banks tend to be conservative in their lending practices and prefer to make loans to established small businesses rather than to high-risk start-ups.
            a) Only 5 to 8 percent of business start-ups get bank financing.
            b) Bankers want to see evidence of a company's successful track record.
            c) They are concerned with a firm's operating past.
            d) They are also want proof of the stability of the firm's sales and about the ability of the product or service to generate adequate cash flows to ensure repayment.
            e) Small banks (those with less than $300 million in assets) are most likely to lend money to small businesses.
        4. Banks also focus on a company's capacity to create positive cash flow because they know that's where the money to repay their loans will come from.
            a) That's why bankers stress cash flow when analyzing a loan request, especially for a business start-up.

    B. Short-Term Loans
        1. Banks primarily are lenders of short-term capital to small businesses.
            a) Short-term loans extend for less than one year.
            b) These funds typically are used to replenish the working capital account to finance the purchase of more inventory, boost output, finance credit sales to customers, or take advantage of cash discounts.
        2. Commercial Loans or ("Traditional Bank Loans")
            a) The basic short-term loan is the commercial bank's specialty.
            b) It is usually repaid as a lump sum within three to six months and is unsecured because secured loans are much more expensive to administer and maintain.
            c) The bank grants a loan to the small business owner without requiring him to pledge any specific collateral.
            d) The owner is expected to repay the total amount of the loan at maturity.
            e) Until a small business is able to prove its financial strength to the bank's satisfaction, it will probably not qualify for this kind of commercial loan.
            f) If the commercial loan exceeds a particular amount, usually about $100,000, the bank may require the entrepreneur to maintain a compensating balance in a bank account as a form of security for the loan.
                (1) The size of this reserve varies from bank to bank, but it often is 10 percent of the total amount approved plus 10 percent of the credit actually used.
        3. Lines of Credit
            a) One of the most common requests entrepreneurs make of banks is for a line of credit, a short-term loan that provides much-needed cash flow for day-to-day operations.

b) With an approved line of credit, a small company can borrow up to a predetermined amount at any time during the year quickly and conveniently by writing itself a loan.

c) Banks usually limit the open line of credit to 40 to 50 percent of the firm's present working capital, although they will lend more for highly seasonal businesses.

(1) It is usually extended for one year (or more) and is secured by collateral.

d) A business typically pays a small handling fee (1 to 2 percent) plus interest on the amount borrowed.

4. Two types of lines of credit are available: seasonal and sustained growth.

a) Seasonal lines of credit are more common and are used to finance a company's seasonal cash needs such as financing inventory or accounts receivable.

(1) Banks allow borrowers to draw on seasonal lines as needed; however, once a year they require business owners to pay them down to zero for a short time.

(2) This standard repayment protects the bank against default by forcing the firm to prove its creditworthiness.

b) Sustained growth lines of credit are designed to finance rapidly growing companies' cash flow needs over a longer time period.

(1) Because they cover a longer time horizon and are designed to finance growth, sustained growth lines usually do not call for a 30-day annual cleanup.

c) Table 14.1 asks seven questions every entrepreneur should be able to answer before approaching a banker.

5. Floor Planning.

a) Floor planning is a form of financing frequently used by retailers of big-ticket items that are easily distinguishable from one another (usually by serial number), such as automobiles, boats, and major appliances.

b) The longer a floor-planned item sits in inventory, the more it costs the business owner in interest expense.

C. Intermediate- and Long-Term Loans

1. Extend for one year or longer and are normally used to increase fixed- and growth-capital balances.

2. Commercial banks grant these loans for starting a business, constructing a plant, purchasing real estate and equipment, and other long-term investments.

3. Loan repayments are normally made monthly or quarterly.

4. Four categories of intermediate and long-term loans exist: unsecured term loans, installment loans, discounted installment contracts, and character loans.

5. Unsecured term loans.

a) Unsecured term loans are granted primarily to businesses whose past operating experience indicates a high probability of repayment.

b) If an entrepreneur is successful in obtaining a term loan to begin a business, the bank will likely require him to provide roughly half of the start-up cost.

6. Installment loans

a) These loans are made to small firms for purchasing equipment, facilities, real estate, and other fixed assets.

b) In financing equipment, a bank usually lends the small business from 60 to 80 percent of the equipment's value in return for a security interest in the equipment.

c) The loan's amortization schedule typically coincides with the length of the equipment's usable life.

7. Discounted installment contracts

a) Banks will also extend loans to small businesses when the owner pledges installment contracts as collateral.

b) The process operates in the same manner as discounting accounts receivable.

8. Character loans
    a) Banking regulatory changes made by the Clinton administration and intended to create jobs by increasing the credit available to small and medium-sized companies now allow banks to make character loans.
    b) Rather than requiring entrepreneurs to prove their creditworthiness with financial statements, evaluations, appraisals, and tax returns, banks making character loans base their lending decisions on the borrower's reputation and reliability (i.e., "character").
    c) Approximately 80 percent of the nation's 12,000-plus banks are certified to make character loans.
    d) To qualify, a loan must be less than $900,000 and cannot exceed 3 percent of the bank's total capital.

GAINING THE COMPETITIVE EDGE - Maintaining a Positive Relationship with Your Banker

Too often, entrepreneurs communicate with their bankers only when they find themselves in a tight spot needing money. How can business owners develop and maintain a positive relationship with their bankers? The first step is picking the right bank and the right banker. After finding the right banker, an entrepreneur must focus on maintaining effective communication. What else can business owners do to manage their banking relationships?

- Invite the banker to visit your company.
- Send customer mailings to the banker as well.
- Send the banker samples of new products.
- Show off your employees.
- Know your company's assets.
- Be prepared to personally guarantee any loans the bank makes to your business.
- Keep your business plan up-to-date and make sure your banker gets a copy of it.
- Address safety and environmental concerns.
- Consider alternative ways of showing the banker why your company needs money.

1. What advantages do entrepreneurs gain by communicating openly with their bankers?
   Answer - It builds trust, they gain the banker's expertise and suggestions for handling any problems, and they give the banker a vested interest in seeing the business succeed.
2. Why do so few entrepreneurs follow Tim Chen's example when dealing with their bankers?
   Answer - Traditionally business and banking have been adversarial. Most business people say, "The bank will only lend you money when you don't need it." Plus entrepreneurs can be a bit defensive about their companies, seeing the need for capital as a weakness on their part.
3. What might be some consequences of an entrepreneur's failing to communicate effectively with a banker?
   Answer - A loss of trust. The banker acting negatively--calling the note due, foreclosing, etc., just as the entrepreneur is turning the situation around, denying future capital, etc.

III. Nonbank Sources of Debt Financing
   A. Asset-Based Lenders
      1. Asset-based lenders, which are usually small commercial banks, commercial finance companies, or specialty lenders, allow small businesses to borrow money by pledging idle assets as collateral.
      2. Even unprofitable companies whose financial statements could not convince loan officers to make traditional loans can get asset-based loans.

3. The amount a small business can borrow through asset-based lending depends on the advance rate, the percentage of an asset's value that a lender will lend.
4. The most common types of asset-based financing are discounting accounts receivable and inventory financing.
5. Discounting accounts receivable
    a) The most common form of secured credit
    b) A small business pledges its accounts receivable as collateral; in return, the commercial bank advances the owner a loan against the value of approved accounts receivable.
    c) A small business usually can borrow an amount equal to 55 to 80 percent of its receivables, depending on their quality.
        (1) In general, banks hesitate to finance receivables that are past due, and no bank will accept accounts that are as much as 90 days past due.
        (2) Many commercial finance companies also engage in accounts receivable financing.
    d) As the firm receives payment from customers on its accounts receivable, it transfers them to the bank.
    e) The bank subtracts an agreed-upon percentage of the proceeds, applies it to the loan balance, and then deposits the remainder in the firm's account.
    f) If an unusual number of accounts are uncollectible, the firm must make up the deficit to satisfy the loan.
6. Inventory financing
    a) The small business loan is secured by the firm's inventory--raw materials, work in process, and finished goods.
    b) Because inventory is not a highly liquid asset in most cases, banks are willing to lend only a portion of its worth--usually no more than 50 percent of the inventory's value.
7. Asset-based financing is a powerful tool.
    a) A small business that could obtain a $1 million line of credit with a bank would be able to borrow as much as $3 million by using accounts receivable as collateral.
    b) It is also an efficient method of borrowing because a small business owner has the money he needs when he needs it.
8. Sometimes, entrepreneurs have no other choice but asset-based borrowing because their young, fast-growing companies cannot qualify for loans from traditional lenders.
9. Asset-based loans are more expensive than traditional bank loans because of the cost of originating and maintaining them and the higher risk involved.
    a) Rates usually run from 2 to 7 percentage points above the prime rate.
    b) The cost of an asset-based loan can be twice that of a typical bank loan.

B. Trade Credit
    1. Because of its ready availability, trade credit is an extremely important source of financing to most entrepreneurs.
    2. Getting vendors to extend credit in the form of delayed payments (e.g., "net 30" credit terms) usually is much easier for small businesses than obtaining bank financing.
    3. It is no surprise that businesses receive three dollars of credit from suppliers for every two dollars they receive from banks as loans.
    4. Vendors and suppliers usually are willing to finance a small business owner's purchase of goods from 30 to 90 or more days, interest free.

C. Equipment Suppliers
    1. Most equipment vendors encourage business owners to purchase their equipment by offering to finance the purchase.

2. This method of financing is similar to trade credit, but with slightly different terms.
3. Usually, equipment vendors offer reasonable credit terms: only a modest down payment with the balance financed over the life of the equipment (usually several years).

D. Commercial Finance Companies
1. Finance companies are second only to banks in making loans to small businesses, and they often specialize in lending to companies in particular industries.
2. Some 135 large commercial finance companies specialize in small business loans ranging from $50,000 to $2 million.
3. Commercial finance companies are usually willing to tolerate more risk than conservative counterparts.
4. They are interested in the quality of the assets the company can pledge as collateral.
5. At their core, commercial finance companies are fundamentally asset-based lenders.
6. Their most common methods of providing credit to small businesses are accounts receivable financing and inventory loans, and they operate exactly as commercial banks do.
7. In addition to such short-term financing, finance companies also extend intermediate- and long-term loans for real estate and fixed assets.
8. Commercial finance companies usually offer many of the same credit options as commercial banks do.
    a) However, because their loans are subject to more risks, finance companies charge a higher interest rate than commercial banks (usually at least prime plus 4 percent).
9. Before taking on higher cost debt from a finance company, an entrepreneur should consider these three questions:
    a) Can my company qualify for a bank loan instead?
    b) Can my company afford the extra cost of this source of financing?
    c) Am I willing to allow lenders to audit my financial statements, and can my company afford to pay for those audits?
10. With proper planning and stringent management, business owners can afford the higher finance charge without putting undue pressure on the financial health of their businesses.

E. Savings and Loan Associations
1. Savings and loan (S&L) associations specialize in loans for real property.
2. In addition to their traditional role of providing mortgages for personal residences, savings and loan associations offer financing on commercial and industrial property.
3. In the typical commercial or industrial loan, the S&L will lend up to 80 percent of the property's value, with a repayment schedule of up to 30 years.
4. Minimum loan amounts are typically $50,000.
5. Savings and loan associations expect the mortgage to be repaid from the firm's profits.

F. Stock Brokerage Houses
1. Stockbrokers are getting into the lending business, too, and many of them offer loans to their customers at lower interest rates than banks.
2. These "margin loans" carry lower rates because the collateral supporting them, the stocks and bonds in the customer's portfolio, is of high quality and is highly liquid.
3. Usually, brokers set up a line of credit for their customers when they open a brokerage account.
4. To tap that line of credit, the customer simply writes a check or uses a debit card.
5. Aspiring entrepreneurs can borrow up to 70 to 80 percent of the value of their portfolios.
6. Brokers typically lend a maximum of 50 percent of the value of stocks and bonds in a portfolio, 70 percent for corporate bonds, and 85 to 90 percent for government securities.

7. There is risk involved in using stocks and bonds as collateral on a loan.
    a) Brokers typically require a 30 percent cushion on the loan.
    b) If the value of the borrower's portfolio drops, the broker can make a margin call; that is, the broker can call the loan in and require the borrower to provide more cash and securities as collateral.
    c) Such a margin call could require an entrepreneur to repay a significant portion of the loan within a matter of days--or hours.
    d) Although there is no limit on the loan term, the interest rate changes from month to month.

G. Insurance Companies
    1. Insurance companies offer two basic types of loans: policy loans and mortgage loans.
    2. Policy loans are extended on the basis of the amount of money paid through premiums into the insurance policy.
        a) It usually takes about two years for an insurance policy to accumulate enough cash surrender value to justify a loan against it.
        b) Once cash value is accumulated in the policy, the entrepreneur may borrow up to 95 percent of the value for any length of time.
        c) Interest is levied annually, but repayment may be deferred indefinitely.
        d) Policy loans typically offer very favorable interest rates, often around 8 percent or less.
        e) Term life insurance, which offers only pure insurance coverage, has no borrowing capacity.
    3. Insurance companies make mortgage loans on a long-term basis on real property worth a minimum of $500,000.
        a) They are based primarily on the value of the real property being purchased.
        b) The insurance company will extend a loan of up to 75 or 80 percent of the real estate's value and will allow a lengthy repayment schedule over 25 or 30 years so that payments do not strain the firm's cash flows excessively.
    4. Insurance companies also make intermediate-term loans in addition to the long-term loans in which they specialize.

H. Credit Unions
    1. Credit unions, nonprofit financial institutions that are owned by their members, are best known for making consumer and car loans.
    2. Many are now willing to lend money to their members to launch businesses, especially since many banks shy away from loans to high-risk start-ups.
        a) Approximately 1,000 are actively making member business loans, those of more than $25,000 granted without personal collateral for the purpose of starting a business.
        b) Most credit union officials believe that business lending makes up a significant part of their loan portfolios, but the majority of loans are personal loans to entrepreneurs who use the proceeds to launch companies.
    3. With credit union membership totaling 71.4 million people and total deposited savings of $295 billion, these financial institutions have plenty of lending power.
    4. To qualify for a loan, an entrepreneur must be a member.
    5. Lending practices at credit unions are very much like those at banks, but credit unions usually are willing to make smaller loans.

I. Bonds
    1. Bonds, which are corporate IOUs, have always been a popular source of debt financing for large companies.

2. Few small business owners realize that they too can tap this valuable source of capital.
3. Many companies raising money through bond issues use zero coupon bonds (or junk bonds) because of their attractiveness to both the investor and the issuing company.
    a) Investors earn a high yield for the duration of the bond.
    b) The issuing company gets the capital it needed but does not have to make periodic interest payments as it would if it had issued regular bonds.
    c) Instead, it sells the bond at a discount from its par value and then repays the investor the full par value at maturity.
    d) The difference between the bond's discounted price and the par value represents the missing interest.
4. Junk bond disadvantages
    a) Unless a company makes its issue under the Securities and Exchange Commission's Rule 144A exemption, it must follow the same regulations that govern businesses selling stock to public investors follow and register the offering with the SEC.
    b) Also, because of the large cash payments they require at maturity, junk bonds can create problems for companies whose actual performances fall behind their financial projections.
    c) Given the costs involved in issuing bonds, selling zero coupon bonds may not be practical for companies with small capital requirements.
5. Industrial revenue bonds (IRBs).
    a) A company must get authorization from the appropriate municipality and the state.
    b) Typically, the amount of money small companies issuing IRBs seek to raise is at least $1 million, but some small manufacturers have raised as little as $500,000.
    c) Costs associated with making an IRB issue can run up to 2 or 3 percent.
6. To open IRBs up to even smaller companies, some states pool the industrial bonds of several small companies too small to make an issue.
7. The issuing companies typically pay lower interest rates than they would on conventional bank loans, often below the prime interest rate.

J. Private Placements
1. Private placements are also available for debt instruments.
2. A private placement involves selling debt to one or a few investors, usually insurance companies or pension funds.
3. Private placement debt is a hybrid between a conventional loan and a bond. At its heart, it is a bond, but its terms are tailored to the borrower's individual needs, as a loan would be.
4. Privately placed securities offer several advantages over standard bank loans.
    a) First, they usually carry fixed interest rates.
    b) Second, the maturity of private placements is longer than most bank loans: 15 years, rather than five.
    c) Private placements do not require complex filings with the SEC.
    d) Finally, because private investors can afford to take greater risks than banks, they are willing to finance deals for small companies.

K. Small Business Investment Companies
1. The small business investment company program was started after Russia's successful launch of the first space satellite, Sputnik, in 1958. Its goal was to accelerate the United States' position in the space race by funding high-technology start-ups.
2. Their function is to use a combination of private capital and federally guaranteed debt to provide long-term capital to small businesses.
3. There are two types of SBICs: regular SBICs and specialized SBICs (SSBICs).

a) Approximately 88 SSBICs provide credit and capital to small businesses that are at least 51 percent owned by minorities and socially or economically disadvantaged people.

b) Since their inception in 1969, SSBICs have helped finance more than 19,000 minority-owned companies, with investments totaling $1.86 billion.

c) Some 194 SBICs are in operation across the United States, and they have invested more than $13 billion in nearly 80,000 small businesses since 1960.

4. Most SBICs prefer later round financing (mezzanine financing) and leveraged buyouts (LBOs) over funding raw start-ups. SBICs invest twice as much in start-up companies as do private venture capitalists.

5. Both SBICs and SSBICs must be capitalized privately with a minimum of $5 million, at which point they qualify for up to four dollars in low-rate, long-term SBA loans for every dollar of private capital invested in small businesses.

6. As a general rule, both SBICs and SSBICs may provide financial assistance only to small businesses with a net worth of under $18 million and average after-tax earnings of $6 million during the past two years.

7. SBICs are limited to a maximum investment or loan amount of 20 percent of their private capital to a single client, and SSBICs may lend or invest up to 30 percent of their private capital in a single small business.

8. SBICs operate as government-backed venture capitalists, providing long-term loans, equity capital, and management assistance to both start-up and existing businesses.

9. By combining their own private capital with government funds, SBICs can provide the equivalent of venture capital to low-tech or no-tech companies that private venture capitalists would never consider.

a) SBICs also accept deals that venture capital companies consider too small.

b) The average SBIC investment is around $583,200.

L. Small Business Lending Companies

1. Small business lending companies (SBLCs) make only intermediate- and long-term SBA-guaranteed loans.

2. They specialize in loans that many banks would not consider and operate on a nationwide basis.

3. Most SBLC loans have terms extending for at least 10 years.

4. The maximum interest rate for loans of seven years or longer is 2.75 percent above the prime rate; for shorter-term loans, the ceiling is 2.25 percent above prime.

IV. Federally Sponsored Programs

A. Economic Development Administration

1. This is a branch of the Commerce Department.

2. It offers loan guarantees to create new businesses and to expand existing businesses in areas with below-average income and high unemployment.

3. Focusing on economically distressed communities, the EDA finances long-term investment projects needed to diversify local economies and to create jobs through loan guarantees.

4. The EDA guarantee reduces the lender's risk. It guarantees the loan balance (up to the ceiling) if the entrepreneur defaults on the loan.

a) The EDA guarantees up to 80 percent of business loans between $750,000 and $10 million.

b) Start-up businesses must contribute at least 25 percent of the guaranteed amount in the form of equity.

        c)   Existing businesses must make equity investments of at least 15 percent of the guaranteed amount.
- 5.   To qualify for an EDA loan, the business must be located in a disadvantaged area, and its presence must directly benefit local residents.
  - a)   Applicants must prove that their business will create at least one job for every $20,000 in EDA loan guarantees.

B. Department of Housing and Urban Development
1. HUD sponsors several loan programs to help qualified entrepreneurs raise needed capital.
2. The Urban Development Action Grants (UDAGs) are extended to cities and towns that, in turn, lend or grant money to entrepreneurs to start small businesses that will strengthen the local economy.
3. Grants are aimed at cities and towns that HUD considers economically distressed. Urban Development Action Grant loan and grant terms are negotiated individually between the town and the entrepreneur.

C. Farmer's Home Administration
1. The U.S. Department of Agriculture provides financial assistance to certain small businesses through the Farmer's Home Administration (FmHA).
2. The FmHA loan program is open to all types of businesses and is designed to create nonfarm employment opportunities in rural areas: those with populations below 50,000 and not adjacent to a city where densities exceed 100 persons per square mile.
3. The FmHA does not make direct loans to small businesses, but it will guarantee as much as 90 percent of a bank's loan up to $10 million (although actual guarantee amounts are almost always far less) for qualified applicants.
   - a)   The FmHA requires much of the same documentation as most banks and most other loan guarantee programs.
   - b)   The FmHA requires an environmental impact statement describing the jobs created and the effect the business has on the area.

D. Rural Economic and Community Development Agency
1. The Rural Economic and Community and Development (RECD) Agency guarantees up to 80 percent of loans up to $10 million to businesses that will stimulate economic growth in economically depressed areas.
2. The RECD also provides grants (with no dollar ceiling) to finance emerging and growing companies with less than $1 million in annual revenues and no more than 50 employees that are located in economically challenged areas.

E. Local Development Companies
1. The federal government encourages local residents to organize and fund local development companies (LDCs) on either a profit or nonprofit basis.
2. After raising initial capital by selling stock to at least 25 residents, the company seeks loans from banks and from the SBA.
3. Each LDC can qualify for up to $1 million a year in loans and guarantees from the SBA to assist in starting small businesses in the community.
4. Most LDCs are certified to operate locally or regionally, but each state may have one LDC that can operate anywhere within its boundaries.
5. Three parties are involved in providing the typical LDC loan: the LDC, the SBA, and a participating bank.

a) An LDC normally requires the small business owner to assist by supplying about 10 percent of a project's cost and then arranges for the remaining capital through SBA guarantees and bank loans.
b) Local development companies finance only the fixed assets of a small business.
c) Funds can be used to acquire land or buildings or to modernize, renovate, or restore existing facilities and sites.
d) Funds cannot be used as working capital.
e) The lessee's payments extend for 20 to 25 years to allow repayment of SBA, bank, and LDC loans.

F. The Small Business Innovation Research Program
1. Started as a pilot program by the National Science Foundation in the 1970s, the Small Business Innovation Research (SBIR) program has expanded to 10 federal agencies and has an annual budget in excess of $100 million.
2. These agencies award cash grants or long-term contracts to small companies wanting to initiate or to expand their research and development (R&D) efforts.
3. The goal is to encourage advanced research and development in science and engineering.
4. The SBIR program operates in three phases.
a) In Phase I, small companies can receive up to $75,000 to perform basic research that establishes the technical merit and feasibility of ideas that have commercial potential. Businesses have six months to complete Phase I research.
b) Companies that complete Phase I successfully may qualify for up to $300,000 in Phase II to continue their research, with the goal of developing it into a commercial product or service. Businesses have up to two years to complete Phase II research.
c) In Phase III, companies no longer qualify for federal funds; by this stage, they should be far enough along in the development of their products and services that they can attract private financing.
5. About one out of four small businesses receiving SBIR awards has achieved commercial success for its products.
6. Several states also have developed their own versions of the federal SBIR program.

G. The Small Business Technology Transfer Act of 1992
1. The Small Business Technology Transfer (STTR) program complements the existing Small Business Innovation Research (SBIR) program.
2. STIR uses companies to exploit a vast new reservoir of commercially promising ideas that originate in universities, federally funded R&D centers, and nonprofit research institutions.
3. Five federal agencies award grants of up to $500,000 in three phases to these research partnerships.

V. Small Business Administration
A. Described
1. In its 40-plus years of operation, the SBA has helped some 14 million companies get the financing they need for start-up or for growth.
2. To be eligible for SBA funds, a business must meet the SBA's criteria for a small business.
3. The loan application process can take from three days to many months, depending on how well prepared the entrepreneur is and which bank is involved.
4. To speed up processing times, the SBA has established a Certified Lender Program (CLP) and a Preferred Lender Program (PLP).
a) Both are designed to encourage banks to become frequent SBA lenders.

b) Certified lenders account for nearly a third of all SBA business loan guarantees. When a bank becomes a preferred lender, it makes the final lending decision itself, subject to SBA review.

c) The SBA guarantees up to 75 percent of PLP loans in case the borrower fails and defaults on the loan.

d) The minimum PLP loan guarantee is $100,000, and the maximum is $500,000.

5. The SBA recently instituted the LowDoc (for "low documentation") Loan Program, which allows small businesses to use a simple one-page application for loans up to $50,000.

a) Loans between $50,000 and $100,000 require the one-page application plus personal tax returns for three years and a personal financial statement from the entrepreneur.

6. To qualify for a LowDoc loan, a company must have average sales below $5 million during the previous three years and employ fewer than 100 people.

a) The LowDoc program focuses on applicants' character and credit history to identify qualified borrowers.

b) Businesses can use LowDoc loans for working capital, machinery, equipment, and real estate.

c) Since its inception, the LowDoc program has made nearly 30,000 loan guarantees totaling more than $1.5 billion.

d) The average loan amount is about $55,500, and account for about half of all SBA loan activity.

7. The FASTRAK Program, in which participating banks use their own loan procedures and applications to make loans of up to $100,000 to small businesses without the SBA's re-viewing the loan applications

a) Because the SBA guarantees up to 50 percent of the loan, banks are often willing to make small loans to entrepreneurs who might otherwise have difficulty meeting lenders' standards.

b) Eighteen SBA lenders across the United States, including many large banks, are authorized to make FASTRAK loans.

B. SBA Loan Programs

1. The SBA offers three basic types of loans in administering its programs: direct, immediate participation, and guaranteed.

2. The SBA makes direct loans directly to the small business with public funds and no bank participation.

a) In general, a direct loan cannot exceed $150,000.

b) The interest rate charged on direct loans depends on the cost of money to the government, and it changes as general interest rates fluctuate.

3. Immediate participation loans are made from a pool of public and private funds.

a) The SBA provides a portion of the total loan, and a private lender supplies the remaining portion.

b) The SBA's general policy is to fund no more than 75 percent.

c) The SBA's portion of an immediate participation loan may not exceed $150,000.

4. Guaranteed 7(a) Loans

a) By far, the most popular type of SBA loan

b) Guaranteed loans are extended to small businesses by a private lender (usually a commercial bank) but are guaranteed by the SBA (80 percent of loans up to $100,000 and 75 percent of loans above $100,001 and up to $750,000, the loan guarantee ceiling).

c) Figure 14.4 illustrates the path an entrepreneur's loan application takes from the local bank to the SBA guarantee program.

5. Qualifying for an SBA loan guarantee requires cooperation among the entrepreneur, the participating bank, and the SBA.

6. The participating bank determines the loan's terms and sets the interest rate within SBA limits.

7. The median loan through the guarantee program is $175,000, and the average duration of an SBA loan is 12 years--longer than the average commercial small business loan.

   a) These longer terms translate into lower payments, which are better suited for young, fast-growing, cash-strapped companies.

8. The CAPline program

   a) In addition to its basic 7(a) loan guarantee program, the SBA provides guarantees to small businesses for start-up, real estate, machinery and equipment, fixtures, working capital, exporting, and restructuring debt through several other methods.

   b) About two-thirds of the SBA's loan guarantees are for machinery and equipment or working capital.

   c) The CAPline program offers short-term capital to growing companies needing to finance seasonal buildings in inventory or accounts receivable under five separate programs:

      (1) seasonal line of credit (provides advances against inventory and accounts receivable to help businesses weather seasonal sales fluctuations).

      (2) contract line of credit (finances the direct labor and materials costs associated with performing contracts).

      (3) builder's line of credit (helps small general contractors or builders finance direct-labor and materials costs).

      (4) standard as-set-based line of credit (an asset-based revolving line of credit that provides financing for cyclical growth and recurring and/or short-term needs).

      (5) small asset-based line of credit (an asset-based revolving line of credit of up to $200,000).

   d) CAPline is aimed at helping cash-hungry small businesses by giving them a credit line to draw on when they need the money.

9. Loans involving Iinternational trade.

   a) For small businesses going global, the SBA has the Export Working Capital Program (EWCP).

   b) Under this program, the SBA will guarantee 90 percent of a bank credit line up to $750,000.

   c) The EWCP is a combined effort of the SBA and the Export-Import Bank.

   d) The International Trade Program is for small businesses that are engaged in international trade or adversely affected by competition from imports.

   e) It offers loans for facilities or equipment, with maturities of up to 25 years.

10. Section 504 Certified Development Company (CDC) Program.

   a) Designed to encourage small businesses to expand their facilities and to create jobs.

   b) Section 504 deals provide long-term, fixed-asset financing to small companies to purchase land, buildings, or equipment.

   c) Three lenders play a role in every 504 loan: a bank, the SBA, and a certified development company (CDC).

      (1) A CDC is a nonprofit organization designed to promote economic growth in a community.

   d) The entrepreneur generally is required to make a down payment of 10 percent of the total project cost.

   e) The CDC puts up 40 percent at a long-term fixed rate, supported by an SBA loan guarantee in case the entrepreneur defaults.

    f)   The bank provides long-term financing for the remaining 50 percent, also supported by an SBA guarantee.

    g)   SBA restrictions on 504 loans:

        (1) For every $35,000 the CDC loans, the project must create at least one new job.

        (2) Machinery and equipment financed must have a useful life of at least 10 years.

        (3) The borrower must occupy at least two-thirds of a building constructed with the loan.

        (4) The borrower must occupy at least half of a building purchased or remodeled with the loan.

        (5) The borrower must qualify as a small business under the SBA's definition, must not have a tangible net worth in excess of $6 million, and must not have had an average net income in excess of $2 million after taxes for the preceding two years.

    h)   Because of strict equity requirements, existing small businesses usually find it easier to qualify for 504 loans than do start-ups.

11. Microloans

    a)   About three-fourths of all entrepreneurs needed less than $100,000 to launch their businesses.

    b)   Indeed, research suggests that most entrepreneurs require less than $50,000 to start their companies.

    c)   In SBA's microloan program, loans range from just a few hundred dollars too as much as $25,000.

    d)   In 1992, the SBA began funding microloan programs at 96 private, nonprofit lenders in 44 states in an attempt to fill the void in small loans to start-up companies.

    e)   Today, more than 500 lenders provide microloans in 49 states.

    f)   The average microloan is for $9,916 over four years (the maximum term is six years), and interest rates are no more than prime plus 4 percent.

    g)   Lenders' standards on microloans are less demanding.

        (1) More than 39 percent of microloans go to minority entrepreneurs, and nearly 42 percent go to women.

12. Minority and women's prequalified loan program

    a)   The program is designed to help minority and women entrepreneurs prepare loan applications and "prequalify" for SBA loan guarantees before approaching banks and lending institutions for loans.

    b)   To be eligible for the program, a business must be at least 51 percent owned, operated, and managed by women or minorities; its annual sales cannot exceed $5 million; and it must employ 100 or fewer workers.

    c)   The maximum loan amount is $250,000 (of which the SBA will guarantee up to 80 percent), and the money can be used for everything from supplementing working capital and purchasing equipment or machinery to buying inventory and real estate.

    d)   Loan terms range from seven to 25 years, depending on the purpose of the loan.

    e)   Since its beginning, the program has guaranteed nearly 700 loans, totaling more than $71.6 million.

13. The 8(a) Program

    a)   This program is designed to help minority-owned businesses get a fair share of federal government contracts.

    b)   The SBA directs about $4 million each year to small businesses with "socially and economically disadvantaged" owners.

    c)   Government agencies cooperate with the SBA in its 8(a) program because the law requires them to set aside a portion of their work for minority-owned firms.

SMALL BUSINESS ACROSS THE GLOBE - Big Results from Small Loans

Microloans are producing phenomenal results all around the globe. From less-developed countries such as Bangladesh and Malawi to industrialized giants such as the United States, microloans--loans as small as $25--are giving global entrepreneurship a tremendous boost. ACCION International, the Trickle Up program, and other organizations have been making microloans to entrepreneurs in developing nations for years in an effort to boost local economies and to create jobs. Rather than merely offering people a handout, these organizations are providing people with a "hand up." Using his own money, Yunus started the Grameen Bank in the early 1970s, lending amounts of $25 or less to peasant women to buy sewing machines or to farmers to buy a tool. Traditional development "experts" dismissed Yunus's idea as an exercise in failure, predicting that the bank would fold when the borrowers could not repay their loans. They were wrong. Today, the Grameen Bank is one of the largest and most successful in Bangladesh, providing more than $6 million each month in microloans to people in 18,000 villages.

In Monterey, Mexico, Aaron Aguilar, an unemployed factory worker, and his wife wanted to start a business making and selling decorative figurines. ACCION International, a nonprofit international development group, loaned the Aguilars the $100 start-up capital they needed to buy clay and glazes to make the figurines. Over the next six years, the Aguilars took out and repaid five loans and built their business to the point where it now employs 18 full-time workers.

In tiny Black Mountain, North Carolina, the Mountain Microenterprise Fund offers loans ranging from $500 to $8,000 to entrepreneurs who cannot qualify for traditional bank loans and other sources of capital. So far, the fund has financed a variety of innovative businesses, including a maker of miniature clay flower jewelry and a door-to-door recycling service. The Mountain Microenterprise Fund has 22 "lending circles" groups of entrepreneurs who band together to learn more about running small businesses successfully.

1. What types of entrepreneurs are most likely to benefit from microloan programs?
   Answer - Those needing small amounts of capital to simply get their businesses started.
2. Would a microloan program be useful as a tool for economic development in your area? Explain. What advantages and disadvantages do you see in setting up such programs?
   Answer - Students' answers will vary based on where they are from. But even those students from affluent areas should be able to see individuals and opportunities that would benefit.
3. Working with a team of your classmates, use the resources of the World Wide Web and your local library to research microloans. On the basis of your research, develop a plan for launching a microloan program in your area.
   Answer - Responses will depend on research efforts.

---

14. Disaster Loans
    a) Disaster loans are made to small businesses devastated by some kind of financial or physical loss.
    b) The maximum disaster loan usually is $500,000, but Congress often raises that ceiling when circumstances warrant.
    c) Disaster loans carry below-market interest rates.
    d) Loans for physical damage above $10,000 and financial damage of more than $5,000 require the entrepreneur to pledge some kind of collateral, usually a lien on the business property.
       (1) Economic Injury Disaster Loans offer companies affected by disasters working capital until they can reopen for business.

(2) Business Physical Disaster Loans are earmarked for repairing and replacing damaged business property.

15. Other SBA Loan Programs
    a) The Small Business Administration also offers several other loan programs for specialized purposes.
    b) For an overview: http://www.sbaonline.sba.gov/financing/indexloans.html>

VI. State and Local Development Programs
  A. Described
    1. State-sponsored loan and development programs are becoming more active in providing funds for business start-ups and expansions.
    2. Many states have decided that their funds are better spent encouraging small business growth rather than "chasing smokestacks" (trying to entice large businesses to locate in their boundaries).
    3. These programs come in a wide variety of forms, but they all tend to focus on developing small businesses that create jobs and economic benefits.
    4. Although each state's approach to economic development is somewhat special, one common element is some kind of small business financing program: loans, loan guarantees, development grants, venture capital pools, and others.
    5. Even cities and small towns have joined in the effort to develop small businesses and help them grow.

VII. Internal Methods of Financing
  A. Factoring Accounts Receivable
    1. Instead of carrying credit sales on its own books (some of which may never be collected), a small business can sell outright its accounts receivable to a factor.
      a) A factor buys a company's accounts receivable but pays for them in two parts.
      b) The first payment, which the factor makes immediately, usually is for 75 to 80 percent of the accounts' agreed-upon value.
      c) The factor makes the second payment, which makes up the balance less the factor's service fee, when the original customer pays the invoice.
      d) Factoring is more expensive than bank and commercial finance company loans.
    2. Begun by American colonists to finance their cotton trade with England, factoring has become an important source of capital for many small businesses.
      a) Under deals arranged with recourse, the small business owner retains the responsibility for customers who fail to pay their accounts.
      b) Under deals arranged without recourse, however, the owner is relieved of the responsibility for collecting them.
        (1) Because the factoring company assumes the risk of collecting the accounts, it normally screens the firm's credit customers, accepts those judged to be creditworthy, and pays the small business owner the value of the accounts receivable.
    3. Factors will pay anywhere from 60 to 95 percent of the face value of a company's accounts receivable, depending on the small company's:
      a) Customers' financial strength and credit ratings
      b) Industry and its customers' industries
      c) Financial strength, especially in deals arranged with recourse
      d) Credit policies
    4. Factoring is ideally suited for fast-growing companies, especially start-ups that cannot qualify for bank loans.

5. A small business should have an adequate volume of accounts receivable before turning to this source of funds.
   a) Most factors prefer to work with companies billing at least $8,000 to $10,000 a month.
   b) Entrepreneurs should use factoring as a short-term financial strategy as they make the transition to more traditional financing.

B. Leasing
   1. Leasing is another common bootstrap financing technique.
   2. By leasing expensive assets, small business owners are able to use them without locking up valuable capital for an extended period of time.
   3. Also, because no down payment is required and because the cost of the asset is spread over a longer time (lowering monthly payments), the firm's cash flow improves.

C. Credit Cards
   1. Unable to find financing elsewhere, some entrepreneurs have launched their companies using the most convenient source of debt capital available: credit cards.
   2. A recent study of entrepreneurs by Arthur Andersen and National Small Business United found that one-third of those with fewer than 20 employees said they use credit cards as a source of financing, up from 17.3 percent in 1993.
   3. Putting business start-up costs on credit cards, which can charge 21 percent or more in annual interest, is expensive and risky, but some entrepreneurs have no other choice.
      a) In the past, women entrepreneurs had difficulty convincing traditional lenders to grant them loans and were forced to rely on credit cards more often than men.

WIRED TO THE WEB - Paving the Way for Financing

Jerry Turner and Michael Clarke met while working for a road-paving company that was constantly experiencing cash flow problems and failing to meet its payroll. That's when they decided to start their own paving company. They began drumming up business in Santa Ana, California, and every time they got a job, the pair would rent all of the equipment they needed to complete it. As they entered their second year of business, the partners knew that they had to buy their own equipment--and soon. Unfortunately, road-paving equipment is not cheap. Turner and Clarke set their sights on purchasing a used dump truck first. They found one in good shape for just under $20,000 at a local heavy-equipment dealership that advertised an attractive financing program. Unfortunately, the vendor would not approve a loan on the truck.

1. Use the information in this chapter and the resources of the World Wide Web to help Turner and Clarke identify potential sources of financing for their business.
   Answer - Responses depend on research efforts.
2. Develop a plan for attracting the $150,000 they need to purchase the equipment for Emerald Asphalt and Concrete. What can they do to make their loan proposal attractive to potential lenders?
   Answer - See #1.
3. Is Turner and Clarke's dilemma common to owners of small start-up companies? Explain.
   Answer - Yes. They have the double bind, they need money to grow, but because they are a "young" company and growing, no one will lend them money. In start-up, since you have to produce the product or provide the service before you get paid, you are always "behind" until you generate enough profit to build up cash reserves.

4. A study by the National Foundation of Women Business Owners (NFWBO) concluded that women entrepreneurs today are almost as likely to have bank loans or lines of credit as are male entrepreneurs.
   a) During that time period, the proportion of women entrepreneurs using credit cards as a source of capital dropped from 52 percent to 23 percent (see Figure 14.5).

D. Other Creative Solutions
   1. Some business owners needing cash to finance growth have found a simple solution: print their own.
   2. This not-so-funny money is legal.
      a) Frank Tortoriello, owner of The Deli, a Massachusetts delicatessen, printed his own currency called "Deli Dollars." He sold $10 worth of Deli Dollars to his customers for $9. They could use the money six months after they bought it to buy anything in the store.
      b) Tortoriello's Deli Dollars were just six-month loans from his customers.
   3. They worked so well that other local merchants began to print their own currencies. Some merged their currencies so that their customers could spend their dollars at various locations around town.

VIII. Where Not to Seek Funds
   A. Cons and Schemes
      1. The swindle usually begins when the con artist scours an area for "DEs" (Desperate Entrepreneurs) in search of quick cash injections to keep their businesses going.
      2. Usually, the small business scheme follows one of two patterns (although variations exist).
      3. Under one scheme, the small business owner is guaranteed a loan for whatever amount he needs from a nonexistent bank with false credentials.
         a) The con artist tells the owner that loan processing will take time and that, in the meantime, he must pay a percentage of the loan amount as an "advance fee."
         b) Of course, the loan never materializes, and the small business owner loses his deposit.
      4. Another common scam begins with a con artist who claims to be a representative of the Small Business Administration.
         a) He promises the cash-hungry small business owner an SBA loan if he pays a small processing fee. Again, the loan never appears, and the small business owner loses his deposit.
      5. Unfortunately, scams by con artists who prey on unsuspecting business owners in need of capital are more common than ever.
         a) The World Wide Web has made crooks' jobs easier.
      6. The best protection against such scams is common sense and remembering that if it sounds too good to be true, it probably is. Experts offer the following advice to business owners:
         a) Be suspicious of anyone who approaches you--unsolicited--with an offer for "guaranteed financing."
         b) Watch out for red flags that indicate a scam: "guaranteed" loans, credit, or investments; up-front fees; pitches over the World Wide Web; Nigerian-letter scams (promises to cut you in for a share if you help transfer large amounts of money from distant locations, such as Nigeria. Of course, the con artists will need the number of your bank account, which they promptly clean out.).
         c) Conduct a thorough background check on any lenders, brokers, or financiers you intend to do business with.

    d) Ask the lender or broker about specific sources of financing.
    e) Make sure you have an attorney review all loan agreements before you sign them.
    f) Never pay advance fees for financing, especially on the World Wide Web, unless you have verified the lender's authenticity.

Chapter Summary

♦ Describe the vital role that banks play in providing small business financing and the types of business loans banks make.
- Commercial banks offer the greatest variety of loans, although they are conservative lenders.
- Typical short-term bank loans include commercial loans, lines of credit, and floor planning.
- Intermediate- and long-term loans include discounted installment contracts and character loans.

♦ Explain the types of financing available from nonbank sources of credit.
- Asset-based financing includes discounting accounts receivable and inventory financing.
- Trade credit is used extensively by small businesses as a source of financing. Vendors and suppliers commonly finance sales to businesses for 30, 60, or even 90 days.
- Equipment suppliers offer small businesses financing similar to trade credit, but with slightly different terms.
- Commercial finance companies offer many of the same types of loans that banks do, but they are more risk-oriented in their lending practices. They emphasize accounts receivable financing and inventory loans.
- Savings and loan associations specialize in loans to purchase real property--commercial and industrial mortgages--for up to 30 years.
- Stock brokerage houses offer loans to prospective entrepreneurs at lower interest rates than banks because they have high-quality, liquid collateral--stocks and bonds in the borrower's portfolio.
- Insurance companies provide financing through policy loans and mortgage loans. Policy loans are extended to the owner against the cash surrender value of insurance policies. Mortgage loans are made for large amounts and are based on the value of the land being purchased.
- Credit unions are nonprofit financial institutions that make loans to their members, many of whom use the proceeds to launch businesses.
- Zero coupon bonds allow a company to borrow the funds it needs without having to make periodic loan payments. But a public bond issue does require the company to make public certain financial information.
- Entrepreneurs can finance their businesses by making private placement of debt instruments with a select group of investors.
- Small business investment companies are privately owned companies licensed and regulated by the SBA. Once they are privately capitalized, SBICs may qualify for SBA loans to be invested in or loaned to small firms.
- Small business lending companies make only intermediate- and long-term loans that are guaranteed by the SBA.

♦ Identify the sources of government financial assistance and the loan programs these agencies offer.
- The Economic Development Administration, a branch of the Commerce Department, makes loan guarantees to create and expand small businesses in economically depressed areas.
- The Department of Housing and Urban Development extends loans to cities that, in turn, lend and grant money to small businesses in an attempt to strengthen the local economy.
- The Farmer's Home Administration's loan program is designed to create nonfarm employment opportunities in rural areas through loans and loan guarantees.
- The Rural Economic Community and Development (RECD) Agency guarantees loans to businesses that will stimulate economic growth in economically depressed areas.

- Local development companies, financed privately, seek loans from banks and from the SBA. They lend this money to small businesses to develop a sound economic base in the local community.

♦ Explain the various loan programs the Small Business Administration offers.
  - The Small Business Administration has three types of loans: direct, immediate participation, and guaranteed. Most SBA loans are not really loans at all but loan guarantees.
  - SBA loan programs include the LowDoc (for "low documentation") Loan Program, the FASTRAK program, the CAPline program, the Export Working Capital Program, the International Trade Program, the Section 504 Certified Development Company (CDC) program, microloans, the Minority and Women's Prequalified Loan program, the 8(a) program and disaster loans. The Small Business Innovation Research (SBIR) program, and the Small Business Technology Transfer (STTR) program.

♦ Discuss state and local development programs.
  - In an attempt to develop businesses that create jobs and economic growth, most states offer small business financing programs, usually in the form of loans, loan guarantees, and venture capital funds.
  - Discuss valuable methods of financing growth and expansion internally with bootstrap financing. Small business owners can find important sources of capital inside their firms. By factoring accounts receivable, leasing equipment instead of buying it, and minimizing costs, business owners can stretch their supplies of capital.

♦ Describe how to avoid becoming a victim of a loan scam.
  - Business owners hungry for capital for their growing businesses can be easy targets for con artists running loan scams. Entrepreneurs should watch out for promises of "guaranteed" loans, credit, or investments; up-front fees; pitches over the World Wide Web; and Nigerian-letter scams.

Discussion Questions

1. Define debt financing. What role do commercial banks play in providing debt financing to small businesses?

   Answer - Debt financing involves the funds that the small business owner has borrowed and must repay with interest. Very few entrepreneurs have adequate personal savings to finance the complete start-up costs of a small business. Commercial banks are the very heart of the financial market, providing the greatest number and variety of loans to small businesses. Business owners consider banks to be lenders of first resort. A recent study by the Federal Reserve concluded that commercial banks provide almost half the financing available to small businesses. The same study found that 80 percent of all loans to existing small businesses come from banks.

2. Outline and briefly describe the major types of short-, intermediate-, and long-term loans offered by commercial banks.

   Answer - Banks primarily are lenders of short-term capital to small businesses. Short-term loans extend for less than one year. These funds typically are used to replenish the working capital account to finance the purchase of more inventory, boost output, finance credit sales to customers, or take advantage of cash discounts. Intermediate- and long-term loans. Extend for one year or longer and are normally used to increase fixed- and growth-capital balances. Commercial banks grant these loans for starting a business, constructing a plant, purchasing real estate and equipment, and other long-term investments. Loan repayments are normally made monthly or quarterly. Four categories of intermediate- and long-term loans exist: unsecured term loans, installment loans, discounted installment contracts, and character loans.

3. Explain how asset-based financing works. What is the most common method of asset-based financing? What are the advantages and the disadvantages of using this method of financing?

    Answer - Asset-based lenders, which are usually small commercial banks, commercial finance companies, or specialty lenders, allow small businesses to borrow money by pledging idle assets as collateral. Even unprofitable companies whose financial statements could not convince loan officers to make traditional loans can get asset-based loans. The amount a small business can borrow through asset-based lending depends on the advance rate, the percentage of an asset's value that a lender will lend. The most common types of asset-based financing are discounting accounts receivable and inventory financing. Asset-based financing is a powerful tool. A small business that could obtain a $1 million line of credit with a bank would be able to borrow as much as $3 million by using accounts receivable as collateral. It is also an efficient method of borrowing because a small business owner has the money he needs when he needs it. Sometimes, entrepreneurs have no other choice but asset-based borrowing because their young, fast-growing companies cannot qualify for loans from traditional lenders. Asset-based loans are more expensive than traditional bank loans because of the cost of originating and maintaining them and the higher risk involved. Rates usually run from 2 to 7 percentage points above the prime rate. The cost of an asset-based loan can be twice that of a typical bank loan.

4. What is trade credit? How important is it as a source of debt financing to small firms?

    Answer - Because of its ready availability, trade credit is an extremely important source of financing to most entrepreneurs. Getting vendors to extend credit in the form of delayed payments (e.g., "net 30" credit terms) usually is much easier for small businesses than obtaining bank financing. It is no surprise that businesses receive three dollars of credit from suppliers for every two dollars they receive from banks as loans. Vendors and suppliers usually are willing to finance a small business owner's purchase of goods from 30 to 90 or more days, interest free.

5. What types of loans do savings and loan associations specialize in? Describe the two types of loans extended by insurance companies.

    Answer - Savings and loan (S&L) associations specialize in loans for real property. In addition to their traditional role of providing mortgages for personal residences, savings and loan associations offer financing on commercial and industrial property. In the typical commercial or industrial loan, the S&L will lend up to 80 percent of the property's value, with a repayment schedule of up to 30 years. Minimum loan amounts are typically $50,000. Savings and loan associations expect the mortgage to be repaid from the firm's profits.

    Insurance companies offer two basic types of loans: policy loans and mortgage loans. Policy loans are extended on the basis of the amount of money paid through premiums into the insurance policy. It usually takes about two years for an insurance policy to accumulate enough cash surrender value to justify a loan against it. Insurance companies make mortgage loans on a long-term basis on real property worth a minimum of $500,000. They are based primarily on the value of the real property being purchased. The insurance company will extend a loan of up to 75 or 80 percent of the real estate's value and will allow a lengthy repayment schedule over 25 or 30 years so that payments do not strain the firm's cash flows excessively. Insurance companies also make intermediate-term loans in addition to the long-term loans in which they specialize.

6. How do zero coupon bonds differ from standard bonds?

    Answer - Bonds, which are corporate IOUs, have always been a popular source of debt financing for large companies. Many companies raising money through bond issues use zero coupon bonds (or junk bonds) because of their attractiveness to both the investor and the issuing company. The issuing company gets the capital it needed but does not have to make periodic interest payments as it would if it had issued regular bonds. Instead, it sells the bond at a discount from its par value and then repays the investor the full par value at maturity. The difference between the bond's discounted price and the par value represents the missing interest.

7. What function do SBICs serve? How does an SBIC operate?
    Answer - The small business investment company function as a combination of private capital and federally guaranteed debt to provide long-term capital to small businesses. There are two types of SBICs: regular SBICs and specialized SBICs (SSBICs). Most SBICs prefer later-round financing (mezzanine financing) and leveraged buyouts (LBOs) over funding raw start-ups. SBICs invest twice as much in start-up companies as do private venture capitalists. Both SBICs and SSBICs must be capitalized privately with a minimum of $5 million, at which point they qualify for up to four dollars in low-rate, long-term SBA loans for every dollar of private capital invested in small businesses. As a general rule, both SBICs and SSBICs may provide financial assistance only to small businesses with a net worth of under $18 million and average after-tax earnings of $6 million during the past two years. SBICs are limited to a maximum investment or loan amount of 20 percent of their private capital to a single client, and SSBICs may lend or invest up to 30 percent of their private capital in a single small business. SBICs operate as government-backed venture capitalists, providing long-term loans, equity capital, and management assistance to both start-up and existing businesses. By combining their own private capital with government funds, SBICs can provide the equivalent of venture capital to low-tech or no-tech companies that private venture capitalists would never consider.

8. Briefly describe the loan programs offered by the following:
    Answer -
    a. The Economic Development Administration
    b. The Farmer's Home Administration
    c. The Department of Housing and Urban Development
    d. Local development companies
    Answer -
    a. Economic Development Administration
        ▪ This is a branch of the Commerce Department.
        ▪ It offers loan guarantees to create new businesses and to expand existing businesses in areas with below-average income and high unemployment.
        ▪ The EDA guarantee reduces the lender's risk.
        ▪ The EDA guarantees up to 80 percent of business loans between $750,000 and $10 million.
        ▪ Start-up businesses must contribute at least 25 percent of the guaranteed amount.
        ▪ Existing businesses must make equity investments of at least 15 percent of the guaranteed amount.
        ▪ To qualify for an EDA loan, the business must be located in a disadvantaged area, and its presence must directly benefit local residents.
        ▪ Applicants must create at least one job for every $20,000 in EDA loan guarantees.
    b. Department of Housing and Urban Development
        ▪ HUD sponsors several loan programs to help qualified entrepreneurs raise needed capital.
        ▪ The Urban Development Action Grants (UDAGs) are extended to cities and towns that, in turn, lend or grant money to entrepreneurs to start small businesses that will strengthen the local economy.
        ▪ Grants are aimed at cities and towns that HUD considers economically distressed.
    c. Farmer's Home Administration
        ▪ The U.S. Department of Agriculture provides financial assistance to certain small businesses through the Farmer's Home Administration (FmHA).

- The FmHA loan program is open to all types of businesses and is designed to create nonfarm employment opportunities in rural areas: those with populations below 50,000 and not adjacent to a city where densities exceed 100 persons per square mile.
- The FmHA does not make direct loans to small businesses, but it will guarantee as much as 90 percent of a bank's loan up to $10 million (although actual guarantee amounts are almost always far less) for qualified applicants.

d.   Rural Economic and Community Development Agency

- The Rural Economic and Community and Development (RECD) Agency guarantees up to 80 percent of loans up to $10 million to businesses that will stimulate economic growth in economically depressed areas.
- The RECD also provides grants (with no dollar ceiling) to finance emerging and growing companies with less than $1 million in annual revenues and no more than 50 employees that are located in economically challenged areas.

e.   Local Development Companies

- The federal government encourages local residents to organize and fund local development companies (LDCs) on either a profit or nonprofit basis.
- After raising initial capital by selling stock to at least 25 residents, the company seeks loans from banks and from the SBA.
- Each LDC can qualify for up to $1 million a year in loans and guarantees from the SBA to assist in starting small businesses in the community.
- Most LDCs are certified to operate locally or regionally, but each state may have one LDC that can operate anywhere within its boundaries.
- Three parties are involved in providing the typical LDC loan: the LDC, the SBA, and a participating bank.

9.   Explain the three basic types of loans the Small Business Administration offers. Which type is most popular?
Answer - The SBA offers three basic types of loans in administering its programs: direct, immediate participation, and guaranteed. Direct loans are made by the SBA directly to the small business with public funds and no bank participation. In general, a direct loan cannot exceed $150,000. The interest rate charged on direct loans depends on the cost of money to the government, and it changes as general interest rates fluctuate. Immediate participation loans are made from a pool of public and private funds. The SBA provides a portion of the total loan, and a private lender supplies the remaining portion. The SBA's general policy is to fund no more than 75 percent. The SBA's portion of an immediate participation loan may not exceed $150,000. Guaranteed 7(a) Loans. By far, the most popular type of SBA loan. Guaranteed loans are extended to small businesses by a private lender (usually a commercial bank) but are guaranteed by the SBA (80 percent of loans up to $100,000 and 75 percent of loans above $100,001 and up to $750,000, the loan guarantee ceiling).

10. Outline the basic programs available to entrepreneurs from the Small Business Administration.
Answer - The CAPline program offers short-term capital to growing companies needing to finance seasonal buildings in inventory or accounts receivable under five separate programs. For small businesses going global, the SBA has the Export Working Capital Program (EWCP). Section 504 Certified Development Company (CDC) Program is designed to encourage small businesses to expand their facilities and to create jobs. Section 504 deals provide long-term, fixed-asset financing to small companies to purchase land, buildings, or equipment. In SBA's microloan program, loans range from just a few hundred dollars to as much as $25,000. In 1992, the SBA began funding microloan programs at 96 private, nonprofit lenders in 44 states in an attempt to fill the void in small loans to start-up companies. Minority and Women's Prequalified Loan Program. The program is designed to help minority and women entrepreneurs prepare loan applications and "prequalify" for SBA loan guarantees before approaching banks and lending institutions for loans.

11. How can a firm employ bootstrap financing to stretch its capital supply?
    Answer - Instead of carrying credit sales on its own books, a small business can sell outright its accounts receivable to a factor. A factor buys a company's accounts receivable but pays for them in two parts. The first payment, which the factor makes immediately, usually is for 75 to 80 percent of the accounts' agreed-upon value. The factor makes the second payment, which makes up the balance less the factor's service fee, when the original customer pays the invoice.

    Leasing is another common bootstrap financing technique. By leasing expensive assets, small business owners are able to use them without locking up valuable capital for an extended period of time. Also, because no down payment is required and because the cost of the asset is spread over a longer time (lowering monthly payments), the firm's cash flow improves.

    Unable to find financing elsewhere, some entrepreneurs have launched their companies using the most convenient source of debt capital available: credit cards. Putting business start-up costs on credit cards, which can charge 21 percent or more in annual interest, is expensive and risky, but some entrepreneurs have no other choice.

    Some business owners needing cash to finance growth have found a simple solution: print their own. This not-so-funny money is legal.

12. How does a factor operate? What are the advantages and disadvantages of using a factor? What kinds of businesses typically use factors?
    Answer - Instead of carrying credit sales on its own books (some of which may never be collected), a small business can sell outright its accounts receivable to a factor. A factor buys a company's accounts receivable but pays for them in two parts. The first payment, which the factor makes immediately, usually is for 75 to 80 percent of the accounts' agreed-upon value. The factor makes the second payment, which makes up the balance less the factor's service fee, when the original customer pays the invoice. Begun by American colonists to finance their cotton trade with England, factoring has become an important source of capital for many small businesses. Under deals arranged with recourse, the small business owner retains the responsibility for customers who fail to pay their accounts. Under deals arranged without recourse, however, the owner is relieved of the responsibility for collecting them. Factors will pay anywhere from 60 to 95 percent of the face value of a company's accounts receivable, depending on the small company's. Factoring is ideally suited for fast-growing companies, especially start-ups that cannot qualify for bank loans. A small business should have an adequate volume of accounts receivable before turning to this source of funds.

Step Into the Real World

1. Visit a local small business owner and ask the following questions:
   a. How did you raise your starting capital? What percent did you supply on your own? What percent was debt capital and what percent was equity capital?
   b. Which of the sources of funds described in this chapter does the owner use? Are the funds used to finance fixed, working, or growth capital needs?
2. After a personal visit, prepare a short report on a nearby factor's operation. How is the value of the accounts receivable purchased determined? Who bears the loss on uncollected accounts?
3. Interview the administrator of a financial institution program that offers a method of financing with which you are unfamiliar, and prepare a short report on its method of operation.
4. Go to the Small Business Administration's World Wide Web site at <http://www.sba.gov>. Choose one of the loan programs the SBA offers and prepare a one-page report on its purpose and method of operation.
5. Contact your state's business development board and prepare a report on the financial assistance programs it offers.

6. Develop a plan for establishing a microloan enterprise in your community. Which community groups, banks, and individuals would you approach for help? How would you establish lending criteria? For more information, contact:

    ◆   The Association for Enterprise Opportunity, 304 N. Michigan Avenue, Suite 804, Chicago, IL 60601 (312) 357-0177

    ◆   The Self-Employment Learning Project, the Aspen Institute, P.O. Box 222, Queenstown, MD 21658 <http://www. aspeninst.orgtdir/polpro/SELP/SELP 1. html>

    ◆   The U.S. Small Business Administration, Washington, D.C. (SBA Answer Desk 1-800-827-5722) <http://www.sbaonline.sba.gov/financing/indexloans. html>

    ◆   Trickle Up, 54 Riverside Drive, New York, N.Y. 10024 (212) 362-7958 <http://www. igc.apc.org/ia/mb/trickle.html>

    ◆   ACCION International, 235 Havemeyer Street, Brooklyn, N.Y. 11211 (718) 599-5170 <http://www. accion.org/>

7. Contact a woman entrepreneur and interview her about how she raised the capital to launch her business. Where did she find the capital? What special problems did she encounter? Was she denied financing from some sources? If so, for what reasons? Did she see evidence of discrimination in her search for capital simply because she is a woman? Prepare a brief summary of your interview.

Chapter 15 - Location, Layout, and Physical Facilities

We've moved our company so many times that we consider relocation one of our core competencies.
The president of a small medical services company

There's no place like home. There's no place like home. There's no place like home.
Dorothy, in The Wizard of Oz

Teaching Objectives

Students will be able to:

1. Explain the stages in the location decision.
2. Describe the location criteria for retail and service businesses.
3. Outline the basic location options for retail and service businesses.
4. Explain the site selection process for manufacturers.
5. Discuss the benefits of locating a start-up company in a business incubator.
6. Describe the criteria used to analyze the layout and design considerations of a building, including the Americans with Disabilities Act.
7. Explain the principles of effective layouts for retailers, service businesses, and manufacturers.
8. Evaluate the advantages and disadvantages of building, buying, and leasing a building.

Instructor's Outline

I. Introduction

   A. The Location Decision

      1. Few decisions have as big and as lasting an impact on a business as the entrepreneur's choice of location.
      2. The location decision plays a major role in many aspects of a company's life--from its cost structure and the quality of its workforce to the size of its customer base.
      3. Unfortunately, many entrepreneurs never consider locations beyond their own hometowns.
      4. The "secret" to selecting the ideal location goes back to knowing who a company's target customers are and then finding a site that makes it most convenient for those customers to do business with the company.

II. The Logic of Location: From Region to State to City to Site

   A. Introduction

      1. An entrepreneur's ultimate location goal is to locate the company at a site that will maximize the likelihood of success.
      2. The more entrepreneurs invest in researching potential locations, the higher is the probability that they will find the spot that is best suited for their company.
      3. Choosing an appropriate location is essentially a matter of selecting the site that best serves the needs of the business's target market.
         a) The better entrepreneurs know and understand their target customers' characteristics, demographic profiles, and buying behavior, the greater are their chances of identifying the right location from which to serve them.
      4. The logic of location selection is to begin with a broad regional search and then to systematically narrow the focus of the site selection process.
         a) See Figure 15.1.

B. Selecting the Region
   1. The first step is to focus at the regional level.
   2. Common requirements include rapid growth in the population of a certain age group, rising disposable incomes, the existence of specific infrastructure, a nonunion environment, and low operating costs.
   3. At the broadest level of the location decision, entrepreneurs usually identify regions of the country that are experiencing substantial growth.
   4. One of the first stops entrepreneurs should make when conducting a regional evaluation is the U.S. Census Bureau.
      a) The Census Bureau publishes a monthly newsletter, "Census and You," which is especially helpful to business owners.
      b) In addition, the Census Bureau makes most of the information contained in its valuable data banks available to entrepreneurs through its easy-to-use World Wide Web site <http:/www.census.gov/>.
      c) At this site, entrepreneurs can find vital demographic information for specific locations.
   5. The Small Business Administration also has valuable aids to help you throughout your location search.
      a) Some of these are "Practical Use of Government Statistics," "Using Census Data to Select a Store Site," and "Using Census Data in Small Plant Marketing."
   6. *American Demographics* magazine has two valuable booklets also: The 1990 Census: The Counting of America and A Researcher's Guide to the 1990 Census.
   7. Four other helpful publications.
      a) *Sales and Marketing Management's Survey of Buying Power*, published annually, provides a detailed breakdown of population, retail sales, spendable income, and other characteristics.
      b) The *Editor and Publisher Market Guide* is similar to the *Survey of Buying Power*, but provides additional information on markets. The guide includes detailed information on key cities.
      c) *Rand McNally's Commercial Atlas and Marketing Guide* reports on more than 128,000 places in the United States, many of which are not available through census reports.
      d) The *Zip Code Atlas and Market Planner* is an extremely useful location and market-planning tool. It combines a breakdown of zip codes (often the basis of psychographic customer profiles) with maps featuring physical features such as mountains, rivers, and major highways.
   8. The Small Business Administration's Small Business Development Center (SBDC) program also offers location analysis assistance to entrepreneurs.
   9. For many businesses, especially manufacturers, cost considerations are driving factors in the location decision.
   10. In other cases, a company's location decision stems from the availability of particular raw materials or natural resources.
   11. The task of analyzing potential locations--gathering and synthesizing data on a wide variety of demographic and geographic variables--is one ideally suited for a computer.
      a) In fact, a growing number of entrepreneurs are relying on geographic information systems (GISs), powerful software programs that combine map drawing with database management capability, to pinpoint the ideal location for their business.
      b) These programs enable users to search through virtually any database and plot the relevant findings on a detailed map of the country, an individual state, a specific city, or even a single city block.

c) Using a GIS program, an entrepreneur could plot her existing customer base on a map, with various colors representing the different population densities.

d) Geographic information system street files originate in the U.S. Census Department's TIGER (Topological Integrated Geographic Encoding Referencing) file, which contains map information broken down for every street in the country and detailed block statistics for the 345 largest urban areas.

C. Selecting the State

1. Every state has a business development office to recruit new businesses to that state.

2. Some of the key issues to explore include the laws, regulations, and taxes that govern businesses and any incentives or investment credits the state may offer to businesses locating there.

3. Other factors to consider include proximity to markets, proximity to raw materials; quantity and quality of the labor supply, general business climate, and wage rates.

4. Proximity to markets

a) Locating close to markets that manufacturing firm's plan to serve is extremely critical when the cost of transportation of finished goods is high relative to their value.

b) Service firms often find that proximity to their clients is essential. If a business is involved in repairing equipment used in a specific industry, it should be located where that industry is concentrated.

c) The more specialized the business or the greater the relative cost of transporting the product to the customer, the more important proximity to the market is.

5. Proximity to needed raw materials

a) A business that requires raw materials that are difficult or expensive to transport may need a location near the source of those raw materials.

b) In situations in which bulk or weight is not a factor, locating close to suppliers can facilitate quick deliveries and reduce inventory-holding costs.

6. Labor supply

a) Two distinct factors are important for entrepreneurs analyzing the labor supply in a potential location: the number of workers available in the area and their level of education, training, and experience.

b) Business owners want to know how many qualified people are available in the area to do the work required in the business.

c) The size of the local labor pool determines a company's ability to fill jobs at reasonable wages.

d) Knowing the exact nature of the labor needed and preparing job descriptions and job specifications in advance will help business owners determine whether there is a good match between their company and the available labor pool.

e) Checking educational statistics in the state to determine the number of graduates in relevant fields of study will provide an idea of the local supply of qualified workers.

7. Business climate

a) What is the state's overall attitude toward your kind of business?

b) Does the state offer small business support programs or financial assistance to entrepreneurs?

c) Some states are more "small business friendly" than others.

(1) *Entrepreneur* magazine recently named Minnesota's Minneapolis/St. Paul as one of the best cities for small businesses, citing its positive attitude toward growing and developing small companies as a major asset.

(2) Table 15.1 illustrates a matrix designed to help entrepreneurs score potential locations they are considering.

8. Wage rates
    a) Entrepreneurs should determine the wage rates for jobs that are related to their particular industry or company.
    b) In addition to published government surveys, local newspapers will give entrepreneurs an idea of the wages local companies must pay to attract workers.

IN THE FOOTSTEPS OF AN ENTREPRENEUR - Mapping the Way to Success

SUMMARY
Sonny Tillman opened his first barbecue restaurant in Gainesville, Florida, in 1968, offering customers a hearty meal for an average of about $3.50, compared with as much as $10 for some of his competitors. The business grew. Tillman began selling franchises.

Sonny's has to define its territories properly and put restaurants in the right locations. Giving franchisees territories that lack the customer bases or the demographic traits to make their barbecue restaurants a success means setting them up for failure--something no franchisor can afford to do. Because defining the right territories and selecting the right locations for restaurants within those territories is crucial to Sonny's Bar-B-Q's success, the company is not willing to leave those decisions to chance. Several years ago, Sonny's began using geographic information systems (GISs) to guide territory and location decisions. Using GISs, Sonny's can superimpose on a map a color-coded representation of virtually any characteristic of the area's population from income levels and age breakdowns to traffic counts and eating habits.

Managers look for regions where people already are familiar with barbecue (primarily the South) but that do not have a high concentration of competing barbecue restaurants. They also cull specific data from the Census Bureau's database and then combine it with census maps to get a picture (literally!) of a site's potential for a new restaurant. Turner can set the minimum criteria for each characteristic and let the GIS display the areas that meet those criteria, or he can outline a geographic area the company is interested in developing and the system will display the traits of the population in it. Turner establishes strict criteria for locations.

Putting together a smoothly functioning GIS was neither easy nor inexpensive for a small company such as Sonny's Bar-B-Q. In just a short period of time, the system has paid for itself many times over.

1. What advantages does GIS give Sonny's in franchising?
    Answer - It saves an immense amount of time and expense. Rather than spending hours looking through various sources, visiting sites, etc. The software does the work. It also enhances the likelihood of success of each franchise.
2. What other types of businesses would benefit from using a GIS program? What other business applications can you think of for GIS? Explain.
    Answer - The list is almost limitless; it's a matter of the cost. There are limited scale GIS software packages available through office supply stores like Staples. Consider buying one (under $100) and demonstrating it to the class.

D. Selecting the City
    1. Population trends and density
        a) By analyzing population and other demographic data, an entrepreneur can examine a city in detail.
        b) Using only basic census data, entrepreneurs can determine the value of the homes in an area, how many rooms they contain, how many bedrooms they contain, what

percentage of the population own their homes, and how much residents' monthly rental or mortgage payments are.

    c) A company's location should match the market for its products or services, and assembling a demographic profile will tell an entrepreneur how well a particular site measures up to her target market's profile.

    d) Trends or shifts in population components may have more meaning than total population trends.

    e) Population density is another important factor for many small businesses.

        (1) Nearly two-thirds of Americans live in high-density, urbanized areas, although these areas make up just 1.7 percent of the nation's land area.

        (2) For owners of businesses that depend on high traffic for their success, determining a city's population density can be crucial.

2. Competition

    a) For some retailers, locating near competitors makes sense because having similar businesses located near one another may increase traffic flow.

    b) Clustering, as this location strategy is known, works well for products for which customers are most likely to comparison shop.

    c) Overcrowding of businesses of the same type in an area can create an undesirable impact on the profitability of all competing firms.

        (1) Consider the specific nature of the competing businesses in the area.

    d) Studying the size of the market for a product or service and the number of existing competitors will help entrepreneurs determine whether they can capture a sufficiently large market share to earn a profit.

        (1) The Census Bureau reports can be a valuable source of information.

        (2) The bureau's "County Business Patterns Economic Profile" shows the breakdown of businesses in manufacturing, wholesale, retail, and service categories and estimates companies' annual payrolls and number of employees.

        (3) The Economic Census, which covers 15 million businesses and is published in years that end in 2 and 7, gives an overview of the businesses in an area, including their sales (or other measure of output), employment, payroll, and form of organization.

3. The Index of retail saturation

    a) For retailers, the number of customers in the trading area and the intensity of the competition are essential factors in predicting success.

    b) One traditional way to analyze potential sites is to compare them on the basis of the index of retail saturation (IRS), a measure that combines the number of customers in an area, their purchasing power, and the level of competition,

        (1) The index is the ratio of a trading area's sales potential for a particular product or service to its sales capacity:

$$IRS = \frac{C \times RE}{RF}$$

        (2) C = Number of customers in the trading area

        (3) RE = Retail expenditures (the average expenditure per person [$] for the product in the trading area)

        (4) RF = Retail facilities (the total square feet of selling space allocated to the product in the trading area)

    c) This computation is an important one for any retailer to make.

    d) Locating in an area already saturated with competitors results in dismal sales volume and often leads to failure.

        (1) See illustration on page 501.

    e)   The amount of available data on the population of any city or town is staggering.

    f)   These statistics allow a potential business owner to compare a wide variety of cities or towns and to narrow the choices to those few that warrant further investigation.

4. Costs

    a)   For many businesses, especially manufacturers, the primary force driving site selection is cost.

    b)   A study by Patrick Howie of Regional Financial Associates found that cities offering the lowest costs experienced the greatest growth in business formations and job creation.

    c)   A growing number of small cities are establishing special technology zones that offer tax exemptions and reduced fees and licensing costs in an attempt to attract high-tech businesses.

5. Local laws and regulations

    a)   Before selecting a particular site within a city, small business owners must explore the local zoning laws to determine if there are any ordinances that would place restrictions on business activity or that would prohibit establishing a business altogether.

        (1) Zoning is a system that divides a city or county into small cells or districts to control the use of land, buildings, and sites.

        (2) Its purpose is to contain similar activities in suitable locations.

6. Compatibility with the community

    a)   One of the intangibles that an entrepreneur can determine only by visiting a particular city is the degree of compatibility a business has with the surrounding community.

    b)   A company's image must fit in with the character of the town and the needs and wants of its residents.

7. Quality of life

    a)   One of the most important, yet most difficult to measure, criteria for a city is the quality of life it offers.

    b)   Entrepreneurs have the freedom and the flexibility to locate their companies in cities that suit not only their business needs but also their personal preferences.

    c)   When choosing locations for their companies, entrepreneurs often consider factors such as cultural events, outdoor activities, entertainment opportunities, safety, and the city's "personality."

8. Transportation networks

    a)   Manufacturers and wholesalers in particular must investigate the quality of local transportation systems.

    b)   For retailers, the availability of loading and unloading zones is an important feature of a suitable location.

        (1) Some downtown locations suffer from a lack of space for carriers to unload deliveries of merchandise.

9. Police and fire protection

    a)   Does the community in which you plan to locate offer adequate police and fire protection?

    b)   Inadequate police and fire services will be reflected in the cost of the company's business insurance.

10. Public services

    a)   The location should be served by some governmental unit that provides water and sewer services, trash and garbage collection, and other necessary utilities.

    b)   The streets should be in good repair with adequate drainage.

IN THE FOOTSTEPS OF AN ENTREPRENEUR - Small Is Beautiful--and Profitable

SUMMARY
Ed Deitrick makes the best pizza in West Fairview, Pennsylvania. In fact, Deitrick makes the only pizza in West Fairview. Not only is his Uni-Mart store the only place to buy pizza, it is the only store in the tiny town (population 1,532). Deitrick's store in West Fairview embodies the strategy that Uni-Mart founder Henry Sahakian has followed to take his chain of convenience stores to the $330 million level of annual sales. His 416 stores are scattered throughout the mid-Atlantic states, and all of them are located in small (often really small) towns.

The typical Uni-Mart carries more than 3,500 items, but local owners and managers can add up to 100 items that are unique to their particular locations. Originally a franchisee of another convenience store chain, Sahakian decided to branch out on his own. As he looked for new locations for his expanding business, he realized that most of the cities and suburban areas he was considering were already saturated with convenience store competitors. The only competition he faced in small towns were the local "mom-and-pop stores" that could not match the lower costs generated by his volume buying power. Thus was born his small-town location strategy. Sahakian plans to expand his connection with fast-food franchises such as Arbys, Burger King, and Blimpies.

1. What advantages does Sahakian's location strategy offer Uni-Mart. What are its disadvantages?
    Answer - He has limited competition. Probably has very low overhead costs--land, buildings, etc. There is limited growth opportunity for each store due to the small populations. He may have difficulty staffing his stores.
2. What tools and techniques should Sahakian use to identify potential sites for future Uni-Mart stores?
    Answer - Refer to the resources outlined on pages 494-495.

    11. The location's reputation
       a) Like people, a city or parts of a city can have a bad reputation.
       b) In some cases, the reputation of the previous business will lower the value of the location.
       c) Sites where businesses have failed repeatedly create negative impressions in customer's minds; customers often view any business locating there as just another one that will soon be gone.

III. Selecting the Site
  A. Introduction
    1. The final step in the location selection process is choosing the actual site for the business.
    2. Each type of business has different evaluation criteria for what makes an ideal location.
      a) A manufacturer's prime consideration may be access to raw materials, suppliers, labor, transportation, and customers.
      b) Service firms need access to customers but can generally survive in lower-rent properties.
      c) A retailer's prime consideration is customer traffic. The one element common to all three is the need to locate where customers want to do business.
    3. Site location draws on the most precise information available on the makeup of the area.
    4. Two additional Census Bureau reports entrepreneurs find especially useful when choosing locations are "Summary Population," which provides a broad demographic look at an area, and "Housing Characteristics," which offers a detailed breakdown of areas as small as city blocks.

IV. Location Criteria for Retail and Service Businesses
   A. Trade Area Size
       1. Every retail business should determine the extent of its trading area: the region from which a business can expect to draw customers over a reasonable time span.
       2. The primary variables that influence the scope of a trading area are the type and size of the operation.
          a) If a retailer is a specialist with a wide assortment of products, he may draw customers from a great distance.
          b) As a rule, the larger the store and the greater its selection of merchandise, the broader its trading area.
       3. The following environmental factors influence the retail trading area size.
          a) Retail compatibility. Shoppers tend to be drawn to clusters of related businesses. The concentration of businesses pulls customers from a larger trading area than a single freestanding business does.
          b) Degree of competition. The size, location, and activity of competing businesses also influence the size of the trading area. If a business will be the first of its kind in a location, its trading area might be extensive. However, if the area already has eight or ten nearby stores that directly compete with a business, its trading area might be very small.
          c) Transportation network. The transportation networks are the highways, roads, and public service routes that presently exist or are planned. An inconvenient location reduces the business's trading area.
          d) Physical, cultural, or emotional barriers. Physical barriers may be parks, rivers, lakes, or any other obstruction that hinders customers' access to the area.
             (1) Locating on one side of a large park may reduce the number of customers who will drive around it to get to the store.
             (2) In urban areas, new immigrants tend to cluster together, sharing a common culture and language.
             (3) One powerful emotional barrier is fear.
          e) Political barriers are creations of law. Federal, state, county, or city boundaries--and the laws within those boundaries--can influence the size of a company's trading area.

   B. Customer Traffic
       1. Perhaps the most important screening criteria for a potential retail (and often for a service) location is the number of potential customers passing by the site during business hours.
       2. Entrepreneurs should know the traffic counts (pedestrian and auto) at the sites they are considering.

   C. Adequate Parking
       1. If customers cannot find convenient and safe parking, they are not likely to stop in the area.
       2. Shopping malls typically average five parking spaces per 1,000 square feet of shopping space; many central business districts get by with 3.5 spaces per 1,000 square feet.
       3. Customers generally will not pay to park if parking is free at shopping centers or in front of competing stores.

   D. Room for Expansion
       1. A location should be flexible enough to provide for expansion if success warrants it.

2. Failure to consider this factor can force a successful business to open a second store when it would have been better to expand in its original location.

E. Visibility
   1. No matter what a small business sells and how well it serves customers' needs, it cannot survive without visibility.
   2. Highly visible locations simply make it easy for customers to make purchases.
   3. A site lacking visibility puts a company at a major disadvantage before it even opens its doors.
   4. Some service businesses, however, can select sites with less visibility if the majority of their customer contacts are by telephone, fax, or the Internet.

V. Location Options for Retail and Service Businesses
   A. Six Basic Areas
      1. There are six basic areas where retailers and service business owners can locate: the central business district, neighborhoods, shopping centers and malls, near competitors, outlying areas, and at home.
      2. According to the International Council of Shopping Centers:
         a) the average cost to lease space in a shopping center is about $15 per square foot.
         b) at a regional mall, rental rates run from $20 to $40 per square foot.
         c) in central business locations, the average cost is $43 per square foot.

   B. Central Business District
      1. The central business district (CBD) is the traditional center of town: the downtown concentration of businesses established early in the development of most towns and cities.
      2. Advantages of a downtown location.
         a) They attract customers from the entire trading area of the city.
         b) They benefit from the traffic generated by the other stores clustered in the district.
      3. Disadvantages
         a) Some CBDs are characterized by intense competition, high rental rates, traffic congestion, and inadequate parking facilities.
         b) In addition, many cities have experienced difficulty in preventing the decay of their older downtown business districts as a result of "mall withdrawal."
      4. Recently, however, CBDs have experienced a resurgence in popularity as increasing numbers of shoppers have grown tired of the sameness of malls and shopping centers.
      5. As shoppers have become more interested in preserving their downtown districts, retailers have returned to Main Street.
      6. One real estate developer experienced in Main Street locations says that his research shows that the best downtown retailing streets are located in densely populated, affluent areas, are one-way, offer on-street parking, and are shaded by mature trees.

   C. Neighborhood Locations
      1. Small businesses that locate near residential areas rely heavily on the local trading areas for business.
      2. The primary advantages of a neighborhood location include relatively low operating costs and rents and close contact with customers.

   D. Shopping Centers and Malls

1.   Shopping centers and malls have experienced explosive growth over the last three decades.
2.   Because many different types of stores exist under a single roof, shopping malls give meaning to the term "one-stop shopping."
3.   There are four types of shopping centers and malls:
     a)   Neighborhood shopping centers. The typical neighborhood shopping center is relatively small, containing from three to twelve stores and serving a population of up to 40,000 people who live within a 10-minute drive. The anchor store in these centers is usually a supermarket or a drugstore.
     b)   Community shopping centers. The community shopping center contains from 12 to 50 stores and serves a population ranging from 40,000 to 150,000 people. The leading tenant is a department or variety store.
     c)   Regional shopping malls. The regional shopping mall serves a much larger trading area, usually from 10 to 15 miles or more in all directions. It contains from 50 to 100 stores and serves a population in excess of 150,000 people living within a 20- to 40-minute drive. The anchor is typically one or more major department stores.
     d)   Power centers. A power center combines the drawing strength of a large regional mall with the convenience of a neighborhood shopping center. Anchored by large specialty retailers, these centers target older, wealthier baby boomers, who want selection and convenience. Small companies must be careful in choosing power center locations to avoid being overshadowed by their larger neighbors. Spillover traffic from the anchor stores is the primary benefit to small businesses locating in power centers.
4.   The cost of locating in a shopping center or mall makes it an important decision.
     a)   Is there a good fit with other products and brands sold in the mall or center?
     b)   Who are the other tenants?
     c)   Demographically, is the center a good fit for your products or services?
     d)   How much foot traffic does the mall or center generate?
     e)   How much vehicle traffic does the mall or center generate?
     f)   What is the vacancy rate? The turnover rate?
     g)   Is the mall or center successful? How many dollars in sales does it generate per square foot?
5.   Although they still account for the majority of retail sales, malls have waned in popularity within the last decade.
     a)   Today, the average mall visit is 76 minutes, down from 106 minutes during the mall heyday of the 1980s.
     b)   Regional malls clearly have a life cycle, and some are in their last throes. The result is "demalling," in which developers renovate old malls by demolishing their interior common space, eliminating most of the small retailers, adding more entrances, and making them more closely resemble power centers.
6.   Mall developers are trying new formulas--often based on adding entertainment and offering a fresh mix of specialty stores catering to customers' changing tastes--to keep shoppers coming back.

E. Near Competitors
    1.   One of the most important factors is the compatibility of nearby stores with you.
    2.   Although some small business owners seek to avoid locations near direct competitors, others want to locate near rivals.
         a)   Restaurateurs know that restaurants attract other restaurants, which, in turn, attract more customers.
    3.   There are limits to locating near competitors, however.

    4. Clustering too many businesses of a single type into a small area ultimately will erode their sales once the market reaches the saturation point.

F. Outlying Areas
    1. In general, it is not advisable for a small business to locate in a remote area because accessibility and traffic flow are vital to retail and service success.
    2. There are exceptions as some small firms have turned their remote locations into trademarks.

IN THE FOOTSTEPS OF AN ENTREPRENEUR - Mall Appeal... or Appall?

The onslaught against the mall, that paradise of shopping pleasure, shows no sign of receding. Mail-order catalogs, television shopping channels, the World Wide Web, toll-free numbers, direct mail, and other methods offer customers the ultimate convenience in shopping: never having to leave home. Many experts predict that, over the next few years, many malls will shut down or be converted into storage.

Many owners across the United States are remodeling, redesigning, and repositioning their malls in an attempt to lure customers back. A common strategy is to add entertainment and attractions. Some 20 million customers visit Canada's West Edmonton Mall, the largest mall in the world, each year to shop at its more than 800 retail stores and to visit the mall's petting zoo, water parks, skating rink, amusement park, and Spanish Galleon in its own lagoon.

The goal is to make malls a destination for shoppers, and to keep them longer once they get there. The more time people spend in a mall, the more money they are going to spend. Entertainment features and attractions serve the same purpose that anchor stores do, generate traffic. Perhaps nowhere has the shift to entertainment become more obvious than in Las Vegas. A recent $90 million, 283,000-square-foot expansion of the Forum Shops, a group of upscale retail shops located next to the hotel/casino complex at Caesar's Palace, offers visitors a chance to stroll back into history. The average mall rings up sales of $278 per square foot, and sales of more than $400 per square foot are considered spectacular. At the Forum Shops, sales average $1,300 per square foot!

1. What advantages and disadvantages does a mall location offer a small business?
   Answer - The other stores draw more customers, better parking and accessibility, longer retail hours and the ability to charge higher prices.
2. Use the World Wide Web to research the malls described here and other malls in your area. What trends are influencing shopping malls and the retailers located there?
   Answer - Responses depend on research. General trends will be shifts in demographics--with more minorities having higher incomes and therefore doing more non-essential shopping; move in the population out of cities and to the South and West in the US. Economic upturn leading to more general disposable income. Working men and women wanting to spend more time with their families, etc.

G. Home-Based Businesses
    1. For 27.1 million people (14 million full-time and 13.1 million part-time), home is where the business is, and their numbers continue to swell.
    2. Home-based businesses represent 25 percent of all newly created small companies.
    3. Disadvantages
      a) Interruptions are frequent.
      b) Presenting a professional image to clients can also be a challenge.
      c) Another problem involves zoning laws.

d) Refer to Table 1.2 in Chapter 1I for advice on issues to consider before setting up a home-based business.

VI. The Location Decision for Manufacturers

A. The Criteria

1. For manufacturers is very different from those of retailers and service businesses.
2. The decision can have just as much impact on the company's success.
   a) Local zoning ordinances will limit a manufacturer's choice of location.
   b) Some cities have developed industrial parks in cooperation with private industry.
3. Location of the plant can be dictated by the type of transportation facilities needed.
4. In some cases, the perishability of the product dictates location.
5. Needed utilities, zoning, transposition, and special requirements may also work together to limit the number of locations that are suitable for a manufacturer.

B. Foreign Trade Zones

1. Foreign trade zones can be an attractive location for many small manufacturers that are engaged in global trade and are looking to lower the tariffs they pay on the materials and parts they import and on the goods they export.
2. A foreign trade zone is a specially designated area that allows resident companies to import materials and components from foreign countries; assemble, process, package, or manufacture them; and then ship finished products out while incurring low tariffs and duties or, in some cases, paying no tariffs or duties at all.
   a) See Figure 15.2 for how a foreign trade zone works.

C. Enterprise Zones

1. Originally created to encourage companies to locate in economically blighted areas, empowerment zones offer entrepreneurs tax breaks on investments they make within zone boundaries.
2. Companies can get federal tax credits for hiring workers living in empowerment zones and for investments they make in plant and equipment in the zones.

D. Business Incubators

1. A business incubator is an organization that combines low-cost, flexible rental space with a multitude of support services for its small business residents.
2. The overwhelming reason for establishing an incubator is to enhance economic development in an area and to diversify the local economy.
3. Common sponsors of incubators include government agencies (49 percent); colleges or universities (13 percent); partnerships among government agencies, nonprofit agencies, and private developers (18 percent); and private investment groups (12 percent).
4. Business and technical incubators vary to some degree as to the types of clients they attempt to attract, but most incubator residents are engaged in light manufacturing, service businesses, and technology- or research-related fields.
   a) See Figure 15.3.
5. The shared resources incubators typically provide their tenants include secretarial services, a telephone system, a computer and software, fax machines, meeting facilities, and, sometimes, management consulting services.
6. An incubator will normally have entry requirements that are tied to its purpose and that detail the nature and scope of the business activities to be conducted.
7. Incubators also have criteria that establish the conditions a business must meet to remain in the facility as well as the expectations for "graduation."

        a) One recent study found that more than 80 percent of companies become profitable within three years of entering an incubator.

8. In addition to shared services, incubators offer their fledgling tenants reduced rents and another valuable resource: access to the early-stage capital that young companies need to grow.

        a) A recent survey by the National Business Incubation Association found that 83 percent of incubators provide some kind of access to seed capital, ranging from help with obtaining federal grants to making connections with angel investors.

9. More than 600 active incubators operate across the United States, and a new incubator opens, on average, every week.

        a) Firms that graduate from incubators have only an 11 percent failure rate. The average incubator houses 17 ongoing businesses employing 55 people.

VII. Layout Considerations: Analyzing the Building

    A. Size

1. A building must be large enough to accommodate a business's daily operations comfortably.

2. There must be room enough for customers' movement, inventory, displays, storage, work areas, offices, and restrooms.

3. Haphazard layouts undermine employee productivity and create organizational chaos.

        a) If an owner plans any kind of expansion, will the building accommodate it?

        b) Will hiring new employees, purchasing new equipment, expanding production areas, or increasing service areas require a new location?

        c) How fast is the company expected to grow over the next three to five years?

4. Some experts recommend that new businesses should plan their space requirements one to two years ahead and update the estimates every six months.

    B. Construction and External Appearance

1. Is the construction of the building sound? It pays to have an expert look it over before buying or leasing the property.

2. Beyond the soundness of construction, does the building have an attractive external and internal appearance?

3. The physical appearance of the building provides customers with their first impression of a business and contributes significantly to establishing its identity in the customer's mind.

4. A glass front enables a retail business to display merchandise easily and to attract potential customers' attention.

        a) A window display can be a powerful selling tool if used properly.

        b) For maximum eye-catching potential, businesses should display small merchandise in windows with elevations of at least 36 inches.

        c) Displays of larger merchandise can start lower: just 12, 18, or 24 inches from the ground.

5. Tips for creating create window displays that sell:

        a) Keep displays simple.

        b) Keep displays clean and up to date.

        c) Promote local events.

        d) Change displays frequently.

        e) Get expert help, if necessary.

        f) Contact the companies whose products you sell to see if they offer design props and assistance.

    C. Entrances

1. All entrances to a business should invite customers in.
2. Wide entryways and attractive merchandise displays that are set back from the doorway can draw customers into a business.
3. Entrances should be lighted to create a friendly atmosphere that invites customers to enter a business.

D. The Americans with Disabilities Act
   1. The Americans with Disabilities Act (ADA), passed in July 1990, requires practically all businesses to make their facilities available to physically challenged customers and employees.
   2. In addition, the law requires businesses with 15 or more employees to accommodate physically challenged candidates in their hiring practices.
   3. The ADA allows flexibility in how a business achieves this equal access, however.
   4. Although the law allows a good deal of flexibility in retrofitting existing structures, buildings that were occupied after January 25, 1993, must be designed to comply with all aspects of the law.
   5. Complying with the ADA does not necessarily require businesses to spend large amounts of money.
      a) The Justice Department estimates that more than 20 percent of the cases customers have filed under Title III involved changes the business owners could have made at no cost.
      b) In addition, companies with $1 million or less in annual sales or with 30 or fewer full-time employees that invest in making their locations more accessible to all qualify for a tax credit.
   6. The Disabilities Act also prohibits any kind of employment discrimination against anyone with a physical or mental disability.
   7. The following are some of the specific provisions of Title III of the act:
      a) Restaurants, hotels, theaters, shopping centers and malls, retail stores, museums, libraries, parks, private schools, day-care centers, and other similar places of public accommodation may not discriminate on the basis of disability.
      b) Physical barriers in existing places of public accommodation must be removed if readily achievable. If not, alternative methods of providing services must be offered, if those methods are readily achievable.
      c) New construction of places of public accommodation and commercial facilities must be accessible.
      d) Alterations to existing places of public accommodation and commercial facilities must be done in an accessible manner.
      e) Elevators are not required in newly constructed or altered buildings under three stories or with less than 3,000 square feet per floor, unless the building is a shopping center; shopping mall; professional office of a health care provider; terminal, depot, or station used for public transportation; or an airport passenger terminal.

E. Signs
   1. One of the lowest-cost and most effective methods of communicating with customers is a business sign.
   2. Signs tell potential customers what a business does, where it is, and what it is selling.
      a) A sign should be large enough for passersby to read it from a distance, taking into consideration the location and speed of surrounding traffic arteries.
      b) The message should be short, simple, and clear.
      c) A sign should be legible both in daylight and at night.
      d) Contrasting colors and simple typefaces are best.

     e) Because signs become part of the surrounding scenery over time, business owners should consider changing their features to retain their effectiveness. Animated parts and unusual shapes can attract interest.

   3. The most common problems with business signs are that they are illegible, poorly designed, improperly located, poorly maintained and have color schemes that are unattractive or are hard to read.

   4. Before investing in a sign, an entrepreneur should investigate the local community's ordinance.

WIRED TO THE WEB - The Applicant

SUMMARY

"Hey, Ramon, what did the guy in the wheelchair want?" "He was applying for the job we advertised in *The Dispatch* this past Sunday." Ramon was the founder and CEO of American Classic Lighting, Inc., a company that manufactures high-quality reproductions of antique and period lighting fixtures. Ramon had started the company after he and his wife had purchased an old home and had difficulty finding lighting fixtures to blend with the house's classic style.

"You mean the manufacturing job? The one in assembly," Pete, who was the company's manufacturing manager, asked. "But a guy in a wheelchair can't assemble lamps, can he?" "To be honest, I've never really thought about it." "But a job in our production department? None of the other 27 people in this company are in wheelchairs. Wouldn't we have to change everything just to accommodate him?" "We have to make some adjustments. . . I'll need to talk with our attorney about our responsibilities under the Americans with Disabilities Act."

1. Use the World Wide Web to research the Americans with Disabilities Act. What obligations does American Classic Lighting have to Jacob Saunders under the act?
   Answer - Ramon is under the full weight of ADA due to the size of his company. He needs to make reasonable accommodation so the applicant could work if he is qualified. Basically Ramon must treat him like any other applicant in the hiring process.
2. On the basis of your research, what advice would you give to Ramon Hernandez about Jacob Saunders application for employment?
   Answer - Treat him fairly, hire him if qualified. Be clear about work expectations, goals, etc., just as he would with any other applicant. Once he's made an offer then he should discuss specifically what accommodations the applicant might need.
3. Is it ever ethical for businesses such as American Classic Lighting to take into consideration a job applicant's physical qualities in a hiring decision? If so, when?
   Answer - Generally no. Only when those physical conditions cannot be accommodated, or they disqualify the applicant from being able to perform the job.

  F. Interiors
    1. Designing a functional, efficient interior is not easy.
    2. Technology has changed drastically the way employees, customers, and the environment interact with one another.
    3. Ergonomics, the science of adapting work and the work environment to complement employees' strengths and to suit customers' needs, is an integral part of a successful design.
      a) An ergonomically designed workspace can improve workers' productivity significantly and lower days lost due to injuries and accidents.

b) One OSHA study found that 62 percent of all workplace injuries are musculoskeletal injuries, most of which could have been prevented by ergonomic designs.

4. When planning store, office, or plant layouts, business owners too often focus on minimizing costs.

a) One extensive six-year study concluded that changes in office design have a direct impact on workers' performance, job satisfaction, and ease of communication.

b) The report also concluded that the savings generated by effective layouts are substantial, and conversely, that poorly planned designs involve significant costs.

5. When evaluating an existing building's interior, an entrepreneur must be sure to determine the integrity of its structural components.

a) Are the building's floors strong enough to hold the business's equipment, inventory, and personnel?

b) Like floors, walls and ceilings must be both functional and attractive. On the functional side, walls and ceilings should be fireproof and soundproof.

6. For many businesses, a drive-through window adds another dimension to the concept of customer convenience and is a relatively inexpensive way to increase sales.

G. Lights and Fixtures

1. Proper lighting is measured by what is ideal for the job being done.

2. Modern advances in lighting technology give small businesses more options for lighting their stores, factories, and offices.

3. Lighting is often an inexpensive investment when considering its impact on the overall appearance of the business.

VIII. Layout: Maximizing Revenues, Increasing Efficiency, and Reducing Costs

A. Introduction

1. The ideal layout contributes to efficient operations, increased productivity, and higher sales.

2. What is ideal depends on the type of business and on the entrepreneur's strategy for gaining a competitive edge.

B. Layout for Retailers

1. Retail layout is the arrangement and method of display of merchandise in a store.

a) It should pull customers into the store and make it easy for them to locate merchandise; compare price, quality, and features; and ultimately to make a purchase.

b) The floor plan should take customers past displays of other items that they may buy on impulse.

2. Customers' traffic patterns give the owner a clue to the best location for the items with the highest gross margin.

a) Merchandise purchased on impulse and convenience goods should be located near the front of the store.

b) Items people shop around for before buying and specialty goods will attract their own customers and should not be placed in prime space.

c) Prime selling space should be restricted to products that carry the highest markups.

d) Table 15.2 offers suggestions for locating merchandise in a small retail store.

3. Layout in a retail store evolves from a clear understanding of customers' buying habits.

4. Retailers have three basic layout patterns from which to choose: the grid, the free-form layout, and the boutique.

a) The grid layout arranges displays in rectangular fashion so that aisles are parallel.

(1) It is a formal layout that controls the traffic flow through the store.

           (2) Figure 15.4 shows a typical grid layout.

      b) Unlike the grid layout, the free-form layout is informal, using displays of various shapes and sizes.

           (1) Its primary advantage is the relaxed, friendly shopping atmosphere it creates, which encourages customers to shop longer and increases the number of impulse purchases they make.

           (2) Figure 15.5 illustrates a free-form layout.

      c) The boutique layout divides the store into a series of individual shopping areas, each with its own theme. It is like building a series of specialty shops into a single store.

           (1) The boutique layout is informal and can create a unique shopping environment for the customer.

           (2) Figure 15.6 shows a boutique layout for a small department store.

5. Business owners should display merchandise as attractively as their budgets will allow.

      a) Retailers can boost sales by displaying together items that complement each other.

      b) Spacious displays provide shoppers an open view of merchandise and reduce the likelihood of shoplifting.

6. When planning displays, retailers should remember:

      a) The average man is 68.8 inches tall, and the average woman is 63.6 inches tall.

      b) The average person's normal reach is 16 inches, and the extended reach is 24 inches.

      c) The average man's standing eye level is 62 inches from the floor, and the average woman's standing eye level is 57 inches from the floor.

7. Retailers must remember to separate the selling and nonselling areas of a store.

8. Certain areas contribute more to revenue than others. The value of store space depends on floor location in a multistory building, location with respect to aisles and walkways, and proximity to entrances.

      a) Space values decrease as distance from the main entry-level floor increases.

      b) Figure 15.7 offers one example of how rent and sales could be allocated by floors.

9. The layout of aisles in the store has a major impact on the customer exposure that merchandise receives.

      a) Items located on primary walkways should be assigned a higher share of rental costs and should contribute a greater portion to sales revenue than those displayed along secondary aisles.

      b) Figure 15.8 shows that high-value areas are exposed to two primary aisles.

10. Space values also depend on the spaces' relative position to the store entrance.

      a) Typically, the farther away an area is from the entrance, the lower its value.

      b) Most shoppers turn to the right when entering a store and move around it counter-clockwise.

      c) Only about one-fourth of a store's customers will go more than halfway into the store.

      d) Figure 15.9 illustrates space values for a typical small-store layout.

11. The decline in value of store space from front to back of the shop is expressed in the 40-30-20-10 rule.

      a) This rule assigns 40 percent of a store's rental cost to the front quarter of the shop.

      b) 30 percent to the second quarter.

      c) 20 percent to the third quarter.

      d) 10 percent to the final quarter.

12. Each quarter of the store should contribute the same percentage of sales revenue.

C. Layout for Manufacturers

    1. Manufacturing facilities have come under increased scrutiny as firms attempt to improve quality, decrease inventories, and increase productivity through facilities that are integrated, flexible, and controlled.

a) Facility layout has a dramatic effect on product mix, product processing, materials handling, storage, control, and production volume and quality.

b) Some manufacturers are using 3-D simulation software (based on the same technology as the 3-D video games people play) to test the layout of their factory and its impact on employees and their productivity before they ever build them.

IN THE FOOTSTEPS OF AN ENTREPRENEUR - When It Comes to Store Layout, She Keeps 'Em Guessing

SUMMARY
What makes people drive up to three hours to this quaint little railroad town about 50 miles north of Kansas City that is surrounded by nothing but farmland? Most of the people who go to Atchinson are looking to buy home furnishings from Mary Carol Garrity's unique shop named Nell Hill's (after Garrity's grandmother). A significant part of the store's success is due to its unique layout and Garrity's effective use of her inventory and props to create a wonderfully warm and friendly environment that makes customers want to linger and shop--and buy. Housed in an old bank building, Nell Hill's gives shoppers the impression that they are in someone's tastefully decorated home rather than a retail shop. Practically everything customers see is for sale.

In addition to the store's welcoming ambiance, Nell Hill's offers customers something new every time they come in. Garrity is constantly changing the store layout. Even customers whose visits are just days apart will see a layout that is completely different. The primary reason Garrity is constantly changing the layout of the store is to keep her customers interested and coming back frequently.

Garrity's recipe for Nell Hill's is a success. The company's net profit margin of 10 percent is well above that of similar shops and is growing at an amazing 20 percent a year. She recently opened a second store in Atchison, G. Dieboldt's (named after her father) that focuses on bedroom furnishings and fabrics, which had formerly occupied the top floor at Nell Hill's. Garrity's plan is to open four or five stores, all with different themes, but with the same spirit as Nell Hill's.

1. Why is layout such an important component in stores, such as Garrity's, that sell home furnishings and decorations?
    Answer - The other stores draw more customers, better parking and accessibility, longer retail hours and the ability to charge higher prices.
2. Use the World Wide Web to develop a demographic profile of the residents of Atchinson, Kansas. On the basis of your analysis, discuss the importance of Garrity's approach to store layout and her overall sales strategy for Nell Hill's.
    Answer - Students' answers will vary according to their research.

---

2. Factors in Manufacturing Layout.
    a) Type of product.
    b) Type of production process.
    c) Technology used.
    d) Ergonomic considerations.
    e) Economic considerations.
    f) Space availability within the facility itself.
3. Types of manufacturing layouts. There are three basic types of layouts that manufacturers can use separately or in combination--product, process, and fixed position--and they differ in their applicability to different levels of manufacturing volume.

    a) In a product (or line) layout, a manufacturer arranges workers and equipment according to the sequence of operations performed on the product.

      (1) See Figure 15.10.

      (2) Conceptually, the flow is an unbroken line from raw materials input to finished goods.

         (a) This type of layout is applicable to rigid-flow, high-volume, continuous or mass-production operations or when the product is highly standardized.

      (3) Product layouts offer the advantages of lower materials-handling costs; simplified tasks that can be done with low-cost, lower-skilled labor; reduced amounts of work-in-process inventory; and relatively simplified production control activities.

      (4) Disadvantages of product layouts include their inflexibility, monotony of job tasks, high fixed investment in specialized equipment, and heavy interdependence of all operations.

    b) In a process layout, a manufacturer groups workers and equipment according to the general function they perform, without regard to any particular product.

      (1) See Figure 15.11.

      (2) Process layouts are appropriate when production runs are short, when demand shows considerable variation and the costs of holding finished goods inventory are high, or when the product is customized.

      (3) Process layouts have the advantages of being flexible for doing customer work and promoting job satisfaction by offering employees diverse and challenging tasks.

      (4) Its disadvantages are the higher costs of materials handling, more skilled labor, lower productivity, and more-complex production control.

    c) In fixed-position layouts, materials do not move down a line as in a product layout; because of the bulk or weight of the final product, materials are assembled in one spot.

4. Designing Layouts

    a) The starting point in layout design is determining how and in what sequence product parts or service tasks flow together.

    b) One of the most effective techniques is to create an overall picture of the manufacturing process using assembly charts and process flowcharts.

    c) Given the tasks and their sequence, plus knowledge of the volume of products to be produced, an owner can analyze space and equipment needs to get an idea of the facility's demands.

      (1) When a product layout is being used, these demands take precedence, and manufacturers must arrange equipment and workstations to fit the production tasks and their sequence.

      (2) If a process layout is used, different products place different demands on the facility. Rather than having a single best flow, there may be one flow for each product, and compromises will be necessary. As a result, any one product may not get the ideal layout.

5. Analyzing production layouts

    a) Although there is not general procedure for analyzing the numerous interdependent factors that enter into layout design, specific layout problems lend themselves to detailed analysis.

    b) Two important criteria for selecting and designing a layout are worker effectiveness and materials-handling costs.

    c) Designing layouts ergonomically so that they maximize workers' strengths is especially important for manufacturers.

(1) Creating an environment that is comfortable and pleasant for workers will pay big benefits over time.

d) Manufacturers can lower materials-handling costs by using layouts designed to automate product flow whenever possible and to minimize flow distances and times.

(1) The extent of automation depends on the level of technology and amount of capital available, as well as behavioral considerations of employees.

(2) Flow distances and times are usually minimized by locating sequential processing activities or interrelated departments in adjacent areas.

e) The following features are important to a good manufacturing layout:

(1) Planned materials flow pattern

(2) Straight-line layout where possible

(3) Straight, clearly marked aisles

(4) Backtracking kept to a minimum

(5) Related operations close together

(6) Minimum of in-process inventory

(7) Easy adjustment to changing conditions

(8) Minimum materials-handling distances

(9) Minimum of manual handling

(10) No unnecessary rehandling of material

(11) Minimum handling between operations

(12) Materials delivered to production employees quickly

(13) Use of gravity to move materials whenever possible

(14) Materials efficiently removed from the work area

(15) Material handling done by indirect labor

(16) Orderly materials handling and storage

(17) Good housekeeping

IX. Build, Buy, or Lease?

A. The Decision to Build

1. Constructing a new facility can project a positive image to potential customers.

a) A new building can incorporate the most modern features during construction, which can significantly lower operating costs.

b) In addition, by constructing a new building, a business owner can incorporate into the layout features that meet the business's unique design needs such as loading docks, laboratories, or refrigeration units.

c) Building a new facility can also improve a company's long-term productivity and efficiency.

2. In some rapidly growing areas, there are only a few or sometimes no existing buildings to buy or lease that match an entrepreneur's requirements.

a) A business owner must consider the cost of constructing a building as a significant factor in her initial estimates of capital needs and breakeven point.

b) Constructing a building imposes a high initial fixed cost that an owner must weigh against the facility's ability to generate revenue and to reduce operating expenses.

c) Building a new structure also requires more time than either buying or leasing an existing one.

B. The Decision to Buy

1. In many cases, there may be an ideal building in the area where an entrepreneur wants to locate.

a) Buying the facility allows her to remodel it without seeking permission from anyone else.

    b) Buying can put a drain on the business's financial resources, but the owner knows exactly what her monthly payments will be.
    c) Under a lease, rental rates can (and usually do) increase over time.
    d) If an owner believes that the property will actually appreciate in value, a decision to purchase may prove to be wise.
    e) In addition, the owner can depreciate the building each year, and both depreciation and interest are tax-deductible business expenses.
2. When considering the purchase of a building, the owner should use the same outline of facilities requirements developed for the building option.
    a) Remodeling can add a significant initial expense.
3. Building or buying a building greatly limits an entrepreneur's mobility, however.
    a) Some business owners prefer to stay out of the real estate business to retain maximum flexibility and mobility.
    b) Plus, not all real estate appreciates in value.

GAINING THE COMPETITIVE EDGE - How to Get the Best Deal on a Lease

SUMMARY
The Lion's Head, a popular Greenwich Village restaurant and bar, recently closed its doors after three decades as the favorite gathering place of writers, artists, and actors. A series of steep increases in the Lion's Head's lease payments put the restaurant in a precarious financial situation.

Rent or lease payments represent one of the largest expenses many business owners pay. As the Lion's Head proves, failing to negotiate a satisfactory lease can push a company's operating expenses so high that ultimately the company fails. What can a business owner do to avoid lease nightmares? The following tips will help.
- Read the lease agreement before you sign it.
- Ask an experienced attorney to review the lease before you sign it.
- Incorporate (or form an LLC) before you sign a lease.
- Try to negotiate a lease term that is as short as possible at the outset.
- Get everything in writing.
- Pay close attention to the details.
- Make sure you have good insurance to cover any damage to the property.
- Verify that the lease's provisions on such issues as parking spaces, improvements, operating hours, air conditioning and heating, cleaning and other services, and maintenance suit your business and its financial situation.
- Ask for the ability to sublease (with the landlord's approval, of course).
- Retailers who lease spaces in shopping centers should try to include a clause that guarantees the landlord will not lease to another competing business (called an "exclusive").

C. The Decision to Lease
    1. The major advantage of leasing is that it requires no large initial cash outlay, so the business's funds are available for purchasing inventory or for supporting current operations.
        a) Also, lease expenses are tax-deductible.
        b) Because leasing is usually the least expensive option, most start-up businesses lease their buildings.
        c) According to one small business expert, entrepreneurs typically begin to consider buying or constructing a building when their companies are about five years old.
    2. One major disadvantage of leasing is that the property owner might choose not to renew the lease.

a) Also, if a business is successful, the property owner may ask for a significant increase in rent when the lease renewal is negotiated.

b) In some lease arrangements, the owner is compensated, in addition to a monthly rental fee, by a percentage of the tenant's gross sales. This practice is common in shopping centers.

c) Still another disadvantage to leasing is the limitation on remodeling.

(1) All permanent modifications of the structure become the property of the building owner.

Chapter Summary

♦ Explain the stages in the location decision.
  ▪ The location decision is one of the most important decisions an entrepreneur will make, given its long-term effects on the company. An entrepreneur should look at the choice as a series of increasingly narrow decisions: Which region of the country? Which state? Which city? Which site?
  ▪ Demographic statistics are available from a wide variety of sources, but government agencies such as the Census Bureau have a wealth of detailed data that can guide an entrepreneur in her location decision.

♦ Describe the location criteria for retail and service businesses.
  ▪ For retailers and many service businesses, the location decision is especially crucial. They must consider the size of the trade area, the volume of customer traffic, number of parking spots, availability of room for expansion, and the visibility of a site.

♦ Outline the basic location options for retail and service businesses.
  ▪ Retail and service businesses have six basic location options: central business districts (CBDs), neighborhoods, shopping centers and malls, near competitors, outlying areas, and at home.

♦ Explain the site selection process for manufacturers. · A manufacturer's location decision is strongly influenced by local zoning ordinances. Some areas offer industrial parks designed specifically to attract manufacturers. Two crucial factors for most manufacturers are the accessibility to (and the cost of transporting) raw materials and the quality and quantity of available labor.

♦ Discuss the benefits of locating a start-up company in a business incubator.
  ▪ Business incubators are locations that offer flexible, low-cost rental space to their tenants as well as business and consulting services. Their goal is to nurture small companies until they are ready to "graduate" into the larger business community. Many government agencies and universities offer incubator locations.

♦ Describe the criteria used to analyze the layout and design considerations of a building, including the Americans with Disabilities Act.
  ▪ When evaluating the suitability of a particular building, an entrepreneur should consider several factors: size (is it large enough to accommodate the business with some room for growth?); construction and external appearance (is the building structurally sound, and does it create the right impression for the business?); entrances (are they inviting?); legal issues (does the building comply with the Americans with Disabilities Act? If not, how much will it cost to bring it up to standard?); signs (are they legible, well located, and easy to see?); interior (does the interior design contribute to our ability to make sales? Is it ergonomically designed?); lights and fixtures (is the lighting adequate for the tasks workers will be performing, and what is the estimated cost of lighting?).

♦ Explain the principles of effective layouts for retailers, service businesses, and manufacturers.
  ▪ Layout for retail stores and service businesses depends on the owner's understanding of her customers' buying habits. Retailers have three basic layout options from which to choose: grid, free-form pattern, and boutique. Some areas of a retail store generate more sales per square foot and are, therefore, more valuable than others.

- The goal of a manufacturer's layout is to create a smooth, efficient workflow. Three basic options exist: product layout, process layout, and fixed position layout. Two key considerations are worker productivity and materials-handling costs.
♦ Evaluate the advantages and disadvantages of building, buying, and leasing a building.
   - Building a new building gives an entrepreneur the opportunity to design exactly what he wants in a brand-new facility; however, not every small business owner can afford to tie up significant amounts of cash in fixed assets. Buying an existing building gives a business owner the freedom to renovate as needed, but this can be an expensive alternative. Leasing a location is a common choice because it is economical, but the business owner faces the uncertainty of lease renewals, rising rents, and renovation problems.

Discussion Questions

1. How do most small business owners choose a location? Is this wise?
   Answer - Many entrepreneurs never consider locations beyond their own hometowns. No, because the "secret" to selecting the ideal location goes back to knowing who a company's target customers are and then finding a site that makes it most convenient for those customers to do business with the company. An entrepreneur's ultimate location goal is to locate the company at a site that will maximize the likelihood of success. The more entrepreneurs invest in researching potential locations, the higher is the probability that they will find the spot that is best suited for their company.

2. What factors should a manager consider when evaluating a region in which to locate a business? Where are such data available?
   Answer - The logic of location selection is to begin with a broad regional search and then to systematically narrow the focus of the site selection process. See Figure 15.1.

   Common requirements include rapid growth in the population of a certain age group, rising disposable incomes, the existence of specific infrastructure, a nonunion environment, and low operating costs. At the broadest level of the location decision, entrepreneurs usually identify regions of the country that are experiencing substantial growth. The Census Bureau publishes a monthly newsletter, "Census and You," which is especially helpful to business owners and has an easy-to-use World Wide Web site <http:/www.census.gov/>.

   The Small Business Administration also has valuable aids to help you throughout your location search. Some of these are "Practical Use of Government Statistics," "Using Census Data to Select a Store Site," and "Using Census Data in Small Plant Marketing." *American Demographics* magazine has two valuable booklets also: The 1990 Census: The Counting of America and A Researcher's Guide to the 1990 Census. Sales and Marketing Management's Survey of Buying Power, published annually, provides a detailed breakdown of population, retail sales, spendable income, and other characteristics. "The Editor and Publisher Market Guide" is similar to the "Survey of Buying Power," but provides additional information on markets. The guide includes detailed information on key cities. *Rand McNally's Commercial Atlas and Marketing Guide* reports on more than 128,000 places in the United States, many of which are not available through census reports. *The Zip Code Atlas and Market Planner* is an extremely useful location and market-planning tool. It combines a breakdown of zip codes (often the basis of psychographic customer profiles) with maps featuring physical features such as mountains, rivers, and major highways. The Small Business Administration's Small Business Development Center (SBDC) program also offers location analysis assistance to entrepreneurs. Entrepreneurs are relying on geographic information systems (GISs), powerful software programs that combine map drawing with database management capability, to pinpoint the ideal location for their business.

3. Outline the factors entrepreneurs should consider when selecting a state in which to locate a business.

Answer - Every state has a business development office to recruit new businesses to that state. Some of the key issues to explore include the laws, regulations, and taxes that govern businesses and any incentives or investment credits the state may offer to businesses locating there. Other factors to consider include proximity to markets, proximity to raw materials, quantity and quality of the labor supply, general business climate, and wage rates.

4. What factors should a seafood-processing plant, a beauty shop, and an exclusive jewelry store consider in choosing a location? List factors for each type of business.
    Answer - Seafood-processing plant--costs, local laws and regulations, compatibility with the community, and transportation networks. A beauty shop--population trends and density, competition, costs, and local laws and regulations. An exclusive jewelry store--competition, costs, quality of life, and police and fire protection.

5. What intangible factors might enter into the entrepreneur's location decision?
    Answer - One of the intangibles that an entrepreneur can determine only by visiting a particular city is the degree of compatibility a business has with the surrounding community. A company's image must fit in with the character of the town and the needs and wants of its residents. Another intangible, one of the most important, yet most difficult to measure, criteria for a city is the quality of life it offers. Entrepreneurs have the freedom and the flexibility to locate their companies in cities that suit not only their business needs but also their personal preferences. When choosing locations for their companies, entrepreneurs often consider factors such as cultural events, outdoor activities, entertainment opportunities, safety, and the city's "personality."

6. What are zoning laws? How do they affect the location decision?
    Answer - Before selecting a particular site within a city, small business owners must explore the local zoning laws to determine if there are any ordinances that would place restrictions on business activity or that would prohibit establishing a business altogether. Zoning is a system that divides a city or county into small cells or districts to control the use of land, buildings, and sites. Its purpose is to contain similar activities in suitable locations.

7. What is the trade area? What determines a small retailer's trade area?
    Answer - The trade area: the region from which a business can expect to draw customers over a reasonable time span. The primary variables that influence the scope of a trade area are the type and size of the operation. If a retailer is a specialist with a wide assortment of products, he may draw customers from a great distance. As a rule, the larger the store and the greater its selection of merchandise, the broader its trade area. The following environmental factors influence the retail trade area size.
    - Retail compatibility.
    - Degree of competition.
    - Transportation network.
    - Physical, cultural, or emotional barriers.

8. Why is it important to discover more than just the number of passersby in a traffic count?
    Answer - Perhaps the most important screening criteria for a potential retail (and often for a service) location is the number of potential customers passing by the site during business hours. Entrepreneurs should know the traffic counts (pedestrian and auto) at the sites they are considering. They need to know if the passersby are customers and whether there is adequate parking. Otherwise they won't sell enough to surpass their breakeven point.

9. What types of information can an entrepreneur collect from census data?
    Answer - Entrepreneurs can find vital demographic information for specific locations.

10. Why may a cheap location not be the best location?
    Answer - It may not have sufficient passerby traffic, it might be inaccessible, it might be hidden by other stores, it might have insufficient parking, etc.

11. What function does a small firm's sign serve? What are the characteristics of an effective business sign?
    Answer - One of the lowest-cost and most effective methods of communicating with customers is a business sign. Signs tell potential customers what a business does, where it is, and what it is selling.
    - A sign should be large enough for passersby to read it from a distance, taking into consideration the location and speed of surrounding traffic arteries.
    - The message should be short, simple, and clear.
    - A sign should be legible both in daylight and at night.
    - Contrasting colors and simple typefaces are best.
    - Because signs become part of the surrounding scenery over time, business owners should consider changing their features to retain their effectiveness. Animated parts and unusual shapes can attract interest.

12. Explain the statement: "The portions of a small store's interior space are not of equal value in generating sales revenue." What areas are most valuable?
    Answer - Retail layout is the arrangement and method of display of merchandise in a store. It should pull customers into the store and make it easy for them to locate merchandise; compare price, quality, and features; and ultimately to make a purchase. The floor plan should take customers past displays of other items that they may buy on impulse.

    The decline in value of store space from front to back of the shop is expressed in the 40-30-20-10 rule. This rule assigns 40 percent of a store's rental cost to the front quarter of the shop, 30 percent to the second quarter, 20 percent to the third quarter, and 10 percent to the final quarter. Each quarter of the store should contribute the same percentage of sales revenue.

13. What are some of the major features that are important to a good manufacturing layout?
    Answer - Factors in manufacturing layout.
    - Type of product.
    - Type of production process.
    - Technology used.
    - Ergonomic considerations.
    - Economic considerations.
    - Space availability within the facility itself.

14. Summarize the advantages and disadvantages of building, buying, and leasing a building.
    Answer - Constructing a new facility can project a positive image to potential customers. A new building can incorporate the most modern features during construction, which can significantly lower operating costs. In addition, by constructing a new building, a business owner can incorporate into the layout features that meet the business's unique design needs such as loading docks, laboratories, or refrigeration units. Building a new facility can also improve a company's long-term productivity and efficiency. Disadvantages. A business owner must consider the cost of constructing a building as a significant factor in her initial estimates of capital needs and breakeven point. Constructing a building imposes a high initial fixed cost that an owner must weigh against the facility's ability to generate revenue and to reduce operating expenses. Building a new structure also requires more time than either buying or leasing an existing one.

In many cases, there may be an ideal building in the area where an entrepreneur wants to locate. Buying the facility allows her to remodel it without seeking permission from anyone else. Buying can put a drain on the business's financial resources, but the owner knows exactly what her monthly payments will be. If an owner believes that the property will actually appreciate in value, a decision to purchase may prove to be wise. In addition, the owner can depreciate the building each year, and both depreciation and interest are tax-deductible business expenses. Disadvantages. When considering the purchase of a building, the owner should use the same outline of facilities requirements developed for the building option. Remodeling can add a significant initial expense. Building or buying a building greatly limits an entrepreneur's mobility, however.

The major advantage of leasing is that it requires no large initial cash outlay, so the business's funds are available for purchasing inventory or for supporting current operations. Also, lease expenses are tax-deductible. Because leasing is usually the least expensive option, most start-up businesses lease their buildings. One major disadvantage of leasing is that the property owner might choose not to re-new the lease. Also, if a business is successful, the property owner may ask for a significant increase in rent when the lease renewal is negotiated. In some lease arrangements, the owner is compensated, in addition to a monthly rental fee, by a percentage of the tenant's gross sales. This practice is common in shopping centers. Still another disadvantage to leasing is the limitation on remodeling. All permanent modifications of the structure become the property of the building owner.

Step into the Real World

1. Ask your librarian to help you with a search of government documents to gain additional insight about a city or town you are familiar with. What did you learn about the area and its residents? What kind of businesses would be most successful there? Least successful

2. Visit a successful retail store and evaluate its layout. What, if anything, struck you about the layout of the store? What suggestions can you make for improving it?

3. Locate the most recent issue of either *Entrepreneur* or *Fortune* describing the "best cities for (small) business." (For *Entrepreneur*, it is usually the October issue, and for *Fortune*, it is normally an issue in November.) Which cities are in the top 107? What factors did the magazine use to select these cities? Pick a city and explain what makes it an attractive destination for locating a business.

4. Spend some time researching the details of creating an attractive window display. On the basis of your research, develop a simple rating system to evaluate the effectiveness of window displays. Then visit an area of your town or city where there is a cluster of small retail shops. Evaluate the window displays you see using your rating scale. Which ones are most effective? Least effective? Why?

Chapter 16 - Purchasing, Quality Control, and Vendor Analysis

Without the right goods, sales are impossible.
Anonymous

Quality is never an accident; it is always the result of high intention, sincere effort, intelligent direction, and skillful execution; it represents the wise choice of many alternatives.
William A. Foster

Teaching Objectives
Students will be able to:
1. Understand the components of a purchasing plan.
2. Explain the principles of total quality management (TQM) and its impact on quality.
3. Conduct economic order quantity (EOQ) analysis to determine the proper level of inventory.
4. Differentiate among the three types of purchase discounts vendors offer.
5. Calculate a company reorder point.
6. Develop a vendor rating scale.
7. Describe the legal implications of the purchasing function.

Instructor's Outline
I. Introduction
  A. Their Importance
    1. Purchasing is not one of the most glamorous or exciting jobs an entrepreneur will undertake, but it is one of the most vital functions to a small company's ultimate success.
    2. When entrepreneurs begin producing products or providing services, they soon discover how dependent their products and services are on the quality of the components and services they purchase from their vendors, or suppliers.
    3. Selecting the right vendors and ensuring that the purchasing process operates efficiently determine a small company's ability to produce and sell quality products at a reasonable price.
    4. The effects of an entrepreneur's decisions on purchasing, quality, and vendor selection ripple throughout the entire company, affecting everything it does and producing a dramatic impact on its "bottom line."
    5. Depending on the type of business involved, the amounts spent by the purchasing department range from 25 to 85 cents per one dollar of sales.

II. The Purchasing Plan
  A. Described
    1. Purchasing involves the acquisition of needed materials, supplies, services, and equipment of the right quality, in the proper quantities, for reasonable prices, at the appropriate time, from the right vendor, or supplier.
    2. A major objective of purchasing is to acquire enough (but not too much!) stock to ensure smooth, uninterrupted production or sales and to see that the merchandise is delivered on time.
    3. The purchasing plan is closely linked to the other functional areas of managing a small business.
    4. A purchasing plan should recognize this interaction and help integrate the purchasing function into the total organization.
      a) See Figure 16.1.

III. Quality
    A. Introduction
        1. Not long ago many companies mistakenly believed that producing, and therefore purchasing, high-quality products and services was too costly.
        2. The benefits companies earn by pursuing quality products, services, and processes come not only in the form of fewer defects but also as lower costs, higher productivity, reduced cycle time, greater market share, increased customer satisfaction, and higher customer retention rates.
        3. W. Edwards Deming, one of the founding fathers of the modern quality movement, always claimed that "higher quality is less expensive to produce than lower quality.
        4. Total quality companies believe in and manage with the attitude of continuous improvement, a concept the Japanese call kaizen.
            a) The kaizen philosophy holds that small improvements made continuously over time accumulate into a radically reshaped and improved process.
        5. Despite the benefits, many managers have yet to get on the quality bandwagon.
            a) 83 percent of managers at midsized companies said that quality was a top priority.
            b) Only 31 percent had actually calculated the cost of quality: the costs associated with scrap, rework, inspections, training, technology, and other factors.

    B. Total Quality Management
        1. Under the total quality management (TQM) philosophy, companies define a quality product as one that conforms to predetermined standards that satisfy customers' demands.
            a) That means getting everything--from delivery and invoicing to installation and follow-up--right the first time.
            b) 99.9 percent level of quality is not good enough--See Table 16.1.
        2. TQM instills the philosophy of doing the job right the first time.
        3. Although the concept is simple, implementing such a process is a challenge that requires a very different kind of thinking and very different culture than most organizations are comfortable with.
            a) Patience is a must for companies adopting the philosophy.
        4. Studies show that it takes at least three or four years before TQM principles gain acceptance among employees, and that eight to ten years are necessary to fully implement TQM in a company.
        5. To implement TQM successfully, a small business owner must rely on 10 fundamental principles:
            a) Shift from a management-driven culture to a participative, team-based one.
                (1) Two basic tenets of TQM are employee involvement and teamwork.
                (2) Modify the reward system to encourage teamwork and innovation.
            b) Train workers constantly to give them the tools they need to produce quality and to upgrade the company's knowledge base.
                (1) One of the most important factors in making long-term, constant improvements in a company's processes is teaching workers the philosophy and the tools of TQM.

IN THE FOOTSTEPS OF AN ENTREPRENEUR - Why Certify?

It took LabChem more than nine months and cost the small specialty chemical manufacturer more than $50,000, but, according to vice president Mike Semon, it was definitely worth it. Once a concern only for major corporations, ISO 9000 certification has attracted the attention of a growing number of small businesses who see the benefits of certification. ISO's standards verify that it has established a functional quality control process and consistently follows it. More than 100 countries have adopted ISO 9000 as their national quality standard.

Why are small companies becoming ISO 9000 certified? One-fourth of all the corporations around the globe require their suppliers to be ISO 9000 certified. Many of the companies that are discovering the benefits of becoming certified are small businesses. The benefits of ISO 9000 certification are both internal and external. A quality survey of ISO 9000-certified companies found that 95 percent had derived internal benefits such as improved quality, more efficient systems, and higher productivity. Nearly 85 percent cited higher quality awareness among workers as an advantage. Externally, ISO certification opens the door to more customers.

Gaining ISO 9000 certification, like most things that are worthwhile, takes time, money, and effort. The average cost for a small business (those with less than $11 million in sales) to earn certification is $71,000-$51,000 for internal expenses and $20,000 for external expenses such as quality consultants and trainers. The average time required is 15 months.

1. What benefits does a small company derive from becoming ISO-certified? What are the costs?
    Answer - They gain a prestige image, it opens doors to markets that require certification, and it may result in more customers. It costs significant time and money and may require significant changes in the way the firm does business.
2. Use the World Wide Web to research ISO 9000 requirements. How many levels of certification are there? What areas does each level cover?
    Answer - Students' responses should show the variety of certifications possible, ISO 9001, 9002, etc.
3. Canvas the businesses in your area. Work with a team of your classmates to develop a list of companies that you believe would benefit from becoming ISO 9000 certified. Develop a second list of companies for whom ISO 9000 certification would offer only limited benefits. What characteristics define the differences between the companies on your two lists?
    Answer - Students' responses will vary but should show a greater focus on quality, more participation by employees, and better cost efficiencies.

      c) Train employees to measure quality with statistical process controls (SPC).
      d) Use Pareto's Law to focus TQM efforts.
         (1) One of the toughest decisions is "Where do we start?"
         (2) The best way to answer that fundamental question is to use Pareto's Law (also called the 80/20 Rule), which states that 80 percent of a company's quality problems arise from just 20 percent of all causes.
      e) Share information with everyone in the organization.
      f) Focus quality improvements on astonishing the customer.
         (1) The heart of TQM is customer satisfaction--better yet, customer astonishment.
      g) Don't rely on inspection to produce quality products and services.
         (1) The only way to improve a process is to discover the cause of poor quality, and fix it.
      h) Avoid using TQM to place blame on those who make mistakes.
      i) Strive for continuous improvement in processes as well as in products and services.
         (1) There is no finish line in the race for quality.
    6. Many of these principles are evident in quality guru W. Edwards Deming's 14 points, a capsulized version of how to build a successful TQM approach
      a) See Table 16.2.
    7. Implementing a TQM program successfully begins at the top.

8. Drastic changes such as these naturally create turmoil. Planned and implemented properly, however, TQM can use the energy from that turmoil to drive the changes a company must make if it is to become truly world-class.

IV. Quantity: The Economic Order Quantity (EOQ)
   A. Introduction
      1. An investment in inventory is not profitable because dollars spent return nothing until the inventory is sold.
      2. A primary objective of this portion of the purchasing plan is to generate an adequate turnover of merchandise by purchasing proper quantities.
         a) Tying up capital in the maintenance of extra inventory limits the firm's working capital and exerts pressure on its cash flows.
         b) The firm risks the danger of being stuck with spoiled or obsolete merchandise.
         c) Excess inventory also takes up valuable store or selling space.
      3. On the other hand, maintaining too little inventory can be extremely costly.
         a) Reordering merchandise frequently escalates total inventory costs.
         b) Persistent stockouts are inconvenient for customers, and many will eventually choose to shop elsewhere.
      4. The analytical techniques used to determine economic order quantities (EOQs) will help the manager compute the amount of stock to purchase with an order or to produce with each production run to minimize total inventory costs.
      5. To compute the proper amount of stock to order or to produce, the small business owner must first determine the three principal elements of total inventory costs: the cost of the units, the holding (or carrying) cost, and the setup (or ordering) cost.

   B. Cost of Units
      1. The cost of the units is simply the number of units demanded for a particular time period multiplied by the cost per unit.

          Total annual cost of units = D x C
         a) where:
            (1) D = Annual demand (in units)
            (2) C = Cost of a single unit ($)

   C. Holding (Carrying) Costs
      1. The typical costs of holding inventory include the costs of storage, insurance, taxes, interest, depreciation, spoilage, obsolescence, and pilferage.
      2. The expense involved in physically storing the items in inventory is usually substantial, especially if the inventories are large.
      3. Many small business owners fail to recognize the interest expense associated with carrying large inventories.
         a) The interest expense is evident when the firm borrows money.
         b) Less obvious interest expense is the opportunity cost associated with investing in inventory. A substantial inventory investment ties up a large amount of money unproductively.
      4. Depreciation costs represent the reduced value of inventory over time.
      5. Spoilage, obsolescence, and pilferage also add to the costs of holding inventory.
      6. Formula
          Total annual holding (carrying) costs = Q/2 x H
         a) where:
            (1) Q = Quantity of inventory ordered

(2) H = Holding cost per unit per year

7. The greater the quantity ordered, the greater the inventory carrying costs.
    a) This relationship is shown in Table 16.3.

D. Setup (Ordering) Costs
    1. The various expenses incurred in actually ordering materials and inventory or in setting up the production line to manufacture them determine the level of setup or ordering costs of a product.
    2. The costs of obtaining materials and inventory typically include preparing purchase orders; analyzing and choosing vendors; processing, handling, and expending orders; receiving and inspecting items; and performing all the required accounting and clerical functions.
    3. Ordering costs are usually relatively fixed, regardless of the quantity ordered.
    4. Setup or ordering costs are found by multiplying the number of orders made in a year (or the number of production runs in a year) by the cost of placing a single order (or the cost of setting up a single production run).
    5. Formula
        Total annual setup (ordering) cost = D/Q x S
        a) where:
            (1) D   = Annual demand
            (2) Q   = Quantity of inventory ordered
            (3) S   = Setup (ordering) costs for a single run (or order)
    6. The greater the quantity ordered, the smaller the number of orders placed.
        a) This relationship is shown in Table 16.4.

E. Solving for EOQ
    1. Clearly, if carrying costs were the only expense involved in obtaining inventory, the small business manager would purchase the smallest number of units possible in each order to minimize the cost of holding the inventory.
        a) See illustrations pages 550-551
    2. Neither minimize the total cost of the manufacturer's inventory.
    3. Total cost is composed of the cost of the unit, carrying cost, and ordering costs:
    4. Formula
        Total cost = (D x C) + (Q/2 x H) + (D/Q x S)
    5. These cost are graphed in Figure 16.2. Notice that as the quantity ordered increases, the ordering costs decrease and the carrying costs increase.
    6. The EOQ formula simply balances the ordering cost and the carrying cost of the small business owner's inventory so that total costs are minimized.
    7. Table 16.5 summarizes the total costs for various values of Q for our lawn mower manufacturer.
    8. As Table 16.4 and Figure 16.2 illustrate, the EOQ formula locates the minimum point on the total cost curve, which occurs where the cost of carrying inventory (Q/2 x H) equals the cost of ordering inventory (D/Q x 33).
        a) Total inventory cost is minimized when carrying cost and ordering costs are balanced.

F. Economic Order Quantity (EOQ) with Usage
    1. The preceding EOQ model assumes that orders are filled instantaneously; that is, fresh inventory arrives all at once.

2. Because that assumption does not hold true for many small manufacturers, it is necessary to consider a variation of the basic EOQ model that allows inventory to be added over a period of a time rather than instantaneously.

3. In addition, the manufacturer is likely to be taking items from inventory for use in the assembly process over the same time period.

4. See pages 553-554 for example.

5. Small business managers must remember that the EOQ analysis is based on estimations of cost and demand.

6. The final result is only as accurate as the input used.

V. Price
A. Introduction
1. For the typical small business owner, price is always a substantial factor in purchasing inventory and supplies.

2. In many cases, an entrepreneur can negotiate price with potential suppliers on large orders of frequently purchased items.

3. The typical small business owner shops around and then orders from the supplier offering the best price.

4. The best purchase price is the lowest price at which the owner can obtain goods and services of acceptable quality.

5. Recall that one of Deming's 14 points is "End the practice of awarding business on the basis of price tag."
   a) Without proof of quality, an item with the lowest initial price may produce the highest total cost.

6. When evaluating a supplier's price, small business owners must consider not only the actual price of the goods and services but also the selling terms accompanying them.

7. Vendors typically offer three types of discounts: trade discounts, quantity discounts, and cash discounts.

B. Trade Discounts
1. Trade discounts are established on a graduated scale and depend on a small firm's position in the channel of distribution.
   a) Figure 16.3 illustrates a typical trade discount structure.

C. Quantity Discounts
1. Quantity discounts are designed to encourage businesses to order large quantities.

2. Quantity discounts normally exist in two forms: noncumulative and cumulative.
   a) Noncumulative quantity discounts are granted only if a large enough volume of merchandise is purchased in a single order.
   b) Cumulative quantity discounts are offered if a firm's purchases from a particular vendor exceed a specified quantity or dollar value over a predetermined time period. The time frame varies, but a yearly basis is most common.

3. Some small business owners who normally buy in small quantities can earn such discounts by joining buying groups, purchasing pools, or buying cooperatives.

D. Cash Discounts
1. To encourage prompt payment of invoices, many vendors allow customers to deduct a percentage of the purchase amount if payment is remitted within a specified time.

2. Cash discount terms "2/10, net 30" are common in many industries.

a) This notation means that the total amount of the invoice is due 30 days after its date, but if the bill is paid within 10 days, the buyer may deduct 2 percent from the total.

b) A discount offering "2/10, EOM" (EOM means "end of month") indicates that the buyer may deduct 2 percent if the bill is paid by the tenth of the month after purchase.

GAINING THE COMPETITIVE EDGE - A Funny Thing Happened on the Way to Your Business

SUMMARY
Every year, U.S. companies spend an amount equivalent to 10.5 percent of the nation's GDP--more than $700 billion--just to package and transport goods from one place to another. Consider, for example, the following (true) distribution horror stories.

The shipping manager at a plant in China is struggling to ready a rush order of men's and women's athletic shoes for shipment to a retailer in the United States. Told to put as many as he can fit into each 40-foot shipping container, he has workers take the shoes out of the cartons, remove them from their individual shoe boxes, and put them into the shipping containers. The Chinese workers didn't even tie the shoes in pairs. The containers are filled with thousands of pairs of shoes--all floating around loose. The company incurs thousands of dollars of unplanned labor expenses and eventually sells the shoes at close to its cost.

A dock worker is handling a shipment of margarine traveling from Denmark to Tacoma, Washington, when he notices a leak in one of the shipping containers. At the warehouse, workers open the containers to find 2,000 cartons of margarine that have experienced a complete meltdown. The shipping document from the company in Denmark failed to specify a temperature setting for the cargo.

One freight company that has contracts with two movie studios mistakenly switches their shipments. Of course, one shipment contains X-rated films, and the other contains family films. The manager at the adult video store is sorely disappointed in the mild films he receives, and the nuns at the convent expecting to watch *The Sound of Music* really get a surprise!

How can business owners avoid shipping problems such as these? Although some shipping foul-ups are inevitable, the following tips can help minimize them:
- Communicate clearly with vendors, suppliers, and shipping companies. Never assume that the other party will do what you expect.
- Specify special shipping instructions when required.
- Make sure all shipping labels and instructions are legible and firmly attached to the package.
- Use pressure-sensitive packing tape to seal packages.
- Try to use single shipments rather than multiple shipments.
- On international shipments, verify that the shipper is familiar with the customs regulations of the destination country and knows how to negotiate them.
- When in doubt about a shipment, contact a shipping professional for advice.

---

3. In general, it is sound business practice to take advantage of cash discounts.
4. There is an implicit (opportunity) cost of forgoing a cash discount.
5. By forgoing a cash discount, the small business owner is, in effect, paying an annual interest rate to retain the use of the discounted amount for the remainder of the credit period.

a) Example formula

$$I = P \times R \times T$$

    b) where:
        (1) I = Interest ($)
        (2) P = Principle ($)
        (3) R = Rate of interest (%)
        (4) T = Time (number of days/360)

6. So, to compute R, the annual interest rate,

$$R = \frac{I}{P \times T}$$

    a) In the Print Shop example on page 558 the cost of forgoing the cash discount is 36.735 percent per year.
    b) Table 16.7 summarizes the cost of forgoing cash discounts offering various terms.
7. Although it is a good idea for business owners to take advantage of cash discounts, it is not a wise practice to stretch accounts payable to suppliers beyond the payment terms specified on the invoice.
    a) Letting payments become past due can destroy the trusting relationship a small company has built with its vendors.

VI. Timing
  A. Lead Time
    1. The owner must schedule delivery dates so that the firm does not lose customer goodwill from stockouts.
    2. Also, the owner must concentrate on maintaining proper control over the firm's inventory investment without tying up an excessive amount of working capital.
    3. When planning delivery schedules for inventory and supplies, the owner must consider the lead time for an order, the time gap between placing an order and receiving it.
    4. Developing a reorder point model involves determining the lead time for an order, the usage rate for the item, the minimum level of stock allowable, and the economic order quantity (EOQ).
        a) The lead time for an order is the time gap between placing an order with a vendor and actually receiving the goods.
        b) The usage rate for a particular product can be determined from past inventory and accounting records.
            (1) The anticipated usage rate for a product determines how long the supply will last.
        c) The small business owner must determine the minimum level of stock allowable.
            (1) To avoid stockouts, many firms establish a minimum level of inventory greater than zero.
            (2) They build a cushion, called safety stock, into their inventories in case demand runs ahead of the anticipated usage rate.
    5. To compute the reorder point for an item, the owner must combine this inventory information with the product's EOQ.
    6. The following example will illustrate the reorder point technique:
        a) L = Lead time for an order = 5 days
        b) U = Usage rate = 18 units/day
        c) S = Safety stock (minimum level) = 75 units
        d) EOQ = Economic order quantity = 540 units
    7. The formula for computing the reorder point is:
        Reorder point = (L x U)+ S

8. In this example,
   a) Reorder point = (5 days x 18 units/day) + 75 units = 165 units
9. Thus, this owner should order 540 more units when inventory drops to 165 units.
   a) Figure 16.5 illustrates the reorder point situation for this small business.
10. The simple reorder technique makes certain assumptions that may not be valid in particular situations.
    a) The model assumes that the firm's usage rate is constant.
    b) The model assumes that lead time for an order is constant.
    c) Third, in this sample model, the owner never taps safety stock.
11. More advanced models relax some of these assumptions, but the simple model can be a useful inventory guideline for making inventory decisions in a small company.
12. Another popular reorder point model assumes that the demand for a product during its lead time is normally distributed.
    a) See Figure 16.6.
13. The area under the normal curve at any given point represents the probability that that particular demand level will occur.
    a) Figure 16.7 illustrates the application of this normal distribution to the reorder point model without safety stock.
    b) The model recognizes that three different demand patterns can occur during a product's lead time.
       (1) Demand pattern 1 is an example of below-average demand during lead time.
       (2) Demand pattern 2 is an example of average demand during lead time.
       (3) Demand pattern 3 is an example of an above-average demand during lead time.
14. If the reorder point for this item is the average demand for the product during lead time, 50 percent of the time, demand will be below average.
15. Similarly, 50 percent of the time, demand during lead time will exceed the average, and the firm will experience stockouts.
16. To reduce the probability of inventory shortage, the small business owner can increase the reorder point above DL (average demand during lead time).
17. But by how much? Rather than attempt to define the actual costs of carrying extra inventory versus the costs of stockouts this model allows the small business owner to determine the appropriate reorder point by setting a desired customer service level.

Safety stock = SLF x SD_L

   a) where:
      (1) SLF = Service level factor (the appropriate Z score)
      (2) SD_L = Standard deviation of demand during lead time

18. Table 16.8 shows the appropriate service level factor (Z score) for some of the most popular target customer service levels.
19. Figure 16.8 shows the shift to a normally distributed reorder point model with safety stock.
    a) In this case, the manager has set a 95 percent customer service level; that is, the manager wants to meet 95 percent of the demand during lead time.
    b) The normal curve in the model without safety stock (from Figure 16.7) is shifted up so that 95 percent of the area under the curve lies above the zero inventory level.
    c) The result is a reorder point that is higher than the original reorder point by the amount of the safety stock:

Reorder point = D_L + (SLF x SD_L)

      d) where:
          (1) D_L = Average demand during lead time (original reorder point)
          (2) SLF = Service level factor (the appropriate Z score)
          (3) SD_L = Standard deviation of demand during lead time

20. Figure 16.9 illustrates the shift from a system without safety stock to one with safety stock for this example.

VII. Vendor Analysis
   A. Vendor Certification
      1. To add some objectivity to the selection process, many firms are establishing vendor certification programs: agreements to give one supplier the majority of their business once that supplier meets rigorous quality and performance standards.
      2. When creating a vendor certification program, a business owner should remember the three Cs: commitment, communication, and control.
         a) Commitment to consistently meeting the quality standards of the company is paramount.
         b) A company must establish two-way communication with vendors. Communication implies trust, and trust creates working relationships that are long-term and mutually beneficial.
         c) Finally, a company must make sure that its vendors and suppliers have in place the controls that enable them to produce quality results and to achieve continuous improvements in their processes.
      3. Creating a vendor certification program requires a small company to develop a vendor rating scale that allows the company to evaluate the various advantages and disadvantages of each potential vendor.
         a) The first step in developing a scale is to determine which criteria are most important in selecting a vendor, e.g., price, quality, prompt delivery.
         b) The next step is to assign weights to each criterion to reflect its relative importance.
         c) The third step involves developing a grading scale for comparing vendors on the criteria.
         d) Finally, the owner must compute a weighted total score for each vendor and select the vendor that scores the highest on the set of criteria.
      4. Consider the Bravo Bass Boats, Inc., example of pages 565-566.

IN THE FOOTSTEPS OF AN ENTREPRENEUR - Fewer Surprises Are a Good Thing

SUMMARY
Tom Thornbury, CEO of Softub, a $15 million maker of hot tubs, understands just how important the right vendors can be to a small company's success. In fact, he learned the hard way that one bad supplier can threaten the health of a growing business. He estimates that the lesson cost his company about $500,000.

The odds of its happening again are slim. Under the direction of Gary Anderson, Softub's purchasing agent, cross-functional teams of 10 employees visit potential vendors on site and use a checklist Anderson developed to evaluate them. The checklist covers everything from safety devices and cleanliness to preventive maintenance and quality processes. They interview everyone from the president to the factory workers and ask lots of questions. Anderson also verifies the accuracy of every potential vendor's claims by contacting at least three of its customers. When all the information is in, the team makes its recommendation to the management team, who selects one vendor. Since beginning to use the form,

Softub is getting fewer defective products from its suppliers, and its vendor turnover rate has been cut in half. Plus, Softub has discovered one more unexpected benefit: closer relationships with quality suppliers.

1.   Why is using a vendor evaluation scale important to companies such as Softub?
     Answer - These small companies don't have the surplus cash, storage space, or margin to absorb faulty components, they have to use everything they order. Getting better quality and fewer bad components lowers their costs, maintains their margins, and makes their customers happier.
2.   What benefits can companies that conduct vendor audits expect to gain?
     Answer - Better quality, better relationships with vendor/suppliers, more accurate production scheduling and therefore lower costs, etc.

   B.   Finding Supply Sources
        1.   One obvious way for entrepreneurs to find vendors for their products is to approach established businesses selling similar lines and interview the managers.
        2.   Another source for establishing vendor relationships is the industry trade association.
        3.   A number of publications offer the entrepreneur a great deal of assistance in locating vendors.
             a)   The telephone directory's Yellow Pages.
             b)   Vendor advertisements in trade publications also offer a good list of information about needed merchandise and materials.
             c)   Library reference books that list national distributors and their product lines.
             d)   Publications such as *MacRae's Blue Book* and the *Thomas Register of American Manufacturers* <http://www.thomasregister.com> provide lists of products and services along with names, addresses, telephone numbers, and ratings of manufacturers.
                  (1)   The *Thomas Register* and its accompanying Web site lists more than 60,000 products from 5,500 vendors selling 124,000 brands.
             e)   The *U.S. Industrial Directory* is similar to the *Thomas Register*, although its coverage is not as broad.
             f)   Business owners also should consult the U.S. Chamber of Commerce publication *Sources of State Information* and *State Industrial Directories*, which lists state directories of manufacturers.
             g)   Entrepreneurs whose product lines have an international flair may look to *Kelly's Manufacturers and Merchants Directory*, *Marconi's International Register*, or *Trade Directories of the World* for information on companies throughout the world dealing in practically every type of product or service.
        4.   The World Wide Web is another rich source of information on potential suppliers.
        5.   Business owners' first stop usually is one of the sites that serves as an "electronic Yellow Pages" for vendors.
             a)   One of the most popular sites is Worldwide Internet Solutions' "WIZnet" site <http://www.wiznet.net>.
                  (1)   WIZnet's site is a "virtual product-catalog library" that lists complete catalogs of manufacturers, distributors, and service providers from around the globe.

   C.   The Final Decision
        1.   Number of Suppliers.
             a)   "Should I buy from a single supplier or from several different sources?"
                  (1)   Concentrating purchases at a single supplier gives the individual attention from the sole supplier, especially if orders are substantial.
                  (2)   Second, the firm may receive quantity discounts if its orders are large enough.
             b)   Using a single vendor also has disadvantages.

(1) The small firm may experience shortages of critical materials if its only supplier suffers a catastrophe, such as a fire, strike, or bankruptcy.

2. The advantages of developing close, cooperative relationships with a single supplier outweigh the risks of sole sourcing in most cases.
3. Reliability.
   a) The most common complaint purchasing managers have against suppliers is late delivery.
4. Proximity.
   a) Costs for transporting merchandise can substantially increase the cost of merchandise to the buyer.
   b) Some vendors offer better service to local small businesses because they know the owners.
   c) In addition, a small business owner is better able to solve coordination problems with nearby vendors than with distant vendors.

WIRED TO THE WEB - The Power of the Web

SUMMARY

"Just what we need," said Jack sarcastically. "Two of those things to tell me how to run a business I've been in for more than 20 years." Jack Lampeer had started Industrial Supply nearly 22 years before to supply other small companies in the area with the industrial equipment, supplies, and materials they needed. The company carried a wide assortment of industrial products--from ladders and generators to mops and cleaning supplies. As long as Jack was at the helm, Industrial Supply had refused to enter the computer age. Jack didn't understand computers, nor did he want to.

"Pop, while I was looking through one of our industry publications yesterday, I came across an article about using the World Wide Web to make purchasing inventory more efficient," he said, tossing an open magazine in his father's direction. "So I started investigating. I've already found some awesome Web sites." Jack glanced at the screen and pretended not to be interested. Although he didn't want to admit it, it sounded like a pretty good idea.

"What are you looking for?" Miles asked. "That catalog from Carswell. I thought I saw one the other day.""We need to order some new ladders, etc." "We can do that right here, Pop." As Jack pulled the chair closer to the computer, he said, "The World Wide Web, huh? Show me how it works, son. Show me how it works"

1. Use one of the search engines on the World Wide Web to help Miles find the information he is looking for. Check out some of the following sites as well:
   National Association of Purchasing Managers <http:www.napm.com>
   W.W. Grainger Company <http://www.grainge.com>
   IndustryNET <http://www.industry.net>
   Worldwide Internet Solutions <http:www.wiznet.net>
2. Which sites did you find most useful? Why?
   Answer - Students' responses will vary based on their research.
3. What advantages does the Web offer purchasing agents in small businesses?
   Answer - Quicker, often less expensive, reduces paperwork, don't have to keep track of catalogs, sometimes the sites also carry technical support and FAQs, etc.

5. Services.
    a) Do salespeople make regular calls on the firm, and are they knowledgeable about their product line?
    b) Will the sale representatives assist in planning store layout and in creating attractive displays?
    c) Will the vendor make convenient deliveries on time?
    d) Is the supplier reasonable in making repairs on equipment after installation and in handling returned merchandise?
    e) Are sales representatives able to offer useful advice on purchasing and other managerial functions?

VIII. Legal Issues Affecting Purchasing
    A. Title
        1. Before the Uniform Commercial Code (UCC) was enacted, the concept of title--the right to ownership of goods--determined where responsibility for merchandise fell.
        2. Today, however, the UCC has replaced the concept of title with three other concepts: identification, risk of loss, and insurable interest.

    B. Identification
        1. Identification is the first requirement that must be met.
        2. Before title can pass to the buyer, the goods must already be in existence and must be identifiable from all other similar goods.
        3. Specific goods already in existence are identified at the time the sales contract is made.

    C. Risk of Loss
        1. Risk of loss determines which party incurs the financial risk if the goods are damaged, destroyed, or lost before they are transferred.
        2. Risk of loss does not always pass with title.
        3. Three particular rules govern the passage of title and the transfer of risk of loss:
            a) Rule 1: Agreement. A supplier and a small business owner can agree to the terms under which title passes. Similarly, the two parties can agree (preferably in writing) to shift the risk of loss at any time during the transaction. In other words, any explicit agreement between buyer and seller determines when title and risk of loss will pass. Without an agreement, title and risk of loss pass when the seller delivers the goods under the contract.
            b) Rule 2: F.O.B. seller. Under a sales contract designated F.O.B. seller (free on board seller), title passes to the buyer as soon as the seller delivers the goods into the care of a carrier or shipper. Similarly, risk of loss transfers to the small business owner when the supplier delivers the goods to the carrier.
                (1) An F.O.B. seller contract (also a shipment contract) requires that the buyer pay all shipping and transportation costs.
            c) Rule 3: F.O.B. buyer. A sales contract designated F.O.B. buyer requires that the seller deliver the goods to the buyer's place of business (or to an agent of the buyer). Title and risk of loss are transferred to the small business when the goods are delivered there or to another designated destination.
                (1) Also, an F.O.B. buyer contract (also called a destination contract) requires the seller to pay all shipping and transportation costs.

D. Insurable Interest
1. Insurable interest ensures the right to either party to the sales contract to obtain insurance to protect against lost, damaged, or destroyed merchandise as long as that party has "sufficient interest" in the goods.
2. In general, if goods are identified, the buyer has an insurable interest in them. The seller has a sufficient interest as long as he retains title to the goods.
3. However, under certain circumstances both the buyer and the seller have insurable interests even after title has passed to the buyer.

E. Receiving Merchandise
1. Once the merchandise is received, the buyer must verify its identity and condition.
    a) When the goods are delivered, the owner should check the number of cartons unloaded against the carrier's delivery receipt so that none are overlooked.
    b) It is also a good idea to examine the boxes for damage; if shipping cartons are damaged, the carrier should note this on the delivery receipt.
    c) The owner should never destroy or dispose of tainted or unwanted merchandise unless the supplier specifically authorizes it.
2. Proper control techniques in receiving merchandise prevent the small business owner from paying for suppliers' and shippers' mistakes.

F. Selling On Consignment
1. Selling on consignment means that the small business owner does not purchase the merchandise carried from the supplier (called the consignor); instead, the owner pays the consignor only for the merchandise actually sold.
2. For providing the supplier with a market for his goods, the small business owner normally receives a portion of the revenue on each item sold.
3. The business owner (called the consignee) may return any unsold merchandise to the supplier without obligation.
4. Under a consignment agreement, title and risk of loss do not pass to the consignee unless the contract specifies such terms.
5. The small business owner who sells merchandise on a consignment basis realizes the following advantages:
    a) The owner does not have to invest money in these inventory items, but the merchandise on hand is available for sale.
    b) The owner does not make payment to the consignor until the item is sold.
    c) Because the consignment relationship is founded on the law of agency, the consignee never takes title to the merchandise and does not bear the risk of loss for the goods.
    d) The supplier normally plans and sets up displays for the merchandise and is responsible for maintaining it.
6. Before selling items on consignment, the small business owner and the supplier should create a workable written contract, which should include the following items:
    a) A list of items to be sold and their quantities
    b) Prices to be charged
    c) Location of merchandise in store
    d) Duration of contract
    e) Commission charged by the consignee
    f) Policy on defective items and rejects
    g) Schedule for payments to consignor
    h) Delivery terms and merchandise storage requirements
    i) Responsibility for items lost to pilferage and shoplifting
    j) Provision for terminating consignment contract

7. If managed properly, selling goods on consignment can be beneficial to both the consignor and the consignee.

Chapter Summary

♦ Understand the components of a purchasing plan.

  ▪ The purchasing function is vital to every small business's success because it influences a company's ability to sell quality goods and services at reasonable prices. Purchasing is the acquisition of needed materials, supplies, services, and equipment of the right quality, in the proper quantities, for reasonable prices, at the appropriate time, and from the right suppliers.

♦ Explain the principles of total quality management (TQM) and its impact on quality.

  ▪ Under the total quality management (TQM) philosophy, companies define a quality product as one that conforms to predetermined standards that satisfy customers' demands. The goal is to get everything--from delivery and invoicing to installation and follow-up--right the first time.

  ▪ To implement TQM successfully, a small business owner must rely on 10 fundamental principles: Shift from a management-driven culture to a participative, team-based one; modify the reward system to encourage teamwork and innovation; train workers constantly to give them the tools they need to produce quality and to upgrade the company's knowledge base; train employees to measure quality with the tools of statistical process control (SPC); use Pareto's law to focus TQM efforts; share information with everyone in the organization; focus quality improvements on astonishing the customer; don't rely on inspection to produce quality products and services; avoid using TQM to place blame on those who make mistakes; and strive for continuous improvement in processes as well as in products and services.

♦ Conduct economic order quantity (EOQ) analysis to determine the proper level of inventory.

  ▪ A major goal of the small business is to generate adequate inventory turnover by purchasing proper quantities of merchandise. A useful device for computing the proper quantity is economic order quantity (EOQ) analysis, which yields the ideal order quantity: the amount that minimizes total inventory costs. Total inventory costs consist of the cost of the units, holding (carrying) costs, and ordering (setup) costs. The EOQ balances the costs of ordering and of carrying merchandise to yield minimum total inventory cost.

♦ Differentiate among the three types of purchase discounts vendors offer.

  ▪ Trade discounts are established on a graduated scale and depend on a small firm's position in the channel of distribution.

  ▪ Quantity discounts are designed to encourage businesses to order large quantities of merchandise and supplies.

  ▪ Cash discounts are offered to customers as an incentive to pay for merchandise promptly.

♦ Calculate a company's reorder point.

  ▪ There is a time gap between the placing of an order and actual receipt of the goods. The reorder point model tells the owner when to place an order to replenish the company's inventory.

♦ Develop a vendor rating scale.

  ▪ Creating a vendor analysis model involves four steps: Determine the important criteria (i.e., price, quality, prompt, delivery, service, etc.); assign a weight to each criterion to reflect its relative importance; develop a grading scale for each criterion; compute a weighted score for each vendor.

♦ Describe the legal implications of the purchasing function.

  ▪ Important legal issues involving purchasing goods involve title, or ownership of the goods; identification of the goods; risk of loss and when it shifts from seller to buyer; and insurable interests in the goods. Buyer and seller can have an insurable interest in the same goods at the same time.

Discussion Questions

1. What is purchasing? Why is it important for the small business owner to develop a purchasing plan?
    Answer - Purchasing is one of the most vital functions to a small company's ultimate success. Selecting the right vendors and ensuring that the purchasing process operates efficiently determine a small company's ability to produce and sell quality products at a reasonable price. The effects of an entrepreneur's decisions on purchasing, quality, and vendor selection ripple throughout the entire company, affecting everything it does and producing a dramatic impact on its "bottom line." Depending on the type of business involved, the amounts spent by the purchasing department range from 25 to 85 cents per one dollar of sales.

2. What is TQM? How can it help small business owners achieve the quality goods and services they require?
    Answer - Under the total quality management (TQM) philosophy, companies define a quality product as one that conforms to predetermined standards that satisfy customers' demands. TQM instills the philosophy of doing the job right the first time.

3. One top manager claims that to implement total quality management successfully, "You have to change your [company] culture as much as your processes." Do you agree? Explain.
    Answer - This is a general opinion discussion question but students should consider the fact that to implement TQM successfully, a small business owner must rely on 10 fundamental principles. These principles often directly affect company culture.
    - Shift from a management-driven culture to a participative, team-based one.
    - Train workers constantly to give them the tools they need to produce quality and to upgrade the company's knowledge base.
    - Shift from a management-driven culture to a participative, team-based one.
    - Train workers constantly to give them the tools they need to produce quality and to upgrade the company's knowledge base.
    - Train employees to measure quality with statistical process controls (SPC).
    - Use Pareto's Law to focus TQM efforts.
    - Share information with everyone in the organization.
    - Focus quality improvements on astonishing the customer.
    - Don't rely on inspection to produce quality products and services.
    - Avoid using TQM to place blame on those who make mistakes.
    - Strive for continuous improvement in processes as well as in products and services.

    Drastic changes such as these naturally create turmoil. Planned and implemented properly, however, TQM can use the energy from that turmoil to drive the changes a company must make if it is to become truly world-class.

4. List and briefly describe the three components of total inventory costs.
    Answer - To compute the proper amount of stock to order or to produce, the small business owner must first determine the three principal elements of total inventory costs: the cost of the units, the holding (or carrying) cost, and the setup (or ordering) cost.

    The cost of the units is simply the number of units demanded for a particular time period multiplied by the cost per unit. The typical costs of holding inventory include the costs of storage, insurance, taxes, interest, depreciation, spoilage, obsolescence, and pilferage. The various expenses incurred in actually ordering materials and inventory or in setting up the production line to manufacture them determine the level of setup or ordering costs of a product. The costs of obtaining materials and inventory typically include preparing purchase orders; analyzing and choosing vendors; processing, handling, and expending orders; receiving and inspecting items; and performing all the required accounting and clerical functions. Ordering costs are usually relatively fixed, regardless of the quantity ordered.

5. What is the economic order quantity? How does it minimize total inventory costs?
    Answer - It is that point where the costs of purchasing, inventory, and set-up are balanced. An investment in inventory is not profitable because dollars spent return nothing until the inventory is sold. A primary objective of this portion of the purchasing plan is to generate an adequate turnover of merchandise by purchasing proper quantities. Tying up capital in the maintenance of extra inventory limits the firm's working capital and exerts pressure on its cash flows. The firm risks the danger of being stuck with spoiled or obsolete merchandise. Excess inventory also takes up valuable store or selling space. On the other hand, maintaining too little inventory can be extremely costly. The analytical techniques used to determine economic order quantities (EOQs) will help the manager compute the amount of stock to purchase with an order or to produce with each production run to minimize total inventory costs. To compute the proper amount of stock to order or to produce, the small business owner must first determine the three principal elements of total inventory costs: the cost of the units, the holding (or carrying) cost, and the setup (or ordering) cost.

6. Should a small business owner always purchase the products with the lowest prices? Why or why not?
    Answer - For the typical small business owner, price is always a substantial factor in purchasing inventory and supplies. The best purchase price is the lowest price at which the owner can obtain goods and services of acceptable quality. Recall that one of Deming's 14 points is "End the practice of awarding business on the basis of price tag." Without proof of quality, an item with the lowest initial price may produce the highest total cost. When evaluating a supplier's price, small business owners must consider not only the actual price of the goods and services but also the selling terms accompanying them.

7. Briefly outline the three types of purchase discounts. Under what circumstances is each the best choice?
    Answer - Vendors typically offer three types of discounts: trade discounts, quantity discounts, and cash discounts. Trade discounts are established on a graduated scale and depend on a small firm's position in the channel of distribution. Figure 16.3 illustrates a typical trade discount structure. Quantity discounts are designed to encourage businesses to order large quantities. Quantity discounts normally exist in two forms: noncumulative and cumulative. Noncumulative quantity discounts are granted only if a large enough volume of merchandise is purchased in a single order. Cumulative quantity discounts are offered if a firm's purchases from a particular vendor exceed a specified quantity or dollar value over a predetermined time period. The time frame varies, but a yearly basis is most common. Cash discounts encourage prompt payment of invoices, many vendors allow customers to deduct a percentage of the purchase amount if payment is remitted within a specified time. Cash discount terms "2/10, net 30" are common in many industries. In general, it is sound business practice to take advantage of cash discounts. There is an implicit (opportunity) cost of forgoing a cash discount. By forgoing a cash discount, the small business owner is, in effect, paying an annual interest rate to retain the use of the discounted amount for the remainder of the credit.

8. What is lead time? Outline the procedure for determining a product's reorder point.
    Answer - The owner must schedule delivery dates so that the firm does not lose customer goodwill from stockouts. When planning delivery schedules for inventory and supplies, the owner must consider the lead time for an order, the time gap between placing an order and receiving it. Developing a reorder point model involves determining the lead time for an order, the usage rate for the item, the minimum level of stock allowable, and the economic order quantity (EOQ). The lead time for an order is the time gap between placing an order with a vendor and actually receiving the

goods. The small business owner must determine the minimum level of stock allowable. To compute the reorder point for an item, the owner must combine this inventory information with the product's EOQ. The formula is:

Reorder point = (L x U) + S
L = Lead time for an order
U = Usage rate
S = Safety stock (minimum level)
EOQ = Economic order quantity

9. Explain how an entrepreneur launching a company could locate suppliers and vendors.
   Answer - One obvious way for entrepreneurs to find vendors for their products is to approach established businesses selling similar lines and interview the managers. Another source for establishing vendor relationships is the industry trade association. A number of publications offer the entrepreneur a great deal of assistance in locating vendors.
   - The telephone directory's Yellow Pages.
   - Vendor advertisements in trade publications.
   - Library reference books that list national distributors and their product lines.
   - Publications such as *MacRae's Blue Book* and the *Thomas Register of American Manufacturers*
   - The *U.S. Industrial Directory* is similar to the *Thomas Register*, although its coverage is not as broad.
   - Business owners also should consult the U.S. Chamber of Commerce publication *Sources of State Information* and *State Industrial Directories*, which lists state directories of manufacturers.
   - Entrepreneurs whose product lines have an international flair may look to *Kelly's Manufacturers and Merchants Directory*, *Marconi's International Register*, or *Trade Directories of the World* for information on companies throughout the world dealing in practically every type of product or service.
   - The World Wide Web is another rich source of information on potential suppliers.
   - WIZnet's site is a "virtual product-catalog library" that lists complete catalogs of manufacturers, distributors, and service providers from around the globe.

10. What factors are commonly used to evaluate suppliers?
    Answer - The number of suppliers--"Should I buy from a single supplier or from several different sources?" Reliability--the most common complaint purchasing managers have against suppliers is late delivery. Proximity--costs for transporting merchandise can substantially increase the cost of merchandise to the buyer. Some vendors offer better service to local small businesses because they know the owners. Service--Do salespeople make regular calls on the firm, and are they knowledgeable about their product line?

11. Explain the procedure for developing a vendor rating scale.
    Answer - To add some objectivity to the selection process, many firms are establishing vendor certification programs: agreements to give one supplier the majority of their business once that supplier meets rigorous quality and performance standards. When creating a vendor certification program, a business owner should remember the three Cs: commitment, communication, and control.

    Commitment to consistently meeting the quality standards of the company is paramount. A company must establish two-way communication with vendors. Communication implies trust, and trust creates working relationships that are long-term and mutually beneficial. Finally, a company must make sure that its vendors and suppliers have in place the controls that enable them to produce quality results and to achieve continuous improvements in their processes.

Creating a vendor certification program requires a small company to develop a vendor rating scale that allows the company to evaluate the various advantages and disadvantages of each potential vendor.

- The first step in developing a scale is to determine which criteria are most important in selecting a vendor, e.g., price, quality, prompt delivery.
- The next step is to assign weights to each criterion to reflect its relative importance.
- The third step involves developing a grading scale for comparing vendors on the criteria.
- Finally, the owner must compute a weighted total score for each vendor and select the vendor that scores the highest on the set of criteria.

12. Explain briefly the three concepts that have replaced the concept of title. When do title and risk of loss shift under an F.O.B. seller contract and under an F.O.B. buyer contract?
    Answer - Before the Uniform Commercial Code (UCC) was enacted, the concept of title--the right to ownership of goods--determined where responsibility for merchandise fell. Today, however, the UCC has replaced the concept of title with three other concepts: identification, risk of loss, and insurable interest.

    Identification is the first requirement that must be met. Before title can pass to the buyer, the goods must already be in existence and must be identifiable from all other similar goods. Risk of loss determines which party incurs the financial risk if the goods are damaged, destroyed, or lost before they are transferred. Risk of loss does not always pass with title. Insurable interest ensures the right to either party to the sales contract to obtain insurance to protect against lost, damaged, or destroyed merchandise as long as that party has "sufficient interest" in the goods. In general, if goods are identified, the buyer has an insurable interest in them. The seller has a sufficient interest as long as he retains title to the goods.

    Rule 2: F.O.B. seller. Under a sales contract designated F.O.B. seller (free on board seller), title passes to the buyer as soon as the seller delivers the goods into the care of a carrier or shipper. Similarly, risk of loss transfers to the small business owner when the supplier delivers the goods to the carrier. Rule 3: F.O.B. buyer. A sales contract designated F.O.B. buyer requires that the seller deliver the goods to the buyer's place of business (or to an agent of the buyer). Title and risk of loss are transferred to the small business when the goods are delivered there or to another designated destination.

13. What should a small business owner do when merchandise is received?
    Answer - Once the merchandise is received, the buyer must verify its identity and condition. When the goods are delivered, the owner should check the number of cartons unloaded against the carrier's delivery receipt so that none are overlooked. It is also a good idea to examine the boxes for damage; if shipping cartons are damaged, the carrier should note this on the delivery receipt. The owner should never destroy or dispose of tainted or unwanted merchandise unless the supplier specifically authorizes it. Proper control techniques in receiving merchandise prevent the small business owner from paying for suppliers' and shippers' mistakes.

14. Explain how a small business would sell goods on consignment. What should be included in a consignment contract?
    Answer - Selling on consignment means that the small business owner does not purchase the merchandise carried from the supplier (called the consignor); instead, the owner pays the consignor only for the merchandise actually sold. For providing the supplier with a market for his goods, the small business owner normally receives a portion of the revenue on each item sold.

Before selling items on consignment, the small business owner and the supplier should create a workable written contract, which should include the following items:
- A list of items to be sold and their quantities
- Prices to be charged
- Location of merchandise in store
- Duration of contract
- Commission charged by the consignee
- Policy on defective items and rejects
- Schedule for payments to consignor
- Delivery terms and merchandise storage requirements
- Responsibility for items lost to pilferage and shoplifting
- Provision for terminating consignment contract

Step into the Real World

1. Interview a number of small business owners and attempt to discover if they have implemented any of the following:
    a. a purchasing plan
    b. a quality management program
    c. a vendor analysis program.
    On the basis of their responses, how would you rate the effectiveness of their programs?
2. Interview two or three retailers and ask about the nature and type of their purchase discounts. Do they normally take advantage of the discounts that are offered? If not, why? Do the businesspersons you interviewed have a formal vendor analysis program? If not, what steps should they take to create one?
3. Contact the owner of a small retail shop in your area. How does the owner determine inventory levels? How does he or she know how many items to keep in stock? Are there certain items that move much faster than others? Does the owner purchase all of a particular type of item from a single vendor or from several vendors? Why?
4. Interview the owner of a small manufacturing company. What percentage of the components in the company's finished product comes from outside vendors and suppliers? How does the owner select those vendors? What problems does he or she normally encounter when buying from vendors? Does the owner use a checklist or vendor rating scale to select vendors? How does the owner judge the quality of incoming shipments from vendors?

Chapter 17 - Managing Inventory

> We've got it if we can find it.
> Sign in hardware store

> Great American axiom: Some is good, more is better. Too much is just right.
> Anonymous

Teaching Objectives
Students will be able to:
1. Explain the various inventory control systems and the advantages and disadvantages of each.
2. Describe how just-in-time (JIT) and JIT II inventory control techniques work.
3. Describe some methods for reducing loss from slow-moving inventory.
4. Discuss employee theft and shoplifting and how to prevent them.

Instructor's Outline
I. Introduction
    A. The Importance
        1. Businesses in the United States spend more than $700 billion a year on inventory and moving it around from place to place.
        2. The largest expenditure most small companies make is for inventory, and entrepreneurs can realize tremendous savings from managing their company's inventory effectively.
        3. Excess inventories "also eat up additional warehouse space; boost personnel needs for security, production, and warehouse staff; necessitate the purchase of extra inventory insurance; and increase borrowing needs."
        4. "Companies can increase their profitability 20 to 50 percent through prudent inventory management," says one expert.

    B. Managing Inventory Effectively
        1. Develop an accurate sales forecast. The proper inventory levels for each item are directly related to the demand for that item.
        2. Develop a plan to make inventory available when and where customers want it. Inventory will not sell if customers have a difficult time finding it.
        3. Build relationships with your most critical suppliers to ensure that you can get the merchandise you need when you need it.
        4. Set realistic inventory turnover objectives. Keeping in touch with their customers' likes and dislikes and monitoring their inventory enables owners to estimate the most likely buying patterns for different types of merchandise.
        5. Compute the actual cost of carrying inventory.
        6. Use the most timely and accurate information system the business can afford to provide the facts and figures necessary to make critical inventory decisions.
        7. Teach employees how inventory control systems work so that they can contribute to managing the firm's inventory on a daily basis.
        8. The goal is to find and maintain the proper balance between the cost of holding inventory and the requirements to have the merchandise when the customer demands it.
        9. Walking this inventory tightrope is never easy, but the following inventory control systems can help business owners strike a reasonable balance between the two extremes.

II. Inventory Control Systems
   A. Introduction
   1. Pareto's law (or the 80/20 rule) holds that about 80 percent of the value of the firm's sales revenue is generated by 20 percent of the items kept in stock.
   2. Owners should focus the majority of their inventory control efforts on this 20 percent.

   B. Perpetual Inventory Systems
   1. Perpetual inventory systems are designed to maintain a running count of the items in inventory.
   2. There are a number of different perpetual inventory systems, but they have a common element, keeping a continuous tally of each item added to or subtracted from the firm's stock of merchandise.
   3. The basic perpetual inventory system uses a perpetual inventory sheet that includes fundamental product information such as the item's name, stock number, description, economic order quantity (EOQ), and reorder point.
      a) Whenever a shipment is received from a vendor, the quantity is entered in the receipts column and added to the total.
      b) When the item is sold and taken from inventory, it is simply deducted from the total.
   4. Sporadic use creates problems.
      a) If managers or employees take items out of stock or place them in inventory without recording them, the perpetual inventory sheet will yield incorrect totals and can foul up the entire inventory control system.
      b) Keeping such records for a large number of items and ensuring the accuracy of the system can be excessively expensive.
      c) Therefore, these systems are used most frequently and most successfully in controlling high dollar volume items that require strict monitoring.
   5. Technical advances in computerized cash registers have overcome many of the disadvantages of using the basic perpetual inventory system.
      a) Small businesses now are able to afford computerized point-of-sale (POS) systems that perform all of the functions of a traditional cash register and maintain an up-to-the-minute inventory count.
      b) Combining a POS system with Universal Product Code (bar code) labels and high-speed scanners gives a small business a state-of-the-art checkout system that feeds vital information into its inventory control system.
      c) These systems rely on an inventory database; as items are rung up on the register, product information is recorded and inventory balances are adjusted.
   6. Using the system, business owners can tell how quickly each item is selling and how many items are in stock at any time.
      a) Their inventory records are accurate and always current.
      b) They also can generate instantly a variety of reports to aid in making purchasing decisions.
   7. Specific Perpetual Inventory Control Systems.
      a) Perpetual inventory systems operate in a number of ways, but three basic variations are particularly common: the sales ticket method, the sales stub method, and the floor sample method.
      b) The Sales Ticket Method.
         (1) Most small businesses use sales tickets to summarize individual customers' transactions.
         (2) These tickets serve two major purposes:
            (a) They provide the customer with a sales receipt for the merchandise purchased.

        (b) They provide the owner with a daily record of the number of specific inventory items sold.

    (3) The sales ticket method operates by gathering all the sales tickets at the end of each day and transcribing the data onto the appropriate perpetual inventory sheet.

IN THE FOOTSTEPS OF AN ENTREPRENEUR - A High-Tech Salvage Yard

In 1983, Ron Sturgeon realized that his auto salvage yard, AAA Small Car World, was growing so fast that he was having difficulty maintaining control over it. The company, which salvaged parts from wrecked cars and resold them, "had an awful lot of parts in stock, with sales doubling almost every year."

Employees labeled each part by hand and filled out another label that they filed in the tiny drawers of an old pharmaceutical filing cabinet AAA had on hand. If a customer requested an alternator for an Acura Legend, a salesperson would have to rummage through the tiny labels on file in the pharmaceutical cabinet. Sturgeon set out to solve the problem by writing his own inventory-tracking program to run on the three microcomputers the company already used. After spending a couple of years and $20,000, Sturgeon realized he was getting nowhere. By 1986, he had begun exploring the possibilities of using inventory-tracking software, but this time he decided to buy a software package rather than attempt to write his own. In 1987, Sturgeon took a great leap of faith and spent $70,000 (company sales then were just $2 million!) on an automated inventory tracking system called Checkmate. (With advances in technology a similar system today costs less than $10,000.)

Sturgeon credits the inventory-control system with giving him the tools he needed to make his company one of the leaders in the industry. Today AAA rings up sales of $8 million, processing 100 cars a week. The system tracks every part in its database and even recognizes interchangeable parts. With the computerized tracking system, Sturgeon can determine the number of times customers request a particular part, so he knows whether AAA is missing sales on parts it should be stocking.

1. What benefits do inventory-tracking systems such as the one AAA Small Car World uses give small businesses characterized by large inventories?
    Answer - An efficient way to track and manage inventory. Helps them make better matches with customer needs, keep inventory levels as low as possible, etc.
2. Can investing in such systems give a company a competitive advantage? How?
    Answer - Yes by helping them be more responsive to customer needs and lower operating costs.

---

    c) The Sales Stub Method.
        (1) The principle behind the sales stub method of inventory control is the same as that underlying the sales ticket method, but its mechanics are slightly different.
        (2) Retail stores often attach a ticket with two or more parts containing relevant product information to each inventory item in stock.
        (3) When an employee sells an item, he removes a portion of the stub and places it in a container. At the end of the day, the owner posts the inventory deductions recorded by the stubs to the proper perpetual inventory sheet.
8. The Floor Sample Method.
    a) The floor sample method of controlling inventory is commonly used by businesses selling big-ticket items with high unit cost.
    b) In many cases, these items are somewhat bulky and are difficult to display in large numbers.
    c) A simple technique for maintaining control of these items is to attach a small pad to the display desk with sheets numbered in descending order from 15 to 1.

      d) Whenever an employee sells a roll-top desk, she removes a sheet from the pad.

C. Visual Control Inventory Systems

  1. The most common method of controlling inventory.

  2. Managers simply conduct periodic visual inspections to determine the quantity of various items they should order.

  3. Such systems are impractical when the business stocks a large number of low-value items with low dollar volume.

  4. This method is also the least effective for ensuring accuracy and reliability.

  5. In general, a visual inventory control system works best in firms where daily sales are relatively consistent, the owner is closely involved with the inventory, the variety of merchandise is small, and items can be obtained quickly from vendors.

D. Partial Inventory Control Systems

  1. The most viable option for inventory management is a partial inventory control system.

  2. Such a system relies on the validity of the 80/20 rule.

      a) If a small business carries 5,000 different items in stock, roughly 1,000 of them account for about 80 percent of the firm's sales volume.

      b) Experienced business owners focus their control efforts on those 1,000 items.

      c) One of the most popular partial inventory control systems is the ABC system.

  3. The ABC method of inventory control. The typical ABC system divides a firm's inventory into three major categories:

      a) An items account for a high dollar usage volume.

      b) B items account for a moderate dollar usage volume.

      c) C items account for low dollar usage volume.

  4. The dollar usage volume of an item measures the relative importance of that item in the firm's inventory.

      a) Note that value is not necessarily synonymous with high unit cost.

  5. The initial step in establishing an ABC classification system is to compute the annual dollar usage volume for each product (or product category).

      a) Annual dollar usage volume is simply the cost per unit of an item multiplied by the annual quantity used.

      b) See example calculation on page 582.

  6. The next step is to arrange the products in descending order on the basis of the computed annual dollar usage volume.

      a) Once so arranged, they can be divided into appropriate classes by applying the following rule:

         (1) A items: roughly the top 15 percent of the items listed

         (2) B items: roughly the next 35 percent

         (3) C items: roughly the remaining 50 percent

      b) Figure 17.1 graphically portrays the segmentation of the items listed in Table 17.1.

  7. The purpose of classifying items according to their annual dollar usage volume is to establish the proper degree of control over each item held in inventory.

      a) Items in the A classification should be controlled under a perpetual inventory system with as much detail as necessary.

      b) Control of B items should rely more on periodic control systems and basic analytical tools such as EOQ and reorder point analysis.

      c) C items typically constitute a minor proportion of the small firm's inventory value and, as a result, require the least effort and expense to control. The cost involved in using detailed recordkeeping and inventory control procedures greatly outweighs the advantages gleaned from strict control of C items.

8. One practical technique for maintaining control simply is the two-bin system, which keeps two separate bins full of material.
   a) The first bin is used to fill customer orders, and the second bin is filled with enough safety stock to meet customer demand during the lead time.
   b) When the first bin is empty, the owner places an order with the vendor large enough to refill both bins.
   c) During the lead time for the order, the manager uses the safety stock and marks the level with a brightly colored line.
9. When storage space or the type of item does not suit the two-bin system, the owner can use a tag system.
   a) Based on the same principles as the two-bin system, the tag system applies to most retail, wholesale, and service firms.
   b) Instead of placing enough inventory to meet customer demand during lead time into a separate bin, the owner marks this inventory level with a brightly colored tag.
   c) When the supply is drawn down to the tagged level, the owner reorders the merchandise.
   d) Figure 17.2 illustrates the two-bin and tag systems of controlling C items.
   e) Table 17.2 summarizes the use of the ABC control system.

E. Physical Inventory Count
   1. Regardless of the type of inventory control system used, every small business owner must conduct a periodic physical inventory count.
   2. A physical inventory count allows owners to reconcile the actual amount of inventory in stock with the amount reported through the inventory control system.
   3. The typical method of taking inventory involves two employees; one calls out the relevant information for each inventory item, and the other records the count on a tally sheet.
   4. There are two basic methods of conducting a physical inventory count.
      a) One alternative is to take inventory at regular intervals. Many businesses take inventory at the end of the year.
      b) The other method of taking inventory, called cycle counting, involves counting a number of items on a continuous basis. The manager counts a few types of items each week and checks the numbers against the inventory control system.
   5. Electronic data interchange (EDI) systems enable business owners to track their inventories and to place orders with vendors quickly and with few errors by linking them to their vendors electronically.
      a) These systems often rely on hand-held computer terminals equipped with a scanning wand.
      b) An employee runs the wand across a bar-code label on the shelf that identifies the inventory item; then he counts the items on the shelf and enters that number using the number pad on the terminal. Then, by linking the hand-held terminal to a personal computer, he can download the physical inventory count into the company's inventory control software in seconds.
      c) In many EDI systems, the vendor is tied directly into a company's POS (point-of-sale) system, monitoring it constantly; when the company's supply of a particular item drops to a preset level, the vendor automatically sends a shipment to replenish its stock to an established level.

IN THE FOOTSTEPS OF AN ENTREPRENEUR - HOG Heaven

SUMMARY
House of Guitars caters to guitarists of all skill levels--from beginning amateurs to professionals in rock bands. Although HOG sells everything from CDs and drums to amplifiers and keyboards, its specialty is guitars. The business occupies an old feed store, which is connected to its five cavernous warehouses by a labyrinth of passages so complex that employees sometimes get lost. The huge selection of guitars the HOG offers attracts many customers. The business stocks practically every make of instrument (and what the store doesn't stock, it can get), whereas most other instrument stores specialize in a single brand. Schaubroeck estimates that he has 9,000 guitars in stock. After taking a guest on a tour, however, he revises his estimate upward to 11,000 guitars.

Schaubroeck's accountant almost panicked when he saw the inventory level the House of Guitars maintains. On paper, it looks like a recipe for disaster. In person, at first glance, the disarray looks like a disaster. Then, the beauty of Schaubroeck's strategy begins to emerge. The HOG, says Schaubroeck's accountant, "doesn't turn its inventory as fast as it should, but they carry older things--so once they become out of stock at other places, [HOG's] prices go up." Although Schauboeck's investment in inventory is what most musical instrument store owners would consider excessive, it is actually an important part of the company's success.

1. What benefits does maintaining a large inventory offer the House of Guitars? What costs are associated with holding a large inventory?
    Answer - Armand offers customers selection that other competitors can't. He can offer products others can't because he has them after they've gone out of stock. But he pays the price of carrying inventory for long periods of time. The upside is that his inventory seems to increase in value as it ages, rather than depreciates.
2. What advice would you offer Armand Schaubroeck about controlling his company's inventory more effectively?
    Answer - Any advice offered shouldn't change Schaubroeck's fundamental strategy. He could use an automated system but it should be one compatible with his strategy. He might try using an ABC system since not all of his guitars are as valuable as others.

III. Just-in-Time (JIT) Inventory Control Techniques
    A. Introduction
        1. Many U.S. manufacturers have turned to a popular inventory control technique called just-in-time (JIT) to reduce costly inventories and turn around their financial fortunes.
        2. The just-in-time philosophy, however, views excess inventory as a blanket that masks problems and as a source of unnecessary costs that inhibit a firm's competitive position.
        3. Under a JIT system, materials and inventory should flow smoothly through the production process without stopping.
            a) They arrive at the appropriate location just in time instead of becoming part of a costly inventory stockpile.
            b) Just-in-time is a manufacturing philosophy that seeks to improve a company's efficiency.
            c) The key measure of manufacturing efficiency is the level of inventory maintained; the lower the level of inventory, the more efficient the production system.
        4. A proliferation of inexpensive programs designed for personal computers gives small companies that ability.
        5. Companies adopting the JIT system look for ways to cut machine setup times, reduce the number of adjustments made during production, redesign parts so that machines involved

in the same processes are closer together, and move parts to each manufacturing station only when they are needed.

6. Today, many suppliers recognize that extremely high quality and absolutely on-time delivery are essential elements of remaining competitive.

    a) Just-in-time systems work because suppliers recognize that if they are unable to meet the demands their customers set forth, some other company surely will.

7. Advocates claim that when JIT is successfully implemented, companies experience five positive results:

    a) Lower investment in inventory

    b) Reduced inventory carrying and handling costs

    c) Reduced costs from obsolescence of inventory

    d) Lower investment in space for inventories and production

    e) Reduced total manufacturing costs from the better coordination needed between departments to operate at lower inventory levels

8. The two primary human elements on which successful JIT systems are built are:

    a) Mutual trust and teamwork.

    b) Empowerment.

9. Experience shows that companies with the following characteristics have the greatest success with JIT:

    (1) Reliable deliveries of all parts and supplies

    (2) Short distance between client and vendors

    (3) Consistently high quality of vendors' products

    (4) Stable and predictable product demand that allows for accurate production schedules

B. Just-in-Time II Techniques

1. An unwanted side effect of JIT programs--increased hostility resulting from the increased pressure they put on their suppliers to meet tight, often challenging schedules.

2. To resolve that conflict, many businesses have turned to an extension of JIT, just-in-time II (JIT II), which focuses on creating a close, harmonious relationship with a company's suppliers so that both parties benefit from increased efficiency.

    a) To work successfully, JIT II requires suppliers and their customers to share what was once closely guarded information in an environment of trust and cooperation.

    b) In many businesses practicing JIT II, suppliers' employees work on site at the customer's plant, factory, or warehouse almost as if they were its employees.

    c) This new alliance between suppliers and their customers forms a new supply chain that lowers costs at every one of its links.

    d) Growing numbers of small companies are forging JIT II relationships with their suppliers and customers.

3. Manufacturers are not the only companies benefiting from JIT II.

    a) In a retail environment, the concept is more commonly known as efficient consumer response (ECR), but the principles are the same.

    b) Because vendors are linked electronically to the retailer's point-of-sale system, they can monitor the company's inventory and keep it stocked with the right merchandise mix in the right quantities.

4. Just-in-time II works best when two companies transact a significant amount of business that involves many different parts or products. Still, trust is the biggest barrier the companies must overcome.

IV. Turning Slow-Moving Inventory into Cash
   A. Turnover
      1. Effective inventory management requires a business owner to monitor the company's inventory turnover ratio and to compare it with that of other firms of similar size in the same industry.
         a) The inventory turnover ratio is computed by dividing the firm's cost of goods sold by its average inventory.
         b) This ratio expresses the number of times per year the business turns over its inventory.
            (1) In most cases, the higher the inventory turnover ratio, the better the small firm's financial position will be.
            (2) A very low inventory turnover ratio indicates that much of the inventory may be stale and obsolete or that inventory investment is too large.
         c) Slow-moving items carry a good chance of loss resulting from spoilage or obsolescence.
         d) Some small business owners are reluctant to sell these slow-moving items by cutting prices, but it is much more profitable to dispose of this merchandise as quickly as possible than to hold it in stock at the regular prices.
      2. The most common technique for liquidating slow-moving merchandise is the markdown.
         a) Not only is the markdown effective in eliminating slow-moving goods, but it also is a successful promotional tool.
         b) Advertising special prices on such merchandise helps the small business garner a larger clientele and contributes to establishing a favorable business image.
         c) Using special sales to promote slow-moving items helps create a functional program for turning over inventory more quickly.
      3. Other techniques that help eliminate slow-moving merchandise include the following:
         a) Middle-of-the-aisle display islands that attract customer attention.
         b) One-day-only sales.
         c) Quantity discounts for volume purchases.
         d) Bargain tables with a variety of merchandise for customers to explore.
         e) Eye-catching lights and tickets marking sale merchandise.

V. Protecting Inventory from Theft
   A. Introduction
      1. Security experts estimate that businesses lose $400 billion annually to criminals, although the actual loss may be even greater because so many business crimes go unreported.
      2. Studies show that small businesses are more susceptible to crime than large companies; a small firm is 35 times as likely to be a victim of employee theft, shoplifting, robbery, or burglary as a business with sales in excess of $5 million.
      3. Certain types of businesses are particularly vulnerable to losses from crime.
         a) The very nature of retail leaves that industry highly susceptible to criminal attacks.
         b) Research shows that retailers foot approximately one-fourth of the national crime bill.
      4. Although they may not want to admit it, small business owners are frequent victims of business crimes.

   B. Employee Theft
      1. Employee theft accounts for the greatest proportion of the criminal losses businesses suffer.
         a) Small business owners simply don't want to believe that the people who work for them would steal from them.

b) One U.S. Justice Department study reports that approximately 30 percent of all employees are hard-core pilferers.

c) The study also estimates that without preventive security measures in place, 80 percent of employees will become involved in theft.

d) Many thefts by employees involve "nickel-and-dime" items.

IN THE FOOTSTEPS OF AN ENTREPRENEUR - The Best Hardware Store in the World

SUMMARY

Customers walking into Harvey's Hardware in Needham, Massachusetts, for the first time have a tendency to be overwhelmed by what they see: a modest-sized store loaded with wall-to-wall and floor-to-ceiling inventory. Harvey Katz started the hardware store shortly after he returned from the Korean War. In the early days Harvey had very little money to invest in the business, and he couldn't afford much inventory. To make his store look well-stocked, he scattered his meager inventory of hardware around the shelves and then filled in the gaps with empty boxes he had taped shut. Business picked up gradually, and Harvey noticed that quite a few customers came in looking for odd items that none of the hardware stores in town--including his own--carried. He also observed that when he did happen to have a hard-to-find item, the customer seemed to be especially pleased and usually came back repeatedly to buy other items. Harvey's competition strategy was born! Stock as much merchandise as you possibly can, and you can build a large base of loyal customers. Today Harvey's strategy lives on through his two sons.

The cornerstone of Harvey's strategy for success led to the second factor that puts the store so far ahead of the competition. Years ago, not long after he began stocking so much hardware, Harvey realized that he either had to move to a much larger building where he could spread his merchandise out so customers could help themselves or he had to hire workers to serve customers. Soon, superior customer service became another hallmark of Harvey's.

Gary and Jeff installed a computer system several years ago to help them maintain control over their extensive inventory but they found that they didn't need most of the features it offered. The sales staff knows and watches the inventory so closely that they know they need to order duct tape before the computer tells them to! Stocking and displaying such a volume of merchandise provides a challenge, but the Katz brothers use the store's crowded look to their advantage as well. Harvey's packs $135 worth of inventory per square foot into its building, whereas the typical hardware store carries just $35 worth of goods per square foot. Harvey's sales are more than three times the average for hardware stores: $503 million, compared with $129 in sales at the average hardware store. Retail experts know that the key to success is rapid inventory turnover. Harvey's average inventory turnover ratio is 4.5 times per year, compared with just 3.7 times per year at the typical hardware store.

1. What factors set Harvey's Hardware apart from its competitors? What role have these factors played in the company's success?
    Answer - His customer service, his comfortable shopping environment, his wide selection of products, all set him apart. Working together they have made him successful by setting his store apart from other hardware stores.

2. What dangers does the company face as a result of its unique retail strategy?
    Answer - His large inventory is expensive to carry. Changes in home repair products and do-it-yourself trends could leave him holding a lot of obsolete inventory. He's susceptible to theft.

---

2. Most thefts occur when employees take advantage of the opportunities to steal that small business owners give them.

3. A recent study by the Association of Certified Fraud Examiners found that small companies (those with fewer than 100 employees) "were the most vulnerable to fraud and abuse."
   a) The study found that the median loss per fraud was $120,000, nearly as large as that for firms with more than 10,000 workers (median of $126,000 per fraud).
4. What causes employee theft?
   a) Some may have a grudge against the company; others may have a drug, alcohol, or gambling addiction to support.
   b) "Employees take from the company for four reasons: need, greed, temptation, and opportunity," says one security expert. "A company can control the last two."
5. These conditions can lead to major security gaps in small companies.
   a) The trusted employee.
      (1) Studies show that younger, less devoted employees steal from their companies most often, but long-time employees can cause more damage.
      (2) In many small businesses, the owner views employees, especially long-time workers, almost as partners, operating the business in a family atmosphere.
      (3) Because of their seniority, these employees hold key positions and are quite familiar with operations, so they know where weaknesses in control and security procedures lie.
      (4) Small business owners should also be wary of "workaholic" employees.
      (5) As a security precaution, business owners should require every employee to take vacations long enough so that someone else has to take over their responsibilities (at least 5 consecutive business days).
   b) Disgruntled employees.
      (1) Employees are more likely to steal if they believe that their company treats employees unfairly, and the probability of their stealing goes even higher if they believe they themselves have been treated unfairly.
      (2) Dishonest employees will make up the difference between what they are paid and what they believe they are worth by stealing.
   c) Organizational atmosphere.
      (1) Failing to establish formal controls and procedures invites theft.
      (2) Four factors encourage employees theft:
         (a) The need or desire to steal.
         (b) A rationalization for the act.
         (c) The opportunity to steal.
         (d) The perception that there is a low probability of being caught.
      (3) The owner must recognize that he sets the example for security and honesty in the business. Employees place more emphasis on what the owner does that on what he says.
      (4) Managers must constantly emphasize the importance of security. Security rules and procedures must be reasonable, and the owner must treat the workers equitably.
   d) Physical breakdowns.
      (1) The owner who pays little attention to the distribution of keys, safe combinations, and other entry devices is inviting theft.
      (2) Owners who fail to lock doors and windows or to install reliable alarm systems are leaving their businesses open to thieves both inside and outside the organization.
      (3) Many businesses find that their profits go out with the trash, literally. When collecting trash, a dishonest employee may stash valuable merchandise in with the refuse and dump it in the receptacle.

  e) Improper cash control.

   (1) Without a system of logical, practical audit controls on cash, a firm will likely suffer internal theft.

   (2) Cashiers clearly have the greatest accessibility to the firm's cash and, consequently, experience the greatest temptation to steal.

   (3) A daily inspection of the cash register tape can point out potential employee theft problems.

    (a) When tapes indicate an excessive amount of voided transactions or no-sale transactions, the owner should investigate.

    (b) A no-sale transaction could mean the register was opened to give a customer change or to steal cash.

    (c) A large number of incorrect register transactions also is a sign of foul play.

6. Preventing employee theft.

  a) Many incidents of employee theft go undetected, and of those employees who are caught stealing, only a small percentage are prosecuted.

7. Screen employees carefully.

  a) Perhaps a business owner's greatest weapon against crime is a thorough pre-employment screening process.

  b) Although state and federal regulations prohibit employers from invading job applicants' privacy and from using discriminatory devices in the selection process, employers have a legitimate right to determine job candidates' integrity and qualifications.

   (1) A thorough background check with references and previous employers also is essential.

  c) Some security experts recommend the use of integrity tests, paper-and-pencil tests that offer valuable insight into job applicants' level of honesty.

  d) Because drug addictions drive many employees to steal, employers also should administer drug tests consistently to all job applicants.

8. Create an environment of honesty.

  a) Creating an environment of honesty and integrity starts at the top.

  b) A positive work environment where employees see themselves as an important part of the team is an effective deterrent to employee theft.

  c) Establishing a written code of ethics and having new employees sign "honesty clauses" offer tangible evidence of a company's commitment to honesty and integrity.

9. Establish a system of internal controls.

  a) The basis for maintaining security on the job is establishing a set of reasonable internal controls designed to prevent employee theft.

  b) The most basic rule is to separate among several employees related duties that might cause a security breach if assigned to a single worker.

  c) Business owners should insist that all company records be kept up to date.

   (1) Sloppy recordkeeping makes theft difficult to detect.

   (2) One subtle way to test employees' honesty is to commit deliberate errors occasionally to see if employees detect them.

10. Finally, business owners should demonstrate zero tolerance for theft.

  a) They must adhere strictly to company policy when dealing with employees who violate the company's trust.

  b) When business owners catch an employee thief, the best course of action is to fire the perpetrator and to prosecute.

  c) Prosecuting a former employee for theft is never easy, but it does send a clear signal about how the company views employee crime.

WIRED TO THE WEB - Stolen Trust

SUMMARY
Owner Michael Powell operates a chain of seven bookstores, but the most famous store is the one in downtown Portland; it is the largest bookstore in the United States, taking up an entire city block. Powell's Books is known not only for its huge selection of books but also for the authority and responsibility it gives its workers.

In most major bookstores, one person, the buyer, is in charge of making all inventory decisions. At Powell's, about 70 percent of the employees have a voice in the company's inventory decisions. Powell practices open-book management, sharing the company's financial statements with his employees. Plus, the business has between 30 and 40 working committees reviewing every aspect of its operation.

Unfortunately, when the employee stole from Powell's, he robbed the company of more than money and books; he also tried to steal the atmosphere of trust Powell had worked so hard to create since launching the business. "My first reaction was a kind of numbness and denial. Once I acknowledged what had happened, I felt angry with myself--angry for having such vulnerable systems. I had a momentary impulse to go out and lock everything up--to start treating everybody as a potential thief." The employee stole simply because he could. The theft pointed out obvious weaknesses in Powell's business system.
Still, Powell resisted the temptation to crack down on his employees' freedom to make decisions. His business philosophy remains the same, but his method of implementing it is more cautious.

1. Evaluate Powell's response to his company's encounter with employee theft. Would the result have been the same if Powell had cracked down and imposed a strict set of controls on all employees, in effect taking back the authority and responsibility he had delegated to them?
    Answer - Probably the worst thing Powell could have done would be to overreact and crack down. While wiser and more cautious, he continues to trust employees, just with some reasonable safeguards in place.
2. Use the resources of the World Wide Web to learn more about Powell's Books and to research ways to reduce the likelihood of employee theft. What recommendations would you suggest Powell implement? Explain.
    Answer - Responses will depend on students' research.

    C. Shoplifting
        1. The most frequent business crime is shoplifting.
        2. Businesses lose an estimated $17 billion to $20 billion to shoplifters each year, and small businesses, especially retailers, suffer a significant share of those losses.
        3. Shoplifting losses account for approximately 3 percent of the average price tag.
        4. Types of shoplifters.
            a) Shoplifters look exactly like other customers.
            b) Fortunately for small business owners, most shoplifters are amateurs who steal because the opportunity presents itself.
            c) Experts identify five types of shoplifters.
                (1) Juveniles. Juveniles account for approximately one-half of all shoplifters. Many juveniles steal as a result of peer pressure.
                    (a) When owners detect juvenile shoplifters, they must not let sympathy stand in the way of good judgment.
                    (b) Juvenile offenders should be prosecuted through proper legal procedures just as any adult shoplifter would be.

      (2) Impulse shoplifters. Impulse shoplifters steal on the spur of the moment when they succumb to temptation.

         (a) These shoplifters do not plan their thefts, but when a prime opportunity to shoplift arises, they take advantage of it.

         (b) Many well-respected individuals are impulse shoplifters.

         (c) The most effective method of fighting impulse shoplifting is prevention.

      (3) Alcoholics, vagrants, and drug addicts. Shoplifters motivated to steal to support a drug or alcohol habit are usually easy to detect because their behavior is usually unstable and erratic.

         (a) Small business owners should exercise great caution in handling these shoplifters because they can easily become violent.

         (b) It is best to let the police apprehend these shoplifters.

      (4) Kleptomaniacs. Kleptomaniacs have a compulsive need to steal even though they have little, if any, need for the items they shoplift.

         (a) In many cases, these shoplifters could afford to purchase the merchandise they steal.

         (b) Kleptomaniacs account for less than 5 percent of shoplifters, but their "disease" costs business owners a great deal.

      (5) Professionals. Although only about 15 percent of shoplifters are professionals, they can severely damage a small business.

         (a) Career shoplifters tend to focus on expensive merchandise they can sell quickly to their "fences."

         (b) Police have apprehended professional shoplifters with detailed maps of a city's shopping districts, showing target stores and the best times to make a "hit."

5. Detecting shoplifters.

   a) Small business owners must always be on the lookout for shoplifters, but merchants should be especially vigilant on Saturdays and around Christmas, when shoplifters can hide their thefts more easily in the frenzy of a busy shopping day.

   b) Shoplifters can work alone or in groups.

   c) Solitary shoplifters are usually quite nervous. To make sure they avoid detection, they constantly scan the store for customers and employees. These shoplifters spend more time nervously looking around the store than examining merchandise.

   d) Shoplifters have their own arsenal of tools to assist them in plying their trade.

      (1) They often shop with booster boxes, shopping bags, umbrellas, bulky jackets, baby strollers, or containers disguised as gifts.

      (2) Some shoplifters use specially designed coats with hidden pockets and compartments that can hold even large items.

      (3) Another common tactic is "ticket switching"; the shoplifter exchanges price tickets on items and pays a very low price for an expensive item.

      (4) One variation of traditional shoplifting techniques is the "grab-and-run" in which a shoplifter grabs an armload of merchandise located near an exit and then dashes out the door into a waiting getaway car.

6. Deterring shoplifters.

   a) By focusing on preventing shoplifting rather than on prosecuting violators after the fact, business owners take a stronger stand in protecting their firms' merchandise.

   b) When a store gets a reputation for being tough on shoplifters, thefts drop off.

   c) Knowing what to look for improves dramatically a small business owner's odds in combating shoplifting:

      (1) Watch the eyes.

      (2) Watch the hands.

(3) Watch the clothing.

(4) Watch for devices.

(5) Watch for loiterers.

(6) Watch for switches.

7. Store owners can take other steps to discourage shoplifting.

   a) Train employees to spot shoplifters. Most security experts agree that alert employees are the best defense against shoplifters.

   (1) All employees should watch for suspicious people, especially those carrying the props of concealment.

   (2) An alert cashier can be a tremendous boon to the store owner attempting to minimize shoplifting losses.

   (3) Employees should be trained to watch for group shoplifting tactics.

   (4) The sales staff should watch for those individuals who consistently shop during the hours when most personnel are on breaks.

   (5) The cost of training employees to be alert to shoplifting "gimmicks" can be regained many times over in preventing losses from retail theft.

   b) Pay attention to the store layout. A well-planned store layout also can be an effective obstacle in preventing shoplifting losses.

   (1) Proper lighting throughout the store makes it easier for employees to monitor shoppers.

   (2) Display cases should be kept low, no more than three or four feet high, so store personnel can have a clear view of the entire store.

   (3) Display counters should have spaces between them.

   (4) Business owners should keep small expensive items such as jewelry, silver, and pocket calculators behind display counters or in locked cases with a salesclerk nearby.

   (5) Cash registers should be located so that cashiers have an unobstructed view of the entire store.

   c) Install mechanical devices. A complete deterrence system can be expensive, but failure to implement one is usually more expensive.

   (1) Tools such as two-way mirrors allow employees at one end of the store to monitor a customer at the other end, and one-way viewing windows enable employees to watch the entire store without being seen.

   (2) Other mechanical devices, such as closed-circuit TV cameras, convex wall mirrors, and peepholes, also help the owner protect the store from shoplifters.

   (3) An owner can deter ticket-switching shoplifters by using tamper-proof price tickets.

   (4) One of the most effective weapons for combating shoplifting is the electronic article surveillance system, small tags that are equipped with electronic sensors that set off sound and light alarms if customers take them past a store exit.

8. Apprehending shoplifters.

   a) About 98 percent of the time, shoplifters are successful at plying their trade.

   b) Business owners detect only 1.2 million shoplifting attempts and, of those shoplifters who do get caught, less than half are prosecuted.

   c) The store owner has to be certain that the shoplifter has taken or concealed the merchandise and has left the store with it.

   d) Although state laws vary, owners must do the following to make the charges stick:

   (1) See the person take or conceal the merchandise.

   (2) Identify the merchandise as the store's.

   (3) Testify that it was taken with the intent to steal.

   (4) Prove that the merchandise was not paid for.

    e)   An owner should never apprehend the shoplifter if she has lost sight of the suspect even for an instant.

    f)   Another primary consideration in apprehending shoplifters is the safety of store employees. The wisest course of action when a shoplifter is detected is to alert the police or store security personnel and let them apprehend the suspect.

    g)   Apprehension outside the store is safest. This tactic strengthens the owner's case and eliminates unpleasant in-store scenes that upset other customers or that might be dangerous.

    h)   Many small business owners fail to prosecute because they fear legal entanglements or negative publicity. In most cases, prosecuting the shoplifter is the best option, especially for juveniles and first-time offenders.

    i)   The small business owner who prosecutes shoplifters consistently soon develops a reputation for toughness that most shoplifters hesitate to test.

IN THE FOOTSTEPS OF AN ENTREPRENEUR - An Error in Judgment?

SUMMARY
Patricia Caldwell was shopping in a retail store. A store security employee became suspicious when he saw that she was carrying a large purse and was handling many small items. As she shopped, Caldwell went into several departments and bent down out of sight of the security guard, removed her glasses to read labels and returned them to her purse several times, etc. The guard accused her of shoplifting. He found none of the store's merchandise. Rather than releasing her, he told Caldwell to return to the store with him, where he escorted her back to areas where she had been shopping. The guard told her six or seven times that he had seen her conceal merchandise in her purse. With no evidence of stolen merchandise, another employee told Caldwell she could leave the store.

Caldwell brought a lawsuit against the retailer for slander (making false defamatory statements about another) and false imprisonment (depriving a person of his liberty without justice). The court allowed the retailer's loss prevention manual to be introduced as evidence. The manual spelled out that an employee "must see the shoplifter take our property." The jury in the case awarded Caldwell $175,000 in total damages and the retailer appealed. The appellate court affirmed the lower court's ruling.
1.   What did the retailer in this case do wrong?
    Answer - Employees did not follow their own procedure manual. They violated the basics of apprehension, not losing sight, seeing the theft, etc.
2.   What guidelines should store employees follow when dealing with a suspected shoplifter?
    Answer - The store manual was good, employees need to simply follow it.

   D. Conclusion

      1.   Inventory control is one of those less-than-glamorous activities that business owners must perform if their businesses are to succeed. Although it doesn't offer the flash of marketing or the visibility of customer service, inventory control is no less important. In fact, business owners who invest the time and the resources to exercise the proper degree of control over their inventory soon discover that the payoff is huge!

Chapter Summary

♦ Explain the various inventory control systems and the advantages and disadvantages of each.
   ▪   Inventory represents the largest investment for the typical small business. Unless properly managed, the cost of inventory will strain the firm's budget and cut into its profitability. The goal of inventory control is to balance the cost of holding and maintaining inventory with meeting customer demand.

- Regardless of the inventory control system selected, business owners must recognize the relevance of the 80/20 rule, which states that roughly 80 percent of the value of the firm's inventory is in about 20 percent of the items in stock. Because only a small percentage of items account for the majority of the value of the firm's inventory, managers should focus control on those items.
- Three basic types of inventory control systems are available to the small business owner: perpetual, visual, and partial. Perpetual inventory control systems are designed to maintain a running count of the items in inventory. Although they can be expensive and cumbersome to operate by hand, affordable computerized point-of-sale (POS) terminals that deduct items sold from inventory on hand make perpetual systems feasible for small companies. The visual inventory system is the most common method of controlling merchandise in small business. This system works best when shortages are not likely to cause major problems. Partial inventory control systems are most effective for small businesses with limited time and money. These systems operate on the basis of the 80/20 rule.
- The ABC system is a partial system that divides a firm's inventory into three categories depending on each item's dollar usage volume (cost per unit multiplied by quantity used per time period). The purpose of classifying items according to their value is to establish the proper degree of control over them. A items are most closely controlled by perpetual inventory control systems; B items use basic analytical tools; and C items are controlled by very simple techniques such as the two-bin system, the level control method, or the tag system.

◆ Describe how just-in-time (JIT) and JIT II inventory control techniques work.
- The just-in-time system of inventory control sees excess inventory as a blanket that masks production problems and adds unnecessary costs to the production operation. Under a JIT philosophy, the level of inventory maintained is the measure of efficiency. Materials and parts should not build up as costly inventory. They should flow through the production process without stopping, arriving at the appropriate location just in time.
- JIT II techniques focus on creating a close, harmonious relationship with a company's suppliers so that both parties benefit from increased efficiency. To work successfully, JIT II requires suppliers and their customers to share what was once closely guarded information in an environment of trust and cooperation. Under JIT II, customers and suppliers work hand in hand, acting more like partners than mere buyers and sellers.

◆ Describe some methods for reducing loss from slow-moving inventory.
- Managing inventory requires monitoring the company's inventory turnover ratio; slow-moving items result in losses from spoilage or obsolescence.
- Slow-moving items can be liquidated by markdowns, eye-catching displays, or quantity discounts.

◆ Discuss employee theft and shoplifting and how to prevent them. Employee theft accounts for the majority of business losses due to theft. Most small business owners are so busy managing their companies' daily affairs that they fail to develop reliable security systems. Thus, they provide their employees with prime opportunities to steal.
- The organizational atmosphere may encourage employees theft. The owner sets the organizational tone for security. A complete set of security controls, procedures, and penalties should be developed and enforced. Physical breakdowns in security invite employee theft. Open doors and windows, poor key control, and improper cash controls are major contributors to the problem of employee theft. Employers can build security into their businesses by screening and selecting employees carefully. Orientation programs also help the employee to get started in the right direction. Internal controls, such as division of responsibility, spot checks, and audit procedures, are useful in preventing employee theft.
- Shoplifting is the most common business crime. Fortunately, most shoplifters are amateurs. Juveniles often steal to impress their friends, but prosecution can halt their criminal ways early on. Impulse shoplifters steal because the opportunity suddenly arises. Simple prevention is the best defense against these shoplifters. Alcoholics, vagrants, and drug addicts steal to supply some need

and are usually easiest to detect. Kleptomaniacs have a compelling need to steal. Professionals are in the business of theft and can be very difficult to detect and quite dangerous.

■   Three strategies are most useful in deterring shoplifters. First, employees should be trained to look for signs of shoplifting. Second, store layout should be designed with theft deterrence in mind. Finally, anti-theft devices should be installed in the store.

Discussion Questions

1. Describe some of the incidental costs of carrying and maintaining inventory for the small business owner.

   Answer - The largest expenditure most small companies make is for inventory, and entrepreneurs can realize tremendous savings from managing their company's inventory effectively. Excess inventories also eat up additional warehouse space; boost personnel needs for security, production, and warehouse staff; necessitate the purchase of extra inventory insurance; and increase borrowing needs. "Companies can increase their profitability 20 to 50 percent through prudent inventory management," says one expert.

2. What is a perpetual inventory system? How does it operate? What are the advantages and disadvantages of using such a system?

   Answer - Perpetual inventory systems are designed to maintain a running count of the items in inventory. There are a number of different perpetual inventory systems, but they have a common element, keeping a continuous tally of each item added to or subtracted from the firm's stock of merchandise. The basic perpetual inventory system uses a perpetual inventory sheet that includes fundamental product information such as the item's name, stock number, description, economic order quantity (EOQ), and reorder point. Sporadic use creates problems. If managers or employees take items out of stock or place them in inventory without recording them, the perpetual inventory sheet will yield incorrect totals and can foul up the entire inventory control system. Keeping such records for a large number of items and ensuring the accuracy of the system can be excessively expensive. Using the system, business owners can tell how quickly each item is selling and how many items are in stock at any time. Their inventory records are accurate and always current. They also can generate instantly a variety of reports to aid in making purchasing decisions.

3. List and describe briefly the four versions of a perpetual inventory system.

   Answer - Perpetual inventory systems operate in a number of ways, but three basic variations are particularly common: the sales ticket method, the sales stub method, and the floor sample method. The sales ticket method--most small businesses use sales tickets to summarize individual customers' transactions. These tickets serve two major purposes: 1) They provide the customer with a sales receipt for the merchandise purchased. 2) They provide the owner with a daily record of the number of specific inventory items sold. The Sales Stub Method--The principle behind the sales stub method of inventory control is the same as that underlying the sales ticket method, but its mechanics are slightly different. Retail stores often attach a ticket with two or more parts containing relevant product information to each inventory item in stock. The floor sample method of controlling inventory is commonly used by businesses selling big-ticket items with high unit cost. In many cases, these items are somewhat bulky and are difficult to display in large numbers. A simple technique for maintaining control of these items is to attach a small pad to the display desk with sheets numbered in descending order from 15 to 1.

4. Give examples of small businesses that would find it practical to implement the four systems described in question 3.

   Answer - Students' suggestions will vary. Sales ticket would work with almost any small business--clothing, hardware, small appliance, office supply, etc. Sales stub is often used with clothing stores and small appliance stores. Floor sample is used with furniture, discount warehouse stores, large appliance stores, etc.

5. What advantages and disadvantages does a visual inventory control system have over other methods?
   Answer - It is the most common method of controlling inventory. Managers simply conduct periodic visual inspections to determine the quantity of various items they should order. Such systems are impractical when the business stocks a large number of low-value items with low dollar volume. This method is also the least effective for ensuring accuracy and reliability.

6. For what type of business product line is a visual control system most effective?
   Answer - In general, a visual inventory control system works best in firms where daily sales are relatively consistent, the owner is closely involved with the inventory, the variety of merchandise is small, and items can be obtained quickly from vendors.

7. What is the 80/20 rule, and why is it important in controlling inventory?
   Answer - Pareto's law (or the 80/20 rule) holds that about 80 percent of the value of the firm's sales revenue is generated by 20 percent of the items kept in stock. Owners should focus the majority of their inventory control efforts on this 20 percent.

8. Outline the ABC inventory control procedure. What is the purpose of classifying inventory items using this procedure?
   Answer - The typical ABC system divides a firm's inventory into three major categories: a) A items account for a high dollar usage volume, b) B items account for a moderate dollar usage volume, and c) C items account for low dollar usage volume. The dollar usage volume of an item measures the relative importance of that item in the firm's inventory. The initial step in establishing an ABC classification system is to compute the annual dollar usage volume for each product (or product category). The next step is to arrange the products in descending order on the basis of the computed annual dollar usage volume. The purpose of classifying items according to their annual dollar usage volume is to establish the proper degree of control over each item held in inventory.

9. Briefly describe the types of control techniques that should be used for A, B, and C items.
   Answer - Items in the A classification should be controlled under a perpetual inventory system with as much detail as necessary. Control of B items should rely more on periodic control systems and basic analytical tools such as EOQ and reorder point analysis. C items typically constitute a minor proportion of the small firm's inventory value and, as a result, require the least effort and expense to control. The cost involved in using detailed recordkeeping and inventory control procedures greatly outweighs the advantages gleaned from strict control of C items.

10. What is the basis for the JIT philosophy? Under what condition does a JIT system work best?
    Answer - The just-in-time philosophy, however, views excess inventory as a blanket that masks problems and as a source of unnecessary costs that inhibit a firm's competitive position. Under a JIT system, materials and inventory should flow smoothly through the production process without stopping. They arrive at the appropriate location just in time instead of becoming part of a costly inventory stockpile. Just-in-time is a manufacturing philosophy that seeks to improve a company's efficiency. The key measure of manufacturing efficiency is the level of inventory maintained; the lower the level of inventory, the more efficient the production system. Just-in-time systems work because suppliers recognize that if they are unable to meet the demands their customers set forth, some other company surely will. The two primary human elements on which successful JIT systems are built are: a) mutual trust and teamwork and b) empowerment.

11. What is JIT II? What is its underlying philosophy? What risks does it present to businesses?
    Answer - An unwanted side effect of JIT programs--increased hostility resulting from the increased pressure they put on their suppliers to meet tight, often challenging schedules. To resolve that conflict, many businesses have turned to an extension of JIT, just-in-time II (JIT II), which focuses on creating a close, harmonious relationship with a company's suppliers so that both parties benefit from increased efficiency. To work successfully, JIT II requires suppliers and their customers to share what was once closely guarded information in an environment of trust and cooperation. In many businesses practicing JIT II, suppliers' employees work on site at the customer's plant, factory, or warehouse almost as if they were its employees. Just-in-time II works best when two companies transact a significant amount of business that involves many different parts or products. Still, trust is the biggest barrier the companies must overcome.

12. Outline the two methods of taking a physical inventory count. Why is it necessary for every small business manager to take inventory?
    Answer - There are two basic methods of conducting a physical inventory count. One alternative is to take inventory at regular intervals. Many businesses take inventory at the end of the year. The other method of taking inventory, called cycle counting, involves counting a number of items on a continuous basis. The manager counts a few types of items each week and checks the numbers against the inventory control system. Electronic data interchange (EDI) systems enable business owners to track their inventories and to place orders with vendors quickly and with few errors by linking them to their vendors electronically.

13. Why are slow-moving items dangerous to the small business? What can be done to liquidate them from inventory?
    Answer - Effective inventory management requires a business owner to monitor the company's inventory turnover ratio and to compare it with that of other firms of similar size in the same industry. Slow-moving items carry a good chance of loss resulting from spoilage or obsolescence. Some small business owners are reluctant to sell these slow-moving items by cutting prices, but it is much more profitable to dispose of this merchandise as quickly as possible than to hold it in stock at the regular prices. The most common technique for liquidating slow-moving merchandise is the markdown. Other techniques that help eliminate slow-moving merchandise include the following:
    - Middle-of-the-aisle display islands that attract customer attention.
    - One-day-only sales.
    - Quantity discounts for volume purchases.
    - Bargain tables with a variety of merchandise for customers to explore.
    - Eye-catching lights and tickets marking sale merchandise.

14. Why are small companies more susceptible to business crime than large companies?
    Answer - Security experts estimate that businesses lose $400 billion annually to criminals, although the actual loss may be even greater because so many business crimes go unreported. Studies show that small businesses are more susceptible to crime than large companies; a small firm is 35 times as likely to be a victim of employee theft, shoplifting, robbery, or burglary as a business with sales in excess of $5 million. Most thefts occur when employees take advantage of the opportunities to steal that small business owners give them. A recent study by the Association of Certified Fraud Examiners found that small companies (those with fewer than 100 employees) "were the most vulnerable to fraud and abuse."

15. Why is employee theft a problem for many small businesses? Briefly describe the reasons for employee theft.
    Answer - Some may have a grudge against the company; others may have a drug, alcohol, or gambling addiction to support. "Employees take from the company for four reasons: need, greed,

temptation, and opportunity," says one security expert. "A company can control the last two." These conditions can lead to major security gaps in small companies.

- The trusted employee.
  - Studies show that younger, less devoted employees steal from their companies most often, but long-time employees can cause more damage.
  - In many small businesses, the owner views employees, especially long-time workers, almost as partners, operating the business in a family atmosphere.
- Disgruntled employees.
  - Employees are more likely to steal if they believe that their company treats employees unfairly, and the probability of their stealing goes even higher if they believe they themselves have been treated unfairly.
- Physical breakdowns.
  - Owners who fail to lock doors and windows or to install reliable alarm systems are leaving their businesses open to thieves both inside and outside the organization.
- Improper cash control.
  - Without a system of logical, practical audit controls on cash, a firm will likely suffer internal theft.

16. Construct a profile of the employee most likely to steal goods or money from an employer. What four elements must be present for employee theft to occur?
    Answer - There is no profile, as any employee can steal. Four factors encourage employees theft:
    - The need or desire to steal.
    - A rationalization for the act.
    - The opportunity to steal.
    - The perception that there is a low probability of being caught.

17. Briefly outline a program that could help the typical small business owner minimize losses due to employee theft.
    Answer - Many incidents of employee theft go undetected, and, of those employees who are caught stealing, only a small percentage are prosecuted.
    - Screen employees carefully.
      - Perhaps a business owner's greatest weapon against crime is a thorough pre-employment screening process.
    - Create an environment of honesty.
      - A positive work environment where employees see themselves as an important part of the team is an effective deterrent to employee theft.
    - Establish a system of internal controls.
      - The most basic rule is to separate among several employees related duties that might cause a security breach if assigned to a single worker.
    - Finally, business owners should demonstrate zero tolerance for theft.
      - They must adhere strictly to company policy when dealing with employees who violate the company's trust.

18. List and briefly describe the major types of shoplifters.
    Answer - Shoplifters look exactly like other customers. Experts identify five types of shoplifters.
    - Juveniles. Juveniles account for approximately one-half of all shoplifters. Many juveniles steal as a result of peer pressure.
    - Impulse shoplifters. Impulse shoplifters steal on the spur of the moment when they succumb to temptation.

- Alcoholics, vagrants, and drug addicts. Shoplifters motivated to steal to support a drug or alcohol habit are usually easy to detect because their behavior is usually unstable and erratic.
- Kleptomaniacs. Kleptomaniacs have a compulsive need to steal even though they have little, if any, need for the items they shoplift. In many cases, these shoplifters could afford to purchase the merchandise they steal.
- Professionals. Although only about 15 percent of shoplifters are professionals, they can severely damage a small business.

19. Outline the characteristics of a typical shoplifter that should arouse a small business manager's suspicions. What tools and tactics is a shoplifter likely to use?

    Answer - Small business owners must always be on the lookout for shoplifters, but merchants should be especially vigilant on Saturdays and around Christmas, when shoplifters can hide their thefts more easily in the frenzy of a busy shopping day.
    - Knowing what to look for improves dramatically a small business owner's odds in combating shoplifting:
      - Watch the eyes.
      - Watch the hands.
      - Watch the clothing.
      - Watch for devices.
      - Watch for loiterers.
      - Watch for switches.
      - Solitary shoplifters are usually quite nervous.
    - Shoplifters have their own arsenal of tools to assist them in plying their trade.
      - They often shop with booster boxes, shopping bags, umbrellas, bulky jackets, baby strollers, or containers disguised as gifts.
      - Some shoplifters use specially designed coats with hidden pockets and compartments that can hold even large items.
      - Another common tactic is "ticket switching"; the shoplifter exchanges price tickets on items and pays a very low price for an expensive item.
      - One variation of traditional shoplifting techniques is the "grab-and-run" in which a shoplifter grabs an armload of merchandise located near an exit and then dashes out the door into a waiting getaway car.

20. Describe the major elements of a program designed to deter shoplifters.

    Answer - By focusing on preventing shoplifting rather than on prosecuting violators after the fact, business owners take a stronger stand in protecting their firms' merchandise. When a store gets a reputation for being tough on shoplifters, thefts drop off. Store owners can take other steps to discourage shoplifting.
    - Train employees to spot shoplifters. Most security experts agree that alert employees are the best defense against shoplifters.
    - Pay attention to the store layout. A well-planned store layout also can be an effective obstacle in preventing shoplifting losses.
    - Install mechanical devices. A complete deterrence system can be expensive, but failure to implement one is usually more expensive.
    - Apprehend shoplifters and prosecute.

21. How can proper planning of store layout reduce shoplifting losses?

    Answer - A well-planned store layout also can be an effective obstacle in preventing shoplifting losses. Proper lighting throughout the store makes it easier for employees to monitor shoppers. Display cases should be kept low, no more than three or four feet high, so store personnel can have a clear view of the entire store. Display counters should have spaces between them. Business owners should keep small expensive items such as jewelry, silver, and pocket calculators behind display counters or in locked cases with a salesclerk nearby. Cash registers should be located so that cashiers have an unobstructed view of the entire store.

22. What must an owner do to have a good case against a shoplifter? How should a suspected shoplifter be apprehended?

Answer - About 98 percent of the time, shoplifters are successful at plying their trade. The store owner has to be certain that the shoplifter has taken or concealed the merchandise and has left the store with it. Although state laws vary, owners must do the following to make the charges stick:
- See the person take or conceal the merchandise.
- Identify the merchandise as the store's.
- Testify that it was taken with the intent to steal.
- Prove that the merchandise was not paid for.

An owner should never apprehend the shoplifter if she has lost sight of the suspect even for an instant. Another primary consideration in apprehending shoplifters is the safety of store employees. The wisest course of action when a shoplifter is detected is to alert the police or store security personnel and let them apprehend the suspect. Apprehension outside the store is safest. This tactic strengthens the owner's case and eliminates unpleasant in-store scenes that upset other customers or that might be dangerous.

Step into the Real World

1. Contact a local small business owner and interview him or her to get answers to the following questions: What type of inventory control system is used? How well does it work? Does the 80/20 rule apply to the entrepreneur's inventory? Does the owner's inventory control system reflect the 80/20 rule? How does the owner liquidate slow-moving merchandise?

2. Visit a small manufacturer and ask if the company is using a JIT or JIT II system to integrate inventory and production. If it is, what have the results been? What problems has the company encountered? How did the company solve those problems? What improvements, if any, has the business experienced by using JIT?

3. Interview a local small business owner who has been a victim of shoplifting or employee theft. What security breaches contributed to the theft? How can the owner prevent a recurrence of the theft? What changes has the owner made in the business since the theft occurred?

4. Contact an attorney and interview him or her about the laws governing the apprehension of suspected shoplifters in your state. What should the small business owner who suspects someone of shoplifting do? Write a policy spelling out the proper procedure.

5. Invite a security consultant, police officer, or security agent from a local business to speak to your class about preventing employee theft and shoplifting. How extensive is the problem? What techniques does he or she recommend to prevent losses due to theft?

Chapter 18 - Using Technology to Gain a Competitive Edge

Improving technology can improve your competitiveness.
Chuck Stegman

A businessman's judgment is no better than his information.
P. R. Lamont

Teaching Objectives
Students will be able to:
1. Explain how technology can help small businesses gain a competitive advantage over their rivals.
2. Describe how to create a technology plan that enables business owners to get the most out of their investments in technology.
3. Explain how computers have transformed the way entrepreneurs do business and how to computerize a small business.
4. Outline the major business software applications, identify guidelines for buying computer hardware, and explain the hardware issues entrepreneurs face.
5. Discuss the peripheral equipment, such as printers, scanners, digital cameras, and personal digital assistants, that enhances the performance of the computer.
6. Discuss the role of communications technology, such as the telephone, voice mail, and e-mail, in small companies.

Instructor's Outline
I. Introduction
    A. Technology as a Competitive Weapon
        1. It can transform the way a small company works, the way it does business, and the way it interacts with its customers.
        2. Technologically savvy entrepreneurs are free to focus more on the strategic and creative sides of their businesses.
        3. Smart entrepreneurs see technology as an investment in making their companies more competitive and more successful.
           a) Figure 18.1 shows the results of a recent survey of the *Inc.* 500 fastest-growing private companies, graphing the areas of these companies that benefit most from technology.

II. Information Technology and Competitive Advantage
    A. Introduction
        1. Small businesses that learn to exploit the ability to use information and technology to serve their customers better will gain a competitive edge.
        2. Small companies that collect and use valuable information to manage their operations effectively will have a competitive advantage over their rivals, whatever their size.
        3. Information--or the lack of it--is fast becoming the competitive edge by which the growing company wins or loses in the marketplace.
        4. More small businesses are discovering ways to create what one expert calls a "techno-edge."
        5. It is not the technology itself that is so important to a company's success but how the entrepreneur behind the business devises creative, innovative ways to use that technology to forge lasting relationships with customers and to surpass their expectations.

III. Developing a Technology Plan
  A. Decide What You Want Your Company to Be Able to Do for Itself and for Your Customers
      1. The tasks you want to be able to perform, to a great extent, determine the level of technology you must buy.
      2. The focus of this first step is not on technology; it emphasizes the tasks entrepreneurs want their companies to perform or the service they want to provide to their customers.

  B. Determine the Technology and the Equipment You Will Need
      1. The next step is finding the appropriate technology to perform those tasks and functions.
          a) The goals established in the first step will drive the technology decisions in this step.
          b) Talking with other entrepreneurs at this step can be extremely helpful.
          c) Research technology reviews.
              (1) These reviews discuss important features such as benefits, performance, advantages, disadvantages, and price.
          d) Technology-related "chat groups" on the Internet are another excellent source of information.

  C. Conduct a Technology Audit
      1. The next step in developing a technology plan is to perform an audit of the company's existing technology.
          a) It is important to include a thorough description of each piece of equipment.
          b) Conducting an audit allows entrepreneurs to know where they are on the road to technology.

  D. Match Goals and Resources
      1. This ensures that the business will get maximum value from its existing equipment, from cellular telephones and fax machines to personal computers and digital cameras.

  E. Develop a Technology Budget
      1. It is best to prepare budgets for two or three years into the future, the useful life of most of today's technology.
      2. One way to stretch a company's investment in technology is to compare the cost and resulting capability of upgrading existing equipment with that of buying new equipment.

  F. Make the Necessary Purchases
      1. Avoid the tendency to buy the fastest, most powerful (and therefore most expensive) technology unless you really need it.
      2. Remember to let the demands of the tasks you want to accomplish drive the technology you buy.
      3. Shopping for the best prices on equipment can be time-consuming for busy entrepreneurs but can pay off handsomely.
      4. Common supply sources for small business owners include major retailers such as Best Buy, Office Depot, or Radio Shack, discount warehouses such as Sam's Club or Costco, direct-mail merchants such as computer makers Gateway 2000.
      5. Using the World Wide Web is an excellent way to locate the best bargains on many kinds of equipment.
          a) The more complex the equipment or the more crucial it is to your operation, the more you should be willing to pay for service and support.
          b) Figure 18.3 shows that cost is the number one barrier to technological advancement that small business owners cite.

IN THE FOOTSTEPS OF AN ENTREPRENEUR - A Technological Edge = A Competitive Edge

SUMMARY
But just how much has the computer changed the way people work? Jennifer Jarratt, a manager in a Washington, D.C.-based think tank that specializes in forecasting the future, says that the computer has only begun to transform the business world. Any new technology progresses gradually through three stages: substitution, adaptation, and revolution. Computers currently are in the last part of Stage 2, adaptation, and are beginning to spill over into the revolution stage.

In Stage 1, Substitution--the new technology replaces existing tools, but people are doing the same things they did before, only faster and better. In Stage 2, Adaptation, people discover that the new technology gives them the ability to do new things they never could do before. Users begin to branch out from their traditional approaches to basic tasks and functions to explore new possibilities the technology opens up. Stage 3 involves using technology to create major shifts not only in the way things are done but also in things to be done. People basically throw out everything they did before and start to rearrange not only the task they're doing but also the entire process that it stems from.

An investment in technology has enabled Dominick Segrete's small architectural design company to revamp the way it designs buildings and deals with its customers. Using an inexpensive conference and document-sharing program called ProShare, architects establish "virtual meetings" to present and to discuss with clients. This communication technology has transformed the design process for them. Segrete recently added 3-D and video capability to its computer system; now architects can take clients on a "virtual tour" through the spaces they design long before they are built.

1. How has Tucci, Segrete, and Rosen's investment in technology changed the way in which it competes in the marketplace?
   Answer - It has changed the design process making it more interactive, it has allowed it to capture jobs it might not have otherwise won, and it permits greater and quicker customization of designs, making them more customer-oriented.
2. In what ways has this technology changed the company's dealings with its clients? What are the benefits of these changes?
   Answer - It has reduced costs by reducing travel by both clients and designers, it has decreased turnaround time of designs, enhanced the ability to have ongoing discussions during the design process therefore keeping them closer to the client.
3. What dangers exist for companies that rely on technology such as this to gain a competitive edge?
   Answer - If the technology doesn't work, they don't work. Technology has a short lifespan so whatever they buy has to be undated continually. And, there are support, maintanence, and training costs that continue beyond the investment in the technology.

IV. Personal Computers
  A. Changing the Face of Business
    1. Products that change the way we live and work don't come along often; but when they do, the world is never the same again.
    2. The ubiquitous PC has transformed the workplace:
      a) sending typewriters the way of the papyrus scroll.
      b) enabling workers scattered across the globe to communicate as if they were in the same room.
      c) giving managers the power to analyze countless financial scenarios in just seconds.
      d) providing small companies the opportunity to become just as "big" in the eyes of their customers as any *Fortune* 500 company.

3. Today's personal computers rival or exceed yesterday's minicomputers and mainframes in power and flexibility.
   a) According to Moore's Law, the speed of microprocessors, the "brains" of a computer, doubles approximately every 18 months, but their prices remain about the same.
4. The transition to computer-based operations has not been easy or smooth for many small companies, and many entrepreneurs find computers frustrating and exasperating at times.

B. How to Computerize Your Business
   1. The key issues facing the small business owner who decides to buy a computer are when to buy a computer, how much to spend, what functions to computerize first, which software to use, which hardware to buy, and where to buy the computer.
   2. The real key to success with any technology is making sure that it fits the company's needs, which might include everything from improving the level of customer service to increasing control over inventory.
   3. The process of choosing a personal computer.
   4. Step 1. Develop a list of current activities.
      a) What is the nature of the business?
      b) After defining the general scope of the business, the owner must break down current business activities into more detailed categories that can be computerized, such as accounting, record keeping, inventory control, file management, etc.
      c) The owner should prioritize these activities. Then computerize the most important activities first.
   5. Step 2. Decide how much and which areas of the business to computerize.
      a) The best approach is to computerize a smooth, well-functioning system first.
      b) This will also show the owner what computerization can do for the company.
      c) Finally, when deciding which functions to computerize first, think about:
         (1) Which activities are critical to success now?
         (2) Which activities will become critical as the business grows?
         (3) Which activities will be critical to maintaining a Competitive advantage?
         (4) Which activities will improve the company's ability to serve our customers?
         (5) Which of these activities could benefit from the speed, accuracy, and timeliness of computerization?
   6. Step 3. Develop a computer budget.
      a) Once an entrepreneur has determined which areas of her business to computerize, she can develop a computer budget to do so.
      b) The budget must consider the cost of the computer system as well as additional costs such as training, peripheral equipment, support, consultants (if necessary), and maintenance.
      c) When preparing their computer budgets, entrepreneurs must consider the total cost of ownership (TCO). Total cost of ownership looks at more than just the cost of the equipment; it considers all of the costs--from software and technical support to training and maintenance--that owners will incur over the life of their computers.
         (1) According to one recent study, the out-of-pocket costs of hardware account for just 15 percent of the total cost of owning a computer.
         (2) The purchase price of the software makes up about 20 percent of total cost of ownership.
         (3) Training, support, and development costs make up between 40 and 60 percent of the total cost.

GAINING THE COMPETITIVE EDGE - How to Lower the Total Cost of Owning (TCO) a Personal Computer

SUMMARY
The majority of the total cost of ownership (TCO) for a computer lies beneath the surface in factors such as software, maintenance, technical support, training, supplies, equipment, and others. Ways to keep TCO down.

- Consider a network. Linking the computers in a business together into a local area network may help keep software costs to a minimum.
- Buy software bundles. All of the major software companies produce "suites" of programs, all in one package at significant discounts compared with purchasing each program separately.
- Consider hiring freelance computer technicians.
- Shop for the best deals on hardware and software purchases.
- Standardize your hardware and software purchases. Although it may not be possible to have all computers exactly alike, basing purchase decisions on a standard system profile will make maintaining your company's computers much easier.
- Consider ways to maximize employees' use of computers.
- Invest in training. The best way to ensure that your employees will be able to get the most out of their computers is to train them.
- Don't hold on to old technology forever. Having several generations of equipment in a company complicates the system and increases TCO. Set up a timetable for replacing old equipment and stick to it.
- Buy new technology for the right reasons. The best reason to purchase new technology is that it will improve your ability to do something that you already do or that it will enable you to do something you could not do before.

7. Step 4. Define the informational needs of the functions to be computerized first.
   a) A company's information needs manifest themselves in a number of ways. For example, if the manager plans to computerize the inventory control system, she should begin by studying the flow of information through the manual inventory recordkeeping system.
   b) Identifying these and other related issues will help the owner define the nature and flow of the information the company needs.
   c) The owner must define the type, the quantity, the flow, and the users of the information needed.
   d) For instance, if the system must make information available to several people in either the same or scattered locations, a business owner will need to set up a local area network.
     (1) A local area network (LAN) is a group of computers linked together in a system that makes all of the data, programs, and resources of one computer available to all of the other computers on the network.
     (2) A peer-to-peer LAN, which links a company's computers to one another
   e) Network computers can lower a company's total cost of computer ownership.
     (1) Because they run applications off of the server, network computers need no local storage devices or software, which means they can be stripped-down, very basic machines.
     (2) Network computers cost as little as $800 to $1,200 to purchase.
   f) Computers linked through a network can change the way a company does business and the way employees do their jobs.

g) Employees can work together on the same project simultaneously even though they may be thousands of miles apart.

h) Everyone on the network can work on the same file rather than giving everyone a copy of his own and then integrating all of the changes into a single file later.

i) Before purchasing a local area network, experts recommend that entrepreneurs consider

   (1) How many PCs do you have ? The number of PCs to be included in a network will determine its structure, the network hardware and software required, and the type of cable used to connect it all.

   (2) How do you plan to use your network? The tasks you expect a network to perform will determine its design and construction.

   (3) Where do you plan to buy it? Most business owners purchase their networks from resellers who handle the installation for them.

   (4) How crucial will the network be to your business? The more dependent a business is on its network, the greater is its need to have a system of controls and a contingency plan in place.

8. Step 5. Shop for software packages that will perform the required functions.

   a) A computer is only as good as the software it is running.

      (1) A computer without proper software is like a car without an engine.

   b) Because not all computers are capable of running all software programs, the best approach is to choose the appropriate software first and then select a computer that will run it efficiently.

   c) The first phase of evaluating software packages is to collect information on those that perform the functions the owner is most interested in.

      (1) Computer magazines contain detailed descriptions of popular programs.

      (2) Computer user groups are another valuable source of information.

      (3) Trade associations also may be able to offer advice on which programs companies in an industry rely on.

      (4) Directories such as the *Datapro Directory of Microcomputer Software* provide detailed listings of thousands of different packages.

      (5) Reference books, such as Donald Hockney's *Personal Computers for the Successful Small Business*, and software catalogs, such as *Business Software* (Elsevier Science Publishing Company) and the *Whole Earth Software Catalog* (Quantum Press/Doubleday) also offer valuable assistance.

9. Step 6. Choose the hardware.

   a) The final decision depends on many features, but the machine's processing power, expandability, compatibility, and serviceability are crucial.

   b) Small business owners must resist the temptation to shop for a computer on the basis of price alone.

10. Step 7. Integrate the system into the business.

   a) Employees who will be using the new system must have time to become familiar with it before putting it into action. In addition, the system must be tested thoroughly.

   b) Computer experts estimate that a user can expect to spend at least four hours learning to use a machine and up to 40 hours learning to use the software.

   c) Conversion also requires a financial investment.

      (1) In addition to the cost of getting the hardware and the software in place, there is the cost of training employees to use the system.

      (2) Cutting corners here is dangerous because employees who are unskilled in running the computer system will render it useless.

   d) Most companies find that a gradual phasing in of the computer system works much better than an overnight change.

e) Typically, with a step-by-step process, each subsequent phase becomes easier than the last.

f) Another advantage of a gradual phase-in is that the small business owner has the ability to run the new system parallel to the old one before relying solely on the new one.

 (1) The owner should compare the results of the two systems for at least a month or two.

g) Small business owners can make the conversion process go much more smoothly by heeding the following suggestions:

 (1) Do not be intimidated by computers.

 (2) Become computing-literate.

 (3) Set a good example.

 (4) Reward employees for becoming computing-literate.

 (5) Be sensitive to employees' feelings.

 (6) Create an appropriate environment for learning.

 (7) Set up a training center.

 (8) Offer incentives for improved performance.

 (9) Set up controls.

V. Choosing Software and Hardware

   A. Software Considerations

   1. Choosing the proper software: whether off-the-shelf or customized, doing the job at hand determines the ultimate success of a computer system.

   2. Small business owners can purchase software for practically any applications from simple spreadsheets or word processors to more complex inventory control systems and 3-D design packages.

   a) See Figure 18.4 for most common software applications used in small business.

   3. Word processing

   a) Some experts estimate that word processing is the primary use for 75 percent of all computer systems.

   b) Modem word processors follow a "what you see is what you get" ("WYSIWYG") philosophy; the system will print out just what you see on the screen.

   c) Most come with helpful features such as spell checkers, grammar checkers, a thesaurus, and an HTML (Hypertext Markup Language) converter, which translates documents into HTML format for publication on the World Wide Web.

   d) Popular word-processing programs include Microsoft Word for Windows, Lotus Word Pro, WordPerfect, PFS: Professional Write, Displaywrite, MacWrite, and Office Writer.

   4. Accounting

   a) Software packages can handle a company's general ledger, accounts payable and receivable, inventory control, purchasing, and financial statement preparation much faster and more accurately than manual systems.

   b) These programs save businesses money on their professional accounting fees by keeping their financial transactions and records more organized.

   (1) They also are a tremendous help when tax season rolls around.

   c) There are two types of accounting software: modular and integrated.

   (1) A modular program is built around a specific accounting application (such as accounts receivable) and can be used alone or combined with other modules.

   (a) A complete accounting system built from modules is more expensive than an integrated system, but it usually is more flexible. In addition, owners can choose only those modules they need in their accounting systems.

         (2) An integrated package is a comprehensive accounting system that usually operates from the transactions entered through the general ledger. Once the owner enters transactions into the general ledger, the integrated accounting package automatically posts them to the appropriate subprogram.

    d) More than 500 accounting programs are on the market; some of the most popular ones are 4-in-1 Basic Accounting, MYOB, The Accounting Partner, QuickBooks, Simply Accounting, Accpac Easy Accounting Series, etc.

5. Database management

    a) These programs are the equivalent of electronic file folders and file cabinets.

         (1) A computer file is merely a collection of individual records, such as a customer list or a schedule of a company's inventory.

         (2) Database programs enable business owners to translate large volumes of pure data into manageable, meaningful information they can use to make more-informed business decisions.

         (3) Database management programs record information into fields, which are accumulated into records, which, in turn, are compiled into files.

    b) Database management programs are spreading quickly because of their flexibility, speed, capabilities, and ease of use.

    c) Popular packages include Microsoft Access, Lotus Approach, Act!, Q&A, dBase, Alpha Four, PFS: Professional File, R:Base 5000, Reflex, PC File, Paradox, Knowledgeman, Dayilo, Data Ease, and FileMaker Pro.

6. Spreadsheets

    a) A spreadsheet is simply a grid of rows and columns, much like an accountant's pad.

    b) Entrepreneurs can enter data, text, and formulas into the cells on the spreadsheet.

    c) Once they set up the format of the spreadsheet, entrepreneurs can take advantage of its powerful "what if" capacity.

    d) Spreadsheets allow an owner to enter data, create formulas, format cells, copy and move entries, and produce a variety of graphs.

    e) Popular spreadsheet packages include Microsoft Excel for Windows, Lotus 1-2-3, Quattro Pro, SuperCalc, PFS: Professional Plan, PC-Calc, Perfect Calc, etc.

    f) By using the "ready-made" functions and features of a spreadsheet, entrepreneurs can create customized sheets to help them manage practically every part of their business, from benefit packages in human resources and cash flow in finance to accounts payable in accounting and raw materials inventory in production.

7. Presentation graphics

    a) These packages can transform a personal computer into a professional slide presentation that looks as though a Madison Avenue advertising agency put it together.

    b) A presentation designed with one of these programs can include special effects such as transitions between slides (fades, blinds, wipes, etc.), clip art, animated graphics, photographs, video clips, sound bites, and many others.

    c) Popular presentation graphics packages include Microsoft PowerPoint, Astound, Lotus Freelance Plus, Harvard Graphics, Windows Draw, Draw Applause, GEM Presentation, 35mm Express, PFS:Graph, Boardroom Graphics, etc.

8. Communications

    a) Communications programs enable small business owners to use their computers to communicate with other computers and to send both faxes and e-mail messages.

         (1) All that is necessary is a modem, which links the computer to the telephone line.

    b) With this system, owners can use computer linkups, remote computer terminals, and large databases such as CompuServe, Prodigy, or the Dow-Jones News/Retrieval service, and, of course, the World Wide Web from almost anywhere.

      c) Telecommunications packages enable owners to tap into their own company's databases from remote locations and to exchange information with branch offices or sales representatives in the field.

      d) They also provide automatic telephone dialing and answering, electronic mailbox services, and access to an unbelievable amount of up-to-the-minute information on a wide variety of topics.

      e) Popular communications and e-mail programs include LapLink, HotOffice, Smartcom II, Eudora Pro, Pegasus Mail, Claris Em@iler, Crosstalk, Datapath, Passport, PFS: Access, Starlink, Lync, Micro Phone, and Dyna-Comm.

9. World Wide Web browsers

      a) Two software packages dominate this market segment: Netscape Navigator and Microsoft Explorer.

      b) With these packages, entrepreneurs use the Web to conduct market research, study their competitors, learn about trends in their industries, locate sources of financing, manage their companies' cash, and perform a host of other important activities.

10. World Wide Web page design

      a) Modern Web page design programs help entrepreneurs create eye-catching, innovative Web sites without having to invest huge blocks of time learning some arcane computer language.

      b) The good news is that these programs allow users to create documents and files for their Web sites using standard programs (such as the word processors, spreadsheets, and presentation graphics packages described earlier) and then automatically handle the HTML coding "behind the scenes."

          (1) Approximately 70,000 small business owners in the United States are doing business online, and the number is growing daily.

          (2) Forrester Research estimates that some 52 million people (up from 27 million in 1996) are now on the WWW, which means that the Web is fast gaining mass media status.

          (3) Web shoppers now spend more than $10 billion a year.

          (4) Figure 18.5 gives a profile of those on the WWW by age.

      c) Companies are discovering that their Web shoppers are beginning to resemble closely their in-store shoppers, and those shoppers are looking for a broader range of products and services.

      d) Popular Web design programs include Microsoft FrontPage, Adobe PageMill, Claris Home Page, IBM's HomePage Creator, and NetObjects Fusion.

      e) Entrepreneurs are capitalizing on the power of this easy-to-use Web design software to give on-line customers ready access to their products and services and to information about their companies. In the process, they are discovering the many advantages of virtual stores.

11. Project management

      a) Project management software is designed to help small business managers plan and control the intermediate steps in completing large projects: introducing new products, entering new markets, launching businesses.

      b) Once the manager outlines the basic steps in the project and identifies their priorities, the computer programs calculate the start and finish dates for each task and for the whole project.

          (1) They also track the resources required and account for total project costs.

          (2) These programs highlight the project's critical path: those tasks that must be completed on time if the entire project is to remain on schedule.

          (3) And, they flag those tasks that lack sufficient resources for on-time completion.

   c) Common project management programs include Harvard Total Project Manager, MacProject, Time Line, and Microsoft Project 4.0.

WIRED TO THE WEB - The Fruit of the Virtual Vineyard

SUMMARY
Bill Knight, owner of the Wine House, a 19,000 square-foot retail wine shop in Los Angeles, has found a very inexpensive way to boost his company's sales and profits: the World Wide Web. Seeing the Web's potential as a marketing tool, Knight established his company's site in 1995 to complement the retail operation and the Wine House direct-mail catalog. Visitors to the site <http://www.winehouse. com> can browse through its 32 pages to choose from the Wine House's on-line catalog of 500 wines, read reviews of wines from experts, and get tips on the fine points of the art of wine tasting.

To make sure his site gets noticed, Knight has forged cross-marketing relationships with other wine-related sites such as WineAccess, which includes an online locator visitors can use to track down almost any wine. Knight's philosophy for attracting visitors to the company's Web site is to provide lots of information. To encourage customers to order right over the Web, Knight has added a secure server, which ensures a customers' credit-card information will not fall into thieves' hands when sent across the Internet. Still, many customers shop for wines using the Web and then place their orders by phone.

The Wine House is reaping many benefits from its Web site, including expanding its mailing list. The company mails a newsletter to about 22,000 customers 11 times a year. Because reaching customers through the Web site is so much more cost-efficient than mailing catalogs and newsletters, Knight hopes to eventually shift his marketing efforts more toward the Web. Since the site came on-line, sales revenue has climbed from $7 million to $10 million, and profits are also up. The site now gets about 20,000 hits a month, and the flow of traffic is rising rapidly.

1. What benefits does marketing on the World Wide Web offer small businesses?
   Answer - A broader audience, instantly updateable "catalog" information, instant feedback from customers, data for mailing lists and databases, low cost advertising, linkages and cross-marketing with other products/companies, etc.
2. What barriers must companies selling products such as wine overcome when they sell over the World Wide Web?
   Answer - The customers' need to taste, smell, and see the product. Also the general fear most consumers have about sending their credit card numbers over the Internet.
3. What advice would you offer a small retailer whose company is not yet using the WWW as a marketing tool?
   Answer - Follow Knight's example. Have links to other sites, provide information, etc. But also some design basics; simple is best, quick downloading time, therefore minimal graphics, etc.

---

12. Software suites
   a) A software suite is an integrated collection of programs from a single maker that look alike; use similar commands, menus, and icons; and interact more smoothly than a set of similar programs from different software companies mixed and matched together.
   b) Software suites typically contain a word processor, a spreadsheet, a database, and a presentation graphics package.
   c) 75 percent of word processors and 85 percent of spreadsheets are sold as part of software suites.
   d) The most popular suites include Microsoft Office, Lotus Smart Suite, and Corel WordPerfect Suite.

13. Industry-specific software
   a) Designed to handle transactions and situations in a specific business, this software has increased productivity and streamlined procedures in a variety of industries.
   b) For example, one of the trickiest elements to manage in any retail business is inventory, and many software companies have developed programs to help.

B. Hardware Considerations
   1. Perhaps no machine since the automobile has spawned a more intense love-hate relationship with its human users than the personal computers.
   2. Although it sounds simple enough--like buying a toaster--buying a computer is no easy task, especially for computer novices.
   3. The key to picking the right computer is identifying which software packages a company will need; determining their speed, power, and peripheral requirements; and then matching the hardware to those requirements.
   4. The following guidelines will be helpful.
      a) Do your homework before shopping for hardware. Take the time to learn the basic components of a computer system and what they do.
      b) Buy enough power and speed. Most small business applications do not require extraordinarily fast or powerful hardware to run them. A good rule here is to buy more power and speed than you currently need.
      c) Plan for expansion. Smart business owners get extra mileage out of their computers by buying hardware with expansion capabilities.
      d) Keep it simple. Avoid buying too much computer. It only increases your total cost of ownership (TCO).
   5. One hardware option many business owners choose is a laptop (or notebook or portable) computer.
      a) For entrepreneurs on the go, a notebook computer is an ideal choice because it gives them the power to work as if they were sitting at their desks from practically anywhere.
   6. Computer manufacturers produce three levels of notebook computers:
      a) Top-of-the-line systems are desktop PC replacements.
      b) Value-notebooks perform most of the same tasks as a desktop machine and have almost as much speed and power.
      c) Ultra-portable notebooks weigh just two to four pounds but, because of their smaller screens and keyboards, are not suitable as desktop replacements.
   7. As computer technology constantly improves, notebook computers continue to grow smaller, lighter, faster, and more powerful.
      a) Figure 18.6 describes what entrepreneurs should look for in a notebook PC.

C. The Dark side of computers
   1. Electronic disasters
      a) Despite their dependence on technology, computer experts say most companies are ill-prepared to handle an electronic disaster.
      b) Always back up valuable data and to have an alternate plan in case the system crashes.
         (1) Many computers include tape drives, which can back up data from floppy or hard disks quickly and easily.

GAINING THE COMPETITIVE EDGE - What to Look for While Buying Computer Hardware

SUMMARY
Today, a small business owner who wants a computer system capable of handling virtually any task should consider purchasing the following equipment:

- A Pentium Il processor that runs at 300 MHz or faster with at least 64 megabytes of RAM (which should be expandable)
- A hard disk drive with a capacity of at least 8 gigabytes
- A 56.6 kb per second fax modem for communications capability
- A noninterlfaced super-VGA 15-inch color monitor with a dot pitch of at least 0.24 mm (easier on the eyes).
- At least one high-density (1.44 megabyte) 31/2-inch floppy disk drive
- A 12x CD-ROM drive or DVD-ROM drive
- A tape backup system (to back up programs and data in case of a system "crash.")
- A color printer (ink-jet, laser, or dot-matrix) capable of handling both text and graphics at a speed of at least 4 pages per minute with resolution of at least 600 x 600 dpi (dots per inch)
- A flatbed scanner with an automatic document feeder capable of inputting a page in no more than 3 minutes (for scanning photos, text, graphics, or anything else into documents)

As with the purchase of any technical piece of equipment, the small business owner must consider a computer's serviceability. Before purchasing a computer, the wise business manager will investigate the manufacturer's after-sale support. What happens when the computer breaks down? Does the computer come with a warranty? If so, what are its terms? Remember that the lowest-priced computer may not be the best deal when it comes to service and support.

2. Computer crime
   a) Computer theft costs U.S. businesses about $1.5 billion each year.
      (1) One study found that just 6 percent of those reported resulted in a criminal prosecution.
      (2) A recent study by the Computer Security Institute for the FBI revealed that 75 percent of the companies surveyed had been victims of computer-related crimes in the preceding year.
      (3) The Computer Security Institute's study found that 49 percent of the companies surveyed had reported some type of unauthorized use of their computer systems within the past year.
      (4) Even more alarming, more than 20 percent of the companies said that their systems provided no way of knowing if criminals had invaded their computers.
   b) The FBI estimates that a computer thief nets $600,000 in the average job.
   c) Security experts say that the most common cyberthieves are loyal employees who misuse the authority their employers give them.
   d) Computer security specialists offer a profile of the potential inside computer criminal:
      (1) A trusted employee of long tenure, but has recently become a gambler, a boozer, or a helpless victim of love.
      (2) Has a sick spouse, hungry kids.
      (3) Overwhelmed, most commonly by debt, but occasionally by an unappeasable longing for the rich life.
      (4) Disappointed, disgruntled, torn apart by resentment and envy.
      (5) Could be anyone, under certain circumstances, could be he or she.

    e) The National Computer Security Association (NCSA) estimates that 67 percent of U.S. companies have their computers infected by viruses each year.

      (1) Like a biological virus, a computer virus invades a system and attacks it, destroying data and wrecking programs.

      (2) At the end of 1997, the NCSA estimated that more than 16,000 computer viruses existed, and that number was growing daily.

    f) To avoid virus problems, entrepreneurs should make sure that their computers are equipped with the latest virus detection programs, which should run automatically every time the computer boots up.

      (1) Popular antivirus programs include VirusShield and NetShield (McAfee Associates), Norton Antivirus (Symantec Corporation), and Interscan VirusWall and ScanMail (Trend Micro Inc.).

      (2) It is important to download the latest versions of these virus detection programs at least once a month.

    g) Most computer security experts agree that the key to computer security is people, and that requires education.

      (1) Encouraging employees to maintain security standards on a daily basis is crucial to the success of a security system.

VI. Other Technology Choices

  A. Printers

    1. Today, entrepreneurs can generate documents, signs, fliers, and advertisements on their own printers that they once had to get professional print shops to design and produce.

      a) The almost endless array of fonts, point sizes, and clip art printers can give business owners the ability to create practically anything they can imagine.

      b) Printer choices range from simple monochrome inkjet printers costing little more than $100 to full-color laser printers priced at more than $6,000.

    2. Selecting the ideal printer for a business boils down to determining exactly its printing needs.

    3. Inkjet printers

      a) Business owners who need to print in color but have limited budgets should consider buying an inkjet printer.

      b) Color inkjet printers spray colored ink onto a variety of paper types, ranging from plain paper to clear transparency film.

      c) Their low prices and versatility make them popular choices for small business owners.

      d) Inkjet printers have a relatively high cost per page and are not the best choice for high-volume printing needs.

    4. Monochrome laser printers

      a) The workhorse printer in most business environments remains the monochrome laser printer, which uses a laser to "burn" images onto paper and clear transparency film.

      b) Although they are more expensive than inkjet printers, laser printers are much faster, print higher-quality text, and cost less on a per-page basis.

      c) They provide 600 to 1,200 dpi (dots per inch) resolution at speeds of up to 24 pages a minute. For business purposes, six pages a minute is the minimum speed to consider.

      d) These characteristics make laser printers ideal for text documents and for high-volume printing.

    5. Color laser printers

      a) Color laser printers produce color images with the same high resolution that monochrome laser printers do; however, their costs are significantly higher.

      b) They also tend to run more slowly than monochrome laser printers, typically at two to six pages a minute.

      c) Companies that print large volumes of graphical images would benefit from a color laser printer.

      d) Because they are more expensive to purchase and to maintain, color laser printers have a high cost per page.

  6. Network printers

      a) Businesses that want to have a central printer networked to multiple computers should choose a network printer.

      b) These printers usually are high-volume monochrome laser printers specially configured to handle the flow of documents channeled to them from multiple sources.

      c) The key determinant of the print quality from any printer is resolution, which is measured by the number of dots per inch (dpi).

        (1) For business purposes, 600 dpi is the minimum standard.

        (2) For most business applications, a printer with 512 kb to 2 MB of memory is sufficient. A network printer needs at least 2 MB of memory.

B. Scanners

  1. Scanners are now common office tools in businesses of all types.

  2. Scanners allow entrepreneurs to make a "digital copy" of an image or a document, which they can then edit, download into other files, or post on Web pages.

  3. Entrepreneurs can purchase either sheet-fed scanners or flatbed scanners.

      a) A flatbed scanner operates much like a photocopier.

        (1) The user places a document or graphic image on the scanning bed; the scanner head moves down the page, reading the image and transferring it into a digital format.

        (2) Because of their design, flatbed scanners can read images from single sheets, books, magazines, and a host of other media.

      b) Sheet-fed scanners take up much less space on a desktop than flatbed scanners, but they can accept only single-sheet documents or images.

        (1) They are much cheaper, however, selling from $150 to $350, and are suitable for most small business or home office needs.

  4. As with printers, an important feature to watch for when shopping for a scanner is its resolution. The higher the resolution, the more detail a scanner can provide.

      a) For business applications, a scanner should have a resolution of at least 300 dpi.

      b) A good scanner should include software that enables a user to scan both images and text.

      c) For text, the scanner should include optical character recognition (OCR) software that transforms the scanned text into a document that any standard word processing package can read and edit.

C. Digital Cameras

  1. Unlike traditional 35 mm cameras, digital cameras capture images in digital codes onto either standard floppy disks or removable memory cards.

  2. Most digital cameras are equipped with small color display screens that allow photographers to view their photos immediately.

  3. These cameras also connect to any computer so that photographers can download their images, view them on the monitor, and even edit them using software.

  4. Most digital cameras include a video-out port, with which users can display their images directly on a television monitor or through a VCR.

      a) Some even have the capacity to send images directly from the camera to a printer without going through a computer.

        b)   The minimum any entrepreneur should consider is 640 by 480 resolution.

        c)   A good digital camera also should have the ability to store at least 60 images and should have a flash.

        d)   An LCD viewfinder that allows photographers to see their pictures and rechargeable batteries also are helpful features.

WIRED TO THE WEB - Post It, and They Will Come

SUMMARY

"The World Wide Web is the place you need to be. That's where the future of retailing is!" Tia wondered how much of Mel's idea was youthful enthusiasm and how much was sound business advice. Tia trusted Mel's opinions. She had spotted his business acumen early on after he had come to her with an idea for a location of another Tie One On center. He had done all of the market research as part of a project in a marketing class, and when Tia saw the results, she knew he was right. After building the new store, Tia watched it reach the breakeven point faster than any of her other locations had, and it was now one of her top-grossing stores.

Mel has been studying the Web for more than a year and has learned how to develop Web pages using both html and software packages such as FrontPage and Page Mill. He has an assignment to develop a Web site. Tia finally agrees but has a series of questions, the last of which is "What does a good web site look like?"

1.   Use the resources of the library and the World Wide Web to convince Tia that she should consider setting up a Web site and to answer Tia's question about doing business on the Web.

2.   Again using your research, write a brief report describing for Tia what a good Web site looks like. Go to the Web, locate a site that meets your criteria, and include some of its screens in your report.

3.   Search the Web for a site that you consider to be poorly designed. Prepare a short report on it and include some of its screens in your report. (Hint: Try <http://www.websitesthatsuck.com> for some leads.)

    Answer - This is the response for 1-3. The authors of the above Web site also have a book by the same name. It teaches how to build an effective Web site by showing both good and bad examples. Consider placing copies on reserve for students to review, especially if your college/university has limited Internet connectivity/access for students.

   D. Personal Digital Assistants and Pagers

      1.   Small, hand-held devices such as personal digital assistants (PDAs) and pagers make it easy for entrepreneurs to keep up with their business from practically anywhere.

      2.   Personal digital assistants are a combination of personal computer, appointment book, pager, organizer, and fax machine, all rolled into one wireless device that fits in the palm of your hand.

          a)   Entrepreneurs routinely use these devices to organize their daily schedules, to send and receive e-mail, to track appointments, and even to create simple spreadsheets (on Pocket Excel) and word-processing documents (on Pocket Word) or make presentations (on Pocket PowerPoint) while away from their offices.

          b)   Personal digital assistants are compatible with either PCs or Apple computers.

          c)   Those equipped to connect to PCs run Windows CE, a compact version of the desktop operating system familiar to millions of computer users.

      3.   Although PDAs incorporate many of the same features as standard portable computers, they are not intended to be portable computer substitutes.

          a)   Their small size limits their ability to function as full-fledged PCs.

        b) When choosing a PDA, entrepreneurs should decide exactly how they intend to use the devices: as a simple pocket organizer and communication tool or as a more versatile (and more costly) hand-held computer.

    4. For entrepreneurs for whom a PDA is more computing power than they need on the road, a pager may be the ideal solution.

        a) Pagers still provide the easiest and most timely way to communicate with the office.

        b) High-end pagers provide entrepreneurs with the ability to not only receive information but to transmit it as well.

VII. Telephone, Voice Mail, and E-Mail Technology

  A. Telephone Technology

    1. Within the next several years, no communication device will undergo more changes than the telephone.

    2. It is already beginning its transformation from a relatively dumb device into a computerized communications tool with video capability to enhance its current audio capacity.

    3. Screen phones (or video phones) have built-in monitors that allow entrepreneurs to conduct video conferences with customers and business associates around the world without ever leaving their offices.

        a) These phones also provide the ability to send and receive e-mail messages and to access the latest business news or sports scores.

    4. Entrepreneurs shopping for a screen phone should ask about the following:

        a) Compatibility with standard e-mail services

        b) Other Internet applications that are available

        c) The phone's ability to download files

        d) The ability to attach a full-size computer keyboard

        e) Which Internet service providers the system can access

    5. Cellular phones are also undergoing an identity transformation, taking on the role of tiny portable computers that do much more than make telephone calls.

        a) The latest models of these "smart phones" come with small screens that can display e-mail and fax messages and information from the World Wide Web.

        b) Some models also double as personal digital assistants and have small keyboards that allow users to input data and infrared ports for wireless hookups with PCs to download data.

        c) More than 43 million people across the United States now use cellular phones, and that number grows by 30,000 every day.

  B. Voice Mail

    1. Voice mail systems:

        a) have the ability to take calls.

        b) they also offer multiple voice mailboxes, pager notification, and the ability to check messages from remote locations.

    2. Two basic types of voice mail systems are available: services purchased through local telephone companies and systems for sale.

        a) The most economical option is to subscribe to a voice mail service through a local telephone company; fees typically range from just $6 to $25 a month, and the business owner lets the telephone company handle equipment repairs and maintenance.

        b) Most systems for sale work through a personal computer but require business owners to purchase and maintain equipment.

3. Perhaps the biggest benefit of voice mail to small business owners is that they no longer miss important business calls and the potential revenue they can generate.

C. E-mail
1. Electronic mail (or e-mail), the messages that people send across the Internet from one computer to another, can be a useful business communications tool.
2. E-mail is a convenient way for employees within a business to communicate.
3. It is vital to employees who telecommute.

Chapter Summary

♦ Explain how technology can help small businesses gain a competitive advantage over their rivals.
- Technology is one of the most powerful tools in an entrepreneur's arsenal of competitive weapons. It can transform the way a small company works, the way it does business, and the way it interacts with its customers. Entrepreneurs who understand how to use technology to make their businesses more efficient and more capable and to serve their customers better and faster will have an edge in the marketplace.

♦ Describe how to create a technology plan that enables business owners to get the most out of their investments in technology.
- Building a workable technology plan includes the following steps:
  1. Decide what you want your company to be able to do for itself and for your customers.
  2. Determine the technology and the equipment you will need to perform those tasks.
  3. Conduct a technology audit.
  4. Match goals and resources.
  5. Develop a technology budget.
  6. Make the necessary purchases.

♦ Explain how computers have transformed the way entrepreneurs do business and how to computerize a small business.
- Computers are the "great equalizer" in business; they give entrepreneurs the power to be as big in the eyes of their customers as competitors many times their size.
- Computerizing a small business involves seven basic steps:
  1. Develop a list of current activities.
  2. Decide how much and which areas of the business to computerize.
  3. Develop a computer budget.
  4. Define the informational needs of the functions to be computerized first.
  5. Shop for software packages that will perform the required functions.
  6. Choose the hardware.
  7. Integrate the system into the business.

♦ Outline the major business software applications, identify guidelines for buying computer hardware, and explain the hardware issues entrepreneurs face.
- The software most small business owners use includes word processing, accounting, database management, spreadsheets, graphics, communications, software suites, and industry-specific software.
- Although there are no magic formulas for selecting the right hardware, the following guidelines will be helpful:
  1. Do your homework before shopping for hardware.
  2. Buy a computer with enough power and speed.
  3. Plan for expansion.
  4. Keep it simple.
- In addition to the powerful desktop computers available, entrepreneurs can choose portable computers that have practically all of the same features. For entrepreneurs on the go, a portable

computer is an ideal choice because it gives them the power to work as if they were sitting at their desks from practically anywhere.

♦ Discuss the peripheral equipment, such as printers, scanners, digital cameras, and personal digital assistants, that enhances the performance of the computer.

- With the right printers, entrepreneurs can generate documents, signs, fliers, and advertisements on their own printers that they once had to get professional print shops to design and produce. Entrepreneurs can choose among the four basic types of printers: inkjet printers, monochrome laser printers, color laser printers, and network printers.

- Scanners, once reserved only for graphics design houses or newspapers, are now common office tools in businesses of all types. Scanners allow entrepreneurs to make a "digital copy" of an image or a document, which they can then edit, download into other files, or post on Web pages.

- On the surface, digital cameras resemble traditional cameras, but inside they are very different. Unlike traditional 35 mm cameras, digital cameras use no film; instead, they capture images in digital codes onto either standard floppy disks or removable memory cards and then download them to a computer file.

- Small, hand-held devices such as personal digital assistants (PDAs) and pagers make it easy for entrepreneurs to keep up with their business from practically anywhere. Personal digital assistants are a combination of personal computer, appointment book, pager, organizer, and fax machine.

♦ Discuss the role of communications technology such as the telephone, voice mail, and e-mail in small companies.

- Communications technology is undergoing major technological changes. The telephone is rapidly becoming a "smart" communications tool, incorporating many of the features of a computer into its design. Screen phones (or video phones) have built-in monitors that allow entrepreneurs to conduct video conferences with customers and business associates around the world without ever leaving their office, and they provide the ability to send and receive e-mail messages and to access the latest business news or sports scores.

- Although voice mail systems record messages just as telephone answering machines do, they offer many more features such as the ability to take calls while an entrepreneur is on the phone with another call, multiple voice mailboxes, pager notification, and the ability to check messages from remote locations. These features can be especially important to small businesses because they create the impression that a company is much bigger than it really is.

- Electronic mail (or e-mail), the messages that people send across the Internet from one computer to another, can be a useful business communications tool. E-mail is an easy way for employees within the same company but in different locations to keep in touch; it is also a useful tool for communicating with customers.

Discussion Questions

1. How can technology help a small company gain a competitive advantage over its rivals?
   Answer - Small businesses that learn to exploit the ability to use information and technology to serve their customers better will gain a competitive edge. Small companies that collect and use valuable information to manage their operations effectively will have a competitive advantage over their rivals, whatever their size. Information--or the lack of it--is fast becoming the competitive edge by which the growing company wins or loses in the marketplace. More small businesses are discovering ways to create what one expert calls a "techno-edge."

2. Why is it important for entrepreneurs to develop a technology plan for their companies? What issues should such a plan address?
   Answer - It is not the technology itself that is so important to a company's success but how the entrepreneur behind the business devises creative, innovative ways to use that technology to forge lasting relationships with customers and to surpass their expectations. The plan should address:
   - what you want your company to be able to do for itself and its customers.

- what technology and equipment will be needed.
- a technology audit--what do you already have?
- goals and resources and ensure they match.
- budget needs.
- how to make the necessary purchases--where, when, how.

3. Explain the statement, "More information does not necessarily mean better information."
    Answer - It is not the technology itself that is so important to a company's success but how the entrepreneur behind the business devises creative, innovative ways to use that technology to forge lasting relationships with customers and to surpass their expectations.

4. "Computers have become the great equalizer, giving small companies the power to be as big in the eyes of their customers as companies many times their size." What does this statement mean? Do you agree with it? Explain.
    Answer - The ubiquitous PC has transformed the workplace:
    - sending typewriters the way of the papyrus scroll.
    - enabling workers scattered across the globe to communicate as if they were in the same room.
    - giving managers the power to analyze countless financial scenarios in just seconds.
    - providing small companies the opportunity to become just as "big" in the eyes of their customers as any *Fortune* 500 company.

    Today's personal computers rival or exceed yesterday's minicomputers and mainframes in power and flexibility. According to Moore's Law, the speed of microprocessors, the "brains" of a computer, doubles approximately every 18 months, but their prices remain about the same. Now small companies have the computing resources for database management, broad market access, even global market access through the Internet, video-conferencing, etc., etc., that before were the domain of big companies because of the expense.

5. What factors should the manager consider in the decision to computerize?
    Answer - The key issues facing the small business owner who decides to buy a computer are when to buy a computer, how much to spend, what functions to computerize first, which software to use, which hardware to buy, and where to buy the computer. The real key to success with any technology is making sure that it fits the company's needs, which might include everything from improving the level of customer service to increasing control over inventory.

6. Explain the steps involved in computerizing a small company.
    Answer - The process of choosing a personal computer.
    - Step 1. Develop a list of current activities.
    - Step 2. Decide how much and which areas of the business to computerize.
    - Step 3. Develop a computer budget.
    - Step 4. Define the informational needs of the functions to be computerized first.
    - Step 5. Shop for software packages that will perform the required functions.
    - Step 6. Choose the hardware.
    - Step 7. Integrate the system into the business.

7. What is a local area network (LAN)? What advantages does a LAN offer business owners?
    Answer - If the system must make information available to several people in either the same or scattered locations, a business owner will need to set up a local area network. A local area network (LAN) is a group of computers linked together in a system that makes all of the data, programs, and resources of one computer available to all of the other computers on the network. A peer-to-peer LAN, which links a company's computers to one another. Network computers can lower a company's total cost of computer ownership. Computers linked through a network can change the way a

company does business and the way employees do their jobs. Employees can work together on the same project simultaneously even though they may be thousands of miles apart.

8. What factors should a business owner consider before setting up a LAN?
   Answer - Before purchasing a local area network, experts recommend that entrepreneurs consider:
   - How many PCs do you have? The number of PCs to be included in a network will determine its structure, the network hardware and software required, and the type of cable used to connect it all.
   - How do you plan to use your network? The tasks you expect a network to perform will determine its design and construction.
   - Where do you plan to buy it? Most business owners purchase their networks from resellers who handle the installation for them.
   - How crucial will the network be to your business? The more dependent a business is on its network, the greater is its need to have a system of controls and a contingency plan in place.

9. What is software? How should the small business manager select software?
   Answer - A computer is only as good as the software it is running. A computer without proper software is like a car without an engine. Because not all computers are capable of running all software programs, the best approach is to choose the appropriate software first and then select a computer that will run it efficiently. The first phase of evaluating software packages is to collect information on those that perform the functions the owner is most interested in.

10. Describe the major types of software packages, explain what they do, and give an example of each one.
    Answer - Choosing the proper software: whether off-the-shelf or customized, doing the job at hand determines the ultimate success of a computer system. Small business owners can purchase software for practically any applications from simple spreadsheets or word processors to more complex inventory control systems and 3-D design packages. See Figure 18.4 for most common software applications used in small business.
    - Word processing. Some experts estimate that word processing is the primary use for 75 percent of all computer systems. Popular word-processing programs include Microsoft Word for Windows, Lotus Word Pro, WordPerfect, PFS: Professional Write, Displaywrite, MacWrite, and Office Writer.
    - Accounting. Software packages can handle a company's general ledger, accounts payable and receivable, inventory control, purchasing, and financial statement preparation much faster and more accurately than manual systems. More than 500 accounting programs are on the market; some of the most popular ones are 4-in-1 Basic Accounting, MYOB, The Accounting Partner, QuickBooks, Simply Accounting, Accpac Easy Accounting Series, etc.
    - Database anagement. These programs are the equivalent of electronic file folders and file cabinets. Database management programs are spreading quickly because of their flexibility, speed, capabilities, and ease of use. Popular packages include Microsoft Access, Lotus Approach, Act!, Q&A, dbase, Alpha Four, PFS: Professional File, R:Base 5000, Reflex, PC File, Paradox, Knowledgeman, Dayilo, Data Ease, and FileMaker Pro.
    - Spreadsheets. A spreadsheet is simply a grid of rows and columns, much like an accountant's pad. Entrepreneurs can enter data, text, and formulas into the cells on the spreadsheet. Popular spreadsheet packages include Microsoft Excel for Windows, Lotus 1-2-3, Quattro Pro, SuperCalc, PFS: Professional Plan, PC-Calc, Perfect Calc, etc.
    - Presentation graphics. These packages can transform a personal computer into a professional slide presentation that looks as though a Madison Avenue advertising agency put it together. Popular presentation graphics packages include Microsoft PowerPoint, Astound, Lotus Freelance

Plus, Harvard Graphics, Windows Draw, Draw Applause, GEM Presentation, 35mm Express, PFS:Graph, Boardroom Graphics, etc.

- Communications. Communications programs enable small business owners to use their computers to communicate with other computers and to send both faxes and e-mail messages. Popular communications and e-mail programs include LapLink, HotOffice, Smartcom II, Eudora Pro, Pegasus Mail, Claris Em@iler, Crosstalk, Datapath, Passport, PFS: Access, Starlink, Lync, Micro Phone, and Dyna-Comm.
- World Wide Web browsers. Two software packages dominate this market segment: Netscape Navigator and Microsoft Explorer. With these packages, entrepreneurs use the Web to conduct market research, study their competitors, learn about trends in their industries, locate sources of financing, manage their companies' cash, and perform a host of other important activities.
- World Wide Web page design. Modern Web page design programs help entrepreneurs create eye-catching, innovative Web sites without having to invest huge blocks of time learning some arcane computer language. Popular Web design programs include Microsoft FrontPage, Adobe PageMill, Claris Home Page, IBM's HomePage Creator, and NetObjects Fusion.
- Project management. Project management software is designed to help small business managers plan and control the intermediate steps in completing large projects: introducing new products, entering new markets, launching businesses. Common project management programs include Harvard Total Project Manager, MacProject, Time Line, and Microsoft Project 4.0.

11. What is hardware? What factors should the small business manager consider when evaluating hardware?

Answer - Hardware is the computer and peripherals that run the software. The final decision as to what hardware to buy depends on many features, but the machine's processing power, expandability, compatibility, and serviceability are crucial. Small business owners must resist the temptation to shop for a computer on the basis of price alone.

12. What advantages does a portable computer offer? Disadvantages? In what situations would a portable computer benefit an entrepreneur?

Answer - For entrepreneurs on the go, a notebook computer is an ideal choice because it gives them the power to work as if they were sitting at their desks from practically anywhere. However, their small screen size and keyboards make long-term use difficult. Figure 18.6 describes what entrepreneurs should look for in a notebook PC.

13. Why is computer security a problem? What can the small business manager do to improve computer security?

Answer - Computer theft costs U.S. businesses about $1.5 billion each year. A recent study by the Computer Security Institute for the FBI revealed that 75 percent of the companies surveyed had been victims of computer-related crimes in the preceding year. The Computer Security Institute's study found that 49 percent of the companies surveyed had reported some type of unauthorized use of their computer systems within the past year.

Most computer security experts agree that the key to computer security is people, and that requires education. Encouraging employees to maintain security standards on a daily basis is crucial to the success of a security system.

14. Explain the differences in the four types of printers, and discuss the circumstances for which each type is best suited.

Answer - Printer choices range from simple monochrome inkjet printers costing little more than $100 to full-color laser printers priced at more than $6,000. Selecting the ideal printer for a business boils down to determining exactly its printing needs.

- Business owners who need to print in color but have limited budgets should consider buying an inkjet printer. Their low prices and versatility make them popular choices for small business owners. Inkjet printers have a relatively high cost per page and are not the best choice for high-volume printing needs.
- The workhorse printer in most business environments remains the monochrome laser printer, which uses a laser to "burn" images onto paper and clear transparency film. Although they are more expensive than inkjet printers, laser printers are much faster, print higher-quality text, and cost less on a per-page basis. They provide 600 to 1,200 dpi (dots per inch) resolution at speeds of up to 24 pages a minute. For business purposes, six pages a minute is the minimum speed to consider. These characteristics make laser printers ideal for text documents and for high-volume printing.
- Color laser printers produce color images with the same high resolution that monochrome laser printers do; however, their costs are significantly higher. They also tend to run more slowly than monochrome laser printers, typically at two to six pages a minute. Companies that print large volumes of graphical images would benefit from a color laser printer. Because they are more expensive to purchase and to maintain, color laser printers have a high cost per page.
- Network printers. Businesses that want to have a central printer networked to multiple computers should choose a network printer. These printers usually are high-volume monochrome laser printers specially configured to handle the flow of documents channeled to them from multiple sources.

15. In what ways can entrepreneurs use the following technology? Give an example of how an entrepreneur might use each type.
    Answer - Use accompanies term.
    Scanners - to place images in brochures or on Web pages.
    Digital cameras - to download pictures for inclusion into documents and Web sites.
    Personal digital assistants (PDAs) - personal appointments, note taking, receiving/sending e-mail.
    Screen and cellular telephones - communication with clients at almost any time from anywhere.
    Voice mail - to receive messages while on the phone.
    E-mail - to provide communication links to employees at remote sites.

Step into the Real World
1. Locate a small business that does not use a computer. What reasons does the owner give for not using one? Help the owner evaluate the firm's computer needs. What business functions, if any, could benefit from computerization? Do you recommend the purchase of a computer? Why? If so, what kind of software and hardware do you recommend?
2. Contact a local small business that uses a computer. How is it used in the firm? What functions does it perform? Can you suggest an expansion of the system into other functional areas? What software does the owner use? Did the owner follow the procedure for purchasing a computer outlined in this chapter? Is the computer well-suited to the firm's needs?
3. Contact a local small business that uses a computer. What steps does the owner take to ensure computer security? Do you spot any problem areas? What recommendations can you make to the owner for improving the level of security?
4. Locate a computer users' group in your area and attend a meeting. What business applications for computers do you find?
5. Select a small business in your area. Assume that the owner wants to computerize his or her company. Locate a recent issue of a computer magazine (e.g., *PC World*, *MacWorld*, *PC Computing*, *Computer Shopper*) and use the product reviews and ads to develop a computer budget for the owner. Which software packages and hardware configurations do you recommend? What percentage of the total budget did you allocate for hardware? For software? For training and support?

Chapter 19 - Staffing and Leading a Growing Company

A leader knows best what to do; a manager knows merely how best to do it.
Ken Arielman

The two things people want more than sex or money are recognition and praise.
Mary Kay Ash

Teaching Objectives
Students will be able to:
1. Explain the challenges involved in the entrepreneur's role as leader and what it takes to be a successful leader.
2. Understand the potential barriers to effective communication and describe how to overcome them.
3. Describe the importance of hiring the right employees and how to avoid making hiring mistakes.
4. Explain how to build the kind of company culture and structure to support the entrepreneur's mission and goals and to motivate employees to achieve them.
5. Discuss the ways in which entrepreneurs can motivate their workers to higher levels of performance.

Instructor's Outline
I. The Entrepreneur's Role as Leader
   A. Introduction
      1. A small business manager's most important role is that of leader.
      2. Without leadership ability, entrepreneurs--and their companies--never rise above mediocrity.
      3. Until recently, experts compared the leader's job to that of a symphony orchestra conductor.
      4. Like the symphony leader, a small business manager made sure that everyone was playing the same score, coordinated individual efforts to produce harmony, and directed the members as they played.
      5. In short, management and leadership are not the same; yet both are essential to a small company's success.
         a) Leadership without management is unbridled; management without leadership is uninspired.
         b) Leadership gets a small business going; management keeps it going.
      6. Stephen Covey, author of *Principle-Centered Leadership*, explains the difference between management and leadership this way:
         a) Leadership deals with people; management deals with things.
         b) You manage things; you lead people.
         c) Leadership deals with vision; management deals with logistics toward that vision.
         d) Leadership deals with doing the right things; management focuses on doing things right.
         e) Leadership deals with examining the paradigms on which you are operating; management operates within those paradigms.
         f) Leadership comes first, then management, but both are necessary.
      7. Leadership and management are intertwined; a small business that has one but not the other will go nowhere.
      8. Effective leaders exhibit certain behaviors. They:
         a) create a set of values and beliefs for employees and passionately pursue them.
         b) set the example for their employees.

      c)   focus employees' efforts on challenging goals and keep them driving toward those goals.

      d)   provide the resources employees need to achieve their goals.

      e)   communicate with their employees.

      f)   value the diversity of their workers.

      g)   celebrate their workers' successes.

      h)   encourage creativity among their workers.

      i)   maintain a sense of humor.

      j)   keep their eyes on the horizon.

9. For an entrepreneur, leadership success is one of the key determinants of the company's success.

10. The new leader is the one who sees clearly the goal, shares repeatedly and forcefully the vision, provides the tools, trains and enables co-workers to manage and improve their processes, remains persistent in the face of adversity, and inspires others to take an ownership position in the completion of the mission--by example.

11. Unfortunately, studies show that managers rate their own leadership skills higher than their employees rate those managers' skills.

12. According to the researchers, the discrepancies in the ratings exist because employees rate leaders on the basis of what they do rather than on what they say.

      a)   One of the most crucial requirements for being an effective leader is consistency in words and in actions.

13. Leadership is an earned honor, not something that comes with the job.

14. To be effective, leaders must establish for their workers an environment in which they can achieve success. One expert identifies six conditions that leaders must create for their followers if a company is to succeed. Followers must

      a)   know what to do.

      b)   know how to do it.

      c)   understand why they are doing it.

      d)   want to do it.

      e)   have the right resources.

      f)   believe they have the proper leadership.

15. To be effective, a small business leader must perform four vital tasks:

      a)   Communicate the vision and the values of the company effectively and create an environment of trust among workers.

      b)   Hire the right employees and constantly improve their skills.

      c)   Build an organizational culture and structure that allow both workers and the company to reach their potential.

      d)   Motivate workers to higher levels of performance.

II. Communicating Effectively

A. Introduction

1. Like all leaders, small business owners frequently must walk the fine line between the chaos involved in encouraging creativity and maintaining control over their companies.

2. As leaders, an important and highly visible part of their jobs is to communicate the values, beliefs, and principles for which their business stands. In other words, a leader's foremost job is to be the communicator of the company's vision.

3. One of the first skills successful leaders must acquire is the ability to communicate.

4. Nowhere is this skill more important than among entrepreneurs, whose organizations are predicated on their founders' ability to communicate a vision and a set of values that everyone in the company can embrace.

B. Improving Communication
   1. Research shows that managers spend about 80 percent of their time in some form of communication:
      a) 30 percent talking.
      b) 25 percent listening.
      c) 15 percent reading.
      d) 10 percent writing.
   2. Sending messages
      a) The primary reasons employees usually don't do what they are expected to do has little to do with their motivation and desire to work.
      b) Instead, workers often fail to do what they are supposed to because:
         (1) They don't know what to do.
         (2) They don't know how to do it.
         (3) They don't have the authority to do it.
         (4) They get no feedback on how well or how poorly they're doing it.
         (5) They are ignored or punished for doing it right.
         (6) They realize that no one ever notices even if they are doing it right.
   3. Barriers to effective communication that small business managers must overcome.
      a) Managers and employees don't always feel free to say what they really mean.
      b) Ambiguity blocks real communication. The same words can have different meanings to different people, especially in modern companies, where the workforce is likely to be highly diverse.
      c) Information overload causes the message to get lost.
      d) Selective listening interferes with the communication process.
      e) Defense mechanisms block a message.
      f) Conflicting verbal and nonverbal messages confuse listeners.
   4. How can entrepreneurs overcome these barriers to become better communicators?
      a) Clarify your message before you attempt to communicate it.
      b) Use face-to-face communication whenever possible.
      c) Be empathetic. Try to put yourself in the place of those who will receive your message, and develop it accordingly.
      d) Be organized. Effective communicators organize their messages so that their audiences can understand them easily.
      e) Encourage feedback. Allow listeners to ask questions and to offer feedback.
      f) Tell the truth. The fastest way to destroy your credibility as a leader is to lie.
      g) Don't be afraid to tell employees about the business, its performance, and the forces that affect it.
   5. Listening
      a) Listening is the most important communication skill an entrepreneur can develop.
      b) Listening is a skill that entrepreneurs must develop if they are to improve the quality of their company and achieve growth.
      c) To improve listening skills, one management consultant suggests managers use the "PDCH formula."
         (1) identify the speaker's *purpose*.
         (2) recognize the *details* that support that purpose.
         (3) see the *conclusions* they can draw from what the speaker is saying.
         (4) identify the *hidden meanings* communicated by body language and voice inflections.

WIRED TO THE WEB - www.helpwanted.com

SUMMARY
The World Wide Web is the latest tool businesses are using to recruit employees. A recent survey of executives conducted by Management Recruiters International found that 37 percent said they are using the Web to recruit employees, up from just 26.5 percent 18 months before. Jean E. West, recruiting manager at Salestar, a company making software for the telephone industry has found the Web to be a powerful and low-cost recruiting tool. Where can companies go to post their ads on the Web? The following are some of the most popular commercial sites:

Career Magazine <http://www. careermag.com>
CareerMosaic <http://www.careermosaic.com>
CareerPath <http://www. careerpath.com>
CareerWeb <http://www.cweb.com>
JobCenter <http://www.jobcenter.com>
The Monster Board <http://www.monster.com>
Online Career Center http://www.occ.com
Minorities' Job Bank <http://www.minoritiesjb.com>
The Catapult <http://www. jobweb.org/catapult>

Although Web-based job postings remain skewed toward high-tech jobs, the mix is becoming more diverse. About one-third of the commercial Web sites do not charge companies for job listings. Those that do charge fees have prices that range from $25 to $150 for listings that run for four weeks.
Companies that expect to do extensive recruiting on the Web should consider not only placing ads on commercial sites but also creating their own Web sites. Recruiting on the Web is growing in popularity and in the next several years will become an even more important source of finding quality workers.

1. What benefits does Web-based recruiting offer small companies?
    Answer - It eliminates travel, taps a labor pool of applicants who are computer literate, provides instant advertising, quickly changed ads, low cost, etc.
2. Visit some of the sites mentioned above and read some of the ads listed there. What recommendations would you make to a small company interested in advertising a job on the Web?
    Answer - Students' advice should parallel that for any good job ad--clear job description with any experience or education requirements, contact information, etc. Placing salary range, benefit information etc., is optional. Companies should also think about the presentation of the ads. Anyone using the Internet to job hunt will be judging the company's computer sophistication, culture, etc., on the quality of the ad.
3. Assume that you are the owner of a small software company that designs and develops Web pages for businesses. You need to hire a new Web designer. Write an ad describing the position and the sites on which you would list it. Visit some of the sites mentioned above and find several candidates whom you think could fill this position. Which ones would you want to interview? Why?
    Answer - Students' responses will vary. Common mistakes they will make--overselling the job or company. Providing too much salary/benefit information. Forgetting to mention being an EEOC employer. They should provide a sense of what their company is like in the ad.

   C. That Informal Communication Network--The "Grapevine"
      1. Despite all of the modem communication tools available, the grapevine, the informal lines of communication that exist in every company, remains an important link in a company's communication network.

2. The grapevine carries vital information--and sometimes rumors--through every part of the organization with incredible speed.
3. In a more recent study, 96 percent of executives said their employees routinely use the company grapevine to communicate and that their workers consider the grapevine to be a reliable source of information.

III. Hiring the Right Employees
   A. Introduction
      1. Every "new hire" a business owner makes determines the heights to which the company can climb--or the depths to which it will plunge.
         a) "Bad hires" are incredibly expensive, and no company, especially a small one, can afford too many of them.
         b) One study concluded that an employee hired into a typical entry-level position who quits after six months costs a company about $17,000 in salary, benefits, and training.
         c) In addition, the intangible costs--time invested in the new employee, lost opportunities, reduced morale among coworkers, and business setbacks--are seven times the direct costs of a bad hire. In other words, the total price tag for this bad hire is about $136,000.
      2. Attracting and retaining qualified employees is an especially acute problem for rapidly growing small businesses.
         a) According to a recent survey by National Small Business United, one-fourth of the CEOs at growing companies said that a lack of skilled workers is a major threat to their business's growth and continued survival.
         b) One expert estimates that of every three employees a business hires, one makes a solid contribution, one is a marginal worker, and one is a hiring mistake.
      3. Even though the importance of hiring decisions is magnified in small companies, small businesses are most likely to make hiring mistakes because they lack the human resources experts and the disciplined hiring procedures large companies have.
      4. The following guidelines can help small business managers avoid making costly hiring mistakes.

   B. Create Practical Job Descriptions and Job Specifications
      1. The first step is to perform a job analysis, the process by which a firm determines the duties and nature of the jobs to be filled and the skills and experience required of the people who are to fill them.
      2. The first objective of a job analysis is to develop a job description, a written statement of the duties, responsibilities, reporting relationships, working conditions, and materials and equipment used in a job.
         a) A results-oriented job description explains what a job entails and the duties the person filling it is expected to perform.
         b) Preparing job descriptions may be one of the most important parts of the hiring process because it creates a "blueprint" for the job.
         c) Useful sources of information for writing job descriptions include the manager's knowledge of the job, the workers currently holding the job, and the *Dictionary of Occupational Titles* (D.O.T.), available at most libraries.
         d) The *Dictionary of Occupational Titles*, published by the Department of Labor, lists more than 20,000 job titles and descriptions and serves as a useful tool for getting a small business owner started when writing job descriptions.
      3. The second objective of a job analysis is to create a job specification, a written statement of the qualifications and characteristics needed for a job stated in such terms as education, skills, and experience.

     a) A job specification shows the small business manager what kind of person to recruit and establishes the standards an applicant must meet to be hired.

     b) When writing job specifications, some managers define the traits a candidate needs to do a job well. Table 19.2 provides an example.

C. Plan an Effective Interview
  1. Conducting an effective interview requires a small business owner to know what she wants to get out of the interview in the first place and to develop a series of questions to extract that information.
  2. Guidelines for gaining insight into an applicant's qualifications, personality, and character.
     a) Develop a series of core questions and ask them of every candidate. To give the screening process consistency, smart business owners rely on a set of relevant questions they ask in every interview.
     b) Ask open-ended questions rather than questions calling for "yes or no" answers. Open-ended questions are most effective because they encourage candidates to talk.
     c) Create hypothetical situations candidates would be likely to encounter on the job and ask how they would handle them.
     d) Probe for specific examples in the candidate's work experience that demonstrate the necessary traits and characteristics.
     e) Ask candidates to describe a recent success and a recent failure and how they dealt with them.
     f) Arrange a "noninterview" setting that allows several employees to observe the candidate in an informal setting.
  3. Table 19.3 shows sample interview questions.

D. Conduct the Interview
  1. An effective interview contains three phases: breaking the ice, asking questions, and selling the candidate on the company.
  2. Breaking the ice
     a) In the opening phase of the interview, the manager's primary job is to diffuse the tension that exists because of the nervousness of both parties.
     b) Many skilled interviewers use the job description to explain the nature of the job and the company's culture to the applicant.
     c) Then, they use icebreakers--questions about a hobby or special interest--to get the candidate to relax.
  3. Asking questions
     a) During the second phase of the interview, the employer asks the questions from her question bank to determine the applicant's suitability for the job.
     b) Effective interviewers spend about 25 percent of the interview talking and about 75 percent listening.
       (1) They also take notes during the interview to help them ask follow-up questions based on a candidate's comments and to evaluate a candidate after the interview is over.
     c) Experienced interviewers also pay close attention to a candidate's nonverbal clues, or body language, during the interview.
     d) Increasingly, companies are moving toward unusual questions that test their creativity, reasoning, and logic.
     e) Avoid asking candidates illegal questions.
     f) At one time, interviewers could ask wide-ranging questions covering just about every area of an applicant's background.

           (1) Today, interviewing is a veritable minefield of legal liabilities waiting to explode in the unsuspecting interviewer's face.

           (2) To avoid trouble, a business owner should keep in mind why he is asking a particular question.

           (3) The goal is to find someone who is qualified to do the job well.

        g) Table 19.4 offers a quiz to help you understand which kinds of questions are most likely to create charges of discrimination.

        h) Table 19.5 describes a simple test for determining whether an interview question might be considered discriminatory.

    4. Selling the candidate on the company

        a) This phase begins by allowing the candidate to ask questions about the company, the job, or other issues.

        b) Again, experienced interviewers note the nature of these questions and the insights they give into the candidate's personality.

        c) Finally, before closing the interview, the employer should thank the candidate and tell him what happens next.

E. Check References

    1. Small business owners should take the time to check every applicant's references.

    2. According to the American Association for Personnel Administration, approximately 25 percent of all resumes and applications contain at least one major fabrication.

    3. Rather than contacting only the references listed, experienced employers call an applicant's previous employers and talk to their immediate supervisors to get a clear picture of the applicant's job performance, character, and work habits.

F. Conduct Employment Tests

    1. Although various state and federal laws have made using employment tests as screening devices more difficult in recent years, many companies find them quite useful.

    2. To avoid charges of discrimination, business owners must be able to prove that the employment tests they use are both valid and reliable.

        a) A valid test is one that measures what it is intended to measure.

        b) A reliable test is one that measures consistently over time.

GAINING THE COMPETITIVE EDGE - How to Hire and Keep Great Employees

SUMMARY

Hiring and retaining quality workers is always a challenge, especially for small business owners, who rarely can match the wages, salaries, and benefits their larger rivals offer employees. How do you make the best hires?

- Make a commitment to hire only the best workers.
- Search out the best and brightest young people.
- Hire older, retired people interested in returning to work.
- Transform help-wanted ads into marketing pieces.
- Offer psychic income.
- Create a dynamic, fun workplace that attracts quality applicants.
- Involve staff members in interviewing prospective employees.
- "Test drive" new employees before hiring them.
- Always be on the lookout for new employees.
- Consider offering employees ownership in the company.

3. Experienced small business owners don't rely on any one element in the employee selection process.
4. They look at the total picture painted by each part of a candidate's portfolio.
5. They also recognize that hiring an employee is not a single event but the beginning of a long-term relationship.

IV. Building the Right Culture and Structure
   A. Culture
      1. Company culture is the distinctive, unwritten code of conduct that governs the behavior, attitudes, relationships, and style of an organization.
         a) It is the essence of "the way we do things around here."
      2. Culture can play as important a part in gaining a competitive edge as strategy does.
      3. Company culture manifests itself in many ways--from how workers' dress and act to the language they use.
         a) In many companies, the culture creates its own language.
      4. Creating a culture that supports a company's strategy is not easy; the entrepreneurs who have been most successful at it "have a set of overarching beliefs that serve as powerful guides for everyday action--and that are reinforced in a hundred different ways, both symbolic and substantive," explains one business writer.
      5. Nurturing the right culture in a company can enhance a company's competitive position by improving its ability to attract and retain quality workers and by creating an environment in which workers can grow and develop.
         a) Respect for work and life balance. Cool companies recognize that their employees have lives away from work.
         b) A sense of purpose. Cool companies use a strong sense of purpose to make employees feel connected to the company's mission.
         c) Diversity. Cool companies not only accept cultural diversity in their workforce; they embrace it, actively seeking out workers with different backgrounds.
         d) Integrity. Many workers take pride in the fact that they work for a company that is ethical and socially responsible.
         e) Participative management. Company owners and managers trust and empower employees at all levels of the organization to make decisions and to take the actions they need to do their jobs well.
         f) Learning environment. Cool companies encourage and support lifelong learning among their employees.
      6. Cool companies find it much easier to attract, retain, and motivate workers. In short, the right culture helps a small company compete more effectively.
      7. Managing growth and a changing culture.
         a) As companies grow, they often experience dramatic changes in their culture.
         b) Procedures become more formal, operations grow more widespread, jobs take on more structure, communication becomes more difficult, and the company's personality begins to change.
         c) As more workers come on board, employees find it more difficult to know everyone in the company and what their jobs are.
         d) Unless an entrepreneur works hard to maintain her company's unique culture, she may wake up one day to find that she has sacrificed that culture--and the competitive edge that went with it--in the name of growth.
      8. Ironically, growth can sometimes be a small company's biggest enemy, causing a once successful business to spiral out of control into oblivion.

        a) The problem stems from the fact that the organizational structure (or lack of it!) and the style of management that makes an entrepreneurial start-up so successful often cannot support the business as it grows into adolescence and maturity.

        b) The signs of trouble--diminishing cash flow, rapid turnover of good people, expanding general and administrative expenses, and increasing distance from the core of the business.

9. In many cases, small companies achieve impressive growth because they bypass the traditional organizational structures, forgo rigid policies and procedures, and maintain maximum flexibility.

        a) Growth produces organizational complexity.

B. Structure

1. Entrepreneurs have traditionally relied on six different management styles to guide their companies as they grow.

        a) The first three (craftsman, classic, and coordinator) involve running a company without any management assistance and are best suited for small companies in the early stages of growth.

        b) The last three (entrepreneur-plus-employee team, small partnership, big-team venture) rely on a team approach to run the company as its growth speeds up.

2. The craftsman

        a) These entrepreneurs literally run a one-man (or one-woman) show; they do everything themselves because their primary concern is with the quality of the products or services they produce.

        b) One disadvantage of the craftsman management style is that the entrepreneur must do everything in the business, including those tasks that she does not enjoy.

        c) The biggest disadvantage is the limitations it puts on a company's ability to grow.

3. The classic

        a) The classic entrepreneur brings in other people but does not delegate any significant authority to them, choosing instead to "watch over everything" herself.

           (1) Tight supervision, constantly monitors employees' work, and performs all of the critical tasks herself.

           (2) Not comfortable delegating the power and the authority.

        b) Therefore, entrepreneurs who choose to operate this way must limit the complexity of their business if they are to grow at all.

        c) An inherent danger of this style is the entrepreneur's tendency to "micromanage."

4. The coordinator

        a) In this type of business (often called a virtual corporation because the company is actually quite "hollow"), the entrepreneur farms out a large portion of the work to other companies and then coordinates all of the activities from "headquarters."

        b) By hiring out at least some of the work (in some cases, most of the work), the entrepreneur is free to focus on pumping up sales and pushing the business to higher levels.

        c) Although the coordinator style sounds like an easy way to build a business, it can be very challenging to implement.

           (1) The business's success is highly dependent on its suppliers and their ability to produce quality products and services in a timely fashion.

5. The entrepreneur-plus-employee team

        a) This approach gives an entrepreneur the power to grow the business beyond the scope of the manager-only styles.

        b) In this style, the entrepreneur delegates authority to key employees, but she retains the final decision-making authority in the company.

(1) Delegating requires a manager to realize that there are several ways to accomplish a task and that sometimes employees will make mistakes.

(2) It allows the manager to get the maximum benefit from each employee while freeing herself up to focus on the most important tasks in the business.

6. The small partnership

   a) As the business world grows more complex and interrelated, many entrepreneurs find that there is strength in numbers.

   b) They choose to share the managerial responsibilities with one or more partners (or shareholders).

   c) The biggest advantage is the ability to share responsibility for the company with others who have a real stake in it and are willing to work hard to make it a success.

      (1) Some of the most effective partnerships are those in which the owners' skills complement one another, creating natural lines for dividing responsibilities.

      (2) The is the necessity of giving up total control over the business and the potential for personality conflicts and disputes over the company's direction.

7. The big-team venture

   a) The broadest-based management style is the big-team venture, which typically emerges over time as a company grows larger.

   b) Once a company reaches this point, managers must expand the breadth of the management team's experience to handle the increasing level of responsibility that results from the sheer size of the company.

      (1) Especially if the company's operations have become global in scope.

8. Any of these management styles can be successful for an entrepreneur if it matches her personality and the company's goals.

   a) The key is to plan for the company's growth and to lay out a strategy for managing the changes the company will experience as it grows.

9. Team-based management

   a) Large companies have been using self-directed work teams for years.

   b) A team approach may be best suited for small companies.

      (1) A self-directed work team is a group of workers from different functional areas of a company who work together as a unit largely without supervision, making decisions and performing tasks that once belonged only to managers.

      (2) Some teams may be temporary, attacking and solving a specific problem.

      (3) Many are permanent components of an organization's structure.

   c) Managers in companies using teams work just as hard as before, but the nature of their work changes dramatically.

      (1) Before teams, managers were bosses who made most of the decisions.

      (2) As facilitators, their job is to support and to serve the teams functioning in the organization and to make sure they produce results.

10. Companies have strong competitive reasons for using team-based management.

   a) Companies that use teams effectively report significant gains in quality, reductions in cycle time, lower costs, increased customer satisfaction, and improved employee motivation and morale.

11. A team-based approach is not for every organization, however.

   a) Teams work best in environments where the work is interdependent and people must interact to accomplish their goals.

   b) Table 19.6 describes some of the transitions a company must make as it moves from a traditional organizational structure to a team-based style.

12. What causes teams to fail? The following errors are common:

   a) Assigning teams inappropriate tasks.

   b) Creating "make-nice" teams.

        c) Inadequate training for team members and team leaders.

        d) Sabotaging of teams by underperformers.

        e) Switching to team responsibilities but keeping pay individually oriented.

13. To ensure teams' success, managers must:

    a) Make sure that teams are appropriate for the company and the nature of its work.

    b) Form teams around the natural workflow, and give them specific tasks to accomplish.

    c) Provide adequate support and training for team members and leaders.

    d) Involve team members in determining how their performances will be measured, what will be measured, and when it will be measured.

    e) Make at least part of team members' pay dependent on team performance.

14. Figure 19.1 shows the four stages teams go through on their way to performing effectively and accomplishing goals.

V. The Challenge of Motivating Workers

  A. Motivation

    1. Motivation is the degree of effort an employee exerts to accomplish a task; it shows up as excitement about work.

    2. Motivating workers to higher levels of performance is one of the most difficult and challenging tasks facing a small business manager.

    3. There are four aspects to motivation: empowerment, job design, rewards and compensation, and feedback.

  B. Empowerment

    1. Empowerment involves giving workers at every level of the organization the authority, the freedom, and the responsibility to control their own work, to make decisions, and to take action to meet the company's objectives.

    2. Empowering employees requires a different style of management and leadership from that of the traditional manager.

      a) Business owners who share information, responsibility, authority, and power soon discover that their success (and their company's success) is magnified many times over.

    3. Empowerment builds on what real business leaders already know: that the people in their organizations bring with them to work an amazing array of talents, skills, knowledge, and abilities.

      a) Workers are willing--even anxious--to put these to use.

    4. The business benefits typically include significant productivity gains, quality improvements, more satisfied customers, improved morale, and increased employee motivation.

    5. Empowerment challenges workers to make the most of their creativity, imagination, knowledge, and skills.

    6. Not every worker wants to be empowered, however. Some will resist, wanting only to "put in their eight hours and go home."

      a) One expert estimates that companies moving to empowerment can expect to lose about 5 percent of their workforce.

    7. Empowerment works best when a business owner:

      a) is confident enough to give workers all of the authority and responsibility they can handle.

      b) plays the role of coach and facilitator, not the role of meddlesome boss.

      c) recognizes that empowered employees will make mistakes.

      d) hires people who can blossom in an empowered environment.

      e) trains workers continuously to upgrade their skills.

    f) trusts workers to do their jobs.

    g) listens to workers when they have ideas, solutions, or suggestions.

    h) recognizes workers' contributions.

    i) shares information with workers.

        (1) The goal of open-book management is to enable employees to understand why they need to raise productivity, improve quality, cut costs, and improve customer service.

        (2) Under open-book management, employees:

            (a) see and learn to understand the company's financial statements and other critical numbers in measuring its performance.

            (b) learn that a significant part of their jobs is making sure those critical numbers move in the right direction.

            (c) have a direct stake in the company's success through profit sharing, ESOPs, or performance-based bonuses.

        (3) In short, open-book management establishes the link between employees' knowledge and their performance.

C. Job Design

    1. Over the years, managers have learned that the job itself and the way it is designed can be a source of motivation.

        a) Job simplification invites workers to "check their brains at the door" and offers them little opportunity for excitement, enthusiasm, or pride in their work. The result can be apathetic, unmotivated workers who don't care about quality, customers, or costs.

        b) To break this destructive cycle, some companies have redesigned jobs so that they offer workers intrinsic rewards and motivation. Three strategies are common: job enlargement, job rotation, and job enrichment.

    2. Job enlargement (or horizontal job loading) adds more tasks to a job to broaden its scope.

        a) The idea is to make the job more varied and to allow employees to perform a more complete unit of work.

    3. Job rotation involves cross-training employees so they can move from one job in the company to others, giving them a greater number and variety of tasks to perform.

        a) Cross-trained workers are more valuable because they give a company the flexibility to shift workers from low-demand jobs to those where they are most needed.

    4. Job enrichment (or vertical job loading) involves building motivators into a job by increasing the planning, decision-making, organizing, and controlling functions--i.e., traditional managerial tasks--workers perform.

        a) The idea is to make every employee a manager--at least a manager of his own job.

    5. Five core characteristics central to job enrichment

        a) Skill variety. The degree to which a job requires a variety of different skills, talents, and activities from the worker.

        b) Task identity. The degree to which a job allows the worker to complete a whole or identifiable piece of work.

        c) Task significance. The degree to which a job substantially influences the lives or work of others--employees or final customers.

        d) Autonomy. The degree to which a job gives a worker freedom, independence, and discretion in planning and performing tasks.

        e) Feedback. The degree to which a job gives the worker direct, timely information about the quality of his performance.

    6. Organizational structures, even in small companies, are flatter than ever before, as the lines between traditional "managers" and "workers" get blurrier.

   a) One expert in organizational change says, "There is going to be a tremendous shift during the next 25 years toward independence, autonomy, and self-directedness, with people and teams accountable for their own performances."
7. Many of these shifts are already taking place in the form of flextime, job sharing, flexplace, and telecommuting.
8. Flextime.
   a) An arrangement under which employees build their work schedules around a set of "core hours"--such as 11 A.M. to 3 P.M.--but have flexibility about when they start and stop work.
   b) Flextime not only raises worker morale, but it also makes it easier for companies to attract high-quality young workers who want rewarding careers without sacrificing their lifestyles.
   c) In addition, companies using flextime schedules often experience lower levels of tardiness and absenteeism.
9. Job sharing.
   a) A work arrangement in which two or more people share a single full-time job.
   b) A relatively small portion of the nation's workforce, it is an important job design strategy for some companies that find it difficult to recruit capable, qualified full-time workers.
10. Flexplace
   a) This is a work arrangement in which employees work at a place other than the traditional office, such as a satellite branch closer to their homes or, in some cases, at home.
   b) Flexplace is an easy job design strategy for companies to use because of telecommuting.
11. Telecommuting studies show that workers say they are from 5 percent to 20 percent more productive when working at home because they encounter fewer distractions.
   a) According to Link Resources, approximately 12 million workers are telecommuters, and the number is growing rapidly; by 2002, the Department of Transportation estimates that 15 percent of the U.S. workforce will be telecommuting.
   b) Before shifting to telecommuting, there are important issues.
      (1) Does the nature of the work fit telecommuting?
      (2) Can you monitor compliance with federal wage and hour laws for telecommuters?
      (3) Which workers are best suited for telecommuting?
      (4) Can you provide the equipment and the technical support telecommuters need to be productive?
      (5) Are you adequately insured?
      (6) Can you keep in touch?
   c) A variation of telecommuting that is growing in popularity is hoteling, in which employees who spend most of their time away from the office anyway use the same office space at different times, just as travelers use the same hotel rooms on different days.
      (1) Businesses that use hoteling have been able to reduce the cost of leasing office space, sometimes by as much as 50 percent.

D. Rewards and Compensation
   1. The key to using rewards to motivate involves tailoring them to the needs and characteristics of the workers.

    a) "The core of successful motivation is tapping into the things that are really important to people: taking the time to find out what those are, and structuring your recognition around those in the context of the job," says one motivation expert.

2. One of the most popular rewards is money.
    a) Cash is an effective motivator--up to a point.
    b) By linking employees' compensation directly to the company's financial performance, a business owner increases the likelihood that workers will achieve performance targets that are in their best interest and in the company's best interest.
    c) One recent survey of small companies by National Small Business United found that more than half rewarded their workers with bonuses and other performance-related incentives.

IN THE FOOTSTEPS OF AN ENTREPRENEUR - How Do You Manage Generation X?

SUMMARY
Are the stereotypes of Generation X true? Not necessarily. The key lies in knowing what Gen. X workers expect in the workplace. How can business owners motivate, stimulate, and reward their Generation X employees? The following suggestions will help:

- Don't rely on the traditional career motivators such as fancy job titles and more pay.
- Give them challenging assignments that allow them to learn more skills.
- Treat them as individuals.
- Avoid an authoritarian approach.
- Trust them.
- Offer them varied assignments.
- Say what you mean, and mean what you say.
- Offer frequent rewards.

Small companies are ideally suited for Generation X employees because they offer workers the chance to get involved in many different aspects of the company and because workers can make a difference in the company's future. One-fifth of all small business owners in the United States are Generation Xers, and this generation has the highest business start-up rate among all the others.

1. How would you respond to a manager who used the techniques described above? Explain.
Answer - Students' responses will vary. This question should help students think through their own motivations. Students should be encouraged to feel motivated by things other than what research says motivates them.
2. Write a one-page paper describing a job you have held in which your manager did *not* use effective management and motivational techniques. What impact did the manager's style have on your level of motivation? On job performance? On morale? What suggestions would you make to improve the situation?
Answer - Students' responses will vary with their experiences.

---

    3. Pay-for-performance systems should meet the following criteria:
        a) Employees' incentive pay must be clearly and closely linked to their performances.
        b) Entrepreneurs must set up the system so that employees see the connection between what they do every day on the job and what they are paid.
        c) The system must be simple enough so that employees understand and trust it.
        d) Employees must believe the system is fair.
        e) The system should be inclusive.
        f) The company should make frequent payouts to employees.

4. Nonfinancial incentives can be more important sources of employee motivation than money!
   a) After its initial motivational impact, money loses its impact; it does not have a lasting motivational effect.
   b) Often, the most meaningful motivating factors are the simplest ones praise, recognition, respect, feedback, job security, promotions, and others--things that any small business, no matter how limited its budget, can do.
5. Small companies find that younger workers, especially Generation Xers, respond best to intangible rewards and not to monetary rewards.
   a) Generation X workers are looking for workplaces that offer challenging assignments coupled with a sense of fun.
   b) They respond best to constant feedback that is specific and accurate.
6. Praise is another simple, yet powerful, motivational tool.
7. One of the surest ways to kill high performance is simply to fail to recognize it and the employees responsible for it.
8. Small business owners must be more creative when it comes to giving rewards that motivate workers.
   a) Rewards do not have to be expensive to be effective, but they should be creative and should have a direct link to employee performance.
   b) Creative rewards that entrepreneurs are using successfully to motivate their workers include:
      (1) A $25 "pot" for the week's "poker hand."
      (2) A trip to Disney World.
      (3) A facial or a massage.
      (4) Company points that employees can redeem for prizes.
9. Whatever system of rewards they use, managers will be most successful if they match rewards to employees' interests and tastes.
10. The goal is to let employees know that "every person is important."

E. Feedback
   1. Business owners not only must motivate employees to excel in their jobs, but they must also focus their efforts on the right targets.
   2. Providing feedback on progress toward those targets can be a powerful motivating force in a company.
      a) To ensure that the link between her vision for the company and its operations is strong, an entrepreneur must build a series of specific performance measures that serve as periodic monitoring points.
      b) For each critical element of the organization's performance (e.g., product or service quality, financial performance, market position, productivity, employee development), the owner should develop specific measures that connect daily operational responsibilities with the company's overall strategic direction.
   3. Getting or giving feedback implies that a business owner has established meaningful targets that serve as standards of performance for her, her employees, and the company as a whole.
   4. One characteristic successful people have in common is that they set goals and objectives, usually challenging ones, for themselves.
   5. For feedback to have impact as a motivating force in a business requires business owners to follow the procedure illustrated in Figure 19.2.
   6. Deciding what to measure
      a) The first step in the feedback loop is deciding what to measure.

  b) Every business is characterized by a set of numbers that are critical to its success, and these "critical numbers" are what the entrepreneur should focus on.

  c) Obvious critical numbers include sales, profits, profit margins, cash flow, and other standard financial measures.

7. Deciding how to measure.

  a) In some cases, identifying the critical numbers defines the measurements the owner must make, and measuring them simply becomes a matter of collecting and analyzing data.

  b) One of the best ways to develop methods for measuring such factors is to use brainstorming sessions involving employees, customers, and even outsiders.

8. Comparing actual performance against standards

  a) In this stage of the feedback loop, the idea is to look for deviations in either direction from the performance standards the company has set for itself.

  b) Managers and employees must focus their efforts on figuring out why actual performance is substandard, discover the cause of the subpar performance, and fix it.

9. Taking action to improve performance

  a) Typically, several suitable alternatives to solving a performance problem exist; the key is finding an acceptable solution that solves the problem quickly, efficiently, and effectively.

10. Performance appraisal

  a) One of the most common methods of providing feedback.

  b) Most performance appraisal programs strive to accomplish three goals:

   (1) to give employees feedback about how they are doing their jobs, which can be an important source of motivation.

   (2) to provide a business owner and an employee the opportunity to create a plan for developing the employee's skills and abilities and for improving his performance.

   (3) to establish a basis for determining promotions and salary increases.

  c) The primary purpose of performance appraisals is to encourage and to help employees improve their performances, too often they turn into uncomfortable confrontations.

   (1) Why? Because most business owners don't understand how to conduct an effective performance appraisal.

   (2) Common complaints include unclear standards and objectives; managers who lack information about employees' performances; managers who are unprepared or who lack honesty and sincerity; and managers who use general, ambiguous terms to describe employees' performances.

  d) Perhaps the biggest complaint, employees do not have the opportunity to receive any ongoing feedback on a regular basis.

   (1) All too often, a manager saves up all of the negative feedback to give an employee and then dumps it on him in the annual performance review.

  e) If done properly, performance appraisals can be effective ways to provide employee feedback and to improve workers' performances.

  f) Guidelines for an effective performance appraisal system.

   (1) Link the employee's performance criteria to the job description.

   (2) Establish meaningful, job-related, observable, measurable, and fair performance criteria.

   (3) Prepare for the appraisal session by outlining the key points you want to cover with the employee.

   (4) Invite the employee to provide an evaluation of his own job performance based on the performance criteria.

   (5) Be specific.

(6) Keep a record of employee's critical incidents--both positive and negative.
(7) Discuss an employee's strengths and weaknesses.
(8) Incorporate employee's goals into the appraisal.
(9) Keep the evaluation constructive.
(10) Focus on behaviors, actions, and results.
(11) Avoid surprises.
(12) Plan for the future.

g) 360-degree feedback.
(1) Studies suggest that 30 percent of U.S. companies use 360-degree evaluations as part of their performance appraisal systems.
(2) Peer appraisals can be especially useful because an employee's coworkers see his on-the-job performance every day.
(3) Disadvantages of peer appraisals include potential retaliation against coworkers who criticize, the possibility that appraisals will be reduced to "popularity contests," and the refusal of some workers to offer any criticism because they feel uncomfortable evaluating others.
(4) Some bosses using upward feedback report similar problems, including personal attacks and extreme evaluations by vengeful subordinates.

Chapter Summary

♦ Explain the challenges involved in the entrepreneur's role as leader and what it takes to be a successful leader.
- Leadership is the process of influencing and inspiring others to work to achieve a common goal and then giving them the power and the freedom to achieve it.
- Management and leadership are not the same; yet both are essential to a small company's success. Leadership without management is unbridled; management without leadership is uninspired. Leadership gets a small business going; management keeps it going.

♦ Understand the potential barriers to effective communication and describe how to overcome them.
- Research shows that managers spend about 80 percent of their time in some form of communication; yet their attempts at communicating sometimes go wrong. Several barriers to effective communication include: Managers and employees don't always feel free to say what they really mean; ambiguity blocks real communication; information overload causes the message to get lost; selective listening interferes with the communication process; defense mechanisms block a message; and conflicting verbal and nonverbal messages confuse listeners.
- To become more effective communicators, business owners should: Clarify their messages before attempting to communicate them; use face-to-face communication whenever possible; be empathetic; match their messages to their audiences; be organized; encourage feedback; tell the truth; not be afraid to tell employees about the business, its performance, and the forces that affect it.

♦ Describe the importance of hiring the right employees and how to avoid making hiring mistakes.
- The decision to hire a new employee is an important one for every business, but its impact is magnified many times in a small company. Every "new hire" a business owner makes determines the heights to which the company can climb or the depths to which it will plunge.
- To avoid making hiring mistakes, entrepreneurs should: develop meaningful job descriptions and job specifications; plan and conduct an effective interview; and check references before hiring any employee.

♦ Explain how to build the kind of company culture and structure to support the entrepreneur's mission and goals and to motivate employees to achieve them.
- Company culture is the distinctive, unwritten code of conduct that governs the behavior, attitudes, relationships, and style of an organization. Culture arises from an entrepreneur's consistent and

relentless pursuit of a set of core values that everyone in the company can believe in. Small companies' flexible structures can be a major competitive weapon.

- Entrepreneurs rely on six different management styles to guide their companies as they grow. The first three (craftsman, classic, and coordinator) involve running a company without any management assistance and are best suited for small companies in the early stages of growth; the last three (entrepreneur-plus-employee team, small partnership, big-team venture) rely on a team approach to run the company as its growth speeds up.
- Team-based management is growing in popularity among small firms. Companies that use teams effectively report significant gains in quality, reductions in cycle time, lower costs, increased customer satisfaction, and improved employee motivation and morale.

♦ Discuss the ways in which entrepreneurs can motivate their workers to higher levels of performance.

- Motivation is the degree of effort an employee exerts to accomplish a task; it shows up as excitement about work. Four important tools of motivation are empowerment, job design, rewards and compensation, and feedback.
- Empowerment involves giving workers at every level of the organization the power, the freedom, and the responsibility to control their own work, to make decisions, and to take action to meet the company's objectives.
- Job design techniques for enhancing employee motivation include job enlargement, job rotation, job enrichment, flextime, job sharing, and flexplace (which includes telecommuting and hoteling).
- Money is an important motivator for many workers, but not the only one. The key to using rewards such as recognition and praise to motivate involves tailoring them to the needs and characteristics of the workers.
- Giving employees timely, relevant feedback about their job performance through a performance appraisal system can also be a powerful motivator.

Discussion Questions

1. What is leadership? What is the difference between leadership and management?

   Answer - A small business manager's most important role is that of leader. Without leadership ability, entrepreneurs and their companies never rise above mediocrity. Until recently, experts compared the leader's job to that of a symphony orchestra conductor. Like the symphony leader, a small business manager made sure that everyone was playing the same score, coordinated individual efforts to produce harmony, and directed the members as they played. In short, management and leadership are not the same; yet both are essential to a small company's success.

   Stephen Covey, author of *Principle-Centered Leadership*, explains the difference between management and leadership this way:
   - Leadership deals with people; management deals with things.
   - You manage things; you lead people.
   - Leadership deals with vision; management deals with logistics toward that vision.
   - Leadership deals with doing the right things; management focuses on doing things right.
   - Leadership deals with examining the paradigms on which you are operating; management operates within those paradigms.
   - Leadership comes first, then management, but both are necessary.

2. What behaviors do effective leaders exhibit?

   Answer - Effective leaders exhibit certain behaviors. They:
   - create a set of values and beliefs for employees and passionately pursue them.
   - set the example for their employees.
   - focus employees' efforts on challenging goals and keep them driving toward those goals.
   - provide the resources employees need to achieve their goals.

- communicate with their employees.
- value the diversity of their workers.
- celebrate their workers' successes.
- encourage creativity among their workers.
- maintain a sense of humor.
- keep their eyes on the horizon.

For an entrepreneur, leadership success is one of the key determinants of the company's success. The new leader is the one who sees clearly the goal, shares repeatedly and forcefully the vision, provides the tools, trains and enables coworkers to manage and improve their processes, remains persistent in the face of adversity, and inspires others to take an ownership position in the completion of the mission--by example.

3. Why is it so important for small companies to hire the right employees? What can small business owners do to avoid making hiring mistakes?

   Answer - Every "new hire" a business owner makes determines the heights to which the company can climb--or the depths to which it will plunge. "Bad hires" are incredibly expensive, and no company, especially a small one, can afford too many of them. One study concluded that an employee hired into a typical entry-level position who quits after six months costs a company about $17,000 in salary, benefits, and training. In addition, the intangible costs--time invested in the new employee, lost opportunities, reduced morale among coworkers, and business setbacks--are seven times the direct costs of a bad hire. In other words, the total price tag for this bad hire is about $136,000.

   The following guidelines can help small business managers avoid making costly hiring mistakes.
   - Create practical job descriptions and job specifications
   - Plan an effective interview
   - Conduct the interview
   - Check references
   - Conduct employment tests

4. What is a job description? A job specification? What functions do they serve in the hiring process?

   Answer - To create a job description and job specification, the firm must perform a job analysis, the process by which a firm determines the duties and nature of the jobs to be filled and the skills and experience required of the people who are to fill them. The first objective of a job analysis is to develop a job description, a written statement of the duties, responsibilities, reporting relationships, working conditions, and materials and equipment used in a job. A results-oriented job description explains what a job entails and the duties the person filling it is expected to perform.

   The second objective of a job analysis is to create a job specification, a written statement of the qualifications and characteristics needed for a job stated in such terms as education, skills, and experience. A job specification shows the small business manager what kind of person to recruit and establishes the standards an applicant must meet to be hired. When writing job specifications, some managers define the traits a candidate needs to do a job well. Table 19.2 provides an example.

5. Outline the procedure for conducting an effective interview.

   Answer - Conducting an effective interview requires a small business owner to know what she wants to get out of the interview in the first place and to develop a series of questions to extract that information.

   Creating the Interview
   - Develop a series of core questions, and ask them of every candidate. To give the screening process consistency, smart business owners rely on a set of relevant questions they ask in every interview.

- Ask open-ended questions rather than questions calling for "yes or no" answers. Open-ended questions are most effective because they encourage candidates to talk.
- Create hypothetical situations candidates would be likely to encounter on the job and ask how they would handle them.
- Probe for specific examples in the candidate's work experience that demonstrate the necessary traits and characteristics.
- Ask candidates to describe a recent success and a recent failure and how they dealt with them.
- Arrange a "noninterview" setting that allows several employees to observe the candidate in an informal setting.
- Table 19.3 shows sample interview questions.

Conducting the Interview
- An effective interview contains three phases: breaking the ice, asking questions, and selling the candidate on the company.
  - In the opening phase of the interview, the manager's primary job is to diffuse the tension that exists because of the nervousness of both parties.
  - During the second phase of the interview, the employer asks the questions from her question bank to determine the applicant's suitability for the job.
  - Selling the candidate on the company. This phase begins by allowing the candidate to ask questions about the company, the job, or other issues.

6. What is company culture? What role does it play in a small company's success? What threats does rapid growth pose for a company's culture?
   Answer - Company culture is the distinctive, unwritten code of conduct that governs the behavior, attitudes, relationships, and style of an organization. It is the essence of "the way we do things around here."

   Culture can play as important a part in gaining a competitive edge as strategy does. Company culture manifests itself in many ways--from how workers dress and act to the language they use. In many companies, the culture creates its own language. Creating a culture that supports a company's strategy is not easy; the entrepreneurs who have been most successful at it "have a set of overarching beliefs that serve as powerful guides for everyday action--and that are reinforced in a hundred different ways, both symbolic and substantive," explains one business writer.

   As companies grow, they often experience dramatic changes in their culture. Procedures become more formal, operations grow more widespread, jobs take on more structure, communication becomes more difficult, and the company's personality begins to change. As more workers come on board, employees find it more difficult to know everyone in the company and what their jobs are. Unless an entrepreneur works hard to maintain her company's unique culture, she may wake up one day to find that she has sacrificed that culture--and the competitive edge that went with it--in the name of growth. Ironically, growth can sometimes be a small company's biggest enemy, causing a once successful business to spiral out of control into oblivion. The problem stems from the fact that the organizational structure (or lack of it!) and the style of management that makes an entrepreneurial start-up so successful often cannot support the business as it grows into adolescence and maturity. The signs of trouble--diminishing cash flow, rapid turnover of good people, expanding general and administrative expenses, and increasing distance from the core of the business.

7. Explain the six different management styles entrepreneurs rely on to guide their companies as they grow (craftsman, classic, coordinator, entrepreneur-plus-employee team, small partnership, and big-team venture).
   Answer - Entrepreneurs have traditionally relied on six different management styles to guide their companies as they grow. The first three (craftsman, classic, and coordinator) involve running a

company without any management assistance and are best suited for small companies in the early stages of growth. The last three (entrepreneur-plus-employee team, small partnership, big-team venture) rely on a team approach to run the company as its growth speeds up.

- The craftsman. These entrepreneurs literally run a one-man (or one-woman) show; they do everything themselves because their primary concern is with the quality of the products or services they produce.
- The classic. The classic entrepreneur brings in other people but does not delegate any significant authority to them, choosing instead to "watch over everything" herself.
- The coordinator. In this type of business (often called a virtual corporation because the company is actually quite "hollow"), the entrepreneur farms out a large portion of the work to other companies and then coordinates all of the activities from "headquarters."
- The entrepreneur-plus-employee team. This approach gives an entrepreneur the power to grow the business beyond the scope of the manager-only styles. In this style, the entrepreneur delegates authority to key employees, but she retains the final decision-making authority in the company.
- The small partnership. As the business world grows more complex and interrelated, many entrepreneurs find that there is strength in numbers. They choose to share the managerial responsibilities with one or more partners (or shareholders).
- The big-team venture. The broadest-based management style is the big-team venture, which typically emerges over time as a company grows larger. Once a company reaches this point, managers must expand the breadth of the management team's experience to handle the increasing level of responsibility that results from the sheer size of the company.

8. What mistakes do companies make when switching to team-based management? What can they do to avoid these mistakes? Explain the four phases teams typically go through.
    Answer - Large companies have been using self-directed work teams for years. A team approach may be best suited for small companies. A self-directed work team is a group of workers from different functional areas of a company who work together as a unit largely without supervision, making decisions and performing tasks that once belonged only to managers. Some teams may be temporary, attacking and solving a specific problem.

    A team-based approach is not for every organization, however. Teams work best in environments where the work is interdependent and people must interact to accomplish their goals. Table 19.6 describes some of the transitions a company must make as it moves from a traditional organizational structure to a team-based style. What causes teams to fail? The following errors are common:
    - Assigning teams inappropriate tasks.
    - Creating "make-nice" teams.
    - Inadequate training for team members and team leaders.
    - Sabotaging of teams by underperformers.
    - Switching to team responsibilities but keeping pay individually oriented.

    Figure 19.1 shows the four stages teams go through on their way to performing effectively and accomplishing goals.
9. What is empowerment? What benefits does it offer workers? The company? What must a small business manager do to make empowerment work in a company?
    Answer - Empowerment involves giving workers at every level of the organization the authority, the freedom, and the responsibility to control their own work, to make decisions, and to take action to meet the company's objectives. Empowering employees requires a different style of management and leadership from that of the traditional manager. The business benefits typically include significant productivity gains, quality improvements, more satisfied customers, improved morale, and increased employee motivation. Empowerment challenges workers to make the most of their creativity, imagination, knowledge, and skills.

Empowerment works best when a business owner:
- is confident enough to give workers all of the authority and responsibility they can handle.
- plays the role of coach and facilitator, not the role of meddlesome boss.
- recognizes that empowered employees will make mistakes.
- hires people who can blossom in an empowered environment.
- trains workers continuously to upgrade their skills.
- trusts workers to do their jobs.
- listens to workers when they have ideas, solutions, or suggestions.
- recognizes workers' contributions.
- shares information with workers.

10. Explain the differences among job simplification, job enlargement, job rotation, and job enrichment. What impact do these different job designs have on workers?
Answer - Over the years, managers have learned that the job itself and the way it is designed can be a source of motivation.
- Job simplification invites workers to "check their brains at the door" and offers them little opportunity for excitement, enthusiasm, or pride in their work. The result can be apathetic, unmotivated workers who don't care about quality, customers, or costs.
- Job enlargement (or horizontal job loading) adds more tasks to a job to broaden its scope. The idea is to make the job more varied and to allow employees to perform a more complete unit of work.
- Job rotation involves cross-training employees so they can move from one job in the company to others, giving them a greater number and variety of tasks to perform.
- Job enrichment (or vertical job loading) involves building motivators into a job by increasing the planning, decision-making, organizing, and controlling functions--i.e., traditional managerial tasks--workers perform. The idea is to make every employee a manager--at least a manager of his own job.

11. Is money the "best" motivator? How do pay-for-performance compensation systems work? What other rewards are available to small business managers to use as motivators? How effective are they?
Answer - The key to using rewards to motivate involves tailoring them to the needs and characteristics of the workers. "The core of successful motivation is tapping into the things that are really important to people: taking the time to find out what those are, and structuring your recognition around those in the context of the job," says one motivation expert.

One of the most popular rewards is money. Cash is an effective motivator--up to a point. By linking employees' compensation directly to the company's financial performance, a business owner increases the likelihood that workers will achieve performance targets that are in their best interest and in the company's best interest.

Pay-for-performance systems should meet the following criteria:
- Employees' incentive pay must be clearly and closely linked to their performances.
- Entrepreneurs must set up the system so that employees see the connection between what they do every day on the job and what they are paid.
- The system must be simple enough so that employees understand and trust it.
- Employees must believe the system is fair.
- The system should be inclusive.
- The company should make frequent payouts to employees.

Nonfinancial incentives can be more important sources of employee motivation than money! Often, the most meaningful motivating factors are the simplest ones--praise, recognition, respect, feedback, job security, promotions, and others--things that any small business, no matter how limited its budget, can do. Small companies find that younger workers, especially Generation Xers, respond best to intangible rewards and not to monetary rewards. Whatever system of rewards they use, managers will be most successful if they match rewards to employees' interests and tastes. The goal is to let employees know that "every person is important."

12. Suppose that a mail-order catalog company selling environmentally friendly products identifies its performance as a socially responsible company as a "critical number" in its success. Suggest some ways for the owner to measure this company's "social responsibility index."
   Answer - The company would first have to specifically define "social responsibility," and then set standards to measure against. They could measure how much money the company donates to the local community. They could evaluate how much time employees give to community-related events. The company could ask customers to rate the company through a questionnaire, etc.

13. What is performance appraisal? What are the most common mistakes managers make in performance appraisals? What should small business managers do to avoid making those mistakes?
   Answer - One of the most common methods of providing feedback is the performance appraisal. Most performance appraisal programs strive to accomplish three goals:
   - to give employees feedback about how they are doing their jobs, which can be an important source of motivation.
   - to provide a business owner and an employee the opportunity to create a plan for developing the employee's skills and abilities and for improving his or her performance.
   - to establish a basis for determining promotions and salary increases.
   The primary purpose of performance appraisals is to encourage and to help employees improve their performances; too often they turn into uncomfortable confrontations. Common complaints include unclear standards and objectives, managers who lack information about employees' performances, managers who are unprepared or who lack honesty and sincerity, and managers who use general, ambiguous terms to describe employees' performances. Perhaps the biggest complaint, employees do not have the opportunity to receive any ongoing feedback on a regular basis.

   Guidelines for an effective performance appraisal system.
   - Link the employee's performance criteria to the job description.
   - Establish meaningful, job-related, observable, measurable, and fair performance criteria.
   - Prepare for the appraisal session by outlining the key points you want to cover with the employee.
   - Invite the employee to provide an evaluation of his own job performance based on the performance criteria.
   - Be specific.
   - Keep a record of employees' critical incidents--both positive and negative.
   - Discuss an employee's strengths and weaknesses.
   - Incorporate employee's goals into the appraisal.
   - Keep the evaluation constructive.
   - Focus on behaviors, actions, and results.
   - Avoid surprises.
   - Plan for the future.

Step into the Real World

1. One leadership development program demonstrates how leaders can overcome resistance within a work group by using the following exercise. Participants are organized into groups and are assigned to a table. At each table, one person is assigned to be the change agent, another to be a change supporter, and two others to be change resisters. On the table sits an unopened carton of buttermilk. The change agent must convince the other members of the group to taste the buttermilk. Only when

the change agent opens the carton does the full challenge of the task become apparent. The buttermilk has been injected with a harmless, but GREEN food coloring. Set up your own buttermilk experiment. How would you convince other members of your group to taste the green buttermilk? What does this experiment say about your leadership style?

2. Visit a local business that has experienced rapid growth in the past three years and ask the owner about the specific problems he or she had to face that were caused by the organization's growth. How did the owner handle these problems? Looking back, what would he or she do differently?

3. Contact a local small business with at least 20 employees. Does the company have job descriptions and job specifications? What process does the owner use to hire a new employee? What questions does the owner typically ask candidates in an interview?

4. Using a search engine such as InfoSeek, Yahoo! or Excite!, conduct a search on the various employment tests that are available to companies as screening devices. The American Psychological Association's Web site <http://wwwapa.org/> may be a good place to begin. Write a one-page summary of what you learn about employment tests.

5. Ask the owner of a small manufacturing operation to give you a tour of his or her operation. During your tour, observe the way jobs are organized. To what extent does the company use the following job design concepts: job simplification? job enlargement? job rotation? job enrichment? flextime? job sharing? On the basis of your observations, what recommendations would you make to the owner about the company's job design?

Chapter 20 - Management Succession and Risk Management Strategies in the Family Business

There is a time for departure even when there no place to go.
Tennessee Williams

When it works right, nothing succeeds like a family firm. The roots run deep, embedded in family values. The flash of the fast buck is replaced with long-term plans. Tradition counts.
Eric Calonlus

Teaching Objectives
Students will be able to:
1. Explain the factors necessary for a strong family business.
2. Understand the exit strategy options available to an entrepreneur.
3. Discuss the stages of management succession.
4. Explain how to develop an effective management succession plan.
5. Understand the four risk management strategies.
6. Discuss the basics of insurance for small businesses.

Instructor's Outline
I. Family Businesses
    A. Introduction
        1. More than 80 percent of all companies in the United States are family-owned.
            a) Family businesses generate 50 percent of the U.S. gross domestic product, employ more than 40 million people, and pay 65 percent of all wages.
            b) One-third of the *Fortune* 500 companies are family businesses.
        2. Unfortunately, 70 percent of first-generation businesses fail to survive into the second generation, and, of those that do, only 13 percent make it to the third generation.
        3. The best way to avoid deadly turf battles and conflicts is to develop a succession plan for the company.
            a) Although business founders want their businesses to survive them, and almost 80 percent intend to pass the business on to their children, they seldom support their intentions by a plan to accomplish that goal.
            b) About 54 percent of all family business owners do not have a formal management succession plan.

    B. Shared Values
        1. The first, and probably most overlooked, quality is a set of shared values.
        2. Without shared values, it is difficult to create a future direction for a business.
        3. To avoid the problems associated with conflicting values and goals, the family should consider taking the following actions:
            a) Make it clear to all involved that they are not required to join the business on a full-time basis.
            b) Do not assume that a successor must always come from within the family.
            c) Give family members the opportunity to work outside the business first to learn firsthand how others conduct business.

    C. Shared Power
        1. Shared power is not necessarily equal power.

        a) Shared power is based on the simple idea that the skills and talents of family members may run in different directions.

        b) Shared power is based on the idea that family members should allow those with the greatest expertise, ability, and knowledge in particular areas to handle decisions in those areas.

    2. Dividing responsibilities along the lines of expertise is an important way of acknowledging respect for each family member's talents and abilities.

D. Tradition

    1. Tradition is necessary for a family business because it serves to bond family members and to link one generation of business leaders to the next.

    2. The key is to select those traditions that provide a solid foundation for positive behavior while taking care not to restrict the future growth of the business.

E. A Willingness to Learn

    1. The family business that remains open to new ideas and techniques is likely to reduce its risk of obsolescence.

    2. In many cases, a formalized family council serves as a mechanism through which family members can propose new ideas.

    3. Perhaps more important than a family council is fostering an environment in which family members trust one another enough to express their ideas, thoughts, and suggestions openly and honestly.

F. Family Behavior

    1. Families that play together operate family businesses that are likely to stay together.

    2. Time spent together outside the business creates the foundation for the relationships family members have at work.

    3. Too often, life in a family business can degenerate into nothing but day after day of work and discussions of work at home.

G. Strong Family Ties

    1. Strong family ties grow from one-on-one relationships.

    2. Shared time conveys the message that the family business is more than just a business; it is a group of people who care for one another working together toward a common goal.

    3. The bond that a family business creates among relatives can be powerful.

    4. The same emotions that hold family businesses together can also rip them apart if they run counter to the company's and the family's best interest.

        a) Conflict is a natural part of any business, but it can be especially powerful in family businesses because family relationships magnify the passions binding family members to the company.

II. Exit Strategies

A. Introduction

    1. Most family business founders want their companies to stay within their families, although, in some cases, maintaining family control is not practical.

    2. Sometimes, no one in the next generation of family members has an interest in managing the company or has the necessary skills and experience to handle the job.

    3. Having a solid management succession plan in place well before retirement is absolutely critical to success.

B. Selling to Outsiders
1. A straight sale may be best for entrepreneurs who want to step down and turn the reins over to someone else.
2. However, selling a business outright is not an attractive exit strategy for those who want to stay on with the company or for those who want to surrender control of the company gradually rather than all at once.
3. The financial terms of a sale also influence the selling price of the business and the number of potential bidders.

C. Selling to Insiders
1. When entrepreneurs have no family members to whom they can transfer ownership or who want to assume the responsibilities of running a company, selling the business to employees is often the preferred option.
2. In most situations, the options available to owners are (1) sale for cash plus a note, (2) a leveraged buyout, and (3) an employee stock ownership plan (ESOP).
3. A sale for cash plus a note
    a) Whether entrepreneurs often finance a portion of the sales price.
    b) The buyer pays the seller a lump-sum amount of cash up front and the seller holds a promissory note for the remaining portion of the selling price, which the buyer pays off in installments.
        (1) Because of its many creative financial options, this method of selling a business is popular with buyers.
        (2) Sellers also appreciate the security and the tax implications of accepting payment over time.
4. Leveraged buyouts (LBOs)
    a) In an LBO, managers or employees, or both, borrow money from a financial institution and pay the owner the total agreed-upon price at closing; then they use the cash generated from the company's operations to pay off the debt.
    b) During the economic boom of the 1980s, financial institutions were willing to accept the risks associated with highly leveraged businesses. Because of the high levels of debt they had taken on, the new management had very little room for error.
    c) If properly structured, LBOs can be attractive to both buyers and sellers.
        (1) Because they get their money up front, sellers do not incur the risk of loss if the buyers cannot keep the business operating successfully.
        (2) The managers and employees who buy the company have a strong incentive to make sure the business succeeds because they own a piece of the action and some of their capital is at risk in the business.
        (3) The result can be a highly motivated workforce that works hard and makes sure that the company operates efficiently.
5. Employee stock ownership plans (ESOPs)
    a) Unlike LBOs, employee stock ownership plans (ESOPs) allow employees or managers, or both, to purchase the business gradually.
    b) An ESOP frees up enough cash to finance the venture's future growth.
        (1) Employees contribute a portion of their earnings over time toward purchasing shares of the company's stock from the founder.
        (2) It is a long-term exit strategy that benefits everyone involved.
6. The third exit strategy available to company founders is transferring ownership to the next generation of family members with the help of a comprehensive management succession plan.

III. Management Succession
   A. Introduction
      1. Experts estimate that between 1993 and 2013, $4.8 trillion in wealth will be transferred from one generation to the next, much of it through family businesses.
        a) A recent study by Arthur Andersen and Mass Mutual Insurance Company found that 43 percent of family business founders expect to transfer leadership within the next five years.
      2. The businesses with the greatest probability of surviving are the ones whose owners prepare a succession plan well before it is time to pass the torch to the next generation.
      3. Succession planning also allows business owners to minimize the impact of taxes on their businesses, their estates, and their successors' wealth as well.
        a) With tax rates on gifts and estates as high as 55 percent, a plan that reduces the bite taxes take out of a business transfer is no small matter.
      4. One barrier to succession planning is that, in planning the future of the business, owners are forced to accept the painful reality of their own mortality.
        a) Many business founders hesitate to let go of their business because their personal identities are so wrapped up in their companies.
        b) Turning over the reins of a business they have scarificed for, fretted over, and dedicated themselves to for so many years is extremely difficult to do--even if the successor is a son or daughter.
        c) Many family business founders believe that controlling the business also gives them a degree of control over family members and family behavior.
      5. Planning for management succession protects not only the founder's, successors', and company's financial resources, but it also preserves what matters most in a successful business: its heritage and tradition.
      6. Management succession planning requires, first, an attitude of trusting others.
        a) Planning is an attitude that shows that decisions made with open discussion are more constructive than those without family input.
        b) Management succession as an evolutionary process must reconcile the entrepreneur's inevitable anguish with her successors' desire for autonomy.
        c) Owners' emotional ties to the business may be as strong as or stronger than their financial ties. On the other side are the successors, who may desire or even crave autonomy. These inherent conflicts can, and often do, result in skirmishes.
      7. Succession planning reduces the tension and stress created by these conflicts by gradually changing the guard.
      8. Management succession involves a lengthy series of interconnected stages that begin very early in the life of the owner's children and extend to the point of final ownership transition.
        a) See Figure 20.1.
        b) If management succession is to be effective, it is necessary for the process to begin early in the successor's life (Stage 1).
        c) During this Stage 2, the individual rotates among a variety of job functions both to broaden his base of understanding of the business and to permit the parents to evaluate his skills.
        d) At Stage 3, the successor becomes a full-time worker and ideally has already earned the respect of coworkers through his behavior in the first two stages of the process. Stage 3 focuses on the successor's continuous development.
        e) As the successor develops his skills and performance, he moves to Stage 4. This is the period when the founder makes a final assessment of the individual's abilities to take full and complete control over the firm.
        f) The skills the successor will need include the following:

(1) Financial abilities.
(2) Technical knowledge.
(3) Negotiating ability.
(4) Communication skills.
(5) Juggling skills.
(6) Commitment to the business.

9. The final stage involves the ultimate transition of organizational leadership.
   a) Often, the successor becomes the organization's CEO while the former CEO retains the title of chairman of the board.

10. Sometimes it may be best for the founder to step out of the business entirely.

IN THE FOOTSTEPS OF AN ENTREPRENEUR - Is Two a Crowd?

SUMMARY

Marshall Palsher, founder of a highly successful car wash chain in Boston, faced a daunting decision: how to handle passing the torch of leadership in the business to the next generation. He had one business and two sons, Bob and Dan, both of whom worked in the company and both of whom were highly capable of doing the job. Ultimately, Palsner and his two sons decided that both of the brothers would lead the company. "A recipe for disaster," said many observers.

A recent Arthur Andersen and Mass Mutual Family Business Survey found that 42 percent of family business owners expected to pass their companies on to co-CEOs, rather than to a single next-generation leader. Palsner and his sons recognized that for a co-leadership arrangement to work, they had to put in place a system to address problems that would arise such as handling disputes. They operate from the "office of the presidency" model. The two receive the same compensation and own the same percentage of the company's stock. They have different titles, however. Bob is CEO; Dan is president. They will also focus on different areas of responsibility. Co-leadership is doomed to an early failure unless these elements are present.

*   Divided responsibilities.
*   A board of advisers that includes members from outside the family.
*   A way to resolve conflict.
*   A formal structure for communication.

Business founders want to make sure that their successors are capable and competent. If they are fortunate enough to have two children who fit that description, then why not let both of them share in leading the company? With the proper safeguards in place, it can work beautifully.

1. What pitfalls and dangers do you see with family businesses run by co-CEOs?
    Answer - The two leaders could differ in values, vision for the company, ideas for running the company, and, as equals, they could keep the company from doing anything as they struggle for control. The company, any inheritance could all be destroyed, if they don't cooperate and trust each other.

2. What steps can business founders and their successors do to avoid these problems? Use the resources of the World Wide Web to research the issue of the co-leaders in family businesses. What other recommendations can you find for making co-leadership work in a family business?
    Answer - Responses will depend on research. Along with the ideas suggested by the text, normal business practices should be considered. Clear lines of authority and responsibility, regular communication about where the company is going, consensus decision making, etc.

IV. Developing a Management Succession Plan
   A. Introduction
       1. Families that are most committed to ensuring that their business survives from one generation to the next exhibit four characteristics:
           a) They believe that owning the business helps achieve their family's mission.
           b) They are proud of the values their business is built on and exemplifies.
           c) They believe that the business is contributing to society and makes it a better place to live
           d) They rely on management succession plans to ensure the continuity of their company.
       2. "Succession works best when parents have enough fortitude to discuss everything with their kids and resolve these issues while they're still alive," says one expert.

   B. Step 1. Select the Successor
       1. Entrepreneurs should never assume that their children want to take control of the business.
           a) It is critical to remember at this juncture in the life of a business that children do not necessarily inherit their parents' entrepreneurial skills and desires.
       2. One of the worst mistakes entrepreneurs can make is to postpone naming a successor until just before they are ready to step down.
       3. The problem is especially acute when more than one family member works for the company and is interested in assuming leadership of it. Sometimes, founders avoid naming a successor because they don't want to hurt the family members who are not chosen to succeed them.
       4. Involving the siblings themselves in the process of identifying the successor can alleviate some of the hard feelings that might otherwise surface.

   C. Step 2. Create a Survival Kit for the Successor
       1. Once he identifies a successor, the entrepreneur should prepare a survival kit and then brief the future leader on its contents, which should include all of the company's critical documents (wills, trusts, insurance policies, financial statements, bank accounts, key contracts, corporate bylaws, and so forth).
       2. The founder should be sure that the successor reads and understands all the relevant documents in the kit. Other important steps the owner should take to prepare the successor to take over leadership of the business include:
           a) Create a strategic analysis for the future.
           b) On a regular basis, the entrepreneur should share with the successor his vision of the business's future direction, describing key factors that have led to its success and those that will bring future success.
           c) Be open and listen to the successor's views and concerns.
           d) Teach and learn at the same time.
           e) Explain the strategies of the business and their link to key success factors.
           f) Discuss the values and philosophy of the business and how they have inspired and influenced past actions.
           g) Discuss the people in the business and their strengths and weaknesses.
           h) Discuss the philosophy underlying the firm's compensation policy, and explain why employees are paid what they are,
           i) Make a list of the firm's most important customers and its key vendors, and review the history of all dealings with the parties on both lists.
           j) Discuss how to treat these key players to ensure the company's continued success and its smooth and error-free ownership transition.

          k)   Develop a job analysis by taking an inventory of the activities involved in leading the company.

          l)   Document as much process knowledge ("how we do things") as possible.

D. Step 3. Groom the Successor

    1. The discussions that set the stage for the transition of leadership are time-consuming and require openness by both parties.

         a)   This is the process by which business founders transfer their knowledge to the next generation.

    2. To implement the succession plan, the founder must be:

         a)   Patient, realizing that the transfer of power is gradual and evolutionary and that the successor should earn responsibility and authority one step at a time until the final transfer of power takes place.

         b)   Willing to accept that the successor will make mistakes.

         c)   Skillful at using the successor's mistakes as a teaching tool.

         d)   An effective communicator and an especially tolerant listener.

         e)   Capable of establishing reasonable expectations for the successor's performance.

         f)   Able to articulate the keys to successor's performance.

    3. Teaching is the art of assisting discovery.

         a)   Teaching also requires letting go rather than controlling.

         b)   When a problem arises in the business, the founder should consider delegating it to the successor-in-training.

E. Step 4. Promote an Environment of Trust and Respect

    1. Trust and respect on the part of the founder and others fuel the successor's desire to learn and excel and build the successor's confidence in making decisions.

    2. Developing a competent successor over a period of five to ten years is realistic. Empowering the successor by gradually delegating responsibilities creates an environment in which customers, creditors, suppliers, and staff members can objectively view the successor's growth and development and gradually develop confidence in him.

F. Step 5. Cope with the Financial Realities of Estate and Gift Taxes

    1. Entrepreneurs who fail to consider the impact of these taxes may force their heirs to sell a successful business just to pay the estate's tax bill.

         a)   In a recent survey of small business owners by researchers at Kennesaw State University, more than half believed that their estates would be hit with a tax bill that would limit their company's growth potential.

         b)   One-third said that paying the expected estate tax would require their heirs to sell either part or all of their businesses.

    2. Although tax laws currently allow individuals to pass up to $1.3 million of assets to their heirs without incurring any estate taxes, the tax rate on transfers above that amount starts at 37 percent.

    3. The tax rate climbs to 55 percent for estates valued at more than $3 million.

         a)   According to the Arthur Andersen Center for Family Business, only 10 to 20 percent of all small business owners have written estate plans, even though they have 70 to 80 percent of their net worth tied up in their business.

    4. Many of these estate planning tools need time to work their magic, so the key is to put them in place early on in the life of the business.

    5. Buy/sell agreement

         a)   One of the most popular estate planning techniques is the buy/sell agreement.

  b) A recent survey by the Chartered Life Underwriters and the Chartered Life Financial Consultants found that 76 percent of small business owners who have estate plans have created buy/sell agreements.

  c) A buy/sell agreement is a contract that co-owners often rely on to ensure the continuity of a business. In a typical arrangement, the co-owners create a contract stating that each agrees to buy the other out in case of the death or disability of one.

  d) The buy/sell agreement specifies a formula for determining the value of the business at the time the agreement is to be executed.

  e) One problem with buy/sell agreements is that the remaining co-owners may not have the cash available to buy out the disabled or deceased owner.

   (1) To resolve this issue, many businesses buy life and disability insurance for each of the owners in amounts large enough to cover the purchase price of their respective shares of the business.

6. Lifetime gifting

  a) The owners of a successful business may transfer money to their children (or other recipients) from their estate throughout their lives.

  b) Current federal tax regulations allow individuals to make gifts of $10,000 per year, per parent, per recipient, that are exempt from federal gift taxes.

  c) Each child would be required to pay income tax on the $10,000 gift, but the children are usually in lower tax brackets than the given.

7. Setting up a trust

  a) A trust is a contract between a grantor (the founder) and a trustee (generally a bank officer or an attorney) in which the grantor gives to the trustee legal title to assets (e.g., stock in the company), which the trustee agrees to hold for the beneficiaries (children).

  b) The beneficiaries can receive income from the trust, or they can receive the property in the trust, or both, at some specified time.

  c) Two broad categories of trusts are available: revocable trusts and irrevocable trusts.

   (1) A revocable trust is one that the grantor can change or revoke during his lifetime.

   (2) Under present tax laws, however, the only trust that provides a tax benefit is an irrevocable trust, in which the grantor cannot require the trustee to return the assets held in trust.

   (3) The value of the grantor's estate is lowered because the assets in an irrevocable trust are excluded from the value of the estate.

  d) Bypass trust. The most basic type of trust is the bypass trust, which allows a business owner to put $600,000 into trust naming his spouse as the beneficiary upon his death.

  e) Irrevocable life insurance trust. This type of trust allows a business owner to keep the proceeds of a life insurance policy out of his estate and away from estate taxes, freeing up that money to pay the taxes on the remainder of the estate.

   (1) To get the tax benefit, business owners must be sure that the business or the trust (rather than themselves) owns the insurance policy.

   (2) The disadvantage of an irrevocable life insurance trust is that if the owner dies within three years of establishing it, the insurance proceeds do become part of his estate and are subject to estate taxes.

  f) Irrevocable asset trust. An irrevocable asset trust is similar to an irrevocable life insurance trust except that it is designed to pass the assets in the parents' estate on to their children.

  g) Grantor retained annuity trust (GRAT). A grantor retained annuity trust (GRAT) is a special type of irrevocable trust and has become one of the most popular tools for entrepreneurs to transfer ownership of a business while maintaining control over it and minimizing estate taxes.

(1) Under a GRAT, an owner can put property into an irrevocable trust for a maximum of 10 years.

(2) While the trust is in effect, the grantor retains the voting power and receives the interest income from the property in the trust. At the end of the trust (not to exceed 10 years), the property passes to the beneficiaries (heirs).

(3) The beneficiaries are required to pay a gift tax on the value of the assets placed in the GRAT.

(4) The primary disadvantage of using a GRAT in estate planning is that if the grantor dies during the life of the GRAT, its assets pass back into the grantor's estate.

8. Estate freeze
   a) An estate freeze attempts to minimize estate taxes by having family members create two classes of stock for the business:
      (1) preferred voting stock for the parents.
      (2) nonvoting common stock for the children.
   b) The value of the preferred stock is frozen while the common stock reflects the anticipated increased market value of the business.
   c) Any appreciation in the value of the business after the transfer is not subject to estate taxes.

9. Family limited partnership
   a) Creating a family limited partnership (FLP) allows business-owning parents to transfer their company to their children (thus lowering their estate taxes) while still retaining control over it for themselves.
   b) To create a family limited partnership, the parents (or parent) sets up a partnership among themselves and their children.
   c) The parents retain the general partnership interest, which can be as low as 1 percent, and the children become the limited partners.
   d) One of the principal tax benefits of an FLP is that it allows discounts on the value of the shares of company stock the parents transfer into the limited partnership.
      (1) Because a family business is closely held, shares of ownership in it are discounted at 20 to 50 percent of their full market value, producing a large tax savings for everyone involved. The average discount is 40 percent, but that amount varies on the basis of the industry and the individual company involved.
      (2) Because of their ability to reduce estate and gift taxes, family limited partnerships have become one of the most popular estate planning tools in recent years.

10. In developing a succession plan and preparing a successor, entrepreneurs often call on their attorneys, accountants, insurance agents, and financial planners to help.
    a) Table 20.1 provides an estate-planning checklist for entrepreneurs.

IN THE FOOTSTEPS OF AN ENTREPRENEUR - Pyrrhic Revenge

SUMMARY
Management succession decisions in family businesses usually are defining moments in the life of the business and the family because they are so filled with emotion. Whenever two or more siblings are involved in a family business and more than one wants to assume the leadership role, the founder faces a tough decision.

Psychologist Steven Berglas has coined the name Pyrrhic Revenge for this phenomenon, referring to the Greek general Pyrrhus, whose string of victories came at a catastrophic cost to his own men. Losers in the battle for succession in family businesses "set out to commit professional suicide." Steven Berglas offers these suggestions to avoid falling victim to Pyrrhic Revenge:

- Raise your children to know the difference between your love for them as people and your respect for them as workers and producers.
- Sensitize your children to the fact that there are multiple forms of intelligence and skill sets and not everyone possesses equal amounts of leadership potential.
- Let your children know that they are not alien beings if they don't love the business as much as you do.

1. Use the resources of your library and the World Wide Web to locate stories about family businesses and management succession. Find an example of a family business that faced the difficult issue of Pyrrhic Revenge. Summarize your findings in a one-page paper.
   Answer - Students' responses will vary based on their research.
2. What can parents and their children do to avoid Pyrrhic Revenge syndrome?
   Answer - Refer to Berglas' recommendations above.

V. Risk Management Strategies
   A. Introduction
      1. Insurance is an important part of creating a management succession plan because it can help business owners minimize the taxes on the estates they pass on.
      2. Insurance plays an important role in many other aspects of a successful business--from covering employee injuries to protecting against natural disasters that might shut a business down temporarily.
      3. When most small business owners think of risks such as these, they automatically think of insurance.
         a) Insurance does not solve all risk problems.
      4. Dealing with risk successfully requires a combination of four risk-management strategies: avoiding, reducing, anticipating, and transferring (or spreading) risk.

   B. Avoiding Risk
      1. This requires a business to take actions to shun risky situations.
         a) Conducting credit checks of customers can help decrease losses from bad debts.
         b) Workplace safety improves when business owners implement programs designed to make all employees aware of the hazards of their jobs and how to avoid being hurt.
         c) Business owners who have active risk identification and prevention programs can reduce their potential insurance costs as well as create a safer work environment.
      2. But avoiding risk altogether usually is not practical.

   C. Risk Reduction
      1. A risk-reducing strategy takes actions that build an extra degree of safety into a situation with an identified level of risk.
      2. Businesses can reduce risk by following common safety practices.
      3. Risk reduction strategies do not eliminate the source of the risk, they lessen the impact of its occurrence. Even with avoidance and reduction strategies, the source of the risk is still present; thus, losses can occur.

   D. Risk Anticipation
      1. These strategies promote self-insurance.

2. Knowing that some element of risk still exists, a business owner puts aside money each month to cover any losses that might occur.
3. Sometimes a self-insurance fund set aside may not be large enough to cover the losses from a particular situation.
4. This raises the necessity of transferring risk.

WIRED TO THE WEB - All in the Family?

SUMMARY
Marie and Mark Henson, both 60, were ready to sell the business they had founded more than 30 years ago with just $4,000. They had contacted a business broker friend. Then, the couple's oldest daughter, Lynn, ask them to sell it to her. The other children weren't interested.

She had worked at Saltillo as a clerk in the front office while completing her MBA, so she could appreciate the long hours and sacrifices her parents had put into building the company. She also recognized their desire to be free from the company while maintaining their financial resources. Lynn had used her parents' company as a case study for several business classes during her college years and was impressed by the potential it offered. As much as Lynn wanted the company, she was not sure if she could afford its $2 million value. She pondered methods of sale that would meet both of their sets of goals--her affording it while her parents were free of it and maintained their assets.

1. Use the resources of the World Wide Web and the local library to research ways that Lynn might be able to buy the family business and allow her parents to achieve their retirement goals at the same time.
    Answer - Students should begin by reviewing pages 701-705 and then go to the Web to seek additional information of these strategies. Consider bringing a family business attorney in to speak.
2. Should Marie and Mark sell the business to Lynn or to an outsider? Explain.
    Answer - Students can argue for either position. If they sell to an outsider, they can probably walk away and have all their money, but the family business will no longer be the family's; they could see it become a very different business. If they sell to Lynn, the business stays in the family, they may have some financial commitment still tied into the business, and it could create tensions between them.
3. What could the Hensons have done to avoid this last-minute proposal?
    Answer - Discussed their plans and desires with the family before contacting the business broker.

E. Risk Transference
    1. Most individuals and businesses therefore include in their risk strategies some form of insurance to transfer risk.
    2. For instance, Ami Cohen, owner of seven pizza and sandwich restaurants, began offering his employees health care insurance when he opened for business in 1964. Cohen knew that a self-insurance strategy alone could be risky. If employees' claims were low in a given year, he would save money over what he would have paid in insurance premiums. If several workers suffered catastrophic illnesses at once, however, his company could face a cash crisis. To minimize the risk, Cohen purchased a "stop-loss" policy, which takes over payment of all claims that exceed a certain level.
        a) For businesses with fewer than 50 employees, self-insurance is usually not a wise choice because there is so much variation in the number of annual claims.
        b) Also, companies using self-insurance should be financially stable and should see it as a long-term strategy for savings.

      c)   Table 20.2 provides a self-test for companies to take to determine whether self-insurance is the best option for them.

  3. Insurance is a risk transfer (or risk-spreading) strategy because an individual or a business transfers some of the costs of a particular risk to an insurance company, which is set up to spread out the financial burdens of risk.

  4. During a specific time period, the insured business or individual pays money (a premium) to the insurance carrier (either a private company or a government agency). In return, the career promises to pay the insured a certain amount of money in the event of a loss.

VI. The Basics of Insurance

A. Described

1. Insurance is the transfer of risk from one entity (an individual, a group, or a business) to an insurance company.
   a) It is estimated that 50 percent of small businesses are either not insured or are grossly underinsured.
2. How can insurance companies assume so much risk?
3. The law of large numbers.
   a) A business owner's premiums of $1,000 per year for fire insurance are pooled with those of thousands of other business owners. Out of this pool, the insurance company pays out benefits to what it hopes is only a small fraction of those paying premiums.
   b) Even if in one year the benefits paid out are greater than the premiums paid in, the law of large numbers says that in the long run, the insurance company will have a surplus of premiums.
4. To be insurable, a situation or hazard must meet the following requirements:
   a) It must be possible to calculate the actual loss being insured.
   b) It must be possible to select the risk being insured.
   c) There must be enough potential policyholders to assume the risk.
5. Most insurance companies also like to be sure that the parties (individuals or businesses) are not concentrated in a single geographic area.
6. The risk management pyramid (Figure 20.2) is designed to help business owners decide how they should allocate their risk management dollars.
   a) Begin by identifying the primary risks your company faces.
   b) Then rate each event on three factors:
      (1) Severity. How much would the event affect your company's ability to operate?
      (2) Probability. How likely is the event to occur?
      (3) Cost. How much would it cost your company if the event occurred?
   c) Rate the event on each factor using a simple scale: A (high) to D (low).
      (1) For instance, a small company might rate a fire in its manufacturing plant as ABA.
      (2) On the other hand, that same company might rank a computer system crash as CBA.
   d) Using the risk management pyramid, the business owner sees that the event rated ABA is higher on the risk scale than the event rated CBA. Therefore, this company would focus more of its risk management dollars on preventing the fire in its plant than on dealing with a computer system crash.

B. Types of Insurance

1. The ability to get adequate coverage and to pay the premiums is a significant factor in starting and running a small business.
   a) Sometimes just finding coverage for their business is a challenge for entrepreneurs.

2. Sometimes entrepreneurs purchase the insurance they need through non-insurance groups like the Small Office Home Office Association (SOHOA), a trade association for home-based businesses in Reston, Virginia.

3. Some types of insurance are essential to providing a secure future for the company; others may provide additional employee benefits.

    a) Figure 20.2 illustrates the risk management pyramid, a tool designed to help business owners decide the risks they should focus their resources on preventing, reducing, or insuring against.

4. The four major categories of insurance are property and casualty insurance, life and disability insurance, health insurance and workers' compensation coverage, and liability insurance.

    a) Each category is divided into many specific types, each of which has many variations offered by insurance companies.

    b) Small business owners should begin by purchasing a basic business owner's policy (BOP), which typically includes basic property, casualty, and liability insurance coverage.

    c) Entrepreneurs should then customize their insurance coverage to suit their company's special needs by purchasing additional types of coverage.

5. Property and casualty insurance

    a) Property and casualty insurance covers a company's tangible assets, such as buildings, equipment, inventory, machinery, signs, and others that have been damaged, destroyed, or stolen.

    b) Business owners should be sure that their policies cover the replacement cost of their property, not just its value at the time of the loss, even if it costs extra.

        (1) Specific types of property and casualty insurance include property, business interruption, surety, marine, crime, liability, and professional liability insurance.

    c) Property insurance protects a company's tangible assets against loss from damage, theft, and destruction.

        (1) It applies to automobiles, boats, homes, office buildings, stores, factories, and other items of property.

        (2) Some property insurance policies are broadly written to include all of an individual's property up to some maximum amount of loss, whereas other policies are written to cover only one building or one specific piece of property, such as a company car.

        (3) In some parts of the United States, business owners must buy separate insurance policies for specific causes of loss.

    d) Extra expense coverage pays for the costs of temporarily relocating workers and machinery so that a business can continue to operate while it rebuilds or repairs its factory.

    e) A similar type of insurance, called business interruption insurance, covers a business owner's lost income and ongoing expenses when the company cannot operate for an extended period of time.

    f) A business may also purchase surety insurance, which protects against losses to customers that occur when a contract is not completed on time or is completed incorrectly.

        (1) Surety protection guarantees customers that they will get either the products or services they purchased or the money to cover losses from contractual failures.

    g) Businesses also buy insurance to protect themselves from losses that occur when either finished goods or raw materials are lost or destroyed while being shipped.

(1) Marine insurance is designed to cover the risk associated with goods in transit. The name of this insurance goes back to the days when a ship's cargo was insured against high risks associated with ocean navigation.

h) Crime insurance does not deter crime, but it can reimburse the small business owner for losses from the three Ds: dishonesty, disappearance, and destruction.

6. Life and disability insurance

a) Unlike most forms of insurance, life insurance does not pertain to avoiding risk; death is a certainty for everyone.

b) Rather, life insurance protects families and businesses against loss of income, security, or personal services that results from an individual's death.

c) Many businesses insure the lives of key executives to offset the costs of having to make a hurried and often unplanned replacement of important managerial personnel.

(1) What would it take to replace a company's top sales representative? Its production supervisor?

(2) Key-person insurance provides valuable working capital to keep a business on track while it reorganizes and searches for the right person to replace the loss of someone in a key position in the company.

d) Pensions and annuities are special forms of life insurance policies that combine insurance with a form of saving.

(1) With an annuity or a pension plan, the insured person's premiums go partly to provide standard insurance coverage and partly to a fund that is invested by the insurance company.

(2) The interest from the invested portion of the policy is then used to pay an income to the policyholder when she reaches a certain age.

(3) If the policyholder dies before reaching that age, either the policy converts to income for the spouse or family of the insured or the insurance proceeds (plus interest) go to the beneficiary as they would in ordinary life insurance.

e) Disability insurance protects against losses resulting from an unexpected, and perhaps expensive, disablement.

(1) Because a sudden disability limits a person's ability to earn a living, the insurance proceeds are designed to help make up for the loss of what that person could have expected to earn if the accident had not occurred.

(2) Sometimes called income insurance, these policies usually guarantee a stated percentage of an individual's income--usually around 60 percent while he is recovering and is unable to run a business.

(3) In addition to the portion of income a policy will replace, another important factor to consider when purchasing disability insurance is the waiting period, the time gap between when the disability occurs and the disability payments begin.

7. Health insurance and workers' compensation

a) One of small business owners' greatest concerns in recent years has been the skyrocketing costs of health insurance.

b) Four basic health insurance options are available to employers:

(1) Traditional indemnity plans. Under these plans, employees choose their own health care providers, and the insurance company either pays the provider directly or reimburses employees for the covered amounts.

(2) Managed care plans. As part of employers' attempts to put a lid on escalating health care costs, managed care plans have become increasingly popular.

(a) Two variations, the health maintenance organization (HMO) and the preferred provider organization (PPO) are most common.

(b) An HMO is a prepaid health care arrangement under which employees must use health care providers who are employed by or are under contract with the HMO their company uses.

(c) Under a PPO, an insurance company negotiates discounts for health care with certain physicians and hospitals. Employees must choose a health care provider from the approved list, but they pay only a small fee for each office visit (often just $10 to $25).

(3) Medical savings accounts (MSAs). As its name implies, a medical savings account (MSA) is a special savings account coupled with a high-deductible insurance policy.

(a) Employees contribute pretax dollars from their paychecks into the fund and use them as they need to.

(b) Withdrawals from an MSA are not taxed as long as the money is used for approved medical expenses. Unused funds can accumulate indefinitely and earn tax-free interest.

(c) Only self-employed individuals or those who work for companies with 50 or fewer employees qualify for MSAs.

(4) Self-insurance. As we have seen earlier in this chapter, some business owners choose to insure themselves for health coverage.

(5) The benefits of self-insurance include greater control over the plan's design and the coverage it offers, fewer paperwork and reporting requirements, and, in some cases, lower costs.

(6) The primary disadvantage, of course, is the possibility of having to pay large amounts.

(7) Many self-insured businesses limit their exposure to such losses by purchasing stop-loss insurance.

c) Another type of health-related coverage is workers' compensation, which is designed to cover employees who are injured on the job or who become sick as a result of a work environment.

(1) Although the details of coverage vary from state to state, workers' compensation laws require employers to provide benefits and medical and rehabilitation costs for employees injured on the job.

(2) The amount of compensation an injured employee will receive is determined by a fixed schedule of benefits based on three factors: the wages or salary that the employee was earning at the time of the accident or injury, the seriousness of the injury, and the extent of the disability to the employee.

d) Only three states, New Jersey, South Carolina, and Texas, do not require companies to purchase workers' compensation coverage once they reach a certain size.

(1) Usually, the state sets the rates businesses pay for workers' compensation coverage, and business owners purchase their coverage from private insurance companies.

(2) Rates vary by industry, business size, and the number of claims a company's workers make.

8. Liability insurance

a) One of the most common types of insurance coverage.

b) It protects a business against losses resulting from accidents or injuries people suffer on the company's property or from its products or services and damage the company causes to others' property.

(1) Most BOPs include basic liability coverage; however, the limits on the coverage are not high enough to cover the potential losses many small business owners face.

      (2) Most insurance experts recommend at least $1 million of liability coverage for businesses.

      (3) A typical BOP does not include liability coverage for automobiles.

GAINING THE COMPETITIVE EDGE - Fighting Workers' Compensation Fraud

SUMMARY
Workers' compensation claims cost taxpayers more than $70 billion each year, and experts estimate that about 10 percent of that total goes to fraudulent claims. Fraud is expensive. It raises companies' insurance premiums, results in higher prices for consumers, reduces employee morale and productivity, and can even drive small companies out of business. Why is workers' compensation fraud so prevalent? It is easy to commit, and it is hard to detect. Fraud typically occurs in four areas of workers' compensation.

- Claimant fraud. Claimant fraud occurs when workers fabricate or exaggerate an injury claim to get paid time off. Another form of claimant fraud is called malingering, in which an employee with a legitimate injury stretches out the recovery time to extend workers' compensation payments.
- Insurer fraud. This type of fraud is often directed at small businesses and involves scare artists who peddle cut-rate, but nonexistent, workers' compensation policies to entrepreneurs with the promise of saving them big money.
- Provider fraud. Provider fraud occurs when a doctor or other health care professional collects payment for nonexistent or unnecessary treatments.
- Premium fraud. Sometimes businesses are the perpetrators of workers' compensation fraud. In a premium fraud scare, dishonest business owners cheat insurers by understating the number of workers they have, misclassifying the nature of workers' jobs to make them sound less risky, or changing the names of their companies to mask poor safety records.

In recent years, employers' cost for workers' compensation per $100 of payroll has actually fallen because insurers, states, and employers have been cracking down on fraud. How can business owners help combat workers' compensation fraud?
- Maintain a safe workplace. Involve workers in identifying and removing safety risks.
- Screen all job applicants carefully.
- Give all workers a written statement of your company's workers' compensation policies and procedures.
- Be wary of insurers offering cut-rate insurance coverage.
- Work closely with your insurer.
- Document all workers' compensation claims thoroughly.
- Listen to your workers. In many cases, they are aware of the fraud and are willing to talk about it.

If you suspect a worker has committed fraud, contact your insurance company and let them handle it. By working closely with their insurers, small business owners can save themselves a lot of money.

---

      c) Another important type of liability insurance for many small businesses is professional liability insurance, or "errors and omissions" coverage.

      d) This coverage protects against damage a business causes to customers or clients as a result of an employee's error or failure to take proper care and precautions.

      e) Employment practices liability insurance provides protection against claims arising from charges of employment discrimination, sexual harassment, and violations of the Americans with Disabilities Act, the Family and Medical Leave Act, and other employment legislation.

          (1) Because awards for this type of lawsuit are quite high (see Figure 20.3A) and such suits are likely to be successful (see Figure 20.3B), this is one of the fastest-growing forms of insurance coverage.

      f) Liability insurance for some small businesses has become increasingly difficult to obtain, and, at the same time, premiums have skyrocketed, pricing some businesses out of the market.

C. Controlling Insurance Costs
1. Business owners must take steps to lower insurance costs, such as:
   a) Pursue a loss-control program, by making risk reduction a natural part of all employees' daily routine.
   b) Increase their policies' deductibles. If a business can afford to handle minor losses, the owner can save money by raising the deductible.
   c) Work with a qualified professional insurance broker or agent.
   d) Work actively with brokers to make sure they understand the business owner's particular needs.
   e) Work with brokers to find competitive companies that want small companies' insurance business and have the proven resources to cover losses when they arise.
      (1) The price of the premium should never be an entrepreneur's sole criterion for selecting insurance.
      (2) The rating of the insurance company should always be a primary consideration.
2. To control the cost of health insurance, the small business owner should consider the following:
   a) Increase the dollar amount of employee contributions and the amount of the employee's deductibles.
   b) Switch to HMOs or PPOs. Although some employees resent being told where they must go to receive treatment, the number of businesses offering the HMO and PPO options to employees is rising.
   c) Conduct a yearly utilization review.
   d) Create a wellness program for all employees. Companies that have created wellness programs report cost savings of $6 for every $1 they invest.
   e) Conduct a safety audit. The National Safety Council (1-800-621-7615) offers helpful information on creating a safer work environment.
   f) Create a safety manual and use it.
   g) Create a safety team.
3. The key to controlling insurance costs is aggressive prevention.
4. The key to dealing with those differences is to identify the risks that represent the greatest threat to a company and then to develop a plan for minimizing their risk of occurrence and insuring against them if they do.

Chapter Summary

♦ Explain the factors necessary for a strong family business.
  ▪ More than 80 percent of all companies in the United States are family-owned. Family businesses generate 50 percent of the U.S. gross domestic product, employ more than 40 million people, and pay 65 percent of all wages. Several factors are important to maintaining a strong family business, including: shared values, shared power, tradition, a willingness to learn, behaving like families, and strong family ties.

♦ Understand the exit strategy options available to an entrepreneur.
  ▪ Family business owners wanting to step down from their companies can sell to outsiders, sell to insiders, or transfer ownership to the next generation of family members. Common tools for

selling to insiders (employees or managers) include sale for cash plus a note, leveraged buyouts (LBOs), and employee stock ownership plans (ESOPs).

- Transferring ownership to the next generation of family members requires a business owner to develop a sound management succession plan.

◆ Discuss the stages of management succession.

- Unfortunately, 70 percent of first-generation businesses fail to survive into the second generation, and, of those that do, only 13 percent make it to the third generation. One of the primary reasons for this lack of continuity is poor succession planning. Planning for management succession protects not only the founder's, successor's, and company's financial resources, but it also preserves what matters most in a successful business: its heritage and tradition. Management succession planning can ensure a smooth transition only if the founder begins the process early on.

◆ Explain how to develop an effective management succession plan.

- A succession plan is a crucial element in transferring a company to the next generation. Preparing a succession plan involves five steps: (1) Select the successor; (2) create a survival kit for the successor; (3) groom the successor; (4) promote an environment of trust and respect; (5) cope with the financial realities of estate taxes.

- Entrepreneurs can rely on several tools in their estate planning, including buy/sell agreements, lifetime gifting, trusts, estate freezes, and family limited partnerships.

◆ Understand the four risk management strategies.

- Four risk strategies are available to the small business: avoiding, reducing, anticipating, and transferring risk.

◆ Discuss the basics of insurance for small businesses.

- Insurance is a risk transfer strategy. Not every potential loss can be insured. Insurability requires that it be possible to estimate the amount of actual loss being insured against and to identify the specific risk and that there be enough policyholders to spread out the risk.

- The four major types of insurance small businesses need are property and casualty insurance, life and disability insurance, health insurance and worker's compensation coverage, and liability insurance.

- Property and casualty insurance covers a company's tangible assets, such as buildings, equipment, inventory, machinery, signs, and others that have been damaged, destroyed, or stolen. Specific types of property and casualty insurance include extra expense coverage, business interruption insurance, surety insurance, marine insurance, crime insurance, fidelity insurance, and forgery insurance.

- Life and disability insurance also comes in various forms. Life insurance protects a family and a business against the loss of income and security in the event of the owner's death. Disability insurance, like life insurance, protects an individual in the event of unexpected and often very expensive disabilities.

- Health insurance is designed to provide adequate health care for business owners and their employees. Workers' compensation is designed to cover employees who are injured on the job or who become sick as a result of a work environment.

- Liability insurance protects a business against losses resulting from accidents or injuries people suffer on the company's property, from its products or services, and damage the company causes to others' property. Typical liability coverage includes professional liability insurance or "errors and omissions" coverage, which protects against damage a business causes to customers or clients as a result of an error an employee makes or an employee's failure to take proper care and precautions. Doctors, dentists, attorneys, and other professionals protect themselves through a similar kind of insurance, malpractice insurance, which protects them against the risk of lawsuits arising from errors in professional practice or judgment. Employment practices liability insurance provides protection against claims arising from charges of employment discrimination, sexual harassment, and violations of the Americans with Disabilities Act, the Family and Medical Leave Act, and other employment legislation.

Discussion Questions

1. What factors must be present for a strong family business?

    Answer - More than 80 percent of all companies in the United States are family-owned. Those factors that make for a strong family business are: 1) The first, and probably most overlooked, quality is a set of shared values, 2) shared power is based on the idea that family members should allow those with the greatest expertise, ability, and knowledge in particular areas to handle decisions in those areas; 3) tradition is necessary for a family business because it serves to bond family members and to link one generation of business leaders to the next; 4) a willingness to learn; family members trust one another enough to express their ideas, thoughts, and suggestions openly and honestly; 5) families that play together operate family businesses that are likely to stay together; 6) Strong family ties grow from one-on-one relationships.

2. Discuss the stages of management succession in a family business.

    Answer - Management succession involves a lengthy series of interconnected stages that begin very early in the life of the owner's children and extend to the point of final ownership transition. See Figure 20.1.
    -   If management succession is to be effective, it is necessary for the process to begin early in the successor's life (Stage 1).
    -   During this Stage 2, the individual rotates among a variety of job functions both to broaden his base of understanding of the business and to permit the parents to evaluate his skills.
    -   At Stage 3, the successor becomes a full-time worker and ideally has already earned the respect of coworkers through his behavior in the first two stages of the process. Stage 3 focuses on the successor's continuous development.
    -   As the successor develops his skills and performance, he moves to Stage 4. This is the period when the founder makes a final assessment of the individual's abilities to take full and complete control over the firm.
    -   The final stage involves the ultimate transition of organizational leadership. Often, the successor becomes the organization's CEO while the former CEO retains the title of chairman of the board.

3. What steps are involved in building a successful management succession plan?

    Answer - There are five key steps.
    -   Step 1. Select the successor. Entrepreneurs should never assume that their children want to take control of the business.
    -   Step 2. Create a survival kit for the successor. Once he identifies a successor, the entrepreneur should prepare a survival kit and then brief the future leader on its contents, which should include all of the company's critical documents (wills, trusts, insurance policies, financial statements, bank accounts, key contracts, corporate bylaws, and so forth).
    -   Step 3. Groom the successor. This is the process by which business founders transfer their knowledge to the next generation.
    -   Step 4. Promote an environment of trust and respect. Developing a competent successor over a period of five to ten years is realistic. Empowering the successor by gradually delegating responsibilities creates an environment in which customers, creditors, suppliers, and staff members can objectively view the successor's growth and development and gradually develop confidence in him.
    -   Step 5. Cope with the financial realities of estate and gift taxes. Entrepreneurs who fail to consider the impact of these taxes may force their heirs to sell a successful business just to pay the estate's tax bill.

4. What exit strategies are available to entrepreneurs wanting to step down from their business?
   Answer - Most family business founders want their companies to stay within their families, although, in some cases, maintaining family control is not practical. Sometimes, no one in the next generation of family members has an interest in managing the company or has the necessary skills and experience to handle the job.
   - Selling to outsiders. A straight sale may be best for entrepreneurs who want to step down and turn the reins over to someone else.
   - Selling to insiders. When entrepreneurs have no family members to whom they can transfer ownership or who want to assume the responsibilities of running a company, selling the business to employees is often the preferred option. In most situations, the options available to owners are (1) sale for cash plus a note, (2) a leveraged buyout, and (3) an employee stock ownership plan (ESOP).
   - The third exit strategy available to company founders is transferring ownership to the next generation of family members with the help of a comprehensive management succession plan.

5. What strategies can business owners employ to reduce estate and gift taxes?
   Answer - Many estate planning tools need time to work their magic, so the key is to put them in place early on in the life of the business.
   - A buy/sell agreement is a contract that co-owners often rely on to ensure the continuity of a business. In a typical arrangement, the co-owners create a contract stating that each agrees to buy the other out in case of the death or disability of one. The buy/sell agreement specifies a formula for determining the value of the business at the time the agreement is to be executed.
   - The owners of a successful business may transfer money to their children (or other recipients) from their estate throughout their lives. Current federal tax regulations allow individuals to make gifts of $10,000 per year, per parent, per recipient, that are exempt from federal gift taxes.
   - A trust is a contract between a grantor (the founder) and a trustee (generally a bank officer or an attorney) in which the grantor gives to the trustee legal title to assets (e.g., stock in the company), which the trustee agrees to hold for the beneficiaries (children). Two broad categories of trusts are available: revocable trusts and irrevocable trusts.
   - An estate freeze attempts to minimize estate taxes by having family members create two classes of stock for the business: 1) preferred voting stock for the parents and 2) nonvoting common stock for the children. The value of the preferred stock is frozen while the common stock reflects the anticipated increased market value of the business.
   - Creating a family limited partnership (FLP) allows business-owning parents to transfer their company to their children (thus lowering their estate taxes) while still retaining control over it for themselves. To create a family limited partnership, the parents (or parent) set up a partnership among themselves and their children.

6. Can insurance eliminate risk? Why or why not?
   Answer - Insurance is an important part of creating a management succession plan because it can help business owners minimize the taxes on the estates they pass on. Insurance plays an important role in many other aspects of a successful business--from covering employee injuries to protecting against natural disasters that might shut a business down temporarily.

   When most small business owners think of risks such as these, they automatically think of insurance. Insurance does not solve all risk problems because not all risk problems are insurance problems. Dealing with risk successfully requires a combination of four risk management strategies: avoiding, reducing, anticipating, and transferring (or spreading) risk. See question #7.

7. Outline the four basic risk management strategies and give an example of each.
   Answer - 1) Avoiding risk requires a business to take actions to shun risky situations. But avoiding risk altogether usually is not practical. 2) A risk-reducing strategy takes actions that build an extra degree of safety into a situation with an identified level of risk. Risk reduction strategies do not eliminate the source of the risk, they only lessen the impact of its occurrence. Even with avoidance and reduction strategies, the source of the risk is still present; thus, losses can occur. 3) Risk anticipation promote self-insurance. Knowing that some element of risk still exists, a business owner puts aside money each month to cover any losses that might occur. 4) Most individuals and businesses therefore include in their risk strategies some form of insurance to transfer risk. Insurance is a risk transfer (or risk-spreading) strategy because an individual or a business transfers some of the costs of a particular risk to an insurance company, which is set up to spread out the financial burdens of risk.

8. What problems occur most frequently with a risk-anticipating strategy?
   Answer - Risk anticipation promotes self-insurance. Knowing that some element of risk still exists, a business owner puts aside money each month to cover any losses that might occur. Sometimes a self-insurance fund set aside may not be large enough to cover the losses from a particular situation. This raises the necessity of transferring risk. The owner needs stop-loss insurance to fill in the gap between self-insurance and the total liability.

9. What is insurance? How can insurance companies bear such a large risk burden and still be profitable?
   Answer - Insurance is a risk transfer (or risk-spreading) strategy because an individual or a business transfers some of the costs of a particular risk to an insurance company, which is set up to spread out the financial burdens of risk. During a specific time period, the insured business or individual pays money (a premium) to the insurance carrier (either a private company or a government agency). In return, the career promises to pay the insured a certain amount of money in the event of a loss.

   How can insurance companies assume so much risk? Through the law of large numbers. A business owner's premiums of $1,000 per year for fire insurance are pooled with those of thousands of other business owners. Out of this pool, the insurance company pays out benefits to what it hopes is only a small fraction of those paying premiums. Even if in one year the benefits paid out are greater than the premiums paid in, the law of large numbers says that, in the long run, the insurance company will have a surplus of premiums.

10. Describe the requirements for insurability.
    Answer - To be insurable, a situation or hazard must meet the following requirements:
    - It must be possible to calculate the actual loss being insured.
    - It must be possible to select the risk being insured.
    - There must be enough potential policyholders to assume the risk.
    Most insurance companies also like to be sure that the parties (individuals or businesses) are not concentrated in a single geographic area.

11. Briefly describe the various types of insurance coverage available to small business owners.
    Answer - Some types of insurance are essential to providing a secure future for the company; others may provide additional employee benefits. Figure 20.2 illustrates the risk management pyramid, a tool designed to help business owners decide the risks they should focus their resources on preventing, reducing, or insuring against. The four major categories of insurance are property and casualty insurance, life and disability insurance, health insurance and workers' compensation coverage, and liability insurance.

- Property and casualty insurance covers a company's tangible assets, such as buildings, equipment, inventory, machinery, signs, and others that have been damaged, destroyed, or stolen. Specific types of property and casualty insurance include property, business interruption, surety, marine, crime, liability, and professional liability insurance.
- Life and disability insurance. Life insurance protects families and businesses against loss of income, security, or personal services that results from an individual's death. Many businesses insure the lives of key executives to offset the costs of having to make a hurried and often unplanned replacement of important managerial personnel. Disability insurance protects against losses resulting from an unexpected, and perhaps expensive, disablement.
- Health insurance and workers' compensation. Four basic health insurance options are available to employers:
    - Traditional indemnity plans. Under these plans, employees choose their own health care providers, and the insurance company either pays the provider directly or reimburses employees for the covered amounts.
    - Managed care plans. As part of employers' attempts to put a lid on escalating health care costs, managed care plans have become increasingly popular.
    - Medical savings accounts (MSAs). As its name implies, a medical savings account (MSA) is a special savings account coupled with a high-deductible insurance policy.
    - Self-insurance. As we have seen earlier in this chapter, some business owners choose to insure themselves for health coverage.
- Another type of health-related coverage is workers' compensation, which is designed to cover employees who are injured on the job or who become sick as a result of a work environment.
- Liability Insurance. One of the most common types of insurance coverage. It protects a business against losses resulting from accidents or injuries people suffer on the company's property or from its products or services and damage the company causes to others' property.

12. What kinds of insurance coverage would you recommend for the following businesses? A manufacturer of steel sheets? A retail gift shop? A small accounting firm? A limited liability partnership involving three dentists?
   Answer - All of the businesses would need a basic BOP with key man/woman life insurance. Things to strengthen in each would be:
   - A manufacturer of steel sheets - property, disability, worker's comp.
   - A retail gift shop - property, business interruption.
   - A small accounting firm - disability, professional liability.
   - A limited liability partnership involving three dentists - disability, professional liability.

13. What can business owners do to keep their insurance costs under control?
   Answer - Business owners can lower insurance costs by:
   - Pursuing a loss-control program, by making risk reduction a natural part of all employees' daily routine.
   - Increase their policies' deductibles. If a business can afford to handle minor losses, the owner can save money by raising the deductible.
   - Control the cost of health insurance by increasing the dollar amount of employee contributions and the amount of the employee's deductibles, etc.

Step into the Real World
1. Interview two local business owners about their companies' management succession plans. Do the owners have succession plans? If so, how are they structured? Who have they designated to take over their business? What is the timetable for implementing the plan? What impact will estate and gift

taxes have on the transfer of ownership? What provisions have they made to minimize the impact of those taxes? Write a two-page report on what you learned from your experience.

2. Contact an attorney and an accountant and ask them what steps they recommend small business owners take to plan for management succession. Are their small business clients well prepared to deal with management succession issues? Why or why not? What are the implications for those who are not well prepared?

    a. Interview two small business owners in the local community and report on the types of insurance coverage each carries. Did they have difficulty finding insurance coverage?

    b. Contact an insurance agent and ask about the insurance coverage he or she would recommend for the types of businesses whose owners you interviewed. Do you see any gaps? If so, how much would the additional coverage cost? If the business owners are underinsured, what are the potential consequences of incurring losses?

Chapter 21 - Ethics, Social Responsibility, and the Entrepreneur

> Reputations are longer in the making than in the losing.
> Paul Von Ringelheim

> Watch your thoughts; they become words.
> Watch your words; they become actions.
> Watch your actions; they become habits.
> Watch your habits; they become character.
> Watch your character; it becomes your destiny.
> Frank Outlaw

Teaching Objectives

Students will be able to:
1. Define business ethics and describe the three levels of ethical standards.
2. Determine who is responsible for ethical behavior and why ethical lapses occur.
3. Explain how to establish and maintain high ethical standards.
4. Define social responsibility.
5. Understand the nature of business's responsibility to the environment.
6. Describe business's responsibility to employees.
7. Explain business's responsibility to customers.
8. Discuss business's responsibility to investors.
9. Describe business's responsibility to the community.

Instructor's Outline

I. Introduction
    A. The Ethical Issue
        1. Earning a profit is one of an entrepreneur's primary reasons for going into business, and it is an essential requirement for staying in business.
        2. But does a small company's responsibility end with earning a profit?
        3. A recent *Business Week*/Harris poll found that 95 percent of adults reject the view that a company's only role is to make money.
        4. Ethics involves the moral values and behavioral standards businesspeople draw on as they make decisions and solve problems.
           a) It originates from a commitment to do what is right.
           b) Ethical behavior--doing what is "right" and "good" as opposed to "wrong" and "bad"--is the result of such a commitment.
        5. An inherent difficulty exists in determining what constitutes ethical behavior.
        6. In most situations, ethical dilemmas are less obvious, cloaked in the garb of mundane decisions and everyday routine.
           a) To make proper ethical choices, an entrepreneur must first be aware that a situation with ethical dimensions exists.
           b) Complicating the issue even more is that, in some ethical dilemmas, no clear-cut, right (or wrong) answers exist.
        7. There is the issue of conflicting interests among the company's various stakeholders, the various groups and individuals who affect and are affected by the company.
           a) These conflicts have forced many businesses to identify their stakeholders and to consider the ways they will deal with them.
           b) The power these stakeholders wield determines to a great extent the degree of success a company can achieve.

       c) To make a decision, an entrepreneur often must balance the needs and the demands of various stakeholders.

   8. Society is demanding a higher standard of behavior from businesses today, and businesses large and small must reevaluate their responsibilities to society as a whole.

       a) A socially responsible business considers not only what is best for the firm but also what is best for society.

II. Ethical Perspective

A. Introduction

1. Business ethics consists of the fundamental moral values and behavioral standards that form the foundation for the people of an organization as they make decisions and interact with stakeholders.

2. Maintaining an ethical perspective is crucial to creating and protecting a company's reputation, but it is no easy task.

3. Although every company confronts ethically charged issues, the limited resources of small start-ups make them extremely susceptible to ethical breaches.

4. Succumbing to unethical temptations ultimately will destroy a company's reputation.

       a) And reputation is one of the most precious, and most fragile, possessions a company has.

5. Building a solid reputation for ethical propriety typically takes a long time; unfortunately, destroying that reputation takes practically no time at all, and the effects linger.

B. Three Levels of Ethical Standards

1. The law, which defines for society as a whole what actions are permissible and which are not.

       a) The law merely establishes the minimum standard of behavior.

       b) Few ethical issues are so uncomplicated and unidimensional that the law can serve as the acid test for making a decision.

2. The policies and procedures of the organization, which serve as specific guidelines for people as they make daily decisions.

       a) Research suggests that some 95 percent of Fortune 500 companies and nearly half of all businesses have written codes of ethics in place.

3. The moral stance individuals take when faced with a decision not governed by formal rules.

       a) The values people learn from an early age in the family, in church or synagogue, and in school are key ingredients at this level.

       b) A major determinant of ethical behavior is training.

4. Every businessperson faces at least one ethical issue every day, and some ethical choices can be tough to make.

       a) "Morals are like muscles. The more we flex them, the stronger they get."

       b) Ethics is a practical skill.

5. The pressure to take shortcuts or to violate ethical standards is always present.

       a) One classic study reported that, at some point in their careers, 75 percent of managers felt a conflict between profit considerations and being ethical.

       b) Another study indicated that 65 percent of managers sometimes felt pressure to compromise their personal ethical standards.

       c) Without a supportive ethical structure, employees in such positions are likely to make the "wrong" ethical choices, and that can be devastating.

WIRED TO THE WEB - The Ethics of Marketing to Kids on the Web

SUMMARY
Brauer Software is a small but innovative producer of educational software targeted at children aged 9 to 14. Al started the company from a spare bedroom in his home 15 years ago, and the company grew steadily over the years. Educational organizations raved about the quality of the company's software, and parents eagerly awaited the release of each package. Products covered a wide range of educational topics, from science and math to English and other languages. Brauer Software relied on a team of experienced education experts to design each program, who then worked closely with teams of programmers to implement their designs.

Recently, Brauer had seen an opportunity to use the company's excellent reputation with both children and parents to move into software that was designed strictly for entertainment, a fast-growing aspect of the software industry. The company had launched seven new games aimed specifically at children. They set up a Web site separate from its educational software site. This new site was designed exclusively for kids, with lots of bright colors, funky music, and action, including demo versions of the games the company was selling. Anyone could enter the site, but those who completed periodic marketing surveys could earn "Kid's Kash" a form of virtual money they could exchange for games, discounts, and prizes.

Parents and educators reacted very negatively to the Web site and Kids Kash. They felt that Brauer was using manipulative advertising techniques on the World Wide Web, and they petitioned the Federal Trade Commission to look into it. Newspaper articles came out, such as, "Companies are acting unethically when they use their Web sites as lures for young children to collect specific information from them without parental approval. No other medium has captured children's interest like the Web, and companies like Brauer Software should be ashamed for abusing it to sell to kids."

1. Use the World Wide Web to research the issue of companies' using the Web to advertise to children. Find at least two sites addressing this issue, and summarize their points of view. What is your view on this issue?
    Answer - Students' responses will vary.
2. Do you think Brauer Software has acted unethically? Explain.
    Answer - Students can argue both sides of this issue legitimately. The central question may be how "informed" a consumer a child is. Our free market system largely depends on the consumer to protect him or herself from exploitation and manipulation. Are these companies targeting kids who are not and cannot be informed sophisticated consumers?
3. On the basis of what you read in this chapter and on what you found on the World Wide Web, what actions would you advise Al Brauer and Kara Hernandez to take? What outcomes do you predict for Brauer Software if Brauer and Hernandez do nothing?
    Answer - Students' responses will vary. One reality check, this company does not have the financial resources for a prolonged court battle against the government or consumers. Practically, the company will probably have to pull the Web site unless they can find an organization to fund the court battle. From a PR standpoint, Brauer should mount a limited media campaign, apologize for the unexpected effect and ask parents for ideas on how to meet their two needs, i.e., market the product but not exploit children. This might win over some of their foes.

C. An Ethical Framework
    1. Step 1. Recognize the ethical dimensions involved in the dilemma or decision.
        a) Before an entrepreneur can make an informed ethical decision, she must recognize that an ethical situation exists.

          b) Too often, business owners fail to take into account the ethical impact of a particular course of action until it is too late.

    2. Step 2. Identify the key stakeholders involved and determine how the decision will affect them.

          a) Every business influences, and is influenced by, a multitude of stakeholders.

          b) Frequently, the demands of these stakeholders conflict with one another, putting a business in the position of having to choose which groups to satisfy and which to alienate.

          c) Analysis may not resolve the conflict; it will prevent the company from inadvertently causing harm to people it may have failed to consider.

    3. Step 3. Generate alternative choices and distinguish between ethical and unethical responses.

          a) Small business managers will find the questions in Table 21.1 to be helpful.

    4. Step 4. Choose the "best" ethical response and implement it.

          a) At this point, there likely will be several ethical choices from which managers can pick.

          b) The final choice must be consistent with the company's goals, culture, and value system as well as those of the individual decision makers.

III. Who is Responsible for Ethical Behavior?

  A. Introduction

    1. Although companies may set ethical standards and offer guidelines for employees, the ultimate decision on whether to abide by ethical principles rests with the individual.

    2. Good ethics starts at the top and works its way downward through the entire organization.

    3. Table 21.2 summarizes the characteristics of the three ethical styles of management: immoral, amoral, and moral management.

  B. The Benefits of Moral Management

    1. One of the most common misconceptions about business is that there is a contradiction between ethics and profits.

          a) Andrew Warner of Nolo Press says, "I've never seen the dichotomy over the long term between running a principled business and a profitable one."

          b) 63 percent of business professionals feel that "a business enterprise actually strengthens its competitive position by maintaining high ethical standards."

    2. Other benefits

          a) First, the company avoids the damaging effects of a reputation as an unethical business.

          b) Second, a solid ethical framework guides managers as they cope with an increasingly complex network of external influence, from government regulation and special interest groups to suppliers and the media.

          c) Finally, ethical companies earn the respect of two essential groups: customers and employees.

          d) The ethics factor is intangible and virtually impossible to quantify but is something that customers and employees clearly recognize and consider when deciding where to shop and where to work.

  C. Why Ethical Lapses Occur

    1. The "bad apple"

          a) Ethical decisions are individual decisions, and some people are corrupt.

    2. The "bad barrel"

          a) In some cases, the company culture has been poisoned with an unethical overtone.

3. Moral blindness
   a) Sometimes, fundamentally ethical people commit ethical blunders because they are blind to the ethical implications of their conduct.
   b) One of the most common mechanisms is rationalization:
      (1) "Everybody does it."
      (2) "If they were in my place, they'd do it too."
      (3) "Being ethical is a luxury I cannot afford right now."
      (4) "The impact of my decision/action on (whomever or whatever) is not my concern."
      (5) "I don't get paid to be ethical; I get paid to produce results."
   c) Training in ethical thinking and creating an environment that encourages considering the ethical impact of decisions can reduce moral blindness.
4. Competitive pressures
   a) If competition is so intense that a company's survival is threatened, managers may begin to view as acceptable what were once unacceptable options.
   b) A study conducted by the Ethics Resource Center found that 30 percent of employees admitted to feeling pressure to compromise their company's ethical standards because of deadlines, overly aggressive objectives, concerns about the company's survival, and other factors.
5. Opportunity pressures
   a) When the opportunity to "get ahead" by taking some unethical action presents itself, some people cannot resist the temptation.
   b) The greater the reward or the smaller the penalty for unethical acts, the greater is the probability that such behavior will occur.
6. Globalization of business
   a) Companies have discovered that there is no single standard of ethical behavior applying to all business decisions in the international arena.
   b) Practices that are illegal in one country may be perfectly acceptable, even expected, in another.

IV. Establishing Ethical Standards
   A. Ethical Tests for Judging Behavior
      1. The utilitarian principle. Choose the option that offers the greatest good for the greatest number of people.
      2. Kant's categorical imperative. Act in such a way that the action taken under the circumstances could be a universal law or rule of behavior.
      3. The professional ethic. Take only those actions that a disinterested panel of professional colleagues would view as proper.
      4. The Golden Rule. Treat other people the way you would like them to treat you.
      5. The television test. Would you and your colleagues feel comfortable explaining your actions to a national television audience?
      6. The family test. Would you be comfortable explaining to your children, your spouse, and your parents why you took this action?
      7. Table 21.3 describes ten ethical principles that differentiate between right and wrong, thereby offering a guideline for ethical behavior.

   B. Implementing and Maintaining Ethical Standards
      1. A workable ethics program recognizes that a company has a greater responsibility to society than just earning a profit.
      2. What can managers do to integrate ethical principles into their companies?
      3. Create a company credo.

      a) A company credo defines the values underlying the entire company and its ethical responsibilities to its stakeholders.

      b) It offers general guidance in ethical issues. The most effective credos capture the elusive essence of a company--what it stands for and why it's important, and can be an important ingredient in the company's competitive edge.

      c) A credo is an excellent way to transform those values into employees' ethical behavior.

4. Develop a code of ethics.

      a) A code of ethics is a written statement of the standards of behavior and ethical principles a company expects from its employees.

      b) They do not ensure ethical behavior, but they do establish minimum standards of behavior throughout the organization.

      c) Workers who will be directly affected by the code should have a hand in developing it.

5. Enforce the code fairly and consistently.

      a) Managers must take action when they discover ethical violations.

      b) If employees learn that ethical breaches go unpunished, the code of ethics becomes meaningless.

6. Conduct ethics training.

      a) One of the most effective ways to display that commitment is through ethical training designed to raise employees' consciousness of potential ethical dilemmas.

      b) Ethics training programs not only raise employees' awareness of ethical issues, but they also communicate to them the core of the company's value system.

7. Hire the right people.

      a) Ultimately, the decision in any ethical situation belongs to the individual.

      b) To make ethical decisions, people must have:

         (1) Ethical commitment--the personal resolve to act ethically and do the right thing.

         (2) Ethical consciousness--the ability to perceive the ethical implications of a situation.

         (3) Ethical competency--the ability to engage in sound moral reasoning and develop practical problem-solving strategies.

8. Perform periodic ethical audits.

      a) These reviews send a signal to employees that ethics is not just a passing fad.

9. Establish high standards of behavior, not just rules.

      a) All employees must understand that ethics is not negotiable.

      b) The role that the entrepreneur plays in establishing high ethical standards is critical.

10. Set an impeccable ethical example at all times.

      a) Remember that ethics starts at the top.

      b) Workers believe managers' actions more than their words.

11. Create a culture that emphasizes two-way communication.

      a) Employees must have the opportunity to report any ethical violations they observe.

12. Involve employees in establishing ethical standards.

      a) Involving employees improves the quality of a firm's ethical standards and increases the likelihood of employee compliance.

V. The Issue of Social Responsibility

  A. Described

      1. Since the 1980s, society has imposed a higher standard on businesses: Companies must go beyond "doing well"--simply earning a profit--to "doing good"--living up to their social responsibilities.

2. Today, customers are increasingly demanding the companies they buy goods and services from to be socially responsible.
   a) When customers shop for "value," they also consider the company's stance on social responsibility.
   b) In a recent survey by the Walker Group, nearly 90 percent of consumers said that when price, service, and quality are equal among competitors, they will buy from the company that has the best reputation for social responsibility.
   c) The survey also revealed that 70 percent of consumers would not buy, at any price, from a company that was not socially responsible.

B. Putting Social Responsibility into Practice
   1. One problem facing businesses is defining just what social responsibility is.
      a) Is it manufacturing environmentally friendly products?
      b) Is it donating a portion of profits to charitable organizations?
      c) Is it creating jobs in inner cities plagued by high unemployment levels?
   2. The specific nature of a company's social responsibility efforts will depend on how its owners, employees, and other stakeholders define what it means to be socially responsible.
   3. Social responsibility is the awareness by a company's managers of the social, environmental, political, human, and financial consequences their actions produce.

VI. Business's Responsibility to the Environment
   A. Described
      1. Driven by their customers' interest in protecting the environment, companies have become more sensitive to the impact their products, processes, and packaging have on the planet.
      2. Environmentalism has become and will continue to be one of the dominant issues for companies worldwide because consumers have added another item to their list of buying criteria: environmental safety.
      3. Socially responsible business owners focus on the three Rs: reduce, reuse, recycle.
         a) Reduce the amount of materials used in your company, from the factory floor to the copier room.
         b) Reuse whatever you can.
         c) Recycle the materials that you must dispose off
      4. Truly progressive companies are creating redesigned, "clean" manufacturing systems that focus on avoiding waste and pollution.
         a) These companies design their products, packaging, and processes from the start with the environment in mind, working to eliminate hazardous materials and byproducts and looking for ways to turn what had been scrap into salable products.
         b) Table 2 1.4 offers a list of questions environmentally responsible entrepreneurs should ask themselves.

VII. Business' Responsibility to Employees
   A. Described
      1. Few other stakeholders are as important to a business as its employees.
      2. How can business owners prove to employees that they really are the company's number one asset?
         a) Listen to employees and respect their opinions.
         b) Ask for their input; involve them in the decision-making process.
         c) Provide regular feedback--positive and negative--to employees.
         d) Tell them the truth--always.

    e) Let them know exactly what's expected of them.

    f) Reward employees for performing their jobs well.

    g) Trust them: create an environment of respect and teamwork.

IN THE FOOTSTEPS OF AN ENTREPRENEUR - Following Nature's Example

SUMMARY

Ray Anderson he launched his own company, Interface, Inc., which soon became the leading manufacturer of modular carpeting in the country. Twenty years later, however, Interface was struggling as its cost had gotten out of control and its customers began to question the company's impact on the environment. An employee gave Anderson a copy of Paul Hawken's *The Ecology of Commerce*, which chronicles a thoughtful plan for business success without sacrificing the environment.

Anderson took the concepts in *The Ecology of Commerce* to heart and used nature itself as the model for conducting business. He hired environmental consultants and created teams of employees to study every process in the company to find ways to "ecologize" them. Winning ideas earned employees bonuses. The changes not only have helped the environment, but they also have saved the company more than $75 million in just three years.

Still, some of the biggest benefits of Interface's new method of doing business come in its marketing efforts. Doing business with a "green" vendor, especially a low-cost green vendor, is an attractive feature to many companies. Interface has attracted the attention of other companies with an interest in the environment as potential customers.

Employees benefit from the company's natural approach as well. The typical carpet mill is a noisy, dusty place, where lint particles can be seen floating in malodorous air. Not so at Interface. The factory is not dusty, and the air is free of both odors and lint particles. Although Interface has a long way to go to reach its environmental goals, the company has come a long way. It is once again the world leader in its market.

1. What benefits does conducting business according to nature's model offer companies such as Interface? What is the impact on a company's stakeholders?

    Answer - It gave the company a means for reengineering all of their processes and win the support of employees and customers alike. In this case, it apparently resulted in lower costs, better products, greater employee and customer satisfaction.

2. What future do you predict for this management philosophy? Explain.

    Answer - While the economy is good, it should grow, especially if it is compatible with lower costs, better quality, and greater employee satisfaction and productivity. But if the economy weakens significantly and these measures do not positively impact these three items, it may be abandoned.

  B. Cultural Diversity in the Workplace

    1. The United States has always been a nation of astonishing cultural diversity, a trait that has imbued it with an incredible richness of ideas and creativity.

    2. The United States is moving toward a "minority majority," and significant demographic shifts will affect virtually every aspect of business.

        a) White, non-Hispanic males, now make up just 43 percent of all employees.

        b) Women and minorities will make up 62 percent of the workforce by 2005.

        c) See the diversity wheel in Figure 21.2.

    3. One of the chief benefits of a diverse workforce is the rich blend of perspectives, skills, talents, and ideas employees have to offer.

4. Molding workers with highly varied beliefs, backgrounds, and biases into a unified team takes time and commitment.
5. How can entrepreneurs achieve unity through diversity?
   a) The only way is by managing diversity in the workforce:
   b) That means employers must create an environment that accepts, even values, those differences, provides equal opportunity, and fosters positive working relationships among all employees."
6. Managing a culturally diverse workforce successfully requires a business owner to:
   a) Assess the company's diversity needs.
   b) Learn to recognize and correct one's own biases and stereotypes.
   c) Avoid making invalid assumptions.
   d) Push for diversity in the management team.
   e) Concentrate on communication.
   f) Make diversity a core value in the organization.
   g) Continue to adjust the company to the workers.
7. Table 21.5 compares the traditional management assumptions that companies must change and the diversity management assumptions needed to replace them.

C. Drug Testing
   1. A recent study of managers concluded that substance abuse (drug and alcohol) is the number one workplace issue across the nation.
   2. Unfortunately, small companies bear a disproportionate share of this burden.
      a) The majority--74 percent--of all substance abusers are employed.
      b) Experts estimate that 23 percent of all American workers use illegal drugs on the job.
      c) Only 3 percent of small businesses have drug-testing programs, and only 12 percent have a formal policy on drug use.
      d) One survey of small business employers found that, although they agree that substance abuse is a serious national problem, only 32 percent believe it is a problem among their own workers.
   3. Frequently, the initial response of an employer dealing with a drug problem is to fire the drug abuser.
   4. Another instinctive action some small business owners take is instituting a drug testing program.
      a) If not planned and implemented properly, drug tests can lead to a variety of legal, ethical, and moral problems for the small business owner, including invasion of privacy, discrimination, slander, or defamation of character.
   5. To avoid these and other problems, employers should develop an effective drug program that includes four key elements:
      a) A written substance abuse policy. The policy should state its purpose, prohibit the use of drugs on the job (or off the job if it affects job performance), specify the consequences of violating the policy, explain any drug testing procedures to be used, and describe the resources available to help troubled employees.
      b) Training for supervisors to detect drug-using workers. The supervisor should identify problem employees early and encourage them to seek help.
      c) A drug testing program, when necessary. Preemployment testing of job applicants generally is a safe strategy to follow, as long as it is followed consistently. Testing current employees is a more complex issue.
      d) An employee assistance program (EAP). An employee assistance program (EAP) is a company-provided benefit designed to help reduce workplace problems such as alcoholism, drug addiction, a gambling habit, and other conflicts and to deal with them when they arise.

D. AIDS
1. One of the most serious health problems to strike the world over the past several years is AIDS (acquired immune deficiency syndrome).
2. The disease costs the nation more than $75 billion annually in medical care and lost productivity and is the leading cause of death for Americans aged 25 to 44.
   a) For most business owners, the issue is not if one of their employees will contract AIDS but when.

IN THE FOOTSTEPS OF AN ENTREPRENEUR - When AIDS Attacks Your Company

SUMMARY
In a small business, the impact of AIDS can be incredibly destructive. One writer explains:

The AIDS virus itself presents a perfect metaphor for its effect on relationships and institutions. AIDS attacks the immune system of personal relationships and organizations like businesses, making them even more vulnerable to weaknesses already there, turning commonplace threats into legal toxins. By the same token, AIDS can bring out the strengths of people and organizations.

After returning from another extended bout with illness, Paul met and told the managers of Circle Solutions, Inc., that he was HIV-positive. Paul's revelation prompted a host of questions about HIV. Managers saw an immediate need for an AIDS education program and called in a local expert to counsel managers first and then to conduct a half-day AIDS education program for all employees. Managers also hired this expert to provide counseling to Paul, who decided to tell his coworkers about his disease. Managers met with employees in small groups to tell them about Paul's illness. AIDS education sessions quickly followed, and management gave employees the chance to meet privately with the doctor directing the employee assistance program.

Circle Solutions' managers also brought in an attorney specializing in AIDS discrimination cases to avoid legal problems. The attorney's advice: Keep Paul's medical information private, provide him with the same benefit as those with any life-threatening illness, allow him to work as long as he is able, and ensure that the company did not discriminate against him in any way. Managers made a commitment to living up to their legal and ethical obligations to Paul. That commitment soon was put to the test as Paul's health began to deteriorate and he missed work frequently. Managers first modified his job duties to accommodate his condition. When Paul's leave was depleted, Circle Solutions' president sent employees a memo announcing the creation of a "leave bank"; to which any employee could donate a vacation day and a sick day. The company also arranged for a pharmacist to provide Paul's costly medications and then picked up the tab and completed the necessary paperwork. Paul died one year after he was diagnosed. What managers learned about AIDS through Paul's experience proved to be valuable when two other Circle Solutions employees contracted the HIV virus. The company is well prepared for this unfortunate reality.

1. What steps should a small company take to deal effectively with AIDS?
   Answer - The answer is basically a review of this case.
2. Evaluate Circle Solutions' response to AIDS.
   Answer - Students should see this response as compassionate and extraordinary. Few small businesses would have the ability to do this, especially in absorbing the costs due to lost work, etc. Some students will raise questions about the commitment of so many resources to one employee, especially now that two other employees are ill. How can a company establish a compassionate approach that it can sustain?

3. When faced with the disease, employers and employees often operate on the basis of misconceptions and fear.
   a) One study found that many of the actions employers said they would take with an employee who had AIDS (including firing and telling coworkers) were illegal.
   b) AIDS is considered a disability and is covered by the Americans with Disabilities Act (ADA), which applies to companies with 15 or more employees.
4. Coping with AIDS in a socially responsible manner requires a written policy and an educational program, ideally implemented before the need arises.
5. As with drug testing, it is important to ensure that a company's AIDS policies are legal. In general, a company's AIDS policy should include the following:
   a) Employment. Companies must allow employees with AIDS to continue working as long as they can perform the job.
   b) Discrimination. Because AIDS is a disability, employers cannot discriminate against qualified people with the disease who can meet job requirements.
   c) Employee benefits. Employees with AIDS have the right to the same benefits as those with any other life-threatening illness.
   d) Confidentiality. Employers must keep employees' medical records strictly confidential.
   e) Education. An AIDS education program should be a part of every company's AIDS policy.
   f) "Reasonable accommodations." These may include extended leaves of absence, flexible work schedules, restructuring a job to require less-strenuous duties, purchasing special equipment to assist affected workers, and other modifications.

E. Sexual Harassment
   1. As the number of women entering the workforce has increased, so has the number of sexual harassment charges filed.
      a) See Figure 21.3.
      b) Estimates of the percentage of working women who have experienced sexual harassment on the job range from 40 to 60%.
   2. Sexual harassment is a violation of Title VII of the Civil Rights Act of 1964 and is considered to be a form of sex discrimination.
   3. Sexual harassment is any unwelcome sexual advance, request for sexual favors, and other verbal or physical sexual conduct made explicitly or implicitly as a condition of employment.
      a) Women bring about 90 percent of all sexual harassment charges.
      b) Jury verdicts reaching into the millions of dollars are not uncommon.
   4. Several types of behavior may result in charges of sexual harassment.
   5. Quid pro quo harassment
      a) The most blatant, and most potentially damaging, form of sexual harassment is quid pro quo ("something for something"), in which a superior conditions the granting of a benefit (promotion, raise, etc.) upon the receipt of sexual favors from a subordinate.
      b) Only managers and supervisors can engage in quid pro quo harassment.
   6. Hostile environment
      a) Behavior that creates an abusive, intimidating, offensive, or hostile work environment also constitutes sexual harassment.
      b) A hostile environment usually requires a pattern of offensive sexual behavior rather than a single, isolated remark or display.
      c) In judging whether a hostile environment exists, courts base their decisions on how a "reasonable woman" would perceive the situation.

7. Harassment by nonemployees.
   a) An employer can be held liable for third parties (customers, sales representatives, and others) who engage in sexual harassment if the employer has the ability to stop the improper behavior.
   b) In recent rulings, the United States Supreme Court changed the nature of an employer's liability for sexual harassment, rejecting the previous standard that the employer had to be negligent somehow to be liable for a supervisor's improper behavior toward employees.

GAINING THE COMPETITIVE EDGE - How Much Do You Know about Sexual Harassment?

SUMMARY

Do you know sexual harassment when you see it? Consider the following true case:
Catherine was exposed to nude photographs posted in various areas. She eventually complained to the plant manager, who made inappropriate personal and sexual remarks to her. Some, but not all, of the pictures were removed, despite the employer's policy to remove sexually explicit materials upon discovery. Other employees (including another supervisor) also expressed to Catherine their annoyance over her complaint, and she was subjected to catcalls and harassing whistles. These instances were also reported by Catherine to her immediate supervisor and the plant manager, who indicated to her that she was somehow encouraging the harassment. Management failed to put an end to the whistling and catcalls. In its defense, the company cited the fact that it had instituted a policy of using gender-neutral terms in its job titles. Did Catherine have a legitimate sexual harassment complaint? Explain.

Answer - Yes, details provided in inverted text in the book on page 747.

One of the primary causes of sexual harassment in the workplace is the lack of education concerning what constitutes harassment. The following quiz asks you to assume the roles of an employee and of a manager when answering the questions.

A Test for Employees
Answer each question as true or false.
1. If I just ignore unwanted sexual attention, it will usually stop.
2. If I don't mean to sexually harass another employee, there's no way my behavior can be perceived by him or her as sexually harassing.
3. Some employees don't complain about unwanted sexual attention from another worker because they don't want to get that person in trouble.
4. If I make sexual comments to someone and that person doesn't ask me to stop, then I guess my behavior is welcome.
5. To avoid sexually harassing a woman who comes to work in a traditionally male workplace, the men simply should not haze her.
6. A sexual harasser may be told by a court to pay part of a judgment to the employee he or she harassed.
7. A sexually harassed man does not have the same legal rights as a woman who is sexually harassed.
8. About 90 percent of all sexual harassment in today's workplace is done by males to females.
9. Sexually suggestive pictures or objects in a workplace don't create a liability unless someone complains.
10. Displaying "girlie" pictures can constitute a hostile work environment even though most workers in the workplace think they are harmless.
11. Telling someone to stop his or her unwanted sexual behavior usually doesn't do any good.

Answer - Answers are in inverted text in the book on page 747.

A Test for Managers

Answer each question as true or false.
1. Men in male-dominated workplaces usually have to change their behavior when a woman begins working there.
2. Employers are not liable for the sexual harassment of one of their employees unless that employee loses specific job benefits or is fired.
3. Supervisors can be liable for sexual harassment committed by one of their employees against another.
4. Employers can be liable for the sexually harassing behavior of management personnel even if they are unaware of that behavior and have a policy forbidding it.
5. It is appropriate for a supervisor, when initially receiving a sexual harassment complaint, to determine if the alleged recipient overreacted or misunderstood the alleged harasser.
6. When a supervisor is telling an employee that an allegation of sexual harassment has been filed against that employee, it is best to ease into being direct.
7. Sexually suggestive visuals or objects in a workplace don't create a liability unless an employee complains about them and management allows them to remain.
8. The lack of sexual harassment complaints is a good indication that sexual harassment is not occurring.
9. It is appropriate for supervisors to tell an employee to handle unwelcome sexual behavior if they think that the employee is misunderstanding the behavior.
10. The intent behind employee A's sexual behavior is more important than the impact of that behavior on employee B when determining if sexual harassment has occurred.
11. If a sexual harassment problem is common knowledge in a workplace, the courts assume that the employer has knowledge of it.
Answer - Answers are in inverted text in the book on the top of on page 748.

8. A company's best weapons against sexual harassment are education, policy, and procedures.
9. Education
    a) Preventing sexual harassment is the best solution, and the key to prevention is educating employees about what constitutes sexual harassment.
    b) Table 21.6 offers guidelines for battling sexual harassment in the workplace.
10. Policy. The policy should:
    a) Clearly define what behaviors constitute sexual harassment.
    b) State in clear language that harassment will not be tolerated in the workplace.
    c) Identify the responsibilities of supervisors and employees in preventing harassment.
    d) Define the sanctions and penalties for engaging in harassment.
    e) Spell out the steps to take in reporting an incident of sexual harassment.
    f) In another case, the United States Supreme Court ruled that an employer was liable for a supervisor's sexually harassing behavior even though the employee never reported it.
        (1) The company's liability stemmed from its failure to communicate its sexual harassment policy throughout the organization.
11. Procedure.
    a) Choosing a person inside the company (perhaps someone in the human resources area) and one outside the company (a close adviser or attorney) is a good strategy. At least one of these should be a woman.
    b) When a complaint arises, managers should:
        (1) Listen to the complaint carefully without judging.
        (2) Investigate the complaint promptly, preferably within 24 hours.
        (3) Interview the accused party and and witnesses who may be aware of a pattern of harassing behavior privately and separately.
        (4) Keep findings confidential.

(5) Decide what action to take, relying on company policy as a guideline.

(6) Inform both the complaining person and the alleged harasser of the action taken.

(7) Document the entire investigation.

F. Privacy

1. Modem technology has given business owners the ability to monitor workers' performances as they never could before, but where is the line between monitoring productivity and invasion of privacy?

2. Experts estimate that 20 million workers in the United States are subject to computer monitoring.

3. Managers use electronic monitoring to track customer service representatives, word-processing clerks, data entry technicians, and other workers for speed, accuracy, and productivity.

4. Almost two-thirds of the major trucking companies now have communications devices in their trucks. Companies use these devices to monitor drivers' exact locations at all times, to regulate their speed, to make sure they stop only at approved fueling points, and to ensure that they take the legally required hours of rest.

5. Electronic communication technology also poses ethical problems for employers.

   a) A study by the Society for Human Resource Management found that, although 80 percent of all organizations communicate via e-mail, only 34 percent have written policies governing the privacy of e-mail messages.

   b) Most employees simply do not know that their bosses can legally monitor their e-mail and voice-mail messages, often without notification.

   c) To avoid ethical problems, a business owner should establish a clear policy for monitoring employees' communications and establish guidelines for the proper use of the company's communication technology.

VIII. Business's Responsibility to Customers

A. The Consumer Bill of Rights

1. Socially responsible companies recognize their duty to abide by the Consumer Bill of Rights, first put forth by President John F. Kennedy.

2. This document gives consumers the following rights.

B. Right to Safety

1. Companies have the responsibility to provide their customers with safe, quality products and services.

2. The greatest breach of trust occurs when businesses produce products that, when properly used, injure customers.

C. Right to Know

1. Consumers have the right to honest communication about the products and services they buy and the companies they buy them from.

2. In a free market economy, information is one of the most valuable commodities available.

3. As a result, companies have a responsibility to customers to be truthful in their advertising.

4. Examples of unethical ads from small businesses:

   a) A "universal coat hanger" for just $3.99. The product: a 10-penny nail.

   b) A "solid-state compact food server" for $39.95. The product: a spoon.

   c) A new "vision dieter." The product: a pair of glasses with one red lens and one blue lens; the lenses were supposed to make food look unappetizing (or at least purple).

       d) "Hide-A-Swat," guaranteed to kill flies and pests, for $9.95. The product: a rolled-up newspaper.

D. Right to be Heard
    1. Socially responsible businesses provide customers with a mechanism for resolving complaints about products and services.
       a) Some companies have established a consumer ombudsman to address customer questions and complaints.
       b) Others have created customer hotlines, toll-free numbers designed to serve customers more effectively.
    2. Another effective technique for encouraging two-way communication between customers and companies is the customer report card.

E. Right to Education
    1. Socially responsible companies give customers access to educational programs about their products and services and how to use them properly.
    2. The goal is to give customers enough information to make informed purchase decisions.

F. Right to Choice
    1. Socially responsible companies do not restrict competition, and they abide by the United States' antitrust policy, which promotes free trade and competition in the market.
    2. The foundation of this policy is the Sherman Antitrust Act of 1890, which forbids agreements among sellers that restrain trade or commerce and outlaws any attempts to monopolize a market.

IX. Business's Responsibility to Investors
  A. Described
    1. Companies have the responsibility to provide investors with an attractive return on their investment.
    2. Although earning a profit may be a company's first responsibility, it is not its only responsibility; meeting its ethical and social responsibility goals is also a key to success.
    3. Many businesspeople believe that managing a firm in an ethical, socially responsible manner is the only way to generate profits.
       a) One study of international companies found that firms practicing ethics on a daily basis had a distinct advantage over their rivals.
       b) The report also found that companies can reduce labor problems and increase productivity by maintaining ethical standards. Similarly, small companies tend to integrate ethics into their strategies for growth.
    4. Companies also have the responsibility to report their financial performances in an accurate and timely fashion to their investors.
       a) Firms that misrepresent or falsify their financial and operating records are guilty of violating the fiduciary relationship with their investors.

X. Business's Responsibility to the Community
  A. Described
    1. Socially responsible businesses are aware of their duty to put back into the community some of what they take out as they generate profits; their goal is to become a neighbor of choice.
    2. These companies are the ones who donate money, time, and personnel to schools, civic clubs, and volunteer organizations such as the Red Cross, the United Way, literacy programs, and a host of other groups.

   3. One study concluded that "companies that increased their community involvement were
       more like to show an improved financial picture than those that did not increase their
       community involvement."
   4. Other research shows that small businesses give more to their communities per employee
       than large ones.
       a) The majority of their donations were in the form of in-kind products and services and
           in volunteer time.

B. Conclusion
   1. Businesses must do more than merely earn profits; they must act ethically and in a
       socially responsible manner.
   2. Establishing and maintaining high ethical and socially responsible standards must be a
       top concern of every business owner. Managing ethics and social responsibility presents a
       tremendous challenge, however.
   3. There is no universal definition of ethical behavior, and what is considered ethical may
       change over time or may be different in other cultures. Many companies are tackling the
       problem with education. "Ethics education may not make people act ethically who want
       to act unethically," says one writer. "However, ethics education can help people act
       ethically who want to do so."
   4. Finally, business owners and managers must recognize the key role they play in influ-
       encing their employees' ethical and socially responsible behavior. What owners and man-
       agers say is important, but what they do is even more vital!
   5. Employees throughout a small company look to the owner and managers as models;
       therefore, these owners and managers must commit themselves to following the highest
       ethical standards if they expect their organizations to do so.

Chapter Summary
♦ Define business ethics and describe the three levels of ethical standards.
   ▪ Business ethics involves the fundamental moral values and behavioral standards that form the
      foundation for the people of an organization as they make decisions and interact with organiza-
      tional stakeholders. Small business managers must consider the ethical and social as well as the
      economic implications of their decisions.
   ▪ The three levels of ethical standards are (1) the law, (2) the policies and procedures of the
      company, and (3) the moral stance of the individual.
♦ Determine who is responsible for ethical behavior and why ethical lapses occur.
   ▪ Managers set the moral tone of the organization. There are three ethical styles of management:
      immoral, amoral, and moral. Although moral management has value in itself, companies that
      operate with this philosophy discover other benefits, including a positive reputation among
      customers and employees.
   ▪ Ethical lapses occur for a variety of reasons:
      Some people are corrupt ("the bad apple").
      The company culture has been poisoned ("the bad barrel").
      Competitive pressures push managers to compromise.
      Managers are tempted by an opportunity to "get ahead."
      Managers in different cultures have different views of what is ethical.
♦ Explain how to establish and maintain high ethical standards.
   ▪ Philosophers throughout history have developed various tests of ethical behavior: the utilitarian
      principle, Kant's categorical imperative, the professional ethic, the Golden Rule, the television
      test, and the family test.
   ▪ A small business manager can maintain high ethical standards in the following ways:

Create a company credo.
Develop a code of ethics.
Enforce the code fairly and consistently.
Hire the right people.
Conduct ethical training.
Perform periodic ethical audits.
Establish high standards of behavior, not just rules.
Set an impeccable ethical example at all times.
Create a culture emphasizing two-way communication.
Involve employees in establishing ethical standards.

♦ Define social responsibility.
- Social responsibility is the awareness of a company's managers of the social, environmental, political, human, and financial consequences of their actions.

♦ Understand the nature of business's responsibility to the environment.
- Environmentally responsible business owners focus on the three Rs: reduce, reuse, recycle: reduce the amount of materials used in the company from the factory floor to the copier room; reuse whatever you can; and recycle the materials that you must dispose of.

♦ Describe business's responsibility to employees.
- Companies have a duty to act responsibly toward one of their most important stakeholders: their employees. Businesses must recognize and manage the cultural diversity that exists in the workplace; establish a responsible strategy for combating substance abuse in the workplace (including drug testing) and dealing with AIDS; prevent sexual harassment; and respect employees' right to privacy.

♦ Explain business's responsibility to customers.
- Every company's customers have a right to safe products and services; to honest, accurate information; to be heard; to education about products and services; and to choices in the marketplace.

♦ Discuss business's responsibility to investors.
- Companies have the responsibility to provide investors with an attractive return on their investments and to report their financial performances in an accurate and timely fashion to their investors.

♦ Describe business's responsibility to the community.
- Increasingly, companies are seeing a need to go beyond "doing well" to "doing good"--being socially responsible community citizens. In addition to providing jobs and creating wealth, companies contribute to the local community in many different ways.

Discussion Questions
1. What is ethics? Discuss the three levels of ethical standards.
   Answer - Business ethics consists of the fundamental moral values and behavioral standards that form the foundation for the people of an organization as they make decisions and interact with stakeholders. Three levels. 1) The law, which defines for society as a whole what actions are permissible and which are not. 2) The policies and procedures of the organization, which serve as specific guidelines for people as they make daily decisions. 3) The moral stance individuals take when faced with a decision not governed by formal rules.

2. In any organization, who determines ethical behavior? Briefly describe the three ethical styles of management. What are the benefits of moral management?
    Answer - Although companies may set ethical standards and offer guidelines for employees, the ultimate decision on whether to abide by ethical principles rests with the individual. Good ethics starts at the top and works its way downward through the entire organization. Table 21.2 summarizes the characteristics of the three ethical styles of management: immoral, amoral, and moral management.

    Benefits of moral management.
    ♦ 63 percent of business professionals feel that "a business enterprise actually strengthens its competitive position by maintaining high ethical standards."
    ♦ First, the company avoids the damaging effects of a reputation as an unethical business.
    ♦ Second, a solid ethical framework guides managers as they cope with an increasingly complex network of external influence, from government regulation and special interest groups to suppliers and the media.
    ♦ Finally, ethical companies earn the respect of two essential groups: customers and employees.

3. Why do ethical lapses occur in businesses?
    Answer - Ethical lapses occur for various reasons. 1) Ethical decisions are individual decisions, and some people are corrupt. 2) In some cases, the company culture has been poisoned with an unethical overtone. 3) Sometimes, fundamentally ethical people commit ethical blunders because they are blind to the ethical implications of their conduct. 4) If competition is so intense that a company's survival is threatened, managers may begin to view as acceptable what were once unacceptable options. 5) When the opportunity to "get ahead" by taking some unethical action presents itself, some people cannot resist the temptation. 6) Companies have discovered that there is no single standard of ethical behavior applying to all business decisions in the international arena. Practices that are illegal in one country may be perfectly acceptable, even expected, in another.

4. Describe the various methods for establishing ethical standards. Which is most meaningful to you? Why?
    Answer - There are six ethical standards one could use. Table 21.3 describes ten ethical principles that differentiate between right and wrong, thereby offering a guideline for ethical behavior.
    ▪ The utilitarian principle. Choose the option that offers the greatest good for the greatest number of people.
    ▪ Kant's categorical imperative. Act in such a way that the action taken under the circumstances could be a universal law or rule of behavior.
    ▪ The professional ethic. Take only those actions that a disinterested panel of professional colleagues would view as proper.
    ▪ The Golden Rule. Treat other people the way you would like them to treat you.
    ▪ The television test. Would you and your colleagues feel comfortable explaining your actions to a national television audience?
    ▪ The family test. Would you be comfortable explaining to your children, your spouse, and your parents why you took this action?

5. What can business owners do to maintain high ethical standards in their companies?
    Answer - What can managers do to integrate ethical principles into their companies?
    ▪ Create a company credo.
    ▪ Develop a code of ethics.
    ▪ Enforce the code fairly and consistently.
    ▪ Conduct ethics training.
    ▪ Hire the right people.

- Perform periodic ethical audits.
- Establish high standards of behavior, not just rules.
- Set an impeccable ethical example at all times.
- Create a culture that emphasizes two-way communication.
- Involve employees in establishing ethical standards.

6. What is social responsibility?

Answer - Social responsibility is the awareness by a company's managers of the social, environmental, political, human, and financial consequences their actions produce. The specific nature of a company's social responsibility efforts will depend on how its owners, employees, and other stakeholders define what it means to be socially responsible.
- Is it manufacturing environmentally friendly products?
- Is it donating a portion of profits to charitable organizations?
- Is it creating jobs in inner cities plagued by high unemployment levels?

7. Describe business's social responsibility to each of the following areas: the environment, employees, customers, investors, and the community

Answer -

Environment. Socially responsible business owners focus on the three Rs: reduce, reuse, recycle.
- Reduce the amount of materials used in your company, from the factory floor to the copier room.
- Reuse whatever you can.
- Recycle the materials that you must dispose off

Employees. How can business owners prove to employees that they really are the company's number one asset?
- Listen to employees and respect their opinions.
- Ask for their input; involve them in the decision-making process.
- Provide regular feedback--positive and negative--to employees.
- Tell them the truth--always.
- Let them know exactly what's expected of them.
- Reward employees for performing their jobs well.
- Trust them: create an environment of respect and teamwork.

Customers. One of the most important groups of stakeholders that a business must satisfy is its customers. Building and maintaining a base of loyal customers is no easy task, however. It requires more than just selling buyers a product or a service; the key is to build relationships with customers. And see question #11.

Investors. Companies have the responsibility to provide investors with an attractive return on their investment. Many businesspeople believe that managing a firm in an ethical, socially responsible manner is the only way to generate profits. Companies also have the responsibility to report their financial performances in an accurate and timely fashion to their investors.

Community. Socially responsible businesses are aware of their duty to put back into the community some of what they take out as they generate profits; their goal is to become a neighbor of choice. These companies are the ones who donate money, time, and personnel to schools, civic clubs, and volunteer organizations such as the Red Cross, the United Way, literacy programs, and a host of other groups.

8. What can businesses do to improve the quality of the environment?

Answer - Socially responsible business owners focus on the three Rs: reduce, reuse, recycle. Truly progressive companies are creating redesigned, "clean" manufacturing systems that focus on avoiding waste and pollution. These companies design their products, packaging, and processes from the start with the environment in mind, working to eliminate hazardous materials and byproducts and looking for ways to turn what had been scrap into salable products. Table 21.4 offers a list of questions environmentally responsible entrepreneurs should ask themselves.

9. Should companies be allowed to test employees for drugs? Explain. How should a socially responsible drug testing program operate?
    Answer - Students responses will vary; most will probably be against it. An interesting discussion would be over why they are against it, given the consequences of drug use on the job. Effective drug program that includes four key elements:
    - A written substance abuse policy.
    - Training for supervisors to detect drug-using workers.
    - A drug testing program, when necessary.
    - An employee assistance program (EAP).

10. Many owners of trucking companies use electronic communications equipment to monitor their drivers on the road. They say that the devices allow them to remain competitive and to serve their customers better by delivering shipments of vital materials exactly when their customers need them. They also point out that the equipment can improve road safety by ensuring that drivers get the hours of rest the law requires. Opponents argue that the surveillance devices work against safety. "The drivers know they're being watched," says one trucker. "There's an obvious temptation to push." What do you think? What ethical issues does the use of such equipment create? How should a small trucking company considering the use of such equipment handle these issues?
    Answer - This is an open-ended discussion question. Students should realize that the business has the right to use such devices regardless of employee concerns. The issue is how to implement them without making it an issue. Also, almost two-thirds of the major trucking companies now have communications devices in their trucks. Companies use these devices to monitor drivers' exact locations at all times, to regulate their speed, to make sure they stop only at approved fueling points, and to ensure that they take the legally required hours of rest. They promote safety and cost savings.

11. What rights do customers have under the Consumer Bill of Rights? How can businesses ensure those rights?
    Answer - Socially responsible companies recognize their duty to abide by the Consumer Bill of Rights, first put forth by President John F. Kennedy which gives consumers the following rights.
    - Companies have the responsibility to provide their customers with safe, quality products and services.
    - Consumers have the right to honest communication about the products and services they buy and the companies they buy them from.
    - Socially responsible businesses provide customers with a mechanism for resolving complaints about products and services.
    - Socially responsible companies give customers access to educational programs about their products and services and how to use them properly.
    - Socially responsible companies do not restrict competition, and they abide by the United States' antitrust policy, which promotes free trade and competition in the market.

Step into the Real World

1. Search the current literature (e.g., periodicals such as *Business Ethics, Inc.*, *Entrepreneur*, *Fortune*, *Forbes*, the *Wall Street Journal*, and other business publications) to find examples of companies using each of the three ethical styles of management: immoral, amoral, and moral. Prepare a brief report summarizing each and explaining the consequences of management's behavior.
2. Obtain copies of codes of ethics from several companies or associations and compare them. What are the similarities and differences among them? Do you think these codes would be useful to an employee facing an ethical dilemma? Explain.

3. Contact several local business owners. How do they view their responsibility to society? Have they altered their management styles and their companies to reflect society's changing demands for responsible companies? What methods do they use to meet their responsibility to the stakeholders discussed in this chapter? "Job safety and performance are more important than the slight invasion of privacy caused by drug testing," says one plant manager. Another, who refuses to test employees, claims, "Drug testing is an outright invasion of employee privacy." Conduct a debate in your class on these two positions.

4. Working in a team with another student, interview the owners of two small businesses with at least 10 employees about their experience with employee substance abuse in the workplace. Do the owners use drug tests? If so, what is their policy? If not, why not? Do the owners have formal drug policies? Why? Write a two-page report on your findings and include at least five specific recommendations you would make to these business owners about preventing substance abuse in their workplaces.

5. Consider the following actual case. Working with teammates, decide how you would handle the situation. What ethical and socially responsible principles guided you?

> David is a former drug user who has spent time in jail. For the past three years, he has been straight, and he now operates a forklift at a small construction company. Lately, however, he's begun having seizures, or "flashbacks," as a result of his earlier use of the drug PCP. He has been carefully evaluated by EAP professionals and found to be clean of current drug use; indeed, they say flashbacks of this nature are quite common in ex-addicts. Mishandling of David's machine could be dangerous to him and his coworkers. However, he has already had flashbacks while at the controls, and in each case the seizure caused him to release a handle, which simply stopped the machine. It is the only work he is qualified to do within this company.*

*Source: Minda Zetlin, "Combating Drugs in the Workplace." *Management Review*, August 1991, pp. 17-24.

Chapter 22 - The Legal Environment: Business Law and Government Regulation

A verbal contract isn't worth the paper it's written on.
Samuel Goldwyn

Most problems don't exist until a government agency is created to solve them.
Kirk Kirkpatrick

Teaching Objectives
Students will be able to:
1. Explain the basic elements required to create a valid, enforceable contract.
2. Outline the major components of the Uniform Commercial Code governing sales contracts.
3. Discuss the protection of intellectual property rights involving patents, trademarks, and copyrights.
4. Explain the basic workings of the law of agency. Explain the basics of bankruptcy law.
5. Explain some of the government regulations affecting small businesses, including those governing trade practices, consumer protection, consumer credit, and the environment.

Instructor's Outline
I. Introduction
   A. The Legal Environment
      1. Entrepreneurs must understand the basics of business law if they are to avoid legal entanglements.
         a) See Figure 22.1.
         b) Routine transactions with customers, suppliers, employees, government agencies, and others can develop into costly legal battles.
         c) One big judgment against a small company in a legal case could force it out of business.
         d) Even when a small business wins a lawsuit, it might lose in the long run because the costs of defending itself can run quickly into tens or even hundreds of thousands of dollars.
         e) Plus, lawsuits are bothersome distractions that prevent entrepreneurs from focusing their energy on running their business.
      2. The best way for business owners to avoid legal problems that can threaten their companies is to equip themselves with a basic understanding of the principles of business law.

II. The Law of Contracts
   A. Introduction
      1. Contract law governs the rights and obligations among the parties to an agreement (contract).
      2. It is a body of laws that affects virtually every business relationship.
         a) A contract is simply a legally binding agreement.
         b) It is a promise or a set of promises for the breach of which the law gives a remedy and that the performance of which the law in some way recognizes as a duty.
      3. A contract arises from an agreement, and it creates an obligation among the parties involved.
         a) It is a promise to be fulfilled.
      4. Although almost everyone has the capacity to enter into a contractual agreement (freedom of contract), not every contract is valid and enforceable.
      5. A valid contract has four separate elements:

a) Agreement. A valid offer by one party that is accepted by the other.

b) Consideration. Something of legal value that the parties exchange as part of a bargain.

c) Contractual capacity. The parties must be adults capable of understanding the consequences of their agreement.

d) Legality. The parties' contract must be for a legal purpose.

6. In addition, a contract must meet two supplemental requirements: genuineness of assent and form.

a) Genuineness of assent is a test to make sure that the parties' agreement is genuine and not subject to problems such as fraud, misrepresentation, or mistakes.

b) Form involves the writing requirement for certain types of contracts.

7. Although not every contract must be in writing to be enforceable, the law does require some contracts to be evidenced by writing.

B. Agreement

1. Agreement requires a "meeting of the minds" and is established by an offer and an acceptance.

a) One party must make an offer to another party, who must accept that offer.

b) Agreement is governed by the objective theory of contracts, which states that a party's intention to create a contract is measured by outward facts--words, conduct, and circumstances--rather than by subjective, personal intentions.

c) In settling contract disputes, courts interpret the objective facts surrounding the contract from the perspective of an imaginary reasonable person.

2. Offer. An offer is a promise or commitment to do or refrain from doing some specified thing in the future.

a) For an offer to stand there must be an intention to be bound by it, reasonably certain terms, and communication of the offer.

b) The party making the offer must genuinely intend to make an offer, and the offer's terms must be definite, not vague.

c) The following terms must either be expressed or be capable of being implied in an offer:

(1) the parties involved.

(2) the identity of the subject matter.

(3) the quantity.

(4) Other terms offerors should specify include price, delivery terms, payment terms, timing, and shipping terms.

d) Courts often supply missing terms in a contract when there is a reliable basis for doing so.

(1) The court usually supplies a time term that is reasonable for the circumstances.

(2) It supplies a price term (a reasonable price at the time of delivery) if a readily ascertainable market price exists.

(3) On rare occasions, the court supplies a quantity term, but a missing quantity term usually defeats a contract.

e) An offer must always be communicated to the other party because one cannot agree to a contract unless she knows it exists.

3. Acceptance. Only the person to whom the offer is made (the offeree) can accept an offer and create a contract.

a) The offeree must accept voluntarily, agreeing to the terms exactly as the offeror presents them.

b) When the offeree suggests alternative terms or conditions, he is implicitly rejecting the original offer and making a counteroffer.

c) Common law requires that the offeree's acceptance exactly match the offer.

d) In general, silence by the offeree cannot constitute acceptance, even if the offer contains statements to the contrary.

e) An offeree must accept an offer by the means of communication authorized by and within the time limits specified by the offeror.

C. Consideration
1. Courts require that consideration be present in virtually every contract.
2. Consideration is something of legal value (not necessarily economic value) that the parties to a contract bargain for and exchange as the "price" for the promise given.
3. For a contract to be binding, the two parties involved must exchange valuable consideration.
   a) The absence of consideration makes a promise not binding.
   b) A promise to perform something one is already legally obligated to do is not valuable consideration.
   c) Past consideration is not valid.
   d) And, under the common law, new promises require new consideration.
4. One important exception to the requirement for valuable consideration is *promissory estoppel*.
   a) Under this rule, a promise that induces another party to act can be enforceable without consideration if the promisee substantially and justifiably relies on the promise.
   b) Promissory estoppel is a substitute for consideration.
5. In most cases, courts do not evaluate the adequacy of consideration given for a promise.
   a) The law recognizes that people have the freedom to contract and that they are just as free to enter into "bad" bargains as they are to enter into "good" ones.

D. Contractual Capacity
1. The third element of a valid contract requires that the parties involved in it must have contractual capacity for it to be enforceable.
   a) Not every individual who enters into a contract has the capacity to do so.
   b) Under the common law, minors, intoxicated people, and insane people lack contractual capacity.
   c) As a result, contracts these people enter into are considered to be voidable; that is, the party can annul or disaffirm the contract at his option.
2. Minors
   a) Minors constitute the largest group of individuals without contractual capacity.
   b) In most states, anyone under age 18 is a minor, although a few states establish 19 as the age of majority.
   c) If a minor receives the benefit of a completed contract and then disaffirms that contract, she must fulfill her duty of restoration by returning the benefit.
   d) Adults enter into contracts with minors at their own risk.
   e) Parents are usually not liable for any contracts made by their children, although a cosigner is bound equally with the minor.
3. Intoxicated people
   a) A contract entered into by an intoxicated person can be either voidable or valid, depending on the person's condition when entering into the contract.
   b) If reason and judgment are impaired so that the person does not realize a contract is being made, the contract is voidable and the benefit must be returned.
   c) However, if the intoxicated person understands that he is forming a contract, although it may be foolish, the contract is valid and enforceable.

4. Insane People
    a) A contract entered into by an insane person can be void, voidable, or valid, depending on the mental state of the person.
    b) Those who have been judged to be so mentally incompetent that a guardian is appointed for them cannot enter into a valid contract.
    c) An insane person who has not been legally declared insane (e.g., someone suffering from Alzheimer's disease) or appointed a guardian is bound by a contract if he was lucid enough at the time of the contract to comprehend its consequences.

E. Legality
    1. The purpose of the parties' contract must be legal.
    2. Because society imposes certain standards of conduct on its members, contracts that are illegal (criminal or tortious) or against public policy are void.
    3. If a contract contains both legal and illegal elements, the courts will enforce the legal parts as long as they can separate the legal portion from the illegal portion.
        a) Usually, the courts do not concern themselves with the fairness and equity of a contract between parties because individuals are supposed to be intelligent.
        b) But in the case of unconscionable contracts, the terms are so harsh and oppressive to one party that the courts often rule the clause to be void.

F. Genuineness of Assent and the Form of Contracts
    1. A contract that contains the four elements just discussed--agreement, consideration, capacity, and legality--is valid, but a valid contract may still be unenforceable because of two possible defenses against it: genuineness of assent and form.
    2. Genuineness of assent serves as a check on the parties' agreement, verifying that it is genuine and not subject to mistakes, misrepresentation, fraud, duress, or undue influence.
        a) Only mistakes of fact permit a party to avoid a contract.
        b) Fraud also voids a contract because no genuineness of assent exists.
            (1) Fraud is the intentional misrepresentation of a material fact, justifiably relied on, that results in injury to the innocent party.
            (2) The misrepresentation with the intent to deceive can result from words or conduct.
        c) Duress, forcing an individual into a contract by fear or threat, eliminates genuineness of assent.
    3. In general, the law does not require contracts to follow a prescribed form; a contract is valid whether it is written or oral.
        a) Most contracts do not have to be in writing to be enforceable, but for convenience and protection, a small business owner should insist that every contract be in writing.
        b) If a contract is oral, the party attempting to enforce it must first prove its existence and then establish its actual terms.
        c) Although each state has its own set of statutes, the law generally requires the following contracts to be in writing:
            (1) Contracts for the sale of land
            (2) Contracts involving lesser interests in land (e.g., rights-of-way or leases lasting more than one year).
            (3) Contracts that cannot by their terms be performed within one year.
            (4) Collateral contracts such as promises to answer for the debt or duty of another.
            (5) Promises by the administrator or executor of an estate to pay a debt of the estate personally.
            (6) Contracts for the sale of goods (as opposed to services) priced above $500.

G. Breach of Contract
1. Occasionally, however, one party fails to perform as agreed. This failure is called breach of contract, and the injured party has certain remedies available.
2. In general, the nonbreaching party is entitled to sue for compensatory damages, the monetary damages that will place him in the same position he would have been in had the contract been performed.
   a) In addition to compensatory damages, the nonbreaching party may also be awarded consequential damages (also called special damages) that arise as a consequence of the breach.
3. For the nonbreaching party to recover consequential damages, the breaching party must have known the consequences of the breach.
   a) The injured, or nonbreaching, party does, however, have a duty to make a reasonable effort to minimize (to mitigate) the damages incurred by the breach.
4. In some cases, monetary damages are inadequate to compensate the injured party for the breach of contract.
   a) The only remedy that would compensate the nonbreaching party might be specific performance of the act promised in the contract.
   b) Specific performance is usually the remedy for breached contracts dealing with unique items (antiques, land, and animals).
   c) Courts rarely invoke the remedy of specific performance.
   d) Contracts for performance of personal services generally are not subject to specific performance.

III. The Uniform Commercial Code (UCC)
A. Introduction
1. For many years, sales contracts relating to the exchange of goods were governed by a loosely defined system of rules and customs called the Lex Mercatoria (Merchant Law).
2. In the 1940s, a group of legal scholars compiled the Uniform Commercial Code (or the UCC or the Code) to replace the hodgepodge collection of confusing, often conflicting state laws that governed basic commercial transactions with a document designed to provide uniformity and consistency.
   a) The UCC <http://www.law.cornell.edu/ucc/table.htm> replaced numerous statutes governing trade when 49 states, the District of Columbia, and the Virgin Islands adopted it. (Louisiana has adopted only Articles 1, 3, 4, and 5.)
   b) The Code unites and modernizes the basic tenets into a single body of law.
3. The Code consists of 10 articles:
   a) General provisions
   b) Sales
      (1) Leases
   c) Negotiable instruments
   d) Bank deposits and collections
   e) Letters of credit
   f) Bulk transfers
   g) Documents of title, warehouse receipts, bills of lading, and others
   h) Investment securities
   i) Secured transactions
   j) Effective date and repealer
4. The UCC creates a "caste system" of merchants and nonmerchants and requires merchants to have a higher degree of knowledge and understanding of the Code.

B.   Sales and Sales Contracts
  1.   Every sales contract is subject to the basic principles of law that govern all contracts: agreement, consideration, capacity, and legality.
  2.   But when a contract involves the sale of goods, the UCC imposes rules that may vary slightly or substantially from basic contract law.
       a)   Article 2 governs only contracts for the sale of goods.
       b)   To be considered "goods," an item must be personal property that is tangible and movable (e.g., not real estate).
       c)   A "sale" is "the passing of title from the seller to the buyer for a price" (UCC Sec. 2-10611).
       d)   The UCC does not cover the sale of services, although certain "mixed transactions," such as the sale by a garage of car parts (goods) and repairs (a service) will fall under the Code's jurisdiction if the goods are the dominant element of the contract.
  3.   The Code imposes special standards of conduct in certain instances when merchants sell goods to one another.
       a)   Usually, a person is considered a professional merchant if he "deals in goods of the kind" involved in the contract and has special knowledge of the business or of the goods; employs a merchant agent to conduct a transaction for him; or holds himself out to be a merchant.
  4.   Although the UCC requires that the same elements outlined in common law be present in forming a sales contract, it relaxes many of the specific restrictions.
       a)   For example, the UCC states that a contract exists even if the parties omit one or more terms (price, delivery date, place of delivery, quantity), as long as they intended to make a contract and there is a reasonably certain method for the court to supply the missing terms.
  5.   Acceptance of an offer. The UCC states that as long as an offeree's response (words, writing, or actions) indicates a sincere willingness to accept the offer, it is judged as a legitimate acceptance even though varying terms are added.
  6.   The UCC significantly changes the common law requirement that any contract modification requires new consideration.
       a)   Under the Code, modifications to contract terms are binding without new consideration if they are made in good faith.
  7.   The Code also has its own Statute of Frauds provision relating to the form of contracts for the sale of goods.
       a)   If the price of the goods is $500 or more, the contract must be written to be enforceable.
  8.   The UCC includes a special provision involving the writing requirement in contracts between merchants.
       a)   If merchants form a verbal contract for the sale of goods priced at more than $500 and one of them sends a written confirmation of the deal to the other, the merchant receiving the confirmation must object to it in writing within 10 days. Otherwise, the contract is enforceable against both merchants, even though the merchant receiving the confirmation has not actually signed anything.
       b)   Once the parties create a sales contract, they are bound to perform according to its terms.
       c)   The seller must make delivery of the items involved in the contract, but "delivery" is not necessarily physical delivery. The seller simply must make the goods available to the buyer.
       d)   The buyer must accept the delivery of conforming goods from the buyer. Of course, the buyer has the right to inspect the goods in a reasonable manner and at any

reasonable time or place to ensure that they are conforming goods before making payment.

    (1) However, C.O.D. terms prohibit the right to advance inspection unless the contract specifies otherwise.

9. The buyer can indicate his acceptance of the goods in several ways.

    a) Usually, by an express statement that the goods are suitable.

        (1) This expression can be by words or by conduct.

    b) Also, the Code assumes acceptance if the buyer has a reasonable opportunity to inspect the goods and has failed to reject them within a reasonable time.

10. The buyer has the duty to pay for the goods on the terms stated in the contract when they are received.

    a) The seller cannot require payment before the buyer receives the goods.

    b) Unless otherwise stated in the contract, payment must be in cash.

C. Breach of Sales Contracts

  1. As we have seen, when a party to the sales contract fails to perform according to its terms, that party is said to have breached the contract.

  2. The law provides the innocent (nonbreaching) party numerous remedies, including payment of damages and the right to retain possession of the goods.

    a) The object of these remedies is to place the innocent party in the same position as if the contract had been carried out. The parties to the contract may specify their own damages in case of breach.

    b) These provisions, called liquidated damages, must be reasonable and cannot be in the nature of a penalty.

  3. An unpaid seller has certain remedies available under the terms of the Code.

    a) Under a seller's lien, every seller has the right to maintain possession of the goods until the buyer pays for them.

    b) If the buyer uses a fraudulent payment to obtain the goods, the seller has the right to recover them.

    c) If the seller discovers the buyer is insolvent, the seller can withhold delivery of the goods until the buyer pays in cash.

    d) In some cases, the buyer breaches a contract while the goods are still unfinished in the production process. When this occurs, the seller must use "reasonable commercial judgment" in deciding whether to sell them for scrap or complete them and resell them elsewhere.

  4. When the seller breaches a contract, the buyer also has specific remedies available.

    a) If the goods do not conform to the contract's terms, the buyer has the right to reject them.

    b) If the seller fails to deliver the goods, the buyer can sue for the difference between the contract price and the market price at the time the breach became known.

    c) When the buyer accepts goods and then discovers they are defective or nonconforming, he must notify the seller of the breach.

        (1) In this instance, damages amount to the difference between the value of the goods delivered and their value if they had been delivered as promised.

    d) If a buyer pays for goods that the seller retains, he can take possession of the goods if the seller becomes insolvent within 10 days after receiving the first payment.

    e) If the seller unlawfully withholds the goods from the buyer, the buyer can recover them.

    f) If the seller breaches the contract, the buyer has the right to rescind the contract; if the buyer has paid any part of the purchase price, it must be refunded.

5. Whenever a party breaches a sales contract, the innocent party must bring suit within a specified period of time.
    a) The Code sets the statute of limitations at four years.

D. Sales Warranties and Product Liability
    1. The U.S. economy once promulgated the philosophy of caveat emptor, "let the buyer beware."
    2. Today the marketplace enforces a policy of caveat venditor, "let the seller beware."
    3. There are two general categories involving the quality and reliability of the products sold: sales warranties and product liability.
    4. Sales warranties
        a) Simply stated, a sales warranty is a promise or a statement of fact by the seller that a product will meet certain standards.
        b) Because a breach of warranty is a breach of promise, the buyer has the right to recover damages from the seller.
    5. Several types of warranties can arise in a sale.
        a) A seller creates an express warranty by making statements about the condition, quality, and performance of the good that the buyer substantially relies on.
            (1) Words or actions can create express warranties.
            (2) An express warranty generally arises if the seller indicates that the goods conform to any promises of fact the seller makes, to any description of them, or to any display model or sample.
        b) Implied warranties take several forms.
            (1) Whenever someone sells goods, the UCC automatically infers certain types of warranties unless the seller specifically excludes them.
            (2) Every seller, simply by offering goods for sale, implies a warranty of title, which promises that his title to the goods is valid (i.e., no liens or claims exist) and that transfer of title is legitimate.
            (3) An implied warranty of merchantability assures the buyer that the product will be of average quality--not the best and not the worst.
            (4) An implied warranty of fitness for a particular purpose arises when a seller knows the particular reason for which a buyer is purchasing a product and knows that the buyer is depending on the seller's judgment to select the proper item.
        c) The Code also states that the only way a merchant can disclaim an implied warranty is to include the words "sold as is" or "with all faults," stating that the buyer purchases the product as it is, without any guarantees.
    6. Product Liability.
        a) At one time, only the parties directly involved in the execution of a contract were bound by the law of sales warranties.
        b) Today, the UCC and the states have expanded the scope of warranties to include any person (including bystanders) incurring personal or property damages caused by a faulty product.
        c) In addition, most states allow an injured party to sue any seller in the chain of distribution for breach of warranty.
            (1) The average size of jury verdicts in product liability cases is $773,500.
        d) Although 70 percent of the products made and sold in the United States cross state lines, each of the 50 states has its own version of product liability laws, complicating matters for businesses.
            (1) Less than 5 percent of product-related injuries result in some type of claim for compensation.

e) A common basis of recovery for those who do file claims is negligence, when a manufacturer or distributor fails to do something that a "reasonable" person would do.

WIRED TO THE WEB - He Bit Off More Than He Could Chew

SUMMARY
On October 28, 1983, Fred Goodman injured himself biting into a Wendy's double hamburger sandwich by biting a triangular bone, one and a half inches long, one-sixteenth to one-quarter inch thick, and one-quarter inch wide. He broke three of his teeth and required extensive dental surgery to rectify the damage.

The restaurant purchased its beef from Greensboro Meat Supply Company (GMSC). Wendy's policy manuals require its beef to be chopped and "free from bone or cartilage in excess of one-eighth of an inch in any dimension." The U.S. Department of Agriculture (USDA) had certified GMSC's processing plant.

Goodman sued Wendy's, claiming breach of an implied warranty of merchantability. Wendy's argued that it should not be held liable because the object that injured Goodman was not a foreign object but was "natural" to the food.

Use the resources of the World Wide Web* and your local library to answer the following questions:

1. Did the hamburger Goodman ate violate the implied Warranty of merchantability under the Uniform Commercial Code? Explain.
    Answer - Students' responses should also consider content on pages 770-771. Students should find that, while standards exist, the resolution of the case will depend more on the ability of the attorneys to argue their positions than on an absolute standard.
2. What standards do the courts use to determine whether food complies with the requirements of an implied warranty of fitness for a particular purpose?
    Answer - Students' responses will depend on their Web research.
3. Is it reasonable to expect that every hamburger served will be "perfect"? What implications does your answer have on the outcome of this case?
    Answer - The obvious answer is no, but what constitutes imperfection? The bone found exceeds USDA standards but sufficiently to make the sandwich imperfect? Also, the extensive amount of damage to Goodman's teeth from "one bite" on that size bone could raise questions about contributory negligence on Goodman's part, regarding the care of his own teeth.

*   Try these Web sites to gather information about this case:
    http://www.phlip.marist.edu/contemcheese/index.htm
    http://www.nolo.com/dictionary/Dictionary_alpha.cfm?wordnumber=211&alpha=1
    http://www.lectlaw.com/files/cos53

---

f) Typically, negligence claims arise from one or more of the following charges.
    (1) Negligent design. In claims based on negligent design, a buyer claims an injury occurred because the manufacturer designed the product improperly.
    (2) Negligent manufacturing. In cases claiming negligent manufacturing, a buyer claims that a company's failure to follow proper manufacturing, assembly, or inspection procedures allowed a defective product to get into the customer's hands and cause injury.

(3) Failure to warn. Although manufacturers do not have to warn customers about obvious dangers of using their products, they must warn them about the dangers of normal use and of foreseeable misuse of the product.

7. Another common basis for product liability claims against businesses is strict liability, which states that a manufacturer is accountable for its actions no matter what its intentions or the extent of its negligence.

   a) Unlike negligence, a claim of strict liability does not require the injured party to prove that the company's actions were unreasonable.

   b) The injured person must prove only that the company manufactured or sold a product that was defective and that it caused the injury.

8. Business owners also have a duty to warn customers of physical dangers on their property under the doctrine of premises liability.

   a) This duty to warn encompasses hazards such as wet floors, icy sidewalks, and broken pavement that might cause physical injuries to customers.

IV. Protection of Intellectual Property
   A. Described
      1. Many entrepreneurs build businesses around intellectual property--products and services that are the result of the creative process and have commercial value. New methods of teaching foreign languages at an accelerated pace, hit songs, books that bring a smile, and new drugs that fight diseases are just some of the ways intellectual property makes our lives better or more enjoyable.

      2. Entrepreneurs can protect their intellectual property from unauthorized use with the help of three important tools: patents, trademarks, and copyrights.

   B. Patents
      1. A patent is a grant from the federal government's Patent and Trademark Office (PTO) to the inventor of a product, giving the exclusive right to make, use, or sell the invention in this country for 20 years from the date of filing the patent application.

      2. The purpose of giving an inventor a 20-year monopoly over a product is to stimulate creativity and innovation.

         a) After 20 years, the patent expires and cannot be renewed.

      3. Most patents are granted for new product inventions, but design patents, extending for 14 years beyond the date the patent is issued, are given to inventors who make new, original, and ornamental changes in the design of existing products that enhance their sales.

         a) Inventors who develop a new plant can obtain a plant patent, provided they can reproduce the plant asexually (e.g., by grafting or crossbreeding rather than planting seeds).

         b) To be patented, a device must be new (but not necessarily better!), not obvious to a person of ordinary skill or knowledge in the related field, and useful.

         c) A device cannot be patented if it has been publicized in print anywhere in the world or if it has been used or offered for sale in this country before the date of the patent application.

         d) A U.S. patent is granted only to the true inventor.

         e) No one can copy or sell a patented invention without getting a license from its creator.

      4. Although inventors are never assured of getting a patent, they can enhance their chances considerably by following the basic steps suggested by the PTO.

         a) Only those attorneys and agents who are officially registered may represent an inventor seeking a patent.

      b) Approximately 98 percent of all inventors rely on these patent experts to steer them through the convoluted process.

      c) A list of PTO-approved patent attorneys and agents is available at the U.S. Patent and Trademark Office's Web site <http://www.uspto.gov/web/offices/dcom/olia/oed/roster/>.

IN THE FOOTSTEPS OF AN ENTREPRENEUR - A Worthwhile Patent Battle

SUMMARY

Robert Kearns sued all of the world's major car manufacturers claiming the automakers owed him millions of dollars in royalties for using his invention on millions of cars without his permission. Kearns invented the intermittent windshield wiper, the stop-and-go system ideally suited for those damp, slightly misty days.

Kearns developed the invention due to an eye injury and subsequent dissertation research he did. By October 1963, Kearns had a working prototype of his blinking wipers mounted on his Galaxy. The device suffered a few bugs, however. When the box housing the circuits got hot, for example, the wipers would switch themselves on, rain or not. While he worked to perfect his invention, he contacted two engineers at Ford to see if they were interested. They were, and thus began a six-year relationship between Kearns and Ford. As soon as he had his wipers working smoothly, Kearns took out the first of several patents on his product. From 1966 to 1969, Kearns worked closely with engineers at Ford, teaching them how his system worked. In 1969, Ford introduced its own intermittent wiper system that incorporated many of Kearns's ideas and designs.

Kearns soon saw every major automaker develop intermittent wiper systems that used his ideas. In 1978, Kearns began filing patent infringement lawsuits against every major automaker in the world, starting with Ford. Finally in 1990, a court ruled that Kearns's patent was valid and that Ford had infringed on it. Kearns and Ford settled out of court for $10.2 million. Shortly afterward, he won $113 million from Chrysler in a similar suit. After decades of legal battles, Kearns has collected more than $30 million from automakers for infringing on his patent.

Use the information in this chapter and on the U.S. Patent and Trademark Office's Web site at <http://www. uspto.gov/> to answer the following questions:

1. What is a patent? What purpose does a patent serve?
   Answer - A patent is a grant from the federal government's Patent and Trademark Office (PTO) to the inventor of a product, giving the exclusive right to make, use, or sell the invention in this country for 20 years from the date of filing the patent application. The purpose of giving an inventor a 20-year monopoly over a product is to stimulate creativity and innovation.

2. What did Kearns have to prove to the U.S. Patent and Trademark Office to receive a patent for his intermittent wiper system?
   Answer - That his product was unique and not the outcome of common knowledge.

3. Is it ethical for an inventor to be able to receive a patent--and therefore a monopoly--on an invention? Explain.
   Answer - Students' responses will vary but they should think through the effort and expense of the invention process and what is reasonable compensation for that effort, i.e., the exclusive rights to the fruit of one's labor. Students should also realize the number of inventions/patents that do not lead to anything.

5. The patent process
   a) Since George Washington signed the first patent law in 1790, the U.S. Patent and Trademark Office has issued patents on everything imaginable.
   b) To date the PTO has issued more than 60 million patents, and it receives more than 230,000 new applications each year.
   c) To receive a patent, an inventor must follow these steps:
      (1) Establish the invention's novelty.
      (2) Document the device. Inventors also can file a disclosure document with the PTO: a process that includes writing a letter describing the invention and sending a check for $10 to the PTO.
      (3) Search existing patents. The purpose of the search is to determine whether the inventor has a chance of getting a patent.
      (4) Study search results.
      (5) Submit the patent application.
      (6) Prosecute the patent. Approval of a patent normally takes about two years from the date of the filing.
6. Defending a patent against "copycat producers" can be expensive and time-consuming but often is necessary to protect an entrepreneur's interest.
   a) The average cost of a patent infringement lawsuit is about $600,000 if the case goes to trial (about half that if the parties settle before going to trial), but the odds of winning are in the patent holder's favor.
   b) More than 60 percent of those holding patents win their infringement suits.

C. Trademarks
   1. A trademark is any distinctive word, phrase, symbol, design, name, logo, slogan, or trade dress that a company uses to identify the origin of a product or to distinguish it from other goods on the market.
      a) A service mark is the same as a trademark except that it identifies and distinguishes the source of a service rather than a product.
   2. A trademark serves as a company's "signature" in the marketplace.
   3. A trademark can be more than just a company's logo, slogan, or brand name; it can also include symbols, shapes, colors, smells, or sounds.
   4. There are 1.5 million trademarks registered in the United States, 900,000 of which are in actual use.
      a) Federal law permits a manufacturer to register a trademark, which prevents other companies from employing a similar mark to identify their goods.
      b) Before 1989, a business could not reserve a trademark in advance of use.
      c) Today, the first party who either uses a trademark in commerce or files an application with the PTO has the ultimate right to register that trademark.
      d) Trademarks last indefinitely as long as the holder continues to use it.
      e) However, a trademark cannot keep competitors from producing the same product and selling it under a different name.
   5. Many business owners are confused by the use of the symbols TM and ®. Anyone who claims the right to a particular trademark (or servicemark) can use the ^{TM} (or ^{SM}) symbols without having to register the mark with the PTO.
   6. Only those businesses that have registered their marks with the PTO can use the ® symbol.
      a) Entrepreneurs do not have to register trademarks or servicemarks to establish their rights to those marks; however, registering a mark with the PTO does give entrepreneurs greater power in protecting their marks.

b) Filing an application to register a trademark or servicemark is relatively easy, but it does require a search of existing names.

7. An owner may lose the exclusive right to a trademark if it loses its unique character and becomes a generic name.

a) Aspirin, escalator, thermos, brassiere, super glue, yo-yo, and cellophane all were once enforceable trademarks that have become common words.

D. Copyrights

1. A copyright is an exclusive right that protects the creators of original works of authorship such as literary, dramatic, musical, and artistic works (e.g., paintings, sculptures, literature, software, music, videos, video games, choreography, motion pictures, recordings, and others).

a) The internationally recognized symbol © denotes a copyrighted work.

b) A copyright protects only the form in which an idea is expressed, not the idea itself.

c) A copyright on a creative work comes into existence the moment its creator puts that work into a tangible form.

d) Just as with a trademark, obtaining basic copyright protection does not require registering the creative work with the U.S. Copyright Office <http://lcweb. loc.gov/copyright>.

2. Registering a copyright does give creators greater protection over their work, however. Copyright applications must be filed with the Copyright Office in the Library of Congress for a fee of $10 per application.

3. A valid copyright on a work lasts for the life of the creator plus 50 years after his or her death.

a) A copyright lasts 75 to 100 years if the copyright holder is a business.

b) When a copyright expires, the work becomes public property and can be used free of charge by anyone.

4. Because they are so easy to duplicate, computer software programs and videotapes are among the most-often-pirated items by copyright infringers.

5. Experts estimate that the U.S. software industry loses $15 billion each year to pirates who illegally copy programs and that Hollywood loses $2 billion to those who forge videotapes and sell them.

E. Protecting Intellectual Property

1. Acquiring the protection of patents, trademarks, and copyrights is useless unless an entrepreneur takes action to protect those rights in the marketplace.

2. The primary weapon an entrepreneur has to protect patents, trademarks, and copyrights is the legal system.

3. The major problem with relying on the legal system to enforce ownership rights is the cost of infringement lawsuits, which can quickly exceed the budget of most small businesses.

4. If an entrepreneur has a valid patent, trademark, or copyright, stopping an infringer often requires nothing more than a stern letter from an attorney threatening a lawsuit. Legal battles always involve costs. Before bringing a lawsuit, an entrepreneur must consider the following issues:

a) Can the opponent afford to pay if you win?

b) Do you expect to get enough from the suit to cover the costs of hiring an attorney and preparing a case?

c) Can you afford the loss of time, money, and privacy from the ensuing lawsuit?

V. The Law of Agency
   A. Described
        1. An agent is one who stands in the place of and represents another (the principal) in business dealings.
        2. Although he has the power to act for the principal, an agent remains subject to the principal's control.
           a) Many small business managers do not realize that their employees are agents while performing job-related tasks, but the employer is liable only for those acts that employees perform within the scope of employment.
        3. Any person, even those lacking contractual capacity, can serve as an agent, but a principal must have the legal capacity to create contracts.
        4. Both the principal and the agent are bound by the requirements of a fiduciary relationship, one characterized by trust and good faith. In addition, each party has specific duties to the other.
        5. An agent's duties include:
           a) Loyalty. Every agent must be faithful to the principal in all business dealings.
           b) Performance. An agent must perform his duties according to the principal's instructions.
           c) Notification. The agent must notify the principal of all facts and information concerning the subject matter of the agency.
           d) Duty of care. An agent must act with reasonable care when performing duties for the principal.
           e) Accounting. An agent is responsible for accounting for all profits and property received or distributed on the principal's behalf.
        6. A principal's duties include:
           a) Compensation. Unless a free agency is created, the principal must pay the agent for her services.
           b) Reimbursement. The principal must reimburse the agent for all payments made for the principal or any expenses incurred in the administration of the agency.
           c) Cooperation. Every principal has the duty to indemnify the agent for any authorized payments or any loss or damages incurred by the agency, unless the liability is the result of the agent's mistake.
           d) Safe working conditions. The law requires a principal to provide a safe working environment for all agents. Workers' compensation laws cover an employer's liability for injuries agents receive on the job.
        7. As agents, employees can bind a company to agreements, even if the owner did not intend for them to do so.
           a) An employee can create a binding obligation, for instance, if the business owner represents her as authorized to perform such transactions.
           b) Employees have implied authority to create agreements when performing the normal duties of their jobs.
        8. When an agent achieves the specific purpose of the agency, the agency ends, and the principal no longer binds the agent.
           a) In addition, the two parties can limit the existence of the agency, or they can cancel the agency by mutual agreement.
           b) Only when the two parties have terminated the agency themselves must the principal notify any third parties who might know of the agency relationship.

VI. Bankruptcy
   A. Defined
        1. Bankruptcy occurs when a business is unable to pay its debts as they come due.

       a) Early bankruptcy laws were aimed at forcing debtors into court, where they were required to give their property to their creditors.

       b) Taking debtors to court prevented them from hiding assets from creditors and escaping repayment of debts.

       c) But in 1978 Congress passed the Bankruptcy Reform Act, drastically changing the nature of bankruptcy law.

       d) The law has removed much of the stigma from being bankrupt; in fact, a bankrupt person is now called a debtor.

2. Filing for bankruptcy, which was once akin to contracting a social disease, is becoming an accepted business strategy.

3. Many of those filing for bankruptcy are small business owners seeking protection from creditors under one of the eight chapters of the Bankruptcy Reform Act of 1978.

4. Under the act, three chapters (7, 11, and 13) govern the majority of bankruptcies related to small business ownership.

5. Usually, small business owners in danger of failing can choose from two types of bankruptcies:

       a) liquidation (once the owner files for bankruptcy, the business ceases to exist).

       b) reorganization (after filing for bankruptcy, the owner formulates a reorganization plan under which the business continues to operate).

B. Chapter 7. Liquidations

1. The most common type of bankruptcy is filed under Chapter 7 (called straight bankruptcy), which accounts for 70 percent of all filings.

2. Under Chapter 7, a debtor simply declares all of his firm's debts; he must then turn over all assets to a trustee, who is elected by the creditors or appointed by the court.

3. Depending on the outcome of the asset sale, creditors can receive anywhere between 0 and 100 percent of their claims.

4. Once the bankruptcy proceeding is complete, any remaining debts are discharged and the company disappears.

5. Straight bankruptcy proceedings can be started by filing either a voluntary or an involuntary petition.

       a) A voluntary case starts when the debtor files a petition with a bankruptcy court, stating the names and addresses of all creditors, the debtor's financial position, and all property the debtor owns.

       b) Creditors start an involuntary petition by filing with the bankruptcy court.

          (1) If there are 12 or more creditors, at least three of them whose unsecured claims total $10,000 or more must file the involuntary petition.

          (2) If a debtor has fewer than 12 creditors, only one of them having a claim of $10,000 or more is required to file.

       c) As soon as a petition (voluntary or involuntary) is filed in a bankruptcy court, all creditors' claims against the debtor are suspended.

          (1) Called an automatic stay, this provision prevents creditors from collecting any of the debts the debtor owed them before the petition was filed.

6. According to the Bankruptcy Reform Act certain assets are exempt, although each state establishes its own exemptions.

       a) Most states make an allowance for equity in a home, interest in an automobile, interest in a large number of personal items and other personal assets.

       b) Federal law allows a $15,000 exemption for ownership of a home, a $4,000 exemption for household items and clothing, and a $400 exemption for other property.

7. The law does not allow a debtor to transfer the ownership of property to others to avoid its seizure in a bankruptcy.
   a) If a debtor transfers property within one year of the filing of a bankruptcy petition, the trustee can ignore the transfer and claim the assets.
   b) The law also enables a judge to dismiss a Chapter 7 bankruptcy petition if it is a "substantial abuse" of the bankruptcy code.

C. Chapter 11. Reorganization
   1. For the small business weakened by a faltering economy or management mistakes, Chapter 11 provides a second chance for success.
   2. The philosophy behind this form of bankruptcy is that ailing companies can prosper again if given a fresh start with less debt.
      a) Under Chapter 11, a company is protected from creditors' legal actions while it formulates a plan for reorganization and debt repayment or settlement.
      b) In most cases, the small firm and its creditors negotiate a settlement in which the company repays its debts and is freed of the remainder.
      c) The business continues to operate under the court's direction, but creditors cannot foreclose on it, nor can they collect any prebankruptcy debts the company owes.
   3. A Chapter 11 bankruptcy filing can be either voluntary or involuntary.
      a) Once the petition is filed, an automatic stay goes into effect and the debtor has 120 days to file a reorganization plan with the court.
      b) Usually, the court does not replace management with an appointed trustee; instead, the bankrupt party, called the debtor in possession, serves as trustee.
      c) If the debtor fails to file a plan within the 120-day limit, any party involved in the bankruptcy, including creditors, may propose a plan.
      d) The plan must identify the various classes of creditors and their claims, outline how each class will be treated, and establish a method to implement the plan.
      e) It also must spell out which debts cannot be paid, which can be paid, and what methods the debtor will use to repay them.
   4. A court will approve a plan if a majority of each of the three classes of creditors--secured, priority, and unsecured--votes in favor of it.
   5. Filing under Chapter 11 offers the weakened small business a number of advantages, the greatest of which is a chance to survive (although most of the companies that file under Chapter 11 ultimately are liquidated).
      a) Creditors frequently incur substantial losses in Chapter 11 bankruptcies.

D. Chapter 13. Individual Repayment Plans
   1. Individual debtors (not businesses) with a regular income who owe unsecured debts of less than $250,000 or secured debts under $750,000 may file for bankruptcy under Chapter 13.
      a) Chapter 13 is less complicated and less expensive.
      b) Proceedings must begin voluntarily.
      c) Once the debtor files the petition, creditors cannot start or continue legal action to collect payment.
   2. Under Chapter 13, only the debtor can file a repayment plan, whose terms cannot exceed five years. If the court approves the plan, the debtor may pay off the obligations, either in full or partially, on an installment basis.
   3. The plan is designed with the debtor's future income in mind, and when the debtor completes the payments under the plan, all debts are discharged.

VII. Government Regulation
   A. Introduction
       1. Most entrepreneurs think that the regulatory process is overwhelming and out of control.
       2. The major complaint small business owners have concerning government regulation revolves around the cost of compliance.
       3. A 1996 law, the Small Business Regulatory Enforcement Fairness Act, offers business owners some hope.
            a) Its purposes are to require government agencies to consider the impact of their regulations on small companies and to give business owners more input into the regulatory process.
       4. Most business owners agree that some governmental regulation is necessary.
       5. It is not the regulations that protect workers and consumers and achieve social objectives that businesses object to but those that produce only marginal benefits relative to their costs.
       6. Owners of small firms, especially, seek relief from wasteful and meaningless governmental regulations, charging that the cost of compliance exceeds the benefits gained.
            a) Figure 22.2 shows the annual cost of federal regulation since 1978.

   B. Trade Practices
       1. Sherman Antitrust Act
            a) One of the earliest trade laws, passed in 1890 to promote competition in the U.S. economy.
            b) This act is the foundation on which antitrust policy in the United States is built and was aimed at breaking up the most powerful monopoly of the late nineteenth century, John D. Rockefeller's Standard Oil Trust.
       2. The Sherman Antitrust Act contains two primary provisions affecting growth and trade among businesses.
            a) Section I forbids "every contract, combination in the form of trust or otherwise, or conspiracy in restraint of trade or commerce among the several states, or with foreign nations."
                 (1) This section outlaws any agreement among sellers that might create an unreasonable restraint on free trade in the marketplace.
            b) Section II of the Sherman Antitrust Act makes it illegal for any person to "monopolize or attempt to monopolize any part of the trade or commerce among the several states, or with foreign nations."
                 (1) The primary focus of Section II is on preventing the undesirable effects of monopoly power in the marketplace.
       3. Clayton Act
            a) Congress passed the Clayton Act in 1914 to strengthen federal antitrust laws by spelling out specific monopolistic activities.
       4. The major provisions of the Clayton Act forbid the following activities:
            a) Price discrimination. A firm cannot charge different customers different prices for the same product, unless the price discrimination is based on an actual cost savings, is made to meet a lower price from competitors, or is justified by a difference in grade, quality, or quantity sold.
            b) Exclusive dealing and tying contracts. A seller cannot require a buyer to purchase only her product to the exclusion of other competitive sellers' products (an exclusive dealing agreement).
                 (1) Also, the act forbids sellers to sell a product on the condition that the buyer agrees to purchase another product the seller offers (a tying agreement).

      c) Purchasing stock in competing corporations. A business cannot purchase the stock or assets of another business when the effect may be to substantially lessen competition.

         (1) This does not mean that a corporation cannot hold stock in a competing company; the rule is designed to prevent horizontal mergers that would reduce competition.

      d) Interlocking directorates. The act forbids interlocking directorates--a person serving on the board of directors of two or more competing companies.

    5. Federal Trade Commission Act

      a) To supplement the Clayton Act, Congress passed the Federal Trade Commission Act in 1914, which created its namesake agency and gave it a broad range of powers.

      b) Section 5 gives the FTC the power to prevent "unfair methods of competition in commerce and unfair or deceptive acts or practices in commerce."

      c) Recent amendments have expanded the FTC's powers.

      d) In addition, the agency has issued a number of trade regulation rules defining acceptable and unacceptable trade practices in various industries.

         (1) Its major weapon is a "cease and desist order," commanding the violator to stop its unfair trade practices.

      e) The FTC Act and the Lanham Trademark Act of 1988 (plus state laws) govern the illegal practice of deceptive advertising.

         (1) In general, the FTC can review any advertisement that might mislead people into buying a product or service they would not buy if they knew the truth.

    6. Robinson-Patman Act

      a) In 1936 Congress passed the Robinson-Patman Act, which further restricted price discrimination in the marketplace.

      b) The act forbids any seller "to discriminate in price between different purchases of commodities of like grade and quality" unless there are differences in the cost of manufacture, sale, or delivery of the goods.

      c) The FTC has had the primary responsibility of enforcing the Robinson-Patman Act.

    7. Other legislation

      a) The Celler-Kefauver Act of 1950 gave the FTC the power to review certain proposals for mergers so it could prevent too much concentration of power in any particular industry.

      b) The Miller-Tydings Act in 1937 to introduce an exception to the Sherman Antitrust Act.

         (1) This act made it legal for manufacturers to use fair-trade agreements that prohibit sellers of the manufacturer's product from selling it below a predetermined fair trade price.

         (2) This form of price fixing was outlawed when Congress repealed the Miller-Tydings Act in 1976. Manufacturers can no longer mandate minimum or maximum prices on their products to sellers.

C. Consumer Protection

    1. The first law, the Pure Food and Drug Act, passed in 1906, regulated the labeling of various food and drug products.

    2. Later amendments empowered government agencies to establish safe levels of food additives and to outlaw carcinogenic (cancer-causing) additives.

    3. In 1938, Congress passed the Food, Drug, and Cosmetics Act, which created the Food and Drug Administration (FDA).

      a) The FDA is responsible for establishing standards of safe over-the-counter drugs; inspecting food and drug manufacturing operations; performing research on food, additives, and drugs; regulating drug labeling; and other related tasks.

4. Since 1976, manufacturers have been required to print accurate information about the quantity and content of their products in a conspicuous place on the package.
   a) In general, labels must identify the raw materials used in the product, the manufacturer, the distributor (and its place of business), the net quantity of the contents, and the quantity of each serving if the package states the number of servings.
   b) The law also requires labels to be truthful.
   c) A 1970 amendment to the Fair Packaging and Labeling Act, the Poison Prevention Packaging Act, required manufacturers to install child-proof caps on all products that are toxic.
5. With the passage of the Consumer Products Safety Act in 1972, Congress created the CPSC to control potentially dangerous products sold to consumers, and it has broad powers over manufacturers and sellers of consumer products.
   a) For instance, the CPSC can set safety requirements for consumer products, and it has the power to ban the production of any product it considers hazardous to consumers.
   b) It can also order vendors to remove unsafe products from their shelves.
6. The Consumer Product Safety Act was created to do the following:
   a) Protect the public against unreasonable risk of injury from consumer products.
   b) Help customers compare products on the basis of safety.
   c) Create safety standards for products and consolidate inconsistent state regulations.
   d) Research the causes and possible prevention of injuries and illness from consumer products.
7. The Magnuson-Moss Warranty Act, passed in 1975, regulates written warranties that companies offer on the consumer goods they sell.
   a) The act regulates only the warranties companies choose to offer.

D. Consumer Credit
   1. Another area subject to intense government regulation is consumer credit.
   2. The primary law regulating consumer credit is the Consumer Credit Protection Act (CCPA), passed in 1968.
      a) More commonly known as the Truth-in-Lending Act, this law requires sellers who extend credit and lenders to fully disclose the terms and conditions of credit arrangements.
      b) The Federal Trade Commission is responsible for enforcing the Truth-in-Lending Act.
      c) The two most important terms of the credit arrangement that lenders must disclose are the finance charge and the annual percentage rate.
      d) The Truth-in-Lending Act applies to any consumer loan for less than $25,000 (or loans of any amount secured by mortgages on real estate) that includes more than four installments.
   3. Merchants extending credit to customers must state clearly the following information, using specific terminology:
      a) The price of the product.
      b) The down payment and any trade-in allowance made.
      c) The unpaid balance owed after the down payment.
      d) Total dollar amount of the finance charge.
      e) Any prepaid finance charges or required deposit balances, such as points, service charges, or lenders' fees.
      f) Any other charges not included in the finance charge.
      g) The total amount to be financed.
      h) The unpaid balance.

        i) The deferred payment price, including the total cash price and finance and incidental charges.

        j) The date on which the finance charge begins to accrue.

        k) The annual percentage rate of the finance charge.

        l) The number, amounts, and due dates of payments.

        m) The penalties imposed in case of delinquent payments. A description of any security interest the creditor holds. .

        n) A description of any penalties imposed for early repayment of principal.

    4. Another provision of the Truth-in-Lending Act limits the credit-card holder's liability in case the holder's card is lost or stolen.

        a) As long as the holder notifies the company of the missing card, she is liable for only $50 of any amount that an unauthorized user might charge on the card (or zero if the holder notifies the company before any unauthorized use of the card).

    5. In 1974, Congress passed the Fair Credit Billing Act, an amendment to the Truth-in-Lending Act.

        a) Under this law, a credit-card holder may withhold payment on a faulty product, providing she has made a good faith effort to settle the dispute first.

    6. The Equal Credit Opportunity Act of 1974, which prohibits discrimination in granting credit on the basis of race, religion, national origin, color, sex, marital status, or whether the individual receives public welfare payment.

    7. In 1971, Congress created the Fair Credit Reporting Act to protect consumers against the circulation of inaccurate or obsolete information pertaining to credit applications.

    8. Congress enacted the Fair Debt Collection Practices Act in 1977 to protect consumers from abusive debt collection practices.

        a) The law does not apply to business owners collecting their own debts, but only to debt collectors working for other businesses.

        b) The act prevents debt collectors from doing the following:

            (1) Contacting the debtor at his workplace if the employer objects.

            (2) Using intimidation, harassment, or abusive language to pester the debtor.

            (3) Calling on the debtor at inconvenient times (before 8 A.M. or after 9 P.M.).

            (4) Contacting third parties (except parents, spouses, and financial advisers) about the debt.

            (5) Contacting the consumer after receiving notice of refusal to pay the debt (except to inform the debtor of the involvement of a collection agency).

            (6) Making false threats against the debtor.

E. Environmental Law

    1. In 1970, Congress created the Environmental Protection Agency (EPA) and gave it the authority to create laws that would protect the environment from pollution and contamination.

    2. Although the EPA administers a number of federal environmental statutes, three in particular stand out: the Clean Air Act, the Clean Water Act, and the Resource Conservation and Recovery Act.

    3. The Clean Air Act

        a) The act targets everything from coal-burning power plants to automobiles.

        b) The Clean Air Act assigned the EPA the task of developing a national air-quality standard, and the agency works with state and local governments to enforce compliance with these standards.

    4. The Clean Water Act

a) Passed in 1972, set out to make all navigable waters in the United States suitable for fishing and swimming by 1983 and to eliminate the discharge of pollutants into those waters by 1985.

b) The EPA has yet to achieve those goals.

c) The Clean Water Act requires that states establish water-quality standards and develop plans to reach them.

5. The Resource Conservation and Recovery Act

a) Passed in 1976 to deal with solid waste disposal.

b) The RCRA sets guidelines by which solid waste landfills must operate, and it establishes rules governing the disposal of hazardous wastes.

6. In 1980, Congress passed the Comprehensive Environmental Response, Compensation, and Liability Act (CERCLA) to deal with already contaminated sites.

a) The act created the Superfund, a special federal fund set up to finance and regulate the cleanup of solid waste disposal sites that are polluting the environment.

Chapter Summary

♦ Explain the basic elements required to create a valid, enforceable contract.

- A valid contract must contain these elements: agreement (offer and acceptance), consideration, capacity, and legality. A contract can be valid and yet unenforceable because it fails to meet two other conditions: genuineness of assent and proper form.

- Most contracts are fulfilled by both parties' performing their promised actions; occasionally, however, one party fails to perform as agreed, thereby breaching the contract. Usually, the non-breaching party is allowed to sue for monetary damages that would place her in the same position she would have been in had the contract been performed. In cases where money is an insufficient remedy, the injured party may sue for specific performance of the contract's terms.

♦ Outline the major components of the Uniform Commercial Code governing sales contracts.

- The Uniform Commercial Code (UCC) was an attempt to create a unified body of law governing routine business transactions. Of the 10 articles in the UCC, Article 2 on the sale of goods affects many business transactions.

- Contracts for the sale of goods must contain the same four elements of a valid contract, but the UCC relaxes many of the specific restrictions the common law imposes on contracts. Under the UCC, once the parties create a contract, they must perform their duties in good faith.

- The UCC also covers sales warranties. A seller creates an express warranty when he makes a statement about the performance of a product or indicates by example certain characteristics of the product. Sellers automatically create other warranties--warranties of title, implied warranties of merchantability, and, in certain cases, implied warranties of fitness for a particular purpose--when they sell a product.

♦ Discuss the protection of intellectual property rights involving patents, trademarks, and copyrights.

- A patent is a grant from the federal government that gives an inventor exclusive rights to an invention for 20 years. To submit a patent, an inventor must: establish novelty, document the device, search existing patents, study the search results, submit a patent application to the U.S. Patent and Trademark Office, and prosecute the application.

- A trademark is any distinctive word, symbol, or trade dress that a company uses to identify its product or to distinguish it from other goods. It serves as the company's "signature" in the market-place.

- A copyright protects original works of authorship. It covers only the form in which an idea is expressed and not the idea itself and lasts for 50 years beyond the creator's death.

♦ Explain the basic workings of the law of agency.
  ▪ In an agency relationship, one party (the agent) agrees to represent another (the principal). The agent has the power to act for the principal but remains subject to the principal's control. While performing job-related tasks, employees play an agent's role.
  ▪ An agent has the following duties to a principal: loyalty, performance, notification; duty of care, and accounting. The principal has certain duties to the agent: compensation, reimbursement, cooperation, indemnification, and safe working conditions.
♦ Explain the basics of bankruptcy law.
  ▪ Entrepreneurs whose businesses fail often have no other choice but to declare bankruptcy under one of three provisions: Chapter 7 liquidations, where the business sells its assets, pays what debts it can, and disappears; Chapter 11 reorganizations, where the business asks that its debts be forgiven or restructured and then reemerges; and Chapter 13, straight bankruptcy, which is for individuals only.
♦ Explain some of the government regulations affecting small businesses, including those governing trade practices, consumer protection, consumer credit, and the environment.
  ▪ Businesses operate under a multitude of government regulations governing many areas, including trade practices, where laws forbid restraint of trade, price discrimination, exclusive dealing and tying contracts, purchasing controlling interests in competitors, and interlocking directorates.
  ▪ Other areas subject to government regulations include consumer protection (the Food, Drug, and Cosmetics Act and the Consumer Product Safety Act), consumer credit (the Consumer Credit Protection Act, the Fair Debt Collection Practices Act, and the Fair Credit Reporting Act), and the environment (the Clean Air Act, the Clean Water Act, and the Resource Conservation and Recovery Act.

Discussion Questions

1. What is a contract? List and describe the four elements required for a valid contract. Must a contract be in writing to be valid?
    Answer - A contract is simply a legally binding agreement. It is a promise or a set of promises for the breach of which the law gives a remedy and that the performance of which the law in some way recognizes as a duty. A contract arises from an agreement, and it creates an obligation among the parties involved. Although almost everyone has the capacity to enter into a contractual agreement (freedom of contract), not every contract is valid and enforceable. A valid contract has four separate elements: agreement, consideration, contractual capacity, and legality. In addition, a contract must meet two supplemental requirements: genuineness of assent and form. Although not every contract must be in writing to be enforceable, the law does require some contracts to be evidenced by writing.

2. What constitutes an agreement?
    Answer - Agreement requires a "meeting of the minds" and is established by an offer and an acceptance. One party must make an offer to another party, who must accept that offer. Agreement is governed by the objective theory of contracts, which states that a party's intention to create a contract is measured by outward facts--words, conduct, and circumstances--rather than by subjective, personal intentions. In settling contract disputes, courts interpret the objective facts surrounding the contract from the perspective of an imaginary reasonable person.

    Agreements must have an offer--a promise or commitment to do or refrain from doing some specified thing in the future and an acceptance--only the person to whom the offer is made (the offeree) can accept an offer and create a contract.

3. What groups of people lack contractual capacity? How do the courts view contracts created by minors? By intoxicated people? By insane people?
    Answer - The third element of a valid contract requires that the parties involved in it must have contractual capacity for it to be enforceable. Not every individual who enters into a contract has the capacity to do so. Under the common law, minors, intoxicated people, and insane people lack contractual capacity. As a result, contracts these people enter into are considered to be voidable; that is, the party can annul or disaffirm the contract at his option.

    Minors constitute the largest group of individuals without contractual capacity. In most states, anyone under age 18 is a minor, although a few states establish 19 as the age of majority. If a minor receives the benefit of a completed contract and then disaffirms that contract, she must fulfill her duty of restoration by returning the benefit. Adults enter into contracts with minors at their own risk.

    A contract entered into by an intoxicated person can be either voidable or valid, depending on the person's condition when entering into the contract. If reason and judgment are impaired so that the person does not realize a contract is being made, the contract is voidable and the benefit must be returned. However, if the intoxicated person understands that he is forming a contract, although it may be foolish, the contract is valid and enforceable.

    A contract entered into by an insane person can be void, voidable, or valid, depending on the mental state of the person. Those who have been judged to be so mentally incompetent that a guardian is appointed for them cannot enter into a valid contract. An insane person who has not been legally declared insane (e.g., someone suffering from Alzheimer's disease) or appointed a guardian is bound by a contract if he was lucid enough at the time of the contract to comprehend its consequences.

4. What circumstances eliminate genuineness of assent in the parties' agreement?
    Answer - Genuineness of assent serves as a check on the parties' agreement, verifying that it is genuine and not subject to mistakes, misrepresentation, fraud, duress, or undue influence. Only mistakes of fact permit a party to avoid a contract. Fraud also voids a contract because no genuineness of assent exists. Duress, forcing an individual into a contract by fear or threat, eliminates genuineness of assent.

5. What is breach of contract? What remedies are available to a party injured by a breach?
    Answer - Occasionally, however, one party fails to perform as agreed. This failure is called breach of contract, and the injured party has certain remedies available.
    - In general, the nonbreaching party is entitled to sue for compensatory damages, the monetary damages that will place him in the same position he would have been in had the contract been performed.
    - In addition to compensatory damages, the nonbreaching party may also be awarded consequential damages (also called special damages) that arise as a consequence of the breach.
    - For the nonbreaching party to recover consequential damages, the breaching party must have known the consequences of the breach. The injured, or nonbreaching, party does, however, have a duty to make a reasonable effort to minimize (to mitigate) the damages incurred by the breach.
    - In some cases, monetary damages are inadequate to compensate the injured party for the breach of contract. The only remedy that would compensate the nonbreaching party might be specific performance of the act promised in the contract. Specific performance is usually the remedy for breached contracts dealing with unique items (antiques, land, animals). Courts rarely invoke the remedy of specific performance.

6. What is the Uniform Commercial Code? To which kinds of contracts does the UCC apply? How do its requirements for a sale contract differ from the common law requirements?
Answer - In the 1940s, a group of legal scholars compiled the Uniform Commercial Code (or the UCC or the Code) to replace the hodgepodge collection of confusing, often conflicting state laws that governed basic commercial transactions with a document designed to provide uniformity and consistency. The UCC <http://www.law.cornell.edu/ucc/table.htm> replaced numerous statutes governing trade when 49 states, the District of Columbia, and the Virgin Islands adopted it. (Louisiana has adopted only Articles 1, 3, 4, and 5.) The Code unites and modernizes the basic tenets into a single body of law.

Every sales contract is subject to the basic principles of law that govern all contracts: agreement, consideration, capacity, and legality. But when a contract involves the sale of goods, the UCC imposes rules that may vary slightly or substantially from basic contract law. Although the UCC requires that the same elements outlined in common law be present in forming a sales contract, it relaxes many of the specific restrictions.
- For example, the UCC states that a contract exists even if the parties omit one or more terms (price, delivery date, place of delivery, quantity), as long as they intended to make a contract and there is a reasonably certain method for the court to supply the missing terms.
- Acceptance of an offer. The UCC states that as long as an offeree's response (words, writing, or actions) indicates a sincere willingness to accept the offer, it is judged as a legitimate acceptance even though varying terms are added.
- The UCC significantly changes the common law requirement that any contract modification requires new consideration.
- The Code also has its own Statute of Frauds provision relating to the form of contracts for the sale of goods. The UCC includes a special provision involving the writing requirement in contracts between merchants.

7. Under the UCC, what remedies does a seller have when a buyer breaches a sales contract? What remedies does a buyer have when a seller breaches a contract?
Answer - The law provides the innocent (nonbreaching) party numerous remedies, including payment of damages and the right to retain possession of the goods. The object of these remedies is to place the innocent party in the same position as if the contract had been carried out. The parties to the contract may specify their own damages in case of breach. These provisions, called liquidated damages, must be reasonable and cannot be in the nature of a penalty.

An unpaid seller has certain remedies available under the terms of the Code.
- Under a seller's lien, every seller has the right to maintain possession of the goods until the buyer pays for them.
- If the buyer uses a fraudulent payment to obtain the goods, the seller has the right to recover them.
- If the seller discovers the buyer is insolvent, the seller can withhold delivery of the goods until the buyer pays in cash.
- In some cases, the buyer breaches a contract while the goods are still unfinished in the production process. When this occurs, the seller must use "reasonable commercial judgment" in deciding whether to sell them for scrap or complete them and resell them elsewhere.
When the seller breaches a contract, the buyer also has specific remedies available.
- If the goods do not conform to the contract's terms, the buyer has the right to reject them.
- If the seller fails to deliver the goods, the buyer can sue for the difference between the contract price and the market price at the time the breach became known.
- When the buyer accepts goods and then discovers they are defective or nonconforming, he must notify the seller of the breach.

- If a buyer pays for goods that the seller retains, he can take possession of the goods if the seller becomes insolvent within 10 days after receiving the first payment.
- If the seller unlawfully withholds the goods from the buyer, the buyer can recover them.
- If the seller breaches the contract, the buyer has the right to rescind the contract; if the buyer has paid any part of the purchase price, it must be refunded.

8. What is a sales warranty? Explain the different kinds of warranties sellers offer.
    Answer - Simply stated, a sales warranty is a promise or a statement of fact by the seller that a product will meet certain standards. Because a breach of warranty is a breach of promise, the buyer has the right to recover damages from the seller. Several types of warranties can arise in a sale. A seller creates an express warranty by making statements about the condition, quality, and performance of the good that the buyer substantially relies on. Whenever someone sells goods, the UCC automatically infers certain types of warranties unless the seller specifically excludes them.

9. Explain the different kinds of implied warranties the UCC imposes on sellers of goods. Can sellers disclaim these implied warranties? If so, how?
    Answer - Whenever someone sells goods, the UCC automatically infers certain types of warranties unless the seller specifically excludes them. Every seller, simply by offering goods for sale, implies a warranty of title, which promises that his title to the goods is valid (i.e., no liens or claims exist) and that transfer of title is legitimate. An implied warranty of merchantability assures the buyer that the product will be of average quality--not the best and not the worst. An implied warranty of fitness for a particular purpose arises when a seller knows the particular reason for which a buyer is purchasing a product and knows that the buyer is depending on the seller's judgment to select the proper item. The Code also states that the only way a merchant can disclaim an implied warranty is to include the words "sold as is" or "with all faults," stating that the buyer purchases the product as it is, without any guarantees.

10. What is product liability? Explain the charges that most often form the basis for product liability claims. What must a customer prove under these charges?
    Answer - Today, the UCC and the states have expanded the scope of warranties to include any person (including bystanders) incurring personal or property damages caused by a faulty product. In addition, most states allow an injured party to sue any seller in the chain of distribution for breach of warranty. A common basis of recovery for those who do file claims is negligence, when a manufacturer or distributor fails to do something that a "reasonable" person would do.

    Typically, negligence claims arise from one or more of the following charges.
    - Negligent design.
    - Negligent manufacturing.
    - Failure to warn.

    Another common basis for product liability claims against businesses is strict liability, which states that a manufacturer is accountable for its actions no matter what its intentions or the extent of its negligence. Unlike negligence, a claim of strict liability does not require the injured party to prove that the company's actions were unreasonable.

    Business owners also have a duty to warn customers of physical dangers on their property under the doctrine of premises liability. This duty to warn encompasses hazards such as wet floors, icy sidewalks, and broken pavement that might cause physical injuries to customers.

11. What is intellectual property? What tools do entrepreneurs have to protect their intellectual property?
    Answer - Many entrepreneurs build businesses around intellectual property--products and services that are the result of the creative process and have commercial value. New methods of teaching foreign languages at an accelerated pace, hit songs, books that bring a smile, and new drugs that fight diseases are just some of the ways intellectual property makes our lives better or more enjoyable. Entrepreneurs can protect their intellectual property from unauthorized use with the help of three important tools: patents, trademarks, and copyrights.

12. Explain the differences among patents, trademarks, and copyrights. What does each protect? How long does each last?
    Answer - A patent is a grant from the federal government's Patent and Trademark Office (PTO) to the inventor of a product, giving the exclusive right to make, use, or sell the invention in this country for 20 years from the date of filing the patent application. The purpose of giving an inventor a 20-year monopoly over a product is to stimulate creativity and innovation. After 20 years, the patent expires and cannot be renewed. Most patents are granted for new product inventions, but design patents, extending for 14 years beyond the date the patent is issued, are given to inventors who make new, original, and ornamental changes in the design of existing products that enhance their sales.

    A trademark is any distinctive word, phrase, symbol, design, name, logo, slogan, or trade dress that a company uses to identify the origin of a product or to distinguish it from other goods on the market. A service mark is the same as a trademark except that it identifies and distinguishes the source of a service rather than a product. A trademark serves as a company's "signature" in the marketplace. A trademark can be more than just a company's logo, slogan, or brand name; it can also include symbols, shapes, colors, smells, or sounds.

    A copyright is an exclusive right that protects the creators of original works of authorship such as literary, dramatic, musical, and artistic works (e.g., paintings, sculptures, literature, software, music, videos, video games, choreography, motion pictures, recordings, and others). The internationally recognized symbol © denotes a copyrighted work. A copyright protects only the form in which an idea is expressed, not the idea itself. A copyright on a creative work comes into existence the moment its creator puts that work into a tangible form.

13. What must an inventor prove to receive a patent?
    Answer - To receive a patent, an inventor must have an item that fits into one of the following categories.
    ▪ Inventors who develop a new plant can obtain a plant patent, provided they can reproduce the plant asexually (e.g., by grafting or crossbreeding rather than planting seeds).
    ▪ To be patented, a device must be new (but not necessarily better!), not obvious to a person of ordinary skill or knowledge in the related field, and useful.
    ▪ A device cannot be patented if it has been publicized in print anywhere in the world or if it has been used or offered for sale in this country before the date of the patent application.
    ▪ A U.S. patent is granted only to the true inventor.

14. Briefly explain the patent application process.
    Answer - The patent process involves:
    ▪ Establish the invention's novelty.
    ▪ Document the device. Inventors also can file a disclosure document with the PTO: a process that includes writing a letter describing the invention and sending a check for $10 to the PTO.
    ▪ Search existing patents. The purpose of the search is to determine whether the inventor has a chance of getting a patent.
    ▪ Study search results.

- Submit the patent application.
- Prosecute the patent. Approval of a patent normally takes about two years from the date of the filing.

15. What is an agent? What duties does an agent have to a principal? What duties does a principal have to an agent?

Answer - An agent is one who stands in the place of and represents another (the principal) in business dealings. Although he has the power to act for the principal, an agent remains subject to the principal's control. Both the principal and the agent are bound by the requirements of a fiduciary relationship, one characterized by trust and good faith. In addition; each party has specific duties to the other.

An agent's duties include:
- Loyalty. Every agent must be faithful to the principal in all business dealings.
- Performance. An agent must perform his duties according to the principal's instructions.
- Notification. The agent must notify the principal of all facts and information concerning the subject matter of the agency.
- Duty of care. An agent must act with reasonable care when performing duties for the principal.
- Accounting. An agent is responsible for accounting for all profits and property received or distributed on the principal's behalf.

A principal's duties include:
- Compensation. Unless a free agency is created, the principal must pay the agent for her services.
- Reimbursement. The principal must reimburse the agent for all payments made for the principal or any expenses incurred in the administration of the agency.
- Cooperation. Every principal has the duty to indemnify the agent for any authorized payments or any loss or damages incurred by the agency, unless the liability is the result of the agent's mistake.
- Safe working conditions. The law requires a principal to provide a safe working environment for all agents. Workers' compensation laws cover an employer's liability for injuries agents receive on the job.

16. Explain the differences among the three major forms of bankruptcy: Chapter 7, Chapter 11, and Chapter 13.

Answer - Bankruptcy occurs when a business is unable to pay its debts as they come due. Many of those filing for bankruptcy are small business owners seeking protection from creditors under one of the eight chapters of the Bankruptcy Reform Act of 1978. Under the act, three chapters (7, 11, and 13) govern the majority of bankruptcies related to small business ownership.

The most common type of bankruptcy is filed under Chapter 7 (called straight bankruptcy), which accounts for 70 percent of all filings. Under Chapter 7, a debtor simply declares all of his firm's debts; he must then turn over all assets to a trustee, who is elected by the creditors or appointed by the court. Depending on the outcome of the asset sale, creditors can receive anywhere between 0 and 100 percent of their claims. Once the bankruptcy proceeding is complete, any remaining debts are discharged and the company disappears.

For the small business weakened by a faltering economy or management mistakes, Chapter 11 provides a second chance for success. The philosophy behind this form of bankruptcy is that ailing companies can prosper again if given a fresh start with less debt. Under Chapter 11, a company is protected from creditors' legal actions while it formulates a plan for reorganization and debt repayment or settlement. In most cases, the small firm and its creditors negotiate a settlement in which the company repays its debts and is freed of the remainder. The business continues to operate under the court's direction, but creditors cannot foreclose on it, nor can they collect any prebankruptcy debts the company owes. A Chapter 11 bankruptcy filing can be either voluntary or involuntary.

Individual debtors (not businesses) with a regular income who owe unsecured debts of less than $250,000 or secured debts under $750,000 may file for bankruptcy under Chapter 13. Chapter 13 is less complicated and less expensive. Proceedings must begin voluntarily. Once the debtor files the petition, creditors cannot start or continue legal action to collect payment. Under Chapter 13, only the debtor can file a repayment plan, whose terms cannot exceed five years. If the court approves the plan, the debtor may pay off the obligations, either in full or partially, on an installment basis. The plan is designed with the debtor's future income in mind, and when the debtor completes the payments under the plan, all debts are discharged.

17. Explain the statement "For each benefit gained by regulation, there is a cost."
     Answer - It is simply cost benefit analysis. While regulation solves one problem, it creates cost in terms of time--completing paperwork, cost--money spent or not earned, loss of people--labor spent doing regulatory things rather than productive matters, etc.

Step into the Real World

1. Interview a local attorney about contract law. What is the difference between a valid contract, a void contract, a voidable contract, and an enforceable contract? What elements must be present for a valid contract to exist? What are the most common mistakes business owners make when creating contracts? What advice does the attorney offer to avoid making those mistakes?
2. Go to the U.S. Patent and Trademark Office's Web site at <http://www.uspto.gov/>. Select a product that interests you and search through some of the patents the office has granted for that product. Write a one-page summary of your search results. Do you see any ways to improve upon existing patents?
3. Contact the Small Business Development Center in your area or a local attorney and ask about the "real world" problems of obtaining a patent and enforcing your rights once it has been granted,
4. Visit a small manufacturing company in your area and interview the owner or manager about the federal and state regulations with which the company must comply. Ask to see the some of the paperwork required to comply with federal and state regulations. Which government agencies regulate the company's activities? How much does it cost the company to comply with these regulations? Which regulations make the most sense to the owner? The least? Why? Write a two-page summary of your interview.

Video Guide

to accompany

Effective Small Business Management,
Sixth Edition

Norman M. Scarborough
and
Thomas W. Zimmerer

To the Professor:

This video guide accompanies *Effective Small Business Management*, *Sixth Edition* and offers guidelines for using the eleven videos drawn from the highly-acclaimed PBS series *Small Business 2000*. Hosted by Hattie Bryant, each specially edited video gives your students insight into the exciting and challenging world of entrepreneurship and small business start-up. Students will see and hear entrepreneurs describe the challenges they faced as they worked to launch their businesses and the rewards of running their own companies.

Each video outline in this guide contains:

➤ The video segment's running time.

➤ The section of the book that relates to each video.

➤ The topic of the video segment.

➤ A synopsis of the video.

➤ Discussion questions designed to focus students' attention on the key concepts in the video and to link those concepts to those in the textbook.

➤ Suggested answers to the discussion questions for each video segment.

The discussion questions for each video segment are printed separately so that you can photocopy them as handouts for your students. Use them as either individual or group assignments. They are designed to help you stimulate meaningful class discussions using the videos as a starting point. The goal is to maximize student involvement and learning. We trust that you will enjoy using these outstanding videos as another important teaching tool in your classroom and that your students will learn many important lessons as they see first-hand what it takes to make a small business successful.

Norman M. Scarborough
Thomas W. Zimmerer

451

Video List

Video #1
Staying Power

Length: 17:17
Introductory Video
Topics: Achieving and maintaining success; overview of entrepreneurship.

Synopsis: In this introductory video, a variety of entrepreneurs discuss what it takes for a small business to have "staying power." Show host Hattie Bryant defines staying power.

The video describes the eight points of staying power:

1. Clear vision
2. Providing an environment in which employees can thrive
3. Formulating a solid business model
4. Flexibility
5. Managing capital, especially cash flow
6. Developing an effective marketing and sales program
7. Creating a board of advisors
8. Offering consistent quality.

For each of the points, the video shows an entrepreneur who has used that principle successfully. Many of these entrepreneurs will appear in other videos in this series.

Staying Power
Discussion Questions

1. What is "staying power"?

2. Explain the seven strategies small companies can use to gain staying power.

3. Explain the role of an entrepreneur's vision in establishing a company's staying power.

Video #2
Jagged Edge Mountain Gear

Length: 16:06
Book Section I: The Challenge of Entrepreneurship
Topic: Entrepreneurship
Company Web Address: http://www.jagged-edge.com/

Synopsis: Paula and Margaret Quenemoen are twin sisters who own Jagged Edge Mountain Gear, a manufacturer of outer wear for extreme sports enthusiasts. They describe the humble beginnings of their business in Telluride, Colorado, their passion for their sports and they emphasize the spiritual element of their company. Margaret explains why the Jagged Edge uses recycled material to manufacture its garments, even though it costs $1.50 more per yard. The sisters also show how they are using their World Wide Web site as a marketing tool.

The company's banker talks about the Quenemoens' "amazing business plan" and the loan package they submitted to the Small Business Administration.

The sisters describe the ups and downs of working together to build a business, offer advice to others considering launching a business and give their view on business failure.

Jagged Edge Moutain Gear
Discussion Questions

1. Which characteristics of the "typical entrepreneur" do the Quenemoen sisters exhibit?

2. How do the Quenemoen sisters view the possibility of business failure?

3. What does Paula Quenemoen mean when she says, "Our competition sells the summit; we sell the journey?" What role does this philosophy play in their business?

Video #3
Auntie Ann's Pretzels

Length: 16:44
Book Section II: Building the Business Plan: Beginning Considerations
Topics: Franchising and business ethics.

Synopsis: Ann Beiler is the owner of Auntie Ann's Pretzels, a business that sells pretzels through 400 franchised outlets across the country. Beiler describes how she started the company and how franchising was the natural way to expand the business. Students learn why she decided to slow the growth of the franchise when it became apparent that the demands of franchisees were outstripping the ability of the company to support them. Ann also brought in a franchise consultant to help manage the company's rapid growth.

Throughout the video, students get a clear sense of Ann's views on ethics and on her company's social responsibility. She discusses the idea of making money to give it away.

During the interview, Ann also describes how she financed her franchise (a loan from a local chicken farmer) and her plans for the company's expansion into international markets. In the closing scenes, Ann teaches the show's host Hattie Bryant how to make a pretzel, and she explains the religious symbolism of the pretzel.

Auntie Ann's Pretzels
Discussion Questions

1. What benefits do franchisees receive when they purchase a franchise such as Auntie Ann's?

2. How did Ann Beiler finance the growth of her franchise?

3. What role does Ann Beiler's view of ethics and her company's social responsibility play in her company's success?

Video #4
Knitz and Pieces

Length: 14:37
Book Section III: Building the Business Plan: Marketing and Financial Considerations
Topic: Building a Business Plan

Synopsis: After she was fired from a retail chain, Laurie Davis decided not to get another job. Instead, she chose to create her own business, Knitz and Pieces, a retail store specializing in knit clothing for women. Laurie describes how she spent three months researching the industry, studying her local market and developing her business plan. The banker who extended Laurie an $80,000 SBA-guaranteed start-up loan explains how her business plan convinced him to approve the loan. Hattie Bryant "flips through" the pages of Laurie's plan, pulling out excerpts from it. Laurie's banker offers advice to other entrepreneurs about how to approach a bank with a business plan. The video closes with Laurie explaining her business philosophy and defining her goals for the future – 10 stores, all located in downtown areas.

Knitz and Pieces
Discussion Questions

1. What role did the business plan Laurie Davis created for her company play in her search for capital?

2. Which elements should Laurie include in her business plan?

3. What advice would you offer an entrepreneur about to start building a business plan for a start-up company?

Video #5
Buckeye Beans and Herbs

Length: 14:29
Book Section III: Building the Business Plan: Marketing and Financial Considerations and **Book Section IV:** Marketing and the Small Business: Building a Competitive Edge
Topics: Marketing and International Business

Synopsis: Entrepreneurs Jill and Doug Smith, owners of Buckeye Beans and Herbs, describe how they market their unique line of food products both in the United States and in Japan. Doug discusses the company's mission, which, in part, is "to make people smile." He also explains Buckeye's niche marketing strategy. Jill describes the importance of customer feedback, and the manager of the company's mail order operation shows how Buckeye attempts to "romance the product in the catalog."

Doug explains Buckeye's presence in international markets, primarily Japan. He emphasizes the need for patience, the expectation of quality, and the important role that trade intermediaries play in helping small businesses sell their products in global markets.

Jill describes the company as "a value-added product company and a values-added people company." She goes on to compare her work at Buckeye Beans and Herbs to her earlier career as an artist. In the closing scenes, she offers other entrepreneurs valuable business advice.

Buckeye Beans and Herbs
Discussion Questions

1. What benefits did Buckeye Beans and Herbs earn by listening to its customers?

2. What barriers did Buckeye Beans and Herbs face when trying to break into international markets?

3. What does Jill Smith mean when she says her company is a "value-added product company and a values-added people company"?

Video #6
Solid Gold Health Products for Pets

Length: 16:03
Book Section IV: Marketing and the Small Business: Building a Competitive Edge
Topic: International Business
Company Web Address: http://www.solid-gold-inc.com/

Synopsis: Sissy Harrington-McGill is a nutritionist and a manufacturer of Solid Gold, a healthy dog food. She explains how she got started as a home-based entrepreneur by becoming an importer of a German dog food product. (At one point, he had three tons of dog food stored in her garage!) She explains the natural and healthy ingredients used to manufacture her own brand of dog food today.

Harrinton-McGill describes the prejudice she had to overcome in the early days simply because some companies did not want to do business with a woman. She also discusses her view of the risks of launching a business.

Harrington-McGill explains her company's success in international markets such as Japan, her biggest market and her approach to advertising. Her ads are actually articles designed to teach her customers about the benefits her dog food offers.

She explains that government is her biggest obstacle in business and offers the following practical advice to other entrepreneurs: make sure there is a need for your product, develop a superior product, and focus on a niche.

Solid Gold Health Products for Pets
Discussion Questions

1. How did Sissy Harrington-McGill get started in international business?

2. What benefits do companies such as Solid Gold Health Products for Pets gain by going global?

3. Summarize Solid Gold's approach to advertising.

Video #7
Raising Money

Length: 14:02
Book Section V: Putting the Business Plan to work: Sources of Funds
Topic: Sources of start-up capital

Synopsis: A variety of entrepreneurs discuss the funding sources they used to launch their companies – from suppliers and customers to friends and private investors. Bill Tobin (PC Flowers and Gifts) explains the role of financial partners and how entrepreneurs view risk. Judi Jacobsen (Madison Park Greeting Cards) reinvested the earnings from her company to finance its growth. Jake Miles (Cultural Toys) invested some of his retirement money and then convinced some old college friends to put money into his company. Tom Gegax and Don Gullett (TiresPlus) financed the growth of their company with retained earnings after nine banks refused their loan request. Dave deVarona (Todo Loco) got the money to launch his restaurant from several private investors. Marty Edelston (Boardroom Inc.) put up $30,000 of his own money to start his business and then used retained earnings from the company to finance its growth. After a dozen banks turned down her loan request, Grace Tsujikawa (Pyro Media) was able to qualify for a loan guaranteed by the Small Business Administration. JoAnn Corn (Healthcare Resources Group) used some of her own money, a loan from her parents, and up-front payments from customers to launch her one-stop health care services firm. Cheryl Womack (VCW, Inc.) kept start-up costs low by launching her business out of the basement of her home.

Raising Money
Discussion Questions

1. List the sources of funds the entrepreneurs in this program used to satisfy their business's capital needs.

2. What is an angel investor? How important are angels as a source of business financing?

3. Why is bank financing so difficult for business start-ups to obtain?

Video #8
The Enterprise Network

Length: 13:47
Book Section VI: Location and Layout: Key Criteria
Topic: Location (a business incubator)

Synopsis: Famous for its high technology start-ups, California's Silicon Valley is home to the Enterprise Network, a business incubator that houses more than a dozen small companies, all working to bring technology products to the marketplace. This video takes students into the fascinating world of high technology startups and shows the benefits of locating a fledgling business in a business incubator. In addition to the inexpensive office space, telephone lines, and equipment, entrepreneurs who choose an incubator gain another important but intangible benefit: the advice and support of a host of other entrepreneurs, many of whom serve as mentors.

Two private investors ("angels") explain that the availability of capital is one of the main reasons Silicon Valley has emerged as the "seedbed of the microelectronics revolution." They also describe the typical high technology investor's view of business failure. ("Failure is not a stigma in Silicon Valley at all. As a matter of fact, they say you're really not seasoned until you've had a few of those [failures] under your belt.")

The Enterprise Network
Discussion Questions

1. What is a business incubator?

2. Explain the advantages a business start-up gains by locating in a business incubator.

3. What factors make Northern California's Silicon Valley an ideal location for high-tech start-ups?

Video #9
Stateline Tack

Length: 5:31
Book Section VII: Controlling the Small Business: Techniques for Enhancing Profitability
Topic: Technology

Synopsis: Steve Day is the owner of Stateline Tack, the largest retailer of equestrian equipment in the world. Since he bought the company, Day has increased revenues by a factor of four. He describes his company's investment in technology over the years. Day also explains how he uses that technology to increase Stateline Tack's efficiency and to offer superior customer service to more than 200,000 customers.

Stateline Tack
Discussion Questions

1. What role has technology played in the success of Stateline Tack?

2. What steps should Steve Day take to develop a technology plan for his business?

3. What advice would you offer to Steve Day as he develops a World Wide Web site for Stateline Tack?

Video #10
Hiring Right

Length: 17:36
Book Section VIII: Staffing and Leading a Growing Company
Topic: Hiring, training, and motivating employees

Synopsis: Hattie Bryant introduces this video by saying, "The more successful a business owner is, the more likely you'll hear them say, 'The single most important factor in this business is the people.'" A variety of entrepreneurs discuss the importance of the selection and hiring process.

One business owner says that he screens 300 to 250 people just to hire one person! Other entrepreneurs discuss the importance of reading an applicant's "body language" in an interview, providing meaningful work for employees, providing stock options as a retention tool, hiring caring people, and recognizing that a candidate's attitude is more important than his or her skill level. Entrepreneur Albert Black says that his job is to "teach, preach, coach, and counsel" his employees. He also describes the three types of income his company offers workers: educational, psychological and financial. Dale Crownover, owner of Texas Nameplate Inc., strives for improved communication with his workforce because it improves both employee and customer satisfaction.

Hiring Right
Discussion Questions

1. Which of these business owners would you most enjoy working for? Explain.

2. Explain the motivational techniques the featured business owners use in their companies.

3. Develop a list of the principles by which you will manage the people in the company you plan to start.

Video #11
Flap Happy

Length: 15:07
Book Section IX: Legal Aspects of Small Business: Succession, Ethics, and Government Regulation
Topic: Family Business

Synopsis: Wanting a floppy hat to protect her infant son from the sun, Laurie Snyder ended up designing and selling a hat of her own. Her company, Flap Happy, is a successful family business selling hats to more than 4,000 customers across the globe, including L.L. Bean. Laurie says she started her business "from zero" and that the business generated no income for the first four years. Flap Happy is the quintessential family business, with Laurie's husband, mother, father, and sister all working for the company. (Her son was the model for the company's logo.) Laurie explains her company's emphasis on quality and why her focus has been on profits rather than on sales.

In closing, Laurie's father describes the meaning of the family in "family business." He says that Flap Happy has helped the family stay together as a unit, something he calls "a mitzvah."

Flap Happy
Discussion Questions

1. What contributions do family businesses make to the nation's economy?

2. What roles do Laurie Snyder's family members play in Flap Happy?

3. What is the greatest threat to family business? What steps can family business owners take to overcome this threat?

Video Discussion Questions
Suggested Answers

1. **What is staying power?**
   Staying power is a company's ability to survive and thrive in a competitive environment. The real measure of success is sustainability. Can a small company create a *sustainable* competitive edge over its rivals? If so, it has staying power.

2. **Explain the eight strategies small companies can use to gain staying power.**
   The seven strategies of staying power are: (1) a clear vision, (2) an environment in which employees can thrive, (3) a solid business model, (4) the ability to stay flexible, (5) the ability to stay on top of financials, especially cash flow, (6) developing an effective marketing and sales program, (7) creating a board of advisors, and (8) offering consistent quality.

3. **Explain the role of an entrepreneur's vision in establishing a company's staying power.**
   An entrepreneur's vision is the basis for everything a company is and does. Notice that in the strategic planning process discussed in Chapter 2, developing a clear vision is the first step. Successful entrepreneurs usually have the ability to communicate their vision to everyone the organization touches, from its employees and its customers to its investors and the local community. A clearly defined vision is crucial to a company's staying power because it focuses everyone's attention on what the business must do well to thrive in the face of competition.

1. **Which characteristics of the "typical entrepreneur" do the Quenemoen sisters exhibit.**
   The Quenemoen sisters are quintessential entrepreneurs. They are moderate risk takers, have high levels of energy, maintain a future orientation, are skilled at organizing the various aspects of their business, and value the challenge of succeeding in business more than money. They also exhibit a high degree of commitment to their company and tremendous tenacity toward making it a success.

2. **How do the Quenemoen sisters view the possibility of failure?**
   Like most entrepreneurs, the Quenemoens are extremely optimistic about their chances of success. Notice that in the video, Margaret says, "It's tenacity . . . Going out of business will never be an option. We don't have anything to fall back on." Even more important than their optimism is the sisters total commitment to making

Jagged Edge a successful business venture. They are not willing to accept failure as an option!

3. **What does Paula Quenemoen mean when she says, "Our competition sells the summit; we sell the journey"? What role does this philosophy play in their business?**

After watching this video, students get a clear sense of the "spiritual element" of Jagged Edge Mountain Gear. This is an ideal time to discuss how a business reflects the values, beliefs, and principles of its founder. As extreme sports participants, the Quenemoens truly are more interested in the experience (i.e. the journey) than they are the destination (i.e. the summit). Like many entrepreneurs, they are relishing the experience of operating a business and the sense of freedom that it brings.

This attitude filters into virtually every decision the Quenemoens make about their company - from their use of recycled materials in their products to the way they treat their employees and their customers.

Video #3: Auntie Ann's Pretzels

1. **What benefits do franchisees receive when they purchase a franchise such as Auntie Ann's?**

Franchisees receive many benefits including:
   - ➤ management training and support
   - ➤ brand name appeal
   - ➤ standardized quality of goods and services
   - ➤ financial assistance
   - ➤ proven products and business formats
   - ➤ centralized buying power
   - ➤ site selection and territorial protection
   - ➤ a greater chance for success

Many franchisees say that franchising offers them the opportunity to be in business for themselves but not by themselves.

2. **How did Ann Beiler finance the growth of her franchise?**

After striking out with bank financing, Ann Beiler did what a growing number of entrepreneurs are doing: approaching private lenders and investors for the capital they need to start their businesses or to finance their growth. Beiler approached a local chicken farmer about extending her company a loan. After a few brief meetings, the farmer agreed to become Beiler's bank.

3. **What role does Ann Beiler's view of ethics and her company's social responsibility play in her company's success?**

In this video, Beiler's strong sense of ethics and social responsibility comes through. This attitude has a great deal to do with her company's success. Note that Ann and her management team decided to stop the growth of the company for a time until they were able to build a management infrastructure that would support the franchisees adequately. Not every franchisor would choose to limit growth that is not in the best interest of its franchisees. It is this attitude of mutual trust and respect that makes Auntie Ann's a popular franchise choice. Franchisees know that Ann Beiler has their best interest at heart.

At several points in the video, Beiler also explains her philosophy of "making money to give it away." In fact, the reason she started the company was to finance her husband's non-profit counseling ministry. She demonstrates an attitude of social responsibility in the way she manages her business by giving back to the community.

Video #4: Knitz and Pieces

1. **What role did the business plan Laurie Davis created for her company play in her search for capital?**
    At this point, it's a good idea to emphasize the two reasons for preparing a business plan: 1). Creating a "road map" to help entrepreneurs guide their companies through the often treacherous, hostile competitive environment, and 2.) developing a tool to help entrepreneurs attract the start-up or growth capital their companies need. Reason #1 is the *primary* reason a business owner should build a business plan; however, any business owner expecting to raise either debt or equity capital from outsiders must prepare a comprehensive business plan. A quality business plan is an important tool when an entrepreneur is trying to sell a business idea to a potential lender or investor. Laurie Davis is proof of that!

    Point out how seriously Laurie took the task of developing her plan. (It became her full-time job for three months.) Notice how impressed her banker was with the quality of her plan. Ask your students, "What would Laurie's chances have been of getting a business start-up loan from Huntington Bank *without* a business plan?" (Answer: Nil.) Laurie got the start-up loan because she was prepared to launch and manage her retail business successfully and because she assembled proof of her ability into a comprehensive business plan.

2. **What elements should Laurie include in her business plan?**
    In the video, Hattie Bryant takes viewers on a brief "tour" of several parts of Laurie's business plan. Although every plan should be tailored to the unique characteristics and strengths of a particular business, the following elements are common to most plans:
    -   executive summary
    -   mission statement
    -   business and industry profile
    -   business strategy
    -   description of the firm's products or services
    -   marketing strategy
    -   competitor analysis

478

> owner's resume
> plan of operation
> financial data
> request for funds

3. **What advice would you offer an entrepreneur about to start building a business plan for a start-up company?**
To be effective, a business plan should be "crisp," long enough to cover the necessary details but not so long that no one wants to read it. Don't let someone else prepare your plan for you. It is a good idea to get input and suggestions from others, but the entrepreneur is the driving force behind the business idea and must be the author of the plan. The executive summary is crucial; it must summarize the plan in just one or two pages and must "hook" the reader. If the executive summary is off the mark, the probability that the person reviewing the plan will read it is minimal. If anyone outside the company is going to see the plan, it should be a professional document free of spelling and grammatical errors. Include a table of contents to make it easy for readers to navigate the plan. Make the document visually appealing and interesting to read. Use computer spreadsheets to generate the necessary financial forecasts, and make sure your forecasts are realistic. ALWAYS tell the truth in a business plan.

Video #5: Buckeye Beans and Herbs

1. **What benefits did Buckeye Beans and Herbs earn by listening to its customers?**
One of the most valuable marketing exercises any business owner can engage in is spending time with living, breathing customers. Point out that some of Buckeye's most popular products and successful marketing strategies are the result of interactions with customers. For instance, Jill Smith explains how Buckeye designed pasta in the shape of a Douglas Fir tree (Oregon's state tree), but at a trade show, customers thought the design was of a Christmas tree. Buckeye Beans picked up on customers' comments and began marketing the product successfully as a holiday pasta.

2. **What barriers did Buckeye Beans and Herbs face when trying to break into international markets?**
Doug Smith describes how difficult it was for Buckeye to get its line of food products into the Japanese market. Buckeye had problems with Japanese quotas on imported food products. Plus, breaking into international markets often requires a great deal of patience. However, as Doug explains, the benefits that a company gains are most often worth the wait. He says that the Japanese market holds tremendous growth for Buckeye.

Other barriers that companies face when going global include finding capital to finance international sales, not knowing how to get started in international business, and the problems posed by tariffs and political, business, and cultural barriers.

479

At this point, an interesting assignment for your students might be to research some of the political, business, and cultural barriers that face companies trying to sell in Japan. The text book offers students numerous resources (both in the library and on the World Wide Web) for gathering this information.

3. **What does Jill Smith mean when she says her company is a "value-added product company and a values-added people company"?**
Buckeye Beans and Herbs has found success by positioning itself as a niche marketer of high quality, "fun" food products. (Point out that the company's direct-mail catalog manager talks about "romancing the product" in the catalog.) The basis for its strategy is *not* to compete on the basis of price; instead Buckeye offers unique, high-quality products that make cooking fun.

Buckeye is also a business that values its employees. Jill and Doug Smith know that the best way to have happy, satisfied customers is to have happy, satisfied employees serving their customers. Point out that Buckeye is yet another example of a small company whose owners see their responsibility as much more than merely earning a profit. At Buckeye Beans and Herbs, values are important!

Video #6: Solid Gold Health Products for Pets

1. **How did Sissy Harrington-McGill get started in international business?**
Sissy Harrington-McGill has been in international business since founding her company. She started by importing a high quality German dog food and selling it to other pet owners at dog shows. As sales grew, she set up a licensing arrangement with the German dog food maker. Because Harrington-McGill was operating the business out of her home at the time, she used her garage as a warehouse, once storing three tons of dog food there. Notice the cultural barriers that Harrington-McGill had to overcome as a woman entrepreneur as she conducted business in other countries. What enabled her to overcome these barriers and to succeed? Sheer persistence! Her persistence has paid off; Japan is now Solid Gold's biggest market.

This is a good time to point out to students that even the smallest companies can engage in international business successfully

2. **What benefits do companies such as Solid Gold Health Products for Pets gain by going global?**
Small companies that "go global" gain many benefits including:
> offset sales declines in the domestic market.
> increase sales and profits
> extend their products' life cycle
> lower manufacturing costs
> improve competitive position and enhance reputation
> raise quality levels
> become more customer-oriented

480

3. **Summarize Solid Gold's approach to advertising.**
   Solid Gold's approach to advertising is a reflection of Sissy Harrington-McGill's background as a teacher. The ads are not of the traditional "hard-sell" genre. All of the company's ads are designed to teach customers or potential customers something about nutrition for their pets. Sissy says that the company gets a good deal of customer feedback from the ads.

Video #7: Raising Money

1. **List the sources of funds the entrepreneurs in this program used to satisfy their business's capital needs.**
   Judi Jacobsen (Madison Park Greeting Cards) reinvested the earnings from her company to finance its growth. Jake Miles (Cultural Toys) invested some of his retirement money and then convinced some old college friends to put money into his company. Tom Gegax and Don Gullett (TiresPlus) financed the growth of their company with retained earnings after nine banks refused their loan request. Dave deVarona (Todo Loco) got the money to launch his restaurant from several private investors. Marty Edelston (Boardroom Inc.) put up $30,000 of his own money to start his business and then used retained earnings from the company to finance its growth. After a dozen banks turned down her loan request, Grace Tsujikawa (Pyro Media) was able to qualify for a loan guaranteed by the Small Business Administration. JoAnn Corn (Healthcare Resources Group) used some of her own money, a loan from her parents, and up-front payments from customers to launch her one-stop health care services firm. Cheryl Womack (VCW, Inc.) kept start-up costs low by launching her business in the basement of her home, a form of bootstrap financing.

2. **What is an angel investor? How important are angels as a source of business financing?**
   Angels are wealthy individuals, often entrepreneurs themselves, who invest in business start-ups in exchange for equity stakes in the company. They are a primary source of capital for companies in the start-up through growth phases. Although it is difficult to determine the exact amount angels invest in businesses, experts conservatively estimate that some 250,000 angels invest $20 to $30 billion a year in 500,000 small businesses. In fact, angels are the largest single source of external equity capital for small companies.

3. **Why is bank financing so difficult for business start-ups to obtain?**
   Banks tend to be conservative in their lending practices, a fact that makes lending to high-risk start-up companies unattractive. Plus, because they provide debt capital, the only reward banks get from a successful business customer is the interest on the loan. Because they provide no equity capital, banks get no benefit from a small company that "hits it big," makes an initial public offering, and sees the price of its shares

climb. Experts estimate that just 5 to 8 percent of business start-ups get bank financing.

This is a good time to emphasize to your students the importance of a quality business plan when searching for capital. What can entrepreneurs do to increase their chances of success in the hunt for capital? Study their industry, their local market, and their business opportunity and then assemble that information into a solid business plan.

Video #8: The Enterprise Network

1. **What us a business incubator?**
   A business incubator is an organization that combines low-cost, flexible rental space with a multitude of support services for its small business residences. About half of all incubators are government sponsored; other sponsors include colleges or universities, nonprofit organizations, and private investment groups. The Enterprise Network is one of more than 600 incubators in operation in the United States.

2. **Explain the advantages a business start-up gains by locating in a business incubator.**
   The benefits of locating a start-up business in an incubator are many, including:
   - affordable rental rates
   - shared resources such as secretarial support, telephone system, computers and software, fax and copier machines and other technologies, meeting facilities, and (sometimes) management consulting services.
   - access to growth capital
   - a support network provided by other entrepreneurs going through the same experiences.
   - a higher probability of success. One study found that more than 80 percent of ompanies become profitable within three years of entering an incubator. Another study reports that "graduates" of business incubators have only an 11 percent failure rate.

   Notice that the entrepreneurs in the video mention several of these advantages.

3. **What factors make California's Silicon Valley an ideal location for high-tech start-ups?**
   According the venture capitalists in the video, one reason that Silicon Valley has become a hot spot for high-tech start-up companies is the availability of capital to finance new and growing companies. Not only is Silicon Valley home to many high-tech start-ups, but it also is home to many private investors and venture capital firms looking to invest in small companies.

   Another reason for Silicon Valley's reputation as a high-tech mecca is its geographic location. There are a number of nearby colleges and universities (such as Stanford and Cal-Berkeley) and high-tech businesses, which results in a large pool of educated,

482

highly-skilled workers. Pacific Rim cities (similarly, Seattle) are also hotbeds of high-tech activity (partially due to relative proximity to the high technology producing Asian nations), and the high-tech businesses already located there act as magnets for other similar companies.

Video #9: Stateline Tack

1. **What role has technology played in the success of Stateline Tack?**
    Technology has played a significant role in Stateline tack's success. Since taking over the company, Steve Day has invested a sizable sum of money into various forms of technology - from a sophisticated telephone system to a computer system capable of handling orders from the company's base of 200,000 customers. Day's goals in investing in this technology are to provide superior customer service and to improve the efficiency of the company. This video offers an ideal chance to discuss the need to constantly update the technology a company relies on to maintain its competitive edge. Failing to keep its technology current in key areas can lead a company to fall behind its competitors in a relatively short time.

2. **What steps should Steve Day take to develop a technology plan for his business?**
    Although small companies have the greatest potential to benefit from technology, most small businesses do not use technology effectively. Why? Because they lack a comprehensive plan for integrating technology in ways that could transform their businesses. The steps involved in developing a technology plan for a company are as follows:
    - Decide what you want your company to be able to do for itself and for your customers.
    - Determine the technology and the equipment you will need to perform those tasks.
    - Conduct a technology audit to determine where your company 's technology currently stands.
    - Match goals and resources.
    - Develop a technology budget.
    - Make the necessary technology purchases.

3. **What advice would you offer Steve Day as he develops a World Wide Web site for Stateline Tack?**
    The World Wide Web is a powerful marketing tool for businesses of *any* size. Approximately 70,000 small companies in the United States are doing business online, and the number is growing daily. Designing an attractive Web site that will attract customers and sell products requires planning, however. The text book offers advice on designing an attractive Web site in several places. For instance, Table 11.5 on page 352 offers eight guidelines for Internet ad campaigns. Some of these principles include advice such as "avoid slow downloads," "change the content of your site often," and "assure customers that paying on-line is secure."

You should also refer your students to the Gaining the Competitive Edge feature, "Designing a Killer Web Site," on page 199. Some of the tips in this feature include the following:

> - Be easy to find.
> - Give customers what they want.
> - Promote your Web site in other media.
> - Establish "hot links" with other businesses, preferably those selling complementary services or products.
> - Include an e-mail option on your site.
> - Offer Web shoppers a special all their own.
> - Use a simple design.

Video #10: Hiring Right

1. **Which of these business owners would you most enjoy working for? Explain.**
   Of course, the answers you get here will be unique to each student. As you discuss this issue, the key is to continue probing for the *reasons* each student would prefer working for a particular owner. As students offer explanations concerning why they chose a particular business owner, ask them to consider the style by which they plan to manage the companies they are planning to start (See question #3). Many students will list Albert Black as their favorite because of his simple, yet highly effective, philosophy towards his workers ("teach, preach, coach, and counsel") is so appealing.

2. **Explain the motivational techniques the featured business owners use in their companies.**
   Point out the importance that several of the featured entrepreneurs place on the selection process. They know that hiring the right people is the first step in creating a caring, motivated, dedicated workforce. Several of the business owners in this video segment rely on empowerment as a motivational tool. For instance, Darby McQuaid explains his philosophy of "let other people be involved." Albert Black also empowers his works and gives them the information they need to do their jobs well. Black embraces open-book management (see page 672 in the text book), in which employees have access to all of a company's records, including its financial statements. At TiresPlus, Tom Gegax explains how his company's pay for performance system (refer to pages 676 to 678 in the text book) works.

   This video is an excellent springboard for launching a discussion about managing and motivating Generation X employees. The "In the Footsteps of an Entrepreneur" feature on pages 677 to 678 provides some useful suggestions. Be sure to point out the differences in what is required to manage Generation X employees successfully and what it takes to manage older workers well.

3. **Develop a list of the principles by which you will manage the people in the company you plan to start.**

Once again, the answers you get will be unique to each student. As your class develops a list, watch for differences in management philosophies. Are some students willing to trust their future employees more than others? Do some plan to rely primarily on money as a motivator while others intend to use empowerment, praise, feedback and other intangibles as their primary motivators?

Ask students how they came up with their list of principles. Many of them will list principles that are the opposite of the principles a current or former boss uses or used on them! Explain that this is also quite common among entrepreneurs. You might even ask some students to share a "horror story" or two about a previous experience.

Video #11: Flap Happy

1. **What contributions do family businesses make to the nation's economy?**
   More than 80 percent of all companies in the United States are family-owned, and their contributions to the nation's economy are significant. These companies generate 50 percent of the U.S. gross domestic product (GDP), employ more than 40 million people, and pay 65 percent of all wages. Not all family-owned businesses are small; one-third of the Fortune 500 companies are family businesses.

2. **What roles do Laurie Snyder's family members play in Flap Happy?**
   Flap Happy is the quintessential family business, with Laurie's husband, mother, father and sister all working for the company. Laurie's husband is the facilities manager ("I do whatever she doesn't want to do, and she does whatever I don't want to do."); her sister Amy is in charge of collections; her mother, Judy, handles customer service; and her father, Marty, is in charge of marketing and advertising. Her son, Cody, was the model for the company's logo.

3. **What is the greatest threat to family business? What steps can family business owners take to overcome this threat?**
   The greatest threat to family businesses is the lack of succession planning – that is, the failure to develop a strategy for passing the torch of leadership. Unfortunately, 70 percent of first-generation businesses fail to survive into the second generation, and of those that do, only 13 percent make it to the third.

   The most effective way to battle this threat is to create a management succession plan. Unfortunately, studies also show that 54 percent of all family business owners do not have a formal management succession plan. Developing a plan involves the following steps:
   - ➤ Select the successor.
   - ➤ Create a survival kit for the successor.
   - ➤ Groom the successor, which requires time, patience and a willingness to teach.
   - ➤ Promote an environment of trust and respect.
   - ➤ Cope with the financial realities of estate and gift taxes.